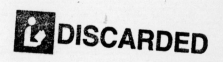

GASPARD DE COLIGNY

ADMIRAL OF FRANCE

Coligny

GASPARD DE COLIGNY

ADMIRAL OF FRANCE

BY

A. W. WHITEHEAD, M.A.

STANHOPE HISTORICAL PRIZE ESSAYIST, 1896

WITH ILLUSTRATIONS AND PLANS

METHUEN & CO.
36 ESSEX STREET W.C.
LONDON

First Published, 1904

CONTENTS

LIST OF ILLUSTRATIONS

GENEALOGICAL TABLE, MAPS, PLANS

GASPARD DE COLIGNY

INTRODUCTORY

THE most important lives of Coligny are those of the late Comte Jules Delaborde and Professor Erich Marcks. The three volumes of M. Delaborde must always form the basis of any study of the Admiral. Besides printing many indispensable documents, he gives either in full or in part the majority of Coligny's letters which are to be found in the Bibliothèque Nationale, Paris, and in the archives of Strasburg, Switzerland, and Turin. They are on the whole correctly copied, and can be trusted. With this the usefulness of the work may be said to end. As a study of Coligny it has little value. It is amorphous, prints hundreds of pages of material —often of questionable importance or easily accessible—which might have been given in as many lines. It is, moreover, laudatory and blindly partisan.

A book of quite another order is Professor Marcks' *Gaspard von Coligny : Sein Leben und das Frankreich seiner Zeit.* Only the first volume has yet appeared, bringing Coligny's life down to the end of 1560. Unfinished as it is, it is perhaps the most scholarly work we have on the France of the sixteenth century. The author has a singular power in sketching the complex movements of the time; he is equally happy in placing Coligny and the life of his age in their true perspective. An example of his accurate scholarship will be found on p. 27, note 1, where he corrects M. Delaborde's misreading of an important document.

Other lives of Coligny have been written by Walter Besant, Sarah Brook, W. M. Blackburn, E. Bersier, J. Tessier, E. Riquet de Caraman, C. Buet, G. Leser, E. Haag, H. Bordier, Stæhelin, and Meylan.

Another work of great value is M. Decrue's *Anne de Montmorency*. It is the outcome of years of original research. We have used it largely in sketching the relations of the Admiral with the Montmorency family. Some of M. Decrue's summaries of political tendencies and events are unequalled.

Two other French writers whose names are indissolubly connected with the history of the sixteenth century, are the late Baron Alphonse de Ruble, and the late Comte Hector de la Ferrière. They have done much of the pioneer work. As compared with the methods of the older historians, such as Martin, who depended almost entirely on printed memoirs and histories, they devoted themselves to exploring new and unpublished sources. They have thus developed and defined many points, and generally enlarged our knowledge. Unfortunately, they have dealt with more material than they could sift. In consequence, their work makes no approach to accuracy. In their narrative of the first war of religion alone we have counted scores of errors more or less serious. A few examples will suffice. M. de Ruble states that on the 29th of March, 1562, Condé divided his cavalry at Meaux into two, he with one part taking the road to Paris, while Andelot with the other advanced by forced marches on Orleans. We can find no authority for this. Equally misleading is his statement that the Dukes of Nevers and Bouillon were among the Huguenot leaders who appeared with Condé before Paris. Neither the Duke of Nevers nor the Duke of Bouillon ever actually joined Condé in the field. Beza's *Histoire Ecclésiastique* is quite decisive on this point. Chantonnay, too, on the 8th of April reported that there were no other members of the Order among the Huguenots except those he had mentioned, " porque el Conde de Hu, que es agora Duque de Nevers, aunque es declarado herege, no se quiere mesclar con ellos " (Arch. Nat. K. 1497). M. de Ruble has, we believe, misread a letter in the *Mémoires de Condé*, said to be from the pen of the Florentine Ambassador. Moreover, the Huguenots arrived before Paris on the 30th of March, and not on the 29th, as M. de Ruble asserts in a note to d'Aubigné's *Histoire Universelle*.

Again, in the negotiations of Talcy in June, the Queen Mother is said to have arrived at St. Simon on the 22nd, and only then directed negotiations, though it is quite certain that she arrived earlier, probably on the 20th; M. de Ruble may have been led astray by a letter of Catherine in M. de la Ferrière's edition of her letters (i. 337, 338), which is incorrectly given as of the 22nd instead of the 12th. Moreover, when the Huguenots moved out from Orleans to Vaussoudun on the 19th of June, they were not divided from the Catholics, as M. de Ruble asserts, by the Loire. Vaussoudun, as a glance at the map of Cassini will show, is on the right bank. Both camps, therefore, were to the north of the river; a report of the English agent Middlemore who visited Orleans, the account of La Noue, and a document printed by M. de Ruble himself (*Antoine de Bourbon*, iv. 411), make this perfectly clear. Then again, M. de Ruble states that Pithiviers was captured on the 8th of November, instead of on the 11th. He also ascribes the defeat of Coligny's final attempt at the battle of Dreux to the efforts of the Swiss, in spite of the fact that Segesser, the biographer of the Swiss Colonel Pfeiffer, Commandant Coynart, the modern historian of the battle, as well as the designs of Tortorel and Perrissin, agree that the Swiss took no part whatever in the second half of the action. In a curious note, too, on d'Aubigné's description of the taking of the Tourelles of Orleans in February, 1563, he explains that the " Bretons" who were to blame for its capture were "habitants de la Grande-Bretagne (Anglais)"! And finally, we would remark that M. de Ruble hardly appreciates the relative value of authorities. Statements made from whatever quarter are received without question. The Spanish Ambassador's opinion as to the number and policy of the Huguenots, as well as of the secret movements of Coligny, is quoted as though it carried weight: we would instance Francis of Montmorency's supposed dealings with Poltrot, and Coligny's supposed secret meeting with Montmorency before his appearance in Paris in 1565. Nor can the oft-repeated assertion that La Popelinière and Beza, in their relation of the first war of religion, " se copient textuellement" be considered satisfactory. Beza's narrative of the first war of religion—the first edition of the *Histoire*

Ecclésiastique is of 1580—is, from a Huguenot standpoint, the most original and important document we possess. On the other hand, La Popelinière in the first editions of his history, which were published in 1571, 1572, and 1579, under the title of *La vraye et entiere histoire*, never dealt with the first war at all; the narrative as it appeared in the later editions of 1581, etc., was taken almost word for word from Beza.

The errors which mar much of the work of M. de la Ferrière are similar to those of M. de Ruble. We might cite as an example his statement that from the 27th to the 29th of June, Condé passed and repassed between Catherine and the Huguenot camp, in fact visited her three times. What actually happened was that Condé visited her on the 28th, accompanied her to Talcy, returned with her to Beaugency on the 29th, and was thence conducted by Coligny and the other Huguenot leaders to their camp. Another example is a letter of Coligny which is given correctly in Forbes and the *Calendar of State Papers* as from Meur (probably Mur, a village a little north of Selles in Berry), 2nd Jan. 1563, but which appears in M. de la Ferrière's *Le XVIme siècle et les Valois* as from Meun, 12th Jan. 1563. In addition, M. de la Ferrière, who was one of the first historians to make use of the documents in the Record Office, is often tempted to rely solely for his facts on the reports of the English agents in France. He thus inaccurately states that the meeting of Toury took place on the 6th instead of the 9th of June, and that by the edict of Amboise the Huguenots were granted the right of service in three towns in each *bailliage*, instead of in one.

We have thought it necessary to draw attention to these facts, as there is a natural tendency to start with the labours of MM. de Ruble and de la Ferrière as a basis. We would add, however, that their work, both from the standpoint of accuracy and knowledge, and much more from that of impartiality, compares favourably with that of another of the principal historians of the sixteenth century: the late Baron Kervyn de Lettenhove. We have examined one of his statements in an appendix: *The Huguenots and the Treaty of Hampton Court.* But it is not necessary to deal with his work here. He has been criticised at length by Mr. Armstrong, Professor Erich Marcks, M. de la Ferrière, and the editors of the *Documents concernant les relations entre le duc d'Anjou et les Pays Bas* (1576–1583). No one who has had to examine carefully M. de Lettenhove's *magnum opus, Les Huguenots et les Gueux*, will seriously question Professor Marcks' opinion that the history of this movement has still to be written.

In addition to the more recent historians already mentioned, there are many others who have done much to give a more accurate and detailed knowledge of the period. Among them are the editors of Beza's *Histoire Ecclésiastique* and the *Calvini Opera*, and MM. Forneron, de Lacombe, Henri Hauser, N. Weiss, Léon Marlet, Tamizey de Larroque, Baguenault de Puchesse, Noel Valois, and the German historians Philippson, Baumgarten, Benno Hilliger, A. Holländer, Maurenbrecher, and Heidenhain.

In writing the following life of Coligny, we have consulted, as far as we are aware, the bulk of the printed matter, both modern and of the sixteenth and succeeding centuries, which touches directly or indirectly on the Admiral, his life and times. It consists of memoirs, histories, philosophic and religious works, collections of historical documents and letters, articles and essays in the various historical reviews, and the publications of the innumerable learned societies of France. They are indicated in part in the bibliographies of MM. Gabriel Monod, Robert de Lasteyrie and E. Lefèvre-Pontalis, and in *Les sources de l'histoire de France* of M. A. Franklin.

We have also drawn largely on unpublished sources. The principal are the Record Office and British Museum ; Archives Nationales and Bibliothèque Nationale, Paris; the Corsini, Barberini, and Vatican Libraries, Rome ; the Vatican Archives, and the state archives of Turin, Parma, Mantua, Modena, Florence, and Naples. We have found the contents of the Italian archives of special importance. They have enabled us to give details of various incidents in Coligny's life which had been practically ignored : we would instance his voyage to Italy 1546–1547, and his friendship with Peter Strozzi. Perhaps the most important are the Archives of Modena, which contain the vast correspondence of Alvarotto, the Ferraran Ambassador in France. He was a man of great experience, for twenty years resident at the Valois court, and as representative of Ferrara followed the doings of the allied house of Guise with the closest attention, and as a necessary consequence the life and career of Coligny. At Mantua is the important correspondence of the Gonzaga family and their agents in France, at Florence that of the Medicis and their agents—very inadequately abstracted by Desjardins in his work on the diplomatic relations of France and Tuscany,—at Parma and Naples that of the Farneses and their agents, in the Vatican that of the Papacy and its Nuncios in France. Moreover, in all these various archives there is a vast mass of other material not to be overlooked.

The published *Calendars of State Papers* (Foreign, 1547–1572) are excellent as a guide to what the Record Office contains, but they certainly do not obviate the necessity of referring constantly to the originals. This fact has not been sufficiently recognised by French writers. The Calendars are admittedly abstracts, and the student will find that subjects which from his standpoint are of the utmost importance have either been merely touched on or wholly ignored. Moreover, the editing, though on the whole satisfactory, considering when it was done, leaves something to be desired. Scores of documents are wrongly placed or not placed at all ; an instance is the calendaring of letters of Coligny and Condé of the 1st and 2nd of April, 1563, under the year 1562. Then, again, the translations are sometimes, though not often, at fault. For instance, the sense of Coligny's explanation that " de raffraischer noz dictz Reistres je les ay mis depuis en autre garnison audessus d'Orleans de ca et de la la riviere " (Record Office, xlix. 131), is not accurately expressed by, " he placed his reiters in garrison both above and below Orleans " (Cal. of 1563, No. 145) ; the same may be said of the phrase " accompaignée de mond. sr. le Prince " (Record Office, xxxix. 231), being given as " in order to meet the Prince of Condé " (Cal. of 1562, No. 329). We have pointed out more serious examples of mistranslation in an appendix : *The Huguenots and the Treaty of Hampton Court.* In the British Museum there are many documents not to be found in the Record Office, among them letters of Coligny and other Huguenots.

From our standpoint, the Bibliothèque Nationale, Paris, is especially valuable. Besides innumerable letters of the Admiral, it contains modern transcriptions of the incomparable correspondence of the Venetian Ambassadors in France. Even more important is the correspondence of the Spanish Ambassadors in the Fonds Simancas of the Archives Nationales. It is a treasure-house of the politics and events of the time. Nevertheless, all statements coming from this quarter must be put to the most careful tests. The Ambassador of Philip II. was invariably the most prejudiced and partisan as well as the most credulous of all foreign observers. In October, 1571, the Papal Nuncio remarked of him: " He is so suspicious and credulous of ill, that not only what he sees and hears but what he thinks and imagines he invariably makes the worst of (*interpreta et crede sempre in male*)."

We have to thank Mr. C. Grant Robertson of All Souls' for kindly looking over this book before publication. We also wish to acknowledge the unfailing courtesy of M. N. Weiss, to whose work we shall have to refer more than once, of M. S. C. Gigon, and of M. Élie Berger, Professor of Palæography at the École des Chartes.

CHAPTER I

THE YOUTH OF COLIGNY

Origin—Connection with the Montmorency Family—Birth, 16th February, 1519
—Tutor the Humanist, Bérauld—Assumes the Title of Châtillon—Court Life—
Influence of Anne of Montmorency—First Public Appearance—His Brother Odet
proposed as Legate of Avignon—Fall of Anne, 1541—Coligny's First Campaigns,
1542–1545—Participation in Court Festivities—Intermediary between Anne and the
Dauphin—Intimacy with Francis of Aumale (later, Duke of Guise) and Peter Strozzi
—Supports Strozzi against Poulin—First Difference with Aumale—Voyage to Italy,
1546–1547—Death of Francis I.

I N the sixteenth century there were three main roads to
distinction : brilliant service, royal favour, and high
birth. With the last, advance, if not the most rapid, was
sure. The prejudices in its favour were strong. Without it,
chance or long years and the exercise of infinite resource
were needed to achieve anything. Here are the words of
that hardy mariner, John Ribaut, to his men, as he lay off
the coast of Florida in the year of 1562. They are the tale
of his struggle for place and glory. " For albeit that from
my tender yeeres, I my selfe have applyed all my industry
to follow them, and have hazarded my life in so many dangers
for the service of my prince, yet could I never attaine thereunto (not that I did not deserve this title and degree of

government) as I have seen it happen to many others, onely
because they descende of a noble race, since more regard is
had of their birth than of their vertue." [1]   This magic gift of
birth, therefore, counted for much in the shaping of a career.

The house of Coligny traced back its origin to the territory of Bresse. Here, forty miles north-west of Geneva, lay
the castle and domain of Coligny. From time to time the
family increased its influence by the acquisition of neighbouring seigneuries such as Andelot and Fromente. But it seems
never to have possessed sovereign power. It was subject to
the steady predominance of Savoy. This position of virtual
dependence is clearly marked throughout the Middle Ages.
With the fifteenth century, however, opened a new chapter.
In the year 1437, the head of the house married Catherine
of Saligny, who brought, among other French possessions, the
castle of Châtillon-sur-Loing. Their son, John III., changed
the centre of family interests, by moving to the soil of France.
Henceforth the house was purely French.

The two sons of John III. best known to history were:
James, Seigneur of Châtillon; and Gaspard, Seigneur of Fromente. The former, following Charles VIII. in his fantastic
expedition into Italy, early won the royal favour. But dying
childless in 1512, his title of Seigneur of Châtillon passed to
his brother, Gaspard. This latter, meanwhile, had not been
idle. He too had served with distinction in Italy. And
evidence of his growing influence is found in the fact that
in 1514 he was considered an eligible suitor for the hand of
Louise, widow of Ferry of Mailly, and daughter of William
of Montmorency, First Baron of the Realm. The year 1516
saw him provisionally Marshal; in 1518 he received all the
dignities of that office, and died on active service in 1522.
His children were: Peter, born in 1515; Odet, in 1517;
Gaspard, the future Admiral, on the 16th of February, 1519;
and Francis, better known as Andelot, in 1521. Louise of
Montmorency had also three children by her former marriage.
They concern us little here, except that, a generation later,
the child of one of them was to marry the Prince of Condé.

It will thus be seen that the Seigneurs of Châtillon had

[1] Hakluyt, iii. 377 (edition of 1809-1812).

won for themselves an assured position. The young Gaspard might reasonably expect a future. Yet the definite turn was given to his career by the new alliance with the Montmorencys. It, in fact, swallowed up the old Coligny traditions, and the Admiral can never be rightly understood, except as a member of this house. He was the son, indeed, of a distinguished warrior; but he was in a more intimate sense the nephew of Anne of Montmorency, Constable and Peer of France.

The family of Montmorency had played an important rôle in French history; but it was Anne who set the seal to its fortunes. His martial ardour in the campaigns of Italy, his championship of the new absolutist theories of the Crown, his real ability, his superficial love for the arts of the Renaissance, all won him the royal favour. Francis I. was generous, and gave largely. For a score of years Anne reaped a veritable harvest. Nothing came amiss. Success and defeat alike consolidated his power. The death of his brother-in-law, Châtillon, made him a Marshal; the terrible defeat of Pavia in 1525 gave him the vacant position of Grand Master of the Realm. Thus at his fall in 1541, not to speak of the cardinalate and ecclesiastical peerage of his nephew, Odet, or the governorship of his brother, La Rochepot, he was by inheritance, grant, or acquisition, Seigneur of Montmorency, Beaumont, Valmondois, Damville, Montbéron, Fère, Conflans, L'Isle-Adam, and a score of other places; he was Governor of the Bastille, Governor of Languedoc, First Baron of France, Knight of the Order of St. Michael, member of the Council, Grand Master, and Constable. He thus gave practical shape to the theory that the servant is worthy of his hire.

It was under the ægis of such splendour that the young Coligny grew up. Born the third son on the 16th of February, 1519, in the castle of Châtillon-sur-Loing, he remained there with his brothers for some eleven years. His half-brother and two half-sisters of the family of Mailly were also at Châtillon, but left during the period. His tutor was Bérauld, the friend of Erasmus and the frequenter of the Humanist circles of Paris. Like so many of their number, though not a little sympathetic to religious reform, he remained

(21 *July*, 1562)

Vre̅ entierement bon et bien
affectionne amy. Chastillon

(25 *April*, 1550)

(5 *June*, 1569)

to the end a Humanist, and a member of the Roman Church. No such definite opinion, on the other hand, can be vouchsafed as to the religious convictions of Coligny's mother, Louise of Montmorency. There is little or no proof that she was a Protestant.[1] She probably belonged rather to the school of thought represented by Margaret of Navarre. Her influence in the education of her son, no doubt, was great. Its nature is indicated in her selection of the liberal-minded Bérauld. Unfortunately, we have but few details to build on. We only know that she lived in semi-seclusion with her children until 1530. In this year, on the suggestion of her brother Anne, she was called to court as lady-in-waiting to the new Queen, Eleanor. With her went the young Gaspard. The second son, Odet, who took orders, was created Cardinal on the marriage of the Duke of Orleans and Catherine de' Medici in 1533, Archbishop of Toulouse in 1534, and in the following year Bishop of Beauvais, and so Peer of France. This and the death of the eldest, Peter,[2] left Gaspard head of the house. Henceforth he assumed the title of Châtillon.[3]

Our knowledge of his early years at court is almost confined to a letter written by him to Bérauld. In it he told how the world was disturbed by wars and rumours of wars, how the King rode eager to the chase, and how he himself was sometimes a witness of these scenes. "But," added he, "I give a greater care to the reading of Cicero and the Tables of Ptolemy under M. du Maine, who, adopting another method than Tagliacarne, has added thereto cosmography, especially in what concerns the longitude of places, and therewith meridians and parallels."[4] This is the letter of a student, and

---

[1] E. Marcks, *Gaspard von Coligny*, 8.

[2] The exact date of Peter's death is unknown. It was probably subsequent to Odet's adoption of an ecclesiastical career. See Marcks, 16, note.

[3] He almost invariably signed his letters "Chastillon," and was spoken of by his contemporaries as "M. l'Admiral" or "M. de Chastillon." In official documents, however, he used the name of "Coulligny"; an exception is the "Chastillon" of the treaty of Hampton Court. He spelt it "Coulligny" until 1563 (though his seal bore the inscription Gaspard de *Colligny*), later "Colligny." It is an open question whether his signature is to be read "G. Coulligny (Colligny)" or "G. d(e) Coulligny (Colligny)," some considering the stroke which passes over the G and cuts the C as a D, others as a mere flourish or part of the C.

[4] Delaborde, i. 33, 575; and Herminjard, iii. 219.

suggests little love of pleasure. But then Coligny was only a boy of fifteen, and moreover was writing as a pupil to his late master. It is clear, too, that this somewnat stoic attitude did not last. The gossipings of Brantôme as well as other records agree that Coligny was not averse to the distractions of court life. What life at the Valois court was, we know. It has been depicted often enough, and no one has given us a truer insight into the ideas which ruled in that delicate, Pagan world, than M. Maulde la Clavière in his faithful if vivacious sketches of the women of the Renaissance. If we turn to the reports of the foreign agents and ambassadors, the impression is the same.[1] All—the more sober as well as the more curious— bear witness to the general moral laxity. It is with something of surprise that we meet Coligny's own brother, Cardinal Odet, among the throng of pleasure-seekers. The patron and protector of Rabelais, he had his Rabelaisian moods. In 1547 he and his uncle, with the King and the Cardinal of Guise, took part in what the shocked Ambassador of Ferrara called a revel of Sardanapalus; the Cardinal of Ferrara, more virtuous or more seemly, refused to be present.[2] Five years later he was still a participant in pleasures which, if comparatively innocent, were at least unclerical. Thus in December, 1552, he was awakened at the dead of night, and swept along in a rout of churchmen and courtiers.[3] But then, in the sixteenth century, a Cardinal's hat did not always hide a monk.

Such scenes, however, by no means show things at their worst. A more melancholy picture is drawn by the Mantuan Ambassador: it is of a King diseased and wearing himself out in the pursuit of pleasure; a mistress, the Duchess of Étampes, handed over by Francis I. to the embraces of his favourite, Brissac; a court from which jealous husbands were dragging their wives; and a Queen, miserable and deserted, trying to lure them back again, hoping thereby to gain the favour of her amorous sons and other gentlemen, " in order

---

[1] In the Farnese collection at Naples, 765 a, is to be found an odd leaf in Spanish without name or date, but evidently written before the fall of the Constable in 1541. It gives a not unrealistic sketch of two bathing scenes where the court disported itself with the unforced gaiety of Pan and the Nymphs.

[2] Modena Francia, 25.

[3] Despatch of 28th Dec. 1552: Modena Francia, 29.

that she too might live, poor woman."[1] This, in a word, was the Valois court, the world in which Coligny lived. It helps to explain why the Admiral, with a temperament naturally austere, only turned to Calvinism late in life. It was hard for a youth to escape from the lax habits and low ideals which were of the very air he breathed.

There were, however, other influences at work, and they proved more lasting. Firstly, there was the New Learning. It was in nearly every instance the starting-point for the great religious reformers. And it cannot be doubted that Coligny's intercourse with the French Humanists prepared his mind for the acceptance of Protestantism. Another and subtle influence was the character and fortunes of his uncle. Anne of Montmorency, stiff and unbending, believed in royal absolutism. He worshipped order and authority. And it is certain that when Coligny emerges from the comparative obscurity of his early life, he bears many of the traits of the Constable. He was to a large extent the inheritor of his qualities and political ideas.

During these early years, as later, Coligny must have been in constant contact with the staid and dark presence of Anne, both at the court and Chantilly. Here his splendid relative in his new Renaissance mansion, rich with the treasures of Italy and Flanders, and in his château of Écouen, "a princely howse and worth the seeinge,"[2] lived in almost regal state. And Gaspard undoubtedly acquired here as well as at the court that taste for art and architecture which was to enrich in after years the castle of Châtillon. At a somewhat later date, Catherine de' Medici wrote "to my cousin the Duke of Florence," begging him to welcome the Seigneurs of Châtillon, "their chief desire being to see your town of Florence and the antiquities which are there."[3]

In 1539, Coligny made his first public appearance. Peace had come. The world-strife of Hapsburg and Valois seemed

[1] Mantua, Archivio Gonzaga, 638.
[2] Howard of Effingham, Wotten, and Throckmorton, 24th May, 1559; Forbes, i. 103. Chantilly was finished in 1530; Écouen was built some time between 1535 and 1547.
[3] 28th Sept. 1546: de la Ferrière, *Lettres de Catherine de Médicis*, i. 17.

ended.   Charles V., impatient of rebellion, was eager to start for the Low Countries.   His route was to lie through the territories of his ancient adversary : through France.   And it was to meet him at the Spanish frontier that on a Wednesday of early November the Dauphin set out from the capital.   In his train was the young Châtillon, dressed in the black and silver livery of his leader.[1]   This, as we have said, and as far as we are aware, was his début before the world.   But it was more.   It was the first recorded intimacy between him and the future Henry II.   In the actual ceremonies that followed at Bayonne, Coligny figured as Ensign of the Company of the Constable.   His position, therefore, was such as to bring him into close contact with the melancholy [2] Emperor, whom he was to meet in such dramatic fashion sixteen years later. But of details we know nothing.   The attention of his contemporaries was absorbed in observing the great actors.   And as yet Coligny was a mere cipher.   And so, we watch him ride out from Paris, and then—he is lost to view among the other twenty thousand French horsemen who are said to have accompanied Charles V. on his way.

Indeed, at this period it is easier to follow the career of Odet.   He was a Cardinal, and so a prominent figure.   He took a distinguished part in all state functions.   He was among those who accompanied Charles V. in his entry into Paris.   He was appointed to receive Cardinal Alexander Farnese, grandson of Paul III. and Papal Envoy.   At a court joust the latter was given a place between him and the Duke of Lorraine ; it was felt to be a special honour.[3]   Time and again he represented his uncle.   And already Anne of Montmorency was proposing to provide his nephew with fresh dignities.   His plan was simple.   Languedoc was his. Provence was his in the person of his relative, the Count of Tende, the Governor.   If only he could establish Odet as Legate at Avignon he would be master of the south of France.

---

[1] Despatch of G. B. da Gambara, 16th Nov.: Mantua, Archivio Gonzaga, 638.

[2] "Mons. Contestabile ha scritto che la M^ta dell' Imp^re sta molto melanconica et retirata con li suoi, et che cura poco alcuno piacere" (Letter from Loches, 10th Dec. 1539) : Modena Francia, 15.

[3] Bishop of Ivrea to Pope, 5th Jan. : Parma, Carteggio Farnesiano.

This was his dream.[1]   And he set to work with his usual
disregard for the feelings or rights of others.   The position,
viewed in the light of later history, was piquant: Anne, the
stubborn and fanatical Catholic, labouring to bestow almost
supreme ecclesiastical power on Odet, the future Protestant.
If he had succeeded, French history might have been different.
Even the immediate consequences might have been great.
The Legation of Avignon in ambitious hands, with a France
close by peculiarly sensitive to all appeals to her Gallican
liberties, might have developed into a national Patriarchate—
into anything!   This Rome saw, and refused her consent.
But even her reluctance might have been worn down in time.
Fortunately for her, the Constable's influence was on the wane.
Already in 1540 the reins were slipping from his grasp.   In
1541 he was no longer dangerous.   And so, on the death of
the old Legate, Cardinal Farnese took his place.[2]

The Constable thus lost a coveted prize.   Nor was this
all.   His disgrace entailed far more.   Family preponderance,
schemes of immediate aggrandisement, hopes, ambitions—all
were shipwreck.   Happily something was saved.   It was the
friendship of the Dauphin.   One of the most curious facts of
sixteenth-century history is this doglike fidelity of Henry II.
It survived good and evil fortune.   The most acute observers
misread it.   They were confident that it must cool.   And yet
eighteen years of stress, appalling defeats like the battle of St.
Quentin, the heresy of the Colignys, could not shake it.   Nothing could shake it.   Viewed from a purely ethical standpoint,
it was a moral quality.   It was equally an intellectual failing.

This affection, however, was as yet only in its initial
stages.   Coligny, nevertheless, had already profited by it.
He was to do so still more, now that he could expect little
direct aid from his uncle.   It was, in fact, his one asset.   It
opened to him the profession of arms.   It gave him his one
chance of a career.   It was not neglected.   In 1542 he made
his first campaign.   It was directed against Luxemburg, and

[1] Bobba to Duke of Mantua, 24th Sept. 1539 : Mantua, Arch. Gonz., 638.
[2] For this question see Decrue, *Anne de Montmorency*, i. 390 ; Parma, Carte Farn.
(letter of 24th Oct. 1539) ; Vatican, Nunz. di Francia Arm., I.A. 209 ; Barberini
Library (copy of corresp. of Card., Farnese, *passim*) ; Naples, Carte Farn., 737.

was under the leadership of the Duke of Orleans, brother of the Dauphin. In 1543 he followed the Dauphin himself in the war of Flanders. He had now a recognised position in the latter's suite. He was Gentleman of the Bedchamber. From the very first, he gave signal evidence of his martial ardour and contempt of danger. We find him thrusting lustily and being thrust at, shot in the trenches of Montmédy, and wounded in the neck at the siege of Binche. And through it all, he was in high spirits. " I make no doubt," he wrote to his aunt, " that you esteemed me the laziest fellow in the world for not having written you, after the promise I made you lately when taking leave, though I am little hindered by the service of the King. I pray you then excuse me. I am not one of the most diligent correspondents you have seen." [1] These lines are worth attention. They are one of the few examples of Coligny in a playful or even humorous mood. Two years later he showed a somewhat similar though more sardonic temper in dealing with Poulin: [2] " As to flight, I replied that I had not spoken of it, nor did I know how he could have been forced thereto, for I had not seen that any one had given chase." [3] But such instances are rare. And their rarity is all the more marked, because he has left behind a large correspondence, a description of the siege of St. Quentin, and a hundred recorded sayings. He was often vigorous, epigrammatic, but seldom humorous. He was far removed from the traditional type of sour-faced Puritan; but he had none of the light and tender touches of La Noue, the irrepressible gaiety of Henry IV., the humour, rooted in vanity, of Sully.

The year 1544 was still further to widen his experience. Tavannes and Martin du Bellay tell how the flower of the young nobility, and among them Coligny, hurriedly left the court for Italy, where they arrived in time to take part in the glorious victory of Cerisole. A few months later, in the struggle with the Imperialists in Champagne, the Dauphin gave him command of a regiment which had lost its leader. This was his first great step upward.

[1] Paris, Bibl. Nat. 3155, 74 (letter to Madame La Rochepot, 11th July, 1543).
[2] Better known to history under the title of Baron de la Garde.
[3] Delaborde, i. 579.

There can be no doubt that Coligny discovered himself for the first time on the field of battle. He was a man of action. He had found his *milieu*. "I heard him once say," wrote Brantôme, "that he was certainly favoured at court because of his uncle, the Constable, yet troubled himself little about its pleasures and favours, but went where blows and honour were given."[1] This, no doubt, accurately expressed his sentiments. It shows where his heart lay. And yet, the events of his life at court have a very real place in his history. Here are a few scenes taken at random. They are among the very few authentic accounts of his appearance in early years in tourneys and pageants, and thus of curious interest.

The first is a description of a court ball. "The King, with Madame d'Étampes on his arm, and with the Admiral following, left his apartments, which are on one side of the courtyard, and came to the banqueting chamber, which was on the other and on the ground floor. On entering, they found the Queen of France, the Dauphin and his wife, Madame Marguerite, and many other ladies. When the repast was over—it lasted a good two hours—they entered another room close by, set apart for dancing. It was hung with beautiful arras, and had a stage at one end for the ladies, and a barrier running its whole length to keep the crowd from impeding the dance. There was a gallery also for the fifers and young ladies of the court wishing to see, of whom there were many. When all had entered, dancing began. Madame d'Étampes led off with M. de Laval, and the Dauphin with the Countess of Vertus. There were many others, too, all dancing Italian measures, while M. de Châtillon had as partner the bride, who was very richly dressed."[2]

Equally striking is an account of a joust at which the King, the Queen, and a great company of ladies and gentlemen were present. "The Dauphin appeared, accompanied by M. de Brissac, M. d'Aumale, and the two Châtillons," wrote Alvarotto. "They were dressed in the German fashion, and armed with beautifully gilt corselets. Over this was a short cape of green velvet with a hood, fastened at the neck, the sides being thrown

[1] Brantôme, iv. 315.
[2] Alvarotto, from Paris, 4 Jan. 1546 : Modena Francia, 22.

2

back over the shoulders, the better to shoulder the lance. The hat was of green silk with white feathers. The lance was of ash. The sash was of white and green velvet, the colours of the Dauphin. They were in single file. Before them were a couple of drummers and fifers, a sergeant dressed in German fashion in green velvet, fifteen arquebusiers . . . and six pages. . . . When they had paraded the ground, they took up their station as defenders of the barrier. There then appeared M. d'Enghien, M. de Laval, four drummers, two fifers, and a great company of cavaliers, who were also on foot. . . . After them came the Signor Pietro Strozzi, the Signor Cornelio Bentivoglio, the Count of Mirandola, M. de Sipierre, and Messer Paris Conegrano. . . . . After their march past, they presented themselves at the barrier, two by two. First came the Dauphin and M. d'Aumale, with drums beating, against M. d'Enghien and M. de Laval. They fought with lances of ash, but very gingerly, it must be confessed, and then with rapiers. MM. de Brissac and Châtillon then met the Count of Nesle, who has been made Marquis by His Majesty on his marriage with Mademoiselle de Rieux, and a brother of M. d'Aumale. Then followed M. de la Bordighiera and the other Châtillon against the Signor Pietro Strozzi and the Signor Cornelio Bentivoglio." [1]

These scenes are historically very suggestive. In the first place, Coligny's position, as revealed here, is little less than astonishing. Not only is he at court, but in the very forefront. The reasons for this lie deep down in the character of Francis I. He was a despot, but of a type far removed from that of his Italian contemporaries. He could never have sat for Machiavelli's Prince. His feelings were shallow rather than evanescent. He was neither very passionate, nor very energetic, nor very sincere. He was active only in his opposition to Charles V., and in his pursuit of pleasure. Even the promptings of jealousy were kept well in hand. He was a kingly Laodicean. And thus it was that the Dauphin was allowed to build up a semblance of a party, and Coligny, the nephew of a disgraced minister, played a rôle at court.

Another fact disclosed by these letters is Coligny's inti-

[1] Alvarotto, from Paris, 1st Feb. 1546: Modena Francia, 22.

macy with the Dauphin. He belonged, it is evident, to the inner circle. He was his friend, and, as Brantôme remarks, his favourite. According to his own statement, he was even the means of gaining a share of this favour for the Count of Aumale.[1] And yet it is easy to misread the significance of this. There is nothing to show that the Dauphin was sensibly drawn toward his young follower. There could hardly have existed between the two any deep or natural sympathy. If there had, the latter would not have slipped so quickly into the background when Anne returned to power in 1547. His real influence, indeed, during these years, was vicarious rather than personal. He was interesting to the Dauphin because he was the representative of his uncle. The Constable strongly appealed to the future Henry II.; he had age and the glamour of military successes.

We now come to Coligny's acquaintance with Francis of Lorraine, Count of Aumale, and later, Duke of Guise. This is by no means the only time we find their names together. They rode in the same jousts,[2] fought side by side in the northern campaigns.[3] Several years earlier, Aumale had made mention of the other in his correspondence.[4] And Coligny himself, on the eve of the Civil Wars, declared—obviously referring to the Guises: " It is well known on what good terms we were at the beginning of the reign of Henry II., and how easy it would have been to continue so."[5] These details, taken together, give a certain colour to the assertions of the contemporary historian of Coligny, and of Brantôme. The former explains that " in their youth they had been linked together with singular familiaritie, insomuch that to testifie their friendship with all, they went appareled in like rayment."[6] Brantôme, with an eye to the picturesque, works in the details. " They

---

[1] Brantôme, iv. 288.

[2] Alvarotto, 3rd Jan. 1546 : Modena Francia, 22.

[3] Decrue, i. 422 (Anne to La Rochepot, 9th Aug.).   [4] Delaborde, i. 36, note 2.

[5] Coligny to Anne of Mont., 6th May, 1562 : Condé, iii. 441.

[6] The author of the work, *Gasparis Colinii Castellonii* . . . *vita*, published in 1575, is probably Hotman : see Delaborde, i. 570. The translation used here appeared in 1576 under the title : " The Lyfe of the most godly, valeant, and noble Capteine and maintener of the trew Christian Religion in Fraunce, Jasper Colignie Shatilion, sometyme greate Admirall of Fraunce." Translated out of Latin by A. Golding.

were both, when young, in the latter years of the reign of
Francis I., and well on into that of Henry II., such great
comrades, friends, and confederates at court, that I have heard
several say who had seen them, that they were wont to dress
in the same livery and attire, and be on the same side in
tourneys, mimic fights, running at the ring, and masquerades,
committing more extravagant follies than all the rest, and
that ill, for they were clumsy players and unlucky in their
games." [1]   These incidents may well be true, especially as the
livery worn was probably that of the Dauphin.[2]   And yet, as
told thus, they are misleading.   They are facts—but out of
perspective.   They give the impression that this intimacy was
in some way out of the common.   Of other early friendships
—not a word!   It stands out alone, baldly, without relief.
And terms are applied to it, especially by Brantôme, which
savour of exaggeration.   The temptation to do so was irresistible.   The change from harmony to strife, love to hatred, was
so startling, so dramatic!   It almost cried aloud for dramatic
handling.[3]   There is no real evidence, however, that Coligny's
relations with Aumale were peculiarly close.   They were
certainly not unique.   They probably differed neither in kind
nor degree from those with others, notably Brissac.[4]   This
error is the more unfortunate, as it has led modern writers to
wholly ignore his deep attachment to another.   This other
was Peter Strozzi.   He belonged to the family which La Noue,
with pardonable enthusiasm, calls " that magnanimous race of
Strozzis." [5]   Though a Florentine and an exile, he was never
mistaken for an adventurer.   Brilliant and resourceful, he was
a thorough soldier.   He was brave, always—sometimes rash.

[1] Brantôme, iv. 286.

[2] For instance, Alvarotto writes on the 19th of March, 1546 : " Sua Altezza capo
di 40 gentilhuomini comparse circa alle 3 hore dopo mezo giorno, vestita di calze di
panno biancho, schiete con taffeta, giupone di raso biancho tagliato, etc. etc. ; del
medesimo concerto erano vestiti Mons. d'Aumala et un' Satiglione." Modena
Francia, 22.

[3] Brantôme, in his sketch of Coligny and Guise, confessedly strove after effect,
seeking for contrasts : " ny plus ny moins qu'un bon lapidaire oppose deux beaux
diamantz l'un contre l'autre pour mieux les aprécier," iv. 285.

[4] Years later Coligny expressed to Brissac his desire "to continue and preserve
our ancient friendship." Paris, Bibl. Nat. 20461, 139.

[5] *Discours politiques et militaires*, 86 (edit. 1587).

Sudden impulses, and the coursing of hot southern blood in his veins, carried him away. "Domenico Ariano," wrote Alvarotto of one who had been with Strozzi in an engagement, "greatly commends the Prior of Capua[1] for his prudence, judgment, and valour, but Peter Strozzi rather for his valour than his judgment."[2] Such was Strozzi. His friendship was the romance of Coligny's early life. Taken in connection with his intimacy with the Constable and Brissac, it throws an interesting light on his character. His grave and deliberate temper led him instinctively to seek the society of those of greater age than himself.

In the spring of 1545 a great naval expedition was organised. The plan was for the Mediterranean and Channel fleets to combine and fall on England. Strozzi was full of the venture. Furnishing a ship at his own expense, he set out alone from Marseilles, and, after many exciting moments, appeared off the Norman coast. Coligny also took part in the expedition. Active operations began. In the middle of August there was a brush with the enemy. Strozzi, daring as ever, was only extricated from an awkward position by his brother, the Prior of Capua. Nothing daunted, however, he gave all the blame to Poulin, the most experienced sailor of the expedition.[3] Coligny, as was only natural, threw himself enthusiastically into the quarrel. Fortunately there is an unsigned account of his action, in his own beautifully clear handwriting.[4] He was bursting with high spirits. His strictures on Poulin were marked by all the vehemence and exuberance of youth. "I would rather be dead and a hundred feet under ground," he cried, "than have acted so." He was evidently a lusty hater.

A few months later, in September, the Duke of Orleans died. And the two friends were chosen to announce the news to Catherine de' Medici, and Margaret, sister of the Dauphin.[5]

---

[1] Leon Strozzi, brother of Peter Strozzi.

[2] 20th Aug. 1545 : Modena Francia, 21.

[3] I hope to publish shortly a detailed account of this expedition and subsequent quarrel drawn from documents in Modena, Mantua, Naples, and Rome.

[4] The original is in Paris, Bibl. Nat. fr. 3157, 31. It is given in full, and curiously misinterpreted by Delaborde, i. 577.

[5] Letter of 14th Sept. 1545 : Modena Francia, 21.

This same Margaret, in after years, married the man who
inflicted on Coligny his first great military defeat: Emmanuel
Philibert, Duke of Savoy, and victor of St. Quentin. She is
even better known as the patron of L'Hôpital and friend of
the Huguenots. And in nothing was her kindliness of heart
shown more than by obtaining for the Admiral in later years
the recession of part of his ancient patrimony in Bresse.[1]
She was one of those rare types, which the late house of
Valois occasionally produced.

Coligny and Strozzi were now almost inseparable. Fortunately, the history of their intercourse is not all of a colour.
It has its lighter side. It reveals the former in his playful
moments. He had his own ideas of the nature of a joke,
which smack more of the camp than the court. They amply
justify Brantôme in his dictum that he was a clumsy player.
On the evening of the 19th of April, 1546, "Châtillon in fun
fired a crossbow at Peter Strozzi, and struck him on the forehead with a pellet of earth. He was dazed for a while; they
even feared for his life; but, thank God! little other damage
was done."[2] If he was a lusty hater, he was a no less
dangerous friend.

Meanwhile, Coligny was steadily gaining in power. He
was becoming a personality. The reasons are obvious.
Hostility between Francis I. and the Dauphin was now a
force in politics. From a passing phase it had grown to a
habit. Their jealousy in regard to Diana of Poitiers, the
discontent of the son at his exclusion from all share in the
government, and the resentment of the father at the appearance
of a hostile party, amply explain this change of feeling. The
Constable, too, was a disturbing factor. He focused their
differences. On the one hand, the King was unalterably
determined never to recall the disgraced favourite. On the
other, the Prince, moved by a natural sympathy and by
disgust at a series of not too brilliant campaigns, was no
less eager for his return. Under these circumstances, it was
inevitable that Coligny should be pushed to the front. He
was prized equally by his uncle and the Dauphin. He served

[1] Haag, iii. 142.
[2] Tomaso Sandrini, 29th April, 1546: Mantua, Arch. Gonz., 640.

as a link between the two. Here is how an acute observer summed up the situation: " His Highness shows himself a more pronounced follower of the Constable every day, and freely come daily recommendations of this and that individual from the Constable, and Châtillon, his nephew, who is with His Highness, bears letters, and publicly presents people to him in the name of his uncle."[1]

So much for royal differences. More interesting, though less remarked at the time, was the first hint of division between Coligny and Aumale. There was nothing like rupture. They still appeared together in attendance on the Dauphin at state ceremonies, at the christening of the child of Catherine de' Medici, at a Spanish duel in July, and on many other occasions. Nevertheless, there was a cleavage. It had arisen out of a proposal to marry Claude of Lorraine, brother of Aumale, to Louise of Brézé, daughter of Diana of Poitiers. The object was plain. It was to gain the ear of the mistress of the heir to the throne. The house of Guise, in fact, were industriously building for the future, and, like so many ambitious families, were not too nice as to means. Coligny was more scrupulous. When questioned by his friend, he expressed himself strongly. " He made more account," he told him, " of an ynch of good name, than of never so great riches,"[2] or, as Brantôme sharpens up the epigram, " of an inch of authority and favour with honour, than an armful without."[3] This could hardly have been the reply expected. It caused deep resentment, and no wonder. Plain speaking has much to recommend it, especially when, as here, Coligny set up a standard of honour to which he himself, both in his own and his daughter's marriage, rigidly adhered. Still, it puts a severe strain on friendship, which the latter, in this instance, did not survive.

Viewed by itself, too, this scene is interesting. Here is the typical Coligny, masterful, passionate, almost brutal in his very directness of speech. He was to be the same through life. Difficulties were met, not evaded. Ends were gained

---

[1] Alvarotto, 5th May, 1546: Modena Francia, 22.
[2] *The Lyfe of Jasper Colignie Shatilion* (1576).
[3] Brantôme, iv. 287.

by overbearing, we might almost say flouting, opposition—
certainly not by finesse or intrigue.

Events now moved quickly. One, so far ignored, and in
fact unknown,[1] we shall give in some detail. It is Coligny's
voyage to Italy. It reminds us irresistibly of the journey of
the young Milton a century later. For both—highly cultured,
lovers of art, and educated in the most "humane" circles in
their several countries—Italy must have had strong attractions.
The appreciation of sensuous beauty, ardour, and youthful
impulses, were still dominant. Neither, as yet, had felt to
the full the austerer teachings of Protestantism.

Coligny, it will be remembered, had already visited Italy,
but only in breathless haste, and as a soldier. Peace, however, which was concluded with England on the 7th of June,
1546, gave him his chance. On the 22nd of August, the
Ambassador of Ferrara wrote as follows: "Tomaso del
Vecchio has told me that Peter Strozzi, after the return of the
Admiral to France, will take post for Italy, and will be
accompanied by Châtillon and his brother Andelot, nephews
of the Grand Constable, and favourites—more especially
Châtillon—of the Dauphin, who has given them leave."[2]
Further details were not long in coming. "Châtillon, who
was to accompany Peter Strozzi to Italy, will leave soon,
and will stop at Ferrara, and then pass on to see Naples,
Rome, and all the other countries. His Eminence[3] would
remind your Excellency,[4] though it seems hardly necessary to
do so, to pay him every attention and make good cheer,
seeing whose nephew he is, and because he is a dependant of
the Dauphin, to whom he is very dear."[5] The news was
still more precise on the 1st of October. "I wrote to your
Excellency, and afterwards confirmed it, that Peter Strozzi
had gone to Germany. This is true. But he may only have
gone to see the armies and to pass thence into Italy to fight
the Count of San Segondo, as I have written. For Châtillon
and the Count of Mirandola have said that they are to be
there all together; that is to say, Peter Strozzi, Andelot, and

---

[1] See Marcks, i. 31.   [2] Modena Francia, 23.
[3] Ippolito d'Este, Cardinal of Ferrara.   [4] The Duke of Ferrara.
[5] Despatch of 19th Sept. : Modena Francia, 23.

they two. Peter Strozzi, I am informed, has got the Dauphin to ask the authorities at Venice for a safe conduct, so as to be able to go there. But I know neither for how long, nor why, nor whether he has obtained it. The reason may be that, as Châtillon and Andelot intend to go everywhere in Italy for pleasure, he wants to be able to accompany them. These latter, I hear, with this end in view, have set aside 14,000 scudi, and propose to be away about a year. All this annoys their uncle the Grand Constable, especially as both will be gone. If it had only been one, he would have stood it. Châtillon, so the Orator of Venice affirms, has letters of introduction from the Dauphin to all the Princes of Italy."[1]

These plans, however, were speedily changed. A little previous to this, Andelot, eager to see the German Protestant army, had slipped away from court with only two companions. Sitting down to dinner one morning in Augsburg, he found himself in the company of some Germans and a Lorrainer who had held high command among the Lansquenets in the French service. The conversation happened to fall on the number and merits of Italian leaders. Andelot, who had heard them name over a few, suggested that they had forgotten Peter Strozzi. The other was up in arms in a moment. He had old scores to pay off. Strozzi, he cried, was a poltroon, and had never done anything for the King. Andelot turned on him hotly. He warned him to be careful; the Italian was his friend, and he would hear nothing to his dishonour. They began to wrangle, then to brawl. The Lorrainer in a rage threw a cup of malmsey in the other's face. Those present did their best to calm matters. They appealed to Andelot. In Germany, they averred, an insult made in one's cups was never taken seriously. It was all in vain. He refused to be pacified. Meeting by chance next day in a hostelry, they again quarrelled, and drew swords. In the mêlée that followed, Andelot, either more skilful or more fortunate, slew his adversary;[2] then, afraid of the consequences, fled to Geneva.[3]

---

[1] Modena Francia, 23.

[2] These details are given by Alvarotto, 3rd Oct. : Modena Francia, 44.

[3] Tomaso Sandrini, 11th Oct. : Mantua, Arch. Gonz., 640.

Here Coligny joined him. But their plans had to be changed.
The younger had now to seek and gain pardon. He therefore returned at once to France. The elder went on alone
to Italy.

His coming created the liveliest concern. It synchronised
suspiciously with Strozzi's appearance on the scene. For this
latter, leaving the Protestant camp on the 6th of October,[1] had
passed through Bâle,[2] and arrived in Venice before the middle
of the month.[3] Don Juan de Vega had assured the Emperor
that they had both come, with the knowledge of the Dauphin,
to seek out the Grand Turk and intrigue. Coligny, therefore,
had no sooner set foot in Milan than he was visited by the
Governor. When he declared that he was travelling with the
sole object of seeing the various cities of Italy, he was not
believed. " I have likewise told off a secret agent," wrote Don
Ferrante Gonzaga to Charles v., " to follow the said Châtillon
everywhere, and watch his movements, in order to discover,
if may be, the reason of his coming. For seeing the number
of coincidences, I think it is with other ends in view than that
of pleasure, as he says." [4]

Leaving Milan, Coligny reached Venice on the 31st of
October,[5] where, some years earlier, his brother Odet had
been received with great distinction.[6] Hardly, however, had
he fulfilled his first duty of visiting the Signory than he fell
seriously ill. He had not recovered by the middle of
November.[7] It is quite certain that, during his stay, he met
Peter Strozzi, who kept flitting backwards and forwards,
absorbed, apparently, in his quarrel with the Count of San
Segondo, but in reality wide awake to the least hint of trouble.
But we can say no more. He was still followed by Don
Ferrante's sleuth-hound—but where ? [8] For nearly two months

[1] 14th Oct., Milan : Parma, Carteggio Gonzaga, 42.

[2] Letter of Nuncio in Switzerland, 29th Oct.: Milan, Doc. Dominio Spagnolo.

[3] L. Tridapale from Venice, 16th Oct.: Mantua, Arch. Gonz., 1478.

[4] Letter of 17th Oct.: Parma, Carteggio Gonzaga, 42.

[5] L. Tridapale from Venice, 31st Oct.: Mantua, Arch. Gonz., 1478.

[6] Paris, Bibl. Nat. Italien, 1715, Regis. 2, p. 22.

[7] V. Amanio to Pier Luigi Farnese from Venice, 13th Nov.: Parma, Carteggio di
Pier Luigi Farnese.

[8] Don Ferrante, in a letter of the 4th of December, mentions Coligny, but does not
say where he is : Parma, Cart. Gonz., 42.

we lose sight of him, though he was probably still in Venice or its neighbourhood, detained by his delicate state of health.[1] When he appears again, it is in Ferrara. It was now January, 1547. Here is an account of his visit from the hand of the Duke: "I would have you know that Châtillon came here. He had expressed a wish to remain four or six days. But things falling out as they did in Genoa,[2] he was warned by the Count of Mirandola and Peter Strozzi that it would be well for him to go and do his best in this revolution for the service of the King. During the short time that he was with me, I did not fail to cultivate him, giving him and his party a lodging to themselves, here at court, and treating him to the best of my ability. It was certainly a disappointment to me that he left so suddenly, for I had planned to give him a banquet and let him enjoy the pleasures of the chase. However, I think he left well satisfied, for he could see the good-will I had to please him. Nor did I fail to provide him at parting with my coaches. I also gave him such advice as I judged to be for the service of the King. I mentioned, among other things, that it was not my pleasure to have recourse to arms, even though Genoa was in tumult, before hearing from the Prince of Melphi[3] whether this would turn to the advantage of His Majesty. I was the more convinced that unreasonable and unseasonable hostilities against the Emperor would not profit the King, inasmuch as it would disturb a real peace, which, if report spoke true, was prized by the King, and, to tell the truth, was very necessary for the good and quiet of the whole of Christendom. This opinion seemed sound to the aforesaid Châtillon, who thereupon went away. I promised to let him know if anything should turn up which might benefit His Majesty."[4]

Thus Coligny drove away in the ducal coach, and is lost to

[1] If he had gone south from Venice in November or December, he would no doubt have broken his journey at Ferrara; yet his first visit there was in January, 1547.

[2] The Count of Fiesco, on his own initiative, had started a revolution in favour of France, which was quickly quelled. For a few hours, however, he had had part of the city in his hands.

[3] French Governor of Piedmont.

[4] Minute of letter of Ercole II., Duke of Ferrara, to Ippolito d'Este, Cardinal of Ferrara, 11th Jan. 1547: Modena, Arch. di Stato.

view. He may have remained in North Italy. A letter we
are about to quote suggests it; the news sent from Milan in
October that the object of his voyage was to see the Lombard
cities [1] suggests it too; and perhaps it was during this period
that he visited Mantua.[2] Yet he may equally have gone to
Florence,[3] or farther south. The letters of Don Ferrante
Gonzaga, Governor of Milan, might throw some light on the
question. Unfortunately, some of them are missing. When
Coligny reappears, it is again in Ferrara, and it is again the
Duke who furnishes the details. "As I wrote you, Châtillon
was here lately, and left unexpectedly, owing to the affair of
Genoa. As he has now returned, besides lodging him and his
company in this my court, I have set myself to provide him
with all the diversions I can, such as country pastimes and the
listening to musical strains. To-day we have had a new, and
to my thinking a most delectable tragi-comedy. It was to
have been performed at carnival time. But when he did not
come as he had said, I had it held over till now, in order that
he might know the desire I had to honour him in all. For
these causes, and because of the goodwill I have shown him
and the gentlemen of his train, I think he will leave here well
satisfied." [4]

He was more than satisfied. What with a present of
horses and a thousand little attentions, he was in a state of
mind bordering on enthusiasm. The Cardinal of Ferrara thus
described his feelings on his return to the French court: "I
shall only tell you that Châtillon has expressed his satisfaction
so loudly, and has spoken and boasted so much of the very
courteous welcome you gave him, that it would be impossible
to say more. The King, the Queen, and all these ladies and
gentlemen, have questioned him, and have asked and heard,
with extraordinary good feeling and satisfaction, all that he

[1] A. Trotto from Milan, 21st Oct.: Modena, Arch. di Stato.

[2] He visited Mantua some time during his Italian voyage. See G. Conegrano from
Paris, 3rd June, 1547 : Mantua, Arch. Gonz., 640.

[3] No mention is made of Coligny's voyage in the despatches of the Florentine
Ambassador in the Arch. Medici. Through an oversight, we omitted to examine the
carteggio of the Duke.

[4] To Cardinal of Ferrara, 20th March, 1547 : Modena, Carteggio dei Principi
Estensi, 16.

had to tell them of your Excellency, your wife, and children. And you may feel assured that the courtesy and signs of love and gratitude, which you have shown this gentleman, have been well employed. For the honour he does you, and the expression of obligations which he says he is under, are beyond compare."[1] There is nothing which causes greater pleasure than the conferring of benefits. In course of time, marriage and politics turned the Duke of Ferrara into the natural enemy of Coligny and the Montmorencys. Yet he still retained pleasant recollections of former intimacy. On no other ground can we explain his real interest in Andelot, during the latter's long imprisonment in Milan, from 1551 to 1556.

Coligny had now finished with Italy. He, Strozzi, and all who had anything at stake, were already, or were soon to be, hurrying back to France. The King, after years of suffering, was nearing his end. On the 31st of March he died at Rambouillet.

[1] To the Duke of Ferrara, 1st May, 1547: Modena, Arch. di Stato.

CHAPTER II

MONTMORENCY *VERSUS* GUISE: STRUGGLE FOR PREDOMINANCE

Coligny Colonel - General of French Infantry — Power and Influence of Rival Houses compared—Knight of the Order of St. Michael—Marriage with Charlotte of Laval—Blockade of Boulogne—Break with Strozzi and Roche-sur-Yon—Dispute in the Boulonnais with Aumale — Military "Ordinances" — Chief Negotiator with England—Voyage to England—Unrewarded—Marriage of Condé with Coligny's Niece—Governor of Paris and Isle of France—Campaign of the Three Bishoprics—Admiral of France, 11th Nov. 1552—Guise fears a Coligny-Montmorency Ascendency in Italy, 1553—Battle of Renty; Quarrel of Coligny and Guise—Governor of Picardy — Chief Negotiator of Peace of Vaucelles — Interview with Charles v.— Resigns Colonelcy of French Infantry to Andelot, and Governorship of Paris and Isle of France to Francis of Montmorency—Renewal of War ; Coligny strikes the First Blow—Defence of St. Quentin, 3rd to 27th Aug. 1557—Coligny a Prisoner.

THE body of Francis I. lay unburied for forty days. And "during all the time between the death and sepulture of the said King, they made of him an effigy, and clothed it in fine vestments, with the crown and sceptre and other royal ornaments. And having placed it on an honoured bed, morning and evening at the accustomed hours they brought wherewith to dine and sup, with the same ceremonies and forms as they are wont with the living person of the King. And when this had been done for some days, they took away those royal vestments, and clothed it in mourning. And forty-eight friars stood by, and each day and all day long chanted Mass, and performed other devout offices for the safety of his soul." [1] It was during these days that the new order was ushered in. There were some changes in the *personnel* of the Government. Diana of Poitiers was installed in the semi-official position of mistress and confidante of the King. De

[1] Ruscelli, *Lettere di Principi*, i. 153, published in Venice 1562 (Casale to Paul III., 25th May, 1547).

Taix, who had engrossed two of the chief military charges,[1] was forcibly retired, Brissac becoming Grand Master of the Artillery, while to Coligny fell the coveted position of Colonel-General of the French Infantry. This was a dazzling prize. For though the Colonel-General officially ranked below the Marshals, in actual power he came next to the Constable. The first hint of war put at his disposal fifteen to thirty thousand men.

It was Coligny's uncle, however, who gained most. By a happy turn of the wheel he was again royal favourite, entrusted with the management of affairs. He had only one disappointment. On the day of the late King's death, the Papal Nuncio had written: "Your Eminence may believe that the real favourites and mignons of the new King are and shall be the Archbishop of Rheims and the Count of Aumale. For His Majesty is seen to love them most cordially, and at the moment has none but them about him."[2] When, therefore, Anne appeared on the scene, he found them ranged in solid phalanx round his master. Scheme as he might, he could never really dislodge them. And thus began the half-century of rivalry between the houses of Montmorency and Guise. The change did not come all at once. One of the Constable's first efforts was to push the claims of the Archbishop of Rheims to a Cardinal's hat.[3] But from the very outset the struggle was seen to be inevitable. One of the acutest observers in France immediately pointed out probable developments. "As to what may come of the rivalry between the Grand Constable and the house of Lorraine, all things are possible and even easy, seeing the natural tendencies of the nation, and the ordinary ways of the court." "The Constable and the younger members of that house, every day and every hour, give expression to their mutual affection. I have seen the Archbishop of Rheims make his court to his Excellency, and go to meet him, and accompany him to table, and dine with him. Yet all are of

[1] News of France (date uncertain, 1546–1547), written to d'Ezcurra: Paris, Arch. Nat. Fonds Simancas, K. 1487.

[2] Vatican, Nunziature di Francia, Arm. I. ii. 318.

[3] Dandino to Cardinal Farnese, 15th April: Naples, Carte Farn., 719, and Vatican, Nunz. di Francia.

opinion that in the end the house of Lorraine will beat him to the ground, though it cannot happen at once." [1]

The contest, however, was not so unequal as this suggests. It was ten years before the house of Guise won a real success. And then it was owing, not to superior force, but to the mistakes of their enemy. Bad generalship on the field of St. Quentin, and the Protestant leanings of the Colignys, lost the Montmorencys their predominance. The military genius of Francis of Lorraine made full use of the one, his brother the Cardinal dealt with the other. And yet, until 1557 the balance was singularly even. Royal favour, marriage, and the skilful manœuvring of sons and nephews, eventually provided the Constable with the resources of half the kingdom. He was supported by, among other families, those of Rohan, La Rochefoucauld, Ventadour, Candale, Nevers, La Tremouille, and Turenne. He and his nephew Odet divided between them two peerages, a cardinalate, and a dukedom. By his position as Grand Master, analogous to that of Prime Minister, he controlled the State. The office of Constable gave him command of the army. The Colonelcy of the French Infantry, the Admiralship of France, and the four great Governorships of Provence, Languedoc, Picardy, and the Isle of France, were also in his or family hands.

The Guises, powerful as they were, had hardly more to show. Their strength lay in their vast clerical influence. They were peculiarly an ecclesiastical house. They had as many as three cardinalates at one time, together with innumerable archbishoprics and bishoprics—eighteen in all.

Equally important was their international position. In the persons of the two Queen Marys they had a lien on Scotland. Another member of the family was head of the reigning house of Lorraine. This added to their dignity in the eyes of France and Europe. It made them born diplomatists. It gave them wide horizons, and equally regal ambitions. On the other hand, it laid them open to the charge of being foreigners, working for foreign ends. In the mouths of Huguenots, this was often mere scurrility. But sometimes it was true, and struck home. Moreover, their interests were too many. The

[1] Alvarotto, 23rd and 29th April : Modena Francia, 24.

consequence was divided energies. Thus at one and the same time they were to arouse a Montmorency and Huguenot opposition, to make Elizabeth their enemy, and almost alienate Philip II. Their supreme ability was shown in extricating themselves from difficulties, and making one policy and ambition support another. The brain of the family was Charles, Archbishop of Rheims and Cardinal of Lorraine. He was an eloquent speaker, a subtle intriguer, a facile theologian, a good administrator, and an experienced diplomatist. In a word, he was a far more able man than the Constable. But he was no more popular. " He is not well beloved," remarked the Venetian Soranzo, " he is insincere, and has a nature both artful and avaricious, equally in his own affairs as in those of the King." [1] Add to these defects that of cowardice, in an age which prized physical courage above all, and you have his personality.

Midway between the Montmorencys and the Guises were the Bourbon Princes and Diana of Poitiers, who devoted her energies to a balancing policy. She avoided all semblance of a breach. She preferred the subtler methods of finesse. With her the feminine passion for intrigue, more fatal in its results in the succeeding centuries, was already a force in French politics.

Thus the two principal houses, with their sounding titles, their ambitions, their illimitable power, stood face to face, and each new accretion of strength was ominous for France. About the year 1558 the Venetian Ambassador remarked that of the fourteen governorships of provinces, no less than nine were in the hands of the rival factions.[2] The " over-mighty " subject had come, and for the time the worst results were only delayed by the unswerving loyalty of Anne. Alvise Contarini might well be pardoned the touch of exaggeration when he exclaimed, with the knowledge come of three civil wars, that " in like manner as Cæsar would have no equal and Pompey no superior, these civil wars are born of the wish of the Cardinal of Lorraine to have no equal, and the Admiral and the house of Montmorency to have no superior." [3] Henry II., though he began to feel the tyranny of the system, bowed before it.

[1] Alberi, ii. 433.   [2] *Ib.* ii. 404.   [3] *Ib.* iv. 244.

3

While he intrigued in secret with Anne, he did not dare offend the Guises. What would it be when the reins of government were in the hands of a woman and child!

Coligny was appointed Colonel-General of the Infantry on the 29th of April, 1547. On the 6th of May he had an interview with the English Governor of Boulogne. France was on the lookout for any infraction of the treaty of peace. Coligny, therefore, protested strongly against the building of a double wall which would command the harbour. The reply was such as one might have expected : the wall was not a fort, only a jetty. It was far from satisfactory. Still, for the time Henry II. confined himself to remonstrance. He was determined to recover Boulogne. But the question of when and how could not be determined off-hand.

Toward the end of May the new Colonel-General and his friend Strozzi were created Knights of the Order of St. Michael, generally known as "the Order" or "Order of the King." Alluding to it in 1558, the Venetian Ambassador explained that "they (the Knights) are bound always to wear, hung from the neck, the figure of St. Michael in the act of wounding with his lance the devil who is under his feet. But on more solemn occasions it is worn attached to a great collar of gold, wrought in a pattern of scollop-shells with links between. It is the gift of the King to each Knight, and must be restored at death."[1] Its dignity steadily declined during the century, owing to the increase in the number of its members.[2] In 1547 its possession was still a distinguished honour.

But the principal event of the year was Coligny's marriage with Charlotte, daughter of Count Guy of Laval, and ward of the Constable. It took place in October. Determined on shortly after 1540, it had been delayed, no doubt owing to the disgrace of Anne. The bride, it was remarked, was somewhat lacking in beauty. But this did not damp the general gaiety. "There were present," wrote the Mantuan Ambassador,

[1] Alberi, ii. 410; cf. Le Laboureur, i. 368.

[2] *Mémoires de Soubise*, 50; letter of 3rd Feb. 1563, in Ehinger's *Franz Hotmann*; Paris, Bibl. Nat., filza 5, 253 ; Record Office, Foreign, xcvi. 1560. For presentation of Collar of Order to Edward VI., see *Papiers de Pot de Rhodes*, 146. In 1559, Condé was chosen to convey the insignia of the Order to Philip II. : Cathala Coture, i. 394. For engraving of Collar, see Ribaut's column of occupation of Florida.

"the King,[1] and all the gentlemen and ladies of the court. As Châtillon had no place suitable for the occasion, they dined sumptuously in the house of his Eminence the Cardinal of Ferrara. During the day there was running at the ring, and a game with dogs; in the evening they held a reception with great festivities, masquerades, and fine dresses. For four days more the revelry lasted; and every day new games and dresses. On the 22nd, Châtillon, with a good troupe of ladies and gentlemen of the court, conducted the bride to Châtillon, where, so they say, they are holding numerous festivities."[2] It is a curious conjunction of names: Châtillon, the wife of the Constable, the Cardinal of Ferrara. In after years no one did more to thwart his plans than the two latter.

Six months later Coligny was entrusted with the blockade of Boulogne. To his duties as Colonel-General of the Infantry he added those of lieutenant to his uncle La Rochepot, acting Governor of Picardy. The official Governor, Anthony of Vendôme, had been quietly set aside. The Constable wished the recovery of Boulogne to be a family matter. Coligny began by attemping a surprise, which failed.[3] His next effort was to build a fort opposite the English Tower of Order. He had to be content with this, and the honour of having it named after himself, Fort Châtillon. Anne of Montmorency was determined to be at hand when the final blow was struck, and at the moment he was busy elsewhere, crushing out the revolt of Bordeaux by "hanging, decapitation, torture, burning, the rack, and other means."[4] Coligny, however, was further solaced by being given command of fifty lances in the Royal Gendarmery, the permanent heavy cavalry force of the kingdom.[5] This was in November.

[1] Neither the King nor Queen was present (Alvarotto, 23rd Oct.: Modena Francia, 25).

[2] G. Conegrano, 25th Oct.: Mantua, Arch. Gonz., 640.

[3] "Intelligences of 2 espiales who were sent into Britanie and Normandie" British Museum, Harley, 353.

[4] Report of expedition of Anne to Bordeaux: Naples, Carte Farnesiane, 737.

[5] It was the ambition of the young noble to enter the ranks of the Gendarmery. See *Les Honnestes Loisirs de Messire François Le Poulchre, seigneur de la Motte Messemé*, 11. At a later date Coligny was in command of one hundred lances: Alberi, ii. 413. The company varied in size from thirty to one hundred, the number being generally reduced in time of peace, or when the treasury was empty. See Chartrier de

Some months earlier, his long friendship with Strozzi came to an end. The fault was not his. Andelot was primarily responsible. He had begun, or rather was continuing, a series of quarrels, which was only to cease with death. In many ways he was the ideal soldier of the sixteenth century. He was resourceful, chivalrous, brave. To a keen sense of honour he added a sincere and generous temper. On the other hand, he was obstinate and passionate to a degree. He was as haughty as Francis of Lorraine, without his compensating charm. He had the further defect of introducing the personal element into differences. If he had possessed some of the diplomatic finesse of his brother the Cardinal, the history of his house and Huguenotism might have been changed. On this occasion the quarrel was final and complete. It took place on the eve of his departure with Strozzi for Scotland in the spring of 1548.[1] The latter at once became the bitterest enemy of Coligny, the Constable, and the whole family. When he was mortally wounded before Thionville in 1558, the arm of Francis of Guise was round his neck.

Still more serious was Andelot's dispute with the Prince of Roche-sur-Yon. It arose over the proposed marriage of René, youngest son of the Duke of Guise, with the younger sister of Andelot's wife, Claude of Rieux. The Prince in a rage threatened to break his head. The other retorted that he wasn't the man to do it. Suddenly Roche-sur-Yon threw himself from his horse—drew—shouted to him to dismount. But Andelot was somewhat sobered by now. It was a serious thing to draw on a Prince of the Blood. While he hesitated, the Duke of Nemours and Enghien, who was with the Prince, tried to ride him down. In the mêlée which followed, a heavy cap and a coat of mail alone saved him. Fleeing wildly, and streaming with blood, he came upon Aumale and Henry, who were hurrying up. The King at once drew his sword, but he had no need to use it. The

Thouars, 86. In a statement in the Barberini Library, Rome (lvi. 96, 840), the men-at-arms are given as 2400, the archers as 3600, making 6000 in all. There were thus three archers to every two men-at-arms. M. Gigon, however, in speaking of the wars of religion, remarks that the "lance" consisted of one man-at-arms and one archer (*La bataille de Jarnac*, 5).

[1] Conegrano, 15th May: Mantua, Arch. Gonz., 641.

Prince with his companions, warned by Aumale, retired to
Paris. The quarrel raised the nice point of the relative
position of a mere noble and a Prince of the Blood.
Eventually a peace was patched up.[1] As was only to be
expected, it was hollow. And the effect of the quarrel can be
seen throughout the reign of Henry II. Some of the friction
between the Montmorencys and the Princes can be traced to
it. If it did not create, it at least accentuated hostility.

In 1549, France was ready. Coligny began operations in
the early spring. An attempt on one of the strongholds of
the enemy again failed. But the combined efforts of the
Constable and Henry resulted in the capture of all the outlying forts round the town. Boulogne was thus cut off from
Calais and isolated. Its only hope of rescue was from the
sea. Its reduction, now seemingly a mere matter of time,
was left to the sole charge of Coligny. On the 9th of
September he was created Lieutenant-General of the King in
the Boulonnais.

These successes rendered the Guise faction furiously angry.
They could not pretend to ignore them. There they were—
very real and substantial. Each explained them in his own
way. Charles, Archbishop of Rheims and Cardinal of Guise,
piously ascribed them to the will of God. Others, with a
better military knowledge, ridiculed the conduct of the
campaign. They declared that the camp, soldiery, commissariat, were in inextricable confusion.[2] We may well
believe it, for M. Decrue is very severe in his strictures on
later operations. Still, capable or not, the Constable had been
favoured by fortune, and that was everything.

So far the enmity between the two houses had been
veiled; it had not got beyond back-stair intrigues and secret
murmurings. It was now to advance a stage. Coligny, as
has been mentioned, was appointed Lieutenant-General in the
Boulonnais. But in addition, Francis of Lorraine was entrusted

---

[1] For this dispute, see Giustiniano, 1st March, 1549, Paris, Bibl. Nat., Regis. 3, 421;
Conegrano, 20th and last of February, 1549: Mantua, Arch. Gonz. ; Alvarotto, 18th
and 27th Feb., 1st June, and 5th July, 1549: Modena Francia, 26; Wotton, 23rd
Feb. 1549: Record Office, Foreign, iii. 589.

[2] Alvarotto, 13th and 25th Sept. : Mantua Francia, 26.

with the general supervision of military operations. Relying
on his somewhat vague powers, he claimed the right to preside
at a duel between two of the captains. Nothing could have
angered the other more. Though never anxious to assume
responsibilities, Coligny resented interference from whatever
quarter.[1] He therefore protested vigorously, and was supported
on an appeal to the King. The question was eagerly can-
vassed at court, and led to a scene in the apartments of Diana
of Poitiers. The Duchess of Aumale complained bitterly.
The King's mistress joined her. But the attack failed. The
Constable met it as he always did when directed from high
quarters: he was servile, apologetic, but hard as flint when it
came to concessions.

Coligny for his part had little time to devote to quarrels.
He was now laying the foundations of his fame as a soldier.
He exercised a sleepless vigilance. He crippled, though he
did not destroy, an important work of the enemy, the Dunette.
By new dispositions he converged on the port; entry became
difficult. Ronsard, with poetic licence, compared him to
Achilles, and the English to the trembling men of Troy.[2]
Another likened these latter to bloodthirsty Moors, whom
Coligny had to bring to reason by acting on the maxim, " to
the cruel, be cruel once and yet again." [3]

But it was in the handling of his own rank and file that he
revealed his genius. It was at this time that he began to
enforce that military code which is known by the name of his
" Ordinances," and which received the royal sanction in 1551.[4]
The soldiery of the sixteenth century was a dissolute, murderous, pillaging rabble. Friend and foe suffered alike. Here
is a lament on a visit of the friendly Imperialists to the town
of Strasburg in 1552—

> "Der Keyser kam auch mit kriegsmacht,
>   Den hat man eingeladen,
>   Blieb in der Statt nicht uber nacht,
>   Sein Volck that drauss viel Schaden." [5]

---

[1] For examples, see Delaborde, i. 80 and 243.   [2] Dubouchet, 364–368.
[3] " A cruel cruel et demy," Brantôme, vi. 18.
[4] Printed by Delaborde, i. 590.
[5] Kleinlawel's *Strassburgische Chronik*, 148. Cf. Sleidan's *Briefwechsel*, 258.

What made his task the more difficult was that he had to deal for the most part with raw levies. Many of the more seasoned troops had gone to Scotland.[1]

His "Ordinances" regulated the daily life of the common soldier. Their value, therefore, was great. They accustomed him to the rule of law. They dealt with his relations to his fellows, his captains, sergeants, merchants, and *vivandiers*. They provided for cases of looting, sack, robbery, desertion, cowardice, mutiny, sleeping while on duty, and cheating at cards. The punishment varied. For robbery, rape, looting of churches, and the graver crimes, it was hanging. Minor delinquencies were generally visited by the penalty of being "passé par les piques," that is to say, beaten with the haft of the pike or the butt of the arquebus. One section reveals the essentially religious temper of the man: "the soldier who shall take the name of God in vain shall be publicly pilloried [2] on three divers days, three hours at a time. And at the end he shall with bared head ask pardon of God." Other points are mentioned by Professor Marcks. No one in a scuffle was to raise the cry of his nation. Here we have a survival of earlier conditions, of a time when Normandy, Poitou, and Gascony were semi-independent kingdoms. Old prejudices were still vigorous. A call to local feeling was sufficient to awake memories and antagonisms difficult to lay. And again, no soldier in a quarrel was to use other weapon than his sword. This witnesses to the fact that quarrels were regulated, not forbidden. Wish as he might, Coligny hardly dared go further.[3]

These "Ordinances" prove him terribly stern. They are of a piece with his whole military career. He had a passionate hatred of disorder. He was the living embodiment of the policy of "thorough." He was "stark" in the old sense of the word; and yet not more so than circumstances demanded. He had his mission. He had, firstly, to break in a wild and turbulent class, civilise them, increase their efficiency. And he appealed to them in the language they knew—that of force.

[1] Alvarotto, 25th Sept. 1549: Modena Francia, 26.
[2] "Sera mis en place publique au carquant."
[3] Marcks, i. 56.

And secondly, he had to protect the ordinary citizen. This he did, and, as Brantôme declares, saved countless lives. In troubled times it is only the strong hand that prevails or accomplishes anything.

He was active, too, in other lines. Circumstances were making of him a diplomatist. England was tired of war. Domestic troubles and the steady pressure on Boulogne were forcing her to treat. Coligny was sounded as early as September, while the English agent, Guidotti, negotiated at court. The French demands, however, proved unacceptable, and nothing was done until the new year. Eventually plenipotentiaries were chosen—La Rochepot, Coligny, du Mortier, and Bochetel—representing France. The first meeting took place on the 19th of January 1550. For two months there was a lively wrangle for terms. The English complained bitterly. " These frenchmen ye see how lofty they be and haultaine in all their proceedings with us. Their orgueil is intolerable, their disputations be unreasonable, their conditions to us dishonourable." It was not until the 24th of March that peace was signed. In return for the surrender of Boulogne with all artillery and munitions of war, France agreed to pay the sum of 400,000 crowns. Coligny and La Rochepot took possession of the town on the 25th of April. On the 15th of May Henry II. made his formal entry, but at his own request first visited the Dunette, one of the engineering marvels of the age,[1] and Fort Châtillon. On the 19th, Coligny left for England. We have full details of the voyage: how he was greeted in the Thames " with honnest peales of ordonance," " saw the pastyme of our beare baytings and bull baytings," dined and supped with the young King, and witnessed the taking of his oath to observe the treaty; entertained, hunted in Hyde Park and at Hampton Court, received presents of gold and gilt plate, " saw both the bear hunted in the river, and also wild fire cast out of boats, and many pretty conceits," and with Andelot captained opposing sides in a game of

---

[1] " La Donnetta, fatta dalli Inglesi nel meggio del porto, la quale e una cosa teribilissima e pare una delle fabriche degli antiqui Romani " (Alvarotto, 19th May). An elaborate plan of it at this time is given by M. A. de Rosny in his *Album Historique du Boulonnais.*

BOULOGNE, 1548

(SHOWING FORT CHÂTILLON, THE DUNETTE, AND THE TOWER OF ORDER)

football.[1] But of how his first visit to a Protestant country affected him, we know nothing. On this head the correspondence is completely silent. Under these circumstances, it is idle to conjecture. On the 8th or 9th of June he was back at the French court.

The recovery of Boulogne was generally acknowledged to be a victory for the Montmorencys. As a consequence, the Guises were in a frenzy. In the latter part of April the Ferraran Ambassador interviewed Francis, now Duke of Guise. He found him both gloomy and suspicious. He insisted that his father, the old Duke, had been poisoned. When pressed by Alvarotto, he replied that he did not know by whom, as he had told the King. Then after a little, " he told me that I should inform your Excellency, but in cipher, that it was generally supposed that the Constable was at the bottom of it. And he bade me beg you, as one who receives advices from all parts, to have the goodness to let him know if you should ever hear anything as to whence came this poison." [2] There is nothing extraordinary in this. It only proves that the Duke of Guise was as credulous as his contemporaries. Charges of poisoning were frequent in the sixteenth century, and, it need hardly be added, generally false. It was credited with the deaths of half the great names in history. The Duke of Bouillon, Andelot, Odet, and Joan of Navarre, are a few of those who were said to be its victims—the three last especially without reason. The popular method seems to have been : " when in doubt, say poison ! "

In this instance, the charges were allowed to drop. In revenge, they centred their attack on the new treaty. France, it was claimed, had paid 400,000 crowns—for what? For something which, with a little more vigour, she could have had for nothing. These assertions had their effect. Coligny waited in vain for some mark of favour. In the first flush, Henry had granted him all unclaimed property in Boulogne. But that was all. He was rewarded with no new dignity or

[1] Council to Mason, 2nd June : Record Office, Mason's *Letter Book* ; Alvarotto, 7th June : Modena Francia, 27 ; Edward VI.'s Journal in Pocock's *Burnet*, v. 19.

[2] To Duke of Ferrara, 28th April : Modena Francia, 27.

Joinville. After a general review of the troops at Vitry, Anne advanced into Lorraine. On the 5th of April, Toul, the first of the Three Bishoprics, opened its gates. Metz was taken by a trick. The Constable had leave of passage for two bands of infantry. These were usually composed of three hundred men. On this occasion he made each seven hundred strong, and the town was his.

When Henry II. arrived before Metz on the 16th, he was specially cordial to the Colonel-General. And in the review which followed, the splendid bearing and accoutrements of his forty-eight ensigns of infantry won general admiration.[1]

As may be imagined, the Constable's rivals were filled with envy. Peter Strozzi in particular distinguished himself by his abuse. He wrangled with Coligny over the question of the fortifications of Metz, while no act of the uncle was allowed to pass without a flood of criticism. "It is clear," he exclaimed, "that the Constable knows nothing of fortresses, nor how to lodge or range an army for battle. In sum, he knows nothing about this army, and little about anything else. He is bewildered, and changes his mind ten times a day." Such strictures naturally defeated their object by their exaggeration. The Constable was certainly more disturbed by his inability to gain possession of Strasburg. His plan was a variant of the ruse employed against Metz. Some hundreds of men were to enter, presumably to renew their outfits, in reality to seize the town. But the citizens were too wide awake, and the French army had to be content with a view of the walls.

This entailed the partial failure of the campaign. For without a base on the Rhine, and with Maurice of Saxony treating with Ferdinand, and an invasion threatening from the Netherlands, retreat was inevitable.[2] It was carried out in

[1] Alvarotto, 22nd April: Modena Francia, 29. At this time "ensign" was the word generally employed to denote a company of infantry, though the word company was also used. An "ensign" varied in strength from 100 to 300 men. A "cornet" was a company of cavalry numbering generally 60 and upwards. Condé and Coligny, in their army regulations of 1568, limited the number of the cornet to 100 and that of the ensign to 200 men.

[2] "A Report of Robert Ascham of the affaires and state of Germany," 31 ; and Holländer, *Strassburg im französischen Kriege*, 1552.

three divisions, the line of march being north-westward toward Luxemburg. Perhaps its most important feature was the occupation, on the 12th of June, of Verdun, the last of the Three Bishoprics. Then Rodemachern, Damvilliers, Ivoy, Montmédy, were taken one by one—all prior to the general disbandment in July. Coligny, as Colonel-General of the Infantry, had been prominent throughout. His force, according to sixteenth-century standards, was well disciplined. His mere presence had been sufficient to save the town of Rodemachern from pillage. The obedience paid him was compounded largely of respect and fear. The more criminal were intimidated by the spectacle of batches of their fellows, " more numerous than birds, hung to the branches of trees." [1]

The outcome of the campaign might have been more brilliant. The dream of making a frontier of the Rhine had not been realised. Nevertheless, much had been done—quite enough for a handsome distribution of rewards. The Montmorencys, as was only natural, were the first to benefit. Their claims were met by a rearrangement of dignities, with some fresh accessions. It was agreed that Andelot, who was still a prisoner, was to have his brother's Colonelcy of the Infantry, Coligny filling the vacant post of Admiral of France. This position did not correspond at all points with that of Constable on land. It was limited to Normandy and Picardy. The Governors of other provinces, such as Brittany, Guienne, and Provence, had control of their own coasts. This was a serious drawback, especially as the Mediterranean galleys, the one permanent fleet of France, were also a separate command. Nevertheless, the Admiral's power was very real. In addition to having the care of the northern harbours, he was administrator-in-chief of maritime affairs. Even more important was the fact that his was one of the great state offices. In Tortorel and Perrissin's engraving of the Estates General held at Orleans,[2] Coligny is seen seated on a long bench with

---

[1] Brantôme, vi. 18.

[2] *Les grandes scènes historiques du* XVIe *siècle*, A. Franklin. In order to show the features, Tortorel has drawn the Admiral and his companions with their backs to the King and Queen Mother, though in reality they faced them (Lalourcé et Duval, i. 30).

the Marshals and the "Grand Écuyer" or Master of the Horse. This is a key to their relative positions. The Admiral never disputed the superior dignity of the Constable or Grand Master. On the other hand, his relations with the Marshals was one long struggle for precedence.[1]

Coligny was appointed Admiral on the 11th of November. Three weeks earlier, the siege of Metz had begun, and with it the great career of Francis of Lorraine as a soldier. His chance had come, so it was stated, through a miscalculation of the Constable. Already, in the summer of 1552, Anne had been revolving plans of how to reward his nephew. One —his entrance into the Council of Affairs [2]—was baulked by the combined opposition of Diana and the Guises. Another, was to obtain for him the Governorship of the new conquests in Lorraine, and especially of Metz. But it was first necessary to remove the Count of Vaudemont, whom Henry had appointed Regent to the young Duke of Lorraine. In trying to do so, the Constable over-reached himself. Guise, instead of entering on an elaborate defence of his cousin, quietly offered to go and see to things himself.[3] In the repulse of the invasion which Charles V. and Alva were directing against Metz, Coligny took little part. As belonging to the covering army, his principal duty was to see that Guise was well supported. In addition, he was told off to treat with Albert of Brandenburg, who was in the French service, but was proving restive. But it was only time lost. For the Margrave pounced suddenly on Aumale, who had been set to watch him, and carried him off to the Imperialist camp.

---

[1] See Marshal's protest against a letter being written by Signory to Admiral and not to them in 1566 (Bibl. Nat., filza 6, 59). On 16th Dec. 1566, Petrucci wrote : " et s'intende che Monsr. l'Admiraglio rinuova il suo antico pensiero di voler precedere alli Maresciali." Florence, Arch. Med., F. vi. 97.

[2] There were two Councils : the Privy Council, an administrative body, consisting of from twelve to thirty members ; and the Close or Secret Council or Council of Affairs, the governing body of the kingdom, and always small in size. Coligny did not belong to this latter until his return to court after the third war of religion. See Noel Valois, *Inventaire des Arrêts du Conseil d'État* (regne de Henri IV.), Intro. xli. What was known as the Grand Council had no connection with these two. It was a court of justice which had been divided off from the Council proper in 1497 and 1498.

[3] Alvarotto to Duke of Ferrara from Soissons, 2nd Aug.: Modena Francia, 29.

l'amiral

COLIGNY

A letter written by Coligny at this time is worth quoting. It is an index of character. It was addressed to the Duke of Guise. As the strict disciplinarian, he was glad to hear of the good behaviour of the soldiers; if it had been otherwise, "the captains would ill do their duty, if they did not make a real and exemplary punishment." Speaking as a general, conscious that his mere presence was a source of strength, he exclaimed, "I could wish nothing better than to have the good fortune to be near, if the Emperor comes to besiege you. For though you have many honest fellows near you, yet would I boast that my men would be none the worse to have me with them."[1] This was written on the 15th of October. On the 19th of December he rounded off his year's work by assisting the Duke of Vendôme in the recapture of Hesdin. Two weeks later, his great rival had become the hero of France. For on the 2nd of January, 1553, the Imperialists were in full retreat.[2] They had certainly not made good their boast that the French "be cockes of courage when thei find no enimie, to shake theme by there combes, but whan the Egle cometh with winges splayde, thei wol in to corners, and hardly be found in the game place."[3]

The defence of Metz was a great achievement. And it is difficult to know which to admire most—the defender's generalship, or his splendid humanity. The former has been fully recognised. Examples of the latter were all too rare in the sixteenth century. We therefore cannot omit a tribute, written a few days after the raising of the siege. "The Duke of Guise thereupon had all the sick brought within, and placed in a hospital, and nourished; while, as to the rest, he had broths and soups given them, and had them cared for till death. He has thus won for himself the reputation of being brave, wise, circumspect, careful, diligent, and pious."[4]

This praise has a copiousness about it which betrays its

[1] Delaborde, i. 111.

[2] The Emperor left on the 1st of January, and not in December, as Sebastian Schertlin says in his *Leben und Thaten*, edited by Schönhuth, 93.

[3] Letter of Morysyn from Germany, 30th Oct. 1552 : Brit. Museum, Galba, B. xi. 114.

[4] Alvarotto, 11th Jan. 1553 : Modena Francia, 30.

origin. Yet, under the circumstances, it was not too exaggerated. And the Duke of Guise, listening to similar encomiums, might have dreamed of another victory, this time over his rivals. But he had scarcely returned to Paris when it was reported that Cardinal Odet was to go to Rome as Ambassador. This news was most unwelcome; and Guise expressed his chagrin freely. He and Tomaso del Vecchio explained to Alvarotto that it was the royal intention to rest for a twelvemonth, and then descend into Italy. As defender of Metz, he was the natural leader. But let Odet once set foot in Rome, and all that was at an end. The upshot would be that either Coligny or Andelot would be called in as Regent. And with Marshal Thermes in the north, and with other creatures of the Constable as Ambassadors at Rome and Venice, Italy would become a Montmorency preserve. These fears were very real. But as it turned out, the mission devolved on Lansac and Cardinal du Bellay. Either from illness, as it was stated, or from reluctance to leave the royal presence, now that he was a favourite, Odet remained in France.[1]

The year 1553 was a sad one for the house of Montmorency.[2] Everything they touched turned to failure. Francis, the eldest son, was captured in Therouanne; the same fate befell Turenne, Villars, and the Vidame of Amiens, in Hesdin. To add to their misfortunes, the Constable's northern operations, with the Admiral leading the vanguard, were miserably inept. His abilities did not lie in waging an offensive war. Coligny's own expeditions, though not characterised by such incompetence, were equally unhappy.[3]

In the following year Anne entered on a new campaign. It promised to be as disastrous as the last. The personal valour of the Admiral, who at Dinan rushed to the assault, "to give heart to the rest,"[4] for "the Constable my maister stod besyd

---

[1] For details of episode see despatches of Alvarotto of 17th and 27th Feb. 1553 : Modena Francia, 30 ; Odet to Duke of Ferrara, 15th Feb. : Modena, Arch. di Stato ; Ercole Strozzi, 17th Feb. : Mantua, Arch. Gonz., 645; Card. of Mantua to Don Ferrante di Gonzaga, 22nd March: Parma, Cart. Gonz., 645; despatches of Santa Croce of 18th Feb., 16th March, and 3rd, 15th, and 20th April: Vatican, Nunz. di Francia, Arm. i. 3.

[2] Decrue, ii. 36–48.   [3] Rochambeau, *Lettres d'Antoine de Bourbon*, 70.

[4] Paris, Bibl. Nat., filza I.A. 20 ; cf. *Mémoires de Soubise*, 23.

crying and boisting in vain," [1] could not make up for a lack of generalship. The honour of France was only saved by the brilliant, if empty, victory of Renty. On the 12th of August, the Constable began the siege of that town, the Imperialists hovering in the neighbourhood. From fear of an attack, the Bois Guillaume, the key of the position, had been occupied by the Duke of Guise, who repulsed the enemy just before daylight on the 13th. The morning broke dark and foggy. Before midday Charles v. launched his vanguard against the Bois Guillaume, and his troops, after occupying the wood, came out into the open. The brunt of the attack fell on the Duke of Guise. At first he was in difficulties, but, collecting his scattered forces, and aided by Nevers and Tavannes, he was able to get the upper hand, though his cavalry could not drive the blow home, as it was exposed to the fire of the Spanish arquebusiers in the Bois Guillaume, for "the plaice of the battaill was a plain valley that lay under the said wood." [2] It was at this juncture that Coligny threw himself from his horse. Then at the head of a thousand or twelve hundred infantry, he rushed on the wood, and cleared out the enemy.[3] This was the turning-point of the day, and the result was a complete victory. Each of the three main instruments attributed to himself the glory. "Monsieur de Tavannes," exclaimed the Duke, "we have delivered the finest charge ever made!" "Yes," retorted the latter, "you have supported me very well." [4] The recriminations between the Admiral and Guise were more bitter. "Ah, mort Dieu!" burst out the Duke, "do not try to rob me of my honour." "I have no wish to," cried the Admiral. "Nor could you," said the other.[5]

The era of hostilities was now nearing its close. The Constable was weary of being held up to public obloquy. "In the squares and courtyards, sonnets and Latin verses were quoted, calling him base and a man of no courage." [6] He was

[1] Sir James Melville's *Memoirs*, 24.   [2] *Ib.* 26.

[3] Jean des Monstiers, 187 ("Discours du progrez de l'armée du roy"); Bianchi, *Alcune Lettere Politiche di Claudio Tolomei*, 28; Brantôme, vi. 22; Rabutin, 622; Ruble, *Antoine de Bourbon*, i. 345.

[4] Tavannes (Pantheon), 201.   [5] Brantôme, iv. 287.   [6] Alberi, ii. 284.

4

tired of war. He was altogether tired of undertaking vast military operations for which he knew himself unfit. Charles V. too, broken down under the weight of empire, was hungering for peace. The way, therefore, was open for a mutual understanding. Even the abortive efforts made at Marc in the spring left France sanguine. " At court," wrote the Venetian Ambassador, "they argue publicly that some agreement will follow." [1] Meanwhile Coligny, who had been created Governor of Picardy on the 27th of June, had now practically control of the war. Owing to his appeal, the men of Dieppe set sail and won a sixteen-hour fight over the Flemings.[2] He himself, with a little army of 6500 men, raided the enemy's territory, and returned laden with booty.[3] In the month of October he revictualled Marienburg with the aid of Nevers.

These operations, however, were only preliminary to peace. Coligny and Lalaing, the Imperialist representative, met to discuss the terms of an exchange of prisoners. The question of a general truce was broached. Compromise on neither head was easy. The Spanish demands were extravagant. In return for the liberation of the Duke of Bouillon and Francis of Montmorency, they asked for the surrender of Boulogne and Marienburg. " Monsieur de Montmorency," retorted Henry II. pithily, " is the son of the Constable, and not of the King of France." [4] Lalaing equally insisted on the mutual restitution of territory as the basis of a truce. That is to say, France was to give up all her conquests of the last few years. Here was ample material for a deadlock. Finally, however, Coligny's firmness and Charles' desire to retire from the world left the victory with France. On the 5th of February, 1556, was signed the truce of Vaucelles, by which the Emperor accepted for the space of five years the general results of the war.[5] As it was an occasion of family rejoicing, the Admiral was accompanied by two of his cousins in his

---

[1] Paris, Bibl. Nat., filza I.A., 88.　　　[2] *Archives Curieuses*, iii. 141, etc.
[3] Paris, Bibl. Nat., filza I.A., 128 (Soranzo from Poissy, 6th Sept.).
[4] *Ib.* 178 (Soranzo from Blois, 23rd Dec.).
[5] For full particulars of negotiations at Vaucelles, see Delaborde, i. *passim* ; Granvelle, iv. *passim* ; and Vertot's *Negocs. de Noaille*, v. 238, 244.

mission to receive the oath of ratification from Charles v. and Philip II.

Fortunately, we have an account of the voyage,[1] alive and vivid. It is a series of pictures, of flashes of humour, and half-hints of personal and national traits. Under the author's handling the past lives again : the galling Spanish pride, which left bare to curious French eyes the tapestries representing the defeat of Pavia; the solemn mass and Philip's taking of the oath, his laughter at the antics of the French jester, and the hesitating, embarrassed silence of the Admiral. Such were some of the scenes. The culmination was the interview of Coligny with Charles V.

It was intensely dramatic. Passing up the staircase between a double row of Spaniards, all in black and "of a grave and venerable bearing," he came to the antechamber. It was hung in black. The royal chamber was in black also. The small table, and the chair on which Charles was sitting, were, like the rest, draped in black. The Emperor seemed old and shrunken. His eyes were those to which tears came quickly. His hands hung limp and nerveless—crumpled with age. He was dressed in the prevailing colour, his simple white collar giving an added touch of severity. Coligny approached, bending low. After a formal address and reply, he handed him a letter, written by Henry II. The Emperor tried to open it, at first vainly. His fingers tore at it feebly ; tears came to his eyes, he was so helpless. He was dispirited and melancholy. He would swear to the truce, he said, though there was no need, for he was past the time for fresh enterprises ; his one wish was to die. Then his mood changed. He inquired sardonically about the King's grey hairs, and wandered off into anecdote. He even exchanged witticisms with the French jester.

All this time Coligny was watching him intently. He was struck, so he wrote Henry,[2] by the Emperor's weak and

---

[1] "Le voyage de l'Admiral devers l'Empereur et le Roy Philippes," probably written by de l'Aubespine, who accompanied Coligny, *Archives Curieuses*, iii. 296–306. Cf. Brantôme, i. 12, and letter of Soranzo, 12th April, Paris, Bibl. Nat., filza I.A. and B.

[2] Letter of Soranzo of the 12th of April.

And yet he knew that, should hostilities ensue, he would find
himself in an intolerable position.   As governor of the frontier
province of Picardy, he would almost inevitably be forced
either to deal or receive the first blow.   He was eager, therefore, to resign.   And it was only at the instance of the King
himself that he consented to retain his position.   His feelings
at this moment are vividly revealed in a letter of the 26th of
August, instinct with a certain proud dignity.

It was not long before the Constable was reconciled to the
alliance with Rome.   This change in his attitude was no
doubt hastened by the need of Papal assistance in straighten-
ing out the tangle in the matrimonial concerns of his son
Francis.   It is even asserted—we confess, on very slender
grounds—that Coligny also was won over to the same view
by the interest which Cardinal Carafa took in the affairs
of Andelot.[1]   But it would be more just to say that the
general political situation, and not the influence of Cardinal
Carafa, produced the change.   Once the King had set his heart
on the new policy, and war threatened, Coligny bowed to the
inevitable.

In November the Duke of Guise left for Italy.   On the
4th of January, 1557, in the dead of night, the Admiral, with
Andelot and a body of horse and foot, made a dash on Douay,
and failed.[2]   In spite of this the Constable was ridiculously
sanguine.   He still hoped that Spain would not or could not
retaliate.   Yet France, especially the northern provinces,
invited attack.   Guise's fruitless expedition to Italy had
tapped her military resources.   A short-sighted economy
aggravated the danger.   Meanwhile Coligny exhibited a
ceaseless activity.   In May he captured Lens.[3]   From April
to the end of August we find him passing from one frontier
town to another.   Among those visited was St. Quentin.
Unfortunately for its safety, the citizens, jealous of their
privileges, were averse to receiving a garrison; moreover, it

[1] *Bulletin du prot. fr.*, 1902, 577–589 (M. Patry).
[2] Archives Nat. 1490 (despatch of 15th Jan.); *Col. de Doc. ineditos*, ii. 463;
Vatican Library, Urbino, 1038, 189.
[3] " Ce que le jeune Feuquières a apporté au Roy de la part de monsieur l'Admiral
touchant la prinse de Lans en Arthois," B.M. 24206, 23.

had been further weakened by the removal of part of its artillery.

During the summer the enemy steadily gathered near Philippeville under Emmanuel Philibert, Duke of Savoy, the Lieutenant-General of Philip II. His plan was by a sudden march to seize either the weakly defended Peronne or St. Quentin, and join with the small army preparing in England. It is quite certain that Coligny did not divine these intentions until too late; it is even doubtful whether he feared a great invasion. In fact, France was completely duped. At the most she expected an attack on one of the frontier fortresses. In the middle of July Savoy was ready. On the 29th he began his march westward. Avoiding the strongholds of Rocroy, Marienburg, and La Chapelle, his advanced troops appeared before St. Quentin on the 2nd of August.

Coligny had warned his uncle that the enemy had designs on the practically defenceless Picardy. All that was now possible was to check them at St. Quentin. France must be given time to prepare. Coligny, therefore, was ordered by the Constable to throw himself into the town. It was a desperate undertaking. But the Admiral did not give himself time to hesitate. Leaving the royal camp at Pierrepont on the 2nd of August, he reached his destination at one o'clock of the following morning.

St. Quentin lay on the summit and side of a hill dipping southwards to the Somme. It was connected on this side by a bridge with its suburb of Isle, which Coligny called the Lower Town. The fortifications of the main town were in the form of a parallelogram and about two and a half miles in extent. They were thus out of all proportion to the population, which did not number more than eight thousand. This was the more serious because they were not of the latest pattern, being survivals of the time of the Hundred Years' War. The north wall was strong, the Gate of St. John commanding most of the fosse. The east wall was a long, straight line, with but one bastion and two weak towers. On the other two sides, the river with its marshes formed an effective natural barrier. The weak points here were the neighbouring heights on the west and the strong bastion in the south suburb, which almost immediately fell into the hands of the enemy.

There were in the town some three hundred regular soldiers. Of the eighteen hundred which Coligny was to have brought with him, not more than eight hundred entered. In time, the civic population supplied fifteen hundred of a sort. Even with the reinforcements which he received later, he probably never had more than two thousand five hundred. With these and an artillery sadly depleted by the late removal of some thirty pieces, he had to keep out an enemy forty-five thousand strong. It was a Herculean task. The spirit in which he carried it through is best given in his own words: " I told all the captains that if they heard me employ language which breathed surrender, I begged them to throw me over the wall into the fosse; and if anyone proposed it to me, I would do no less to him."

He began his work by calling on the inhabitants for service, flogging the idle, strengthening the fortifications, and clearing away the trees on the north side. At the same time he determined to retain his hold on the suburb of Isle. Its strategic point was a bastion, which had been half built and deserted by the townsmen on the 2nd. His hope was that if he could only seize on this, he might delay the Imperialists. Moreover, with this and the bridge in his hands, his relief was easy. The enemy, however, were not to be dislodged. And it was only in the teeth of his officers' opposition that he still clung to the part of the suburb within the old wall. On the 4th a sortie failed, miserably. An attempt of Andelot to enter with succours failed also. On the 6th he was forced to abandon the suburb of Isle. Fortunately, a tremendous breach, made by an explosion, was hid for some time by the smoke. Three days later, seven to eight hundred idle were turned out of the town; his grip was beginning to tighten. And every evening he ascended the great church tower to watch the enemy.

The next move lay with the Constable. He, if we may believe his faithful follower, Sir James Melville, like every other unfortunate character in history, received his inevitable

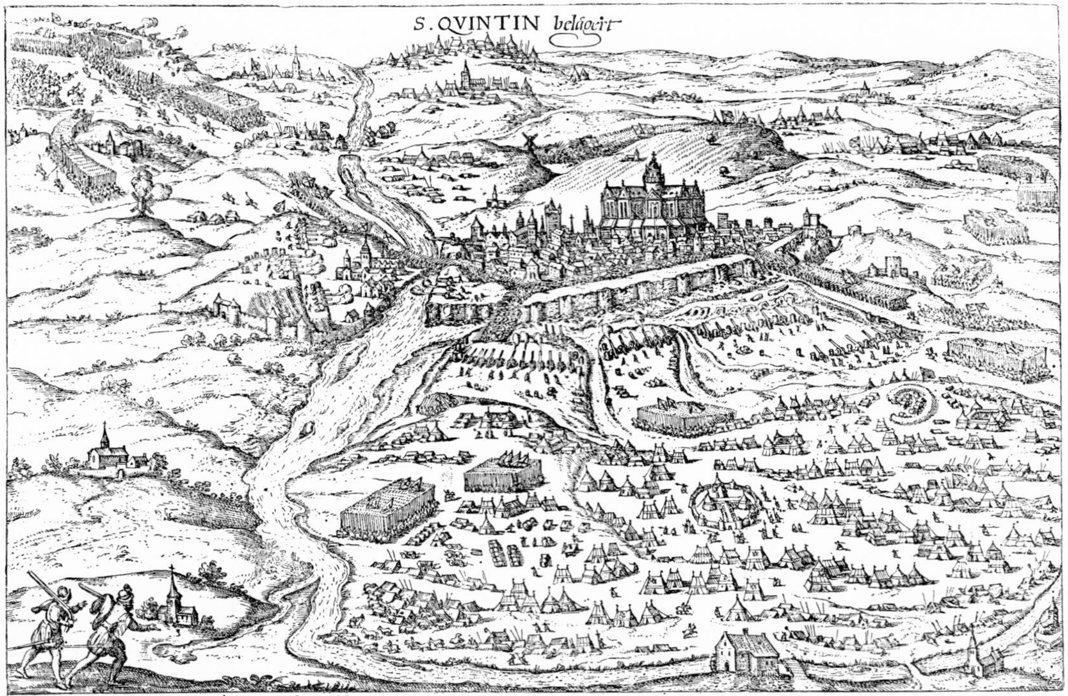

S. Quintin nach gehaltner schlacht
Belegert wirdt mit heeres macht.
Die burger auff dasselbe mael
Den Andelot vnd Admirael

Die furnembst heupter bey sich hatten
So gentzlich wolten nit gestatten
Das sie die Stat aufgeben solten,
Ein sturm sie gern erwarten wolten.

Damit hand die Burgundsche knecht
S. Quintin hefftig angefecht,
Vff vier seiten besturmet hart,
Das ander jm eins gerathen wardt,

Heimlich durch einen thurn inkumen,
Mit gwalt vnd gluck die Stat gewunnen.

Anno des 1557, 27 Julij.

SIEGE OF ST. QUENTIN, 1557

warning. For "ryding to the huntis, there came a man in grave apparell folowing him upon fut, crying for audience for Godis saik. Wherupon the Constable stayed willing him to speak; wha said, ' The Lord said, seeing that thou will not knaw me, I sall lykwayes not knaw the. Already I see the reak of thy glory spred athort the luft in dust.' " Little disturbed by these gloomy vaticinations, he set about his task. On the 7th, the 8th, and the 9th, the French were hovering on the horizon. On the 10th they again appeared. Succours were to enter the town on the side of the marsh. The attempt resulted in the disastrous battle of St. Quentin. It was just one of those defeats which, with a little more care, could so easily have been avoided. By an egregious error, the boats which were to ferry Andelot across, arrived last. When, after some hours, they were got ready, they were found to be over-loaded, and stuck in the mud. Precious time was thus lost—just sufficient to give the Spaniards time to recover from their surprise. The cavalry, under Egmont and Horn, crossed to the south side of the river above the town, the infantry below. When Anne began to retire, it was too late. Two leagues from St. Quentin the Spaniards were on him. His retreat became a rout. The slain amounted to three thousand. All but two of his cannon were taken. There were seven thousand prisoners. Among these was the flower of the French nobility—Anne himself, Montpensier, St. André, Longueville, La Rochefoucauld, Villars, and the Rhinegrave.

The defeat of the Constable was only known with certainty in St. Quentin on the 13th. The Admiral's reception of the news was characteristic. When the Spanish musketeers planted the captured flags on their entrenchments, half in bravado, half with a secret hope of raising drooping spirits, he had the walls lined, the trumpets blown, and the muskets fired off " as a sign of rejoicing." His government of the town was now a veritable reign of terror. It was his will against the panic of a multitude. Townsmen and soldiery were equally disaffected. He did not even dare call his officers together; they might mutiny. He tried the effect of a stirring proclamation. More efficacious, no doubt, was the threat of the gallows for any proposal to yield. It was even stated that two gibbets were raised in the public square as a warning. Already, on the 15th of August, the people clamoured for surrender. Coligny replied by forbidding the assembling of more than three persons on pain of death. When the English archers shot into the town an offer of life and liberty, he sent back in the same manner the laconic answer: "Regem habemus." A further batch of those who refused to work were ejected on the 21st. Two thousand women and children, who by their tears might have still further weakened the nerves of the defenders, were shut up in the great church. Even the priests and monks were pressed into the defence. He knew of what value to France were not only "the days, but the hours that we could guard this place." His greatest solace was his brother Andelot, who had entered on the 10th with about five hundred men, and the company under the Scotsman Hume.

On the 21st of August the last attempt at relief was made by Nevers, and failed. Only some hundred and twenty unarmed soldiers straggled in. His numbers were now too few for sorties. The enemy had long dominated his artillery. At first they had opened fire from the south and west. After a few days they had begun approaches from the east. On the 14th, this side had to bear the brunt of the attack. The walls were crumbling. The ingenious idea of Andelot, of hoisting boats, filled with earth, on to the wall, as a protection against the deadly fire, countermines, and the skilful defence of bastions, had only delayed the Spaniards. Their outworks were now close to the walls. The breaches— there were eleven of them, ten on the east side, and one at the south gate where the English were stationed—were ready. Coligny had at the most eight hundred regular troops to man them. A thousand had died or been killed during the siege, while the townsmen were not suited for this work. The enemy, with new accessions, was probably fifty-five thousand strong.

The Admiral in person directed the defence of a breach almost in the centre. Next him, to his left, were the men-at-arms of the company of the Dauphin. To his right and south of him, Andelot commanded at a breach, not far from the corner of the south and east wall.

At half-past three in the afternoon of the 27th of August, twenty-four days after the disaster of St. Quentin, the trumpets sounded the assault. Philip II., who had arrived on the 13th with a further reinforcement, stood watching the scene, four hundred paces away. Turning to his chaplain, he confessed that he did not like the whizzing of the bullets. His men advanced to the attack in three columns; one against the south gate, and the others against the two ends of the east wall. At almost all points they were beaten back. Andelot for a full hour kept up a successful and heroic defence. But the weak spot had been found. It was where the company of the Dauphin was posted. Not even waiting for a pike thrust, it fled in wild panic. Coligny, seeing something wrong, ran to the threatened point. But, deserted by all but a page, he found the enemy already far into the town. Surrendering to a Spaniard, he was handed over to the Duke of Savoy, and finally sent to the fortress of Sluys.

The sack of St. Quentin is one of the historic events of the sixteenth century. It was a horrible orgy. The cruelty and lust of the soldiers were appalling. Andelot was more fortunate than his brother. Taken prisoner like him, he was able to effect his escape through his knowledge of Spanish, acquired during his captivity in Milan. He had the melancholy task of detailing the disaster to a terror-stricken country.[1]

Such in brief is the history of this memorable siege. As to whether Coligny saved France, that perhaps is a question. It is none the less true that he did all that was humanly possible. As to whether the term " heroic " can be applied to it, depends somewhat on where one draws the line between courage and heroism. One thing, however, is certain. There were few captains who, with the common knowledge of the fate meted out to stormed towns, would have faced the ordeal. There were also few who could have done so much, with such slender resources. Without him, St. Quentin would have fallen within a week. There were fewer still who could

---

[1] Alvarotto, 31st Aug.: Modena Francia, 33 ; E. Strozzi, 29th Aug.: Mantua, Arch. Gonz., 649.

have bridled a disaffected populace. But even more unique than gifts of leadership was his sense of duty. It was rare indeed to find anyone, with his career made, willing to risk all in a forlorn hope.[1]

[1] For the defence of St. Quentin, *La Guerre de* 1557 *en Picardie*, published by the Soc. des Sciences, etc., of St. Quentin, is very important. It includes, among many other documents, Coligny's own description of the siege, written while a prisoner in the Netherlands. I have largely used the admirable introductory sketch of M. E. Lemaire.

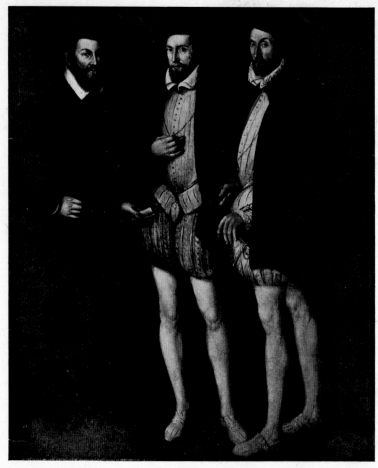

ODET   GASPARD   FRANCIS

THE THREE COLIGNYS

CHAPTER III

COLIGNY'S FIRST CONNECTION WITH PROTESTANTISM

The Reformation in France; its Early History—Possible Stages in Coligny's Attitude toward Protestantism—Villegaignon's Expedition to Brazil—Conversion of Andelot—Calvin's First Letter to Coligny—Coligny's Religious Studies while a Prisoner—His Conversion Religious rather than Political.

THE battle of St. Quentin has a very distinct place in French history. It opened the epoch of forty years' subservience to Spain. It had its influence, too, in the lives of individuals. What strikes one most in the career of Anne of Montmorency is his extraordinary recuperative powers. His was, in a very special sense, a chequered career. Capture, imprisonment, disgrace, favour, authority, followed one another in kaleidoscopic change. Yet there was one event from which even his buoyant fortune never wholly recovered. It was the fatal tenth of August. A diplomatic reverse might have been retrieved; but a *débâcle* in the field struck at the very root of his power. It lost him the confidence both of the army and the nobility, and with them the support of France. He struggled manfully, indeed, against his misfortunes, for he was not easily discouraged. And when later he was supported by the Bourbon interests, and his rivals had lost Francis of Lorraine, he was able to make his influence felt. But he was no longer the commanding figure he had been in the reign of Francis I. and the early years of Henry II.

The Admiral, as was only natural, felt the altered conditions. It is certain that he was influenced. The question is: how far? For instance, had the battle of St. Quentin any part in his change of faith? Did the consequences flowing from the defeat, taken in conjunction with the general situation, lead him to seek a new basis for political influence in Protestantism? In a word, was his conversion religious, or political, or both? A wholly satisfactory answer is perhaps impossible. It is always difficult to discover the springs of human action. And success is still more uncertain when, as here, the subtle eccentricities of character were warped and confused by an age in which the old order was crumbling, and the new as yet was on a shifting basis. Still, a glance at the religious movement, as it developed in France, will at least prepare the way.

The fifteenth and sixteenth centuries witnessed the break-up of mediævalism. A new spirit was stirring. From Italy, herself in inevitable decline, spread a quickened intelligence and the Renaissance. Out of the cold North, brooding over the supposed subjection of centuries, came Luther and the Reformation. The Reformation in France, though partly indigenous—the outcome of the spiritual strivings of Lefèvre of Etaples, his disciples and contemporaries—was essentially Lutheranism working on French soil. In its earlier stages it was on the whole colourless in tone. So far as it was active, it was so among its more humble exponents. But, for the most part, it was a vague yearning, a reasoning appeal, a protest not too robust, against ecclesiastical abuses and the sins of the world. It was in this spirit that it found its protector in the enlightened Margaret of Navarre, and its sympathisers among scholars and literary men. The original members were hardly of the stuff to face a severe ordeal. It was only when the Frenchman Calvin, heir to the full of that passion for logic, that genius for an orderly uniformity so characteristic of his race, had methodised German thought and developed the church as a highly organised religious, and almost of necessity political, republic, that French Protestantism became virile and a force. By his indomitable will, he changed the whole current of a movement. He created a moral mould that could shape men. He sounded the clear call to combat. He banned the works of the " Nicodemites ": those who would conform outwardly to Rome. He rejected all compromise. His creed was a fighting creed. In his *Institutio Christianæ*

Religionis he provided a religious charter, in his government
of Geneva a citadel, " whair," wrote the still more grim Scottish
Reformer, " I nether feir nor eschame to say is the maist perfyt
schoole of Chryst that ever was in the erth since the dayis of
the Apostillis." [1] And it was here that was engendered that
spirit which raised up a new race of " martyrs in Gaul, whose
blood is the testimony of thy doctrine and thy church." [2]

In the earlier years, the victims of persecution had come
from the lower ranks of the nation. They had been the poor
Vaudois with their pasteurs or, as they were called, " barbes,"
drapers, masons, jewellers, labourers, lawyers, students, Jacobins,
but rarely gentlemen.[3] After 1550, however, and especially
1552, aristocratic names were more frequent, not only among
those imprisoned or burnt, but among the members of the new
congregations. In 1555 the Protestants of Paris organised
themselves into a church, an example followed by one
community after another, until the Reformed Church of France
took form and substance in the first national synod of 1559.
Two years previously, the scheming Anthony of Navarre gave
in a covert adhesion, and Huguenotism had a leader. From
that moment it was seldom free from the malign influence of
one or other great personality or party, endeavouring to
utilise the strength inherent in all true convictions for purposes
in which ends other than spiritual were in view. In the
inevitable train came the nemesis of all deflected causes :
clouded purpose, disseminated energy, aims no longer pure
and lofty, and, in the end, half failure.

Coligny's early connection with Protestantism is at least
indefinite. There seems to have been no fixed stages, no
point at which it can be said that here is the break with
Catholicism, here the crisis. Such change as is apparent, is
in the nature of an imperceptible drifting away from old
moorings. It is thus difficult to dogmatise. It is easy to
misinterpret. Indeed, some of the facts we shall give may

---

[1] John Knox to Mrs. Locke, December, 1556 : *Calvini Opera*, xvi. 333.

[2] Hotman to Calvin in Latin, 25th March, 1556 : *Calvini Opera*, xvi. 83. See
also list of 121 Calvinists sent by Geneva into France, 1555-1566, *Bulletin du prot.
français* of 1859, p. 72.

[3] *La Chambre Ardente* of M. Weiss, cxlv.

have been no more than the deeds of a somewhat indifferent Catholic. And we are almost persuaded that they are, when we take them singly. Yet, looked at from the standpoint of the Admiral's later life, they seem unconsciously to slip into place—links in a chain of gradual evolution.

The Humanistic tendencies of Coligny's teacher, Bérauld, and the supposed Protestant sympathies of his mother, have already been mentioned. The latter would be important, if true. But is there any proof that Louise of Montmorency was a sectary? The first hint of it is in the *Life of the Admiral*, published in the year 1575. It is there stated that she refused to see a priest on her deathbed, fortifying her resolution with pious confessions. The author, who is probably Hotman, may be here only retailing what he actually heard from the lips of Coligny; for he was an intimate, and even stayed with him in his home at Châtillon. This is in favour of its accuracy. On the other hand, similar reports were common. One was even spread in regard to the fanatical Anne of Montmorency himself. Added to this is the singular reticence, not only of the whole of the contemporary correspondence, but also of the Guises. They were never slow to remind the Constable of the apostasy of his nephews, if not the proverbial hundred times a day, at least too often to be pleasant; but never a word about his sister. And it was not as though deathbed repentances were easy to keep secret. They had a curious way of passing through closed doors. Within a month that of Anthony of Navarre was common property. But even accepting the chronicler's account, her words, as given by him, do not necessarily suggest her conversion to the new faith. They are in harmony with the sentiments of many of the courtly readers of the Psalms of Marot—but scarcely more.

The next incident was Coligny's visit to Protestant England. At most we can but record it. To draw conclusions would be to fall back on pure conjecture. The following year witnessed a somewhat singular proceeding. The parish services at Châtillon had for centuries been held in the parish and collegiate church which was within the radius of the château, and leaned against the great tower. With the consent of the chapter and burgesses, they were now discon-

tinued; and a new building in the town, erected by the
Admiral's father, became the parish church. As a sop, no
doubt, to public feeling, Coligny presented it with two new
bells.[1] Curiously enough, it was about this time that Sir
William Pickering reported that " Cardinal Chastillion, as I
hear, is a great aider of Lutherians." [2] Neither of these
circumstances, however, must be taken too seriously. In 1553,
Cardinal San Giorgio remarked on the devotion of Odet to
the Holy See.[3] We also find both brothers taking part in a
peculiarly Catholic ceremony : a memorial service at St. Denis
in honour of three saints.[4] And in 1554, Odet took measures
in his diocese to counteract the growth of heretical opinions.
In fact, the eldest of the Châtillons so far was only one of
that school of tolerant and enlightened French churchmen to
which Cardinal du Bellay and Marillac belonged. Moreover,
as late as March, 1556, Coligny was advised to avail himself
of a Papal dispensation to eat meat, and in the same month
he heard Mass with Philip II. in Brussels.

Nevertheless, a few months later we come to an event of
prime importance. The year before, the first colonising effort
of Coligny had begun. The leader, and indeed the originator
of the expedition, was Villegaignon, Knight of the Order of
St. John of Jerusalem. Hasty and unstable by nature, experience had made of him a good soldier but an indifferent
leader. At the time, his religious convictions were in a state
of flux. As a number of the original colonisers were
Protestants, he wrote from Brazil to the Admiral and Calvin,
asking for fresh recruits. Coligny's choice for leader of those
who were to come from Switzerland fell on a Protestant
gentleman, Philip of Corguilleray ; and this contingent visited
him at Châtillon, in September, 1556. Unfortunately, the
naïve and delightful narrative of Jean de Léry is very brief.
A little detail lavished here might have revealed to us one
of the most interesting pages in the development of the great
Huguenot. Instead, we have a few meagre lines : " we travelled and passed to Châtillon-sur-Loing. Here we found the

[1] Becquerel, 18, 42.   [2] Tytler, i. 420.
[3] To Card. Monte, 5th June, 1553 : Vatican, Nunz. di Francia Arm., i. 3, 165.
[4] Alvarotto, 4th Jan.: Modena Francia, 30.

5

Admiral (in his home, which is one of the most beautiful in France). And he not only encouraged us to pursue our enterprise, but promised to aid us in sea-causes. And he gave us many reasons to hope that God would give us grace to see the fruit of our labour."[1] And that is all. But Beza, the historian of the French churches and intimate of the Admiral, wrote of the latter, in connection with Villegaignon's expedition, as one " since then favouring, as much as he was able, the party of the religion."[2] It is clear that this expedition marked the first great step forward. Moreover, almost concurrently, Coligny was undergoing other influences, all tending in the same direction. In July, 1556, Andelot returned from Italy, seemingly imbued with the new faith, and his weight with his brother was always great. It is to be remembered, too, that Coligny's handiwork, the truce of Vaucelles, was soon recognised as essentially an anti-Papal move. The opposition to Rome, of course, was political rather than religious. Yet it is impossible to deny that this political antagonism must have powerfully affected the spiritual outlook of one on whom the bonds of the ancient church were already loosening.

But be that as it may, in April, 1557, Coligny was formally mentioned by Beza as one of those who were not hostile to the Protestant cause. This statement is important. All the probabilities are in favour of its accuracy, since at this very time we begin to discover a deeper religious tone in the Admiral's correspondence, and three months later we have from his hand a letter which seems to mark a turning-point. " Since you are pleased," he wrote to Cardinal Carafa on the 17th of July, " to offer to employ yourself for me in such matters as you can, the opportunity now offers, and, as you have the means, I would readily beg your aid. It is for a monk of the Jacobin Order. He is a man of letters, and I have kept him and had him by me now for a long time. For

---

[1] *Histoire d'un voyage fait en la terre de Bresil*, 1578, p. 8. The words in brackets only appeared in a later edition.

[2] The doubt cast on Beza's authorship of the *Histoire Ecclésiastique* by its most recent editors has on the whole been dispelled by recent criticisms in the *Bull. du prot. fr.*, xxxix. 285 and xlix. 89.

this cause I would ordinarily very willingly keep him by me, if it were not for his habit, which, as you know, is hardly suitable among men of war. I therefore beseech you for the love of me to request His Holiness that it may please him to give him permisson to change the said habit, and do me a favour." [1]

Such is the letter. M. Patry has pointed out its significance. Identifying this "Pierre Marcatel" of Coligny with a monk mentioned by Madame de Mornay, "who in the wars of Picardy preached the truth under cover of his habit," and with a certain Pierre Mercatel who as "minister of the word of God" figured among the refugees in Lausanne, he suggests, and we believe correctly, that he was already in 1557 virtually the Protestant chaplain of Coligny.

Thus we see that the year July 1556 to July 1557 seems to have witnessed a gradual evolution in the religious character of the Admiral. In a word, he crossed the line which divided off the indifferent Catholic from the more or less conscious Protestant. Nevertheless, no absolute proof is forthcoming until the second year of his captivity in the Low Countries. And until then the story of his spiritual life can best be studied in the experiences of his brothers. In April, 1557, a Papal bull had appointed the Cardinals of Lorraine, Bourbon, and Châtillon as Grand Inquisitors in France. Owing to a protest of the German Protestants, the war, and other causes, it failed of its effect. If we may believe Beza,[2] it was the work of the Cardinal of Lorraine, and was directed against his rival, Cardinal Odet. It was the ordinary manœuvre dear to the heart of this intriguer: an attempt to place the enemy on the horns of a dilemma. If Odet served on the commission, he would lose the favour of the Protestants; of the King, if he did not.

More interesting were the difficulties encountered by Andelot. Brantôme asserts that this latter was converted to Protestantism during his captivity in Milan. Other proof, however, is not forthcoming. The first instance of revolt was his absence from Mass at the siege of Calais. His attitude

---

[1] Barberini Library, xliii. 163, fol. 6 (263). For comments of M. Patry see *Bull. du prot. fr.*, li. 577-585.
[2] *Hist. Eccl.*, i. 137.

became still more pronounced in the April of 1558. Borrow-
ing a minister from the church of Paris, he held a series of
services during a tour in Brittany. The court, though informed of these proceedings, did not act at once. The blow
only fell in the third week of May. In this month the
Cardinal of Lorraine met and discussed terms of peace with
Christina of Denmark. When bidding farewell, the Spanish
commissioners explained that peace was less to their interest
than to that of France, threatened as she was by religious
divisions. And Ruy Gomez added that Philip II. had proof
of this in a letter now in his hands, and written by one of
the most distinguished members of the French court. Pressed
by the Cardinal, Granvella divulged the name of the writer.
It was that of Andelot. The letter itself was an exhortation
to the Admiral to persevere, presumably in his Protestant
opinions. The latter, Granvella went on to say, was a
Lutheran of the Lutherans. "He never heard Mass, and
lived a most wicked life, so that, if these Châtillons did not
change their tune, they should be made to pay the cost." [1]
On the 17th of May [2] the Cardinal of Lorraine was back in
France. Andelot was at once summoned to the royal presence.
The memorable interview took place on the morning of the
19th. He was perhaps the last man in France to weather
the storm. Haughty, passionate, outspoken, he had little of
the diplomat and less of the courtier. When Henry accused
him of his Huguenot practices, and especially of sending the
Admiral a Calvinistic tract, he denied nothing, except having
been present at services in the Pré-aux-Clercs. Thrice the
King charged, thrice Andelot justified. [3] At last, in an out-
burst of passion, [4] Henry ordered him to retire, when he was at
once hurried to prison. But though he had bearded the King,
he was not proof against steady pressure. After a time his
wife and Odet had their way. He consented to be present
at Mass, and was liberated.

---

[1] Alvarotto, 23rd May and 11th July : Modena Francia, 34.

[2] Strozzi, 20th May : Mantua, Arch. Gonz., 650.

[3] Desp. of Alvarotto of 20th May, and *Hist. Eccl.*, i. 168.

[4] Alvarotto says that the King struck him on the head ; de Thou states that
Henry lifted a plate, and by mistake wounded the Dauphin.

Thus, as we see, Coligny had gone far on the road to a change of faith. This had begun in the early days of his imprisonment. For, being "vexed fortie dayes with an agewe, as his fits lefte him, he commaunded a Byble to be brought unto him, to ease the griefe and sorrowe of his minde with reading of it. And he studied so much upon it, that he began from thensforthe to have a taste of the pure religion and trew godlinesse, and to lerne the right maner of calling uppon God." [1] Then followed his refusal to hear Mass, Andelot's letter and disgrace, and lastly, a letter from the hand of Calvin. It was of the 4th of September, 1558, and may be said to mark the Admiral's definite though informal acceptance of Protestantism. Calvin was a born leader. He never let slip an opportunity to gain a friend or hold a waverer. He was no doubt moved in this instance by the known intimacy of the two brothers, and between them and their niece, Eleanor of Roye, a convert of this year. The letter itself was such as he might have written to the shifty Anthony of Bourbon. It breathed an exhortation, and echoed a hope: "seeing that God has given you this opportunity to profit in His school, as though He had wished to speak to you, privately into your ear." [2]

And now to sum up. All the facts point in one direction. The Admiral's conversion was religious; it was sincere; it was non-political. Opportunism, tradition, family sentiment, and the promptings of self-interest, were all ranged against any move in this direction. In the year 1556–1557, when he first began to show signs of wavering, he and his uncle were still at the zenith of their power. They were loaded with honours. They had met their rivals, on the whole, successfully. And as they, or at least the Constable, had the King's favour, there was no need to bid for new support. In fact, change meant political suicide. Nor could the battle of St. Quentin have influenced him greatly. For he had to judge of Protestantism as he had known it. And until the middle of 1557, in spite of its rapid growth during the last three years, it was an uncertain quantity. It was only during

[1] *The Lyfe of Jasper Colignie Shatilion.*
[2] Bonnet, *Lettres de Calvin*, ii. 230–233.

his detention in the Netherlands that its progress became really alarming; in 1558 its numbers were given by Calvin as 300,000. And of this fact the Admiral must naturally have been comparatively ignorant.

As with so many men of action of the sixteenth century, imprisonment gave him a chance to think. For the first time his predilections had full play. Calvinism appealed to him. He found in its austerity, its unbending will, its moral aspect of the world, the revelation of his ideals. The authors of the military "Ordinances" and the *Institutio Christianæ Religionis* may have been socially poles apart. They were none the less intellectually and spiritually akin. The reaction, too, from the natural feelings of self-interest and caution played, no doubt, a certain if very minor part. Moreover, as time passed, and the Guises more and more adopted a Catholic cry, Coligny instinctively fell into an attitude of opposition. While policy, therefore, did not originate his religious change, it had its influence on later developments.

I. CALVIN.

CHAPTER IV

COLIGNY AS HUGUENOT LEADER

Return from Captivity—Death of Henry II.—The House of Guise in Power—
Meeting at Vendôme—Desire for an Alliance with Catherine premature—Failure of
Anthony to assert himself—Anne resigns the Grand Mastership and Coligny the
Governorship of Picardy—Persecution—Dangers of the Situation—Condition of
France : King, Nobility, Peasantry, Townspeople, Clergy—Ill-advised Measures of the
Government, and Feud between Guises and Montmorencys and Princes of the Blood
precipitate Revolt—Conspiracy of Amboise—Attitude of Coligny, his Policy and
Advice—Was Condé the *Chef Muet*?—Coligny entrusted by Catherine with Mission
in Normandy—His Reply—Connection with Catherine—Her Appearance—Assembly
of Fontainebleau.

IN March, 1558, Coligny was removed from Sluys to Ghent.
In October, negotiations were seriously begun between
England, Spain, and France, at Cercamp. They resulted in
the peace of Cateau Cambrésis of the 2nd and 3rd of April,
1559. On the 20th of November, 1558, the Duke of Savoy
had signed a passport for the Admiral, but it was not delivered
until some months later. Early in February, however, he was
liberated, and set out for the frontier. He was there to be set
free on the part payment of his ransom of fifty thousand écus.
On the 9th he arrived at Arras, on the 10th at Lille. Here,
unfortunately, he was detained on the order of Philip II. as
security for the good faith of Marshal St. André. His uncle,
who had shown an exemplary solicitude throughout, at once
sent his secretary to Brussels. Savoy's own agent at Cateau
Cambrésis wrote advising compliance with the Constable's
wishes. At last, Spanish scruples were satisfied, and Coligny
left for France.[1]

But he was not destined to find it as he had left it. His

---

[1] Delaborde, i., and Granvelle, v. 437 ; Turin, Francia Lettere Ministri, i. (letters
of 13th, 14th, and 15th Feb.) ; Naples, Carte Farn., 715.

own position was profoundly changed; that of Anne of Montmorency was changed also.   The splendid capacity which the
Admiral had shown at St. Quentin was hardly recognised.   He
had to bear the stigma of all unsuccessful generals.   The
condition of the Constable was even worse, for his loss of
prestige was greater and more deserved.   The treaty of Cateau
Cambrésis added still further to their discomfiture.   Anthony
of Bourbon was angered by the neglect of his claims to Spanish
Navarre.   Marshal Brissac, whose great military qualities made
him a valuable ally, was alienated by the signing away of his
conquests in Piedmont.   His passionate resentment surged up
in the apostrophe : " O miserable France ! into what loss and
ruin art thou fallen, thou who wert wont to triumph over all
the nations of Europe ! "   In this phrase popular rage and
disappointment, national sentiment groping for expression,
were made articulate.   The Constable was certainly more
responsible for the humiliating terms of the treaty than the
other commissioners, St. André and the Cardinal of Lorraine.
In consequence, he had to bear the brunt of the very widespread indignation.

      This was a poor record with which to challenge the
brilliant Francis of Lorraine, fresh from his conquest of Calais—
won, so it was said,[1] from the plans of Coligny—and Thionville.   Nor were other events calculated to cheer them.   In
April, 1558, Mary Queen of Scots, and niece of the Duke
of Guise, was married to the Dauphin.   More threatening
still was the religious attitude of the King.   He was sincerely
a Catholic.   It needed in a French king either a very strong
or very weak character to accept Protestantism.   Henry was
neither.   He clung to Catholicism in much the same spirit
as he clung to the Constable.   It was ancient and venerable.
It represented the might of tradition and the type of stability.
It was a safe harbour for an honest, inelastic, and not too
dogmatic mind.   His zeal had long chafed under the curb of
a war and a Protestant alliance.   He had sworn, a year before,
" that were he able to set his affairs in order, he would make
the streets run with the blood and heads of this artisan
canaille." [2]   And now, by the peace of Cateau Cambrésis, which

[1] Brantôme, iv. 213–215.   [2] Alvarotto, 22nd May, 1558 : Modena Francia, 34.

opened the age of the political counter-Reformation, he was free, and prepared to strike. He was eager to vindicate his right to the title of the Most Christian King.

It was at this critical juncture that Coligny reappeared. His state of mind can best be gauged from an incident related by Throckmorton in a despatch from Paris of the 30th of May. "The said Admiral, in conducting of Mr. Wotton and me to the churche of Nostre Dame, toke occasion to question with me toching the state of religion in England ; and supposing he wold have remayned still in our compeny, after I was entered into the quire, and masse ones begonne, I loked for him ; but I could by no meanes understand him to be there, but that he was slipped away from masse : nothwithstanding, he was ready after to bring us home againe." There was nothing equivocal in this ; one step more, and he was an avowed Protestant. Collision with the King seemed inevitable. Their interests, sentiments, ideals, policy, all clashed. Coligny was only saved by an accident. Henry II. was mortally wounded in a tourney on the 9th of June, and died eleven days later.

The sixteenth century was rich in dramatic surprises. None were more startling than the death of Henry II. Few had more far-reaching effects. For the Guises, it was a chance in a thousand. Their dreams were realised. At a stroke, they were virtual regents of the kingdom. Francis II. was a cipher. His anæmic personality bent before the intellectual and, more especially, physical vigour of his consort, Mary, Queen of Scots. And she in her turn was the creature of her uncle, the Cardinal of Lorraine.

It took the new rulers but a short time to oust their rivals. Anne with Coligny was set the task of guarding the dead. His apartments in the Louvre were occupied by the Cardinal of Lorraine. He was deprived of the privy seal of the King. Of his positions of Constable and Grand Master only the titles were left him. The Duke took over the direction of the army, his brother the civil administration. In face of these repeated humiliations Anne retired to Chantilly, " and many," remarked the Spanish Ambassador, Chantonnay, who had his own private grudges against the Guises, " are filled with a great compassion." Condé was got rid of by entrusting him with an embassy, while his brother, Anthony of Bourbon, had not yet appeared at court.

This attack of the Guises was hard to meet. One serious attempt, however, was made. At a meeting of the Montmorency and Bourbon interests at Vendôme, at which Coligny was not present, it seems to have been decided to leave the assertion of their rights to Anthony of Navarre. They no doubt hoped to gain the aid of the Queen Mother. But as yet the step was premature. Her position was too precarious. She dared not respond. She clung to the Guises, not from inclination, but from the instinct of self-preservation. Of power she had little or none. Even after the conspiracy of Amboise, when she had begun to assert herself, she was still, at least to the outside world, scarcely more than one of two queens, the dominating presence of the Cardinal of Lorraine being always in the background.[1] The plan, therefore, of the opposition had small chance of success. And what little it had was jeopardised by the character of Anthony. Irresolute and shifty as ever, drifting helplessly between the general plan of asserting the rights of the Princes of the Blood and his own pet project of regaining Spanish Navarre, he could do nothing. Received coldly at court, he was glad to escape from his hopeless task on the pretext of conducting Princess Elizabeth to her spouse, Philip II.

This preliminary skirmish put heart into the Guise faction. They renewed the offensive. The Duke and the whole family were confessed pluralists. Still, that was no reason for tolerating the failing in others. They therefore pressed the Constable to resign the office of Grand Master. He protested, spent several melancholy months, and then yielded. He was in some sort consoled by the sop of a Marshalship for Francis of Montmorency. He had, in fact, wished to see the Grand Mastership descend to his eldest son ; for the latter, in the event of his father's death, might have found himself stranded. He was only Governor of the Isle of France, and " Governors hold office during the good pleasure of the King, but the Constable,

[1] For this see the account of the mission of the Genoese Ambassadors, June, 1560 : Genoa, Lettere Ministri, 2.

the Grand Master, the Great Chamberlain, the Master of the Horse, and the Chancellor, are given the title, not 'of the King,' but simply 'of France.' In consequence, they hold for life, even though the King dies and another reigns in his stead." [1]

Coligny was approached in a somewhat different manner. The generally accepted account is as follows : Guise hinted to the Admiral that Condé was intriguing to oust him from his government. There was nothing incredible in this, for Condé was poor, turbulent, and had family claims on Picardy. Coligny, however, discovered the ruse. At the same time he recognised the difficulty, if not anomaly, of holding two great offices. He determined, therefore, to abandon Picardy. It would still remain in the family, as it would necessarily fall to his nephew, Condé, who was the most likely claimant. The first part of the plan was carried into effect by his resignation in the month of January, 1560; but the second failed utterly. Brissac, and not Condé, was thrust into the vacant place.

The Ferraran Ambassador, however, gives another reason, which seems more probable.[2] According to him, Coligny stated that the fortifications of many of the towns, such as Calais, Abbeville, Peronne, and St. Quentin, would have to be rebuilt and garrisoned. "And only 6000 francs being offered him on this head, which he refused as insufficient, and fearing that some day shame would come of it, he resigned."

These first months of the reign of Francis II. were a period of unrelieved gloom. The Protestants felt the full force of persecution. The Florentine Ambassador wrote from Paris in August that "one is continually burning someone of the lower class." In November a new edict, that of Villers-Cotterets, enforced the penalty of death. In December, Du Bourg, one of the most distinguished members of the Parliament, was put to death. This deed, which aroused the Huguenots and even moderate men to frenzy, was characterised by Philip II. as "profitable to the service of Our God." Unhappily for France, the Spanish King had definitely entered the arena of French politics. He urged the Government to the last excesses, mind-

[1] Chantonnay, 2nd Dec. 1559: Paris, Arch. Nat., K. 1492.
[2] 3rd March, 1560: Modena Francia, 36.

ful of " the place in which Our Lord has set us, and the obliga-
tion under which we are to desire the increase of the authority
of the Holy Apostolic See, as its obedient son, and the common
good of Christendom." His Ambassador was invariably
gloomy at the thought of sparing heretics. " All manner of
speed and rigour," he protested to Marshal St André, " was
laudable in the present necessity; vigour should be shown
without respect of persons, for this would bruit abroad the
punishment, and make all tremble." [1]

The Guise position, however, was weaker than it seemed.
France, in fact, was ripe for rebellion. Professor Marcks, in his
luminous sketch of its condition, brings into full relief the
hidden dangers. Crowning the social edifice was the King,
gradually centring in himself the legal, administrative, and
financial organisation of the kingdom. Below him stood the
aristocracy, as yet unreconciled to its new position. It had
fallen on evil days. It groaned under the stress of poverty;
at the very time that the gold-mines of America were quad-
rupling prices, and the Renaissance, by cultivating taste, was
creating a love of luxury, its income, derived from land,
remained stationary. But it felt above all the steady pressure
of royalty. It resented the filching away of its powers one
by one. Representing the spirit of localism, it clung
desperately to the tatters of mediæval feudalism, and craved
independence. At last, in the Estates of Orleans and Pontoise
of 1560–1561, it gave voice to its accumulated discontents.
It protested against the attack of the peasantry on aristocratic
rights, demanded permission to engage in commercial pursuits
without the loss of its privileges, insisted on the claims of the
provincial estates, and urged the necessity of reorganising the
judicial, administrative, and financial system on lines which
would virtually restore the old order—in a word, it cried out
against centralisation.

Below the aristocracy, again, came the peasantry, who,
though scarcely actuated by the bitter opposition which was
to produce the French Revolution, felt that they could only
rise in the social and economic scale at the expense of their

[1] This and the other quotations are from letters of January, 1560: Paris, Arch.
Nat., K. 1493.

immediate superiors. Perhaps the most contented section of the community was the citizen class. All the changes of the last half-century had played into its hands: the Renaissance, the discovery of America, the expansion of trade, the rise in prices, and the decline of the nobility. Moreover, the extension of royal influence had on the whole told in its favour, especially as it provided the instruments of the new régime: the legal and administrative class. But even here there was cause for uneasiness. It was sensitive to any interference of the Crown with its privileges, and it might at any moment develop a policy which would prove as dangerous as aristocratic pretensions to the central power. Moreover, in its midst there was a chronic struggle for authority of merchants and lawyers, office-holders and the mass of the community. And, lastly, there was a scarcely disguised hostility between it and the nobility, and between these two and the ecclesiastical order. Even the Church had hidden within it seeds of discord. It was not, like the aristocracy, reactionary in the sense of opposing the centralising tendencies of the monarchy. The Concordat had bound it to the King, and it submitted to, if it was not content with, its lot. Nevertheless its abuses, its corruption, its unwillingness, or rather inability, to reform itself quickly, were a social menace.

It was on such a France—divided, agitated, though seemingly at peace—that the Reformation descended with all its disturbing influences. Originally non-political in tone, counting its converts among every class, it was inevitably drawn into the vortex. Nevertheless, there might have been peace, at least for a time, had not the death of Henry II. let loose other factors. It was soon apparent that the accession of the Guises to power had not only embittered the feud with the Montmorencys, but had alienated the Bourbons. In consequence, the general unrest was soon revolving round this antagonism as its centre.

It can hardly be said that the measures adopted by the Government tended to allay opposition. War had created a military class. By the peace of Cateau Cambrésis it was thrown on its own resources. Without occupation, indigent, largely aristocratic, and therefore turbulent and chafing at

restraint, it was willing to voice every floating discontent.
Many had already joined the ranks of Protestantism; more
followed. They needed delicate handling. The Cardinal of
Lorraine, on the contrary, dealt with them severely. He
struck at them by persecution. His honourable attempts to
keep down expenses were resented still more. Many needy
gentlemen, aggrieved by these economies, eager for pensions
and posts, unpaid, crowded the court. One device to get rid
of them was to flee them like the pest. "The court,"
Chantonnay reported on the 23rd of January, "will go ten miles
from here to Amboise, the King meanwhile hunting for twelve
or fifteen days to escape the importunities of captains and
others, to whom one owes much and does not pay." Another
was to drive them away by threats. This was the surest
means of spreading sedition broadcast.

Such conduct brought its nemesis. Huguenots, soldiers,
disappointed office-seekers, Montmorencys, Princes of the
Blood, all were thrown into opposition. The more violent
were eager to strike. And their impatience led to the
conspiracy of Amboise.[1] Its object, as given by the Duke of
Guise, was: to kill him and the Cardinal of Lorraine, to
present an armed petition, and dictate terms to the King, even
murder him.[2] His statement, however, cannot go unchallenged.
He was a prejudiced witness, and unfortunately a type of most
of those who were best able to throw light on the subject.
The bulk of the evidence was extorted by torture, and from
men in the fear of death. It is this which makes the
conspiracy of Amboise so difficult to fathom. It is easy to
generalise on causes and results. The problem is to discover,
with any degree of certainty, the actual intentions of the
conspirators. One piece of evidence is undoubtedly genuine.
It is the documents, partly in cipher, found on La Bigne,
servant of the ringleader, La Renaudie. If we accept the
abstract given by La Planche, it seems to clear the movement
from the charge of anti-royal tendencies. The first article,

[1] Ruble, in his *Antoine de Bourbon*, ii. cap. viii., has collected most of the material
dealing with the subject; see also de la Ferrière's *Lettres de Catherine de Médicis*, i.
Intro. lxiv.

[2] Alvarotto from Amboise, 20th March : Modena Francia, 36.

which was in cipher, began with the words: "Protestation made by the chief and all those of the council to attempt nothing against the Majesty of the King, nor the Princes of the Blood, nor the state of the realm."[1]

But let us take the accusations of Guise one by one. Firstly, did the conspirators purpose killing the Duke and the Cardinal of Lorraine? That they did so, rests on the declaration of one of the prisoners, Raunay, and the supposed confession of another, the Baron of Castelnau. We say supposed, for the Baron de Ruble[2] was hardly justified when he stated that "the English Ambassador says positively that Castelnau avowed the project of killing the Duke of Guise and the Cardinal of Lorraine." What Throckmorton actually did say was: "Castelnovo hath confessed, as I here say, . . . that the cause of their haste was, to dispeche their first enterprise for the killing of the Duke of Guise and the Cardinall of Lorrein."[3] Nevertheless this hearsay evidence of Throckmorton is quite credible, especially when we remember that Calvin wrote to Sturm on the 23rd of March: "totum cardinem verti in conficiendo Antonio[4] recte judicas."[5]

We see, therefore, that the first accusation of Guise is at least plausible and even probable. The second—namely, that the conspirators intended to present a petition with arms in their hands—cannot be contested. The third, on the other hand, has the least substance of the three. There is an almost complete absence of proof that there was any design against the life of the King. The Guises did their best, by question and torture, to extract confessions of an anti-royal conspiracy, but in vain. In fact, the charge was a mere manœuvre on the part of the King's uncles to identify his cause with their own. It met with scant success. Chantonnay and Throckmorton had remarked on the attempt in the early days of March. By the end of the month, the facts of the conspiracy, so far as they were ever known, were common property. Yet the public remained sceptical as to the conspirators being actuated by any anti-royal bias. Andelot assured the Queen Mother, in a voice too loud to please her, that the rising was directed

[1] La Planche, 255.   [2] Vol. ii. 194, note 3, of *Antoine de Bourbon*.
[3] Forbes, i. 381.   [4] Francis of Guise.   [5] *Calvini Opera*, xviii. 39.

neither against the King, nor his brothers, nor the order of the kingdom.[1] The Mantuan Ambassador took practically the same view. He reported that it was generally held that nothing would ever have happened, if it had not been for the wish to kill the Cardinal of Lorraine.[2]

To sum up: all that can be stated with certainty is that the conspirators intended to force their way into the presence of the King, and present petitions in favour of the free exercise of both religions, the removal of the Guises, and the summoning of the Estates General, in which the Cardinal of Lorraine and his brother were to be formally accused. The evidence of a plan of more summary treatment of these latter is, as we have said, probable, while there is little or no evidence that an attack on the King was ever contemplated.

The Guises were more successful in their efforts to implicate the Huguenots. Without doubt a very large number, if not the majority, of the conspirators were Protestant. One at least of the petitions was Protestant also. And in some localities the ministers seem to have organised the revolt. Yet there is much in favour of the contention that " the Huguenot party as such, both in its principal chiefs and their adherents, remained a stranger to it." [3]   Certainly this applies to the case of Calvin.[4] To the first proposals of armed resistance he had objected " that if one drop of blood were shed, rivers would run with it throughout Europe." [5]   He was equally firm in rejecting the solicitations of La Renaudie. Coligny, too, seems to have been innocent. The only evidence,

[1] Alvarotto, 27th March : Modena Francia, 36.

[2] 18th March : Mantua, Arch. Gonz., 652.

[3] Ehinger's *Franz Hotmann*, 17.

[4] Ruble (ii. 139, note 4) wrote of Calvin and the conspiracy of Amboise : "du moins la blâma-t-il après coup (Lettre du 16 avril, 1561 ; Bonnet, *Lettres de Calvin*, t. ii. p. 382)." This was quite uncalled for, as M. de Ruble would have recognised if he had consulted the complete works of Calvin, instead of M. Bonnet's edition. For, on the 23rd of March, 1560, Calvin wrote to Sturm, obviously referring to the conspiracy, though as yet he had no news of the result : " Quum me principio consulerent qui primi ad hoc negotium agitandum aliis fuerunt autores, libere respondi, mihi non placere totam agendi rationem, rem vero ipsam multo minus probari." *Calvini Opera*, xviii. 38, 39.

[5] Calvin to Coligny, 16th April, 1561 ; Bonnet, *Lettres de Calvin*, ii. 382. This was written by Calvin in reply to a demand from Coligny for a public disavowal.

direct or indirect, against him, comes from the tainted source
of La Renaudie, who assured Calvin that the Admiral was
mixed up in the affair.   But immediately afterwards he spread
similar reports about Calvin himself.   This was evidently an
ordinary ruse of the volatile intriguer for gaining recruits.
La Renaudie was evidently quick of resource, active, and
intelligent ; but he was without character.   His condemnation by the French courts for bolstering up a case by forged
documents, his relations with Calvin, and his subsequent
direction of the conspiracy, prove him to have been untruthful,
reckless—one who would stop at nothing.   We may, therefore,
assert that neither Calvin nor Coligny had any share in the
conspiracy of Amboise.

The same confidence cannot be felt in regard to Condé.
At the time he was almost universally considered as the *chef
muet*, who was to declare himself after the first success.
Castelnau, La Planche, and almost all the others, speak of him
time and again as the leader.   And modern writers, such as
M. Decrue and the Baron de Ruble, have popularised this
view.   Yet in reality, after sifting the evidence, it comes to
this, that the one solitary fact against him is the confession
of one of the conspirators, Mazères.   Now Mazères did not
pretend that he had either seen or spoken to Condé.   His
evidence was mere hearsay.   La Renaudie had told him that
under certain circumstances the Prince would take over the
command.   This assurance may have been sufficient to
convince Mazères and his friends, but it is certainly not a
solid basis on which to build up a theory of Condé's guilt,
though we are willing to believe that, given a first success,
he would very easily have been prevailed on to lead the
movement.   Nor, in the absence of facts, can we accept the
statements or suspicions of his contemporaries.   La Planche,
for instance, was admirably equipped as an historian of the
conspiracy.   Yet he had no inside information ; he was not
one of the conspirators.   And he is obviously very often at
fault.   In the case of Condé, he and the other writers and
statesmen seem to have been influenced, firstly by the
statements of La Renaudie, secondly by the known turbulence
of the Prince and his hatred of the Guises.   Rumour and

6

suspicion did the rest. In truth, very few could have known the real facts, probably only La Renaudie himself.

Personally, we believe that the *chef muet* never existed. He was a pure figment of the brain of La Renaudie. Nothing is more curious in the religious wars in France, than the Huguenot passion for legality. Legists, divines, commanders, the author of the *Vindiciæ contra Tyrannos*, and a score of others, all sought a legal basis for their action. They must have leaders who could make a fair claim to the right to resist. When, therefore, the King or the heir to the throne failed them, they fell back on " magistrates," and Princes of the Blood. La Renaudie knew their weakness. He created the *chef muet*.

From the very beginning, the conspiracy was doomed to failure. The Guises had received a first warning on the 12th of February. By the 20th or 21st they had the plan, at least in outline, from a lawyer named Pierre des Avenelles. On the 17th of March an ill-concerted attempt against Amboise was easily frustrated. Yet the uncertainty had been quite sufficient to shake their nerves. On the 7th of March, Throckmorton reported, with what truth we do not know, that the Guises " are in such feare as themselfs do were privy coatis, and are in the night garded with pistoleers and men in arms." The Cardinal of Lorraine, fearful as ever, was haunted, so it was said, by the mumblings of some Jewish astrologer, who had prophesied his death for this year.[1] His brother, however, was of another mould. He revelled in a very orgy of blood. The scaffold was not quick enough. Countless victims were swung gaunt from the battlements ; ten, twenty, fifty, were thrown in sacks into the Loire. In so far as mercy was shown, it was by sparing some for the galleys. Under the Guisard impulsion, the court crowded to the château windows to take in the details. Condé, sickened by the butchery, burst into fiery denunciation : " I am astonished," cried he, " that the King is counselled to put so many honest lords and gentlemen to death."[2] D'Aubigné, who was later to become the inspired interpreter of Huguenotism, gives us, as a memory of his childhood, the scene where his father, wending his way through the bustling

---

[1] Chantonnay to Philip II., 19th March : Paris, Arch. Nat., K. 1493.
[2] La Planche, 268.

throng of Amboise, came suddenly on the withering heads of his friends. "They have slaughtered France, the butchers!" cried he. The son, riding after him, saw that he had been moved. Then the father, laying his hand on the boy's head, exclaimed, "My child! thy head must no more be spared than mine, in avenging these honoured leaders whose heads you have seen. If thou dost, my curse be on thee!"[1] The Admiral made a determined effort to save one of the conspirators, the Baron of Castelnau. But this aged and distinguished nobleman was hurried off to the shambles.

During the latter half of February, the suspicious Guises determined to summon the Colignys. The Admiral was probably called on the plea of an expedition to Scotland. He arrived on or before the 24th. When consulted by the Queen Mother, he was frank to the verge of recklessness. He went minutely into the causes of unrest, political as well as religious. He inveighed bitterly against his enemies. He cried out against their monopoly of power. He pointed to the general discontent. Protestantism, he assured her, was too far advanced to be suppressed by persecution. Appeasement would only come with toleration. As a temporary expedient, he advised the immediate publication of an edict which should give relief to Huguenots. The religious question might then be finally settled by a general or national council. These representations, no doubt, coincided in the main with Catherine's own opinions. They were therefore communicated to the Council, and resulted in the edict of the 8th of March. It was certainly not what the Admiral had hoped for; it was still less what he had counselled. It was strongly Catholic. It condemned Geneva and all her ways. It insisted on conformity with the Catholic Church. Nevertheless, by passing a sponge over past religious offences, in issuing a general pardon to all—preachers, conspirators, and a few others alone excepted—it was something gained. It was issued under the form " Par le Roy estant en son conseil auquel estaient messieurs"; then followed the names of the Privy Councillors. Among them were those of Coligny and Odet. By this means the court was able to make use of the popularity of these two with the malcontents. Andelot's

---

[1] *Mémoires de d'Aubigné* (Lalanne), 5.

name does not appear in the list. He only arrived at court on the 15th of March. His brothers had already proposed to retire, but had been detained as a measure of precaution. Coligny's destination was Normandy, where he was to organise a Scottish expedition. Immediately before leaving, he was charged by Catherine to pacify local disturbances. In addition, he was to give her his opinion on the general situation. The Queen Mother had thus unwittingly set him on the road which led directly to his dramatic appearance at the assembly of Fontainebleau.

About this time the term " Huguenots "—derived from the German word " Eidgenossen," a party name of the Swiss Protestants—was first heard. And from the Admiral's standpoint, their future was not unpromising. For though they had suffered serious losses at Amboise, progress had been steady. " Religious matters," wrote the Spanish Ambassador on the 23rd of March, " grow more disturbed every hour; many declare themselves, who until now dissembled." The Florentine Tornabuoni remarked, " I am more than ever doubtful of this kingdom." In May, Protestantism received partial relief by the edict of Romorantin. During the summer Coligny felt strong enough to hold open services at Dieppe. And he must have watched with grim satisfaction the tide of hatred rising steadily against his enemies. " So extreme is the hatred revealed by the nobility and people against these gentlemen," exclaimed Alvarotto, " that it is impossible to express it in writing." Attempts were made to burn their houses; the effigy of the Cardinal of Lorraine was hung, head downwards, in Paris; twelve mounted arquebusiers guarded his person; two hundred thousand men of Dauphiné and Provence, so it was said, were ready to die in wreaking vengeance on their rulers.[1] The fiery Hotman, dipping his pen in vitriol, gave tongue to the public rage in his savage pamphlet, addressed to the Cardinal of Lorraine, *The Tiger of France—*

> "Tigre enragé ! Vipère venimeuse !
> Sépulchre d'abomination ! Spectacle
> de malheur !"[2]

---

[1] These details are from despatches of Alvarotto of 19th April and 7th June : Modena Francia, 36.

[2] *Le Tigre,* edited by Charles Read.

To the ancient causes of complaint were now added their recent cruelty, their pitiless revocation of the merciful ordinance of the 17th of March, and their egoism, which forced from the King a virtual abdication in favour of the Duke, henceforth the royal Lieutenant-General. Then, too, they had surrounded Francis II. with a bodyguard. Nothing was more calculated to arouse popular indignation. "There is not a Frenchman," wrote Tornabuoni, "who is free of his tongue, who does not say that it is a great shame that a King of France, accustomed to go everywhere with a couple of lacqueys, should be reduced, for love of the Guises, to drag after him a guard, without the least reason in the world."[1] Their seeming unwillingness, again, to summon the Estates was a fresh goad to fury. "Many believe that the true remedy for rebellion in this kingdom would be the convocation of the Estates, which are wont to meet when the King ascends the throne, especially when he ceases to have a guardian and comes of age. The end in view is, that the Government, at the very beginning, may be established amid general acclaim. Those who now govern, however, fear nothing more than this convocation of Estates, for they are hated, and are strangers."[2]

It was in the midst of these commotions that Coligny replied to the request made by Catherine on his departure for Normandy. His plan was that the Guises should be removed, that she herself should take over the government of the kingdom, that the Protestants should be tolerated, and that the edicts, which should embody these measures, should be religiously kept. This résumé of Coligny's policy is interesting. He would have been quite content, if circumstances had let him, to work all his life with and through the King and Queen Mother. In this particular instance he proposed too much. Catherine did not dare take things into her own hands. The Guises were too strong—and she was timid. She was to show in the future remarkable courage and self-confidence; but they were acquired gifts, come of the exercise of power. Nevertheless, Coligny's proposal was to bear fruit. It was the origin of a

---

[1] Desjardins, iii. 423.

[2] G. de Vega and Chantonnay, from Chartres, 27th June: Paris, Arch. Nat., K. 1493.

connection with Catherine, which, 'begun in hope, ended in tragedy. His life henceforth was never free from the influence of this sinister figure. It may therefore be worth while to give a sketch of her appearance, drawn by one of the naïve and downright Swiss emissaries in 1557. Her personality, with all its feline subtlety and complexity, was only fully revealed later. " The aforesaid Queen Catherine de' Medici, a Florentine, is a large, tall, and powerful woman, with a full, round, red face like the Dauphin. Her hair is curly, and lies well forward on her head before her cap, which makes some think it false. It is yellow, as are her eyebrows. She has light eyes, a somewhat large and colourless mouth, and large, long teeth. Her speech is unfeminine, almost that of a rough country-woman. She had on a dark robe of fine texture. Her bust is well formed, and her whole figure—for she stood upright—reminds me, with the exception of her face, of Frau Agnes Kollerin." [1]

Coligny was more successful in another direction. With the aid of the new Chancellor, L'Hôpital, he impressed the Queen Mother with the wisdom of summoning the Notables of the kingdom. This plan was accepted by the King's guardians and carried out. The assembly was to meet at Fontainebleau in August. The Constable arrived on the 17th, accompanied by his four sons, Coligny, Andelot, Odet, La Tremouille, Villars, and a cavalcade five hundred strong. It was noted that he was aged and melancholy, perhaps at the thought that Navarre and Condé by their absence had lost him the opportunity of overawing his opponents.

The opening ceremony took place on the 21st. L'Hôpital delivered the introductory address, while Guise and the Cardinal of Lorraine explained the military state of the kingdom. The second sitting was held on the 23rd. Monluc, Bishop of Valence, had just been called on to address the meeting, when Coligny suddenly rose from his seat, and approached the King. And after he had twice made a deep obeisance, he presented two petitions, one addressed to Francis II. and the other to Catherine. They were then handed to the secretary, de l'Aubespine, who read them aloud in a clear voice. They

---

[1] Tagebuch of one of the emissaries, published by Holländer, *Hist. Zeitschrift*, lxix. 403.

CATHERINE DE' MEDICI
(*Clouet*)

were on behalf of those who styled themselves faithful Christians, scattered in divers parts and places of the realm. Their contents were briefly: a strong disapproval of the conspiracy of Amboise, a passionate expression of abhorrence of disobedience to the royal will, and a plea for their complete toleration and for the grant of buildings for Protestant worship.

Amid the astonishment caused by their reading, Coligny begged the King to take his action in good part. On the demand of the Queen Mother, he said, he had grappled with the religious difficulties while in Normandy. And he had promised to present these requests on finding that the petitioners had some grounds for their complaints. To this the King replied in courteous, though vague, terms. On the morrow the Admiral dealt with the general situation. He explained that when he had expressed a wish to have the petitions signed, it had been answered that if the King so wished, fifty thousand signatures could be found. He then plunged into the question of Francis II.'s bodyguard. There was nothing, he exclaimed, more hurtful to a King than to be reared in the fear of his subjects. He therefore urged their dismissal, closing with a plea for the reformation of abuses in the Church, and for the summoning of the Estates General.

Guise and his brother followed. Their speeches were, on the whole, moderate in tone. The Cardinal remarked that if fifty thousand could be found to sign the petitions, the King could meet them with a million. He was against a council to discuss religion, but was inclined to agree to the convocation of the Estates General. On the 26th it was resolved to call the Estates together for December. The suggestion of summoning a national council to discuss religion also found favour, but only if the proposal for a general council fell through. With this the assembly closed.[1]

[1] For details of assembly, see La Place, 53; Condé, ii. 645; Turin, Lettere Ministri Francia (Girolamo della Rovere, 21st Aug.); Florence, Arch. Med., 4594, 342 (Tornabuoni, 18th Aug.).

CHAPTER V

PREPARATIONS FOR CIVIL WAR

Imprisonment of Condé—Death of Francis ii.—Cause of Unpopularity of House of Guise—Coligny's Policy of supporting Catherine—His Antagonism to Guise—His Rôle as Protestant Leader—The Triumvirate—Edict of July—Colloquy of Poissy—Flood-tide of Huguenotism—Alliance with the Court—Failure of the Colloquy—Cardinal of Ferrara in France—Defection of Anthony of Navarre—Massacre of Vassy.

THE assembly of Fontainebleau was the first step toward civil war. The political disputes were grave, but might have been bridged over. The national party, headed by the Constable and Anthony of Bourbon, was menacing the Guises. But compromise was still possible. Their enmity was personal, and might have disappeared. But no skilful diplomacy, no amiable concession, no vague yearnings after peace, could smooth out the tangle of religious differences. So far, Huguenotism had lurked in dark places and cried from dungeons. On the rare occasions when it had struck back, it had done so under the cloak of conspiracy, and in despair. With the assembly of Fontainebleau it changed its attitude. Under the verbal expression of reverence for the royal person brooded the accents of menace. When the Admiral claimed that his petition could be signed by fifty thousand souls, the thought lay behind : could be supported by fifty thousand swords ! In a word, they had the power, and, if need be, the will to resist. And the retort of the Cardinal of Lorraine was the answer of threat to threat.

The ruling idea of this petition is to-day a mere commonplace ; it is of the very texture of modern thought. It was an appeal for toleration. Yet, to sixteenth-century France, it came with the abruptness of a challenge. A people bred and moulded in the tradition of " un roi, une loi, une foi," were suddenly called on to cut themselves off from their sheet-anchor. And the demand was all the more anomalous when we remember that it was not a plea for general toleration. The petitioners insisted on the duty of the Crown to see that the pure service of God was established and abuses exterminated. They themselves were to receive State recognition because their doctrine was that contained in the Old and New Testaments. The only glimmer of a wider view was a reference to the limited toleration of the Jews, whose services, however, they averred, were "abominable before God." In fact, Protestantism in France differed little from Protestantism elsewhere. Wherever triumphant — in England, in Switzerland, in the Empire—it had by sheer force imposed the theory: "cujus regio, ejus religio."

The assembly of Fontainebleau thus prepared the way for conflict, and in so doing influenced the future history of France. It had its place, too, in the life of Coligny; it marked a turning-point in his fortune. It was here that, in the eyes of the world, he formally accepted the Reformation. From that moment he became the heart, the brain, the directing force of Huguenotism. One or other of the Bourbon Princes played a rôle at times; the most strenuous was Joan of Navarre. But it was not until the third war of religion that she became a principal factor; and even then her sex fettered her. Her influence was inevitably second to that of the man of action. As for the rest, the fickle, shifty, foppish, ear-ringed Anthony of Navarre was less than useless. His connection with Huguenotism was a mere intrigue, crowned with betrayal. He was never sincerely a Protestant except in death. His brother, the Prince of Condé, was more faithful; but he was often distracted, sometimes—as in 1564—wavered, and never represented the more sober element among his followers. Coligny, on the other hand, was the party. He created it, inspired it, breathed into it his dominant personality. In the new struggle he was about to undertake he was supported by his brothers. On the 16th of October a Papal bull directed Tournon to take action against Cardinal Odet. He was accused of favouring heresy in his Archbishopric of Toulouse and in the late assembly of Fontainebleau. And what further aroused Catholic resentment was his satirical remark on one occasion, "that he spoke, not as Cardinal, but as Christian."[1] For the moment, however, the religious question was crowded out of view. The struggle between the Bourbon Princes and the house of Guise was nearing a definite issue. The latter were thoroughly alarmed. They feared a vast Montmorency-Bourbon intrigue. Navarre and Condé, who were plotting in the south, were induced or rather terrorised into coming to court. Elaborate precautions had been taken in Orleans. The population was disarmed; there was scarcely a knife left for table use.[2] The town was alive with soldiery. The two princes entered through a lane of hostile pikes. Condé was at once hurried off to prison. The Admiral was soon summoned by the news that his half-sister, Magdalen of Roye, was a prisoner. Condé, it is alleged, had been actually condemned to death, and was only saved by the illness of the King. Francis II. died on the 5th of December.

The feeling of relief was general. "The King is dead," Coligny is reported to have said; "this means life to us."[3] "Behold the Lord our God has awakened," wrote Beza triumphantly, "and removed that boy." A great stream of Protestant exiles flowed back from Geneva. The aged Constable, forgetful of his gout, his political ailments and all, came hurrying to court. Andelot resumed his duties of Colonel of the Infantry, "which he had not done in the time of the late King."[4] "The Queen," suggests Sir James Melville, "was blyeth of the death of King Francis hir sone, because she had no guiding of him."[5] As for Anthony of Navarre, he said little. The danger he had run had for the moment sobered him. Condé, on the contrary, took back his sword and dagger, cursing the Guises.[6]

The rule of the Cardinal of Lorraine had not been without its merits. It was certainly no more corrupt, and was probably more capable, than any possible substitute. Its legal reforms,

[1] "Processo e Sentenza contro il Cardinale Chatillione": Rome, Corsini Library, cxci. 141–147.

[2] Vatican Library, Urbino, 1439, 213.　[3] Bibl. Nat., Cinq Cent de Colbert, 488,749.

[4] Girolamo della Rovere, 15th Dec.: Turin, Francia Lettere Ministri, i.

[5] Melville's *Memoirs*, 86.

[6] Chantonnay, 28th Dec.: Paris, Arch. Nat., K. 1494.

its financial methods, its earnest desire to restrict expenses, its refusal to arm Catholics in the provinces, were both statesmanlike and patriotic. But the Guises lacked one great essential : popular support. Their very last act was received coldly. For reasons of economy, Francis II., their creature and victim, was buried with an unusual absence of pomp. Someone pointed the lesson by writing on the velvet coverlet of the bier : "Where is Messire Tanneguy du Chastel ? but he was a Frenchman ! " This was a reference to a gentleman who had beggared himself to bury his master, Charles VIII. Indeed, at no time in the half-century of their ascendancy were the Guises less in touch with national sentiment. Arbitrary procedure, violence, cruelty, might have been forgiven them. Their fault lay in the fact that they made no appeal to France. Self-interest and a passionate hatred of their enemies had reduced them to the condition of a faction.

Charles IX. was the new King. Coligny had to decide on a policy. There were two claimants to the regency : the Queen Mother and Anthony of Bourbon, First Prince of the Blood. Which of the two, then, was he to support ? Calvin and the bulk of the Protestants had no doubts on the matter. The former was thoroughly hostile to Catherine. His plan was to summon the Estates, who would appoint a council of regency, Anthony presumably directing affairs. Let Catherine have all possible honour, wrote he ; but to allow her, a stranger and an Italian, to rule, would be a dishonour.[1] A few months later, Hotman still wrote of the ambition and tyranny of Semiramis."[2] And in their belief in the advisability of excluding her from power, the public was with them. " Though in all these cases," wrote the Venetian Soriano, " there may be diversity of opinion, the one commonly held is that the government of the kingdom belongs to the Princes of the Blood, and especially to those nearest the crown, while the charge of the person of the King falls to the Queen Mother."[3] But Coligny shared neither their ideas nor their prejudices. He knew the King of Navarre as they did not. Anthony was unstable, untrustworthy, and absorbed in the chase of that

[1] *Calvini Opera*, xviii. 282.   [2] *Ib.* xviii. 424.
[3] Alberi, iv. 141.

tempting mirage, Spanish Navarre. He had failed at every crisis. He had delayed until too late in the summer of 1559. He had refused to appear at the assembly of Fontainebleau. And now, on the death of Francis II., he was intimidated by Catherine, contenting himself with the command of the army. It was idle to try to galvanise him into action. He was an impossible leader.

Coligny had other reasons also for working with Catherine. Protestantism had now become the passion of his life. He was determined to make the nation accept it, but to do this royal support was necessary. Everything in France began and ended in the Crown. It was the one permanent force in politics. He therefore set himself to win it over. His chief hope lay in the character of the sovereign and his mother. Charles IX. was young, while Catherine, though she was less impressionable, was an opportunist, and so open to conviction. These, no doubt, were his views on the situation. They were perfectly sound, but to put them into practice, in face of the half-concealed hostility of friends, needed courage and self-reliance of a high order. But this alliance did not come all at once. For the first few months Catherine's attitude was strictly neutral. She allowed the rival factions to find their level. In this contest the Montmorency-Bourbon interest was able to boast an initial advantage in gaining control of the Council of Affairs and the Privy Council. But with this their success ended. The Guises quickly recovered their influence, and with the aid of Nemours, Brissac, St. André, and Tournon, they were soon on equal terms. The struggle was a severe one. Guise exclaimed that some day they would be at one another's throats.[1] When the court moved to Fontainebleau, both parties came fully armed. They wrangled over the amours of Françoise de Rohan, the question of precedence, and of the castle keys. Guise then proposed the somewhat desperate remedy of a duel of "man against man, or of so many against so many."

The acknowledged leader of the anti-Guise party was Anthony of Bourbon; the real leader was Coligny. He was the heart and soul of the movement. He had to bear the brunt of the storm. He had a violent quarrel with the Duke

---

[1] Alvarotto, 30th Jan. 1561 : Modena Francia, 36.

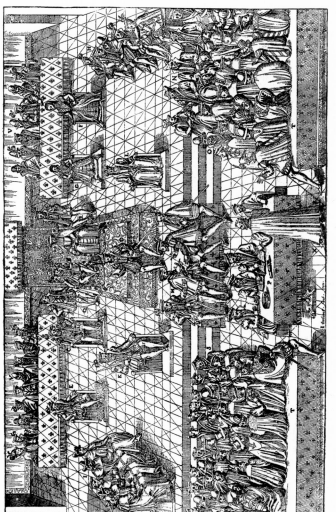

ESTATES-GENERAL OF ORLEANS, JAN., 1561

(*Vorterei*)

A—KING   B—QUEEN MOTHER   C—BROTHER OF KING   D—SISTER OF KING   E—KING OF NAVARRE   F—DUCHESS OF FERRARA
G—GUISE AS GREAT CHAMBERLAIN   H—PRINCES   I—CARDINALS   K—CONSTABLE   L—CHANCELLOR   M—THE ADMIRAL AND
MARSHALS   N—PRIVY COUNCILLORS   O—KNIGHTS OF THE ORDER OF ST. MICHAEL   P—THE FOUR SECRETARIES OF STATE
Q—CIPIERRE   R—CRUSOL   S—CLERGY   T—DEPUTIES OF NOBILITY AND THIRD ESTATE   V—GENTLEMEN AND OTHERS
X—QUINTIN, ORATOR OF CLERGY, SPEAKING

of Guise in the Council; the latter longed to poniard him.[1]
He was attacked in the Estates General by the orator of the
clergy.   In 1561, a fanatic of Paris, playing on the root-mean-
ing of the name Châtillon, whipped the mob to fury with the
text: "'Go ye into the castle which is over against you.'   Over
against you is this Châtillon, who will be your ruin if you do
not take care."[2]   The proud and arrogant Chantonnay brooded
darkly over his doings. "The Cardinal of Châtillon, the Admiral,
and Andelot," he reported on the 28th of December, "are continually in the palace.   When once the gates are open, the King
and Queen Mother are never without one of them.   Already
this has attracted attention, and raised a fear that little by
little they may spread the opinions with which they are generally said to be infected."   No wonder, then, that Coligny was
hailed by Huguenotism as a deliverer! "There is one among
the chiefs," wrote Calvin enthusiastically, "who acts wisely."

Thus, as we see, his action was no longer solely or indeed
distinctly political.   He was vigorously pushing the religious
question to the front.   On the 11th of February Bedford
informed Cecil that "the wife of the Admiral was lately
delivered of a child, which he caused to be baptised in the
vulgar tongue, after the manner of Geneva; the Admiral was
present thereat himself; the doing of the same was much
commended by many."   Two weeks later he reported a conversation with the Duchess of Ferrara on the chances of Protestantism.   "To be plain," said she, "its chief promoters in this
Court are the Admiral and the Cardinal of Châtillon, for if it was
not for them, no good would be done; the one travails with
the Queen Mother, and the other with the King of Navarre."
When at court he held Protestant services in his apartments
in the palace.   The Spanish Ambassador complained, but the
only satisfaction he received was that "whereas formerly the
Admiral held his preaching with closed doors, on Palm Sunday
he held it with open ones."   "And they began their ceremonies like those of Geneva, singing aloud their psalms until
the whole courtyard was filled with the sound."[3]

---

[1] Chantonnay, 8th Dec. 1560 : Paris, Arch. Nat., K. 1493.
[2] Labitte, *Les Prédicateurs de la Ligue*, 84.
[3] Paris, Arch. Nat., K. 1494 and 1495 (2nd and 9th April).

So much for his personal example; more important was his general defence of Protestantism. France was in turmoil. For a whole year, the Bishop of Orleans wrote sadly, there had been nothing to chronicle but troubles and seditions, Catholics massacring Protestants, Protestants threatening bishops and magistrates.[1] Already, before the death of Francis II., the Estates of Normandy had proposed a sweeping confiscation of ecclesiastical property.[2] At Orleans the orator of the Third Estate had been particularly bitter against the Church. In Provence the Huguenot stalwart, Mouvans, had pillaged the churches and broken the images. In April, 1561, Odet had to flee Catholic vengeance in his own city of Beauvais. Coligny threw himself into this struggle with characteristic energy. He became the Protestant champion. He insisted on the rigorous punishment of Catholics.[3] He served, moreover, as intermediary between the Reformed churches and the Council. In all this he was no doubt aided by the tolerant views of the Chancellor, L'Hôpital, and by Catherine. And it is to these three that we must ascribe several minor edicts, leading up to the important one of the 19th of April. This latter was the first great concession to Huguenotism. The right of private worship was granted, and all religious prisoners were liberated.

But this policy of Coligny was having its inevitable result. It was accentuating religious differences. Creeds, even more than political cries, were becoming the badge of party. One of the first to be affected was the Constable. His life had been spent in persecuting heretics. As an absolutist, he despised the democratic Calvin. As a votary of authority, he hated sedition. Religious division seemed to him to be a wedge driven into the body politic; political unity, that great essential of national well-being, was threatened. Thus honour, tradition, prejudices, state theories, all seemed to urge him in one direction. His break with the Admiral became inevitable. And yet it was hard for him to turn his back on the past and the policy of years, to shatter family solidarity, to shun old

---

[1] Jean de Morvillier to Bp. of Rennes, 22nd May : Brit. Mus., Egerton, 23, 303.
[2] Chantonnay, 8th Sept. 1560: Paris, Arch. Nat., K. 1493.
[3] Ruccellai to Card. Farnese, 15th April, 1561 : Naples, Carte Farnesiane, 738.

friends, and hold out the hand to those who had plotted his
ruin. An unexpected event decided him. In March, 1561,
the Estates of the *bailliage* of Paris formulated a scheme
of government. Navarre was to be regent. Coligny and the
Constable were to be the chief figures in a Council, from
which the Guises, St. André, and all ecclesiastics were to be
excluded. In addition, those who had administered the State
were to give an account of their charge. These extraordinary
demands wound up with a claim on behalf of the Estates
General to a large share in the Government.[1] Such as they
were, they were sufficient to work the Constable into a state
of fury. In vain Coligny tried to reason with him. The
expostulations of his son Francis, that they were not aimed
at him but at his enemies, and that his true rôle was to act
as arbiter of France, were unheeded. His prejudices, his
fears, the jealous whisperings of his wife, the promptings of a
generous disregard of possible consequences, spurred him on.
On the 6th of April, the Duke of Guise, the Constable, and
Marshal St. André took the sacrament together in the little
chapel of Fontainebleau. This was the new Catholic league,
the ill-omened Triumvirate. It was the first threatening
rearrangement of parties for war. Its object was not one of
defence, but of intimidation. Its temper was shown in the
retort of Guise that he would be faithful to His Majesty so
long as His Majesty was a Catholic.

The defection of Anne was undoubtedly serious. The
Admiral had now only to count on Condé, Navarre,—who had
now a larger share in the Government,—and in a less degree
on Catherine and L'Hôpital. He still, however, fought
strenuously. He quarrelled with Tournon and his uncle in
the Council. "A little before the departure from Fontainebleau, he and his brother entered the Supreme Council at the
rising of the King, which scandalised greatly all the Catholics
of this realm," wrote Chantonnay. If we may believe the
same somewhat credulous witness, Coligny gave precedence
over his own wife to Isabella of Hauteville, who was dubbed
satirically "Madame la Cardinale," and who was later the wife
of Odet. He publicly attached to himself a minister. He

[1] Summary in Arch. Nat. Paris, K. 1494.

formally absented himself from the Catholic ceremonies of the coronation. In a word, many "were dismayed and gave up all for lost, while the heretics were prouder than ever."[1] Yet Coligny was careful not to push his advantages too far. The Portuguese Ambassador who went to visit him at Châtillon wrote back that the townspeople zealously took part in all the Catholic processions on the day of Corpus Christi."[2]

The great event of the summer of 1561 was a conference between the Council and the Parlement. They met to consider the religious question. There were four sets of opinion. A few of the lawyers demanded an "interim"; some leaned to the moderate policy of the late edict of Fontainebleau; others to that of Romorantin, which had decreed penalties against preachers only. The majority, however, favoured the old rigorous and persecuting spirit of Henry II., expressed in the edict of Chateaubriant.[3] Both sides strained every effort. Guise and Coligny were especially bitter. The latter turned on the Bishop of Paris, who had advised extreme measures against heresy, his strictures finally developing into an attack on bishops in general;[4] and so in the hot, pest-ridden Paris of that summer he struggled on. But Catholic influence was too strong. A policy of toleration was rejected by eighty votes to seventy-two,[5] and the result was the persecuting edict of July. Fortunately for the Protestants, the opposition of their leaders had been so vigorous that the latter remained a dead letter.[6]

The contest as yet had only begun. More important events were to follow. The Estates General met at Pontoise, and Coligny was able to give Catherine a practical example of his influence and goodwill. He was able to persuade the Estates quietly to accept the division of power between her and Anthony as arranged in April. His attention, however, was principally directed to the proposed colloquy of Poissy.

---

[1] The above facts were given by Chantonnay, 9th April and 12th May : Paris, Arch. Nat., K. 1494.

[2] Letter to Borromeo from Paris, 17th July : Vatican, B. ix. 13.

[3] Girolamo della Rovere from Paris, 10th July : Turin, Francia Lettere Ministri, i.

[4] *Arcana Seculi*, ii. 125, 126.

[5] Letter of Hotman, 6th Aug.: Heidenhain, Beilagen, 178.

[6] Kluckhohn, i. 205.

This assembly was to resolve the religious question. Its composition and exact scope, therefore, became of vital interest. The French hierarchy, who were preparing to attend the Council of Trent, were willing to debate the question of ecclesiastical discipline at Poissy. But they were determined not to discuss it with heretics, and were unwilling to touch on matters of faith. Coligny's attitude is defined in an eloquent tribute paid him by the Venetian Ambassador: " Those, however, who profess the new opinions, do all they can to bring into the discussion matters of faith. And the Admiral, who shows himself more concerned than the rest,— not because he is a lover of strife, but because he is persuaded that what he believes is the true faith,—would have one arrange a colloquy of a certain number of learned men of either side, whereby one might know which opinions be the best." [1] Coligny had yet to learn that, when once religious division has gone beyond a certain point, discussion only brings into fuller relief irreconcilable differences.

Interest in the colloquy of Poissy is largely theological. But it is important for other reasons. It was there, and during the subsequent months, that Huguenotism made its supreme effort to capture France. The King and Queen of Navarre, the Prince of Condé, the Admiral, Andelot, and Odet, set to work to organise victory. They expected to gain at least toleration. They hoped, no doubt, to found a new national Protestant church. The court was infected. It was Huguenot, heretic, Laodicean, anything but Catholic. There was a wild craving for newness and excitement. The time for reflection came later. A galaxy of noble dames—Renée of France, Duchess of Ferrara and mother-in-law of the Duke of Guise, Magdalen of Mailly, Eleanor of Roye, the Countess of La Rochefoucauld, the Countess of Senyngham, the Princess of Portien, Jacqueline of Rohan, the Baroness of Crussol, and many others, worked and strove; and, as ever in French politics, feminine influence was not small. Calvin, at the instance of Catherine and Coligny, had stayed away. But in his stead came the eloquent and aristocratic Beza. He was an able substitute. Daily, and with infinite address, he expounded

[1] *Huguenot Society Publications*, vi. xl.

7

detractors. "I do not consider," wrote he, "that wisdom consists in only predicting ill, for in that case Nostradamus would have to be reputed the wisest of all."[1]

Another fact which militated against success at Poissy was the profound cleavage in Protestantism. Calvinist and Lutheran mixed as oil and water. The zealous Lutheran, Duke Christopher of Wurtemberg, had already in this year advocated sending an embassy to France to ensure the triumph of his own creed over the rival one of Geneva. But the Saxon Elector had assured him that it was useless; Condé and Coligny were confirmed Calvinists.[2] This divergence between the French and German schools of thought naturally told heavily against Protestantism. The Cardinal of Lorraine skilfully insisted on it at Poissy. The Huguenots were at a loss to know how to counter him. The attempt to do so, made by Navarre, was a mistake. He summoned German theologians. Fortunately, they arrived when the colloquy was over; but the mere possibility of their coming, with its inevitable threat of divided counsels, proved disconcerting. Another check which French Protestantism suffered at this time was the defection of Anthony of Bourbon. He had been won over by the vague promises of Philip II. of some compensation for his claims on Spanish Navarre. He threw in his lot with the Triumvirate, and by February, 1562, he had become, in the phraseology of Huguenotism, Julian the Apostate. The blow was a severe one. It deprived the party at a stroke of the prestige and legal standing which the support of the First Prince of the Blood had given it; and at the same time it lost it the command of the army.

The consequences of these two events—the failure of the colloquy of Poissy and the defection of Navarre—were soon apparent. They quickened the crisis which was rapidly approaching. In the provinces, the Huguenots took the remedy into their own hands, and seized the churches. At court, the breach between the Protestant leaders and the Triumvirate steadily widened. Already in November the Englishman

[1] 30th Dec. 1561 : Modena Archivio di Stato. Ferrara's opportunist policy was severely criticised in Rome ; see *Nuntiaturberichte*, 2 Abt., 1 Band, 333.
[2] Kugler, *Christoph Herzog zu Wirtemberg*, ii. 297.

Shakerley had written: "These things cannot end without some little civil war." And Peter Martyr, looking out anxiously over the France before him, confided to his friend, Bishop Jewel, that he saw "no appearance of an approaching war, and yet that matters could be settled in no other way."[1] In fact, the Huguenots were determined to be no longer treated as legal outcasts; while the Triumvirate were equally resolved to allow of no equality. Each day, too, the opposition of Philip II. to Coligny was becoming more bitter. He had the double fault of being an enemy of the faith and an enemy of Spain. He was even now organising his expedition under Ribaut to colonise Florida, and was, it was feared, urging Charles IX. to interfere in the Netherlands.

The crisis was reached in January 1562. Catherine made one last despairing effort for peace. On the 17th of that month, spurred on by Condé, Coligny, and L'Hôpital, she promulgated an edict which recognised the legality of Protestant worship outside the walls of towns. This edict, known to history as the Edict of January, was, as Pasquier wrote, "dead from birth."[2] And it is a nice question whether, from the standpoint of Catherine and the Chancellor, who were sincerely anxious for peace, it was not a sad miscalculation and blunder in statecraft. As a piece of legislation, it had two flaws: it went far beyond the political and moral conceptions of the bulk of Frenchmen, and the central power had no means to enforce it. Its immediate effect was a Catholic reaction. During the discussion which had preceded it, hot words had passed between the Admiral and the Constable. Spanish complaints now rose to a menace. On the 17th of February, Coligny was obliged to retire to Châtillon. The complexion of the court became Catholic. As an off-set, Catherine ordered St. André to his Government, but he refused to go. In fact, the Triumvirate was ready. As a preparatory step, the Cardinal of Lorraine had set out with his brother to meet the Duke of Wurtemberg at Saverne. Their object was to cut off from French Protestants all hope of aid from across the Rhine. On the return journey, the Duke of Guise, while

[1] *Zurich Letters* (Parker Society), 118.
[2] *Lettres de Pasquier*, ii. 96.

passing through the village of Vassy, determined to overawe, perhaps disperse, a Huguenot congregation. Those whom he sent on to announce his coming seem to have been over zealous. A fracas began; it was soon a massacre. For France, the Massacre of Vassy was the herald of civil war.

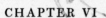

CHAPTER VI

CIVIL WAR BEGINS

Ineffectiveness of L'Hôpital—Result of Vassy—Indecision of Catherine—Entry of Guise into Paris and Departure of Condé—Coligny decides to join the Prince at Meaux—The Huguenot March to Orleans.

THE Edict of January, with its appeal to the social qualities of man, had foreshadowed a time of peace. Within some forty days occurred the Massacre of Vassy—its practical commentary. L'Hôpital, honourable, well-meaning, possessed with a visionary and pathetic belief in the binding force of law, had in the edict besought all subjects not "to abuse, reproach, nor provoke one another because of religion." The slaughter of the worshippers of Vassy came as answer, and the hoarse cry of Protestant France for vengeance. Only a year before, the same L'Hôpital, in proud and opulent phrase, had claimed that on "the seal of France is stamped the figure of the King, not armed and horsed as on many a one of other lands, but sitting on his royal throne, distributing and executing justice."[1] Here, all unconsciously, the Chancellor put his finger on the weak spot of the system he was upholding. France had less need of a judge and lawgiver than of a King —in L'Hôpital's own phrase—"armed and horsed." It was to the lack of a strong central power that much of the confusion of the second half of the sixteenth century was due. If the King had been a warrior, or if he had been possessed of ample military resources, there might have been no Massacre of Vassy, no helpless, impotent drifting, no civil war, with its crop of misery and tears. As a statesman, L'Hôpital dealt in noble sentiments, when an army and party were needed. Politically, he might be said to have been beating the air.

[1] *Histoire Ecclésiastique*, i. 457.

Perhaps no intellect, however alert, could have greatly changed
the issue; but a more powerful personality, with a finer gift
of caution, might have effected more.   There are indeed some
strange analogies, both in character and career, between this
deep-browed, amiable Chancellor of the sixteenth century and
the brilliant Turgot.   In the development of political and
legal ideas, and, above all, in the modern conception of toleration, the chancellorship of L'Hôpital was a landmark.   But
it was less noteworthy as an example of practical statesmanship.

The news of the Massacre of Vassy spread like wildfire
through France.   It was received by Protestantism as a modern
instance of the lament of the Psalmist : " The dead bodies of
Thy servants have they given to be meat unto the fowls of the
heaven, and the flesh of Thy saints unto the beasts of the
earth." [1]   Everywhere rage, horror, fury, struggled for expression.   The more turbulent among the Huguenots seized
their arms.   Little bands of tens and twenties went galloping
along country roads, pressing on for the capital ; Condé or the
Admiral might have need of them.   In Paris itself the effect
was magical.   The leaders ran to Catherine, who was at
Monceaux, and cried for vengeance.   The interview was a
telling one.   When Beza presented himself, and demanded
justice, the King of Navarre " mocked him in pungent and
contemptuous words."   Stung to the quick, the fiery Calvinist
struck off in the heat of the moment one of the great phrases of
history.   " Sire," said he, " it is, I confess, for the Church of God,
in whose name I speak, to endure blows and not to give them.
But may it please you remember, it is an anvil which has worn
out many hammers." [2]   It was in this high and jubilant note,
not without gravity, that the best in Huguenotism prepared
for the coming struggle.   The phrase itself, read in the light
of future events, ranks almost as prophecy.   Some few months
later, the same vain, erratic, visionary Anthony of Navarre lay
dying, winding slowly up the Seine in his cumbrous barge,
again a Protestant.

Catherine received these representations more courteously.
But she dared not act.   The attitude of the Triumvirate

---

[1] *Archives Curieuses*, iv. 103.   [2] *Histoire Ecclésiastique*, ii. 6.

thoroughly alarmed her.   On the 8th of March, the Constable, St. André, and Navarre met in Paris.   On the 13th, the Duke of Guise, ignoring her request to come to her direct, joined with the other Triumvirs at Nanteuil.   On the 16th he entered the capital amid the acclamations of the populace.   It had been Catherine's intention to visit Fontainebleau ; but in face of these events she was urged to retire to the Loire, and put herself and her children in safety.   For a time she hesitated, then yielded.   It was given out that she would proceed directly to Orleans.   But she wavered at the last moment.   She was afraid to defy the Triumvirate, and so went no farther than Fontainebleau.

Condé, meanwhile, failed in his attempt to beat up a Protestant opposition in Paris.   Crowds flocked to hear Beza, " who preaches in a garden, and in place of a pulpit stands on a wall for all to hear." [1]   But for the most part they were non-combatants.   And in a struggle with his enemies, Condé would have to depend on a few hundred scholars and townsmen.   There was no place in the kingdom on which Huguenotism had less hold than on the capital.   This was a disagreeable fact, and Condé would not acknowledge it at once. Indeed, his enemies had some difficulty in edging him out. But his position was fast becoming untenable.   The one man on whom he could have relied, the Governor Francis of Montmorency, had been set aside.   Moreover, the Triumvirate was organising the city on a military basis.   At last, therefore, on the 22nd of March, the Prince, in company with Stuart, Séchelles, Pérussel, and Beza, stole quietly off—in deferene, said he, to the royal commands ; in reality, because the place was hopelessly Catholic.   His followers were filled with fore-bodings.   To them he was a Pompey leaving Rome for ever. He, with a lighter heart, but equally enamoured of classical analogy, sent off post haste to the Admiral, requesting him to come to Meaux, " for," wrote he, in reference to Guise's arrival in Paris, " Cæsar had not only crossed the Rubicon, but had already seized Rome." [2]

This message found Coligny undecided.   He had urged Catherine to retire to Orleans.   He had vigorously denounced

[1] Vatican Library, Urbino, 1039, 352.   [2] La Noue, 545.

the Massacre of Vassy. But it was another matter to unite with Condé. Such a step, he knew, would be irrevocable. It is doubtful whether military glory ever had the same attractions for him as for the other great generals of the sixteenth century: Bayard, Peter Strozzi, Guise, Monluc, and Tavannes. They were warriors pure and simple. They lived in an atmosphere of war. With Coligny, on the other hand, the pursuit of it—at least after the siege of St. Quentin—was always secondary to his interest in the fortunes of Huguenotism; while in the shape in which it offered itself now—that most lamentable of all its forms, civil strife—it was abhorrent to his very nature. Moreover, he was not fitted for the rôle of revolutionary. Character, training, a clear understanding of the value of ordered progress, led him to reject violent measures. At every crisis he had set his face against a resort to arms. Nevertheless, things were now wholly different. The Massacre of Vassy, seen through the haze of rumour, exaggeration, and partisan hatred, appeared as a direct challenge to Protestantism. The further action, too, of Guise did not tend to dispel the impression. His ignoring of the commands of the Queen Mother, his solemn entry into Paris, his military organisation of the capital, seemed to suggest that he was preparing to suppress the Edict of January. Moreover, Catherine had shown her fear of him, and had encouraged Condé, if not actually to resort to force, at least to be ready to help her.

And yet in the face of all this the Admiral hesitated. It was only after the repeated importunities of the Huguenot leaders assembled at Châtillon that he took to horse and reached Meaux on the 27th of March. Here he found things well-nigh desperate. To have begun operations with the handful of men which surrounded Condé would have been worse than madness; yet it was not safe to remain idle. As it was, they had delayed too long. Either they must have more men, he declared, or prepare for flight. Fortunately, large reinforcements rode in unexpectedly. They were now able to move. Their plan was to gain possession of the King, or, failing that, to retire to Orleans. They at once, therefore, wrote to Catherine to ask her intentions, and on the 29th of

March proceeded to Claye on the road to Paris.[1] At their approach on the 30th the capital was in confusion. The drawbridges were raised, and one broken; some of the gates were closed, others guarded; "and everywhere it seemed like a city besieged." Passing by Montmartre, in full view of the city, eight hundred to fifteen hundred strong and "all mounted,"[2] they slept that night at St. Cloud.[3] They had received on the way the bad news that the Triumvirate and Navarre had left Paris on the 26th and arrived at Fontainebleau on the 27th. The King was now in the hands of the enemy.

"The taking of the King or Paris," the younger Tavannes remarked acutely, "is half the victory in civil war."[4] Coligny and his nephew had failed in both. Their hope now lay in seizing the rich and populous Orleans. Leaving St. Cloud, therefore, on the 31st, they arrived the same evening at Montlhery. Here they received advices from Orleans which induced them to send on three gentlemen in advance. Their duty was to prepare the way for the army. One of them may have been Andelot, for he was sent on by Condé for the same purpose. He slept at Cercottes, an hour's distance from Orleans, on the 1st of April, and entered the town unperceived early on the morning of the 2nd. But Monterud, lieutenant of Roche-sur-Yon, had scented danger, and was introducing a Catholic garrison from Beaugency. Suddenly the gate was closed. Andelot, however, with a band of Huguenots who had been prepared beforehand, rushed on the scene, drove Monterud back, forced it open, and waited anxiously for Condé.

---

[1] Ruble's account of Condé's march to Orleans (iv. 139, etc.) is extremely faulty. In addition to authorities quoted by him, we have used: *Journal de Jehan de la Fosse*, 46 ; Turin, Francia Lettere Ministri, ii. (Montfort to Savoy, 4th April) ; Naples, Carte Farn., 758 (Lolgi, last of March) ; Vatican Library, Urbino, 1039, 354 (Avvisi of 1st April).

[2] Jehan de la Fosse, 46. The description of Condé's army given by Beza (*Hist. Ecclé.* and *Calvini Opera*, xix. 383, 387), La Noue, Mergey, Bruslard, d'Aubigné, and the author of the *Journal de* 1562, would lead one to believe that the Prince had no infantry. Others, however, and among them the Cardinal Santa Croce and the Savoyan Montfort, affirm—though we think incorrectly—that there were five hundred foot.

[3] Bruslard remarks that Condé was refused an entry into Paris for his troops, and that Bussy, one of the leaders, made an ineffectual attempt to force his way in.

[4] Tavannes, 250.

Fortunately, the Prince was close at hand. He had lain that night at Angerville. But instead of hurrying on, he allowed himself to be inveigled into negotiations by Gonnor, while d'Estrées, another follower of the Triumvirate, was hastening to seize Orleans in their name. Thus some precious hours were lost. At last, however, he moved forward. His force had been greatly strengthened by reinforcements at St. Cloud and between Étampes and Angerville. When close to Toury, urgent messages began to pour in from Andelot. " Then all, unwilling to lose so tempting a morsel, . . . not content with a trot, demanded a race. No sooner said than done! Some six leagues off the stir began. For the Prince, who had with him some two thousand gentlemen and valets, putting himself at their head, set off at full gallop for the gate, and the whole pack after him. It so happened that innumerable strangers and others were on the road on their way to Paris. Seeing the strangeness of this chase—for no questions were asked, and as yet there was no news of war—most of them thought that it was an assembly of all the fools of France, or a wager. . . . For on the road were valets unhorsed, steeds lamed and spent, and trunks overturned, which drew from the racers themselves shouts of laughter." [1]

One might search in vain to find quite such another scene as this Huguenot ride to Orleans. In the wild, grim multitude of Marseilles, groping blindly on to Paris in the summer of 1789, mumbling vague shibboleths and crying for vengeance, we have revolution and the breath of change. So, too, in many a Puritan host, praying under the cold stars, and waiting for victory and the dawn, we have the temper of men who compel victory. But this mad, fantastic, Gilpin-race to Orleans —was it revolution or comedy? La Noue, who paints the scene, does so with laughter. To him it appeared as a pleasing interlude in the grey monotone of war. Nevertheless, there was something ominous in the light-hearted gaiety of this entry on civil strife. It is too suggestive, to be pleasant, of the spirit which culminated almost a century later in the hollow Fronde.

[1] La Noue, 554, 555.

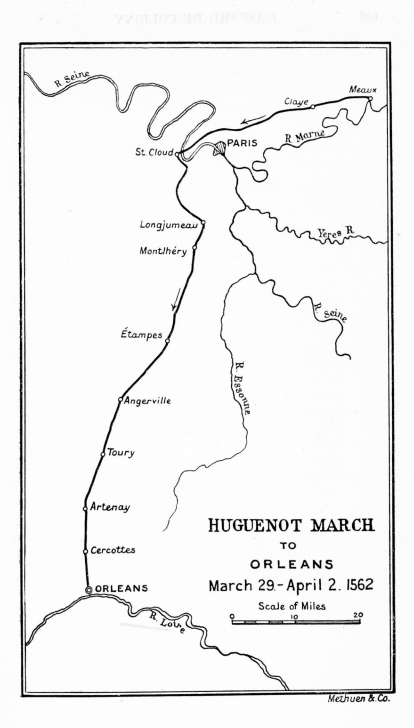

R. Seine

Meaux

Claye

R. Marne

St. Cloud

PARIS

Longjumeau

Montlhéry

Yeres R.

R. Seine

Étampes

R. Essonne

Angerville

Toury

Artenay

Cercottes

ORLEANS

R. Loire

HUGUENOT MARCH

TO

ORLEANS

March 29.– April 2. 1562

Scale of Miles

0   10   20

Methuen & Co.

CHAPTER VII

THE FIRST WAR OF RELIGION: ORGANISATION
AND NEGOTIATIONS

Condé and Coligny compared—Condé's Manifesto—Coligny opposed to soliciting
Foreign Aid—Act of Association—Creation of an Army ; its Moral Tone ; its Speedy
Deterioration and Excesses—Huguenot Party preponderatingly Aristocratic—Huguenot
Fanaticism ; Condé and Coligny try to check it—Catholic Excesses—Coligny's Appeal
to the Constable—Negotiations—Meeting of Toury—Meeting of Talcy—Partial
Disbandment at Orleans—Catholic Plan of Campaign ; its Success—Character of
Monluc—Huguenots hard pressed—Treaty of Hampton Court—Coligny's Fortitude
—Suggests the Sack of Paris—Coming of Andelot with German Reinforcements.

FROM the very first, the Admiral was marked out as the
organising and directing genius at Orleans. Not that
Condé was by any means a mere figure-head. On the contrary, he was alert and energetic; he had a will and ideas of
his own; and his position as Prince of the Blood, important
in itself, was further strengthened by his natural vivacity and
popularity with the young nobility. None the less, Coligny,
by his standing as uncle of the Prince, his greater age, his
experience and character, exercised a dominant influence.
Here is a comparison of the two, all the more interesting for
being drawn by the Papal Nuncio, Santa Croce : " Yet the
pursuits and talents of each are different. The Admiral
excels in counsel, the Prince in action. The strength of the
latter lies in a certain impetuosity of mind, that of the former in
a steady constancy. The one is shrewd, the other still shrewder.
Just as the Prince has a more pleasing character, the Admiral has
one more austere. The Prince, too, is a lover of racing, jumping,
exhibitions of wrestling, hunting, public shows, every kind of
armed contest, horses, sports, jests, the dancing of girls, and the
singing of women. But with the Admiral there always seems to
be a certain seriousness of thought and action. Then again, the

Prince is a most graceful speaker, while the eloquence of the Admiral is of a graver kind, since he has become familiar with the Latin tongue, and devotes himself earnestly to theological pursuits. The latter, also, is zealous in State affairs and swift to punish wrongs, the former being more easy-going. And while the Admiral consults as to what must needs be done, the Prince does it. Then, too, the former gives audience to ambassadors, busies himself with supplies and finance, decides points of law, fortifies positions, draws up the line of battle, pitches the camp, reviews the army, chooses the place and time of battle, and superintends religious affairs. The Prince, on the other hand, asks for dangers and the fight; and while he is small and of elegant figure, the former uses a toothpick and has it in his mouth day and night. Yet both, by their graciousness and generosity, are a power with all." [1]

One of the first duties which fell to the leaders was to publish a defence of their conduct. This was done by the Prince in his own name on the 8th of April, and again on the 25th. In his first manifesto, which was the more moderate of the two, he accused the Triumvirate of beginning the war. In proof of this he cited the Massacre of Vassy, Guise's disobedience of Catherine, the gathering of the Catholic leaders in Paris, and their evident intention of destroying the Edict of January. His purpose, he declared, was to guard the latter, free the King, who was now a captive, and disarm, if the Triumvirate would do so too. It may at once be stated that neither his action in taking up arms nor his subsequent apologias won the universal approval of French Protestants. The great Huguenot centre of La Rochelle, and warm sympathisers such as Nevers, Bouillon, and Longueville, refused to follow him. Belleville, who was a power among the Saintonge nobility, fell off from him before the year was out, and protested against waging war against the King. Yet it would be unwise to condemn Condé too hastily. His position had been a difficult one. Catherine had encouraged him. In four undated letters, written in the latter half of March, she had hinted, and not obscurely, that he was the only barrier between her and the tyranny of the Triumvirate. He

[1] Martène and Durand, *Veterum Scriptorum Collectio*, v. 1478.

had also good grounds for supposing, at least at first, that the Queen Mother and the King were virtually prisoners. Moreover, the action of Guise and his friends throughout March and April certainly justified Condé's belief that they were concerting an attack on the Edict of January. On the 29th of March the Huguenots were forbidden to hold the service of the Lord's Supper. On the 4th of April the Constable in person saw to the destruction of their places of worship; and on the 11th it was decreed that the edict was no longer to apply to Paris and the suburbs.

This manifesto of the 8th of April was only one of the means by which appeal was made to the sympathies of France and Europe. Condé and Coligny despatched embassies and wrote innumerable letters to England, Switzerland, Savoy, and Germany. Most of the leaders, however, wished for something more substantial than sympathy. They were in favour of asking for foreign aid. But in this they met with the uncompromising hostility of the Admiral. He confessed that he would rather die than let the Huguenots first call in the stranger. He had his way for the moment; and if his views had only prevailed with both parties, France might have been saved from the fate of becoming the cockpit of Europe. Unhappily, his own party soon found it impossible to stand alone, while the Triumvirate furnished it with an excuse by negotiating with the Catholic States. As a result, Huguenot emissaries were soon busy abroad, raising men and money.

Meanwhile, Condé's followers in Orleans were being organised into a party. On the 11th of April was signed, first by the Prince and then by Coligny and the rest, an act of association, which was at once a religious brief and a declaration of policy. It declared Condé to be their leader and lawful protector of the crown; it announced their unalterable determination to set free the King, enforce the Edict of January, and maintain the honour of God and His pure service. An even more formidable task was to create an army. From the very outset the two leaders were heavily handicapped. They had no *cadre* to start from. The artillery and most of the permanent forces were in the hands of the enemy. Nothing daunted, however, they set to work. Already, before leaving Meaux, Condé had written to the various churches, and he followed this up on the 7th of April by an urgent appeal for either reinforcements or funds. On the 21st of April, La Rochefoucauld arrived with four hundred horse; Grammont brought with him four thousand men from Gascony; others came from Provence and Languedoc. Cannon were cleverly brought by river from Tours; an arsenal was formed; horses were provided; provisions were largely supplied by forced contributions from Catholics; townsmen, and even monks and priests, were set to work on the walls; royal revenues, ecclesiastical ornaments, and offerings from the different Huguenot centres, went to fill the treasury; regiments were raised in various towns, while, not to tax the resources of Orleans too severely, troops were quartered in the adjacent country.[1] In two months' time the Prince and Admiral were ready to take the field.

But perhaps the most astonishing fact was the discipline of the army. Dice, cards, robbery, pillage, foraging, oaths, loose women—that scourge of every army—were almost unknown. One day Teligny and La Noue remarked on this when the Admiral was present. "Thereupon he said to us, it is truly a fine thing, provided that it lasts. But I fear that these men will suddenly throw aside their goodness, and in two months' time malice alone will remain. I have long commanded the infantry, and I know it; it often proves the proverb: 'In youth a hermit, in age a devil.'"[2] This prophecy was only too true. At the storming of Beaugency, early in July, the Provençals got out of hand, and thenceforth there was steady decline. There was no longer that spirit which moved two companies of Huguenots earlier in the year, who, when pillaging began, went out into the fields to pray.[3] Unfortunately, too, a similar deterioration took place among the Catholics, who till then had preserved a semblance of restraint.

"The civil wars," remarked La Noue sadly, "are the factories of all wickedness."[4] If not so inhuman or bloody as the Thirty Years' War, the difference was not so much of kind as of degree.

---

[1] For the organisation of the army see Lacombe's *Catherine de Médicis entre Guise et Condé.*

[2] La Noue, 575.   [3] D'Aubigné, i. 324.   [4] La Noue, 708.

The soldiery set the standard of military ethics. Murder, mutiny, pillage, massacre, rape, the refusal of quarter, broken promises, were common. The defeat of the Huguenot host at Vergt in August, 1562, was described by a Protestant as a just judgment of God upon an unholy, pillaging rabble.[1]   In June of 1562 a corps of Cevennes mountaineers descended on Languedoc, " but instead of planting religion there, it only pillaged and burnt."[2]   The track of the Protestant champion, des Adrets, was marked by a trail of blood. The Catholic Monluc broke his word and slaughtered the people of Graves —hence the phrase, "the faith of Graves," a local example of Punic faith. The Protestant Duras retaliated by slaying five hundred men, a quarter of whom were priests.[3] And lastly, to this general stock of horrors the German mercenaries were to add their quota.

Naturally, this licence had its limits, and the presence of the leaders, and especially of Coligny, guaranteed a certain order. In some directions, indeed, the Admiral was unalterably stern. He allowed no trifling with the pledged word or the etiquette of war. Thus, when the garrison of Caen had been guaranteed terms in March, 1563, a Huguenot, who took away the sword of one of them and picked his purse, was condemned to be hung, with the superscription : " For having broken the public faith." So, too, he strove to curb the lust for pillage. But even he, with a hatred of disorder rising to the height of passion, had to acquiesce more or less in the general laxity. The choice, indeed, sometimes only lay between pillage and mutiny. He was bound hand and foot by the voluntary nature of military service, and by the knowledge of his empty coffers. It was difficult to enforce an iron discipline when the soldier was practically free to return home, or was crying out for arrears of pay.

Thus, as we see, Condé and Coligny were only able to preserve discipline for a short time. They were even less successful in checking religious excesses. The Huguenot party both at Orleans and throughout the country was preponderatingly aristocratic. In a list of its leaders, endorsed by

[1] *Histoire Ecclésiastique*, ii. 844.   [2] *Ib.* iii. 224.
[3] D'Aubigné, ii. 90, 91.

8

Cecil,[1] there are over two hundred names, and among them many
of the most illustrious in France. There are Knights of the
Order, Privy Councillors, captains, and military leaders : Condé,
Rohan, Portien, Coligny, Andelot, La Rochefoucauld, Senarpont,
Genlis, Soubise, Piennes, Montgomery, the Vidame of Chartres,
the Vidame of Chalons, Mouy, Morvillier, Bouchavannes, Du
Vigen, Dammartin, La Suze, Avaret, La Noue, Teligny, Bussy,
Briquemault, Duras, Puygreffier, Esternay, Feuquières, Ste.
Foy, St. Remy, St. Auban, La Fayette, Mouvans. Moreover,
in one of the original manuscripts of the Oath of Association
of the 11th of April, after the signatures of the leaders is the
phrase : " and four thousand gentlemen of the best and most
ancient houses in France."[2] From the very first Condé and
his uncle were determined to respect the susceptibilities of
Catholics, and they could, no doubt, have seen that their
commands were respected by this aristocratic section of their
followers, or at least by such as were under their immediate
supervision at Orleans. Indeed, some of these were hardly of
the stuff of fanatics. Castelnau remarks in this connection,
that " seeing that he (Coligny) evidently observed his religion
more strictly than another, he held in check, like a censor, the
immoderate appetites of the young Protestant lords and gentlemen by a certain natural severity which fitted him well."[3]
And we continually come on instances of this temper, ranging
from the crime of rape of Courtenay, the fifth son of the Count
of Dammartin, to the gay indifferentism of Genlis at Gien, who
" lived a scandalous life, and even wished to take in hand the
reformation of the prayers, which, said he, were too long."[4]

But it was not only with aristocrats and gentlemen that
the Prince and Admiral had to deal. There was the rank
and file of the party. And they soon found themselves power-
less before its fanaticism. Condé had promised the Catholics
in Orleans his protection, and they were left in possession of
their churches, at least until the 21st of April. Then the
Huguenot zealots, goaded to fury by massacres at Sens, began

---

[1] Record Office, Foreign, xli. 436. It is dated, not 7th Sept., as given in the
Calendar of State Papers, but simply Sept.

[2] Delaborde, ii. 69.   [3] Castelnau, 142.

[4] *Hist. Ecclésiastique*, ii. 536.

their work of destruction. Church after church was either defaced or pillaged. News was brought to Condé and Coligny that the rabble was wreaking its vengeance on the Cathedral of Ste. Croix. Snatching up their swords, they ran to the scene. " As it happened, a man was seen high up in the act of breaking an image. When the Prince seized an arquebus, intending to shoot him, the man called out, ' Sir! have patience until I have broken this idol, then I shall die if it so please you.' " [1] Before such a spirit no protest, no threat, no entreaty was of any avail. And Huguenot writers fell to confiding to the King that image-breaking was the secret working of God against idolatry.[2]

Unfortunately, this outbreak in Orleans was by no means an isolated instance. The *Histoire Ecclésiastique*, the official history of Huguenotism, gives innumerable others during the years 1560–1563. Calvin had deprecated all violence, even the seizure of places of worship.[3] The ministers, too, generally counselled moderation, but they were not listened to. All that even remotely suggested Rome—missal and crucifix, wood and masonry—were battered down or cast to the flames. Sometimes the local leader, such as Mouvans, headed the movement. De Foix, writing of his own diocese before the civil wars, described how the Huguenots, though in no way provoked, destroyed altars, copes, seats, and organ.[4] The Protestants of Castres were certainly more self-contained than the majority of their fellows, when they covered up the images to prevent all disorder.[5] The *Histoire Ecclésiastique* speaks of the good order preserved at Valence on the outbreak of war in 1562, but when news came to hand of the destruction of images throughout the realm, it was no longer possible to save them in Dauphiné. The invaluable library of Cluny was destroyed ; the soldiery said they were all books of the mass. In the abbey church of Caen the beautiful tombs of William the Conqueror and Matilda were shattered.[6] At Rouen, manuals, missals, psalters, were ruined. Even the Huguenot

---

[1] *Hist. Ecclésiastique*, ii. 51. [2] Condé, iii. 355.
[3] *Calvini Opera*, xviii. 63, 378. [4] British Museum, Harley, 7016, 5.
[5] Gaches, 15.
[6] *Bourgueville de Bras* (edition of 1833), 253, 254.

writers and ministers, opposed though they were on principle to such proceedings, waxed merry in the recital of this destruction as time went on. At Dives, the Protestant army in February, 1563, discovered a crucifix, revered by the mariners from ancient times, "which had come out of the sea, said they, several hundred years before, and which had spoken, but no one could tell what it had said; and when it was thrown into the fire with several others, it took to burning without a word." [1]

An even more evil spirit was often found. The Catholic Bruslart reports on the 4th of May that the Huguenots of Rouen had trampled the host under foot, and then stuck it on a dragon-headed lance, saying that the dragon had eaten the mass.[2] At Bressols, in 1561, the Huguenots, finding the priest at mass, "made him mount—vestments and all—on a donkey with his face to the tail, which he held with one hand, while the other grasped the chalice; on his forehead was the host, and bulls on his shoulders, the missal being borne on the point of a halberd; and thus he was led to the public place in Montauban." [3] At Angers, in April, 1562, "they carried off the image of the Trinity, and that of Our Lady, and dragged it through the streets, and whipped it, and burnt it; and they took the holy and sacred host and threw it in the fire." [4] Beza, who was sent at this time to Angers from Orleans, wrote to Calvin as follows: "Nothing disturbs us more than the baseness of the Church, not to give it a harder name. I have been as far as Angers, in peril of my life, but I was able to do little or nothing. Their violence in the destruction of altars is incredible, and we have been quite unable to prevent it here. In short, all things are suddenly changed, so that I am amazed at the spectacle; for the enemy in a hundred years, even if victorious, could not restore, in this one city alone, what has been destroyed in the space of two hours." [5] Even the dead were not sacred. At Vendôme the princely tombs of the

---

[1] *Hist. Ecclésiastique*, ii. 334.   [2] Condé, i. 85.

[3] *Hist. Ecclésiastique*, i. 935.

[4] Journal de Louvet, *Revue de l'Anjou* of 1854, p. 202.

[5] Salomon Cyprian, i. 240. A German translation is given by Baum (Beza, ii. 11), which is quoted by Duhr (*Stimmen aus Maria Laach*, xxix. 120).

Bourbons were defiled;[1] at Craon the remains of Anne of Tremouille were strewn about the floor.

To the credit of their cause, be it said, these worst excesses were sternly reproved by all that was best in Huguenotism. And it is therefore the more lamentable that, as the war proceeded, the leaders gave the soldiery a free hand in their treatment of priests. At the storming of Sully, in January, 1563, thirty-six priests were slain; two months earlier, at Pithiviers, " as to the priests, they slew all of them they met."[2] At Mortagne, remarks the same work with dry brevity, " some (of the priests) having fled to the tower, came down after another fashion."

It must not be supposed that such methods were confined to one party. The Catholics were even more guilty. It often happened that the Huguenots expended their rage in demolishing images, while their enemies, when once aroused, were only satisfied when they had shed blood. This aspect of the question is well brought out by a letter of Pasquier, himself a moderate. " It would be impossible," he writes, " to tell you what barbarous cruelties are committed by both sides. Where the Huguenot is master, he ruins the images and demolishes the sepulchres and tombs. On the other hand, the Catholic kills, murders, and drowns all those whom he knows to be of that sect, until the rivers overflow with them."[3] Moreover, the Catholic leaders set a very evil example. Early in July, 1562, that is to say, before Condé had begun to take harsh measures against ecclesiastics, the Constable ordered La Tremouille to execute the minister, whom he had caught at Thouars, either by hanging him or throwing him into the water in a sack.[4] But it is unnecessary to deal further with this question of religious excesses. Those of Huguenotism cause regret rather than surprise, for it was inevitable that a persecuted minority would strike back. They have been given at some length, because in this way only can be explained the ferocious spirit which characterised the religious wars.

These and kindred matters fully occupied the Admiral

---

[1] Haton, i. 277.   [2] *Hist. Ecclésiastique*, ii. 235.   [3] Pasquier, ii. 99.
[4] *Mémoires de la Société de Statistique des Deux Sevres*, 11me, partie xix. 197 (Anne to La Tremouille from Blois, 23rd July).

during the months of April and May. He was especially
moved by the massacres of Protestants, which were now
common throughout the country, and they drew from him a
protest to the Queen Mother.[1] But what touched him even more
nearly was the family schism. Some of the friendships of his
life seem to have been made only to be broken. His intimacy
with Guise, with Brissac, and Anthony of Navarre, had only
played with the surface of things. His feelings, however, toward the Constable were profoundly different. To some extent
he had inherited Anne's peculiar temper. And throughout his
career he had owed much to his uncle's sleepless generosity.
Moreover, he had been marked out as his political successor.
It was no doubt with these thoughts in mind that he sat down
to make a last appeal to him on the 6th of May. He reminded
him that he had loved him as a father; he told him that he had
broken with the Guises for his sake; and he warned him that he,
Anne, was now the tool of those who had sworn his ruin, and
whose success could only end in the ruin of his family. To this
the Constable replied on the 12th of May in a letter instinct with
dignity and high feeling. He assured his nephew that nothing
was further from his wish than to see him receive harm or
shame; and he expressed the hope that if he only considered
the evil which had fallen on the kingdom since the troubles had
begun, he would be moved to the quick, and long to see an
end of it. The tone of the correspondence is clear enough: no
hope and no solution, only vain appeals known to be vain!

Other negotiations, however, were more promising. There
was one soul in France who, above all others, hoped against
hope. It was the Queen Mother. She longed for peace.
War, she knew, would inevitably lead to her practical super-
session as regent; already there were hints from the Catholic
crowd of her forced retirement to Italy.[2] She had at her
command a little army of negotiators: the Sieur de Gonnor,
the Abbé of Saint Jean de Laon, Robertet, Claude de l'Aubespine, Losses, Lioux, Morvillier, Villars, Vieilleville, and lastly,
the keeper of the Queen's conscience, Monluc, Bishop of
Valence. Innumerable messages passed between the court
and Orleans. The main difficulties in the way of a settlement

[1] Ruble, iv. 174.　　　　　　　　[2] Heidenhain, Beilagen, 101.

ANNE OF MONTMORENCY

were the Huguenot demand for the retirement of the Triumvirate, and the strict observance of the Edict of January.
Moreover, some untoward incident was constantly creating a
deadlock.   At one time it was the violent tone of the letters
or manifestoes of Condé, at another the intractable attitude of
the Triumvirate, or the murder by the Huguenots of La Mothe-
Gondrin, the savage lieutenant of Guise in Dauphiné.   Yet, in
spite of all, Catherine remained hopeful.   On the 14th of
May she started for Monceaux, partly to demonstrate the
falsity of the Huguenot assertion that she was a prisoner,
partly in the expectation of meeting Condé at Milly in the
Gatinais.[1]   And though the interview fell through, she had
real grounds for confidence.   On the 2nd of June she was
informed of the Prince's willingness to meet her at Toury in
Beauce.   On the 3rd she left Vincennes.   Early on the 5th she
set out from Étampes for Toury—but no Condé!   She had
come with more than the stipulated escort, and the suspicious
Protestants had refused to allow him to appear.   A meeting,
however, was finally arranged for the 9th.

It took place at Château Gaillard, between Toury and
Angerville, a bare, level, melancholy spot, swept by a cold,
wintry rain.   Condé, acting under orders, showed his distrust
of the enemy by refusing either to retire to a barn which was
close by, or even to dismount.   His brother, Navarre, was in
command of the Catholics.   Eight hundred to a thousand
paces divided the sides.   Each was a hundred strong, fully
armed with cuirass and lance.   They had already adopted the
colours which were to distinguish them during the religious
wars.   The Huguenot gentlemen wore surcoats of white,
the Bourbon colour of Condé.   The Catholics were similarly
attired, but in the distinctive crimson of the house of Lorraine.
The Huguenot pennons were also white, those of their opponents being crimson.   After the ordinary courtesies had
passed between Condé and Navarre, the real interview began
between the Prince and Queen Mother.   It lasted for two
hours.   But from the very first there was very little chance of
a settlement.   Condé had come without powers, and confessed
that he must refer proposals back to the Colignys, none of

[1] Montfort to Savoy, 14th May: Turin, Francia Lettere Ministri, i.

whom were present. Catherine, for her part, had nothing to offer. Her terms—or shall we say the terms of the Triumvirate? —which were naturally rejected, were practically the abolition of the Edict of January. Indeed, the only feature which lifts the conference of Toury above a hundred other abortive interviews, was the scene where some of the opposing gentlemen streamed across the space which divided them, and greeted one another —perhaps for the last time. One thing, however, was gained. A fresh meeting was to be held, at which the Triumvirate and the Colignys were to be present. But, like the proposed conference of the 5th of June, it never took place. Condé wrote rejecting the terms offered, while the Catholic leaders were, under any circumstances, averse to an interview. Catherine, therefore, had to be content with forwarding to the Prince what was to all intents and purposes an ultimatum, and starting on her return journey.[1]

She had, however, scarcely reached Vincennes, before she was recalled by Navarre. And though suffering from a fall from her horse, she set out again on the 17th, just three days after her arrival. The change in the situation, it appears, had been brought about by two conciliatory letters from Condé. Navarre had then arranged a suspension of arms without reference to Guise. Beaugency was to be the place of meeting, and was neutralised with this end in view, and occupied by troops of Navarre as soon as the Huguenots had withdrawn. Instead of going to the royal camp, which was now only a day's march from Orleans, Catherine determined to settle at St. Simon, between the two armies, where she arrived on the 20th—an assumption of impartiality and independence which the Triumvirate bitterly resented.

A first conference was to have taken place between Condé and Navarre on the 19th, but it was postponed, as the Huguenots issued from Orleans with two thousand horse and six thousand foot, and took up their position at Vaussoudun, on the road to Beaugency. They met, however, the next day.

---

[1] For details of meetings of Toury and Talcy see despatches of Alvarotto, Fiaschi, Ippolito d'Este, Girolamo della Rovere, Montfort, Lolgi, Tornabuoni, in Archs. of Modena, Turin, Naples, Florence; see also authorities quoted by Ruble, *passim.*

After the interview, Condé was to have visited the Queen
Mother, but, owing to indisposition, failed to appear before the
21st.   The argument between the three lasted for four hours.
The Prince's demands were briefly the recognition of the Edict
of January, and the disarmament of both parties; Navarre,
however, to retain command of the royal troops.   These were
at last drawn up and sent to the Catholic camp in charge of
Morvillier and de l'Aubespine.   But the Triumvirate would
not hear of them.   They even indulged in threats of forming
a Catholic association.   When, therefore, Condé arrived on
the 22nd, he and Catherine parted sadly within the hour.
Catherine, however, made a last desperate effort on the
23rd.   She had heard that some of the Protestants had
complained that they had not been shown the articles
offered by her and Navarre on the 4th of May.   She
determined, therefore, to send them a copy, hoping at the
least to sow dissension in their ranks.   Francis of Montmorency was entrusted with the mission.   But his reception
was other than she expected.   The Huguenot army, drawn
up in squadrons, greeted the articles with tumultuous cries
of " Battle! battle!"   The Queen had now nothing to do
but to become reconciled to the angry Triumvirate.   All hope
of peace was at an end.   Even Navarre, who originally had
been pacifically inclined, now adopted a stiffer attitude, won
over by the unexpected arrival of a promise of Sardinia from
Philip II.

With the evening of the 24th, however, came a dramatic
change.   During the day, Coligny, with fifteen of his friends,
had drawn up and signed a document, wherein it was stated
that, provided that the Triumvirate retired to their houses, they
would obey the commands of Catherine and Navarre, and
would beg Condé to put himself into her hands as a pledge of
their good faith.   This move was viewed by the Catholics as a
virtual surrender.   Guise wrote off jubilantly to the Cardinal of
Lorraine.   Moreover, he, St. André, and the Constable at once
agreed to retire, and started out on the 27th, but only went as
far as Châteaudun.   In fact, their action throughout was
thoroughly dishonest.   The Ferraran Ambassadors declare
categorically that the Triumvirate were to be recalled at the

end of eight days [1]—a contravention of the spirit if not of the letter of the agreement.

On the 28th, Condé made his appearance, and was conducted by Catherine and Navarre to Talcy. Here he begged her for permission for Coligny and the others to come and kiss hands. Navarre vigorously, and as it turned out wisely, combatted this request. He was equally opposed to allowing Condé to appear at the interview. But Catherine agreed to both proposals, and the Prince accompanied her on the 29th, under the promise, however, of returning with her to Talcy. A house had been set aside for the meeting in Beaugency; but Coligny refused to enter a walled town. It was held instead in a barn, in the open country. When the Admiral approached and dismounted, Catherine received him courteously, and " kissed him on the mouth, as is the custom of the queens of France with the great officers of the King." [2] The Protestants opened proceedings by demanding the Edict of January, and when this was flatly refused, begged leave to quit the country, their only proviso being that those whom they left behind should enjoy complete religious liberty. Such, at least, is Coligny's and Andelot's version of the affair.[3] But most of the Catholic accounts say that they went further, and that they, or Condé in their name, proposed an unconditional retirement from France. Catherine, who at first either felt or feigned reluctance, at last fell in with their views, and they parted on this understanding. The Prince, however, was not allowed to accompany her back to Talcy. Coligny insisted on his return to the Huguenot camp. The excuse given for this breach of faith was the alleged discovery of a Catholic plot either to kill him or keep him prisoner.

The next morning the leaders had to consider the best means of escaping from the rash promise of the day before. Coligny proposed that it should be communicated to the army. This was done, with the natural result that the soldiery cried

[1] In a despatch in cipher of the 3rd of July, Alvarotto and Fiaschi declare that they had seen a letter of Catherine to the Duchess of Guise to this effect: Modena Francia, 37.

[2] *Journal de l'année* 1562 (*Revue reprospective*, v. 178).

[3] *Bull. du prot. fr.*, li. 393 (Coligny to Rhinegrave, 21st July, 1562), and Condé, iii. 533, etc.

out that it was a base betrayal. Much the same views were
expressed by Coligny, Andelot, and Boucard in the Council.
Fortunately for them, the jubilant letter of Guise of the 25th
fell into their hands, together with a *précis* of a strongly
anti-Huguenot policy, drawn up for Navarre by the Triumvirate
at Châteaudun. This provided them with an excuse, and
Catherine's agent, who had come to arrange their voluntary
banishment, could do nothing.

In reviewing the action of Coligny throughout, we are
astonished by his lack not only of caution but of common
sense. The document of the 24th of June was undoubtedly
largely his work. And there is no disguising the fact that
although it showed him in an amiable light, as keenly desirous
of peace, it was none the less a political blunder. It mis-
calculated not only the character of Catherine and Navarre,
but the general situation. For even supposing that the
Triumvirate had retired straight to their homes, Coligny and
his friends would have gained nothing. The troops would
have remained in the hands of Anthony, who was liable to be
bought up at any moment by Philip II. Moreover, neither
Anthony nor Catherine, however favourably inclined, could
have dared to tolerate Protestantism. The force behind the
Triumvirate was too overwhelming, and for practical purposes
it mattered little whether they were at the court or not. In a
word, if the Huguenots had carried out their engagements,
they would have annihilated their party. As it was, they only
escaped by a side-wind. Then again, the Admiral must bear
part of the blame for the offer made to Catherine at Beaugency.
It is generally held that Condé proposed this voluntary banishment. It is none the less true that no word of protest fell
from the Admiral at the time. And Beza, who was at Orleans,
and was well acquainted with the inner working of affairs, held
all the leaders equally responsible.

Somewhat disillusioned and humiliated, the leaders
determined on a bold stroke. It was nothing less than a
night-surprise of the Catholic army which lay round Talcy.
The camp was therefore moved up on the 1st of July, and
by dusk all was ready. And when they had said public
prayers, "as is the custom of those of the religion," and the

summer night had come, the whole army stole out, stirred,
says La Noue, by a high and buoyant courage. Coligny rode
at the head with eight hundred horse. The march lay across
the level stretches of Beauce, now a sea of tall, undulous corn.
Hour after hour they pressed on, ghost-like in the white shirts
thrown over their armour. Unhappily, when day broke, they
were still far from the enemy's camp; the guides had lost their
way in the dark. A surprise was now impossible. So that
day and the next they offered battle, but it was refused.
Condé, therefore, turned aside, stormed Beaugency, and returned
to Orleans.

Their difficulties were now, in reality, only beginning.
The ranks were visibly thinning. Some had gone, or were
going, over to the enemy; some had stolen away; many who
remained turned in thought homeward, as tales of local battle
and strife came in. Soon Condé and Coligny would be
generals without an army. They were unable to check what,
from a military standpoint, was the bane of the civil wars:
their local character. Each civil war carried along with it a
host of petty provincial contests, disconnected, and raging
round some town or district. Often the forces in Languedoc,
Guienne, Dauphiné, or Provence far outnumbered those in
Orleans. The leaders, therefore, accepted the inevitable, and
despatched the various local magnates to their provinces.
Duras was sent to Guienne, La Rochefoucauld to Poitou and
Saintonge, Soubise to Lyons, Yvoi to Bourges, Portien to
Champagne, and lastly, Montgomery to Normandy. By this
means they hoped to occupy, possibly even defeat, the Catholics,
and so allow their followers to return.

But what was even more serious than this partial disbandment of the central army at Orleans, was the fact that they
were everywhere losing ground. At one time they had had
the lower, and so the most important, half of the Loire in their
hands. They had been strong in the south; Poitiers, Bourges,
and Lyons had kept a way open between it and Orleans.
Rouen had given promise of serving as a link with England.
But the inevitable reaction set in. The Triumvirate soon recognised that these successes were out of all proportion to the
enemy's strength. Their plan of action was simple. It was

to isolate Orleans. It was to be cut off from all succour, and then reduced before England or the German Princes could interfere. Haunted, therefore, by few fears of losing touch with their base at Paris, they moved down the Loire from Talcy early in July against Blois. Town after town was recovered. When Poitiers fell on the 1st of August, their preliminary move had succeeded. Then came the surrender of Bourges on the 1st of September, the defeat of Duras by Monluc at Vergt on the 9th of October, and the storming of Rouen on the 26th of the same month. With these terrible reverses the fate of Orleans seemed sealed.

The name of Monluc, who saved the south-west for Catholicism, tempts us to turn aside to sketch his character. For he was the type of leader which the religious wars were to raise or nourish in every corner of France. He was self-reliant to a degree. He believed in his destiny. Catherine de' Medici had her moments of doubt, and consulted her astrologers. Monluc was his own astrologer. He cast a preparatory glance at the heavens, found them propitious, and started on his career, hewing men and weaving his stratagems, while the stars trembled their acquiescence. " All the world," cried he, with naïve exultancy, " is not so lucky as Monluc." [1] Toward the end of his life, when all was not well with him, and he had to content himself with the empty honour of a marshal-ship, he had cravings after hair-shirts and monastic solitudes. But this was only a temporary aberration. Cautious by nature, he had a nice perception of the dividing line between the possible and impossible: " I am not such a fool," wrote he, " as to spit against the sky." [2] *Rusé* above his fellows, he favoured a bluff exterior: " all that is in my heart can be read in my face." [3] Poor, and so by necessity a half-adventurer, he was not averse to dipping his hands in the coffers of all and sundry. In the year 1568, Bordeaux only voted him a paltry thousand écus for expenses, " which did not content him," remarks the chronicler drily, " and was the reason why he was not very nice to the town." [4] His most salient trait, however, was the high estimate he had of himself and his

[1] Monluc, iii. 55.   [2] *Ib.* iii. 199.   [3] *Ib.* iii. 139.
[4] *Chronique Bordelaise de Jean Gaufreteau*, 148.

abilities. " Monluc," wrote Alva to Philip II. in 1565, "came
up to speak to me. As he is as vain as can be, the way to
approach him seemed to me to be through his vanity." [1]

His reputation was great, and justly so. His defence of
Sienna in the fifties is one of the feats of French history. His
resource, and it alone, in this the first war of religion, created
a Catholic ascendancy in Guienne, the cradle of Huguenot
influence. Ten years later, the appearance of his black cornet
was sufficient to demoralise his enemies, "that cornet which
had achieved such great exploits, and which, its master said,
all the Huguenots dared not handle, even should they find it
in a ditch." [2] His treatment of the enemy, especially as given
in his own words, had its note of individuality. " If God
grants you the favour to run your fortunes through, and escape
with the crown on your head," he wrote to Charles IX., " you
can say that it is a great greyhound escaped in a wood from
five hundred wolves." [3] It was much in this spirit that
Monluc entered on the first war; only not the hound, but the
five hundred Huguenot wolves were his quarry. Shortly after
the battle of Vergt he wrote to Pius IV. that " all the lands of
Low and High Guienne have taken again to the Mass. When
they have not wished to do it out of piety, I have made them
do it by force of arms." And he went on to mention that
" more than forty ministers of the false law were killed in the
battle. Your Holiness can be certain that when they fall into
my hands I take good care that they never again spread
their heresies." [4] Again, at Terraube, he first broke faith with
the garrison, then slaughtered them and threw them into " the
well of the town, which was very deep, and which they filled
up so that you could touch them with your hand—a very
good despatch," he remarked, " to a very bad lot." [5] At
Monsegur, " Captain Héraud, who had been a member of my
company at Moncallier, as brave a soldier as there was in
Guienne, was a prisoner. Many wished to spare him for his
bravery. But I said, ' If he escape, he will fight us in every
village,' for I well knew his worth; and that was the reason

[1] *Papiers d'État de Granvelle*, ix. 286.   [2] D'Aubigné, iii. 385.
[3] De la Ferrière, *Deux années de mission à S. Pétersbourg*, 232.
[4] Vatican, B. ix. 622 (copy of letter of 16th Nov.).   [5] Monluc, iii. 23.

why I hung him." [1] With these instances in mind, one is not surprised at the remark of a Protestant gentleman in 1567, that "the name of Monluc was feared greatly among our troops who remembered the first civil war." [2]

But to return to Orleans. These summer and autumn months of 1562 were a time of mourning for those who remained, and especially for Coligny. On the 14th of July he lost his eldest son. Moreover, he was deprived of the Admiralship of France, which was given to his cousin Damville, while his company of a hundred men-at-arms was divided between another cousin, Meru, and Givry. [3] On the 27th of July the Parlement declared guilty of rebellion all those who were in arms in Orleans and elsewhere, with the exception of Condé. Coligny, of course, was one of them. This was followed up on the 18th of August by the issue of a writ of imprisonment against the Admiral and other leaders. And finally, on the 16th of November, he was condemned to death. It was the general situation, however, which was disquieting. After the fall of Poitiers, and again after that of Bourges, Orleans was threatened with a siege. A general exodus of the Gascons and Dauphinois was only avoided by the stirring appeals of Grammont and Condé. Every day brought the tale of some fresh disaster. All efforts seemed vain. For instance, Coligny led a most brilliant sortie, and on the 1st of September cut off an ammunition train on its way to the beleaguering host before Bourges. But "tears followed close upon laughter"; that very day Bourges had fallen. Then, too, the town itself was a veritable charnel-house. A plague was raging; ten thousand is given by Beza as the number of its victims. And outside, the Catholics were increasing daily. Spain, the Papacy, Savoy, were either promising or preparing help. German mercenaries, by no means all Catholics, as well as Swiss, were passing through Paris, or had already arrived at the royal camp. And as against this Condé and Coligny had little to show.

---

[1] Monluc, iii. 447.   [2] *Mémoires de Fabas, Vte. de Castets.*
[3] Letter of Card. Ferrara of 15th Aug. : Arch. di Stato, Modena. The Ambassador of Ferrara on 20th Aug. (Modena Francia, 37) divides the company between Damville and Montberon, another cousin, who was slain at Dreux.

A few thousand Swiss came to their aid in the Rhone valley. It was the only occasion during the whole course of the religious wars on which the Swiss Protestants took the field in favour of their co-religionists, and even then it was not official. But they did nothing. English aid, again, was disappointing. The treaty of Hampton Court was signed on the 20th of September. By it Elizabeth was to garrison and receive the joint control of Havre and Dieppe, aid Rouen if it was threatened, and provide a loan. In addition to this, the Vidame of Chartres, the Huguenot emissary, going beyond his instructions, allowed Cecil to insert an article by which it was agreed that the English were to remain at Havre until Calais was restored to them. The action of the Admiral and his nephew was, we believe, patriotic. They never intended that Elizabeth should have complete control of the two great seaports, and would certainly never have consented to her holding Havre as a lien on Calais.[1] None the less, the treaty, looked at from its result, was possibly a mistake. Firstly, it created odium by calling in the hereditary enemy. Secondly, from a military standpoint, it accomplished little. Elizabeth had driven a hard bargain. True, the threat of the landing, which only took place in the first week of October, drew off the royal army from the projected siege of Orleans. On the other hand, it led directly to the storming of Rouen. This the Huguenots, released from garrisoning the seaports, and the few hundred Englishmen thrown into the town, were unable to avert. The salvation of the party, indeed, seemed destined to come from Germany. In the very first days of his residence at Orleans, Coligny had inquired eagerly as to the resources of the Princes.[2] And he especially expressed his indebtedness to the Landgrave Philip of Hesse, who was the most vigorous champion of Huguenotism.[3] In July his brother Andelot started for Heidelberg, and with the aid of his half-sister, Magdalen of Mailly, Beza, Louis of Bar, and others, set to work to raise an army. But there were innumerable difficulties to overcome, and those in Orleans were worn out with waiting.

---

[1] For the whole question of the treaty of Hampton Court see Appendix I.

[2] *Arcana Seculi*, ii. 217.   [3] Heidenhain, Beilagen, 104.

Yet, in spite of these disappointments and reverses, Coligny never wavered. He laughed at the danger of the siege of a town so strongly held as Orleans. And he justified his confidence by an appeal to the lessons to be drawn from the sieges of Padua and Metz. Let the enemy only give them a little time, he wrote to Andelot on the 3rd of August, and they would have a warm reception.[1] All through these months, indeed, he and Condé were tireless, preparing the town against attack. Cannon were cast, provisions collected, the walls strengthened, at the last of which, so it was said, the Princess of Condé and the wife of the Admiral helped with the rest.[2] When at last the terrible news came of the defeat at Vergt and the loss of Rouen, Coligny remarked stoically that "one misfortune was always followed by another; one must await the third event."[3] In a word, he was the born leader of a minority.

Unfortunately, his record in other lines was not blameless. Several of his actions laid him open to criticism. Two of them were the execution of the curé of Saint Paterne at the end of July, and of the abbé of Gastines and of Sapin, a member of the Parlement of Paris, on the 2nd of November. Both these events must be laid at the door of Coligny and Condé, as they were the responsible leaders. The case of the curé of Saint Paterne has certainly not as yet been probed to the bottom. M. de Lacombe, who had the materials to do so,[4] has thrown little light on the question. As to the strangling of Sapin and the abbé of Gastines, it was admittedly a reply to the execution of the distinguished Huguenot minister Marlorat and others at Rouen, and only as such, if at all, was it justifiable. Condé and Coligny had to make the enemy fear reprisals. Otherwise, their position would have become impossible.

A much more questionable matter, we think, is contained in a letter of his of the 3rd of August, addressed to his brother Andelot.[5] It was the offer of the sack of Paris, to be

---

[1] *Kervyn de Lettenhove*, i. 502, etc.
[2] Fiaschi and Alvarotto, 21st Aug. : Modena Francia, 37.   [3] La Noue, 583.
[4] *Catherine de Médicis entre Guise et Condé.*
[5] *Kervyn de Lettenhove*, i. 402, etc.

given as an inducement to the German mercenaries. It is easy to explain the reasons of this almost incredibly callous suggestion. They are to be found in the letter itself. The cruelty of the Paris mob had become a byword throughout France. On the 15th of June, Ercole Strozzi thus described its methods: " This people is so exasperated against those of this new religion, that, if they find one of them anywhere, they slay him without more ado, and drag him through the place as though he were a dog."[1] Just eight months later, Smith wrote to Cecil as follows: " They in Paris every day murder one or other for Huguenots. It is enough if a boy, when he sees a man in the street, but cries ' Voyla ung Huguenot,' and straight the idle vagabonds, and such as cry things to sell, and crocheters, set upon him with stones; and then out come the handicraftsmen and idle apprentices with swords, and thrust him through with a thousand wounds; then they spoil him of his clothes, and the boys trail him down to the river and cast him in." Yet in spite of this the Admiral is not to be justified for a moment, the less so when we remember that he was a soldier. He knew well what the sack of a town meant: the butchery of innocent victims, rape, pillage, and its thousand and one horrors. He was aware, too, that of all soldiers the German mercenaries were the most lawless. And this was the mob which he was proposing to let loose on the great and populous Paris, the capital and very heart of France! Of all actions of his life, this one is the most to be regretted.

Moreover, it seemed to fail of its effect. Andelot and his Germans did not come. It was not even known where they were. Toward the end of October things looked serious. Something had to be done. Condé and Coligny decided that one of them must leave for Germany; the former for choice, as his position as Prince of the Blood would carry greater weight. Suddenly news was received that the Germans were well on their way. On the 6th of November Andelot himself entered Orleans. He had shown a splendid audacity. Sick, and carried in a litter, he had led his men from the Rhinelands across France, in spite of the royal armies under St. André,

[1] Mantua, Arch. Gonz., 653.

Nevers, and Tavannes, who were to bar his passage. La Rochefoucauld had already arrived on the 1st with three hundred gentlemen and the débris of Duras' army which had escaped from the battle of Vergt. Condé was now ready to move.

CHAPTER VIII

THE FIRST WAR OF RELIGION: CAMPAIGNS OF DREUX AND NORMANDY

March on Paris—Negotiations—Battle of Dreux—Condé a Prisoner—Coligny chosen Leader—Retires Southwards—Marches into Normandy—Murder of Guise—Edict of Amboise—Coligny returns to Orleans—His Dissatisfaction with Edict—Retires to Châtillon.

CONDÉ left Orleans on the 8th of November. His objective was Paris. It was hoped that by embarrassing the capital the enemy would be forced either to sue for peace or give battle. Throckmorton, who accompanied the army and was only captured at Dreux, estimated its strength as 2000 horse and 6000 foot. When reinforced by the foreign levies—that is to say, 3500 reiters and 4000 lansquenets—it gave a force of 5500 cavalry and 10,000 infantry, or 15,500 in all.[1] As to the artillery, La Noue wrote that it consisted of eight pieces of varying calibre.

The first town which was reached was Pithiviers. After a short siege, it surrendered unconditionally on the 11th, the priests being slaughtered wholesale. It was here that the German mercenaries joined the main army. "The Marshal of Hesse," Throckmorton remarked drily of their leader, "is the moost moderate and advised Almayn that I have seene; but the people under his charge be verey Almain souldiors, which do spoyle all thinges where they go." The same day Gonnor entered the camp with proposals from Catherine. He had already been in correspondence with the Admiral, who had replied to him on the 28th of October.[2] But though

[1] Beza, who was also with the army, gave the number as 6000 horse and 9000 foot: *Calvini Opera*, xix. 598.

[2] Condé, iv. 55.

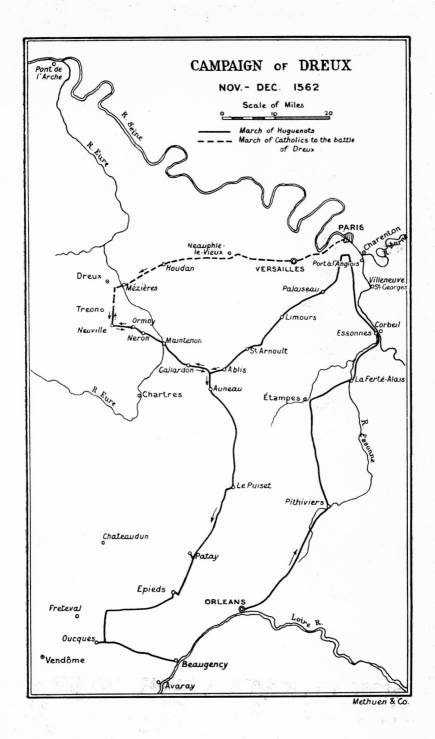

CAMPAIGN of DREUX

NOV.- DEC. 1562

Scale of Miles

0   10   20

——— March of Huguenots
– – – March of Catholics to the battle
of Dreux

Pont de
l'Arche

R. Seine

R. Eure

PARIS   Charenton
Neauphle·   Port à l'Anglois   R. Marne
le-Vieux
Houdan   VERSAILLES
Dreux   Villeneuve
Mézières   Palaiseau   St Georges
Treon   Limours   Corbeil
Neuville   Ormoy   Essonnes
Neron   Maintenon   St Arnoult
Callardon   Ablis   La Ferté-Alais
R. Eure   Auneau
Chartres   Étampes

R. Essonne

Le Puiset

Pithiviers

Chateaudun

Patay

Epieds

Freteval   ORLEANS
Oucques   Loire R.
Vendôme   Beaugency

Avaray

Methuen & Co.

willing to treat, the leaders determined to push steadily
forward. Their appearance under the walls of Étampes on
the 14th was sufficient to induce the townsmen to surrender
the keys. But without entering they pushed on to La Ferté-
Alais and Corbeil, where they arrived on the 16th. They
had thus, it will be seen, turned aside from the direct road to
Paris. They were convinced that they could never capture
it, while to pillage the suburbs would gain nothing, and
might seriously affect both the morale and discipline of the
mercenaries. On the other hand, if they could only seize
Corbeil, which commanded the river, they would cause real
distress in the capital, and so make her more amenable to
reason. The plan, however, miscarried, and a week was
wasted. Corbeil was now well garrisoned by St. André, and
its capture was quite beyond the resources of the Huguenots
with their few cannon. Coligny, therefore, refused to press
the siege ; he feared the effect of a disaster. When someone
cried out that it was shameful cowardice, he turned on him
with the retort " that he would rather be mocked unjustly by
friends, than justly by enemies." [1]

But there was another reason for this apparent lack of
vigour. Negotiations were again in full swing. Saint Mesme,
on behalf of the Queen Mother, came with the news of the
death of Navarre on the 17th. In addition, he was instructed
to sound Condé. This was followed up on the 22nd by
another visit from Gonnor. On the 23rd the Prince was
again on the march for Paris. Only the Seine divided him
from St. André, the armies exchanging shots and shouts of
defiance as they took a parallel course down the river. On
the 24th Condé was at Juvisy, on the 25th at the nunnery
of La Saussaie, where it was arranged that he should meet
Catherine on the morrow near Charenton.[2]

On the 26th the Queen Mother duly arrived from
Vincennes, but, as so often before, she was disappointed by

[1] La Noue, 593.

[2] Ruble (*Jeanne d'Albret*, 201), following the *Journal de l'Année* 1562, says that
Catherine went to meet Condé at St. Maur-les-Fossés. This seems doubtful, taking
into consideration the position of the Huguenot army. Another account (Vatican
Library, Urbino, 1039, 390) gives the proposed place of meeting as between Charenton and Villeneuve St. Georges—that is, near Port à l'Anglois, mentioned by Beza.

Condé. This time he was ill. But, not to lose the occasion, the Admiral and the Constable agreed to an interview. It was cordial, but neither would give way. Anne would not listen for a moment to his nephew's proposal of a religious "interim," or the Edict of January. On the other hand, he drew attention to the real weakness of the Protestant forces, though he seems to have passed over in silence Condé's claim to be considered political heir of Anthony of Navarre.

On the 27th, Catherine again appeared, and again Condé failed her. It was finally arranged that the Admiral should see her, while the Constable visited the Prince. Coligny crossed the river in a small boat. Catherine received him with every demonstration of affection. She embraced and kissed him, and presented him with a horse, as he was on foot. He assured her earnestly that the sole reason of his taking up arms was his regard for the honour of God and the rights and safety of the Princes of the Blood. He affirmed that he and his friends were loyal subjects—more faithful than many who were near His Majesty. He protested that their swords were at the King's service. And lastly, he stated that he could easily see to the retirement of the foreigners, presumably English and German. On other subjects he and the Prince reiterated the views of the day before, adding a request for the retirement of the Guises. On one question Catherine made her intentions perfectly clear. She would not hear of any plan of sharing the supreme power with Condé.

The interview, on the whole, was disappointing. On the next day, therefore, Condé moved his camp nearer Paris. After a brisk skirmish, which was carried by the vanguard under Coligny to the very walls of the town, he settled at Gentilly, Arcueil, Montrouge, and the surrounding villages. On the morning of the 29th he offered battle, but it was refused. In the afternoon he met Catherine at a mill four or five hundred paces from the suburb of St. Marcel. There was another conference on the 1st of December, though Catherine and Condé were absent. But they met again on the 2nd, the 4th, and the 5th, most of the principals also

being present, but not the Duke of Guise. Things were now
shaping well. Progress was especially good on the 3rd, when
there was no meeting, but an active interchange of views.
Condé had now definitely dropped his claims as candidate to
the position of First Prince of the Blood, in favour of his elder
brother, the Cardinal of Bourbon, and was concentrating his
attention on the religious issues. Both sides seemed inclined
to moderation, a state of mind produced largely, no doubt, by
their empty coffers. When they met on the 4th, peace seemed
assured. The Prince had compromised on almost every
question. Protestantism was to be confined to those places
where it had been exercised before the outbreak of hostilities.
But even there it was only to be tolerated when asked for.
Moreover, it was to be excluded from frontier-towns—though
other places would be set aside instead—and Paris. Finally,
it was agreed that the treaty should be sworn to by the Privy
Councillors instead of being guaranteed by hostages, as the
Huguenots had originally demanded. But before parting,
Condé presented Catherine with the sum of his demands in
writing. His intention was to clear up all obscure points,
preparatory to a treaty. But the result was not what he
expected. For it was her reply to this which shattered all
chances of an agreement. The crucial points were: the King
should declare the Protestant army to be his army, and so
presumably undertake its payment; cases at law in which
Huguenots were involved should, if they so wished, be called
before the Grand Council, as the various Parlements were
notoriously hostile; Huguenots should be reinstated in all
offices and honours; and both parties should disband. All
of these Catherine either directly or indirectly refused. Yet
on the last three, especially, Condé and the Admiral could
not compromise. To have done so would have been to put
themselves at the mercy of their enemies. Matters thus came
to a deadlock, and though negotiations were still continued—
indeed, until the Protestants were well on their way to Dreux—
nothing was done. For the Triumvirate were less inclined
than ever that anything should be done. Genlis, who had
been weakening for some time, and had enjoyed a long interview with Guise, deserted to them on the night of the 6th,

while on the 7th strong reinforcements arrived from Gascony and Spain.

Who then, it may be asked, was responsible for the failure of negotiations? Certainly not the Prince and Admiral. Cipierre, a Catholic gentleman, recounted to the Venetian Ambassador a somewhat truculent saying of theirs, to the effect that, if their demands were not conceded, they would sharpen well their swords, as it was meet to make trial of them. But this was a mere flourish of trumpets, intended to impress. In reality they showed themselves keenly anxious to come to an understanding, if for no other reason than because they had thousands of mercenaries whom they had not paid and could not pay. Catherine, again, there can be no doubt, would have sacrificed almost anything except power to obtain peace. She had early moved from Vincennes to the city, the better to negotiate. Day after day she had gone out to the conferences, ill, chilled to the bone, and so hoarse, wrote one, that you could scarcely hear her speak. And at night she had ridden back, her way lit by torches, and through streets where the angry Parisians thrust out their heads to jeer. Everything, indeed, points to Guise as the real obstructor. It is possible that the Constable, also, was not too willing to compromise; for, in so doing, his son Damville would lose the Admiralship of France. None the less, it was Guise who proved the stumbling-block. Condé indirectly charged him with the failure. The Venetian and Florentine Ambassadors took practically the same view. In fact, he had shown himself unbending throughout. He had never once appeared when Condé and Coligny were present, yet all the while he and the Spanish Ambassador were bringing pressure to bear on the Queen. He felt, no doubt, a supreme confidence in his own capacity as a general to crush the enemy, and was only waiting for the Gascons and Spaniards to force an issue.[1]

---

[1] For negotiations before Paris, see Condé, iv. 144, etc. ; Forbes, ii. 217, etc. ; *Hist. Ecclé.*, ii. 240, etc.; *Calvini Opera*, xix. (Beza, 14th Dec.) ; *Huguenot Society Publications*, vi. lxxxi., etc.; Vatican Library, Urbino, 1039, 390 (letter of 4th Dec.) ; Vatican, B. xiv. 170 (letter of 14th Dec.) ; Florence, Arch. Med. (several despatches of Tornabuoni) ; Modena, Arch. di Stato (Card. Ferrara to Borromeo, 9th Dec.) ; Modena Francia, 37 (Alvarotto, 24th Nov., 9th and 13th Dec.) ; Naples, Carte Farn., 765 (Lolgi to Card. Farnese, 2nd Dec.) ; Paris, Arch. Nat., K. 1496, 102.

Diplomacy had now done its utmost, and failed.   The way of arms failed also.   The night of the 6th was chosen by Condé for a *camisade*, or night-surprise of the enemy; but, like a similar plan arranged for the last of November, it came to nothing.   This time it was the desertion of Genlis which at the last moment upset calculations.   The only move now left them, therefore, was to decamp.   All the arguments which Coligny had used as to the danger of besieging Orleans applied with even greater force to his own and Condé's present position.   At any moment they might be surprised, and suffer a disaster.   On the other hand, there was little hope of blockading Paris effectually, still less of taking it by storm   Then, too, they had to take into account that with an army such as theirs, living from hand to mouth, settling on the land like a swarm of locusts and eating it up, movement was a necessity of existence.   And the resources of the neighbour-hood of Paris would soon give out.   These reasons, together with the need of somehow finding pay for the Germans, induced them to turn their faces toward Normandy.   When once there, they might hope to draw on Elizabeth for both men and money.   This course was certainly hazardous, for they were divided from the English by the Seine, with all its towns and bridges in the hands of the enemy.   Nevertheless, it was not desperate.   Their plan was to capture Chartres, then by a rapid move northwards seize on Pont de l'Arche, and so eventually get in touch with Warwick, who was at Havre.   Their best chance of success lay in speed.   The question resolved itself into who—they or the Triumvirate— should arrive in Normandy first.

Early on the 10th Condé was on the move, Coligny, as always, commanding the vanguard.[1]   Their march, if not dilatory, was deliberate.   The Prince spent the night at Palaiseau ; the nights of the 11th and 12th at Limours ; those of the 13th, 14th, and possibly 15th at St. Arnoult, which was taken by assault.   Here the false news that the enemy were on their way to Étampes threatened to derange his plans. It was now too dangerous to attack Chartres, strongly held as

[1] *Hist. Ecclé.*, ii. 274.   The vanguard may have left on the 9th.   Throckmorton and Smith give it as the date of the departure of the army.

it was, and with a hostile force within striking distance. But Condé was ready with a scheme. It was characteristic of his rash and sanguine nature. It was to make a dash back on Paris, carry the suburbs, terrify the citizens, and at the same time isolate the Catholic army, which would be forced to make a long detour to regain the capital. But Coligny was not long in exposing its futility. To throw themselves on Paris, he explained, would be to cut themselves off from their base of supplies in Orleans, which would invite a siege. Moreover, they themselves might be attacked and taken at a serious disadvantage, with the Triumvirate in front and a hostile town in rear. Then again, the mercenaries were crying out for their pay, which was only to be obtained by a march on Normandy. These arguments prevailed, especially as a Huguenot gentleman named Baubigny promised to surprise Dreux.

On the 16th, Gallardon was stormed with the now usual holocaust of priests. In the evening of the 17th, it was found that, after having crossed the Eure, Condé, with the " battle " or main army at Ormoy, was in advance of Coligny, who was with the vanguard at Neron. The 18th, therefore, was set aside to rectify this mistake of the camp-marshals. But necessary as the delay was, it dealt a final blow to their plans. Already valuable time had been wasted. They had spent several days at St. Arnoult in hesitating and providing fresh transport for their artillery, then more hours in storming Gallardon. Thus the initial advantage of starting in advance, of having a smaller force and less artillery, was thrown away. For the Triumvirate, leaving Paris on the 11th, and passing through Versailles and Neauphle, had arrived at Mezières on the Eure during the 18th. Their march, in relation to that of Condé, had formed the string of the bow.[1] They were thus in a position to threaten his advance, while effectually blocking his way to the Seine. Moreover, by keeping to

---

[1] Florence, Arch. Med. 4595, 147 (Tornabuoni from Paris, 16th Dec.). The route, suggested by Coynart, of Chevreuse, Rambouillet, and Épernon, is almost certainly wrong. Alvarotto on 13th Dec. (Modena Francia, 37), as well as the *Journal de l'Année* 1562, mentions the Triumvirate as being at Neauphle. This march due west in the direction of Houdan and Dreux is also to be inferred from the accounts of the Venetian Ambassador (*Hug. Publications*, vi.) and Chantonnay (from Paris, 16th Dec. : Paris, Arch. Nat., K. 1496).

ORDER OF THE ARMIES AT THE BATTLE OF DREUX, 19 DEC., 1562

(*Tortorel at Perrissin*)

A—CONDÉ WITH MEN-AT-ARMS   B—COLIGNY AND PORTIEN WITH MEN-AT-ARMS   C—LA ROCHEFOUCAULD WITH MEN-AT-ARMS
D—MOUY AND AVARAY WITH MEN-AT-ARMS   E—FIVE CORNETS OF REITERS IN TWO SQUADRONS   F—SIX CORNETS OF REITERS
G—DE LA CURÉE WITH SIX CORNETS OF ARGOULETS   H—LANSQUENETS   I—FRENCH FOOT   K—' FORLORN HOPES '   L—ARTILLERY
M—CONSTABLE WITH CAVALRY   N—DAMVILLE WITH CAVALRY   O—ST. ANDRÉ WITH CAVALRY   P—GUISE WITH CAVALRY
Q—OTHER MEN-AT-ARMS   R—SWISS   S—BRETON AND FRENCH FOOT   T—GERMAN FOOT   V—FRENCH FOOT   X—SPANISH FOOT
Y—' FORLORN HOPES '   Z—ARTILLERY   A A—ARTILLERY

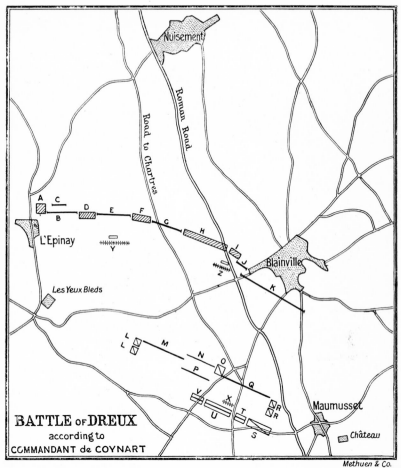

Nuisement

Road to Chartres

Roman Road

A C
B
D E F G H I J
L'Epinay
Y
Blainville
Z
K

Les Yeux Bleds

L
L M N O Q R R
P
V X
U T R R
S
S

Maumusset

BATTLE of DREUX
according to
COMMANDANT de COYNART

Château

Methuen & Co.

CATHOLIC ARMY

A—2,500 SPANISH FOOT   B—GUISE WITH 350 MEN-AT-ARMS   C—150-200 VOLUNTEERS   D—2,000 FRENCH AND GASCON FOOT (10 DEEP)   E—ST. ANDRÉ WITH 300 LIGHT-HORSE   F—3,000 LANSQUENETS (10 DEEP) G—DAMVILLE AND AUMALE WITH 350 MEN-AT-ARMS   H—6,000 SWISS FOOT (10 DEEP)   I—MARTIGUES WITH 3,000 FRENCH AND GASCON FOOT   J—SANSAC WITH 200 LIGHT-HORSE   K—CONSTABLE WITH 600 MEN-AT-ARMS   Y—14 CANNON BEFORE 'VAN' WITH 250 'FORLORN HOPES'   Z—8 CANNON BEFORE SWISS WITH 250 'FORLORN-HOPES'

HUGUENOT ARMY

L L—2 SQUADRONS OF REITERS (16 DEEP)   M—CONDÉ WITH 400 MEN-AT-ARMS   N—MOUY AND AVARAY WITH 200 MEN-AT-ARMS   O—DE LA CURÉE WITH 200 ARGOULETS (16 DEEP)   P—LA ROCHEFOUCAULD WITH 300 MEN AT ARMS   Q—COLIGNY AND PORTIEN WITH 600 MEN AT ARMS   R R—2 SQUADRONS OF REITERS (16 DEEP)   S—1,200-1,400 REITERS IN RESERVE (16 DEEP)   T—2,000 LANSQUENETS OF COLIGNY (10 DEEP) U—5,000 FRENCH FOOT (10 DEEP)   V—2,000 LANSQUENETS OF CONDÉ (10 DEEP)   X—5 CANNON

broken country, they were able to neutralise their great inferiority in cavalry.

But these were only a few of the Huguenot errors and misfortunes. The attempted surprise of Dreux failed. Then again, Coligny was insisting that their opponents had no intention of giving battle at the very time that the Triumvirate was preparing to attack in the plain of Dreux. And though Condé did not share in this delusion, he was negligent. Thus in the afternoon of the 18th he set out against the enemy, who were reported to be crossing the Eure. Yet, strangely enough, when this news proved false, he returned to his quarters, and took no steps to keep in touch or occupy the villages along the river.

On the 19th, the Prince, who had a presage of battle, rose two hours before daylight, and made his preparations. He had been hailed by hags and dreamed dreams. And portents played an important part in the imagination of the sixteenth century, as can be gauged from the work of the distinguished Protestant divine, Louis Lavater, *Of ghostes and spirites walking by nyght, and of strange noyses, crackes, and sundry forewarnynges, whiche commonly happen before the death of menne, great slaughters and alterations of kyngdomes.*[1] But Coligny would have none of them, and, convinced of the remoteness of a fight, loitered on the way. Furthermore, some of those with him, lulled to sleep by his confidence, failed to put on their heavy armour. In consequence, Condé was not under way before eight in the morning. The proposed line of march was north-west across open country to Treon. It was specially suited to Huguenot tactics, with their large preponderance of cavalry. But beyond Treon the ground was broken, and would, as Coligny himself confessed on passing through some months later, have given the whole advantage to the Catholic infantry. But, fortunately for the Protestants, they never got more than half-way. On the 18th, in the deep silence of night, with neither trumpets sounding nor drums beating—"à la sourdine," as one chronicler quaintly puts it—the Triumvirate had crossed the Eure, and now, on the morning of the 19th, came down the plain in extended line from

[1] Translated into English by R. H. in 1572.

Nuisement. They were thus directly north of Condé. Before midday both sides heard the other's drums beating. The Prince, eager for battle, and alive to the danger of exposing his flank, halted his men, and went forward with Coligny and Andelot to reconnoitre the enemy.

The Catholic line ran east and west for some two thousand yards between the villages of Blainville and Épinay. But in marching down south from Nuisement, the Triumvirate had found their front too extended, and Guise on the right with the vanguard had fallen to the rear, and now lay concealed from view behind Épinay. He and St. André, with some French horse, lansquenets, Gascons, and Spanish foot, were thus the right wing of the Catholic army. In the centre, and forming part of the "battle" or main army, were the Swiss, while the Constable was on the left. As they were weak in cavalry, they adopted the novel mode of interspersing it in small bodies among the infantry, a form warmly recommended by the experienced La Noue. Throughout, however, they clung to the old French tactics of the *haie*, or single line of cavalry. Before the centre and left wings were parks of artillery, which, however, did not play a large part in the main struggle.

The Protestant leaders at once saw that this position was a strong one. Firstly, it was impossible to take it in flank. Secondly, should the Huguenots attack, they would have to cross a valley and arrive spent, and probably shaken by the Catholic artillery, which was twenty-two in number. And thirdly, their smaller force, with its less extended front, might be enveloped. It was therefore decided to resume the march to Treon. But though the army began to move, it was found impossible to avoid an engagement, especially as some of the cavalry was put to flight by a volley from the Catholic fieldpieces. Condé, therefore, drew up his "battle" opposite the Swiss; while Coligny, with the vanguard, in reversal of its true order, formed the Protestant right wing, and so faced the Constable. This was owing either to the fact that the "van" had not yet regained its ordinary position in advance, or, as seems more likely, that Coligny had already started for Treon, and on hurrying back came in behind Condé, and took the right in order to complete the line.[1]

The Huguenot extreme left was made up of two squadrons of reiters, sixteen deep, "each horseman carrying two or three pistols at his saddle-bow." [2] Their tactics were to advance to within pistol-shot, when the first line fired and wheeled to the left and rear, where it re-formed and re-charged its weapons— each line in turn repeating the manœuvre. Next to the reiters came the French cavalry in *échelon*, then a squadron of argoulets, a kind of light cavalry sixteen deep, and armed with an arquebus two or two and a half feet in length. All these were under Condé. Coligny, commanding the right, had under him 600 men-at-arms in *haie* or single line, the form ordinarily adopted by the French horse, and two squadrons of reiters. The second line of the army was formed by the artillery and foot and a reserve of 1200 to 1400 reiters. Thus it will be seen that the Huguenots, as they were superior in cavalry, had placed it in front: the battle was to be a cavalry battle. The formation of the French argoulets into a compact body, probably in imitation of the reiters, and, on the Catholic side, the infantry line interspersed with cavalry, are novel and interesting features.

The Huguenots had perhaps 4500 cavalry. As to the infantry, "the Prince hath not past seven thousande, whereof his three thousand Frenchmen be very ill armed." [3] The wear and tear of the campaign, sickness, desertion, and the garrisoning of towns, had thus greatly reduced their numbers. The Triumvirate had probably 14,000 to 16,000 foot, but not more than 2000 horse.

Coligny, as he looked northwards, saw before him an undulating plain, sloping gently up to Nuisement, and streaked by the uneven line of the enemy, with the village of Épinay

---

[1] *L'Année* 1562 *et la bataille de Dreux*, by Commandant de Coynart. This work is an admirable interpretation of the valuable plans of the battle published by Tortorel & Perrissin in 1570. I have followed it throughout, merely correcting a few obvious errors.

[2] Venetian Amb., Paris, 21st Dec. 1562 (*Hug. Soc. Publications*, vi.).

[3] Throckmorton to Elizabeth, 13th Dec. : Forbes, ii. 227. Beza, who was also present at the battle, gives the number as 4000 horse and less than 5000 foot : *Hist. Eccl.*, ii. 289.

perched high in the west. On either hand of him the
Protestant horse made a gay front of colour, and contrast, and
glittering steel, the Huguenot gentlemen in the centre, with
their armour and lances and flutter of white scarves and
surcoats, being edged on both flanks by the imposing squadrons
of the reiters.

There was no preliminary skirmish, generally so dear to
the heart of sixteenth-century captains. Condé was eager for
the fray. Though his plan would ordinarily have been to
engage and defeat the right wing of the enemy, he failed to do
so, as it was hid from view behind the village of Épinay. His
whole energies, therefore, were directed to breaking up the
Swiss, 6000 strong. Around this squadron was the most
obstinate struggle of the day. Again and again attacked, first
by Mouy, Avarey, and La Curée, then by Condé himself, then
by the reiters, on flank and front and rear, each time they
re-formed. La Rochefoucauld, who had lain idle with some
horse, also made an attempt, but was thrown back in confusion.
Condé's lansquenets failed equally. They set out against them,
but when the Swiss showed signs of meeting them half-way,
they fled in terror. At last, however, before a final dash of
the reiters and the horse of Mouy and Avaray, probably on
their return from pillaging the baggage at Nuisement, these
hardy mountaineers fell back sullenly westward under Épinay,
broken but not scattered.

Meanwhile Coligny had been triumphant on the right.
With a rush that nothing could stay, he fell on the enemy's
left wing headed by the Constable. Charge followed charge.
The victory was decisive. Damville, a son of the Constable,
who had ridden across the field to help the Swiss and rescue
his father, was roughly handled; Montberon, another son, was
slain; Aumale, the brother of Guise, was wounded; many
Catholic gentlemen lay dead, and the old warrior himself was
finally taken amid the hoarse cries of the reiters.

The rout of the Catholic left was complete. The whole of
their main army was a fleeing rabble. Some went running to
the very gates of Paris, crying that all was lost. The plain
near at hand was almost clear of Catholics. The Swiss had
fallen back under Épinay, while the rest were either re-forming

behind Guise, or were flying toward Nuisement. The battle
was now being fought at right angles to its original position.
Thus Condé and Coligny, who were breathing their horses
close to Blainville, were now facing west instead of north.   A
great part of their reiters were scattered in pursuit of the
enemy.   The battle seemed won.   Some of the Huguenot
gentlemen were already congratulating Coligny on the victory.
But he was too cautious to be carried away by their enthusiasm.
During the pause he watched uneasily.   Seeing the Catholic
vanguard appearing on the heights of Épinay, he replied in
alarm, "That heavy cloud will fall on us yet."[1]   His fore-
bodings were well founded.

Guise from his shelter at Épinay had watched the battle
raging below.   An hour and a half passed.   His own men
were anything but steady.   He stiffened them by a more
compact order.   At last he had his opportunity.   The
Huguenot horse were scattered in pursuit.   Little more than a
remnant remained to their leaders.   The artillery and infantry
of the vanguard was virtually unprotected.   Guise, therefore,
exhorting his men with the cry, " Now, friends, the day is ours ! "
came down from the crest of the hill.   With his right he
seized the Protestant artillery and put their infantry to utter
rout.   With his centre he drove back the loose bands of
Huguenot cavalry upon Condé and Coligny ; while with his
left he temporarily cut off the rest who were in the direction
of Nuisement.   The Huguenots were utterly helpless.   The
reiters, seeing the foot in disorder, made for the rear with
the French cavalry, Condé on the way being taken prisoner.
Coligny made desperate efforts to rally his men, and when
once across a little valley behind Blainville, a halt made
by Guise to receive the surrender of 2000 lansquenets gave
him his chance.   He was able to collect a body of 1200 horse.
Appealing to them, calling on them as their leader, crying,
" Courage, my friends ; he who rallies last bears off the fruits
of victory ! "[2] he led them again to battle.   He himself was in

[1] La Noue, 594.

[2] This address of Coligny as given by d'Aubigné (ii. 113) seems fairly plausible,
though he could only have made it to the French cavalry.   He was forced to
communicate with the reiters through an interpreter.

the centre, Portien and La Rochefoucauld with their cavalry, as well as the reiters, being on either hand. And though those on the left still hung back, he threw himself on the enemy with the rest. The Catholic cavalry was drawn up in three squadrons. The Admiral drove it before him with terrible execution. All was going well; it looked like victory. But as the Duke retired, the Gascon bands were uncovered, and opened fire. Coligny was forced to turn his attack on them, but they were solid as a wall; it was impossible to break them. Moreover, the Spaniards were coming up. The Admiral was now in danger of being hemmed in. Forced to choose between defeat or disaster, he fell back at a foot-pace, slowly and in perfect order. Then the darkness came down, and the battle was over.

Guise was thus left victor of the field. The Triumvirate was no more. The Constable was on his way to Orleans as a prisoner. St. André, the nominal leader of the vanguard, was dead. And of the other side Condé was a captive, destined to sleep that night in the bed of the conqueror. The two great actors alone remained. The perplexing cross-currents introduced by the formation of the Triumvirate ceased. The old rivalry came out clear again : Coligny against Guise.

The Huguenot losses have been variously estimated. The most responsible calculation has come from Beza.[1] It was based on a review held a few days later. Of 2500 French foot, 1000 were left, and of 3000 lansquenets only 900. This would give a loss of 3600. But if, as Throckmorton wrote, the number of the infantry before the battle was 7000, the killed, wounded, and prisoners would then amount to 5000. Beza's estimate, however, is probably the more correct. Of this total many were prisoners—among them a batch of 1400 cowardly lansquenets of the "battle." The losses among the cavalry were trifling. Coligny put them as low as 60.[2] To these must be added four fieldpieces. The baggage and the three heavy cannon were saved, though a culverin was abandoned later. Thus, it will be seen, Coligny had by no means suffered a crushing defeat. This was the view taken

[1] *Hist. Ecclé.*, ii. 306.
[2] De la Ferrière : *Le XVIme siècle*, 93 (Coligny to Montgomery, 28th Dec.).

by himself and by Throckmorton. For his cavalry, the most important arm in the sixteenth century, was practically intact. The Catholic losses may not have scaled 2000. Yet, on the other hand, they were largely among their *corps d'élite*: the Swiss and the French men-at-arms.

The Admiral spent the night of the 19th at the village of Neuville, a few miles away from the field of battle. He proposed to set out again in the morning and recommence the struggle. But the reiters would not move. They never descended to the methods of the Italian mercenary, who, at different stages of his history, had reduced the saving of his own life to a fine art. In the late battle they had covered themselves with glory. Nevertheless, their first object in coming to France was to pillage and make their fortune, and there were risks they did not care to run. They were opposed, therefore, to taking the offensive, shattered as they were, and with some of their number not yet come in. Such being the case, Coligny had to be content on the 20th with making a demonstration, and then moving south-east to Gallardon. On the 21st he arrived at Auneau, where he was unanimously chosen as leader.

The position of commander-in-chief of the Huguenot forces had few attractions, and the Admiral pleaded with them to choose someone else. But in reality he was all that was left to them. He had made grave mistakes in the late campaign; he had been obstinate; occasionally his generalship had been at fault. But in the battle itself and after, he was the one man who had stood between them and ruin. They felt, and he felt, though unwillingly, it is true, that, by position, by character, and by his extraordinary influence over the foreign troops, he alone could make their prospects something more than a forlorn hope.

From Auneau Coligny passed to Le Puiset, arriving on the 23rd of December. On the 24th he reached Patay, where he busied himself in hanging some lawless followers, and where, on Christmas Day, the sin-hardened Germans received communion after the Lutheran fashion. Continuing his march to Epieds, he called up all spare troops from Orleans to repel a feared attack from Guise. Then, on the 27th, hearing that the latter

was despatching reinforcements to Blois, he pursued them as
far as Freteval. This move thoroughly perplexed the enemy.
It was thought that he was marching on Poitou, thence, perhaps,
to fall back on Gascony and Navarre.[1] His real intention,
however, was to rest his troops and make a fresh attempt to
reach Normandy; the victorious Montgomery was there, and
the English. Therefore, crossing the Loire at Beaugency, he
marched toward the Cher, " with the wish," wrote he, " of re-
freshing this army, and especially the reiters." [2] This meant,
in less euphemistic language, to storm some of the enemy's
towns and villages, and give the mercenaries the chance of
emptying the surrounding country. On the 7th of January,
1563, Selles capitulated, and the relics of gold and silver, as well
as other property collected by the priests of the surrounding
country, went to pay the army. St. Aignan and Montrichard
were also occupied.

Nevertheless, the Admiral's position was insecure. At any
moment he might have been cut off from Orleans. This, in
fact, is what Guise proceeded to do. Having cleared Beauce,
he arrived at Beaugency, and some of his troops soon appeared
on the south side of the Loire. This forced Coligny to bring
up his men and throw him back across the river. The reiters
were then settled at Jargeau, the infantry being in Orleans
under Andelot.

Throughout January he became increasingly anxious at the
general situation. Guise was evidently bent on the siege of
Orleans. It was the only means of bringing the Protestants to
their knees. For with their large superiority in cavalry they
were able to do as they pleased in the open country, " and we
have been unable to stop them," wrote a Catholic gentleman
to Mary Queen of Scots, " for they have neither artillery nor
foot to stop them trotting here and there." [3] And for this very
reason Coligny hesitated to throw himself into Orleans, and
so sacrifice his one great advantage: mobility. Moreover, he
would be risking all on the defence of one town. If it fell, the
party would be annihilated. Thus everything was urging him
imperiously back to Normandy. It was clear that, if the party

[1] Ruble, *Jeanne d'Albret*, 386.   [2] Condé, iv. 243.
[3] Dalendouze from Blois, 6th Feb.: Brit. Museum, 19401, 79.

was any longer to remain a military factor, it must receive pay
and recruits. In addition, such a retreat, combined with a
few successes, might draw off Guise from the neighbourhood of
Orleans. But immediate action was necessary. The Catholic
leaders might get a firmer grip on the maritime province and
cut him off permanently from the sea. Everything, however,
depended on the temper of Elizabeth and the reiters. They
called for the most delicate handling. In dealing with the
former, he used all the arts of entreaty and flattery. On the
morrow of the battle he had sent her an account, minimising
his defeat. He promised to enter on no negotiations without
her consent. He begged her to get ready infantry and
pay for his reiters, and so prepare the way for his projected march. " Madam," he wrote, " we have our chief
hope in your aid and succour after God, who, you well know,
has placed you in this high station and given you knowledge
of Himself, and put the sword in your hand to succour those
unjustly oppressed, to defend religion, and oppose those who
would abolish His true and pure service, as is the duty of all
princes and potentates of the earth, among whom you hold so
great a place." [1]

A more difficult task was to appease the reiters. There are
few pages in history more curious than the relations between
the two. He was a master, of a kind, among untamed bar-
barians. They raged and clamoured for their pay, now
months in arrear. The loot of the country round Selles and
Jargeau failed to satisfy them. They threatened to take him
prisoner. And all the time Guise menaced them and intrigued.[2]
But the Admiral, with unfailing tact and persistence, humoured,
appeased, restored his influence, until they swore anew to stand
by him to the end. As a last strain on their allegiance, he
begged them to leave everything behind and follow him to
Normandy. It was impossible to take them with him, loaded
as they were. With their thousands of carts to carry past and
future pillage, they were almost as immobile as infantry, and
they would prove an easy prey to so alert a general as Guise.

---

[1] 2nd Jan. : de la Ferrière, *Le XVIe siècle*, 95.
[2] Chantonnay to Philip II., 9th Jan.: Paris, Arch. Nat., K. 1499. Cf. *Calvini
Opera*, xx. 19.

The difficulty was solved with the aid of their commander, Rollshausen, Marshal of Hesse, and they were cajoled into placing their baggage in Orleans under the care of Andelot with the main army. " He had a subtle judgment," Brantôme wrote enthusiastically of Coligny, "wherewith he knew better how to hold and treat them than any captain or anyone in the world without means has done or shall do." [1]

Coligny was now ready. Catherine tried to divert him with a promise of negotiations, and failed. On the 30th of January, therefore, he sat down to pen a last letter to the imprisoned Condé. In addition to other matters, it was full of commendations of his constancy. " We all praise God," he wrote, " for the grace which He gives you to persevere in the holy vocation to which He calls you. Thus shall you receive the recompense which He promises to His own. But "——here we have the presentiment of all that was changeful in the nature of the Prince——" we all beseech you in the name of God to have naught before your eyes but what turns to His glory, for thus shall you and we be happy indeed." [2] Two days later he set out on his journey. He had a force of about 4000 mounted men, made up of 2000 reiters, 500 French cavalry, 1000 arquebusiers, and a few hundred valets. In addition there were 1200 baggage animals, but no artillery. In six days he had left the enemy far behind, having covered the astonishing distance of fifty French leagues. And it looked, too, as though he were about to accomplish the double feat of eluding pursuit and at the same time enticing away the Catholic army now closing in on Orleans. It was only the generalship and eloquence of Guise that held them to the siege.

On the 8th of February Coligny was already at Touques, having passed through Treon, scattered the peasantry at Bernay, and skirted Evreux. He finally settled at Dives, which was convenient for communication with Havre. His great difficulty was the reiters. He waited impatiently for the expected aid from Elizabeth. " But the winds were persistently contrary between England and Havre, which angered the Admiral not a little, for he had Orleans ever before his eyes,

---

[1] Brantôme, iv. 320.   [2] Delaborde, ii. 201.

while the reiters ceaselessly importuned him to keep his promise. His final answer was to point to the waves of the sea." [1] This, of course, was hardly calculated to content them. In revenge they burnt and destroyed the surrounding villages, irrespective of party. They even considered the advisability of murdering him, La Rochefoucauld, and the Marshal of Hesse. And he was only able to quell this incipient mutiny by producing on the 17th letters which he had received from the English. Fortunately, too, Throckmorton disembarked at Havre from England on the 19th. But even then the Admiral's anxieties were not at an end; for before paying out any monies to Huguenot representatives, Throckmorton insisted that he and the other Huguenot leaders should sign a document, promising to observe all the stipulations of the treaty of Hampton Court. It was only after the arrival of Throckmorton at Caen on the 27th that Coligny learnt for the first time that by one of the articles of the treaty Elizabeth was to remain in Havre until France had restored Calais.

The siege of the château of Caen was now pushed vigorously forward. Its commander was the Marquis of Elbœuf, brother of Guise. The town had been occupied by part of the Huguenot army as early as the 14th and 15th, while Coligny himself had personally inspected the château on the 19th. On the 27th and 28th 2000 English arrived, also cannon, munitions of war, a first instalment of pay for the reiters, and some companies of French under Montgomery and others. Equally welcome was the news, which came to hand on the 28th, of the death of the Duke of Guise. "Whereupon thanks were given to God, solemnly and with great rejoicings, without knowing by whom and how the deed had been done." [2] In fact, the Duke, on the 18th of February, the eve of a final assault on Orleans, had been shot by a Huguenot spy, Poltrot de Meré, and died on the 24th. On the 2nd of March Caen yielded on terms. A week later the camp was electrified by the tidings that the murderer had accused Coligny of being his abettor. His confession had been sent by the Catholics to the reiters, in the hope of shaking their loyalty. The Admiral, therefore, at once drew up a minute reply, and wrote to the

[1] *Hist. Ecclé.*, ii. 335.　　　　[2] *Ib.* ii. 378.

Queen begging her to guard the life of the prisoner until such time as he could confront him in person.

With the exception of this unfortunate incident, his prospects were good. Almost the whole of lower Normandy was in his hands; Granville, Cherbourg, and St. Michel alone remained to the enemy. Bayeux and Honfleur had been captured; St. Lo, Avranches, and Vire had fallen before the victorious Montgomery. It was now his intention to march south through Maine and Anjou, and then turning east secure the course of the Loire. But it was not to be. A draft of proposals for peace had come from Condé, and it called Coligny imperatively back to Orleans. He was thoroughly dissatisfied with their terms. For with St. André and Guise dead, and the Constable a prisoner, he had hoped for great concessions. Dividing his force, therefore, into two, he left Caen on the 16th with great regret, as he told Castelnau later. He himself passed by Falaise, Argentan, Seez, Mortagne, and Brou, the second column taking a more easterly route by way of Lisieux. On the 23rd he arrived at Orleans—too late! The Edict of Amboise had been promulgated in that town on the 19th, and published in the royal camp on the 22nd.

It granted to the great Huguenot aristocracy (" barons, chastellains, hauts justiciers, et seigneurs tenans plein fief de haubert ") free exercise of their religion for themselves, their families, and dependents. Other gentlemen were to enjoy the same privilege, but with two important restrictions: it was to apply only to themselves and families; and should they live in a town or village belonging to a high justiciar other than the King, they had to receive permission from their overlord. In addition, Protestant worship was to be permitted in all towns which had been Huguenot on the 7th of March, and in the suburbs of one town in each *sénéchausse* and *bailliage*.

From a Protestant standpoint this edict suffered from three great defects. It was frankly aristocratic in tendency; it restricted the future growth of Protestantism, in stating where, and where only, it might be exercised; and it did not apply to Paris. In accepting it Condé seems to have been moved by, among other reasons, a hope of assuming the rôle of Anthony of Navarre. And he may have known that, if war continued, he would be in imminent danger of losing his chances ; for the Catholics were proposing to his elder brother, the Cardinal of Bourbon, that he should renounce his ecclesiastical career, and so actively take up the position of First Prince of the Blood.[1] The leaders in Orleans, on the other hand, who were eager to return home, and who saw the party diminishing before their eyes, agreed to it on the theory that " what one must have is cheap at any price." [2] Catherine's reasons were very similar. They were given very tersely in reply to Papal protests : lack of means; Imperial demands for the surrender of Metz, Toul, and Verdun ; the presence of the English on French soil ; and a threatened new invasion of German mercenaries.[3]

Coligny did his best to have the articles modified in a Protestant sense. He spoke in the council and interviewed Catherine. He was not slow to point out the inconvenience to the great nobility of being practically forced to turn their houses into conventicles. But he was especially opposed to limiting Protestantism to specified towns. " With this stroke of the pen," he exclaimed with pardonable exaggeration, " they had ruined more churches than the enemy could have razed in ten years." As to the nobility who had pushed the treaty through, " the towns had been an example to them, and the poor had shown the way to the rich who, instead of sticking to their party until the end, and employing all their substance for the same, went to the war to pillage and enrich themselves, and at once talked of retreat if things turned out a little otherwise than they had fancied." [4]

These words are a revelation of character. They interpret, as nothing else can, the spirit in which the Admiral battled for his cause. But they do more. They amply explain why he, an aristocrat, became at once the trusted leader and hero of the bourgeois and artisan. But protest as he might, he could do nothing, and on the 5th of April he retired to Châtillon.

[1] Ferrara to Borromeo : Rome, Corsini Library, 399, 464, 465.
[2] Ehinger's *Franz Hotmann* (letter of March).
[3] Santa Croce from Blois, 25th March : Vatican, B. xiii. 419.
[4] *Histoire Ecclésiastique*, ii. 423, and *La Popelinière*, i. 362.

CHAPTER IX

COLIGNY AND THE MURDER OF THE DUKE
OF GUISE

Poltrot's Accusations and Retractations—Coligny's two Written Defences—Was Catherine the Instigator of Poltrot? Arguments for and against—De Ruble's Suggestions ; their Improbability—Poltrot's Charges examined—Coligny's Innocence—His Attitude toward the Murder.

WAR, it is often claimed, and at times with justice, tries a nation like fire. Even that most pathetic of its forms, civil strife, has failed on occasion to dull the moral sense and conscience of a people. Thus, the England of 1645, in spite of the steady degradation of the royalist forces, and in spite of the shattering of some ideals, scarcely fell below the young, the impetuous England of 1642. But it was otherwise with France, groping towards peace in the early months of 1563. It had little permanently heroical to show—instead, character deteriorated, cruelty become a habit, fanaticism a creed. But savage and callous as this first struggle had been, it had recognised certain conventions. It was still war, even if brutal war. With the murder of the Duke of Guise it became a blood feud. It introduced that tragic element which had made the France of the early fifteenth century a world of chaos. From the 21st of February 1563, when the murderer Poltrot accused the Admiral of being his abettor, the chain of events led inexorably to the massacre of St. Bartholomew. This was a new development. It affected Coligny vitally. What, then, was his connection with Poltrot? Was he innocent or guilty?

The events connected with the murder may be briefly summarised as follows. Jean Poltrot, Sieur de Meré, a Huguenot fanatic and native of Angoumois, was twenty-six

FRANCIS OF LORRAINE, DUKE OF GUISE

(*Dumoust'er?*)

years of age. In the summer of 1562 he appeared at Orleans; during the autumn he served in the Lyonnais under Jean de Parthenay, Sieur de Soubise; and in January, 1563, he became the spy of Coligny. On the evening of the 18th of February he dangerously wounded the Duke of Guise with a pistol-shot as the latter was returning to his headquarters in the château of Cornay or Vaslins from the Portereau, the suburb of Orleans on the south bank of the Loire. No sooner had Catherine de' Medici heard the news at Blois, than she offered 2000 crowns for the name of the assassin, and double the sum for his capture alive.[1] On the 20th Poltrot was taken. Examined at the bidding of the Duchess of Guise, he would confess nothing, but begged for an interview with his victim. This, however, was denied him by Catherine, who had arrived in the camp the same day and had visited Guise. She decided, in agreement with the surgeons, that such an interview would be too disturbing to the patient. She therefore determined to see Poltrot herself. The examination took place on the 21st of February. Besides the Queen Mother, the Cardinal of Bourbon, and eight others who had accompanied her from Blois, were present.

The prisoner declared that in the June or July of 1562 he came to Orleans, and there met two followers of the Admiral with whom he was acquainted. They were Feuquières and Brion. They questioned him covertly as to whether he was willing to do a deed to further the cause; but without further developing the matter, they introduced him a few days later to Coligny himself. The latter proposed to him to slay the Duke of Guise, who was at Beaugency. When Poltrot demurred, Coligny begged him to keep the suggestion secret. Poltrot then accompanied Soubise to Lyons. But shortly after the disastrous defeat of Dreux, he was sent for by Coligny, and met him at Villefranche in Berry in January, 1563. Thence he passed to Orleans. Here the subject of assassination was again broached. But it was only when Beza and another pasteur had added their prayers to those of

---

[1] Copy of a despatch of the Cardinal of Ferrara, 24th Feb.: Rome, Corsini Library, 399, 444, 445; cf. *Avvisi varii*, based on letters of 23rd and 27th Feb.: Florence, Arch. Med., 4850.

the Admiral that he allowed himself to be persuaded. Once persuaded, he met with the unstinted praise of the great leader, who told him that fifty other gentlemen were bent on like enterprises.   He also received a gift of twenty écus or crowns. He then visited the Catholic camp; but his courage failing him, he returned to Orleans. Coligny again exerted his influence, and again Poltrot promised. This time his reward was a hundred crowns. It was to buy a fast horse to effect his escape. The result was a fresh visit to the besieging army and the assassination of the Duke.

Having confessed so far, he went on to warn Catherine against the designs of the Admiral. The latter, as every Huguenot, was greatly incensed against her since the fatal day of Dreux, because she had made many promises in the negotiations before Paris which she had not kept. And he had heard the Admiral declare that when Guise was gone his successors would undergo the same fate, as well as six or seven Knights of the Order. He also added that he had seen some of the gentlemen chosen by Coligny for these enterprises lurking about the court and royal camp. And finally, in reply to a question, he threw some doubt on La Rochefoucauld, though he excepted Condé, Soubise, and Andelot by name from all charge of guilt.[1]

Such was his confession. Unfortunately, it was not taken down at the time, but was written out some hours later by a Guisard lawyer, Vailliard, and only signed by the prisoner himself on the 22nd. On the 23rd Poltrot was sent to Paris. On the 24th the Duke died. On the 27th of February and the 7th of March Poltrot was examined for the second and third time, and on each occasion clung to his charges against Coligny. On the 15th of March, however, he retracted the accusations which he had made before Catherine on the 21st of February. On the 18th of March he was condemned to death. After sentence had been pronounced, he was questioned, and declared that his first confession of the 21st of February was false, and had only been made in the hope of prolonging his life. The only fact which was correct was that Coligny had given him

---

[1] Poltrot's confession is printed in E. Fournier's *Variétés historiques et litteraires*, iv. 1-29.

first twenty écus, and then a hundred to buy a horse. He had murdered Guise of his own accord, and no one had persuaded him thereto. But after praying for a little while, he implicated the Admiral anew on two separate occasions, though acknowledging that most of the details of the confession of the 21st of February were untrue. Brought to the place of execution, he cried out that he wished to clear his conscience. Coligny and Andelot, said he, were innocent. Then, with almost his last breath, he accused him again—and died.

Thus, we see, Poltrot accused Coligny on some half-dozen occasions: namely, once on the 21st and 27th of February, once on the 7th of March, and thrice on the 18th. On the other hand, he declared him innocent three times: once on the 15th of March, and twice on the 18th.

Meanwhile, the Admiral at Caen received news of the death of Guise on the 28th of February. A few days later a German gentleman arrived in camp. The Catholics had taken him prisoner at the battle of Dreux, and he was now released by the Duke of Aumale and supplied with a copy of Poltrot's confession, in the hope of sowing dissensions among the German mercenaries. At first Coligny thought it a forgery, but soon perceiving its gravity, he assembled the Marshal of Hesse with the chief captains, and protested his innocence. The confession of Poltrot was taken by him point by point, and the reply was sent to the Queen Mother.[1]

He had never, he asserted, met or heard of Poltrot in the summer of 1562. The first time he had seen him was at Selles in the early days of 1563. But he had not sent for him; he had come as the messenger of Soubise, who was anxious to have news of the battle of Dreux. Nor had he sent him to Orleans; he had only given him permission to go. As commander-in-chief he had need of spies. Wishing, therefore, for intelligence of the Catholic camp, he had employed him on the recommendation of Feuquières who had found him very useful as a spy in Picardy, and had given him twenty écus. But he had never spoken to him of killing or not killing the Duke. And before the war, when he had known

[1] It is printed in the *Mémoires de Condé*, iv. 285–304.

of some who were bent on slaying the latter, he had done his best to dissuade them, and had informed the Duchess of Guise of the fact. But since he had heard that Guise and St. André had hired bravos to assassinate him, Andelot, and Condé—a fact he had revealed to Catherine before Paris and to his uncle the Constable at Orleans—he had never tried to dissuade anyone who had talked of killing the Catholic leader. (In a letter to Catherine of the 12th of March, we learn that one of those whom he had heard propose the murder of Guise was Poltrot.) None the less, he had never solicited or induced anyone to commit such a deed, neither by words, nor money, nor promises, direct or indirect. And so far had he been from entrusting such an enterprise to Poltrot, that he had had doubts of his loyalty, as he had told Grammont. Poltrot, it had seemed to him, had entered the Catholic camp with suspicious ease. Coligny added that he had often prayed that the kingdom might be delivered from Guise, and that he considered it God's providence that he had been removed; but he insisted that he had never named him in public, and certainly not to Poltrot, either personally or through anyone else.

When Poltrot had returned to Orleans from the enemy's camp, Andelot at first had thought of putting him under arrest, as his account seemed confused; but he had finally sent him on to Coligny. The latter found that his information was plausible, and agreed with what he had heard from other quarters. And as it was very important to know accurately the Catholic plans, he sent him back as a spy, and gave him a hundred écus to buy a fresh horse; for his own was spent, and speed was absolutely essential.

In conclusion, Coligny informed Catherine that in due time he would confront Poltrot. He therefore begged her to see that the prisoner should be carefully guarded, and not intimidated or suborned or executed by the Parlement of Paris, who might wish to see its enemy deprived of the means of proving his innocence.

On the 5th of May, Coligny published a second defence.[1] It was more of a pamphlet than the first. It pointed out that

[1] Condé, iv. 339–349.

the depositions of Poltrot had been written down by his enemies, and so were open to suspicion. It complained of the execution of the assassin as depriving him of the best means of proving his innocence. It remarked on the absurdity of thinking that he could procure the murder of Guise for a paltry twenty écus, or any like sum. And it went on to explain more fully the military reasons for giving various sums of money to Poltrot, one of his many spies. He had been told that Guise intended to follow him into Normandy with 3000 to 4000 mounted arquebusiers. The latest and quickest information, therefore, was essential. And as he had no good horses himself, and Poltrot's was worn out, the latter received a hundred écus to buy a new one.

Such, in brief, are the facts as we know them. We have now to solve the problem of Coligny's responsibility. This would be easy if we could accept the annotations of F. W. Ebeling on one of the documents which appeared in his *Archivalische Beiträge zur Geschichte Frankreichs unter Carl IX.* It is a letter written by "Albanus tuus," partly in ordinary characters, partly in cipher, to someone unknown.[1] At the beginning of last century someone deciphered it and jotted down the transcription between the lines, at the same time translating the signature "Albanus tuus" as Arnoldus Sorbin, a Catholic priest who became a notorious disputant during the later civil wars. Ebeling declared that on comparing this letter with two others of Sorbin, he was confident that they were by the same hand. Unfortunately, by 1887 he had lost or parted with it, and the efforts of Professor Erich Marcks to trace it have been vain.

Various names given by "Albanus" are obviously pseudonyms. The whole interest and importance of the letter, therefore, lie in interpreting these aright. Ebeling, in assigning the letter to 1563, translated "Domina" as Catherine de' Medici, "Patronus" as Poltrot de Meré, "Patruus" as the Duke of Guise, "Pater" as Coligny, and "Cognati" as the Huguenots. Read in this light, the letter is an irrefutable

---

[1] This letter in the original Latin, together with a translation in French, is given in the *Bull. du prot. français* of 1891, p. 144, and is accompanied by a criticism from the pen of Professor Erich Marcks.

proof of the guilt of Catherine de' Medici as instigator of the murder of Guise. Having received your advice, writes Sorbin, evidently to an ecclesiastical superior, in regard to the questions put to me by the Queen Mother, I returned to her yesterday evening and expressed my hesitation to give an answer, as I was young, had spent my time in the religious duties of our order, and was a stranger to civil and political questions. Even when I did answer, she declared that my replies lacked sincerity and clearness. Her design is that Guise shall lose his suit (it is under this euphemism that Sorbin speaks of Guise's murder). But in order to turn away suspicion from herself, and at the same time prevent the Huguenots and especially Coligny from limiting her power when the Duke is gone, she wishes to saddle them with the crime, and so paralyse them by raising up against them the implacable hatred of the Guises. As I approved of this, I saw Poltrot. He is a spare, sickly, poverty-stricken, yellow-complexioned, bony little man of twenty or thereabouts, but looks older. He is of moderate capacity, yet set in his opinions. He is ambitious, and devoted to the interests of the heretics. Though no proof of our meeting could be produced, I made him swear on the Bible not to reveal it, even if menaced with torture and death. I then told him I was speaking on behalf of Catherine, and that she was delighted with this project of getting rid of a man who was the sole cause of friction between the two parties; once he was removed, she would concede to the Huguenots all their demands. Moreover, she would protect and reward him, Poltrot. When I asked him whether he had consulted with the Huguenot leaders about the matter, he replied that he had. Some, said he, had pointed out the difficulties, some had encouraged, none discouraged. As to Coligny, with whom Poltrot was very discontented, he had pretended not to understand or wish to discuss the question. To this I replied that the Admiral cared not at all for the interests of his party; he was moved solely by self-interest; and since it was to his advantage that Guise should die (or, as the writer puts it, lose his suit), it was only pride and the dictates of prudence which had prevented him from giving in an open adhesion. When at last I persuaded Poltrot that this was the true view of the situation, he could scarce contain his rage. The result was that he fell in with my plan : namely, that he should publicly accuse the Huguenot leaders, and especially Coligny, of being instigators of the crime ; for in this way he would thwart Coligny's intrigues. And on my assurance that, should he be taken, we and the Queen Mother would snatch him from the hands of his enemies, he promised to stand by his accusations.

Now, once admitted that Ebeling's interpretation is the true one, the letter, as Professor Marcks points out, fits to perfection into the historical framework of 1563. It is at one in every detail with the facts such as we know them. It reflects faithfully the character and appearance of Poltrot, his relations with Coligny, the attitude of the Admiral and the Huguenot leaders towards Guise's murder in face of the loose talk of some of their supporters, and lastly, Catherine's machiavelian wiles and jealousy of Guise. Even the revelation of Catherine's determination to murder the Duke hardly comes as a surprise. On the 21st of February, Smith, the English Ambassador, reported that " some are so cancard that they would say it was the Queenes doeng and now she had hir desier." [1] Moreover, suspicion is thrown on Catherine by the fact that when Poltrot was captured, and begged to see his victim, she—in consultation with the doctors, so it was said— refused his request, and examined him herself.

As to the letter itself, it does not appear to be an ancient forgery, and still less a modern one; for Ebeling consulted several authorities, among others Jacob Grimm. [2]

These, in brief, are the arguments in favour of its genuineness and Ebeling's interpretation.

Nevertheless, there is an imposing array of facts on the other side. In the first place, the Latin is bad. Secondly, there is a contradiction—easily explainable, it is true—between the writer's first statement that he had seen the " Domina " last night, and his second that he had not seen her for two days. Thirdly, the whole letter is marked by a verbose prolixity, which is, to say the least, surprising in an affair so secret and

---

[1] Record Office, li. 326 (Calendar of 1563, No. 361).
[2] Bull. du prot. fr., year 1891, p. 163.

dangerous. Fourthly, is it not strange to read that the writer has the " Patronus " (Poltrot) watched ; for this told strongly against the secrecy of the plot. Fifthly, it is very remarkable that Poltrot, during his innumerable twists and tergiversations, not only on the rack but during his last moments, when all chance of rescue was gone, never once charged the Queen Mother. Personally, we give little credence to the suggestion that he may have been influenced by the oath he took on the Bible. A man who was willing to lie outrageously about Beza, one of the most distinguished ministers of his religion, was hardly the one to be bound by oaths, however solemn.

The above five reasons are taken from the article of Professor Marcks. We shall add some others which are at least equally weighty. To begin with, if Catherine was Poltrot's instigator, how are we to explain her offer of a reward for his capture ? She would have known that it would seem to him nothing less than treason, and would be the surest means to drive him to accuse her. Moreover, her plan, as revealed in Sorbin's letter, was primarily for Poltrot to accuse Coligny from a safe retreat. It was not to her interest to have him captured. It may, of course, be submitted that her offer of a reward was to avoid suspicion. But we believe that, had she been guilty, she would have seen that the disadvantages of such a step far outweighed its advantages. Then again, Catherine examined Poltrot in the presence of nine of the most distinguished Councillors and Knights of the Order, who, though they may be classed as members of her party, were by no means her creatures. Moreover, as de Ruble explains, the proceedings were virtually under the control of a Guisard lawyer named Vailliard. These were certainly fearful risks to take.

This brings us to another point of still greater importance. Catherine, instead of keeping Poltrot near her at Orleans or Blois, where she might have been able to exercise some kind of control over him, let him pass into the hands, none too friendly, of the Parlement and Paris—Paris, to whom the dead Duke was a martyred hero. But not only did she do this, but she actually delayed giving her assent to his execution. And yet she must have been well aware that if anything leaked out to the Paris mob, there would have been a revolution. In a word, those who believe her to have been the instigator of Poltrot, will find it very difficult to give a satisfactory explanation of her conduct here. Then again, we know that within a few weeks of the death of Guise, Catherine spoke in a very disparaging way of him to at least three persons: Condé,[1] and the Ambassadors of Savoy and Venice. This was certainly not typical of her and her crafty ways—always supposing, of course, that she had had a hand in his assassination.

We have to remember, too, that one of Catherine's most trusted counsellors was Guise's uncle by marriage, Ippolito d'Este, Cardinal of Ferrara.[2] This, we believe, would have weighed with her and deterred her from extreme measures, however discontented she might have been.[3] Another fact we must not pass over, is the terrible risks of such a plan as is revealed in this letter. The least slip would have involved her in a struggle with one or both of the great factions in the State. Someone may object that she actually did adopt this or a somewhat similar plan in 1572. To this we would reply that the Catherine of 1572 was a more desperate and at the same time more arbitrary and self-confident woman than the Catherine of 1563.

In face of these arguments, it would be rash, we think, to accept this letter as interpreted by Ebeling. At the best, the case in its favour is not proven. We fully recognise the ease with which it fits into its historical surroundings. We will even admit that Catherine might conceivably have plotted against Guise, though we believe that facts do not favour this assumption. The real difficulty is reached when we have to explain her action and the action of her supposed accomplice subsequent to the attempt on the life of Guise: that is

---

[1] Smith reports in a despatch of the 30th of March, that Catherine had told Condé that Guise's death "had no less redemyd hir owt of prison then the same had sett him, the prince, at lybertye": R.O. liii. 481 (Calendar No. 539).

[2] Catherine's relations with the Card. of Ferrara are treated at some length by Hilliger in the *Hist. Taschenbuch* of 1891 (Cath. von Medici und die Zusammenkunft von Bayonne).

[3] We may mention that we found no hint of Catherine's guilt in the Cardinal's correspondence now in Modena and Rome, and we believe that he never entertained a doubt of her innocence.

11

to say, the course of events from the 18th of February to the 18th of March. Personally, we confess we cannot explain it. Her action only becomes clear to us when we assume that she was a stranger to the designs of Poltrot. And therefore we must find other means of dealing with the charges against Coligny than by transferring the guilt to other shoulders. Professor Marcks has suggested that, apart from the statement of Ebeling, there is nothing to prevent us from ascribing the letter to some other than Sorbin. We would add, there is nothing to make us believe that Ebeling's interpretation is the only possible one. It is plausible, certainly; and we frankly confess that, though we have tried, we have failed to find another. Nevertheless, we are not convinced that another cannot or will not be found.

But to return to the question with which we set out: was Coligny innocent or guilty? was Poltrot his paid assassin, or did the latter murder Guise on his own initiative? The judgment of historical scholars, from Ranke to Professor Marcks,[1] was on the whole favourable to the Admiral. All that could be said had been said. It was no longer a burning question, when suddenly in 1897 there appeared a work which awoke new interest in the problem. It was *L'Assassinat de François de Lorraine, duc de Guise*, by Baron Alphonse de Ruble. It is an examination of the murder and its effect on the history of the years 1563–1572. Though the author does not formally range himself among those who consider the Admiral guilty,[2] he nevertheless seems to lean to their point of view.

These latter, of course, do not pretend that all Poltrot's assertions are exact; that would be impossible, since they so often conflict. But they consider that there is a residuum of truth, and that, taken in connection with Coligny's feeble defence and half-admission, it marks out the Admiral as his instigator. Now, such critics are at once faced by the awkward question, why did Poltrot on several occasions exculpate Coligny? They find this very difficult to explain satisfactorily, especially as Coligny's own defence and Poltrot's exculpation are in

[1] *Historische Zeitschrift*, lxii. 48.
[2] Lacombe (*Catherine de Médicis entre Guise et Condé*, p. 316) states that he does.

substantial agreement. De Ruble, however, considers that a
story of the Spanish Ambassador, Chantonnay, is plausible.
The despatch which contains it is the one really new fact which
de Ruble contributes to the discussion, though not so new as
he seems to suggest. Professor Marcks knew of it and spoke
of it as " une lettre pleine de renseignements suspects ou
faux." [1] The original, which is to be found in Paris (Arch.
Nat., K. 1499, 56), related that a letter had been found written
by Marshal Montmorency to Poltrot. In it the Marshal urged
the assassin to retract the declaration which he had made before Catherine, and to stop at nothing to clear the name of
Coligny. In return he promised to save him. And it was
in consequence of this — so Chantonnay asserts — that the
murderer recanted ; but finding at the last that he was really to
be executed, he began again to confirm and amplify his original
deposition, accusing in addition Coligny's brother, Andelot.

It is difficult to take this report of Chantonnay seriously,
especially as the rest of the letter, with its luxuriant details of
plot and intrigue, is grotesquely impossible. It is harder still to
understand why de Ruble gave it credence. It is absurd on
the face of it. As is seen, it stands or falls on the theory that
a letter passed between Marshal Montmorency and Poltrot.
Now the whole Catholic faction—Parlement, Paris, Guisards—
hated the former. He destroyed Catholic unity. As leader
of a middle party which later developed into that of the
" Politiques," he was the natural ally of the Huguenots. As
Governor of Paris he had control of the heart of France. His
enemies, therefore, would have given much to have had it in
their power to remove or ruin him. Such a letter as Chantonnay reports to have been found would have been a godsend.
It would have disgraced him ; it would also have been a strong
card to play against Coligny. Why, then, was it never produced? Why was it never published? There could only have
been one reason : namely, that it had never existed.

But even were we to admit that Montmorency might have
written to Poltrot or communicated with him by some other
means, we would find ourselves entangled in a maze of
improbabilities. For instance, if Poltrot was induced by

[1] *Bull. du prot. fr.*, 1891, p. 160, note 3.

Montmorency to exculpate the Admiral, how are we to explain the fact that he again accused him on the 18th of March before his chances of a rescue were gone—that is to say, before he had been taken to the place of execution? Is it probable, is it possible, that after having been promised his life he would throw it away so lightly? For he well knew that, if he again accused Coligny, Montmorency would never raise a hand to save him. That is too much to expect even from the notoriously unsteady intellect of Poltrot. Secondly, if Coligny's defence is false, and Poltrot's exculpation of him is false, how is it that they agree in the main? We can only explain this by supposing that they were in collusion: that is, that Coligny had informed Montmorency what line Poltrot was to take up. Now Coligny was not in a position to state definitely the points of his intended defence until the 12th of March, the date on which he wrote and forwarded it to the Queen Mother. The first exculpation of Coligny by Poltrot took place on the 15th. We have not the particulars of that confession, but we may feel sure that it did not differ materially from that of the 18th. Therefore Poltrot must have heard from Montmorency not later than the 14th. So that a messenger starting from Coligny in Caen on the 12th would have had to arrive in Paris on the 14th, a distance of 150 miles through a thoroughly hostile country, where every Huguenot would be cut off!

Let us now examine for a moment Poltrot's charges quite apart from his later recantations. It is clear that the whole texture of the confession of the 21st of February arouses the strongest suspicions. For instance, besides the Admiral, some four or five others are accused, and later Soubise and Andelot. De Ruble states that his, de Ruble's, aim is to concentrate his attention on the charges against Coligny alone. But he should not omit to say that the fact that Poltrot incriminates so many greatly weakens the force of the latter's accusations. Then, too, consider the vague patter of this confession: "the man of middle height with a light beard, etc.," and the sweeping assertion that Coligny had in his pay a little army of bravos. Again, Brion, whom he declared to have been the first to hint at murder, joined the Catholic party. Surely it is more than probable that, if there had been any truth in Poltrot's charge,

Brion would either have been afraid to join them, or, if he had, would have curried favour by revealing the plot, throwing all responsibility on the Admiral and others. The fact is, that to prove the guilt of Coligny one is met at every turn by almost insuperable difficulties.

On the other hand, if we accept Poltrot's retractation of his charges against the Admiral, the difficulties vanish. The assassin's conduct then becomes explicable, and there is no need of elaborate special pleading to bridge over interstices in the argument. Poltrot declared that his first confession of the 21st of February, accusing Coligny, had only been made in the hope of prolonging his own life. This was reasonable, for he might hope to gain time by confusing the issue, or by being used as a convenient weapon by the Admiral's enemies; there was even a chance that peace would intervene, and he might escape altogether. This first confession, then, was the effort of a desperate man clutching at any straw; it was not wholly logical in his own interests. He accused too many; but then he was not originally clear-minded, and fear had further clouded his intellect. As time went on, we consider that remorse began to develop, and that on the 15th of March he cleared his conscience by withdrawing his accusations. Then on the 18th, the day of his condemnation, he cleared his conscience a second time; but the fear of death again seizing him, he again accused the Admiral to gain a delay. Lastly, on the scaffold he finally freed Coligny, but made one last desperate attempt to avoid his doom by again accusing him and begging for a last interview with Catherine. This, we believe, is the only simple and logical explanation of his many changes of front.

The Admiral's own defence bears out this view. It is clear and straightforward. It declares his pleasure at the death of Guise; it glozes over none of his relations with Poltrot; indeed, de Ruble asserts that he almost defends himself as though he were guilty. De Ruble's attitude, however, is curious. It is, of course, quite other than that of the pro-Catholic historian, Baron de Lettenhove; yet it is patent that in dealing both with the intricate subject of Coligny's character and Huguenot character and affairs in general, he occasionally shows a lack of sympathy, or rather a lack of comprehension, that makes his judgment fall short of impartiality. Coligny's own explanation of his defence, as reported by Beza, was as follows: "Such was this reply. Some of those present objected to the Admiral so freely confessing some points. But the Admiral . . . replied that if when confronted with Poltrot the latter should confess something more, some might think he had not yet revealed the whole truth." And in this opinion, we believe, he was more than justified. His defence certainly was no legal brief; it was the last one to propitiate the enemy, and did not conceal enough for his friends. But this is only a further proof of its sincerity. Let us take an instance. One of the most damaging admissions made by Coligny was that he had paid Poltrot two several sums of twenty and one hundred écus. Poltrot also, in his exculpation of Coligny, makes the same statement. De Lettenhove, however, considers that this gift of money is an irrefragable proof of Coligny's guilt. But surely if Coligny's defence was false, or Poltrot's exculpation was false, this is just one of those points one or both of them would have concealed.

To recapitulate: No sound reason has been furnished by the accusers of Coligny for his exculpation by Poltrot. No collusion between Coligny at Caen and Poltrot at Paris was probable or even possible. Yet Coligny's defence and Poltrot's exculpation of him do not conflict. Both defence and exculpation are natural and clear. On the other hand, Poltrot's accusation against Coligny of the 21st of February breathes the spirit of falsehood. Finally, Beza, Soubise, and La Rochefoucauld, who had also been implicated, all declared their innocence.

Yet though all tends to show that Coligny cannot be charged with suggesting, soliciting, or procuring the death of Guise, he is not absolved from all responsibility. His attitude is explained in his letter and defences of the 12th of March and the 5th of May. He confessed to having heard Poltrot remark that he could easily slay the Duke, and to having done nothing to dissuade him. In fact, he had been perfectly neutral. And he added that he was not in the least grieved at the death of Guise, for he considered it a blessing to religion, the King, and kingdom.   To have brought it about, he would have trained a cannon on him in battle or made him the mark of ten thousand arquebusiers.

This was a frank confession truly.   It estranged the moderates of his time, and to-day it has received severe censure, and not unjustly.   For neutrality in a question of murder, under any condition whatever, saps the basis of moral and social order.   And the expression of joy over a dead foe is a sin against its chivalrous instincts which the world does not easily condone.   But allowing for all this, to our mind de Ruble places Coligny's action in quite an unnecessarily odious light.   His attitude was clear enough.   He was neutral because he believed that Guise was plotting against him and richly deserved running the risk of being caught in his own net.   As to his expression of joy over the death of an enemy, it was typically Huguenot, or shall we say Protestant.   Quite such a remark might have come from some Puritan of England if such a fate had befallen Charles Stuart, " that man of blood." Distinguished Protestant teachers such as Christopher Goodman and Bishop Poynet recognised the justice of the murder of tyrants.[1]   Bishop Jewel, on the 5th of March, 1563, wrote : " The death of the Guisian Pharaoh, which I have to-day heard as an ascertained and undoubted fact, has, believe me, affected my inmost heart and soul.   It was so sudden, so opportune, so fortunate, and so far exceeding all our hopes and expectations."[2] Coligny had still greater cause to regard Guise as the scourge of God's elect.   He had been at Amboise in 1560 when the latter had seemed for the moment drunk with carnage.   We have related how d'Aubigné, the inspired poet and historian of Huguenotism, passed through Amboise as a boy, and how his father, on seeing the heads of his co-religionists, like Hasdrubal of old bade him avenge the dead.   If such were the feeling of the rank and file, what must have been those of their leader ! And on Amboise had followed Vassy and the desolation of a religious war.

Nevertheless, it would be vain to assert that the attitude of Coligny was a noble attitude, was admirable, was even free

---

[1] Max Lossen : *Die Lehre vom Tyrannenmord in der christlichen Zeit*, 24.
[2] *Zurich Letters*, published by the Parker Society, i. 124.

from moral laxity.   There was a certain humane and Christian chivalry lacking in him of the kind which gave so rare a distinction to La Noue and his friend Sir Philip Sidney.   Coligny approximates more closely to another Protestant type — to the stern type of Calvin and John Knox.   His language has sometimes the violence of the fanatic, as when in 1562 he spoke of the bestial cruelty of the Catholics at a time when his own troops were fresh from the pillage of Beaugency. Still, his action did not lack a certain sombre dignity and sincerity.

This, then, in brief, is the Admiral's connection with the murder of the Duke of Guise.   Of that murder, we believe, a close examination of documents shows him to be innocent. Blame, too, of his position of neutrality and of his unconcealed relief at his rival's death ought to be measured.   At the same time, we must be careful not to misjudge the Guises.   From 1563, it is true, they persecuted Coligny with a persistence that made some form of St. Bartholomew only too probable ; but it is none the less true that they believed, and sincerely believed, that they were pursuing one whose hands were red with the blood of the head of their house.   There were points in Coligny's defence that filled even his own supporters with suspicion.   How much more black, then, would they seem to a family who regarded him as the arch-enemy, who found him to have had the murderer in his pay, and who were to see in the Catholic, Charry, only another of his victims.

CHAPTER X

PEACE, 1563–1567

FROM the Huguenot standpoint the drawbacks of the peace of Amboise were more than balanced by the net gains. Their military feats had scarcely entitled them to generous treatment. War had proved a heavy flail. The Triumvirate had swept them from the Loire, except from Orleans. Monluc had hunted them from the greater part of Guienne. Tavannes had cleared them from his province of Champagne.

And now, after a year of stress and turmoil, France was again at peace. Yet already the thought uppermost in men's minds was : how long will it last ? The charlatan Nostradamus, who lived on the fears and superstitions of his contemporaries, hazarded the guess : fifteen days ! Even the most sanguine scarcely hoped that it could be permanent. There was real cause for anxiety. It was hard for a Catholic majority to tolerate a heretic opposition ; it was hard for a spirited minority to exercise a nice moderation ; it was equally hard for the Queen Mother to refrain from restricting the action of a treaty only extorted by the fear of foreign invasion ; and it was above all hard for the Guises to see the supposed murderer of their chief unpunished.

The body of the murdered Duke still lay in the church at Blois when his brother Aumale cried out for vengeance. Turning to his nephew, the young Henry of Guise, and finding

him of the same mood, he swore by the Body of God that he
would have slain him had he found him otherwise.[1] This
was on the 2nd of March. Toward the end of April he
followed this up by applying to the Parlement of Paris for a
summons against the Admiral. Coligny, therefore, was forced
to act. On the 5th of May he published his second defence,
and on the 11th set out for the court, which was at St.
Germain. But he only reached Essonnes. There he was met
by Condé, who bore the royal commands for him to return
home. He obeyed reluctantly, the Prince and Andelot going
on alone to St. Germain as representatives of his interests.
The Council assembled on the 15th of May. Condé eloquently pleaded his relative's cause, both in a written declaration and by word of mouth. The peace of Amboise, he insisted,
had forbidden the raking up of old disputes; yet so eager
was his uncle to prove his innocence that he would waive his
rights, would thresh out the question provided that the judges
were " not suspect." But—and here he threw out the covert
threat later developed by Andelot of raising charges against
the dead Duke—his enemies must be called upon to do the
same. And he concluded with the impressive warning that
he who struck at the Admiral struck also at him.

Of even greater significance were the remarks of Marshal
Montmorency. He declared that the Constable his father was
determined to support his nephews. This meant that the
breach in the family ranks had been closed, and that the old
rivalry between the Montmorencys and Guises was again a
factor. Catherine, though generally credited with a balancing
policy and a desire to sow distrust between the great families,
viewed this recrudescence of hostility with alarm. When,
therefore, Montpensier urged Andelot to particularise his
charges against Guise, she broke in hastily with the remark
that he had spoken in general terms, and that there was no
need to specify anything. On the next day the Council postponed all further action until war was at an end.

This truce imposed on the two parties did not last long.
The operations against England, in which Coligny and Andelot
took no part, were soon over. In July Havre fell. In August

[1] Alvarotto, 9th March: Modena Francia, 37.

Odet appeared at court, and at once exerted a marked influence. On the 26th of September the widowed Duchess of Guise, with great dramatic display, clad in deep mourning and surrounded by her children and the members of her house, threw herself on her knees before the King at Meulan, and pleaded for authority to prosecute her husband's murderers. Coligny, however, was ready for the move, and presented a protest against the jurisdiction of the Parlement of Paris, notoriously inimical to his interests. To the chagrin of the Guises, both petitions were granted, and the charges against Coligny were called before the King in his Grand Council. In either camp there was unrest, the assembling of troops, and threats of coming strife. Catherine, always fearful, always ready with shifts and expedients, extracted promises to adopt only legal means and to be accompanied by an ordinary train. Then followed dexterous manœuvres of the Duchess to evade, and equally persistent efforts of Coligny to insist on his right to be heard by the Grand Council. It is unnecessary to give the history of their appeals and counter-appeals. Only two proposals seemed promising. The first was made by the Duchess, who suggested that the case should be tried by a local Parlement. As a compromise, the Crown offered a mixed tribunal composed of members of the Grand Council and of a local Parlement in equal numbers. In the end the King, impatient to start on a tour through the kingdom, and finding that an arrangement was hopeless, took matters into his own hands. By a decree of the 6th of January, 1564, he reserved the case to himself, deferring judgment, however, for the space of three years.

In order the better to defend himself, Coligny had come to court in November. Catherine, either intimidated by the Guises or well satisfied with the freedom his absence gave her, tried to stop him. But this time he refused to listen to her. Overtaking the court at Chailly, not far from Fontainebleau, he escorted it a day's journey toward the capital. On the 20th of November, accompanied by Odet, Andelot, and a large following, he rode into Paris. By a tactical blunder the Guises gave the game into his hands. When the Admiral arrived at the Louvre to take up his residence with the King,

Aumale, the acting Grand Master, with the Duchess and her coterie, fled precipitately to the Hôtel de Guise. This was intended, no doubt, to express their horror of a supposed murderer; in reality, it was interpreted as a sign of fear.

Outwardly, at least, Coligny regained his old position. The Ferraran Ambassador related that on one occasion he was the first to enter the King's chamber and assist at his dressing. In another despatch he told how, when Charles IX. went to Mass outside the Louvre, Coligny, Andelot, and Condé walked up and down somewhat ostentatiously in full view of the public. Granvella's report of the great Huguenot's influence was more lugubrious still, and, however exaggerated, reflected in attractive fashion Catholic fears. " I know," he wrote from Brussels on the 5th of December, " that while the Admiral has been at court, he and his brothers have hardly ever been away from the King's side, endeavouring by pestiferous talk to incite him to think ill of priests and ecclesiastics. And to this end they read him story-books such as Pantagruel and others, full of jests on the things of Holy Church and the ecclesiastical order—which is the way in which the sacramentalists corrupted King Edward of England." [1] The Spanish Ambassador at Paris was still more detailed, and, what is of importance, more exact. He sketched vividly the daily scenes at court. " This King," wrote he, " shows the Admiral great consideration and favour. He jests with him, goes to seek him and Andelot in their room with torches to greet them on Innocents' Day,[2] after the manner that is in vogue here. The Queen pretends and gives out that she does not speak to the Châtillons, and that she treats the Huguenots with great disfavour, and they have to bear with it all. But I see that from morning till night they are about her, and when she retires she speaks with them many hours in secret. Every evening, when all are ordered to withdraw from her chamber, the Châtillons remain until she begins to disrobe;

---

[1] Vatican, T 32, p. 264. The word "sacramentalists" was applied by the Catholics to all Protestants in general, the Lutherans, in their turn, applying it to the Zwinglians and Calvinists. It was, of course, a term of reproach, intended to point to unorthodox opinions on the sacrament.

[2] The Spanish is "darles los Innocentes."

thence they pass to that of the Most Christian King, and are with him until he retires and the curtains are drawn for sleep. Thereupon they enter the great hall, which lies before the royal apartments, and there, accompanied by a hundred, sometimes a hundred and fifty, chosen men, while away an hour." [1]

But in reality this anxiety of the Catholic party was scarcely warranted. Catherine was the ruler of France, and had no mind to share her responsibility. The Venetian Ambassador diagnosed the situation more accurately than his fellows when he declared that it was impossible to interpret her action. All he knew was that she flattered both sides to their faces, and cursed them behind their backs ; of the Admiral she had remarked that she hated him so that she would be glad to hear of his murder. And he went on to say that some thought that she was plotting a *coup*, which would be easy at the moment, as the Huguenot chiefs slept in the royal palace.[2] This is the first, far-off hint of a St. Bartholomew. It is certain that Coligny's position was far from secure. As he confessed to the English Ambassador, the difficulties arising out of the murder of Guise tied his hands. These were still further increased by a tragic event of the 31st of December. Andelot, it was known, as Colonel of the Infantry, strongly resented the attempt of Charry, Captain of the King's Guard, to escape from his jurisdiction. Relations had become strained, when suddenly the murder of the latter, about eight in the morning on the Pont St. Michel, fell like a thunderbolt on Paris. The assassin, Chastelier-Portaut, had been accompanied by two others, as Charry had with him a Captain Tourette and a soldier. Chastelier was one of Andelot's ensigns, and a close friend of Coligny ; he had even slept in the Admiral's room the night before. Suspicion at once fell on the Colignys. Fortunately, Chastelier left behind him a letter at his lodgings, and subsequently wrote a second, declaring that he had taken his revenge on Charry because the latter had slain his brother some years before, and had recently made an attempt on the honour of his sister. It also leaked out that one of Chastelier's fellow-assassins had old scores to wipe out. As, therefore,

[1] Despatch of 31st Dec., post-dated 3rd Jan. : Paris, Arch. Nat., K. 1501.
[2] 30th Nov. : Gar, *Instituto Veneto di Scienze*, atti 1870.

there was no proof whatever that Coligny or Andelot had incited to or been cognisant of the deed, the matter was allowed to drop. De Ruble, however, has hinted that Coligny, " so gravely compromised by the murder of the Duke of Guise, does not appear so complete a stranger to this new crime as one could wish for the honour of his memory." [1] It may be well, therefore, to examine the question more closely.

The first point which arrests attention is the peculiar nature of the crime. It was not of the ordinary type of assassinations. A Huguenot pamphlet asserts that Chastelier first challenged Charry when some paces away, and that the latter failed to draw. If this is true, it was not so much a murder as a street fight. But be that as it may, one fact is clear: the deed was committed in broad daylight. Detection was a practical certainty. Now both enemies and apologists of Coligny agree that he was, above all, cautious. If this is, as we believe, a true estimate of his character, it is in the last degree unlikely that his chosen assassin would have acted at such a time and place. It is still less likely that he would have chosen as instrument his own closest intimate. To do so would have been to invite suspicion.

These facts by themselves are strongly in favour of his innocence. But they are not alone; there are others all pointing in the same direction. In December he was in a precarious position. He was engaged in deadly feud with the Guises over a charge of murder. The greatest circumspection was demanded on his part. And he well knew that a fresh crime was the one fact above all others which, humanly speaking, would give the game into their hands. To repeat, however much he may have hated Charry, he would never have faced the risks. Moreover, it is expressly stated that he had dissuaded the Caumonts, who had a private quarrel with Charry, from taking any action. And there is still another aspect of the question. Coligny was well aware that at the moment royal support was absolutely essential. Yet there was no way of losing it more effectually than striking at the Captain of the King's Guard. Therefore, the murder of Charry must have been ruled out of the list of possible courses. In

[1] Ruble, *Mémoires de la Société de l'Histoire de Paris*, vi. 237.

fine, the only logical conclusion is that the murder of Charry was the spontaneous act of Chastelier, neither connived at, nor instigated, nor prompted from outside. The time of day, the suddenness of the attack, the fact that Chastelier alone, and not the friends by his side, dealt the blow, suggest a piece of personal revenge carried out on a sudden impulse, and not a well-conceived conspiracy.[1]

The next two years Coligny spent quietly at home or in visiting his friends. His presence at court was not desired, for Catherine and her son were making a tour of the kingdom, and one of her objects was to meet and conciliate the Catholic rulers, especially Philip II. During this period there were many changes in the Coligny family. Andelot took as his second wife Anne de Salm, and Granvella gravely reported that he passed with her through Châtillon, "where, contrary to his usual custom, he danced with the ladies."[2] It was at Châtillon, too, that took place the somewhat bizarre wedding of Odet in his cardinal's robes and Isabelle de Hauteville. Of more immediate interest, however, was the Admiral's connection with his other relatives. In spite of the Constable's periods of Catholic fervour, the relations between him and his nephew were cordial. The only danger to family harmony came from the equivocal policy of Damville and the character of Condé. Damville was always a somewhat incalculable factor. He was connected by marriage with Aumale, and probably did not relish being deprived of the dignity of Admiral which he had enjoyed during the late war. As to Condé, ever since the peace of Amboise, he had thrown himself into the gaieties of the court with an ardour and abandon which only Henry IV. was to rival. Gossip was busy with his name, whispering of amours more than platonic. Naturally, such conduct could not but be offensive to Coligny both as Huguenot and uncle of the wronged wife. As a consequence,

---

[1] For murder of Charry see Florence, Arch. Med., 4595, v., parte seconda, fo. 1 (Tornabuoni, Paris, 4th Jan.); Record Office, lxvi. 1345 (Calendar No. 1553); Cimber et Danjou, vi. 153; *Arcana Seculi*, ii. 284; Melville's *Memoirs*, 101; *Mémoires de Condé*, v. 34–37; Kluckhohn, i. 512, 691, 692; and Ruble in *L'Assassinat de François de Lorraine*, and *Mémoires de la Soc. de l'Histoire de Paris*, vi.

[2] *Papiers d'État de Granvelle*, viii. 358.

their relations became less cordial, and with the death of the neglected Princess in July, 1564, the last link seemed broken. At the same time Condé's designs on the office of Constable embroiled him with the aged Anne of Montmorency, " for he is quite sure, if the Constable dies, that they can give it to none other than to him." [1]

To the intriguing mind of the Cardinal of Lorraine, this division suggested the possibility of winning over the official head of Huguenotism. It was a pleasing prospect, offering much to attract him : a field for exquisite finesse, and, as a result, revenge, power, and satisfied ambition. Therefore, in December, 1564, all France was startled by the news that the Cardinal of Lorraine had visited the Prince at Soissons. The meeting gave rise to a swarm of marriage rumours. Condé, so it was said, was to seal the new alliance by making his choice of a wife from among the brilliant galaxy of Guise princesses, one of whom, at least, Mary Queen of Scots, had already expressed anything but joy at the prospect of such a union. Nowhere was this news less welcome than in the *entourage* of Francis of Montmorency, Governor of Paris. He was sworn enemy of the Guises and rival of Condé for the succession to the position of Constable. When, therefore, the Cardinal of Lorraine appeared with a large following in the capital with the intention of evoking a popular demonstration against the Governor, his way was blocked. Though specially provided with a royal permit to ride accompanied, he scorned to produce it. In consequence, there was a scuffle, and several Guisards were slain. The next day the Cardinal saw fit to slip away from Paris, " before sunrise and by the light of torches." Aumale, however, hovered in the neighbourhood to avenge, if possible, the insult to his family. Under this threat, the Marshal summoned Coligny to his aid. When the hated Admiral appeared before the Parlement haughtily, with sword on thigh, the First President de Thou likened him to Pompey ; the stern eye of the Governor reduced the authorities to a becoming courtesy. But Coligny's visit was short. He arrived on the 22nd of January, 1565, and left on the 30th. Thus it was but a week's stay. But it was a week too long for

[1] Paris, Arch. Nat., K. 1501, 55.

Catherine. It was currently reported at court that the tumult in Paris was a Huguenot plot to get rid of the Guise leaders, a project which, quite apart from the danger of civil war, did not in the least fit in with her plans. The fact, too, that Aumale was scheming, did not tend to reassure her. Coligny, therefore, as well as the Catholic leaders, was commanded not to approach the capital. Matters, however, did not mend. The Admiral especially seems to have viewed the split in the Huguenot ranks with alarm, and he despatched a gentleman to the German princes, presumably to secure their goodwill should there be a crisis.[1] He also visited Condé in Picardy. But this did not remove all friction, at least as between the Prince and the Marshal. The former insisted on visiting Paris, and chafed under the vigilance of the Governor. " Certain kinds of men have taken to contend with princes," he cried in a rage. " This is not to be borne ; they must be given a taste of the stick." [2]

In December, 1565, Coligny set out for the court, which was at Moulins. In the following month, after but a superficial examination of his case by the Council, he was declared innocent of the murder of Guise. He was only too glad to accept this decision. Yet it could scarcely be considered as final, as it had been largely based on political considerations. It was the result of Catherine's views of expediency. The young Duke Henry of Guise showed his contempt for it by refusing to acknowledge it for more than five years ; even the rest of his house, though more compliant, undoubtedly accepted it with mental reservations. And yet a judgment of the Parlement of Paris would not have carried greater weight. Its action during the last few years, its attempt to coerce and control the Government, its declared hostility to the Admiral, had fully justified the latter in refusing its jurisdiction. It had committed that worst fault of a legal body, of confusing political with judicial functions.

Thus it came about that the decree issued at Moulins veiled rather than eradicated an evil. It was at the best a temporary expedient, not a remedy. Nevertheless, this

---

[1] Editorial note in Kluckhohn's *Briefe Friedrich des Frommen*, i. 585.

[2] Paris, Bibl. Nat. Italien, 1725, filza 5 b, 83.

12

restlessness among the great might, under ordinary circumstances, have remained quiescent.   Unfortunately, during these
same years, the situation was no less acute in other spheres.
A meeting on an island in the Loire had sufficed to lay the
foundations of the treaty of Amboise.   It demanded something more to give it reality.   It is true that the more
desolating traces of civil war had disappeared like magic.
The Spaniard, Chantonnay, travelling through the most disturbed districts in 1564, was struck by the general air of quiet
and prosperity.[1]   Yet trouble was brewing.   Lansac wrote to
Catherine from Bordeaux in 1564 in despair of the attempt
to reconcile the rival factions.   Catholics for the most part
showed a contempt for the provisions of the Edict of Pacification.   Protestants attempting to return home or to Paris were
attacked.   Aumale formed a Catholic league; others sprang
up in Guienne.   The Jesuits, the arch-enemies of Protestantism,
were given permission to open a college at Paris.   At Dijon a
member of the Parlement openly protested against the toleration of two religions.   In Languedoc, Damville harried the
Huguenots, hung their pasteurs, and treated them as a conquered people.   In Toulouse, Protestants were compelled to
decorate their houses on Catholic festivals.   It was with the
greatest difficulty that Huguenot lawyers and officials were
reinstated in their various offices.   Monluc, who had at first
enforced the edict with even-handed justice, later lapsed into
the position of unofficial adviser to Philip, and pleaded for
Catholic pressure to be brought to bear on Catherine to sweep
away Huguenot privileges; he even approached the Queen
Mother herself with a proposal for a vast Catholic league.
Sometimes no place was appointed for Protestant worship;
sometimes, as in the case of Dax, services were forbidden as
being too near the Spanish frontier.   Murder was frequent.
Coligny declared to the Parlement in January, 1565, that
already five hundred of his co-religionists had been slain.
The Protestants, for their part, were slow to restore the
churches to the Catholics.   At times, when in the ascendant,
they insisted on holding their services illegally within the
town walls or in places not specially set apart.   Thus, in

[1] British Museum, 30625, 125.

the spring of 1565, the Duchess of Ferrara broke the letter of
the edict at Chartres, while a few weeks later large Huguenot
congregations assembled in Paris. Almost simultaneously
statues and images were thrown down in the cemetery of
St. Sulpice. At Montauban they refused admittance to the
bishop; they seized Caussade, and committed the worst excesses at Pamiers.[1]

Catherine for her part made strenuous efforts to bring
order out of chaos. She threatened the Parlement of Paris.
She upheld the Protestants at Toulouse and Bordeaux. She
appointed peace commissions and nominated moderate
Catholics such as Vieilleville to carry out her wishes. She
refused to listen to Catholic suggestions of a meeting at Nancy
to consider the question of the extirpation of heresy. And she
was at least always ready with promises of redress. But it
was difficult to steer straight amid political and religious
dissensions, with a Catholic Spain on the border. Perhaps the
task was beyond human powers. It is none the less certain
that to the miscalculations of the Queen Mother must be
directly traced the resurgence of civil war in 1567. Much
would have been forgiven her by the Huguenots on the score
of inability,—for the central power was known to be weak and
badly organised,—but she gave them cause to doubt first her
goodwill, then her sincerity. The Edict of Amboise, by
restricting Protestantism to certain specified towns and localities,
greatly weakened its evangelising power. Catherine should
have been content with this. Unfortunately, she was eager to
impress Philip with her orthodoxy and gain an interview.
Therefore from 1563 to 1565 interpretations were put upon
the Edict of Amboise, culminating in that issued from Roussillon,
limiting it sometimes in the letter, sometimes in the spirit.
Thus Coligny, the Duchess of Ferrara, and all Huguenots were
not permitted the exercise of their religion at court; the King
forbade Protestant services on his route, thus depriving whole
districts of their undoubted rights; towns, which had once
been ecclesiastical property, were excluded from the operation

[1] These facts about the state of France are drawn from the *Histoire Ecclésiastique*,
the *Mémoires de Condé*, d'Aubigné, de Thou, Monluc, Bruslart, de la Ferrière,
Marcks, Delaborde, de Ruble, and a few letters in the Bibl. Nat., Paris.

of the edict; the freedom of ministers, the opening of schools, and the holding of synods were interfered with; converts to Huguenotism during the late war were forced to return to their convents; foreigners, of whom there were many in the Protestant ranks, were to enjoy no privileges. These were but some of the restrictions. Moreover, the fortifications of the great Huguenot strongholds of Orleans, Montauban, and Sisteron were thrown to the ground, at the very time that royal fortresses were rising on all sides. Then, as a climax, in the June of 1565 came the unhappy interview of Bayonne, between Catherine, Alva, and the Queen of Spain. Two of the latest students of this complex problem, Professor Erich Marcks and the late Comte de la Ferrière,[1] though they differ somewhat as to Catherine's designs, agree that she elaborated here no plot to murder the Huguenot chiefs. Nevertheless, she does seem to have been forced against her will to promise to set aside the late edict. And for the Huguenots, the fact of the interview was enough. It gave form and consistency to what had been before undefined suspicion. It was to them positive proof of her ill-will.

The year 1566 and the early months of 1567 passed without serious incident. Coligny's position was becoming more commanding year by year. On the 26th of August, 1566, Hugh Fitzwilliam, the English representative, wrote of him: "Surely the Admirall is of great power and welbeloved of all the best soldiers in ffraunce . . . and for chivalry these 2 bretherne (Coligny and Andelot) are counted the fflowers of fraunce without comparison. And for my simple opinion, the Admirall were the metest man to be Emperor of any I do knowe on this syde the sea in Europe, he is of suche governement and counsell, in all respectes wyse and provident, who wynnes so many with his vertues, that other wayes cannot be wonne with rewardes and gyftes."[2] And yet it was a time of unrest. Attempts on his life, warnings from friends in high places, effectually banished the feeling of even personal security. And he had other troubles. He quarrelled in the Council with the Cardinal of Bourbon, who was destined, many years later,

---

[1] *Die Zusammenkunft von Bayonne* and *Revue des Questions Historiques*, xxxiv.
[2] Record Office, lxxxv. 548 (Calendar, No. 676).

to be hailed by a faction as King Charles X. His every appearance at court called forth Spanish intrigues or protests. Catherine's jealousy of him, too, was increasing. She had watched with some complacency the partial estrangement of Condé from his friends. But the latter's marriage in the autumn of 1565 with the daughter of the Protestant Marquise de Rothelin put an end to her hopes. It was only natural, therefore, that she should show resentment at the large assembly at the wedding ceremony, and the occasional meeting of the Admiral with his brothers and friends. In Catholic and court circles there was always profound suspicion of Coligny's aims. And in the August of 1566 a disreputable criminal, Le May, played upon this feeling in accusing the great Huguenot of urging him to murder the Queen Mother. The upshot was that Le May was executed, and a tax put on his land in favour of the two gentlemen whom he accused of being intermediaries between him and the Admiral. There is no doubt that the charge was false; it was less plausible than that brought against him in connection with the assassination of Guise and Charry. But it is significant that it should have been made; the accusations of Poltrot had sown a terrible crop of suspicion.[1]

Few, perhaps, hoped to preserve peace for long. It was the unexpected, however, which precipitated the crisis. The almost concurrent news in 1566 of the massacre of Coligny's expedition to Florida and the revolt of the Netherlands produced a profound sensation. The Admiral, the Huguenots, Condé, were all eager for hostilities. But Catherine, though consumed with hatred of Spain, always drew back before the shadow of war. And in this instance she was supported by the Constable; for his enmity against Condé was growing, and his Catholic and absolutist sympathies condemned the giving of help to the heretic rebels in the Low Countries. But as the year 1567 advanced, things seemed for the moment to play into Coligny's hands. The rumour that Philip, on his way to Brussels, was to

---

[1] For details of the affair of Le May, see Fitzwilliam's despatches in the R.O. (Foreign, vols. 85 and 86); Paris, Bibl. Nat. Italien, 1726, filza 6; Florence, Arch. Med., F. vi. p. 84–87; Paris, Bibl. Nat., 15882, p. 167; *Messager des Sciences Historiques*, 1880, p. 388; *Journal de Jehan de la Fosse*, 80. Delaborde (ii. 375, 419, 420) is at fault in dealing with the question.

pass by way of Italy to interview the Pope and Emperor, had filled Catherine with alarm. And she acquiesced in the proposal to raise 6000 Swiss to be on hand during Alva's progress north from Italy to suppress the Low Country rebels. In June an important assembly met at St. Germain. Coligny was not present; but the Huguenots were well represented by Condé, Andelot, and Odet. It was decided that Condé and Anjou should operate in the direction of Luxemburg, that Coligny should raise 3000 horse, and that the Swiss should line the eastern frontier. Suddenly the Queen's mood changed. Condé was treated with chilling coldness. He met with threats from Anjou. All movements which could be construed as a menace to Spain were laid aside. The Huguenots were both perplexed and anxious. They were afraid that Catherine's object was to destroy them; for, though Alva had reached the Netherlands, the order to raise the Swiss was not countermanded. Her interpretations of the edict, her interview with Alva in 1565, and now the recruiting of the Swiss, seemed but so many links in a chain.

The chiefs met secretly at Valery and Châtillon. They recalled the suspicious acts of the last few years, and the warnings which the Prince of Roche-sur-Yon had secretly imparted to Coligny of the hostile nature of the interview of Bayonne. The question to decide was whether it would be better to anticipate the enemy. Coligny in particular pleaded against civil war. As a last resource, they appealed to the Constable to disband the Swiss. "What would you that we did with these Swiss," came the blunt response, "now that they are well paid, unless use them?" For a third time there was a meeting at Valery. The Admiral, still fearful, still possessed with a lively sense of the horrors and uncertainty of war, was carried away by the more impetuous temper of Andelot. A few of the strongest towns were to be seized; the King was to be captured; the Swiss, before they could hurry up, were to be cut to pieces; and the Cardinal of Lorraine banished from court. Such was the programme. The place of assembly was to be Rozay in Brie, the date the end of September.

CHAPTER XI

THE SECOND WAR OF RELIGION

Flight of the Court from Meaux—Blockade of Paris—Negotiations—Battle of St. Denis—Death and Character of the Constable—Retreat from before Paris—Junction with German Reinforcements—Coligny's Army Organisation—Siege of Chartres—Peace of Longjumeau.

WHEN once the Huguenots had determined on war, no secret was ever better kept. The Catholics, however, became uneasy. As a consequence, the regiment in Paris was warned to keep good guard; the Parisians themselves favoured the walling up of four of the city gates; and on entering the capital the English Ambassador found the drawbridges up.[1] Yet the old Constable, though suspicious by nature and a life of intrigue, scouted danger. His one precaution was a vain attempt to probe the meaning of the mysterious meetings at Châtillon and Valery. But when his son Thoré, charged with the mission, reached Châtillon, he found the Admiral peacefully tending his vines.[2] A little later, the Huguenots were congregating in Brie, " four by four, three by three, two by two, so that their movements might escape notice." [3] The King, who was at the château of Monceau, was within an ace of being surprised. Castelnau, a royalist leader, who came with the news of a probable rising, was covered with ridicule. Then on the 22nd of September some cavalry were spied in a little wood where the King was to hunt on the following day. On the 24th, " in great fear and, so to say, in full flight," the court reached Meaux. The Swiss were at once hurried up, and arrived on the 26th. On the 27th, Francis of Mont-

---

[1] Paris, Arch. Nat., K. 1508, 55; Paris, Bibl. Nat., filza 6, 140; Record Office, xciv. 1303 (Calendar, No. 1683).
[2] Pasquier, i. 272.   [3] Claude Haton, i. 432.

morency was sent forward to Condé to ask for explanations. The night of the same day the Council met to determine whether to remain at Meaux or retire on Paris. A vigorous appeal of Pfeiffer, Colonel of the Swiss, decided the matter. "May it please your Majesty," he cried passionately, "to confide your person and that of the Queen Mother to the valour and fidelity of the Swiss. We are 6000 strong, and with our pikes we shall open you a way through the army of your enemies wide enough to pass through." [1] Two hours before daybreak on the 28th, the King, with a numerous court, stole out from Meaux. Pfeiffer's men had already started, singing at the top of their bent and encouraging one another. "I freely confess," declared the Venetian Ambassador, "never to have seen a more disreputable *canaille*. They looked like a lot of porters, who possessed neither the knowledge nor power to use or shoulder arms. But when ranged in battle, they seemed to me to be other men. Thrice they turned and faced the enemy; they threw at them whatever came to hand, even to bottles; and, lowering their pikes, they ran at them like mad dogs at full speed more than four times the length of this room; yet no one outstripped his fellow; and they did it with such a show of readiness and desire for the fight, that the enemy dared not attack." [2] Condé and the Admiral had come upon them near Lagny; the most they could do was to skirmish. La Noue relates that if only the horse from Picardy had arrived in time, they would have pressed the attack home. Happily, they were saved from this last folly. That night the Protestants encamped at Claye, a disappointed army.

They had thus lost the first move in the game. Their programme was to have developed with simple regularity. How fantastic it must have seemed now in the dry light of accomplished facts! They had failed to cut the Swiss to pieces, or capture the King, or weaken the Guises; and, for aught they knew, they might likewise fail to seize Lyons or Toulouse. In the midst of the general discouragement, they had to cast about for a new plan, and at last fell on one of astonishing daring. They determined to strike at Paris, to

[1] De la Ferrière, *Catherine de Méd.*, iii., quoted from Zurlauben.
[2] Alberi, iv. 219.

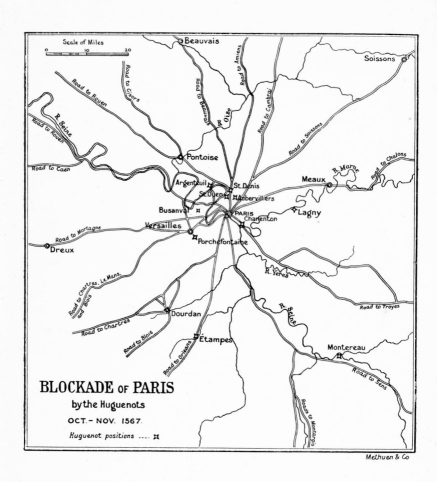

Scale of Miles
0   10   20

Beauvais

Soissons

Road to Amiens

Road to Gisors

Road to Rouen

Road to Beauvais

R. Oise

Road to Cambrai

R. Seine

Road to Rouen

Road to Soissons

Road to Caen

Pontoise

Argenteuil

St.Denis

Meaux

R. Marne

Road to Chalons

St.Ouen

Aubervilliers

Busanval

PARIS

Charenton

Lagny

Versailles

Road to Mortagne

Porchefontaine

Dreux

R. Yères

R. Seine

Road to Chartres, Le Mans, and Blois

Road to Troyes

Road to Chartres

Dourdan

Road to Blois

Etampes

Montereau

Road to Orleans

Road to Sens

Roads to Montargis

BLOCKADE of **PARIS**

by the Huguenots

OCT. - NOV. 1567.

Huguenot positions ....

Methuen & Co

starve and harry it, and so force on a battle or peace. A
similar plan had been found hazardous enough in the first war
with a well-equipped force; now, they were a mere handful
of men hardly deserving the name of army. Yet there was
safety in their very audacity. It confused the Catholics, led
them to suspect treachery within their own ranks, made the
Constable unwilling to crush his nephews, and finally gave
Condé what he desired: a battle.

It is impossible not to admire the skill with which the
Huguenots set to work. Waiting for a few days at Claye
for reinforcements from Picardy, Champagne, and Burgundy,
they occupied St. Denis on the 2nd of October. In a little
more than a month they had ravaged the country, burnt the
mills, and had in their hands most of the strategic points on
the great high-roads and rivers which supplied the capital:
Charenton, Aubervilliers, St. Denis, St. Ouen, Busanval,
Argenteuil, Dourdans, Étampes, Orleans, and Montereau.
And yet, even with the little army which Montgomery
brought them, they were never more than a few thousand strong.
If it is asked why a force of over twenty thousand allowed
itself to be besieged and cooped up by a fourth of its number;
the answer will be found in the character of the Constable.
While the populace, driven by humiliation and the fear of
hunger, clamoured for action, he was content to wait. He was
cautious. He had all his life favoured Fabian tactics. They
appealed with special force to him now, when to risk a battle
was to hazard everything. Even victory would have had its
drawbacks. It would at least have ruined his nephews. For
the moment, therefore, he was one of the strongest influences
making for peace.

While the Huguenots were still at Claye, the Chancellor,
L'Hôpital, visited their camp. He was presented with a
defence of their resort to arms. It was one long diatribe
against the house of Guise. On the 3rd he reappeared, this
time at St. Denis. At his request, they drew up a summary
of their grievances. It was a curious mixture of the religious
and political, of the personal and public. It gave L'Hôpital
his opportunity a little later of pointing out to the Palatine
envoy, who was sent to report on the situation, the political

complexion of the rising.[1] For in addition to demanding the free exercise of religion without any restriction whatever— thus going far beyond what had been granted them by the Edict of Amboise—they cried out against the avaricious Italians about the King ; as an aristocracy, they claimed their right to exemption from taxation, and begged for a fair distribution of the honours and dignities of the State ; and lastly, they advised the convocation of the Estates-General. This was an unfortunate opening. It touched Catherine in her tenderest points : her love of power and sympathy with her fellow-Italians. It therefore met with a prompt response. On the 7th of October a herald arrived at St. Denis, and, with a triple blast of his trumpet and a thrice-repeated summons, commanded Coligny, Condé, and their companions to appear before the King. The result was that, though they refused to obey, they replied in a more humble strain, and negotiations were resumed. But the irascibility of the Constable spoiled everything. He had been accustomed to rule the family circle like a patriarch : his eldest son had been forced to contract a distasteful marriage ; his nephews had been so many pawns in the political game. And though the first war had changed all this, he had been too old to learn. At the first conference, therefore, with his nephews and Condé, he was unable to control his temper. He burst in with the remark that the Edict of Amboise, with its recognition of two distinct religions, was never intended and never could be a permanent settlement. This statement was enough ; it only too fully justified Protestant fears.

With November affairs shaped for a definite issue. The Catholics had several successes following closely on one another. By the 8th the Huguenot boats at St. Ouen were sunk, Argenteuil and the château of Busanval captured, and the bridge of Charenton occupied. This and the arrival of reinforcements compelled Anne to take action, for already, as the Florentine Ambassador declared, popular indignation had risen to dangerous heights. A chance was not long in coming. The Huguenots committed the fault of scattering their forces, Andelot and Montgomery being detached to occupy Poissy

[1] Kluckhohn, *Zwei pfälzische Gesandschaftberichte*, 191.

and Pontoise.   On the 9th the Constable made a reconnaissance, on the 10th the army marched out from Paris to the
plain of St. Denis.   The Huguenots were not ready.   Coligny,
cautious as ever, would have been satisfied with a skirmish
in force.   This would have given Andelot time to return.
Condé, however, was eager to fight, and carried the day.   The
form of battle was simple yet effective.   Three points had to
be protected : St. Denis, and its advanced and flanking villages,
St. Ouen and Aubervilliers.   The army, therefore, was divided
into three, each division being composed of part of the cavalry
supported by arquebusiers.   It lay, as La Popelinière remarks,
spread out like a crescent moon.   The ground to be covered
being so great, the cavalry were in single line.   Coligny
commanded the right at St. Ouen, Genlis the left at
Aubervilliers, and Condé the centre covering St. Denis.   The
plan of the Constable was to overwhelm the enemy's wings,
while he in person pierced the centre, preparatory to the
capture of St. Denis.[1]   He himself with heavy cavalry [2] faced
Condé.   Before him was his son, the Marshal, with the flower
of the men-at-arms.   To his right were the Swiss, and to
their right again were infantry and the bulk of the cavalry,
all facing toward Aubervilliers ; for it was here that the most
stubborn resistance was expected.   In front, to the right of
the Swiss, was the artillery.   To the Constable's left and
opposite the Admiral were some cornets of horse with their
supports of arquebusiers, and well to their rear were the 6000
infantry of Paris.

As the great Catholic battalions, with their artillery and
splendidly " barded " and accoutred horse, drew up to the north
of Montmartre, 19,000 strong, the Huguenot leaders must
have had serious misgivings.   They had at the most 2000 to
3000 men at their disposal, and not a single cannon.   A
month earlier they had not a lance among them.[3]   On the
day of battle they had perhaps 300, which they had made

---

[1] Duc d'Aumale, *Hist. des Princes de Condé*, i. 307.

[2] From the accompanying sketch of the battle, it will be seen that, as later at
Moncontour, the bulk of the Catholic cavalry, possibly even the men-at-arms under
the Constable and his son, was in masses and not in single line.

[3] Paris, Arch. Nat., K. 1508, 69.

from the poles of a local fair; the rest of the cavalry carried sword and pistols. No one was fully armed; the horses were without protecting "bards" because of their feeble stature, for they were "almost all cobs and such like small-made mounts." They were indeed a sorry company. As it turned out, audacity, the fury of their charge, the skilful use of what infantry they had, the digging of a ditch to protect Aubervilliers, above all, the fall of night, saved them from destruction.

The battle opened with several salvoes from the Catholic artillery. This was followed by an attack by Biron and Cossé on Aubervilliers. But by the furious charges of Genlis and the withering fire of infantry which had been placed in a mill and in a ditch connecting the latter with the village, the Catholics were thrown back in disorder. Almost simultaneously, Coligny was victorious on the right. Bringing up his arquebusiers, which followed close upon his cavalry, he shook the cornets of Nemours. Then charging vigorously, he scattered all before him, and came on the Parisians in the rear. But the latter refused to await the shock. Decked out in all their martial finery, "gilt like chalices," as the Huguenot d'Aubigné put it, they broke madly towards the city. Meanwhile, Condé was driving home an attack in the centre. This brilliant cavalry leader, finding that he was unable to slip by the Marshal Montmorency, who commanded the first line, left a third of his force to engage him, and with the other two-thirds fell on the second line under the Constable. Here the impetuous rush of the Huguenot gentlemen carried all before it; the whole Catholic line was broken up, thrown back, and the Constable himself mortally wounded. It was no doubt at this moment that the Turkish envoy, looking out over the battlefield from the heights of Montmartre, and seeing half the Catholic army in rout, exclaimed, "Oh! if the Grand Signior had two thousand men like these in white"—the colour of Condé—"to place at the head of each of his armies, in two years the world would be his." [1] It was indeed a sight to stir the blood of an onlooker. Rarely, if ever, has a mere handful of men, with no special superiority of tactics or arms, so nearly

[1] D'Aubigné, ii. 249.

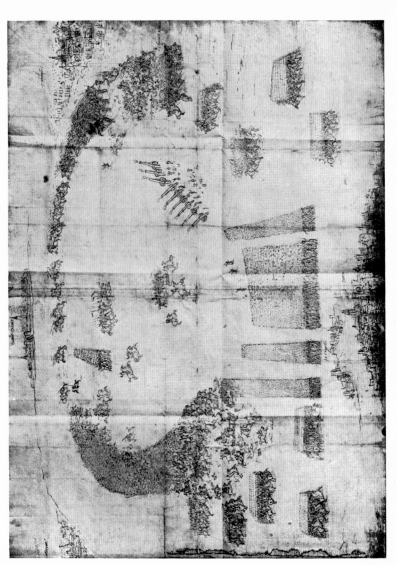

La Chapelle   *Paris*

BATTLE OF ST. DENIS, 10 NOV., 1567

(Record Office)

wrested victory by sheer force of valour and *élan*. But the Huguenot advance was bound to wear itself out. The Marshal Montmorency was carrying all before him; sweeping away the cavalry in front of him, he fell on the infantry, and put them to flight. Cossé was also getting the upper hand at Aubervilliers. The Constable had been extricated and Condé thrown back. Part of the Admiral's command was attacked and shaken by Chavigny, while Coligny himself had disappeared; carried away by an unmanageable horse, he was twice among the Catholic fugitives. Condé's forces were in imminent danger. Suddenly, the report spread that the Constable had fallen. The Catholics hesitated, and pursued half-heartedly. This, with the failing light, gave the Prince and Admiral a chance to withdraw to St. Denis. As for the Catholics, the three sons of the Constable, taking up their father, moved off, a mournful procession, to the capital.

On the 11th the Constable died. With him passed away a great and interesting figure. His death was yet another link broken between the period of Francis I. and the age of the civil wars, between the France of unquestioned autocracy and the France of popular and aristocratic strivings. His faults were many. They are easy to point out. He had lived on tradition, and had attempted by the light of tradition to solve a revolution. His son Francis, *politique* and hater of Guise, if not more admirable as a man, was probably wiser. Yet it was something to have ideals, to scorn to accept family and personal interests as the measure of duty. It is impossible to guess what were the inner feelings of Coligny: possibly a sorrow lightened by awakening hopes of effecting something now that Marshal Montmorency was the family head; more probably a lasting regret at the loss of one to whom he owed position, character, and even, lately, support in the face of the house of Guise. But of the sentiments of France at large there could be no question. The feeling of relief was universal, scarcely hid under the empty ritual of an elaborate funeral. Catherine had escaped from an irksome tutelage, the Catholics from a too aged and moderate leader, while for the Huguenots it was a persecutor the less.

The battle of St. Denis had one immediate result : it made
the Huguenot position untenable.   Their object had been
either so to harass the capital as to force on a peace, or to
be able to receive or join Casimir, son of the Elector Palatine,
who seemed the only Protestant in Europe ready or likely to
aid them.[1]   The drawn battle of the 10th advanced neither.
Indeed, the chances of a successful retreat to Lorraine, with
the Catholic army still unbeaten, were considerably lessened.
Yet it was equally dangerous to remain where they were.
Moreover, they must have reinforcements, and it was too much
to expect that the Germans would seek them out at St. Denis.
Their retreat, however, was not that of a disorganised or
beaten army.   The day following the battle, Andelot, now
returned from Poissy, ravaged and burnt to the very gates of
Paris.   On the 13th they were on the move.   Paris thought
they were making for Soissons.   In reality, passing through
Lagny, Rozay, and Nangis, they arrived at Montereau.
About the 1st of December they were again marching southward.   At Pont-sur-Yonne they coalesced with 5000 men of
Poitou and Guienne under La Rochefoucauld.   These reinforcements were all the more welcome, as they brought
with them six cannon from Orleans, and thus filled up a
great deficiency.   Pont-sur-Yonne and some of the surrounding
villages being taken, Coligny made a feint on Sens.   This
allowed the rest of the army to seize Bray and Nogent and
cross the Seine.   They had now to arrange their plans for
the future.   One point was soon settled.   Coligny and Condé
were determined to continue the negotiations which they
had begun.   A more difficult problem was to decide what
to do with their army : whether to remain on the Yonne and
Seine, or turn eastward to meet Casimir.   The latter seemed
the more obvious course.   But Coligny refused to recognise
the necessity.   His imperious nature little relished the
semblance of flight.   His reluctance, too, was no doubt
reinforced by his experience of a volunteer army, which was
peculiarly sensitive to every retrograde movement.   He therefore urged that they should remain where they were and await
the Germans, in the meantime collecting pay for them,

[1] Kugler, ii. 540, etc.

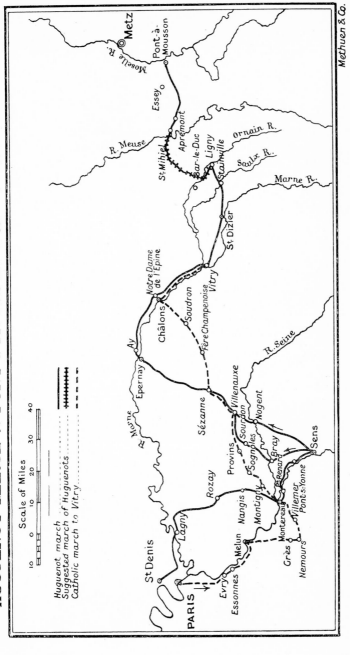

HUGUENOT MARCH TO PONT-à-MOUSSON after the battle of ST DENIS

Scale of Miles

Huguenot march
Suggested march of Huguenots
Catholic march to Vitry

Methuen & Co.

Metz
Pont-à-Mousson
Moselle R.
Essey
R. Meuse
Apremont
St Mihiel
Bar-le-Duc
Ligny
Stainville
Ornain R.
Saulx R.
Marne R.
St Dizier
Notre Dame de l'Epine
Vitry
Soudron
Châlons
Fère Champenoise
Ay
Epernay
R. Marne
Sézanne
Villenauxe
R. Seine
Nogent
Sourdon
Provins
Rozay
Sognoles
Bray
Renard
Sens
Lagny
Nangis
Montigny
Pont-s-Yonne
Montereau
Villemer
Grès
Nemours
St Denis
Evry
Melun
Essonnes
PARIS

guarding the passages of the rivers, and informing Casimir of their reasons. Happily these arguments were rejected. But on his advice it was agreed to march with the whole army. By this means it was thought that Anjou, who had come out from Paris,[1] might be induced to pursue; this would save Orleans until it was garrisoned by the " Viscounts," who were coming from the south. On the other hand, if the infantry had been left behind in the various towns, it might have been cut off and overwhelmed.

Their march lay through Villenauxe and Sézanne, straight to Épernay. Here they arrived about the middle of December, a three days' truce having been arranged to discuss terms of peace. Crossing the Marne and marching up the right bank, they encamped near Châlons. They were now in imminent danger. Anjou, who had been reinforced by Spanish troops from the Low Countries, was on their heels; Guise was concentrating a force at Troyes; Nevers was hurrying out of Piedmont with Italians. An attack on their left wing at Sarry gave Condé and the Admiral the needed warning. Suddenly they decamped " a little before day; the moon was bright, the air very fresh." [2] La Noue relates that in three days they marched twenty long leagues through such rains and bad roads that it was a wonder how the artillery was able to follow. Their passage was marked by a trail of abandoned waggons; many of the soldiers were barefoot and the horses unshod.[3] At last the Meuse was crossed, and they were safe. But the Huguenot nobility, which had shown such heroic qualities at St. Denis, was now unstrung, and it had required all the influence of their leaders to save the situation. In this we have a glimpse of national character: quick to act, sensitive to feel, distrusting its leaders, hasty with criticism, and passing in swift succession through all the stages from exaltation to despair. One day as La Noue fell to discussing the general depression with Coligny, the latter said that a battle must be avoided at all hazards until they had coalesced with the Germans and regained their morale. " But if they are not there,"

[1] For the Catholic line of march during this and the following campaigns, we have used the maps in Segesser's *Pfeiffer*, altering them, however, in places.

[2] Jean de Fabas, *Vicomte de Castets*, 36. [3] Castelnau, 218.

interrogated someone, "what will the Huguenots do?" "I think they will blow on their fingers," came the ironical response, "for it is very cold."

The forces of Casimir numbered 6500 reiters and 3000 lansquenets. Their arrival caused a general feeling of relief; much feasting and merry-making followed. The question now was how to provide the promised pay. The party, as usual, was in financial straits. They had early cast about for support. Norris, the English Ambassador, had been approached as early as July,[1] while on the 13th of November Berne had been besought to provide a loan of 100,000 thalers.[2] But their efforts in these directions proved fruitless; they had to depend on themselves. Condé and Coligny were thus in a desperate situation. They had no treasury—only an army, poor, miserably equipped, and of flagging zeal. The Admiral, however, with his accustomed resource, found a way out of their difficulties. He visited the German camp and remained six days negotiating. And it was owing to his efforts that an agreement was come to which found expression in the capitulations signed later at Arc. Together with Condé, with tears in his eyes, he entreated his followers to contribute something, he himself setting the fashion by giving 500 écus. His example was contagious. A wave of self-sacrifice swept through the army. For the time, at least, they were possessed by that generous and eminently French spirit which was to make the nobility of the Revolution vote away in a night their privileges. Seigneurs and gentlemen, captains and soldiers, pages and lacqueys, vied with one another in their enthusiasm to give. Vessels of gold and silver, rings, earrings, coins, were heaped together, a sum of 80,000 livres.

The whole army now set out well content in the direction of Paris. Whether the leader was Condé, Coligny, or Henry of Navarre, Paris was always the chief objective—a tribute to the predominating importance of the capital. But though the ultimate goal was Paris, "the plan of the Protestants was to

---

[1] Record Office, xcii. 1148 (Calendar, No. 1463).
[2] A. Gobat's *La République de Berne et la France pendant les Guerres de Religion.*

turn aside their Germans from the country of Châlons, become a desert through the insolence of the two armies, and lead them through Burgundy, the valley of Aglan, Hurepoix, and Gâtinais. It was a fine rich country, for it had not tasted of the miseries of this war; and above all—a fact which two-thirds of these troops did not hate—it was laden with the rarest and most excellent wines of France." [1] Thus, this southerly route solved some of the problems facing the leaders. It made the provisioning of the army possible. Still, there remained the questions of how to do it methodically, how to avoid defeat with a Catholic army near, how to preserve some semblance of discipline while compromising with the lax military spirit resulting from the civil wars. It was Coligny who took the task in hand. The fact that no serious hitch occurred during this march in the depth of winter is a witness to his energy and abilities. La Noue gives an interesting sketch of his leader's measures. Coligny well understood the importance of the commissariat.[2] The infantry was divided into two: the "van" and "battle." The cavalry always lodged in the outlying villages. Each cornet of horse—there were probably forty—was provided with a baker and two pack-horses, and the bread was distributed from these various centres to the infantry by means of the pack-horses and carts. All this was under the strict supervision of picked transport officers. The army—as indeed all the armies of the civil wars —was spread over a vast extent of country. The reason was the necessity of finding provisions and complying with the desire of the soldiers to sleep under cover. This was the worst feature in its organisation, for it left it open to surprise. Coligny did his best to minimise the danger. The cavalry was accompanied by mounted arquebusiers. A cornet, on entering a village, roughly fortified itself for the night. If attacked, it held out till relief came. An alarm was the signal for a concentration at headquarters, whence aid was sent to the threatened point.

The march was uneventful save for a small engagement

[1] La Popelinière, I. pt. ii. 42.
[2] " Souloit dire, quand il estoit question de dresser corps d'armée, commençons à former ce monstre par le ventre."—La Noue, 627, 628.

13

near Mussy on the upper Seine,[1] a useless attempt on Cravant,
and the cruel storming of Irancy. It was never seriously
contested by the royal troops lingering round Troyes, for
Condé had now a formidable army. A still more cogent
reason was the hopeless division among the Catholics. At the
death of Anne of Montmorency, Catherine had had her heart's
desire, "being now quite freed," as the eighteenth-century
translator of Davila puts it, "from the power and authority of
the Grandees." She refused to appoint a new Constable, and
the young Duke of Anjou, the future Henry III., was created
Lieutenant-General of the Realm. As a result there were
many generals, but no leader. The Council was a faithful
reflection of the army. Francis of Montmorency, relying on
the ancient rule of France that the First Marshal, in the
absence of the Constable, should lead the "van," insisted on his
rights. When they were refused, he retired from court. Then
there were quarrels between Montmorency-Meru and Martigues,
differences between Martigues and Nemours, hints that Coligny
knew too much of the royalist plans, and murmurings among
the people lashed to fury by excitable preachers.[2]

Instead of making direct for Paris, the Huguenots determined to spread through the rich lands of Beauce. At
Auxerre, as so often before, the army divided, Coligny going
to Châtillon for a few days' rest. On the 23rd of February
it appeared before Chartres. It was explained that the
siege was undertaken by Condé as a threat to Paris. Many
believed, however, that he was prompted by a desire to cover

---

[1] The best authorities for the Huguenot march from Châlons to Pont-à-Mousson
are La Noue, Castelnau, La Popelinière, the English Ambassador (Record Office),
who several times mentions Vitry and Ligny, the *Journal of the Prince of Condé's
Army* (Record Office, xciv. 1589), and two letters of Condé of the 27th December
and 3rd January from Apremont and Essey (Aumale, i. 569, and *Calendar of State
Papers*, Foreign, 1566–68, No. 1911). The exact route from Ligny to St. Mihie
is doubtful. Moreover, the whole army did not go to Pont-à-Mousson, but only
some of the leaders. On the return journey to Chartres the combined forces passed
in the neighbourhood of Commercy and Joinville; the Marne was crossed at Marnay,
the Seine at Étrochey and above Châtillon near St. Seine; the route was then
Auxerre, Châtillon-sur-Loing, Montargis, and Beauce.

[2] Details are given by Luca Mannelli (Naples, Carte Farn., 759), Alava (Paris,
Arch. Nat., K. 1509), Correr (Paris, Bibl. Nat., filza 6), Norris (R.O. xcv. *passim*),
and La Noue.

his family possessions of Vendôme. He had now at his command a force as large or larger than his army at Dreux, for he was reinforced by the "Seven Viscounts" of Quercy, who, after one of the most skilful marches of the civil wars, had succoured Orleans and captured Blois. Yet the siege did not progress.[1] The defence was stubborn, the spot selected for the breach ill-chosen. The one brilliant feat was a swoop of the Admiral, who commanded the covering army, on a detachment of the enemy's cavalry. As it turned out, the siege was never carried through. On the morrow of the battle of St. Denis, Teligny had appeared before the King, beseeching him "to cast his pitiful eyes upon his subjects." And throughout the succeeding months negotiations had been constant, at Bray, Châlons, and Paris. They were now continued, and with increased chance of success. Catherine was more conciliatory, now that the German mercenaries were in the very heart of the country. Coligny, on the contrary, was violent in his opposition. He insisted that the enemy would never forget the humiliation of Meaux; they offered this mere husk of a treaty to save Chartres and to divide and then crush them at leisure. But the force of events was too strong for him. The Germans were unpaid, and might mutiny; the troops were disappearing in shoals, going home to Xaintonge and Poitou. Therefore, on the 23rd of March, 1568, peace was signed at Longjumeau. It was roughly a reproduction of the Edict of Amboise. But from the Huguenot standpoint it had one advantage: it applied for the first time to Provence.

[1] For the siege of Chartres see Lépinois, *Histoire de Chartres*; H. Lehr in *Bull. du prot. fr.*, 1897; Métais, *La défaite de Condé et des Protestants devant Chartres en* 1568.

CHAPTER XII

THE THIRD WAR OF RELIGION

Catherine determines to seize Condé and Coligny—Flight to La Rochelle—Army Regulations—Autumn Campaign of 1568—Battle of Jarnac—Death of Condé.

WHEN the Italian captains who had fought in the late war returned to Turin, they had piteous tales to tell of the ruin of France.[1] One of the most lamentable features of the struggle had been that the country had become the resort of the foreign mercenary. And it soon looked as though he was to be called in again. It was evident that the peace of Longjumeau was only the simulacrum of a peace, mere hollow words and empty phrasing. It in nowise expressed an intellectual or moral compromise. It rather marked a stage of momentary exhaustion and fatigue. It was based on insincerity and hedged about with mental reserves. The far-sighted Admiral, slow to draw the sword and equally slow to sheathe it, had felt all this, and struggled, though in vain, with the too sanguine expectations of his friends. He was now to be justified. "We are knee-deep in peace," wrote a satirical Catholic in May, and with that plunged into an account of the massacre of Protestants.[2]

It is unnecessary to picture the scenes of violence of the period of six months which divide the second from the third religious war, that "covert war," as La Noue described it, or, as Coligny branded it, that "bloody peace full of infidelity." They were of the pattern only too familiar to the France of that age: robbery, murder, rapine, and legal chicane. Massacres of the Huguenots at Amiens, Auxerre, Blois,

[1] News from Turin, 27th May: Naples, Carte Farn., 283.
[2] Vatican Library, Cod. Vat. 6436, 209.

Bourges, Sens, Troyes, and other places, were only one, although the worst, feature of the situation. Even Catherine, naturally sanguine, was distracted by the general unrest. She was bewildered by Huguenot complaints, charges, and counter-charges. Finally, rendered desperate, she determined to clear away the tangle. Her scheme was to seize Coligny and Condé. She hoped to be able to do this, as La Rochelle, which had refused to receive a Catholic governor, gave her a specious pretext under which to mature her plans. Coligny was the first to take alarm. Finding the Italian Martinengo stationed at Gien near Châtillon, he retired to Andelot at Tanlay, and thence passed to Condé at Noyers in Burgundy. The Catholic troops were disposed as follows : Brissac was concentrating on the north at Montereau ; artillery was coming from Paris ; to the west large forces were massing at Orleans ; to the south infantry and cavalry were marching from Lyons toward Dijon.[1] It was given out that the object of all this activity was to guard the frontier and reduce La Rochelle. Coligny and Condé saw at a glance that they would probably be seized on the way. Intelligence of Catherine's plans is said to have come from several sources. These were one or more members of the Council, the Marquise de Rothelin, who was then at court, and two persons of less importance, Gragnan and Créquy ; the son of Marshal Tavannes claims that his father, though one of Catherine's instruments, also gave Condé warning. However this may be, on the 22nd of August, Coligny wrote a letter to the Queen Mother charged with menace and warning. He declared that these violations of the edict could not go on for ever. " It must be confessed," said he in calm disdain, " that if you have the good will you have not the power." On the 23rd, Condé, evidently with his companion's assistance, drew up a veritable "Grand Remonstrance." It breathed the spirit of Coligny's impressive warning of a month earlier : " God will not leave unpunished the shedding of so much innocent blood, which cries continually before Him for vengeance." All their grievances were catalogued : the

[1] For these details see A. Gobat, *La République de Berne*, 54 ; the discourse of Odet ; Brantôme, v. 115 ; Tavannes ; Kluckhohn, ii. 242 ; de la Ferrière's *Catherine de Médicis*, iii. ; Ruble, *Mémoires de Jeanne d'Albret*, 197.

murder of Rapin, a gentleman of Condé, and of the Count of
Cipierre; the garrisoning of bridges and towns, the formation of
the Catholic League of the Holy Ghost,[1] the intended surprise
and assassination of themselves—the long list closing with a
cry for vengeance against the Cardinal of Lorraine, the "source,
root, and origin of the ruin and subversion which menaces this
crown."[2]

When the document was despatched, Condé professed his
intention of awaiting a reply. That very night, however, he
set out with Coligny for La Rochelle. They had with them
their children as well as those of Andelot, the Princess of
Condé, and the wife of Andelot. Coligny's own wife, Charlotte
of Laval, had died on the 3rd of March. It was a perilous
adventure. Before them was nearly the whole breadth of
France. The Loire alone, with its crossings in the enemy's
hands, was a formidable barrier. Fortune, however, was on
their side. A ford was found near Sancerre. When they had
crossed over, the river rose in sudden flood, and cut off pursuit.
Falling on their knees, they broke into the psalm: "When
Israel came out of Egypt: and the house of Jacob from
among a strange people." The sentiment here—the conviction that they were a chosen race—was not unique; it was the
heritage of all Protestant peoples and more than half their
strength. In Berry they were joined by various gentlemen.
Vieilleville, the royalist leader in Poitiers, let them pass. In
the first days of September they entered La Rochelle.

Of all the wars of religion the third was perhaps the
most creditable to the Huguenots, if the most disastrous.
With hardship and a growing sense of inferior numbers, they
had shed many of their looser elements. The timid had
sunk to a pale neutrality. The ambitious, the courtier, the
mere looter and free-lance, looked for their chances elsewhere.
The net result was to deepen their character. Huguenotism,
from being a fashion, became a faith. And therefore at the
first summons to arms, "with a joy and ardour incredible,
they abandoned their wives, their children, their homes, and

---

[1] It had been signed 25th June. It is to be found in full in Boutiot's *Histoire de la
ville de Troyes*, iii. 622.

[2] These letters, etc., are in Delaborde, iii. 34, 43, 496-516.

came in daily to join the Prince."[1] This was a spirit essentially different from that of the crowd which had laughed and jostled into Orleans in the spring of 1562. Yet though the rank and file had not failed them, Condé and the Admiral had no easy task. For the first time they had not taken the offensive, and, therefore, could scarcely hope for initial success. In La Rochelle, however, they had an invaluable base, difficult to capture, rich in the spoils of Huguenot sea-rovers, and above all, in touch with England and possible succour. The unpreparedness of the enemy and their own indomitable resolution did the rest. Day by day they added to their numbers: the unconquerable Joan, Queen of Navarre, arrived from the south; Andelot, after an exciting journey from Brittany, reached Poitou. With fierce energy they seized on Thouars, Parthenay, Niort, and other towns. The Catholic gentleman Messire François de Poulchre, Seigneur de la Motte Messemé, gives us a piquant scene at Niort, where the great Admiral wandered through the stables in quest of a war-horse for his brother Andelot.[2] Then, after the capture of these northern strongholds, they swept down on Angoulême. Unhappily, from the very outset of the campaign the soldiery had a tendency to get out of hand.[3] It disobeyed its chiefs, violated military etiquette, slaughtered surrendered garrisons. The Admiral was in a fury. He treated them to " prayers, remonstrances, insults, and bastinados."[4] As to one of the most prominent of his followers, who ignored the commands of Condé and went looting, " he was near striking him with a stick, and had his arm already raised to do it, if the Princes and other lords had not appeased him."

This slack spirit among his followers had already drawn from Condé at Saintes a set of army regulations which were no doubt inspired by Coligny. They were confessedly complementary to the rules which already governed the royal gendarmery, and the Admiral's earlier " Ordinances " for the French infantry. They differed in scope from these latter in that they dealt solely with troops actually campaigning. They thus throw a vivid light on the condition of things

---

[1] De Thou, iv. 147.
[2] *Les Honnestes Loisirs*, 119.
[3] *Histoire du Langon*, i. 111.
[4] La Popelinière, pt. ii. 67.

during the religious wars. An army constantly tended to
degenerate into an unorganised, undisciplined, pillaging mob,
with another mob of useless hangers-on at its heels. Even
worse was the vast baggage train, made up for the most
part of stolen animals and pillage, which choked the roads,
destroyed mobility, and made confusion worse confounded.
These regulations of 1568, therefore, made a desperate effort
to cope with abuses. Soldiers were no longer to ramble
from company to company. They were to be enrolled
under definite officers, and take an oath, which was to be
renewed monthly. Camp-followers were also to be enrolled
and restricted in number, while the train was to be reduced
in size. Private quarrels, as well as private enterprises, were
forbidden; pillaging was severely dealt with, especially the
robbery of beasts of tillage; and the bulk of the booty was to
go to the support of the army, an eloquent testimony to the
straits, monetary and other, to which Huguenotism was reduced. And all this was to be done, because, as an army of
the reformed faith, " they ought to serve as an example to
others in all righteousness and justice." [1]

The Protestants had now some of the richest lands of the
west, and a front secured by a line of towns. No one was
more surprised at these successes than Coligny. " I have
heard the Admiral," remarked La Noue, " make use of the fine
saying of Themistocles : ' our destruction had been certain had
our danger been less.' " [2] But this promising beginning had a
less brilliant sequel. In fact, the campaign of the autumn of
1568 was in no way decisive. It will therefore suffice to give
it in broad outline. It was a campaign of lost opportunities.
After the capture of Angoulême in October, the obvious course
was either to crush the small royalist column under Montpensier,
which had moved up the Vienne from Châtellerault, or join
with Acier and Mouvans coming from the south. The plan
actually followed was to turn west and besiege Pons. This
gave Montpensier his chance. Marching rapidly south to
Perigueux, he fell on Mouvans at Mensignac, and slew him
with more than 1200 men. Again, when once the two

---

[1] Delaborde, ii. 522.

[2] " Nous estions perdus si nous n'eussions esté perdus."—La Noue, 644.

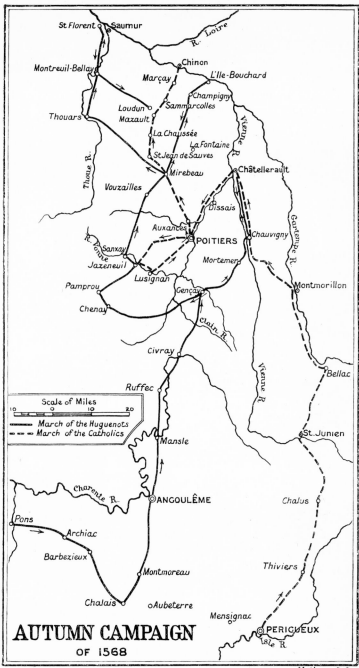

Huguenot forces had coalesced at Chalais and Aubeterre, they failed to isolate Montpensier and cut him off from the main Catholic army under Anjou.

In a long race from Perigueux to Châtellerault[1] Montpensier was the first to arrive. When Coligny came up with the Huguenot "van," he found himself confronted by Anjou with an army 27,000 strong. The position was too formidable to attack, and the Admiral vainly offered battle. On the 11th of November, therefore, he was back again at Chauvigny. Condé and he now found themselves in a somewhat difficult position. It was scarcely possible to make direct for the Prince of Orange, who was to enter France from the north-east, for Anjou barred their way to the north, while the Creuse was high and the crossings guarded. Yet it was dangerous to remain on the right bank of the Vienne. If attacked and beaten by Anjou, they would have to escape across the river, with the chance of a second attack from the garrison of Poitiers. They therefore determined to fall back south-westwards into open country. This might induce Anjou to give battle; under any circumstances, it would allow them to join Boucard, who was marching to their aid with the infantry left behind at Pons. Almost at the same moment Anjou decided to throw himself between them. The result was that on the 16th the hostile armies came into touch at Pamprou. Then followed several skirmishes, affairs of outposts, and small combats. Many details have come down to us in the letters of George North and Henry Champernowne, two Englishmen fighting under Condé. Others are to be found in the pages of La Noue, who dashes in little touches of his own. He tells us how the Admiral, with only a handful of men, skilfully concealing his weakness, made a brave show, as it was neither safe nor honourable to retire in the presence of a hostile force; and how the Catholics, in imminent danger, beat their drums Swiss-like to deceive the enemy; and finally how the inoffensive camp-followers, clustering round the fires, " warming

---

[1] See de Serres' Commentaries; Coustureau's *Histoire de la vie de Montpensier*, Aumale, ii. 371 (North to Cecil—the word "truge," as given by Aumale, is wrong; the original in the Record Office gives it "touke").

themselves, singing, and making good cheer," frightened a whole army.

The object of Condé and Coligny throughout had been to gain a passage on the Loire. On the 17th, the day of the inconclusive combat at Jazeneuil, where Anjou had his headquarters, Coligny had found Sanxay abandoned. On the 19th the whole Huguenot army was on the road for the north. Mirebeau was then captured, the Catholic quarters at Auxances beaten up by an unexpected raid of the Admiral, and Saumur threatened. But the Protestants were again to suffer a disappointment. Anjou, who had retired to Poitiers, marched out, stormed Mirebeau, and besieged Loudun. To save the latter, Condé retraced his steps. The hostile forces were thus once again brought face to face, "their courage as high as their looks were brave, and some were only awaiting the signal for combat. . . . But, on the other hand, you must know that it was the severest winter experienced for twenty years. Not only did it freeze hard, but the frost was so terrible that even the foot could not march without falling, much less the horse." [1] And thus they stared idly at one another for three days, only a few of the skirmishers daring to attack. But this could not last. The severe weather, with its consequent sickness, and the loud complaints of the soldiery, drove both sides into winter quarters. Anjou settled himself at Chinon, while Condé retired south-westward. Thus ended the campaign of 1568. If there are no great successes to chronicle, and if the Protestants were unable to break through the hostile barrier, still the balance of success was with them. They had secured a strong position with La Rochelle as base, and they had suffered no defeat.

With 1569 the change was sudden. It was the year which witnessed the nadir of Huguenot fortunes. In February their army was busy preparing for a move.[2] They had two alternatives : either to await their German auxiliaries, behind

---

[1] La Noue, 659.

[2] The following account of the campaign and battle of Jarnac is a résumé of M. Gigon's admirable and detailed article in the *Mémoires de la Société arch. et hist. de la Charente*, 1895. This article, "La bataille de Jarnac," is accompanied by a map of the theatre of war and a plan of the battle.

their rampart of fortified towns and the river Charente, or meet them half-way. They declared for the latter. Its success depended largely on getting a long start in the race across France. At the moment this seemed feasible, for the Catholics as yet were not stirring. But an ill-considered attack on Confolens in the first half of February ruined their chances. Tavannes, the principal adviser of Anjou, divining the move, marched up the Creuse to La Roche-Posay, his object being to make for Limoges should the Huguenots be found in the valley of the Vienne. At La Roche-Posay, however, he learned that the latter had retired, and were supposed to be concentrating in Angoumois. He determined, therefore, to approach the Charente. Entering Montmorillon on the 18th of February, he advised a stay until the army could move forward at full strength. The younger and more impatient leaders, however, thought otherwise, and Confolens was reached on the 22nd, and Verteuil on the 28th. This last stage of the advance had been made on his express advice, as he had resolved to get into touch with Condé and prevent if possible the latter's march southwards.

The Huguenots, who were concentrating about St. Jean d'Angely, thus found themselves cut off from the east. A southern route was still open through Cognac, Barbezieux, and Chalais, where they might hope to pick up the " Viscounts," and then turn toward the upper Loire. But even this was now difficult, for Tavannes, with his superiority in cavalry, and consequently greater mobility, could threaten their line of march. Coligny, who commanded the " van," was aware of the danger, and did his best to inveigle the Catholics southwards. The Huguenots might then, with their 4000 horse and 18,000 foot, slip southwards from St. Jean d'Angely to Cognac and Chalais, while the enemy—since the Charente from Saintes to Angoulême was Protestant—would be forced to march back and cross the river to the north before they could pursue. But Tavannes was too wary to fall into the trap. Moreover, he perceived that the Protestant march southwards was about to begin, for the Catholic leader La Rivière, who had made a raid on Jarnac and Cognac, came on the enemy near the latter town on their way from St. Jean d'Angely, and was shut

up in Jarnac and compelled to surrender on the 6th of March.
As a counter-move, he proposed to make a circuit round
Angoulême and seize Châteauneuf. Crossing to the left bank
of the Charente, he encamped at Montignac, where all his
firmness was needed to keep his army from returning to the
right bank in response to the enemy's feints. Then, further
strengthened by the arrival of the reiters, he encamped south
of Angoulême on the 8th with 8000 horse and 15,000 foot,
reaching Châteauneuf the following day. He was now south
of the Huguenots, whom he threatened to attack by way of
the bridge at this latter place. So unwelcome indeed was
this news, that Coligny, hearing of it on the 10th of March at
Jarnac, where he was with the "van," at first refused to believe
it. Its accuracy, however, was soon brought home to him.
On the 11th the Catholics made a vigorous attack on Cognac,
with the double object of reconnoitring and containing the
enemy. The Huguenots had now to decide on a new plan.
The one that found most favour was to march to the north,
now open, and, seizing a passage on the Loire, join hands with
the Germans. The day of the 12th, however, slipped by.
Coligny made an elaborate reconnaissance, and placed cavalry
and infantry in the loop formed by the river opposite
Châteauneuf. They were to keep in touch with the enemy,
and resist any attempt to cross. As Coligny's "van" was now
the rearguard, the only way to give Condé with the "battle" a
good start was to keep Anjou, or rather Tavannes,—for the
latter was the real leader,—on the other side. His dispositions
having been made, the Admiral himself retired to the village
of Bassac, midway between Châteauneuf and Jarnac.

On the 13th, two hours before daybreak, the royal army,
by the light of a glorious moon, were crossing by the old
stone bridge and a pontoon of boats. The Huguenot guard,
except for a few horse, had disappeared; they had little relish
for a night in the open. Coligny, as soon as he had news of
the surprise, ordered a concentration on Bassac; he intended
to delay the enemy's advance at the various defensible points
on the way to Jarnac. When once the Catholics were across,
they had to mount due north to gain the plateau, and then
swing round west and march parallel with the river. Before

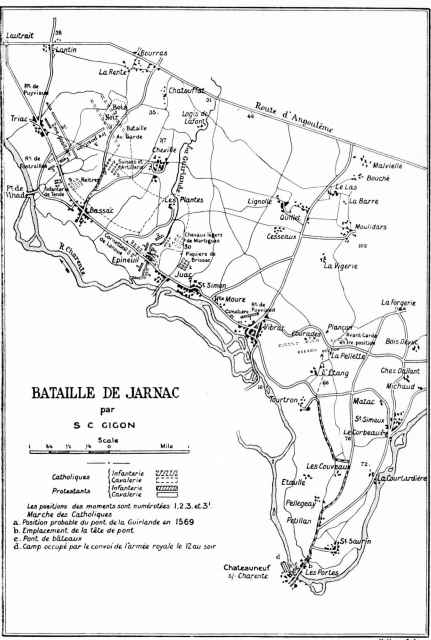

BATAILLE DE JARNAC

par

S C GIGON

Scale

Les positions des moments sont numérotées 1, 2, 3, et 3¹.
Marche des Catholiques

Catholiques { Infanterie
            { Cavalerie
Protestants { Infanterie
            { Cavalerie

a. Position probable du pont de la Guirlande en 1569
b. Emplacement de la tête de pont
c. Pont de bâteaux
d. Camp occupé par le convoi de l'armée royale le 12 au soir

Methuen & Co.

them were several villages, a stream named the Guirlande, then the village of Bassac, with a marshy pond behind, and beyond it again the village of Triac. A fight at each of these points is in a word the battle of Jarnac.

The struggle began seriously at Vibrac. Here the hardy warrior Puyviaud, with his infantry, which should have been watching opposite Châteauneuf, was swept back by the light horse of Martigues and the young Duke of Guise, and was only saved by the spirited charges of a few cavalry under La Noue. After Vibrac came another stand at the little stream of the Guirlande. But this in its turn was forced by the Catholic pikemen in front, while Martigues and Guise crossed higher up, and were able by this movement to crush the mounted troops of La Noue. The triumphant Catholics now dashed upon and through Bassac. Andelot, however, falling on them suddenly with a squadron of 120 horse, slew Monsalez with his own hand, and threw them back in disorder on the Guirlande. Their flight was only arrested by the timely arrival of the reiters.

It was at Triac that the Huguenots made their last stand. Coligny, finding himself in imminent danger, had already summoned to his assistance Condé, who had set out north-westwards that morning from Jarnac. Appearing on the scene with seven cornets of horse, he drew up his little army at right angles to the Charente behind an excellent line of defence, formed by a little valley almost impassable owing to streams and the marshy nature of the ground. He had at his disposal perhaps 2000 infantry and 1000 horse. On his right he placed part of the infantry to defend the road crossing the valley; the rest lay at Triac in his rear to keep open a way of retreat. The cavalry was drawn up in a long line, Montgomery being on the right, Coligny on the left, and Condé himself in the centre. The Catholic army, aware of the strength of this position, at once adopted the tactics that had just been so successful at the Guirlande, and spread north-wards with the intention of sweeping round and outflanking the enemy. To meet this new development, Condé swung round his cavalry until it was at right angles to its old position.

The Huguenots were now pressed in, their back to the river, and retreat difficult. The end was not long in coming. A few of the cornets on the extreme left were routed. Coligny and Andelot, with the cavalry of the "van," tired out by a day's marching and fighting, came on, says Tavannes, "without dash, for when they were a lance's length away, the greater part turned to the left," and galloped off the field. Montgomery on the right, though he had shown more spirit, was equally unsuccessful. The issue of the fight now depended on Condé. Perhaps retreat would have been the wisest course, but this accorded little with his sanguine and fiery temper. Turning to his little band, and with the touching motto of his standard in mind, " PRO CHRISTO ET PATRIÂ DULCE PERICULUM,"[1] he called on them for a final effort. " See !" cried he, " here is the chance we have longed for. Come ! let us follow up the first charges and remember how Louis of Bourbon goes to the combat ' for Christ and country ! ' "[2] His onset was irresistible. He broke and scattered all before him, even reaching the enemy's " battle," which the Duke of Anjou led in person. But numbers and weight told. He was at last surrounded, and, while in the act of surrendering, or immediately after, was slain by someone unknown.[3] His followers still fought on

---

[1] *Troisième Guerre Civile*, 323.   [2] D'Aubigné, iii. 51.

[3] The official Huguenot version of the death of Condé is to be found in letters of Henry of Condé and Coligny of the 11th and 13th of April to Louis of Wurtemberg (Schott, *Herzog Ludwig von Württemberg und die französischen Protestanten*, 1568– 1570), and of Cardinal Odet to the Elector Palatine, 10th June (Kluckhohn, ii. 335). They state that Condé had surrendered to two gentlemen, Argence and St. Jean, squire of Anjou, when Montesquiou, Captain of the Guards of Anjou, arrived on the scene and slew him in cold blood. But M. Denys d'Aussy, in the *Revue des Questions Historiques*, xlix. 573, shows good reason for thinking that Montesquiou was not the murderer, but some other Gascon gentleman. We would add that Alfonso Giannelli, an agent of Ferrara, writing from Lyons on the 28th of March (Modena Francia, 56), stated that Condé was slain by an Italian, who, on being acknowledged to be the murderer by Anjou, had passed through Lyons post haste for Italy, where he hoped to pick up some reward. De Losses, however, who brought the news of victory from Anjou to the court at Metz, though he had seen and touched the body of Condé (Vatican, Polit. xxxii. 209), was ignorant of the name of the slayer (Gasparo Foglie, Metz, 22nd March : Modena Francia, 59). Florentine advices (Florence, Arch. Med., 4598, Fa. viii. 67), which seem to us to be founded on those of Ferrara, state that an Italian slew Condé. At Metz, the accepted account, which was no doubt that given by de Losses, was that Condé in the fight had his

LVIS·III·DE·BOVRBON·PRINCE·DE·CÔDE.
Ludwig von Bourbon Furst zu Conde ~ Cùm Gra,
tia & Priuilegio 1568 Mathis Zündt

LOUIS OF BOURBON, PRINCE OF CONDÉ

heroically. "It was the fiercest and most stubborn combat of the civil wars," says d'Aubigné, himself a witness of the scene. "Among others we noticed an old man named La Vergne, who fought that day in the midst of twenty-five nephews, he and fifteen of them being slain, all in a heap." So ended the career of Louis of Bourbon, Prince of Condé. "He died," as the Queen of Navarre expressed it, "on the true bed of honour,"[1] and with greater credit to himself than to his enemies. "For the same night that the battle was fought, the Duke of Anjou, pursuing the enemy, victoriously entered into Jarnac, whither the body of the Prince was carried in triumph on the back of a miserable ass, to the infinite joy and diversion of the whole army, which made a joke of this spectacle, though while he lived they were terrified at the name of so great a man."[2] This scene bears eloquent witness to the rapid deterioration produced by the civil wars. It seems a glimpse of another world to that where Condé, a captive at the battle of Dreux, shared the couch of the victor.

The day of Jarnac had thus proved fatal to the Prince. More fortunate than he, Coligny indeed escaped, but with a somewhat tarnished reputation. It is difficult to free him wholly from responsibility for the disaster. It is possible that in a few particulars M. Gigon's strictures may be too harsh; M. Patry suggests extenuating circumstances.[3] As he took excellent measures to keep in touch with the enemy at Châteauneuf and prevent surprise, he can scarcely be blamed for his men, contrary to his orders, forsaking their posts. Again, as M. Patry points out, proof is lacking that Coligny received orders from Condé to retire on Jarnac at daybreak of the 13th; therefore the criticism that he ought to have informed his advance guard opposite Châteauneuf on the night of the 12th, and in consequence would have discovered their

horse killed under him, his hand almost severed, and had also received a wound in the breast or thigh. Being surrounded by some soldiers, he offered them 200,000 crowns. Thereupon, some unknown coming up and recognising the Prince on the latter's vizor being raised, shot him in the face with his pistol and blew out his eye.

[1] British Museum, Harley, 7016, 1.   [2] Davila.

[3] *Bull. du prot. fr.*, 1903, p. 143, etc. It seems to us rather hazardous for M. Patry to suggest that Coligny left Jarnac unprotected as a feint to deceive the enemy. It was too dangerous.

negligence, falls to the ground. Nevertheless, he seems to
have been less watchful and less alive to the true position of
affairs than the Catholic generals, Biron, Montpensier, and
Tavannes. Nor is it easy to meet fully the criticism of the
duc d'Aumale, that Coligny's recall of Condé was risking all
to extricate himself. Equally weighty is the dictum of M.
Gigon, that, had he given orders to concentrate, not at Bassac,
but farther back, he would have given time and opportunity
to his squadrons to collect, and, with his whole force drawn
up and resting on Jarnac, there would have been no battle.

CHAPTER XIII

THE THIRD WAR OF RELIGION—*continued*

Coligny virtually succeeds Condé as Leader — Death of Andelot — Coming of William of Orange and Zweibrücken — Combat of Roche - l'Abeille — Coligny's Severity in Perigord — Siege of Poitiers — Battle of Moncontour — "Voyage of the Princes" — Battle of Arnay-le-Duc — Need of Peace — Miserable State of France — Edict of St. Germain.

THE result of the battle of Jarnac was known in the court at Metz in the early hours of the 21st. "Sire!" said Anjou's messenger, on entering the King's chamber, "I bring you good news." As the tale of victory was unfolded, the satisfaction of the ill-balanced, excitable Charles knew no bounds. He exclaimed that his greatest enemy was dead; he fell on his bare knees, and offered up a short prayer; then, throwing on a dressing-gown, he rushed off in his slippers to the Queen Mother, and finally carried her off with the court to hear a Te Deum in the cathedral church. The Cardinal of Lorraine, still more enthusiastic, wrote to Rome, promising to send the ensigns captured in the battle, if the Pope would only agree to have them hung in St. Peter's as a perpetual memorial. And in due time they arrived, twelve in all, "the which," reported an eye-witness on the 23rd of April, "the Pope hath joyfullie receivede and this daie triumphethe for the victorie."[1]

The joy of the Catholics, however, was somewhat premature. As a military event the battle of Jarnac did not rank high. The Protestant losses were inconsiderable, perhaps four hundred in all. Moreover, they had gained as an effective force by having the command concentrated in the hands of one person. To keep up the old fiction that they were the

[1] British Museum, Lansdowne, 94, 61.

constitutional party, Henry of Navarre and Henry of Condé were accepted as chiefs. Yet round the camp-fires the latter were known as " the pages of M. l'Amiral." Coligny, in fact, was formally appointed their lieutenant and adviser. He was entrusted with the handling of negotiations and the conduct of war. He, in a word, was in command. Fortunately, at this critical moment an unsuccessful attack of Anjou on Cognac gave time to organise and prepare. The morale of the troops had been shaken. But at a grand review held at Tonnay-Charente, the indomitable Joan of Navarre presented her son Henry to the army and delivered an inspiriting address.

The Huguenots had thus found their leaders. They had now to seek a policy. Some, whose nerves were unstrung, advised retiring on La Rochelle, the troops being thrown into the islands of Maillezay and Marans. At best this was a counsel of despair, and met with Coligny's instant opposition. His plan, more hazardous in appearance, offered not only better chances of success, but was the only means by which the party could be kept together. The towns of the Charente were to be held and strengthened in anticipation of the coming of the German mercenaries. Foreign succour indeed at last seemed at hand. In the autumn of 1568, William of Orange had crossed the frontier with an army composed of his own followers and a large body of Huguenot gentlemen. But the intrigues and threats of Catherine, together with the risks attending a journey across France, made them, says d'Aubigné, " cold theologians." In January, therefore, William had been forced to retire into Germany. On the 6th of April he joined Zweibrücken, already on his way towards the Loire with reiters and lansquenets ; on the 26th the combined force appeared under the walls of Dijon, and on the 20th of May captured La Charité. From his retreat at Saintes Coligny had anxiously watched the advance. He had hardly dared hope for success. But when once they had reached the Loire, the Admiral sent a promise to meet them in Limousin. Starting eastward, he made his will at Archiac on the 5th of June, wrote to Cecil from Angoulême on the 6th, detached Montgomery at Nontron for a campaign in Navarre, and finally reached Cars on the 10th. The same

day the tireless Zweibrücken, who had eluded the royalist
forces, was carried in his coach to Nexon, booted and spurred,
in a dying condition. Coligny arrived on the 11th. But
the Duke was too ill to see him, and died in a few hours. On
the 12th the Admiral and his principal followers were granted
the sad privilege of seeing his remains. The success of his
march had been due in large measure to the divisions in the
royal camp. Nevertheless, it was a brilliant feat of arms,
and remained with the Huguenots one of the great memories
of the religious wars. And one would have thought that he
would have been left quiet in his grave. But learned wit was
not to be denied. In playful allusion to his name and the
supposed cause of his death was spun off—

"Pons superavit aquas, superarunt pocula Pontem."

His loss was all the more keenly felt because it followed
so close on that of Andelot. The brilliant, impetuous
Colonel-General of the French Infantry, the beloved brother
of Coligny, the Protestant "chevalier sans peur," as his
followers and friends affectionately called him, one of the great
figures of his time, died at Saintes on the 7th of May, and
was ultimately buried in the Huguenot centre of Nîmes. His
end gave rise to the suspicion of poisoning, probably without
cause. Unfortunately, in the sixteenth century any suggestion
of foul play found ready acceptance. In this instance it fed
on the supposed apophthegm of the Italian and royalist
Birague, to the end that the war could be brought to a speedier
close by means of cooks. In this connection we might quote
an incident which was passed on by the Spanish Ambassador
to Philip II. It may or may not be true, probably not. Its
interest lies in the curious glimpse it gives of the manners and
sentiments, or rather superstitions, of the age. This is the
story: "An Italian offered this Queen to kill the Prince of
Condé, the Admiral, and Andelot from Paris. In the end
they put such faith in the said Italian, that for six months he
has been closeted in a room with a German craftsman he
brought from Strasburg, and he has had him make three
bronze figures of the Prince of Condé, the Admiral, and
Andelot, full of screws in the joints and breasts with which to

open and shut them, and work the arms, thighs, faces, and hair, which is very abundant and turns upwards. Day after day the said Italian does nothing but study their birth and with an astrolabe turns and unturns screws. When the Prince of Condé died, they say that his thigh gave clear signs of his death, the like also happening in the case of Andelot. Two weeks ago, they aver, similar signs were observed in the statue of the Admiral, which may have given rise to the rumour here of the last few days of his death. To-day, when they find out their mistake, and know that he is alive, the authors of this silly work give out that the signs were not so much those of death, as in the case of Condé and Andelot, but rather to indicate the serious illness of the said Admiral and the death of his eldest son. . . . When the Queen left this town for the camp, she wrote the Cardinal of Lorraine and the Bishop of Sens that they would very soon hear news which would give the Pope and Christendom greater joy than any they had had these twenty years. This must be the result of the good hope they have of the working of the said charm." [1]

After the death of Zweibrücken the Catholics and German Protestants marched on parallel lines as far as Roche-l'Abeille and St. Yrieix. Here the main Huguenot army joined its allies. Coligny had now a force of at least 17,000 of all arms. This is the number given in a valuable narrative of the campaign from an Italian standpoint,[2] though other calculations have placed it well over 20,000. It divides them into 5000 reiters, 5000 lansquenets, 2000 French horse, and 5000 French foot. Still more satisfactory than these mere numbers was the spirit of the troops. Coligny was able to provide the Germans with a month's pay, while the courtly abilities of Cardinal Odet, who had fled to England, and the fear of what might follow a Huguenot *débâcle*, promised to triumph, at least partially, over Elizabeth's notorious unwillingness " ever to advance her money for an ill-assured enterprise.[3]

[1] Alava to Philip, Paris, 8th June : Paris, Arch. Nat., K. 1514, 122.
[2] *Narrative of the Campaign of the Italian troops under Santa Fiore* : Rome, Barberini Library, lv. 34, p. 76.
[3] La Mothe-Fénelon, i. 15.

BATTLE OF ROCHE-L'ABEILLE, 25 JUNE, 1569

(*Tortorel*)

O—THE ADMIRAL ON HORSEBACK   X—PHILIP STROZZI TAKEN PRISONER
A, F, G, H, I, M—HUGUENOT POSITIONS AND FORCES   T—STROZZI'S INFANTRY

One incident of this time is worth mentioning. The Queen of Navarre had had twenty massive gold chains made at La Rochelle, and medals struck with the inscription : " ou paix asseurée, ou victoire entière, ou mort honneste." They were presented to the German captains by Coligny. This fact has a melancholy interest, for when, on the day of St. Bartholomew, the Admiral's assassins turned to rifle his clothing, they found one of these, or a similar medal, attached to his cap.

On the 23rd of June the Italians sent by the Pope entered the royal camp. Both sides now felt that something must be done. The country was mountainous and sterile. To gain even the scantiest subsistence it was necessary to scatter, thereby running the risk of surprise. Coligny, therefore, determined to anticipate the enemy. This resulted in the battle of Roche-l'Abeille of the 25th of June. As a military event it was of little or no importance. Only the Catholic " van," more especially the infantry of Philip Strozzi, the new Colonel-General, was engaged. Such interest as it arouses is largely owing to two facts. It figures in Tortorel & Perrissin's unique collection, published in 1570, of historic scenes of the sixteenth century, particularly of the first three religious wars. It was also one of those smaller combats, so often quoted, in which Coligny, uniformly unfortunate in larger engagements, was successful. The two armies were only separated by a valley. The Huguenots, with their cavalry and 3000 arquebusiers, made an attack on an outpost of the royalist camp. In the result Philip Strozzi's infantry was rolled up, some hundreds killed, and he himself taken prisoner. Thus vanished into air the hopes of Rome, together with the pleasing vision of that ancient and learned friar who, gazing in a mirror, had seen therein a bloody victory for the King for the Feast of St. John.[1]

On the 27th, Coligny was on the march for Perigord. He was forced to seek out a country where the dangers of surprise were less, and which would provide better quarters and more food for his troops, especially the Germans. But before setting out, he indulged in one of those extravagances of knight-errantry which the European soldier abandoned only with his

---

[1] Avvisi di Roma, 29th June : Vatican Library, Urbino, 1041, 101.

relinquishment of armour. Sending to the royal camp, he offered to pit eighty of his reiters against a hundred of Santa Fiore's Italians, and boastfully promised a hundred sous to the trumpeter who should bring a favourable answer. Not to be outdone, the Italian scornfully proposed a hundred to a hundred, and a hundred and fifty sous for the messenger coming with the Admiral's assent.[1]

In sharp contrast with the Coligny of this episode is Coligny the terrible avenger of the wrongs of his followers. After their defeat at Mensignac on the 25th of October, 1568, the Provençals had been slaughtered wholesale by the peasants of Perigord. At the time the Admiral had been too busy following Montpensier to turn aside to punish them. But he had now his chance, and he determined not only to exact a signal retribution, but to terrorise them into some show of moderation for the future. As a consequence, there was a veritable carnage. When Brantôme suggested that the executions should be confined to the districts of Mensignac, Coligny replied with impassive imperturbability that it was the same country, and they were all peasants of Perigord.[2] It is therefore with a feeling almost of astonishment that, in the midst of these wild scenes, we come on one of Brantôme's most vivid pen-sketches. The subject is William of Orange, the founder of Dutch liberties and the future husband of Louise of Coligny. "It was at that time," he writes, "that I saw these foreign princes, and conversed for quite a time with the Prince of Orange in an alley of my garden. I found him, to my thinking, a very great personage. He spoke well on all subjects. He talked of the ineffectiveness of his army, giving the blame to a lack of money and the foreigners who loved him to excess. But he would never halt, he said, in so good a cause, and would soon be speeding back again. He had a fine carriage and figure, Count Louis his brother being smaller in size. I found him sad, and his mien showed that he felt overwhelmed by fortune. As to his brother Louis, he was of a more gay and open countenance, and held to be more daring

---

[1] *Narrative of the Italian troops under Santa Fiore* : Rome, Barberini Library, lv. 34, 129.

[2] Brantôme, vi. 18, 19.

WILLIAM OF ORANGE

and venturesome than the Prince of Orange, but the latter
wiser, more mature, more discreet." [1]

In the first week of July, the Protestant army, under
Coligny, William of Orange, Louis of Nassau, and Mansfeld,
the newly chosen leader of the Germans, turned towards the
Vienne. It had little to fear from the Duke of Anjou. His
reiters were openly disaffected. The Secretary, de l'Aubespine,
ascribes the failure to contest Zweibrücken's crossing of the
Vienne to their unwillingness to march.[2] Their excuse was
that they had neither wine nor bread. It was certainly not
ill-founded, for we find that "the kinges rasters have dronke
no wine theis 6 daies; a pot of wine is worthe 8 or 9
soubz, and the loafe of breade which was wont to be solde for
one soubz is now woorthe 6 soubzes in Limoges." [3] Nor, from
a military standpoint, were things greatly bettered by leaving the south and the neighbourhood of Roche-l'Abeille and
Limoges. Anjou's army was literally disappearing before his
eyes. The French had already left or were leaving the camp
to gather the harvest, while such of his force as remained was
wasting away with disease.[4] A summer campaign, in fact, was
out of the question. Coligny, meanwhile, was pushing north
and westward. His intention was first to save Poitou, the
richest and most populous centre of his influence. Thence he
intended to make for Saumur on the Loire. With it in his
hands he could threaten Paris. Confolens was left on the
10th. On the 20th the château of Lusignan was taken. His
aim was now to march to the Loire. The nobility, however,
especially the Poitevins, insisted on an attack on Poitiers.
Unfortunately, they had their way. "In civil wars," says La
Noue quaintly, "the plough sometimes draws the oxen." The
prize was undoubtedly tempting. Its capture would have
secured Poitou, and placed in their hands the young Duke of
Guise. But Coligny clearly saw the dangers of the plan;
experience was against it. When, therefore, his too sanguine

---

[1] Brantôme, ii. 166.   [2] Limoges, 10th June: British Museum, 21405, 68.
[3] News from Strasburg, 11th July, founded on a letter from Lyons: British
Museum, Lansdowne, 94, 61.
[4] Avvisi di Roma per lettere del campo cattco. di 22 Luglio: Vatican Library,
Urbino, 1041, 101; Relation de la guerre en France: Paris, Arch. Nat., K. 1529, 19.

followers dragged him off to the siege, he was dark and moody. "These great cities," he protested, "are the sepulchres of armies." This was only too true a prophecy. On the 25th the leaders held a final council of war. On the 27th the Catholic La Motte-Messemé, leaning idly on the walls of Poitiers, watched the Huguenots streaming down from the heights. Failure dogged them from the outset. The Admiral chose the point of attack badly. Instead of making his approaches from the south-west, the one spot unprotected by water, he settled on the valley of the Clain, on the east side, where the town, though dominated by the neighbouring heights, was well shielded by the river. He also omitted to occupy the suburb of Rochereuil. The effect of these initial mistakes was soon apparent, especially as the garrison had been strengthened by the timely arrival of 500 Catholics from St. Maixent on the 31st of July. When a breach was made and a bridge thrown across the Clain, the besieged cut it during the night; finally, they flooded the meadows by causing the river to overflow, crying derisively that the Admiral's command did not extend to this sea of fresh water. And though Coligny made new preparations, he never felt justified in giving the word to storm. Too late he turned his thoughts to the suburb of Rochereuil, which lay to the north. But here the attack was insufficiently prepared; the Catholic works commanding the breach were not destroyed; and the grand triple assault of the 3rd of September was thrown back with slaughter.[1] The Admiral now only waited for an excuse to withdraw. It was not long in coming. Anjou, who had been inactive for some time, having disbanded most of his troops at Loches, was ready to renew the offensive. He therefore moved out against Châtellerault, captured by the Huguenots on the 12th of July. On the 7th of September the Admiral had left Poitiers behind and was marching to save Châtellerault. After following the retreating Anjou,[2] he retired across the Vienne to

---

[1] For siege of Poitiers see Colonel Babinet, *Mém. de la Soc. des ant. de l'ouest*, 2nd series, vol. xi.

[2] The map of Segesser is incorrect. Anjou recrossed the Creuse and settled at La Selle, north-west of La Haye, and not south-east of the latter, as marked by Segesser.

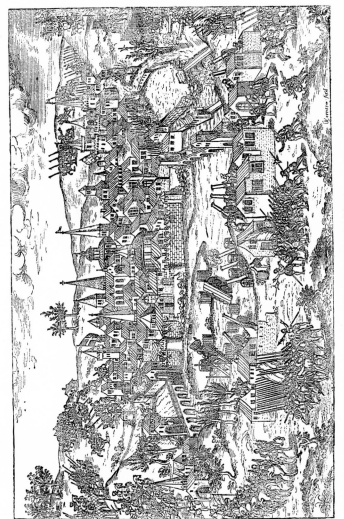

SIEGE OF POITIERS, 1569

(Perrissin)

Faye-la-Vineuse. Those who had overruled him had now to cast up their account: 2500 stricken down by disease, their leaders ill, Coligny near to dying and carried in a litter, and the young Henry of Guise, by his brilliant defence, become the popular hero.[1] Such were the evil results of the interference of subordinates with the plans of the General.

The Admiral did not wait long at Faye. After seeing William of Orange depart with a small escort for Germany, he resolved to march into southern Poitou, place himself behind a barrier of friendly towns, and then, if he wished, join the Viscounts and the victorious Montgomery. A battle was out of the question. His troops were wearied and discouraged; their numbers were not what they had been; many of the gentlemen had retired, and gave no signs of returning. But to sustain the morale of his troops he pretended to make preparations to meet Anjou. The plan was excellent. Yet the desire of his men to risk all in a battle, and the late arrival of his artillery horses at Faye, and, in consequence, his own late departure, were destined to produce another disaster. Anjou quitted Chinon with the deliberate intention of cutting off the Huguenots from lower Poitou and forcing an action. On the 29th of September the Catholics crossed the Vienne and camped the same day at Loudun. On the 30th Coligny was on the move southward; then swinging round to the right, he made for his real goal, Moncontour. In the plain of St. Clair his rearguard under Mouy stumbled on the royal army, and was roughly handled. It was only by good fortune that the Admiral was able to get his army safely over a marshy stream and line the banks; the crossing was narrow, only twenty horse could advance abreast.[2] Then, thinking he had only to do with the "van," he cheered on his men, and charged the enemy. But the whole Catholic army had come up, and he was forced to retire. His troops were then put to a final test. The enemy brought up their guns and played on the heavy masses of the reiters. It was only the influence of Coligny and their leaders which kept them steady

---

[1] See poems in his honour in Liberge, *Le Siege de Poitiers*, 1569.

[2] An Italian account in the Barberini Library states that the French and Italian Catholics actually crossed the stream, but were thrown back.

and prevented a rout. Darkness at last saved them. And that night, without beat of drum, the Admiral led his dispirited troops a league on the way to Moncontour.

Next day the two forces stood facing one another on opposite sides of the deep but narrow Dive. Coligny was now comparatively safe. The Catholics could not attack him in front; should they attempt to turn his position by marching round the head-waters of the Dive, he would have time to escape south-westward. During the 1st and 2nd of October the advisability of retreat was brought home to him. Two Catholic gentlemen warned a Protestant outpost to tell him to avoid a battle; the forces of Anjou had been largely reinforced, and were flushed with anticipations of victory. This advice undoubtedly appealed all the more to him when reinforced by the opinion of La Noue and Teligny, who had carried out a reconnaissance. But, in reality, the decision rested less with him than with his army. And there was no doubt as to its views. French and German alike cried for battle. The Huguenot gentlemen, already a year from home, would wait no more. Disaffected bands threatened to retire. The ill-paid and mutinous foreign levies called for death or victory. When Louis of Nassau was summoned to the Admiral's room some hours before daylight, he fell into a rage at the mere suggestion of avoiding battle. For a second time the conduct of the campaign was taken out of Coligny's hands. But he did what was possible. The Princes had already been called up from Parthenay to inspirit the men. The army was warned to be ready to march at dawn for Airvault. His hope undoubtedly was to cross the Thouet before the arrival of the Catholics. On the morning of the 3rd of October all was ready; the troops were on the move, when suddenly the German foot chose the moment to mutiny for pay. Nearly two hours passed before they were pacified, and kissed the ground, swearing to die with honour. It was now too late to think of reaching Airvault. The Catholic army had turned the Dive during the night of the 2nd–3rd, and was now streaming north into the plain of Moncontour. It was here that Coligny had to give battle. As he watched the enemy spreading out their "battle" westward under the guidance of

Cossé, he divined their plan of cutting him off from Airvault. His counter-move was to throw forward his "battle"; this effectually frustrated the Catholic attempt, and kept a way of retreat open.

In accordance with sixteenth-century tactics, each army was divided into two divisions: "van" and "battle." In addition, the Catholic general, Tavannes, left a reserve of horse under Biron. Behind the Protestant "battle" there was also a special force surrounding the young Princes, but it was rather a retinue or guard. Coligny, as always, led the Protestant "van." In this instance it brought up the rear, and was less advanced toward the south than the "battle." From this station, with the army stretching away toward the Thouet, the Admiral was well able to control its general movements. He entrusted the "battle" to Louis of Nassau.

The Huguenot line was from north-east to south-west: from the Moulin du Titre to Douron. Its formation was as follows: On the extreme east were thirty mounted arquebusiers and a company of foot also armed with the arquebus. These were thrown out on the left as a cover to two companies of men-at-arms of Coligny and Acier which had to their right two cornets of reiters. Next came two companies of arquebusiers covering four French cornets of horse under Coligny, who had on his right four or five cornets of reiters under Wolrad of Mansfeld. In front were two companies of French horse under Mouy and La Loue, who had to their right two cornets of reiters. The lansquenets,[1] with six pieces of

---

[1] Colonel Babinet ("Episodes de la troisième guerre civile en Poitou" in the *Mém. de la Soc. des antiquaires de l'ouest*, year 1893) states that the lansquenets were divided between the "van" and "battle." His authority for this is undoubtedly the faulty and confused phrase in the official account (Record Office, cviii. 381): "Et departoient lesd. Rebelles toutes leurs forces en deux Leurs Regimentz de lansquenetz avec des trouppes de Reystres et des gens de cheval françois flanqué led. Regiment de grosses trouppes de harquebouziers," etc.—and la Popelinière, these two being obviously copied by d'Aubigné, who was not present at the battle, and Castelnau, who, though present, wrote many years later. The words of La Popelinière are to the effect that Coligny led the "van" and had with him Puygreffier and others "qui avoyent charge de deux Canons, deux Longues, et deux Mousquets: et le Comte de Mansfeld pour Chef de Reitres: desquels il avoit distribué près de la moitié a la Bataille: comme aussi des Lansquenetz, que Granvillars conduisoit." We personally believe that the translation is not that he had distributed some

artillery before them, and surrounded by five regiments of French arquebusiers, and flanked on each side by two cornets of horse, ended the "van." The "battle" was similarly arranged, the bulk of the German and French cavalry coming first; then five regiments of French arquebusiers, flanked by four cornets of horse, and having before them three cannon and a culverin. On the extreme west, but behind the two cornets flanking the foot, were Henry of Navarre and the Prince of Condé with six cornets of French horse.

The Catholics were arranged as follows: The "van," under the Duke of Montpensier, was on the east and opposite the Protestant "van." The Catholic cavalry leader, Martigues, was thrown out in front, his duty being to begin the battle. The extreme east of the line was formed by the Italian cavalry under Santa Fiore, the eighteen cornets of reiters under Bassompierre, Schomberg, and the two Rhinegraves, being somewhat behind. Next came half of the Swiss foot surrounded by five regiments of French infantry; in front and a little to their right were seven pieces of artillery, while behind came Montpensier and his son, the Prince Dauphin, with their French horse. To the west of the Swiss and ending the "van" was the cavalry of Guise and La Valette. The east wing of the "battle" was formed of the *élite* of the French cavalry under Anjou, Longueville, and Aumale. In front rode Carnavalet with fifty chosen horse; behind, Baden with five cornets of reiters. Next came the second half of the Swiss, flanked by Spanish, Walloon, Burgundian, and French foot. They were also protected on the east by their baggage, while before them were five pieces of artillery.

lansquenets under Granvillars to the "battle," but rather that he had with him in the "van" Puygreffier, Mansfeld, and his reiters (half of whom he had distributed to the "battle"), and some lansquenets under Granvillars. This reading is supported by the design of Tortorel & Perrissin, by the Swiss Clery, and Urs zur Matten, who wrote shortly after the battle (Segesser, i. 64, etc.), and the Catholic official account, apart from the phrase we have quoted above. It is the only one, too, which seems to fit in with La Popelinière's own explanation a few pages farther on : "Pour le regard de l'infanterie, celle de l'Avante garde estoit en masse tenant forme d'un gros Bataillon que faisoyent les Lansquenetz sous la charge du Baron de Greleseé et de Granvillars. . . . L'infanterie de la Bataille faisoit un autre Bataillon composé d'harquebuziers des Regimens de Beaudiné, Mombrun, Blacons, Mirabel, et Virieu." . . .

Ernest of Mansfeld with five cornets of reiters formed the extreme west of the line. Behind him rode the cavalry of Cossé. In second line and behind Anjou was a reserve under Biron.[1]

The " van " and " battle " of each army had thrown out in front " forlorn hopes," who acted as skirmishers. Each side had, as far as possible, made use of the ground to shelter its men from the effects of artillery fire. The number of the Protestants was, approximately, 6000 horse, 8000 French foot, and 4000 lansquenets, or 18,000 in all; that of the Catholics, 24,000—that is to say, 8000 horse and 16,000 foot.

Perhaps the most remarkable feature of the battle was that Coligny, instead of placing a supporting line of arquebusiers immediately behind a line of French cavalry, as he had done previously, now for the first time formed them into separate bodies, and placed them to the left of each few companies of the men-at-arms and of the light horse. He also, it will be seen, alternated French with German horse; they were thus, owing to the difference in their tactics, a protection to one another. The extent of his line has been criticised; Colonel Babinet, however, suggests that it was owing to the fact that the mutiny among the German foot had given the " battle " a long start. The comparative weakness of his " battle " was probably owing to his intention of giving a decisive blow with his " van," which would enable him to continue his march on Airvault. It is to be noted, too, that the Huguenot cavalry was in single line; Tavannes, on the contrary, ranged his in compact squadrons.[2] Moreover, Coligny's followers either disdained or their horses were too small to carry the lance; the rank and file of the French infantry, also, had not one single pike among them; they were all arquebusiers. These facts, together with the absence of any Huguenot reserve, the poor quality of the horses, and the lack of courage evinced by some of the cavalry and foot, explain Coligny's defeat.

Meanwhile, the cannonade had been furious on both sides

---

[1] The plan of the battle, published by Tortorel & Perrissin in 1570 (and re-published by A. Franklin in 1885), is, as far as the Catholic army is concerned, approximately correct.

[2] La Noue, 290 ; Tavannes, 270.

the Huguenots doing the greater damage. The battle began between the two "vans." It was now long after midday.[1] Tavannes had reconnoitred, and promised Anjou the victory. But Montpensier was loath to move, hoping, says the young Tavannes, to play the brilliant rôle of Guise at Dreux. Twice Anjou ordered him to charge, and twice he hesitated; at last, however, he was forced to "drain the cup." The cannon were withdrawn to the rear, the trumpets sounded the advance. The Protestant "van," wearing the Huguenot white, sent an answering challenge. Martigues dashed forward, but, met by a galling fire from a body of Huguenot arquebusiers, turned suddenly to his right and fell on Mouy. The latter, deserted by the two supporting cornets of reiters, was thrown into confusion. Renel and Autricourt came to his assistance, but were met by the fire of the Catholic arquebusiers and the vigorous charges of the Italians. In the result Autricourt was left on the field, while the cavalry fell back on the infantry and threw it into disorder. Guise also had charged successfully on the Catholic left. Seeing that the issue was doubtful, Coligny sent to Louis of Nassau for a reinforcement of three cornets of reiters. The latter, with ill-considered zeal, came himself, and left the "battle" without a leader. Moreover, the Admiral, alarmed for the safety of the Princes, had already ordered them to retire. A crowd of faint-hearted warriors threw themselves into their retinue, thereby weakening and dispiriting the fighting line.

Meanwhile the Catholic reiters were advancing. They were met by the sustained fire of the arquebusiers, and Coligny charged them in person with his men-at-arms. Twenty paces before his followers he pistolled the Rhinegrave, but was in turn wounded in the cheek. The reiters began to give way. The Protestants cried victory! but their leader was at last hemmed in, and only rescued by the spirited charge of Wolrad of Mansfeld. Unfortunately, the Admiral could fight no more. Choking with blood, he was led from the field by his page. This was the crowning disaster.

The struggle between the "battles" had been equally

---

[1] The Venetian Ambassador reported from Tours, on the 4th of October, that the actual battle lasted from one to four: Bibl. Nat. Italien, 1727.

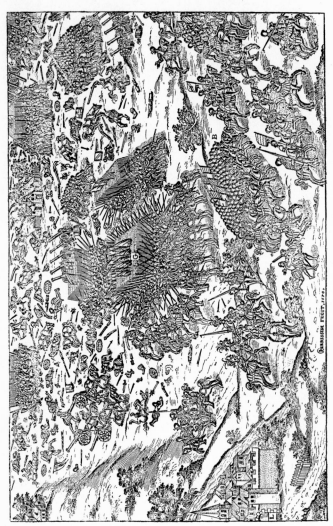

SLAUGHTER OF THE LANSQUENETS AT THE BATTLE OF MONCONTOUR, 3 OCTOBER, 1569

G—LANSQUENETS ATTACKED BY CATHOLIC CAVALRY AND SWISS   B—RETREAT OF THE REITERS

furious. The Duke of Anjou, impatient with the undecided
conflict of the "vans," rashly hurried forward, outstripping the
Swiss. In consequence, Carnavalet was routed; Anjou's own
troop was thrown into confusion, and his horse slain under him;
while Aumale and Baden were pressed back by the fire of the
Huguenot infantry and mounted arquebusiers and the charges of
their horse. Things looked black when Ernest of Mansfeld and
Cossé charged on Anjou's left, the Swiss were brought up at
the double, Biron with the reserve placed himself at their right,
and Anjou was horsed. This was the preliminary to victory.
The Protestants were unable to withstand the steady pressure
of these new forces. And their reiters—part of whom had
made a mistaken and disastrous charge on the Swiss, who had
been protected by baggage—from both "van" and "battle"
formed into a body some thousands strong and retired from
the field. The lansquenets were thus left to the tender mercies
of the Swiss, their rivals in the trade of arms. They threw
up their pikes; several, with hands clasped and on their
knees, cried, "Bon Papiste! Bon Papiste, moy!" It was all to
no purpose. The slaughter was terrible. Only 200 survived
out of 4000. The French arquebusiers, more fleet of foot and
granted quarter by Anjou, suffered less. Perhaps 1500 were
slain.

Judged by ordinary standards of endurance, it might have
been supposed that neither Coligny nor Protestant France
could recover from such a blow. For, as far as Coligny was
concerned, it had not come singly. The defeat of Jarnac; the
deaths of Condé and Andelot; murderous attempts on his
own life; the judgment of the Parlement of Paris sentencing
Gaspard de Coligny "to be hung and strangled on a gallows
to be placed for the deed in the Place de Grève before the
Hôtel of this town of Paris, his dead body there to remain
hung the space of twenty-four hours, and afterwards to be
carried and hung to the gibbet of Montfaucon on the spot
most high and eminent"; the setting of a price of 50,000
crowns on his head, alive or dead;—all these he had had to
bear, and now he was the vanquished in the bloodiest battle of
the civil wars. Happily, there is no need to speculate as to
how he faced the crisis. D'Aubigné, with affecting and

reverent pen, paints us a scene which speaks with simple pathos : " The Admiral saw falling to his share, as is the fate of leaders of peoples, blame for accidents, silence as to merits. He saw, too, the remnant of an army which even before the last disaster had been in unutterable despair, two princes still young, towns feeble, garrisons fearful, enemies powerful and without pity—least of all for him,—himself abandoned by all the great except a woman (Joan of Navarre) who, having of woman only the name, had advanced to Niort to stretch out her hand to the afflicted and deal with affairs. Thus it was with this aged sire, stricken with fever, and suffering from the thought of these and other afflictions, more painful than his troublesome wound. As he was being carried in his litter, L'Estrange, an aged gentleman and one of his principal councillors, wounded and travelling in like manner, had his litter brought abreast of the other, when the road was wide enough. Then, pushing his head through the curtains, he looked fixedly at his chief, and, with tears in his eyes, left him with these words : ' Surely God is very gentle ! ' This great captain has confessed to his friends that this little friendly speech braced him up and set him on the way to good thoughts and resolutions for the future." [1]

It was now, at this moment of physical suffering and universal discouragement, that Coligny saved Protestant France. The 3rd of October saw him at Parthenay ; in the early months of 1570 he was on the frontiers of Spain ; in the summer he was at La Charité. The object of this move was simple. It was to avoid destruction, provide for the reiters, and join hands with Montgomery, fresh from his victories in Bearn. It was undoubtedly greatly aided by the Catholic generals, who wore themselves out in the arduous attempt to reduce St. Jean d'Angely.

The " voyage of the Princes," [2] as it was called, can be briefly sketched. Taking with him Henry of Navarre and the young

---

[1] *Histoire Universelle*, iii. 130.

[2] For the "voyage of the Princes" see *Journal de F. de Syreuilh* (edited by C. Simon) ; *Histoire générale de la province de Quercy*, by G. Lacoste ; Paul Courteault *Revue de l'Agenais*, 1898, p. 234) ; *Histoire générale de Languedoc*, by de Vic and Vaissete ; La Popelinière ; and E. Arnaud's histories of the Protestants of Dauphiné and Vivarais.

Condé, Coligny left Parthenay and arrived at Niort on the 5th of October. Here Sir Henry Champernowne with a body of English horse rode in, his trumpets sounding, and his black standard fluttering proudly its motto: "DET MIHI VIRTUS FINEM." On the 6th the Admiral set out for St. Jean d'Angely, passing thence to Saintes. A month later he had successfully crossed a great network of rivers—the Dronne, the Isle, the Vezère, the Dordogne, the Lot, the Aveyron—and was within the walls of Montauban. His men arrived in the direst extremities. "They had not a horse who could put one foot before the other, as many of them have confessed to me since," wrote Monluc. Fortunately, the Catholics of the south were without unity, for their leaders, Monluc and Damville, did not work well together. After resting at Montauban, Aiguillon and Port Sainte Marie were seized at the end of November. A junction was now possible with Montgomery, who was at Condom. For a month the Huguenots ravaged and emptied the country south of the Garonne. But Monluc was on the watch, and, by the ingenious device of throwing a mill into the river, broke the bridge. Coligny at once became anxious about his communications, and recalled his troops to the north bank. Montgomery joined him on the 3rd of January, 1570, and together they crossed the Tarn, and swept down on Toulouse. Here the country houses of the members of the Parlement were burnt as a punishment for their execution or rather murder of Rapin, a gentleman of the Prince of Condé who had announced to them the conclusion of the peace of Longjumeau. After an interview with his cousin Damville, which came to nothing, Coligny led his men towards Caraman, where several towns were sacked. One part of the army now went to Castres, the reiters into the Albigeois, "where the Germans drank to their hearts' content, for this country is extremely rich in wine."[1] Then renewing their march, the Huguenots appeared under the walls of Carcassone, Montpellier, Lunel, and entered Nîmes. One of the most stirring incidents of the late advance had been a sudden raid by Pilles from Barbayran toward the Spanish border.

As a military fact, as an expression of the indomitable

[1] *Histoire de Languedoc*, v.

15

courage of Coligny and the French Protestants, the "voyage of the Princes" is a unique event; as a stage in the evolution of the military ethics of the religious wars, it has an unenviable reputation. The army had deteriorated; the reins of discipline had loosened; the line of march was marked by rapine and plunder. And the worst of it was that all this slaughter was so much blood spilled on the sand. The Admiral must have been well aware that he was no nearer peace than when he had set out from Parthenay. It was no doubt with this thought in mind that he determined to strike at the centre of France. Leaving Nîmes, therefore, the Princes with the reiters took a westerly route through Alais, St. Ambroix, Aubenas, and Privas, while Coligny himself directed his course towards the Rhone. After he had thrown Louis of Nassau across the river to help the Huguenots on the left bank, he settled at La Voulte. On the 22nd of May, however, he was again on the move. Leaving his cannon at Pouzin and Grane under Mombrun, he threw himself into the mountainous country of the Vivarais, and arrived at St. Étienne. He was now in high fever. When the negotiations which were in train were suspended, some of his more impatient followers were for treating without him. But the reply of the Catholic emissary, Biron, effectually damped their self-confidence. "Should he die," said he, "not even a glass of water would we offer you. His name alone is worth to you more than a new army added to your own." When he recovered, Biron in vain demanded a truce. The Admiral pushed rapidly northwards. The chances were in favour of his outmanœuvring the enemy, as his troops were all mounted, and he had no cannon. On the 26th of June he was a little north of Arnay-le-Duc and face to face with Cossé, who had marched eastwards to intercept his advance. The Huguenots probably did not number 6000— a third of the enemy. But the Admiral, by rare generalship, was able to equalise the chances. A rolling hillside provided ample shelter from the royal artillery. His front was protected by a stream and two mills, these latter being strongly held by his arquebusiers. Every attempt of the enemy to cross the river was met by a heavy fire and charges of the cavalry, which was drawn up, French and German alike, in compact masses.

The result was that Cossé fell back, shaken though not routed. The Admiral never showed his military instinct more than by forbidding all pursuit.

The victory had important consequences. In the first place, following closely as it did on the brilliant success of La Noue at Luçon, in the west, it encouraged the Protestants. In the second, it opened the way to La Charité, and finally to peace. The terrible mobility of this elusive foe, whose day's march was "of eight or ten good leagues through mountains where artillery can scarce go";[1] the danger of more active intervention from England;[2] the fear of a new invasion from Germany, now that Coligny was more in touch with them at La Charité; an empty treasury; dissatisfied mercenaries—all these inclined Catherine to compromise. Coligny had already made proposals in June, 1569; and during the following winter and spring innumerable letters, messengers, and ambassadors passed between the Queen Mother, Joan of Navarre, and Coligny. Both sides recognised that peace must be had at all costs. It is impossible to exaggerate the depth of misery and desolation during the third war of religion. "But in effecte," wrote an Englishman in 1569, "the face of ffrawnce is lamentable at this season, the meaner subjects spoiled every where, and the greater neither sure of liffe nor lyvinge in any place, wherebye murther is no crueltie, nor disobedyence any offence, bathing one in another's blood, makinge it custome to dispise religion and justice, or any more sacred bond, either of devyne or humayne constitution. Where the victorer maye bewaile his victorie, and the naturall lastlie in dainger to be over rune by the stranger whome he provides nowe for his defence. Havinge consumed the store of the laste yere and wastinge that on the ground which should serve for the yere to come, so as a present desperacion and a piteous mournynge doth invade every sorte, as thoughe their calamyties shold have none end, but with the ende of their lives togeather. And that withall the dreadfullest cruelties at once of the world, plague, honger, and the sworde, which god of his goodnes cease in them, and preserve from us; and to this is joyned

[1] Letter of Cossé in de la Ferrière's *Lettres de Catherine de Médicis*, iii. lxiii.
[2] De la Mothe-Fénelon, iii. 120, 121.

as far as words are concerned, of which she is very liberal.
Her industry in affairs causes a general wonder and astonishment. No step, however unimportant, is taken without her.
Scarcely has she time to eat or drink or sleep, so great are her
harassing cares. She runs here and there between the armies,
doing a man's work, without a thought of sparing herself. Yet
she is beloved by no one in the land—or at least by few.
The Huguenots say that she has given them fine words and
feigned welcomes, while all the time she has been treating
with the Catholic King and scheming their destruction. The
Catholics, on the other hand, declare that if she had not exalted
and favoured the Huguenots, these latter would not have been
able to do what they have. Moreover, this is an age in France
when every man presumes. He thinks of something, then
passionately asks for it. If his request is refused, he grumbles
and throws the blame on the Queen Mother. And as she is a
stranger, though she were to give all, they would only say that
she gave nothing of her own.

"All resolutions taken in peace and war which have not
given satisfaction have been attributed to her, as though she
governed absolutely without the advice and counsel of others.
I do not say that the Queen is a Sybil and cannot err, and
that she does not sometimes rely too much on herself; but I
do say that I know of no other prince, whatever his wisdom
and experience, who would not have lost his head with a war
on his hands in which it was difficult to tell friend from foe,
and in which, to provide a remedy, he would have to make use
of the aid and counsel of those around him, all of whom were
interested, and part not too faithful. I repeat, I know of no
prince, however prudent, who would not have been lost with
so much against him—not to speak of a woman, a stranger,
without confidants, fearful, and always kept in ignorance of the
truth. Indeed, it has been a marvel to me that she has not
been confused, and given herself up altogether to one of the
parties, a course of action which would have ended in the total
ruin of that kingdom. She has thus preserved that royal
majesty, small though it is, which one sees to-day in that court.
I have therefore rather pitied than blamed her, as I told her
once when I had the chance. And in talking over the diffi-

culties which beset her, she confirmed me in my opinion, and has reminded me of it several times since. I know, too, that she has been seen weeping in her cabinet more than once. Then forcing herself, she has dried her eyes and appeared in public with a smiling countenance. And so those who judged how things were going from her face were not disturbed. Then resuming her conduct of affairs, when she has not been able to have her way, she has compromised here and there. Thus have been arranged those ill-considered measures which have redounded little to her honour and set all the world talking." [1]

Such is one, and not the least pleasing, interpretation of the character of this extraordinary woman—offspring of an upstart house, child of the callous and brilliant Renaissance, and student in a very real sense of the political teachings of Machiavel.[2] During the long years of the civil wars, she had seen her enemies swallowed up one by one: Navarre, St. André, Guise, Montmorency, Condé. And partly as a consequence, partly as the result of increased experience, she had grown in self-reliance, in ambition, in the love of power. In her scheme of things there was no room for Coligny in his rôle of Huguenot leader, with its tendency to develop into a form of unofficial kingship. The haunting sense of this danger had only to be reinforced in her mind by the fear of his growing ascendancy over her son, and we have the lamentable chain of events culminating in St. Bartholomew.

To Catherine, then, for political reasons, as to Catholics for religious reasons, Coligny was the enemy. " There remains now but one root which can make this (Protestant) religion long endure in France," wrote a Florentine on the death of the Admiral's elder brother Odet. " But as it is old, we may believe that it also will soon dry up." [3] As was inevitable, the successful issue of the third war had enhanced his reputation. " No one," related the Venetian Contarini, " in these wars has been more talked about and made his influence more felt than the Admiral. And it is astonishing how, whereas in the wars with Spain when serving the King he did nothing worthy of

---

[1] Alberi, iv. 202–204.
[2] See Lord Acton's Introduction to Burd's *Machiavelli*.
[3] Petrucci, 2nd April, 1571: Florence, Arch. Med., 4600, F. x. 82.

praise, in these against him he has won such reputation and
made himself so feared! It is astonishing, too, that he, a
private gentleman with little means, has sustained so long and
important a struggle not only against the whole might of his
own sovereign, but against all the help the latter has had of
Spain, of many princes of Italy, and some of Germany. And
the wonder grows when we remember that though he has lost
many battles, he has preserved his reputation with all." [1] It
was no doubt under the influence of this feeling that Noailles
wrote him on the 22nd of October, 1570: " I have not only
heard you say that patience surmounts all difficulties, but seen
you practise the same." [2]

These were the two protagonists. But there was another
who deserves a passing notice. It was the foul-mouthed,
melancholy, neurotic Charles IX. It was indeed a strange
freak of fortune which chose him out to play a rôle in one
of the great tragedies of history. He comes to us from the
merciless dissection of the Venetian Ambassadors half beast
and wholly a child. His mind moved vaguely ; the least
intellectual effort wore him out. His soul was in martial feats
and violent exercise. He was never in repose; a demon of
unrest had hold of him. Scrambling to his horse, he would
ride the day long, tireless, seemingly immune from fatigue.
His hunting was a very orgy of physical endurance ; brief
moments only were snatched for food and sleep. When not
at the chase, he was playing tennis or perfecting his skill in
arms. Often, too, he would enter the forge which he carried
about with him, and swing a great hammer hour after hour,
shaping morions and cuirasses. To tire out his following gave
him incredible delight. When he spoke, which was seldom,
what struck the beholder most were his beautiful, furtive eyes.
Stooping slightly like his father, he would raise them suddenly,
then let them fall in a flash ; he dared not encounter the glance
of others. When he lied, it was written on his face; deceit as
yet had not become a second nature. [3] And all the time, day
and night, he was dreaming of glory and the things of war.

[1] Alberi, iv. 238.   [2] Lettres de Noailles (edited by T. de Larroque), 23.
[3] A remark of the Spanish Ambassador Alava, quoted by Baumgarten in Vor der
Bart., 33, and Bezold in Hist. Zeitschrift, 1882.

(*Thomas de Leu*)

Perhaps the most pathetic touch about him was his longing to fall some day on the field of battle. Under more favouring circumstances he might have been known to history as an amiable if not brilliant king. Reared as he was in the fetid atmosphere of the Valois court, neglected, with all that was best in him undeveloped, he has become a warning of the dangers of an irresponsible monarchy. The one strong and invigorating influence in his life—that of Coligny—was to be shattered on a woman's jealousy.

The first duty which fell to the Admiral after the conclusion of the peace of St. Germain, was to rid himself of his troublesome friends, the reiters. This done, he turned his steps to Châtillon, lying sad and desolate by the Loing, gutted during the late war. But his stay there was brief. Accompanied by the young Princes and Louis of Nassau, he retired to the safer refuge of La Rochelle. There are few more interesting periods in his private life than the ten months which followed. They witnessed great changes in his family relations: the death in England of his elder brother, Cardinal Odet, whose remains now lie in Canterbury Cathedral; the marriage of his daughter Louise with the young Huguenot diplomatist, Teligny; and his own second marriage with the Savoyan, Jacqueline d'Entremonts. This latter, fired by the story of his heroism, had offered him her hand, and taken a perilous journey to seek him at La Rochelle. The wedding ceremony, which took place on the 25th of March, 1571, has a touch of the picturesque. After the bride and bridegroom had been conducted to the service by Joan of Navarre and her son, and the ceremony had been completed, the old war-worn Admiral fell on his knees before the young King. And the latter, taking a drawn sword from Montgomery, created him his knight; and Teligny buckled on him a pair of golden spurs, and placed a golden helmet on his head. And as a last touch, Henry with his own hands decorated him with the collar of the order "which the followers of Navarre now wear as of their supreme prince." [1]

It is worth remarking that the Catholic party throughout

[1] Modo che si tenne nelle cerimonie delle nozze dell' Amiraglio nel 1571 : Rome, Barberini Library, lviii. 12, fol. 143a.

Europe had followed this marriage with the closest attention. They believed that Coligny had chosen a wife in Savoy because her possessions at the door of France, Italy, and Geneva would offer an excellent centre for intrigue.[1] And therefore when Jacqueline wrote to her cousin on the 1st of December, 1571,[2] that her husband intended to visit her parents in the near future, the Pope expressed the liveliest anxiety, and warned the Duke of Savoy to be on his guard.[3] During this period, too, Coligny's share in the religious life of his time was very real. He corresponded with the foreign churches, participated in a Huguenot national synod, and saw the new college of La Rochelle grow under his eyes, with his own arms as well as those of Joan and Condé placed conspicuously above the main entrance, as a recognition of his liberality in founding various chairs.[4]

But even more interesting was his rôle as leader in what was to all intents and purposes a veritable republic. For the time being, La Rochelle was an *imperium in imperio*. Louis of Nassau's fleet swept the seas in search of the shipping of Philip II., with whom France was nominally at peace. Joan and Coligny negotiated with the Crown almost as equals, protesting vigorously against every infraction of the edict, demanding a readjustment of the burdens of taxation for meeting the claims of the reiters, and refusing to come to court until their demands were satisfied. In a word, the royal authority stopped sharply outside the walls of the city. Both sides were aware that this could not last. Happily, a ground of reconciliation seemed to offer in a common hostility to Spain. The Admiral was the inspirer of the policy. His hatred of civil war had risen to the heights of a passion. He was eager to give the people a new interest, to turn their gaze outward and away from brooding over ancient wrongs, the friction of daily intercourse, and the jealousy of family against family, class against class, town against town. All this might be done if he could only direct the immemorial instinct for martial glory against Spain — Spain, the persecuting power,

[1] Vatican, Nunz. di Francia, iv. 34.
[2] Turin, Roma Lettere Ministri, 6.   [3] *Ib.* (letter of 25th Feb., Rome).
[4] Barbot, *Hist. de La Rochelle*, Arch. Hist. de la Saintonge, xviii. 102.

his own inveterate and sleepless foe, and the one shadow on
his dreams of a new France over sea.   For his part, the young
King, Charles IX., though perhaps incapable of grasping so
intricate a problem, was fired by thoughts of conquest and the
extension of his frontier.   He had no doubt been cut to the
quick, too, by the contemptuous insolence of the Spanish
Ambassador.   With almost inconceivable irony, he had informed Charles that he had often mentioned to Philip what a
knight he was, and what a beard he had; but as yet he had
failed to announce that he clipped it![1]

As to Catherine—to her also Spain was the enemy.   As
a Florentine she hated that monarchy; as a mother she
was wounded by the rejection of her petitions for a marriage
alliance; as a queen she was galled by Spanish airs of
dictation and by the slaughter of Coligny's expedition to
Florida.   Nor was she without her ambitions.   And it was
difficult to find a more tempting prize than the rich and
populous Netherlands.   But above all, what she desired was
any policy which might give a chance of internal quiet.
When a special envoy, sent from Rome, protested against
the peace of St. Germain, she replied vehemently.[2]   She was
utterly sceptical of the theory that religion was in any way
bound up with the fate of parties in France.   And Charles,
no doubt inspired by her, declared to the Nuncio that not
heresy but private interests were at the bottom of all the
trouble.   The name of Catholic and Protestant were merely a
convenient cloak, adopted much in the same spirit as the
ancient party-cries of Guelph and Ghibelline.[3]   Catherine,
therefore, was willing to consider, though not necessarily adopt,
any course which offered.

This, then, was the policy which was taking shape during
the long months that Coligny waited in La Rochelle.   Its
chances of success were not diminished by a proposed double
marriage alliance, that commonest instrument of sixteenth-
century statesmanship.   Henry of Navarre was to wed
Margaret of Valois, while the Queen of England was to link

[1] Baumgarten, *Vor der Bart.*, 19.
[2] Turin, Francia Lettere Ministri, iii. (letter of Montfort, 5th Nov.).
[3] Philippson, *Deutsche Zeitschrift für Geschichtswissenschaft*, year 1892, p. 44.

her fortunes with those of the victor of Jarnac and Moncontour, the young Duke of Anjou, later Henry III. The reconciliation of French and English claims on the Netherlands and a common policy against Spain would then naturally follow. Such, in brief, was the trend of events. There were other variants of these schemes, now or later: for instance, the marriage of Elizabeth and Henry of Navarre, and a great league of Florence, France, and Protestant Germany against Spain. There was even a counter-proposal: France, Spain, and the Empire were to descend on Italy, and envelope Florence and the Papacy. But these plans never formed an integral part of French policy, though it seemed at one time as though Florence were about to throw herself definitely into the balance against Spain.

It was a pleasing prospect: a France pacified, national jealousies moderated if not forgotten, and a humiliated Spain. But it was a difficult task to harmonise the various interests. Catherine was profoundly suspicious of the Montmorencys[1] and their natural ally, Coligny; while he, for his part, dared not trust the court. The situation was succinctly summed up by Catherine in an interview she had with the Ambassador of Savoy on the 4th of November, 1570. She had a great desire, she told him, but little hope that the peace would continue. The cause of her anxiety was the Admiral. He saw that he was hated for what he had done, counselled, or permitted. He was well aware that he had gained the enmity of the paternal relatives of the two young Princes, by detaining these latter almost as hostages. The Queen of Navarre, too, had been far from pleased by his omitting to bring her son and nephew to her on his return from Burgundy. This being the case, Catherine added, he was afraid to trust promises, and, so long as this continued, he would be a storm-centre. She therefore begged that the Duke of Savoy should use his influence to bring about a better understanding.[2]

In the summer of 1571 things moved quickly. Coligny expressed a wish to be reconciled with the court and keep the Queen Mother in power. In July, Louis of Nassau had a

[1] Vatican, Nunz. di Fr., iv. 67 (Gaiazzo, 22nd Oct. 1570).
[2] Turin, Francia Lettere Ministri, 3 (Montfort, 29th Nov.).

secret interview with the King. On the 7th of August, Biron,
Teligny, Briquemault, La Noue, Gian Galeazzo, and the
Florentine Ambassador met to discuss a proposal of the
Grand Duke of Tuscany for immediate hostilities. But La
Noue, in this instance the mouthpiece of the Admiral, was
opposed to a move that year, and carried the meeting with
him. He pointed out that the Nassau Princes were exiles,
Catherine ill-disposed, Charles ix., William of Orange, and the
Huguenots without money, England unwilling to join, and the
season too far advanced.[1]

More successful was Coligny's visit to the court. It was
a pet project of the King, who intended it as an assertion of
his own authority and individuality.[2] Coligny fell in with his
views. His only conditions were that Joan should agree,
that Charles ix., Catherine, Anjou, and Alençon should
promise that he could come without danger and be welcome,
and that the King should order Damville, Marshal Montmorency, and Philip Strozzi to see to his safety.[3] There
was no lack of vaticinators, but his only reply was : " Better
die by a bold stroke than live a hundred years in fear." [4] His
entry into Blois on the 12th of September was shorn of all
display. The historic meeting with the King took place by
the bedside of the Queen Mother. Grouped round were the
Queen, Margaret of Valois, Cardinal Bourbon, and the Duke
of Montpensier. Here is the scene : " No one entered the
room with the Admiral but Marshal Cossé. When he had
twice made obeisance to His Most Christian Majesty, they
were seen to change countenance, both being pale. At the
third obeisance the King raised his cap aud embraced him.
The Admiral then said a few words into his ear. When he
advanced toward the Queen Mother, he was greeted with
more warmth, but without the usual kiss. Told by her to
make his reverence to her daughter, the Most Christian
Queen,[5] he fell on his knees and would have kissed her
hand, but she flushed and drew back and would never even

[1] Hauser, *François de la Noue*, 25.
[2] Pio Rajna, Archivio Storico Italiano, 1898, 100.
[3] Baumgarten, *Vor der Bart.*, 86.   [4] Brantôme, iv. 317.
[5] Elizabeth of Austria, wife of Charles ix.

have him touch her. . . . Since then he is to be found each
day at the rising of the King, as well as when he dines and
sups. At all hours he is close to his chair, and with the same
freedom as those who never left the court. And the King
reasons and discourses with him as he does with the rest, so
that it truly seems as though the past were buried in perpetual oblivion."[1] In fact, no sooner did Charles come in
contact with the stronger nature than he succumbed to its
influence. For Coligny was not only a dominating character;
he was also a warrior. And what this meant to the King
may be gauged by the lines written of him ten years earlier
when he was a mere boy: "Above all, he gives indications of
a preference for the things of war; of naught else does he
show a greater willingness to speak ; and for no other sorts of
men does he evince so great a fondness as for captains and
soldiers."[2] Thus all seemed to be telling in Coligny's favour.
But in reality success depended on Catherine. Five weeks
before his arrival at Blois, it had been remarked of her
that "she holds the poor King in such subjection that
he appears to be under a spell."[3] And until the 24th of
August 1572, though this influence was by no means steady,
and had its periods of fluctuation, in the end it always
made up the ground lost. In a word, it was the supreme
factor.

For a time the latent antagonism of Catherine did not
come to the surface. She had no wish to send the Admiral
back to La Rochelle. Though he studiously avoided pushing
his personal claims,—a fact which the Papal Nuncio instances
as a sign of his dissimulation and devouring ambition,—he
was granted the right of search for his stolen treasures of
Châtillon, and the benefices of Cardinal Odet were also be-
stowed on him for the space of a year. In the absence of the
King he presided at the Council. Many of the Huguenot
complaints were listened to and satisfaction promised.[4] The

---

[1] Paris, Bibl. Nat., filza 7, 294, 295. Another interesting account comes from the
Ferraran Fogliano, 14th Sept. (Modena Francia, 59) ; he no doubt had it from the
Card. of Este, who was present.

[2] Alberi, iii. 430.   [3] Paris, Arch. Nat., K. 1520, 43.

[4] For this and his reception at Blois see a letter of his : Paris, Bibl. Nat., 15553,
203.

cross of Gastines at Paris, which was especially offensive to
Huguenot sentiment, as commemorating the destruction of a
meeting-house and the execution of two of their number, was
removed. Yet danger-signals were not wanting. Catherine
had never more than played with the thoughts of war. The
great Spanish victory of Lepanto in October, and the failure
of negotiations for the marriage of Anjou and Elizabeth,
together with the growing influence of Coligny with her son,
made her regard it with still less favour. For in case of
defeat, as now seemed likely, she would lose all ; in case of
victory, the fruits would fall not to her but to the Admiral
as warrior and soldier. The Spanish representative at Blois
recounted a tale which, whether true or false,—the cryptic
phrase with which it closes suggests fiction or rumour,—interpreted the general opinion of the somewhat strained
relations between the two. It was to the effect that when
the King wished to consult with Catherine on questions
dealing with war, " the Admiral told him very politely that
they were not questions to be discussed with women and
clerks. When the Queen Mother heard of this, she was on
very bad terms with the said Admiral, as was also Anjou.
Someone asked her since why her son the King received the
Admiral so well and she so ill. Her reply was that they
knew what they were doing." [1]

In fact, Coligny was face to face with a powerful opposition.
Catherine was against him, and the Papal Nuncio insisted
that she favoured the marriage of Margaret with Henry in the
hope of dividing the latter from the great Huguenot chief.[2]
Anjou was against him, and Coligny's attempt to turn him
into a friend by offering him the leading rôle in a war with
Spain clearly failed. His proposal had been that when Louis
of Nassau, aided by French gold, had invaded the Netherlands
through Friesland and established himself, Anjou should lead
the final and victorious expedition.[3] Philip II., too, had
marked the Admiral down as the enemy. " Here," it was
reported from Spain on the 16th of November, " suspicion is

[1] Paris, Arch. Nat., K. 1524, 47.

[2] Vatican, Nunz. di Francia, iv. 126, etc.

[3] Baumgarten, *Vor der Bart.*, 99.

rife. It is perfectly well understood that the Admiral sleeps not, and that in the end every design will be turned against the states of the Catholic King."[1] When it was reported in Rome in the summer that negotiations were well advanced for the reconciliation of Henry and Coligny with the court, the Pope exclaimed that it was the worst news they could have brought him.[2] And the representatives of these two powers at the French court did their best to thwart Coligny at every turn. Montpensier, too, openly quarrelled with him. The Duke of Nevers bitterly attacked him in the presence of the King.[3] The young Duke of Guise, still unreconciled, was his most determined enemy, and begged to be left alone with him for a little while with a sword, when they would settle their differences without troubling His Majesty.[4] The court, in fine, was a mass of jarring factions, no three holding together.[5] Murder was of almost daily occurrence, and went unpunished.[6] Every event, in fact, was justifying the practical wisdom—we will not say morality—of the Admiral's plan of obtaining peace at home by war abroad. Even his bitterest enemies recognised its expediency. They only differed as to the object of attack.[7]

Toward the end of November, Coligny, who had already momentarily absented himself from court, retired to Châtillon. From odd letters come down to us we get an occasional glimpse of his life. There was no faltering. The loss of his brothers and Condé, the growing hostility of Catherine, the furious menaces of the Catholic faction, the hourly danger of assassination, the sum of his responsibilities as guardian of a cause hallowed by persecution, seem only to have deepened the fine repose of his nature. "If, Sire, it had not been for the promise I made your Majesty on leaving Blois," he wrote in ironical scorn of the threatening movements of the Guises at Troyes, "I should well have liked to have saved trouble to

---

[1] Philippson, *Deutsche Zeitschrift für Geschichtswissenschaft*, 1892, 116.
[2] Florence, Carte Strozziane, xxxii. 151.
[3] Turin, Francia Lettere Ministri, 3 (17th Oct.).
[4] *Ib.* (27th Dec. 1571). [5] *Ib.* (16th Feb. 1572). [6] *Ib.* (18th Dec. 1571).
[7] For instance, Gaiazzo after Lepanto urged Catherine to draw off the ill humours of the country by a crusade against the Turk : letter of 3rd Nov., Vatican, Nunz. di Francia, iv. 142.

those who were saying that they were coming to besiege me in my house by meeting them half-way."[1] In a different strain, more suggestive of the profoundly religious texture of his mind, he unbosomed himself to the ministers of the Church of Zurich. "I pray you, Sirs," he wrote, "that seeing how the Devil sleeps not in ill-doing, you may for your part be vigilant to defeat his designs and practices and remember me in your good prayers."[2]

As time went by, his prospects continued to improve. The Papal embassy of Cardinal Alessandrino, which arrived at the court early in 1572, with the intention of inducing Charles IX. to join the Holy League, of protesting against the toleration of two religions in France, and furthering the proposed marriage of Margaret with the King of Portugal as opposed to one with Henry of Navarre, proved a failure. In April three other events told strongly in his favour. The "Beggars," forced to quit the ports of England, made a descent on the Dutch coast at Brielle, and so opened the period of the freeing of the Netherlands. A defensive alliance was concluded with England, and with some prospect of stability now that Alençon had been substituted for Anjou as suitor for Elizabeth's hand. And lastly, the negotiations for the marriage of Henry of Navarre and Margaret of Valois took definite shape. Already a powerful fleet had collected at Bordeaux, "to go," as the first vague rumour had it, "to China, sailing by the Frozen Sea, which is found to be the shortest route, and which the English have been the first to try."[3] Its destination was then variously given as Scotland, the Portuguese Indies, Genoa, Spain, or the Netherlands. Catherine and Philip Strozzi were probably thinking of the conquest of Peru or some undiscovered country, while Coligny and Charles IX. favoured a descent on the Low Countries. In reality its ultimate goal depended on the course of events. In May, Louis of Nassau slipped north from Paris and seized on the important strongholds of Valenciennes and Mons.

This seemed of splendid omen. Even the recapture of

---

[1] Lettenhove, ii. 337 (letter of 13th Dec.).
[2] *Bulletin du prot. français*, xxii. 463 (letter of 13th Jan. 1572).
[3] Paris, Arch. Nat., K. 1525, 28 (9th Jan. 1572).

Valenciennes by Don Juan de Mendoça on the 29th of May,
though it is said to have sobered the Huguenots, was far
from causing a panic. Coligny had entered Paris the day
after Corpus Christi, that is to say, the 6th of June.
Meeting Philip Strozzi and Brantôme by chance in the outer apartments
of the royal château, probably the château of Madrid in the
Bois de Boulogne, "he started to walk with us and discuss
the affairs of Flanders, now going well, owing to the surprise
of the towns of Valenciennes and Mons which caused him the
liveliest joy. Then he spoke to us of our embarkation which
we were about to make in Brouage, and of the commands
which he had sent to all those within his jurisdiction as
Admiral to assist us in all things. 'God be praised!' said he,
'all goes well. Soon we shall have chased the Spaniard from
the Low Countries and made our King the master, or we shall
all die there, and I the first. And I shall not complain if I
lose my life in so good a cause.' And with this end in view
he was very eager that Strozzi should change his design of
going toward the Isles of Peru, and should make a descent by
sea on Flanders, while he himself would come by land. And
he said that if we could only arrange matters so, all would
turn out as well as one could wish." [1]

He had an even more important interview with his old
acquaintance, Henry Middlemore, on the 10th of June, six
days before the great banquet at which, as Admiral of France,
he feasted the Earl of Lincoln, come to receive the royal oath
to the new treaty. It affords a luminous view of Coligny's
policy, and, as related by Middlemore, contains one of the last
and fullest expressions of his opinion on record. Beginning
with a declaration of his devotion and gratitude to Elizabeth,
he turned to the question of Flanders. His wish was for
joint action. "Yow know, sayde he, how mightye the kynge

---

[1] Brantôme, iv. 297. De la Ferrière (*La Saint Barthélemy*, 63) seemingly places
this interview in July. We believe that it took place between Coligny's arrival at
court on the 6th of June and Strozzi's departure on the 8th (Salviati from Paris, 9th
June : Mantua, Arch. Gonz., 656 ; Gaiazzo from Paris, 9th June : Vatican, Nunz. di
Francia, v. 10–12), and at the château of Madrid, where the court was stationed
during most of June and July. Brantôme, however, incorrectly mentions the house
at St. Cloud, where Henry III. was assassinated, that is to say, the one belonging to
Jerome Gondi (Bayle, viii. 49, edit. 1820).

of spaigne ys, how rytche he is, and what an ennymye he is
to your state.   We also knowe the smale good-will he bearethe
us.   How daingerous a neighboure he maye shortlye growe
unto yow and us, yf he prevayle at this tyme in the lowe
contreys, we bothe maye easelye see.   He will not then
content him selffe with smale matters, nor yet with commen
amitye, but (having in his coffers the XVII millions of crownes
which he seakethe to leavy, and will leavye of the lowe
contreys, yf he be not withstode, togeathers with his other
supplyes from the Indes) will eyther gyve lawe to us and yow
bothe, or els make warre upon us, with such advantage as we
maye hardly sustayne.   His desseing in sight of the wisest
at this daye is to make him selffe monarche of christendome,
or at the least to rule the same.   How necessarye then it shal
be for yow and us to brydle that daingerous affection in him
is easye, me thinkethe, to be perswadyd, and never more easye
to be executyd then by the occasion presently offeryd of the
lowe contreys so greatlye garboylyd.   In the enterprisinge of
which matter, I doo wishe a resolute and determinyd order to
be sett downe and agreed on betwext bothe our princes, and
that suche, so perfect, certayne, and good intelligence maye
be had on bothe sydes, and so apt and mete ministers usyd
and employed with bothe parties, as all good, sincere, and
trewe dealynge might be assueryd, all gealousye, suspition, and
mistrust taken awaye and avoydyd.   Otherwise and withowt
this mutuall accorde and consent, yf we or yow or bothe shall
take in hand to attempt any greate matter that waye, lett us
assuer ourselffs that no good successe canne come therof.
Here he stayed and prayed me to speake my opinion.   I sayd
they were matters owt of my reache and farre from myne
acquayntawnce, and that I knewe least of hir majesties dis-
position that waye.   Neverthelesse he reaquyryd me by waye
of pryvate speache betwene him and me to speake that I
thowghte in the matter.   I sayd I colde only tell him of an
opinion commenly receavyd emongst us in england from the
beginninge of these cyvell warres.   We dyd desyer that
eyther prince might enjoye his owne, as well spaigne as
frawnce, and eyther state to stande in like propertion and
degree of governement as before, and not that the kynge of

spaigne shulde take any thinge from frawnce, or they any thinge from him, wherby any of them bothe might growe the greater and so prove a more daingerous neighboure to us of england. That we thowghte that god had alreadye made so good and even a division of these parts of christendome, settelynge them of longe tyme in the howsses and hands of them that presently dyd possesse them, as it shulde shewe very daingerous to every state to suffer the same any waye to be innovatyd or alteryd. That of all other things we colde least lyke that frawnce shulde commaunde flawnders or brynge it under theyr obedience, for therein we dyd see to apparawntlye the greatnes of our dainger, and therfore in no wyse colde suffer it. He confessyd I had reason to speake as I dyd, but sayd it was not now so ment in any sort, but that the Quenes majestie shulde have (yf it pleasyd hir to joyne with the kynge in that enterprise) as good a parte at the least in the same as the frenche kynge shulde have, and suche and so muche as reasonably she colde desier. And so he wolde undertake. He sayed further that there was inowghe for them bothe, and yf he dyd not thinke it for the Quenes greatnes, honor, and suertye, he protestyd he wolde never have openyd his mowthe in it; marye the only dainger was in the protractinge of tyme in lettynge slipp good occasion and in to late reasolvinge. And so ended that parte of his talke." Then expressing his great joy and gratification with the new treaty and league with England, he broached the subject of the proposed marriage of the Duke of Alençon with Elizabeth. And he not only expatiated on the desirability of the match, but on the fitness of Alençon : " He is of so good a nature, so wise, so vertuous, and so well stayed. I protest unto yow I think he will make as rare a prince as any is in christendome "[1] —an estimate of Alençon's character singularly falsified by later events.

Here, in the replies of Middlemore, we find one of the main obstacles which faced the Admiral : Elizabeth's unwillingness either to interfere actively herself in the Netherlands or allow France to interfere. Another difficulty, which Coligny conveniently ignored, was the personal appearance of Alençon.

[1] British Museum, Vespasian, F. vi. 89, 90.

JOAN, QUEEN OF NAVARRE

(*Clouet*)

Walsingham alluded to the subject a month later in writing to Burleigh. "To be playne with your Lordship," said he, "the only thinge that I feare in this matche is the consyderatyon of the delycasye of her majestyes eye and of the harde favor of the gentleman besydes his dysfygurynge with the smaule pockes: which yf she shoolde see with her eye, I mysdowbt mych yt woolde withdrawe her leekyng to proceade." [1]

The day before this interview with Middlemore, Huguenotism had suffered an irreparable loss. The heroic Joan of Navarre had died in Paris on the 9th of June, in the forty-fourth year of her age. "The Papalists," wrote Hohensax on the 23rd of June, "truly derive great joy from her death." [2] To few of the great leaders of the sixteenth century could be applied so truly the words of the Psalmist, which lose none of their beauty in their old French setting: "La mort des debonnaires du Seigneur est en estime envers luy." [3] The noblest tribute to her memory is from the pen of d'Aubigné, who speaks of her as "having of woman only the sex, with a soul given to things that rather become men, with an intelligence at home in great affairs, and a courage invincible in adversity." [4] On her deathbed she had confided her son to the care of the Admiral, and in her will, drawn up on the 8th of June, she had laid her commands on Henry to cherish in his turn the Admiral, in addition making a last appeal to him, with an earnestness which deserved better success, "to live all the course of his life according to the rule which God has mercifully given him in His Word, conforming his ways to it and never permitting himself to be turned aside an hair's breadth by the allurement of the ordinary pleasures and corruptions of this world." She could ill be spared. If she had lived, the events of the following August might have been other than they were. Catherine would have hesitated twice before murdering a woman, as she would also before sparing one, who could and would have exacted vengeance.

[1] British Museum, Vespasian, F. vi. 107 (13th July, Paris).
[2] *Jahrbuch für schweiz Gesch.*, 1876, iii. 108.
[3] This verse is prefixed to the work, *Brief Discours sur la Mort de la Royne de Navarre advenue a Paris le IX jour de Juin* 1572.
[4] D'Aubigné, iii. 291.

The burden of upholding Huguenotism now fell on Coligny alone. And it was therefore nothing less than a misfortune that he fell seriously ill. The plan of bleeding him twice was tried, with the usual consequences. His illness was all the more trying because war seemed imminent. Philip II. had countermanded his order for his great fleet at Messina under Don John of Austria to sail against the Turks. The Duke of Savoy's representative had strict orders to urge Catherine to keep the peace. Venice was working to the same end; within a few weeks she would be ready to despatch a special embassy. Florence, for long the hope of the Huguenots, was preparing to provide Alva with a loan. Salviati, the Papal Legate, arrived in Paris during the last week of June. To show his independence, he had abused Philip roundly before leaving Rome,[1] but that was all forgotten in face of the enemy. His instructions singled out Coligny for special attack. After detailing various objects of the mission,—namely, to exhort the King to enter the Holy League, and to protest against the marriage of Henry and Margaret and the despatch of a French Ambassador to the Porte,—they go on to declare that though a pacification may have been necessary, Catholics "cannot excuse the fact that the Admiral and his like have been made so bold that it is he, so it is said, who commands and the King who obeys. For he is a brain so unquiet that so long as he lives, his whole thoughts will be turned to causing sedition, sloth, war, and the ruin and destruction of the kingdom. And His Majesty should consider how the poor Catholics who have exposed their life and substance for his service now think and feel at seeing the Admiral exalted and favoured, who has been the cause of such loss, burnings, robberies, and ruin of churches and other buildings sacred and profane."[2]

At the court itself sides were evenly balanced. The Savoyan St. Pol gave an interesting sketch of how they were constituted in despatches of the 11th and 15th of June.[3] At the head of the war party was of course Coligny. On arriving at court early in June, he had tried to persuade

[1] Turin, Roma Lettere Ministri, 6 (letter from Rome, 13th June).
[2] Vatican, Pio, 231, 1.   [3] Turin, Francia Lettere Ministri, 3.

Charles to take the offensive. When he failed, he begged for
a cavalry escort for twelve companies of foot which he intended for the succour of Mons. And he solemnly warned the
King that he had to choose between war in Flanders or at
home ; meaning by this, as he explained later, that when Alva
had finished with the Protestants in the Low Countries, he
would infallibly turn his attention to France, the *fons et
origo* of trouble. In these efforts Coligny was ably seconded
by Huguenots such as La Rochefoucauld and Briquemault,
and by the leaders of the " Politiques," Damville and Cossé.
Nevers and Birague were also in favour of war, though
personally hostile to the Admiral. The opposition was
formed by Montpensier, his son the Prince Dauphin, Morvillier,
Bellegarde, and the Bishop of Limoges. Lansac and de Retz
were undecided, and the same may be said of Aumale and
Guise. They were afraid to declare themselves too plainly ;
to do so would be to turn the rumour into a conviction that
they were pensioners of Spain. Guise, especially, was in a
difficult position. On the 12th of May, he, with the rest of his
family, had finally signed a document accepting the decision
of the Council at Moulins of the 24th of January, 1566, which
declared Coligny innocent of the murder of Duke Francis.[1]
And when the Admiral came to court three weeks later, it was
decided that they should be formally reconciled, Coligny, as
inferior in dignity, first saluting the other.[2] Guise was thus
hardly able to carry on a vigorous opposition. Coming to the
royal family itself, the King was averse to active hostilities ;
for the moment the equivocal success of Louis of Nassau had
somewhat disillusioned him. The same may be said of
Catherine and Anjou. None the less, the former was in a
more neutral spirit than she had been earlier and was destined
to be later. The threats of the Duke of Alva[3] and the action
of the Spanish Ambassador had alienated her. She therefore
not only acquiesced in the necessity laid on France to arm, but
was unwilling fully to exercise her influence in opposing the
Huguenots.

---

[1] *L'Assassinat de François de Lorraine*, 153.
[2] Gaiazzo, 9th June (Vatican, Nunz. di Francia, v. 10–12).
[3] Letter of Catherine of 29th May : De la Ferrière, *La St. Bart.*, 52.

Matters, then, had arrived at this critical juncture when Coligny fell ill. Plans for succouring Mons were suspended. He was still in Paris on the 24th of June, the day Genlis arrived at the court from Mons to beg for aid for Louis of Nassau. Three days later we find him at Châtillon.[1] But he was back again in the capital in the first week of July.[2] About the same time[3] there arrived from England a young Huguenot gentleman of twenty-three, who had been lately travelling in the Low Countries. It was the young Duplessis-Mornay, a name destined to become a household word among French Protestants. When, therefore, " it was concluded in the Council of the King that all those called to consult whether there should be war or not should give their opinion in writing, as well the Marshals as Morvillier, the Bishop of Limoges, the Count of Retz, the Princes who were present, and the Admiral,"[4] the latter in collaboration with Mornay drew up a pamphlet for presentation to Charles IX.[5] It was a complete exposition of his views. After a preliminary mention of the pitiable state of the kingdom, it at once introduces the *motif* of French policy: the need of a war without in order to preserve peace within. This, it adds, has been the immemorial custom of statesmen when dealing with a warlike people, and it is well known how a Frenchman who has tasted of arms can with difficulty lay them aside, and how, often in gaiety of heart, when no enemy is to be found, he falls on his companion, even his friend. Yet such a war can only be defended on the grounds of its inherent justice, its usefulness and ease.

The enemy is the King of Spain. A struggle with him is just because he has massacred your troops in Florida, invaded the Marquisate of Finale for no other reason than to keep you out, filched from you your precedence at Vienna, and

---

[1] Coligny to Cecil, 27th June, from Châtillon : British Museum, Lansdowne, 14, 74.
[2] He attended a Council on the 6th : Vatican, Nunz. di Francia, v. 52.
[3] In *La Vie de Mornay*, by de Licques, and the *Memoires de Mornay*, by his wife, it is stated that Mornay returned from England to France at the end of July. A glance at the context will show that June should be read. Montmorency, to whom Mornay had attached himself while in England, arrived in Paris on the 7th of July : Brit. M., Vesp., F. vi. 82.
[4] Salviati, 16th July : Vatican, Nunz. di Francia, v. 63.
[5] As to the authorship of this pamphlet, see Appendix II.

tried to do the same at Rome; moreover, he is addressed as
"the King," as though he were the only one in the world,
while the aid he has given you in your civil wars was only to
weaken you and keep you occupied, waiting, Sire, but to see
your sceptre broken and your crown in pieces, in order to
collect the splinters and gather the leaves. If he should raise
the cry of being attacked while fighting the Turk, that is only
an old trick of his ancestors. A struggle with him is necessary,
for you have shown your inclinations by your reception of
Louis of Nassau and Genlis, and he will treasure this up
against you. And your Majesty should remember that the
first blow struck is equal to two. And, in declaring yourself, you
will not be making an enemy, but fighting one already made.
A struggle, too, with him is easy, for war is made rather with
iron than with gold, with men rather than with money. You
have a numerous, warlike, and experienced people. Spain, on
the other hand, sparsely populated and with so many diverse
interests, is inevitably—from a military standpoint—inefficient.
A host of her men are swallowed up in garrisoning Low
Country towns, and she is unable to draw on the nobility
there, as many are either banished or beheaded. The Indies,
also, are a weakness, as she is depopulated to hold them. As
for her fleet, it can do you little harm. And remember,
France has never been injured by Spain alone, but by Spain
in conjunction with England, Germany, and Italy. All that
is now changed. England is your ally and will be forced to
agree to your plans. Scotland cannot hurt us, because of our
ancient alliance, their hatred of the Inquisition, and the factious
condition of the kingdom. As to Germany, the Emperor and
the Catholic States will remain neutral, the one owing to fear
of the Turk, the others owing to their geographical position
and other causes; while the Protestant states offer to league
themselves with us. Then again, the Swiss are yours, the
Venetians neutral, Savoy neutral, Rome harmless, Florence
not ready to budge, Ferrara and Mantua friendly. Briefly
put, Germany and England are in your favour, and Italy
neutral, while Spain is depopulated by the Indies, her war with
the Turk, and distant garrisons.
     As to the financial question, your credit is good, hers bad.

And she can no longer draw on the Low Countries—especially in the way of a loan on Antwerp—for the " Beggars " hold the sea.   Then, too, the mines of the Indies have dried up.   On the other hand, war will cost you little, for the nobility, which provides the cavalry, will be practically self-supporting, while the expenses of the infantry will be little above what they are on a peace footing, as the war will to some extent pay for itself.   Then, too, the ecclesiastics, no doubt, will be liberal ; if not, the way of confiscation is open.

In beginning hostilities, we must concentrate, and strike at one point, and one only.   Evil fortune has dogged us when we have scattered our forces.   Where, then, is to be the theatre of war ?   Not Spain, where the mountainous nature of the country favours defence, nor Italy, rich with the blood spilt by us in vain.   It must be the Low Countries, where the people call you, and you have claims on Hainault, Flanders, and Artois.   But see to it that the army is large, so that the blow may be effectual.   It would be well to begin with the capture of a large town such as Bruges, for by showing mercy and restoring their privileges you would encourage others to join you.   But, as a preliminary, come to an understanding with the Prince of Orange, who has an army and is hailed as a liberator by the people.   Then make war as friend of the land and enemy of the enemies of it, avenger of tyranny, and restorer of liberty.   For if you would conquer well you must begin by the conquest of hearts—the rest is easy.   And lastly, war is inevitable—either now, when you are ready, or later, when Spain is ready.

The Catholic and anti-war case was drawn up by Jean Morvillier, Bishop of Orleans.   He remarked firstly that there was no proof forthcoming that Philip's subjects in the Low Countries had any desire to submit to Charles ; secondly, that, whatever French claims might be, Flanders and Artois were hostile ; thirdly, that the King could only hold those territories at vast expense, and that he would have to treat them worse than they were treated now in order to make both ends meet ; fourthly, that an attack on Spain would mean a long and bloody war ; fifthly, that Philip II. was wise, powerful, and rich, and one could hardly hope to do better now than Francis

I. and Henry II. against Charles V.; sixthly, that though William of Orange had an army, he had an empty treasury, and without money no army could march; seventhly, that it was unwise to aid subjects against their prince; eighthly, that Elizabeth was a broken reed, for, in case of hostilities, she would infallibly be bought off, while the German princes would remain neutral; ninthly, that war was ravenous of treasure which at the moment could not be found, for the country was ravaged, poverty general, and new taxes would cause trouble: even the nobles, who could not be taxed, were so impoverished that they could not horse themselves, while the King and the Huguenots were overwhelmed with debt; lastly, that when it was said that the country was full to overflowing with soldiers, he thanked God for it, but they must be made to obey the rule of law, and not provoke civil war: one could be certain that a King who could not govern his subjects in peace would have no better success with them in time of war. As to the contention that if France did not attack Philip now he would attack her later, Morvillier replied that it was impossible to read the future. All that was needed was to be ready.[1]

In considering the relative value of these two documents, it may at once be said that the work of Coligny and Mornay was one of the most brilliant political pamphlets of the times. Nothing could have been abler. It developed every argument which could possibly tell with Charles and his mother. At the same time it was the work of a statesman. Morvillier did well to point out its weak spots. Coligny undoubtedly underestimated the cost of war. The future attack of Spain on France was at least problematical; so was the action of Germany and England. Yet, viewed in the light of later history, Coligny was in almost every instance right and the other wrong. When France did interfere in the Netherlands, England did not come to terms with Philip. Spain did interfere in France. The army of William of Orange did march, though generally with an empty treasury. The French nobility were not so impoverished as not to be able to horse themselves, as twenty years of civil war was to prove. More-

[1] We have used an Italian translation of Morvillier's pamphlet, No. 705, p. 196, Corsini Library, Rome. We believe it to be correct.

over, the leaders in the Low Countries, such as William of Orange, were not, as Morvillier hinted, mere private persons who could not answer for communities. And again, France —now that the Low Countries were in revolt and the "Beggars" swept the sea—had much better chances than in the reigns of Francis I. and Henry II. But it is when we come to the question of the necessity of war to avoid civil strife that Coligny's justification is the most striking. It was all very well for an ecclesiastic with a legal turn of mind to talk of what ought to be, and of how subjects must be disciplined and brought under the rule of law. As a matter of fact, that had not been done and could not be done. Within two months of Morvillier's dictum, France was in turmoil, which lasted for a quarter of a century. And there can be little doubt that she would naturally have slipped back into chaos even without the impulse given by the massacre of St. Bartholomew. Coligny's policy was beset with dangers, but it at least offered some chance of escape.

Caution, however, in the person of Morvillier, carried the day. The Council decided against war, though the royal consent seems to have been given—covertly, it is true—to the succour of Mons. Catherine was either willingly neutral or did not care to risk a trial of strength at the moment. On the 12th of July Genlis left Paris. On the 16th he crossed the border. He had with him forty-two bands of infantry, —that is to say, about 4000 men and 800 horse. On the 17th he was annihilated by Fadrique de Toledo. 3000 Huguenots were wounded or lay dead. Many were slaughtered by the peasants. Not a hundred escaped. Genlis himself was among the 600 prisoners.[1]

[1] Baumgarten, *Vor der Bart.*, 201 ; cf. *Coleccion Doc. Ined.*, vol. lxxv. 56–59, and Vatican, Nunz. di Francia, v. 91.

CHAPTER XV

THE MASSACRE OF ST. BARTHOLOMEW

Coligny and Defeat of Genlis—Resumes Ascendancy over King—Return of Catherine—Council declares against Coligny—His Warning—Prepares Reinforcements for William of Orange—Catherine determines to rid herself of him—Huguenots assemble in Paris—Marriage of Henry of Navarre and Margaret of Valois—Coligny's Hopes ; refuses to doubt Good Faith of Charles—His Wounding—His Fortitude—Huguenot Indignation—Visit of the King—Catherine compels her son to order General Massacre—Massacre of St. Bartholomew—Death of Coligny.

THE defeat of Genlis ushered in the last stage of Coligny's life. It was the crisis. It led up to the massacre of St. Bartholomew by an inexorable chain of events. It put fresh heart into the opponents of war. It induced Catherine once for all to join the opposition. Already in April the Spanish representative had stated that her protestations of peace rang true.[1] Still she had hesitated, haunted by dreams of a new kingdom, worked upon by astrologers' tales, and shaken by the sentiments of the Montmorencys and a court faction eager for glory. With the disaster to Genlis, however, the risks of defeat were added to the risks of losing her influence over her son and in the Government. Henceforth she was a bitter opponent of war.

Coligny first heard of the disaster on the 21st. " Poor Genlis ! " he exclaimed, and then turned his attention to make good the loss. He must have fully recognised the enormous increase in his difficulties, yet he never wavered. It was even reported of him that he had told Gondi to let the Spanish representative know that should any of the prisoners be put to death, it would go hard with the Spanish in France and with him the first. Preparations, too, still continued. On the 27th

[1] Paris, Arch. Nat., K. 1526, 36.

he despatched Teligny to the King. On the 30th the latter arrived in Paris. Alva's insolence, and especially the report that he had wrung from Genlis a confession of Charles's complicity, threw the King into transports of fury. Coligny at once resumed his old ascendancy. " He was made absolute master of affairs, just as was the Constable in the time of King Henry; and so the whole court followed in his wake." [1] He was given a free hand. From eleven in the evening until two in the morning a secret Council was held, composed of the King, Coligny, Marshal Montmorency, and the four Secretaries of State.[2] War was generally held to be imminent, when suddenly, on the 3rd of August, Catherine reappeared on the scene. She had been recalled firstly by a letter of Charles, and later by an urgent summons of her creatures at court. She had gone to meet her daughter, the Duchess of Lorraine. On her return she did not take long to intimidate and shake the King. But he dared not tell the Admiral. He merely informed him that he would leave the decision to the Council. When Coligny complained that it would be composed of lawyers, who naturally abhorred war, Charles replied that he would only summon the Duke of Montpensier, the Duke of Nevers, Marshal Cossé, and one other. The meeting took place on the 6th of August, and was adjourned to the 9th. Coligny marshalled his facts with consummate ability; but it was of no use. The decision was uncompromisingly against a break with Spain. When he knew that he was beaten he made a last appeal to the King. " Your Majesty," he explained, " will not take it ill if, having promised the Prince of Orange every aid and favour, I attempt to keep that promise with such friends, relatives, and servants as I can, and even with my own person if the need arise. Then turning to the Queen, he said : ' Madam, the King refuses to enter on one war. God grant that another may not befall him from which perhaps he will not have it in his power to withdraw.' " [3] And with this ominous prophecy on his lips, which his enemies

[1] *Relazione* of G. Michiel : Alberi, iv. 284.

[2] Gar, *Instituto Ven.*, etc., 1870, p. 1843 ; cf. despatch of Salviati of 5th Aug., Vatican, Nunz. di Francia, v. 99.

[3] Alberi, iv. 285.

were not slow to interpret as a threat of civil war, but which he probably intended as a warning that Orange would be thrown back on France and it would need force to dislodge him, he set about organising fresh succours for the Netherlands. Gondi informed Cuniga that leave had not been given to Coligny to aid William of Orange. Nevertheless it is impossible to find any evidence that preparations already begun were discontinued. William wrote on the 11th: " I have to-day received letters from the Admiral, informing me that in spite of the rout and past defeats of the French, he is bestirring himself and preparing anew about 12,000 arquebusiers and 3000 horse." [1] The same day Walsingham spoke of him as one " whose mind is invincible." [2] On the 13th the Venetian Ambassadors reported that there were 3000 Huguenots on the frontier, who were to be reinforced by those who had assembled for the approaching wedding.[3] His chief anxiety was the rumour of England's withdrawal of her soldiers from Flushing.

Yet all this energy and resource, this imperturbable calm in face of defeat, was only bringing one step nearer the final disaster. The brain of Catherine was already busy, weaving deft plans for his destruction. " The dead do not make war," [4] a Spaniard exclaimed sententiously in 1568 of the imprisoned Egmont and Horn. In this phrase was contained a rule of state never long absent from the mind of the sixteenth-century statesman. It was a commonplace of Spanish and Italian politics, and it appealed with especial force to the crafty Italian Queen Mother, now that her enemy, by coming to Paris, seemed delivered into her hand. Assassination was to be her method of cutting the Gordian knot.

And now all France was crowding into Paris: Catholic and Protestant gentlemen, merchants, soldiers, German students, and Archers of the Guard, summoned " by sound of trump and public cry." [5] All that was stout-hearted and distinguished in Protestant France had come : the quick, the brilliant, sym-

[1] Van Prinsterer, iii. 490.   [2] Digges' *Compleat Ambassador*, i. 233.
[3] Gar, *Instituto Ven.*, etc., 1870, p. 1845.
[4] *Correspondence de Granvelle*, iii. 255.
[5] Mandement du Roy enjoignant à tous les archers de sa garde eux trouver la part où il sera dans le XXII jour du present mois de Juillet. À Paris, 1572.

pathetic Henry of Navarre; the more stubborn and sincere
Prince of Condé, heir of factious traditions and later the
dreamer of a new middle kingdom; the ill-fated Montgomery,
born to slay a king and end his life at the hand of the executioner; Pilles, the heroic defender of St. Jean d'Angely; La
Rochefoucauld, nephew of the Admiral, with his winning
manners, beloved of the King; the grave and chivalrous
Teligny; the Vidame of Chartres, negotiator of the hated
treaty of Hampton Court, who was to die like Montgomery,
a captive; Montclar, one of the "Seven Viscounts"; and
lastly, the Marquis of Renel, Lavardin, Guerchy, Caumont,
Briquemault, Beauvoir-la-Nocle, Puyviault, Berni, Soubise,
Bernard d'Astarac, Brion, Grammont, Duras, the two Par-
daillans, Charles du Bec-Crespin, Baron of Bourry, Beaudiné,
Montaumar de Rouvray, son of the Baron des Adrets. These
were some of the trusty band who upheld Huguenotism
during these years, and on whom St. Bartholomew was to
descend with its havoc of death. There were also some who
had yet to be tried: Mornay, La Force, d'Aubigné, and
Maximilien de Bethune, the future Duke of Sully, whose father
had predicted darkly that "if these nuptials took place in
Paris, the wedding favours would be very red."[1]

It was the eve of the marriage of Henry of Navarre and
Margaret of Valois. The former had entered the capital on
the 8th of July. From time to time it was rumoured that
the wedding would take place immediately. But the Papal
dispensation for which the court was hoping never came. The
result was that Navarre's uncle, Cardinal Bourbon, was
unwilling to perform the ceremony. The Queen, Marshal
Tavannes, Biron, all visited him, but he refused to move. At
last Villeroy brought him back with him to the Louvre, and
the betrothal took place on the 17th of August.[2]

The wedding followed on the 18th. It took place at six
in the evening on a dais raised before the door of Notre Dame
and hung with superb tapestries. The square and windows
were thronged with people, fed on the rumour that a dispensation had been granted. The Ambassadors alone were absent;

---

[1] *Œconomies Royales*, i. 10.
[2] Vatican, Nunz. di Francia, v. 113 (Salviati, 18th Aug.).

it had been thought better not to summon them owing to the attitude of two of their number, the representatives of Spain and the Holy See.   The young Princess came accompanied by the King, the Queen, the Queen Mother, Anjou, Alençon, the Guises, Nevers, the Marshals of France, and other great nobles.   Navarre had with him the Princes of Condé and Conty, Coligny, La Rochefoucauld, and a great suite of Protestant lords and gentlemen.   The Venetian Michiel confessed that the marriage far outshone in splendour those of her two sisters.   The jewellery, brocades, and dresses cost fabulous sums.   Geizkofler, who was present, declared that Margaret's crown alone was valued at 100,000 crowns.   After the ceremony Henry led the bride to the altar of the church, and then retired with his suite.

Such was the act which was to heal all divisions.   A royal coin was struck with the legend: "vobis annuncio pacem."[1] The historian de Thou tells us that after the Mass he entered the choir of Notre Dame and watched Coligny converse with his cousin Damville.   Then suddenly he saw him wave his hand toward "the flags of the battles of Jarnac and Moncontour, hanging on the church walls—sad monument of the defeat of their party!—and I heard him say these words: 'Soon shall they be pulled down from there and others put in their place, more agreeable to see.'"[2]

Such were his hopes—never to be realised.   Already there were strange rumours in the air.   From all quarters warnings had been streaming in against going to Paris and trusting the King.   La Rochelle and La Charité had pleaded with him and expressed their fears of Strozzi's fleet and Nevers' army.[3] He had been reminded of the fate of John Huss, of the unstable character of Charles IX., of the hatred and falsity of the Queen Mother—all to no purpose.   To show his confidence in the King, he had handed over the surety-towns in May, three months before the time of their surrender was due. He undoubtedly knew the risks, but he determined to take them.[4]   Mornay made a last appeal to him to flee the city,

---

[1] Ebeling, *Archivalische Beiträge*, 102.   [2] De Thou, iv. 569.
[3] Ehinger, *Franz Hotmann*, 118.
[4] Corbinelli, 8th Oct.: Archivio Storico Italiano, 1898, 78.

17

for " all good men were in great fear of these nuptials." But the Admiral replied, " I know well, my son, that the Queen Mother and the Duke of Anjou feel no good-will toward me, but the frankness with which the King does me the honour to speak to me, prevents me from having sinister thoughts of His Majesty. Moreover, I know the ills which are attendant on civil wars. If I retire, I shall at once be overwhelmed with calumnies. If I think of the welfare of the churches while the King shows me such favour, I shall be reproached with being carried away by ambition and as hating nothing so much as peace. This is why I am resolved to suffer all which it shall please God to send me."[1] It was in this spirit that Coligny lingered on. His cousin, Marshal Montmorency, more prudent than he, retired to Chantilly. On the 19th of August a Huguenot gentleman took leave of him with the pithy phrase : " I am going because of the good cheer they are giving you. I prefer to be classed with madmen than with block-heads ; you can cure the one and not the other."[2]

The 19th, 20th, and 21st were given over to banquets, jousts, and masquerades. It was only with Friday, the 22nd, that the court began to resume its everyday appearance. Between ten and eleven in the morning the Council was ended, and Coligny was in the act of quitting the Louvre when he met the King, who had been attending service in a little chapel opposite the eastern entrance. Charles was on his way to a game of tennis, and the Admiral turned back to watch him. Teligny, his son-in-law, the King, and the young Duke of Guise all took a hand in the play. After remaining for some time, he at last retired with a following of some twelve or fifteen gentlemen. The house he was then occupying, which belonged to the family of du Bourg, was in the Rue de Béthisy, next the corner formed by that street and the Rue de l'Arbre Sec—now the site of No. 144, Rue de Rivoli.[3] To gain it, he had to make a detour round the Hotel de Bourbon. He

---

[1] La Vie de Mornay, by de Licques, 18. [2] D'Aubigné, iii. 303.
[3] Henri Bordier, La Saint Barthélemy et la critique moderne, 36, etc. ; de Ruble, Mémoires de la Soc. de l'histoire de Paris, xiii. 15, 16 ; Henri Bordier, Bull. du prot. fr., xxxvi. 105 ; Mareuse and de Ruble, Bull. de la Soc. de l'histoire de Paris, xiv. 38.

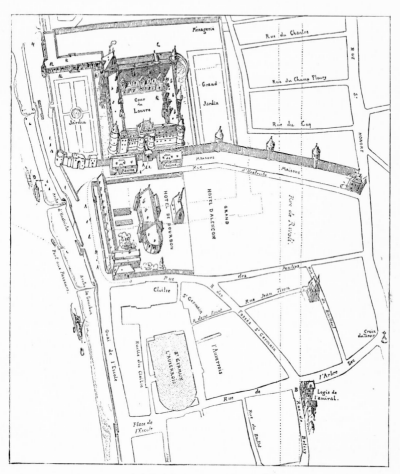

ENVIRONS OF THE LOUVRE, 1572

A—ROUTE TAKEN BY THE ADMIRAL, 22 AUGUST
a—SPOT WHERE THE ADMIRAL WAS WOUNDED
B—THE ADMIRAL'S LODGING

walked slowly, absorbed in reading a petition which had just been handed him. On entering the Rue des Poulies, he made a half - unconscious movement which saved his life. For, finding his overshoes troubling him, he hung back with the intention of either removing them or stamping them into place. Suddenly there was the report of an arquebus. He felt himself hit. But instead of receiving the charge in the breast, one bullet smashed his right forefinger, while the same bullet or another entered at the wrist of his left arm and passed out at the elbow. In a moment all was confusion. His followers were utterly bewildered. They were at a loss where to turn, what to do. Coligny alone was unmoved. " The shot came from the window where the smoke is," he cried, indicating a barred window of a house in the cloisters of St. Germain l'Auxerrois, which looked out obliquely on the street and was by design covered with a cloth. He was then half supported, half carried home. The assassin, meantime, made good his escape. Racing through to the back, he leaped on a horse which was in waiting, and galloped out by the gate of St. Antoine into the open country. He had been chosen by Catherine and Anjou for the deed, and had only failed by a hair's breadth. His name has been given variously as Bême and Peter Paul Tosinghi, both of whom took a prominent part in the final murder of Coligny, and Maurevel, the assassin of Mouy. Bême was indicated by the Florentine Ambassador Petrucci, and Peter Paul Tosinghi by the Venetian Michiel. The weight of evidence, however, points to Maurevel.

No sooner had Coligny arrived at his destination than the famous surgeon, Ambroise Paré, was sent for. This is how the author of the *Life of Coligny* described the scene in the sick-chamber: " He that was witnesse of the things insewing [1] did both see them and also hold up the Admiralles arme as he laye uppon his bed. The sayd Ambrose began his cure at the broozed finger, and did cut it of not without putting his patient to great peyne. For inasmuchas his pinsons were not sharpe ynowgh, he was fayne to open them thryce, and

---

[1] The author of the *Mémoires de l'Estat sous Charles IX.* identifies this witness, and we think rightly, with a gentleman named Cornaton.

thryce to grype them ageine togither. Afterward he launced
bothe the sids of his left arme where the pellets had perced
through : the peyne wherof the Admirall abode, not only
with a stowt corage, but also with a stedfast contenance. Yea
and wheras they that hild up his armes and behild those
launcings were not able to forbeare weeping : the Admirall
perceyving them too bee dismayd, sayd unto them. Why
weepe yee my freends ? I thinke my self blissed in suffering
these wounds for Gods name sake. And therewithall looking
uppon Merline a minister of God's word, my freends (quoth
he) these are Gods benefits. In deede I am full of peine : but
I acknowledge this to bee the will of our Lord God, and I
thinke [1] his majestie that he hath voutsafed me so greate
honour, as to lay somme crosse uppon mee for his most holie
names sake. Therfore let us pray him to graunt me the
gyft of perseverance. Then beholding Merlyne moorning and
lamenting. My Merlyne (quoth he) why dost thou not rather
comfort mee ? Yee say truth sir (aunswered Merlyne) nother
is there any greater or surer comfort for you, than to thinke
continually that God doth you greate honour, in demming
you worthye to suffer these greefes for his name and religions
sake. My Merlyne (replyed the Admirall) if God should
handle mee according to my deserts and worthynesse, and
deale with me according too his justice : I shoulde have farre
other manner of greefes too indure. But blessed bee his Name
for using his mercie and clemencie towards mee his moste
unworthie servant. . . . And when the same Merlyne told him
that the calamities and myseryes which happen too godly
men in this lyfe, do comonly stirre them up to pray unto
God the more earnestly, and quicken them up to reverence
Gods power : byandby the Admiral did burst out into these
words with a lowd voyce and vehement corage, saying : Lord
God, heavenly father, pitie me of thy mercie and clemencie,
and remember not the wickednesse of my former life. If thou
looke uppon our faults, and uppon our lightnesse and unfayth-
fulnes in breaking of thy Lawes, Lord who shall abide it ?
who shal be able to indure the force of thy wrath ? Setting
aside all fabulous Gods, I call uppon thee alone, acknowledging

[1] Thank.

and worshipping thee the eternal father of the eternal God Jesus Christ, Throwgh him I beseech thee to graunt mee thy holy spirit, and the gift of pacience. In thine only mercy do I trust. In that only is my whole hope repozed. Whither it be thy will to give me present death, or to prolong my life yit longer, behold, I protest myself to bee readie unto bothe: nothing dowting but that if I must die out of hand, thou wilt take mee out of hand intoo thy blessed and heavenly rest. And if thow suffer mee too continewe longer in this life, graunt me, O heavenly Father, that I maye spende the rest of my time, all wholly in spreading abrode the glorie of thy name, and in the reverencing and observing of thy most holy religion." [1]

Meanwhile, the Huguenots were running to the Rue de Béthisy from every quarter—with drawn swords, announced one authority.[2] When they had heard the details, they vented their feelings in threats and denunciations. Coligny's own suspicions were not calculated to calm them. In conversing with Damville and Cossé, he could think of no other as the possible instigator than Guise. So great was his followers' rage that they were eager to go to the Louvre and slay the young Duke on the spot. It needed all the influence of Briquemault to keep them back. Some of them even paraded before the Hôtel de Guise, shouting anathemas.

The King was equally moved. When he heard of the catastrophe he turned suddenly pale, and without a word went to his rooms. Catherine, who was about to sit down to table, retired also. Then the palace was cleared and the gates closed. Charles was not content with a merely passive attitude; he showed his sympathy in a very practical manner. He could not bear the sight of the Duke of Guise, who was almost universally suspected and was now secreted in the Louvre. When Navarre and Condé came to him, he assured them warmly that he would exact an exemplary vengeance, though he begged them not to carry out their threat of retiring from the city. He was equally cordial to Damville, who brought him a request from the Admiral to see him. He appeared in the Rue de Béthisy at two in the afternoon. He

---

[1] *The Lyfe of Jasper Colignie Shatilion* (trans. of 1576).
[2] Cavriana from Paris, 27th Aug.: Desjardins, iii. 812.

had already imprisoned the only two people found in the house
in the cloisters of St. Germain l'Auxerrois, which belonged
to a former teacher of Guise, and he was preparing to hand
over the examination of the whole affair to the First President,
de Thou. With him were Damville and the two younger
Montmorencys, Marshal Cossé, the Duke of Montpensier,
Cardinal Bourbon, the Duke of Alençon, and the arch-con-
spirators: Tavannes, de Retz, Nevers, Anjou, and the Queen
Mother. As the King entered, he ordered all of the Admiral's
household except Teligny, with his wife Louise, and another,
from the sick-chamber. Then approaching Coligny's bedside,
he greeted him warmly. The Admiral in reply assured him
of his unalterable devotion to the Crown, then—never long
able to keep his mind off the affairs of Flanders—he warned
him that there were traitors in the Council who divulged the
royal plans to the Duke of Alva, and finally appealed for a
stricter observance of the Edict of St. Germain, or " pacification," as it was generally called.

The King's reply was conciliatory, though he passed over
in silence the reference to the Low Countries. When Coligny
showed some warmth on the question of the suitability of the
commissioners chosen to enforce the edict, declaring that they
were the very men who had placed 50,000 crowns on his
head, the King interrupted him, begging him not to excite
himself unduly, for, said he, " the hurt is yours, but the
despyte is myne." He also requested the Admiral to name
those whom he would like to sit on the commission he was
forming to examine into the whole circumstances of the
attempt on his life. Then followed a conversation between
Catherine, Charles, and Coligny which the Huguenot who had
been left in the chamber was unable to catch. It probably
referred to the supposed share of the Duke of Guise in the
morning's work. Before leaving, the King expressed a desire
to have the Admiral removed to the safer lodging of the
Louvre, but the surgeons vetoed the proposal. Then came
the last incident. He asked to be shown the bronze bullet
which had caused the wound.[1] Here Catherine cynically

---

[1] The bullet was almost an ounce in weight, and had been found buried in the
wall: Cavriana, 27th Aug.; Desjardins, iii. 813.

intervened. "I am glad (quoth she) that the pellet is owt of his flesh," and she proceeded to illustrate her point, with conscious or unconscious irony, from the fate of the murdered Francis of Lorraine.

No sooner had the King left than the Huguenot chiefs assembled in a room under that in which Coligny was lying. Their object was to discuss the advisability of retiring from Paris. The Vidame de Chartres put the case for such a course with great eloquence. He exclaimed that no one could doubt that the event of the morning was the prologue to a tragedy. Teligny, however, opposed him hotly; he was willing to answer for the good intentions of Charles IX., and his views prevailed. A similar scene was witnessed the following day, which was Saturday, this time the minister Merlin taking the place of the Vidame de Chartres, and with a similar result. During Saturday, the King, still ignorant of his mother's and brother's plotting, sent frequently for news of the sufferer. Even the newly married Margaret of Valois came to visit him. Nevertheless, the Huguenots were becoming increasingly uneasy. Something mysterious was in the air; people and armed men were moving to and fro. What did it mean? Henry of Navarre, who with his cousin Condé had been demonstrative in expressing his concern, and had sent almost hourly for news, despatched five of his Swiss to the Rue de Béthisy. In addition, he gave secret orders to his followers to lodge in the quarter;[1] but only some of them came. The King also was entreated to provide a guard, and acceded readily. Anjou, who was by, suggested Cosseins, Colonel of the French Guards, the deadly enemy of Coligny; and so Cosseins, with fifty arquebusiers, was sent, and took up his position in the street and the surrounding buildings. From the very first he was aggressive. He interfered with free entry into the house; he refused to allow the cuirasses of Guerchy and Teligny to be taken to their owners. In consequence, there were hot disputes, which, however, were smoothed over. When night had

[1] *Lyfe of Jasper Colignie Shatilion.* The *De Furoribus Gallicis*, on the other hand, says the Huguenots were ordered to lodge in the neighbourhood of the Rue de Béthisy by command of Anjou; the *Dialogue* (first edition of *Reveille-Matin*) says by command of the King.

come, Guerchy and others begged to be allowed to sleep near the Admiral. But Teligny, blind to all danger, affectionately dismissed them. Then he and his wife Louise retired to a house adjoining, and Coligny was left with the five Swiss of Navarre, Labonne, Yolet, the Admiral's Master of Horse, Nicolas Muss, his German interpreter, half a dozen servants, and three others, who eventually escaped through a window in the attics: the surgeon Ambroise Paré, the minister Merlin, and a Huguenot gentleman named Cornaton, who later furnished Hotman, the author of the *Life of Coligny*, with an account of the events of the 22nd to 24th of August.

At midnight the Rue de Béthisy was silent and deserted; only Cosseins and his fifty arquebusiers were awake and waiting. Catherine was now ready. Her failure to murder Coligny on the 22nd had driven her to the plan of a general massacre. As we read over the scenes of the 22nd and 23rd of August, we are struck by the deadly certainty with which the Huguenots plunged to destruction. An inextricable net of circumstances was gathering them in. Their ill-considered threats, springing from a generous anger, their splendid devotion to their chief and anxiety for his safety, their blind confidence in the word of an unstable king, all dovetailed into Catherine's suddenly conceived plan for their extermination. She had already begun to plot on Friday. Three of the conspirators were, like herself, Italians: Louis of Gonzaga, Duke of Nevers, the Count de Retz, and Birague. Another was the half-Italian Duke of Anjou; the one purely French name was that of Marshal Tavannes. It is easy to dissect the motives of her policy. She was disappointed that Alva was not suspected of originating the attempt on Coligny's life, as she had hoped; she was dismayed at the thought of the crime being brought home to her; she was goaded to desperation by the threats which had been launched against the unknown instigator; she was tormented by the fear of a Huguenot exodus from Paris; she was resolved to prevent a struggle with Spain; and lastly, jealousy tortured her and a devouring hatred of a great rival with whom she was determined never to share the government. Whatever happened, Coligny was not to be allowed to escape; he and his followers were to be swallowed up together. Late on Saturday Catherine entered the King's private room, either alone, as Corbinelli related, or accompanied by the Duke of Anjou.[1] She urged him to a massacre. She begged him to rid himself once for all of this insubordinate sect, now that he had them in his grip. Coligny had done his best to force him into a foreign war; his followers would now surely seek revenge for his wound; one feasible course only was open: it was to anticipate them! Charles resisted her importunities for an hour and a half—vainly. He appealed to his honour, his word. But he was weak, rudderless, shifty; Catherine wore him down. She threatened to leave the court; she insisted, and brought in others to witness, that the Huguenots were already plotting; the figment was built up on the supposed revelations of the Huguenot Bouchevannes, who had reported faithfully to Catherine all that had gone on at the secret meetings of the Rue de Béthisy. With this the last spark of the King's reason and better nature went out. He was seized by an ungovernable fury. There was no longer any need to hound him on.

Marcel and Le Charron, the former and present Provost of the Merchants, were called in to organise the mob and citizen soldiery. The royal commands were that in each house there was to be an armed man provided with a torch and white kerchief tied round his left arm, while a light was to be placed in each window. To Guise was entrusted the supreme task. He was to slaughter the Admiral. Similar work was to be done by other distinguished Catholics. Condé, Navarre, Grammont, Bouchavannes, and a few others alone were to be spared.

Many of the Huguenot gentlemen were with the King until a late hour. Moved by a last impulse of pity, Charles tried to keep by him his friend and intimate, the gallant La Rochefoucauld, but he laughingly took his leave with the rest. A little before midnight Catherine entered the King's apartment. The hours went by. The signal was to be given at dawn by the bell of the Palais de Justice. But the Queen

---

[1] Margaret of Valois relates that Gondi first approached the King; it may have been so, but it is remarkable that four of the most dependable witnesses—Anjou, Corbinelli, Michiel, and Cavalli—never allude to it.

Mother, driven by a demon of impatience, doubtful of the
constancy of her son, could not wait. It was now after
two in the morning, perhaps even as late as between
three and four. The guard had already begun a fracas
with the Huguenots, who had been roused by the noise
of hurrying feet and the flash of lights, and had sallied
out to discover the cause. Quick to seize her opportunity,
Catherine induced her son to give the order to sound the
alarm with the bell of the church of St. Germain l'Auxerrois,
opposite the palace gates. This was the tocsin of St. Bartholomew.

It was dark, though Paris was stirring like a drowsy bee-
hive, as the Duke of Guise set out from the Louvre for the
Rue de Béthisy. He had with him the Duke of Aumale, the
bastard Angoulême, and a band of French and Italian gentlemen. Cosseins knocked at the gate; Labonne ran with the
keys, and, being informed that there was a message for the
Admiral from the King, threw it open. With a sudden movement Cosseins grasped him with one hand and plunged his
dagger into him with the other. Then the Catholics rushed
pell-mell into the courtyard. A few of the servants were
slain, but the Swiss, rushing back, closed the inner door, and,
aided by Cornaton, barricaded the staircase. Aroused by the
noise, Coligny knew that his end had come. Too weak to
rise, he was lifted from his bed and dressed simply in his
gown. In the room itself Merlin was praying; on the staircase the din was increasing: Cosseins was breaking through.
Then the Admiral, " calling upon Christ our God with vehement
sighing, fell to commending of his spirit intoo his hands, which
he had received of God to injoy." Suddenly Cornaton rushed
in with the intelligence that there was no way to withstand
the assassins. Coligny was unmoved. " As for mee (quoth
the Admirall) I have prepared myself untoo death afore hand."
Then turning to his followers, with supreme self-forgetfulness
he entreated them to save their lives—his they could not save.
And so they left him, carrying with them the memory of his
grave and untroubled countenance. Nicolas Muss alone remained—faithful to the last.

The barrier was now broken through. One of the five

Swiss had fallen. Their Catholic fellow-countrymen hesitated to murder the rest, but Cosseins insisted. At last one of them was shot dead, and the band of assassins, surging up the staircase, burst into the sick chamber. Nicolas Muss was slaughtered on the threshold. The light was dim; the dawn as yet was scarce filtering through. Coligny stood by his bed, waiting for death. His assailants hung back, when Martin Koch, a Swiss, stepped forward and struck him with his battle-axe. Bême or another dealt him the second blow; another Swiss, Conrad Bürg, the third. At the seventh he fell against the chimney. Besides the wounds from swords and battle-axes, he seems to have been pistolled as well. Running to the window, they cried out that he was dead. Those below, sceptical to the very last, demanded proof. Whereupon their friends in the room—Tosinghi or Petrucci, Bême or Sarlabos—took him in their arms to throw him down. But the body, gaping with wounds, still resisted, clutched at the casement, then fell at the very feet of Guise. The face was horribly disfigured. Guise—so Hotman in his *De Furoribus Gallicis* alleges; Angoulême according to de Thou—to make certain, wiped away the blood from the features. With that they dispersed in search of a new victim, the redoubtable Montgomery.

For three days Paris was swept by a hurricane of death. No one was safe. Neither age, nor sex, nor nationality was spared. Catholics ran through the streets crying kill, kill, and drunk with slaughter. Huguenots, in the last ecstasies of fright, fled half dressed, on horse, on foot, how they could, seeking vainly for shelter. Fathers fought desperately, pistol in hand, clutching their children. Men and women died heroically rather than renounce their faith. Some tried to escape by wearing the Catholic badges of a white cross in the cap and a kerchief on the left arm, but as often as not they were recognised, or could not give the password. It was enough to cry "There is a Huguenot!" to have a fresh victim. Sometimes a house held out stubbornly; when it was carried, it was pillaged and the defenders massacred. Those who threw themselves into the river were chased and slain also. The Catholic leaders rode about the streets with artillery, infantry, and 800 horse. "Everywhere," wrote Father Panicarola enthusiastically to Rome, "we have seen rivers of blood and mountains of dead bodies."[1] With equal elation the Papal Nuncio, Salviati, described how "nothing is to be seen in the streets but white crosses in hats and caps, of all indifferently, and a beautiful sight it is."[2]

Few of the leaders escaped. Montgomery, however, with the Vidame de Chartres and some others who lived in the Faubourg St. Germain, managed to get away. Guise, who evinced an unexpected humanity, and subsequently the King, saved some others. But in the first flush Charles was deaf to the promptings of pity. When the tocsin was sounded, Navarre and Condé were at once summoned to the royal presence. "Turn out all these scoundrels," he cried, indicating Pilles and the rest of Navarre's following. Whereupon they were thrust out and massacred below almost to a man. Those who had been attracted to the neighbourhood of the Louvre by the stir and bustle were slaughtered mercilessly. An Italian relates that, passing by the château early on Sunday morning, he saw a dozen of the leading Huguenots dead or dying ; two days later another counted more than forty stretched stark and naked on the ground. La Rochefoucauld greeted the brother of Chicot the jester and his masked assassins smiling ; he thought they had come to play a jest on him. Teligny, who escaped by the roof, was eventually despatched with daggers. Not even the inoffensive and distinguished savant, Peter Ramus, nor the lawyer La Place, was spared. "Scrivere le particularità," wrote Corbinelli, who realised more fully than his fellow-Italians the lamentable nature of the scenes he was witnessing, "scrivere le particularità più notabili non è possibile : ὀλοὰ λέγειν, ὀλοὰ δ' ὁρᾶν."

Meanwhile, the body of Coligny lay in the courtyard of his house in the Rue de Béthisy. It was the object of every insult and indignity—kicked, spat upon, mangled—by the passers-by, among whom the women distinguished themselves by their vile inhumanity. From here—so de Thou relates—it was removed to a neighbouring stable. On the 25th the people were cheered by a miracle ; all Paris crowded to the

[1] Vatican, Armadio, 64, 31.　　　　　[2] Theiner, i. 329.

cemetery of the Innocents to gaze on a hawthorn which had flowered suddenly and out of season. Some of them on their way back, fired by religious fanaticism, came to where the dead Admiral lay, and, putting a halter round his neck, hauled him off in triumph to the Seine. Here he was thrown in and pulled out again. The remains—the right breast and arm and the left hand had been hacked off, and the head severed from the body, a present, so it was alleged, for the Pope or Savoy or Spain; and there were other mutilations—were then dragged through the mire to the gibbet of Montfaucon, where they were hung in chains, head-downwards, a prey, as a Florentine remarked, for crows. And there they remained many days, until some servants of the house of Montmorency removed them secretly by night. Now, after three centuries, they find their final resting-place in the château of Châtillon. " On a stone slab, eight feet high by twenty inches broad," wrote Walter Besant, " is an inscription which is here reproduced in full."

Les précieux restes de
l'AMIRAL GASPARD DE COLIGNY,
recueillis après la Saint Barthélemy
par les soins du Maréchal de
Montmorency son cousin furent,
lors de la réhabilitation de
l'amiral qui eut lieu par lettres
patentes du Roy Henri IV données
le 10 juin 1599, successivement déposés
à Chantilly, à Montauban,[1] puis à
Châtillon-sur-Loing duché dépendant
de l'apanage de la maison de Coligny
transférés en 1786 à Maupertuis
dans un monument élevé en son
souvenir par M. le marquis de
Montesquiou, retirés ensuite de ce
monument en 1793, ils ont été conservés
par sa famille jusqu'en 1851, époque
ou M. le comte Anatole de
Montesquiou en a fait la remise à

---

[1] Becquerel, in his *Souvenirs historiques sur l'Amiral Coligny*, p. 33, says that Coligny's remains were taken from Montauban to Holland, where they remained in the possession of his daughter Louise, Princess of Orange, until brought back and deposited at Châtillon by his grandson Henry ; cf. d'Aubigné, iii. 318.

M. Charles-Emmanuel-Sigismond de
Montmorency-Luxembourg, duc
de Luxembourg, de Piney, et de
Châtillon-sur-Loing, ancien
pair de France, capitaine des gardes
du corps des Rois Louis XVIII
et Charles X, qui pour honorer la
Memoire de l'amiral de Coligny,
a déposé le 29 septembre 1851 ces
dépouilles mortelles dans les ruines
du château (Duché de Châtillon-
sur-Loing) à l'endroit même ou
l'amiral a pris naissance dans le
séjour objet de son affection.

Ici reposent
les restes de
GASPARD DE COLIGNI
Amiral de France,
Tué à la Saint Barthélemi
le 24 Août 1572.[1]

---

[1] The above corrected form has been kindly supplied to me by the authorities at Châtillon, who add that the original in the château of Châtillon is all in capitals.

CHAPTER XVI

PROBLEMS OF ST. BARTHOLOMEW

Arrival of the News in Rome—Papal Enthusiasm—Gregory XIII. and Philip II. ignorant of Catherine's Plans of Assassination and Murder—St. Bartholomew not long premeditated ; Plan to assassinate Coligny of first Ten Days of August ; Plan of General Massacre of 22nd to 23rd August—King ignorant of Plan to assassinate, but 23rd August consents to General Massacre—Was there a Huguenot Plot ? Reasons against—Minor Problems.

THE news of the massacre of St. Bartholomew spread like wildfire. No sooner had letters, written in Paris on the 24th of August, reached Lyons on the 27th, than the secretary of Mandelot, the Governor, sent off post-haste to a friend in Rome, acquainting him with the facts and entrusting him with the mission of informing Gregory XIII. The account which had been received was to the effect that the Admiral had been wounded in the shoulder and had subsequently died, and that, when the Huguenots, in consequence, had begun to assemble and seize their arms, the Catholics had fallen on them and slain the principal leaders, Montgomery alone escaping. The special courier, sent from Lyons with this intelligence, also carried a despatch of the 22nd for the Cardinal of Ferrara from his agent in Paris, and another for the Cardinal of Lorraine from one who had actually seen Teligny dead. Travelling at great speed, he arrived in Rome on the 2nd of September, that is to say, nine days after the massacre. The friend of Mandelot's secretary at once informed the Cardinal of Lorraine, and was by him presented to the Pope.[1] The latter could not contain

---

[1] These details are from Florence, Arch. Med. 3291, 32 (Francesco Gerini, Rome, 4th Sept.) ; Vatican, Urbino, 1043 (Advices from Rome, 3rd Sept.) ; *Copia di una lettera venuta novamente da Lione*, printed in Florence, 1572.

his joy. He was eager to illuminate Rome, but the French Ambassador, Ferralz, refused to countenance any public rejoicing until he had received official information, and was looked at askance in consequence. The Pope had thus to content himself with a gift of a thousand crowns to the Lyons courier, to which the Cardinal of Lorraine added another two hundred. Further news filtered through from Savoy. But as yet there was nothing official from Paris. Early on the 5th, however, the long-deferred despatches of the Nuncio arrived. Though still dark, the Cardinal of Como at once informed the Pope, in order, as he said, to relieve him from suspense. That morning a consistory was held; "therefore his Holiness, wishing to impart such fortunate news to the Sacred College, had the letters publicly read, and he himself gave a discourse on their substance, concluding that one could not desire better nor greater news in these times so full of turbulence, and that God seemed to be beginning to turn His pitiful eyes upon us. And his Holiness and all the College received great consolation and were full of gladness at the reading of this intelligence. . . . That same morning, when the consistory for giving the cross to the Legate was over, his Holiness, with the whole College of Cardinals, went to the church [1] of St. Mark to sing the Te Deum and thank God for so signal a favour shown to Christian people." [2]

The same day, Beauville, nephew of Ferralz, arrived with a simple letter of credence written by Charles IX. to Gregory on the 24th of August, and another addressed to Ferralz, explaining that the massacre had been caused by the hatred between Coligny and the house of Guise, and by the late attempt on the Admiral's life. [3] Beauville was warmly received, and the Pope in conversation with the uncle on the 10th exclaimed that the events of the 24th of August were

---

[1] Ferralz in his despatches always calls it the chapel of the palace of St. Mark. In fact, Paul II. had included the original basilica of St. Mark in his new palace of that name (Gregorovius, VII. 642).

[2] Cardinal of Como to Salviati, Rome, 8th Sept.; Philippson, *Deutsche Zeitschrift für Geschichtswissenschaft*, 1892, p. 135.

[3] On the same or following day the version of the massacre which ascribed it to a desire to anticipate a Huguenot plot on the King's life was known in Rome.

more agreeable than fifty victories of Lepanto.[1] On the
evening of the 5th or 6th the guns of the castle of St.
Angelo were fired, and the illumination of the city only
ceased with the 8th. On the same day a still more striking
manifestation of Papal satisfaction was a solemn procession
from St. Mark's to the French church of St. Louis. The
Pope was on foot, accompanied by all the Ambassadors and
thirty-three Cardinals pontifically robed. The crush was great.
For two hundred yards round the church there was a sea of
people. Above the principal entrance was hung a cloth of
purple silk, decked out with ribands and festal garlands, and
shining in letters of gold was a Latin inscription composed
by the Cardinal of Lorraine. In rounded and high-sounding
phrase it told of the joy of Charles IX., the Most Christian
King, who, burning with zeal for the Lord God of Hosts, now
that the heretics and public enemies had been suddenly cut
off as by an avenging angel, augured well from this happy
success, and, joining his prayers to theirs, was present in
spirit in this the church of his ancestor St. Louis.[2] The
author, it was noted, was in a gay and self-confident humour.
To another French Cardinal, the notorious Pellevé, fell the

duty of chanting the Mass, while the choir broke out in the
triumphant strains of the 21st Psalm. A few days later a
solemn jubilee was proclaimed. A Papal medal was also
struck to commemorate the massacre. And though in the

---

[1] Paris, Bibl. Nat., 16,040, 192 (Ferralz, Rome, 11th Sept.).

[2] La Mothe-Fénelon, vii. 341. Other copies, with slight differences of phrasing,
are in the Barberini Library (lviii. 12, fol. 146) and the Medici Archives in Florence
(3291, 32).

18

month of September the Nuncio, Salviati, had specially reported that no Huguenot conspiracy had ever existed, the painter Vasari was set to work on the walls of the Vatican. His frescoes are to be seen to-day in the Sala Regia. They represent the wounding of Coligny on the 22nd of August with an avenging angel appearing in the sky, his body being thrown from a window on the 24th, and the presence of Charles IX. and his brothers in the Parlement on the 26th.

Such, then, was the manner in which Rome hailed the massacre. To express joy over a fallen enemy—butchered though he may have been—seemed both natural and right. It was only later apologists who showed and continue to show nervousness as to the Papal attitude. Yet, in spite of subtle reasonings, the broad facts remain : the Vatican was aware of the horrible cruelty exercised against the heretics ; it is impossible to point to one word of disapproval in any letter or document despatched from Rome ; on the 2nd of September, when details were as yet too scanty to pretend to any knowledge of the justice of the massacre, Gregory XIII. was eager to illuminate the city ; and he allowed Vasari to decorate the Sala Regia, though he had been informed by his Nuncio that the suggestion of a Huguenot plot was a pure figment. If a defence of the Roman Curia is deemed necessary, it must be conducted on quite other lines. Its best excuse is that it was aware that the success of Huguenot policy entailed the failure of the crusade against the Turk, and would produce a great European war. Its apologists, too, may fairly claim that it sincerely believed in Coligny's guilt as instigator of Poltrot ; while to the crime of heresy his followers had added that of ten years of rebellion. Then, again, the Protestant world itself showed a callous disregard, on occasion, of the means by which a tyrant could be removed. It is doubtful whether the bulk of Huguenots sincerely disapproved of Poltrot's murder of Francis of Lorraine. It is certain that it was only the influence of Mornay which restrained the Protestants of La Rochelle from greeting the assassination of Henry of Guise with the lighting of bonfires. But in spite of all that can be pleaded on her behalf, Rome remains gravely compromised. Perhaps the severest commentary on her action was the detestation of the massacre expressed by French Catholics. Hotman, Walsingham, and Languet all bear witness to its sincerity. Morvillier and de l'Aubespine did not try to hide their feelings. Some of the governors and towns exercised a real humanity. No one brought out more unsparingly all the horror of the massacre than the Catholics Corbinelli and de Thou. English Romanists, Zuniga, the Emperor, joined in a chorus of disapprobation. In fine, the action of the Roman Curia fell far below the best ethical standards of the time. In the words of Lord Acton, it was only in Spain and Italy, where hearts were hardened and consciences were corrupted by the Inquisition, in Switzerland, where the Catholics lived in suspicion and dread of their Protestant neighbours, among ecclesiastical princes in Germany, whose authority waned as fast as their subjects abjured their faith, that the massacre was welcomed as an act of Christian fortitude.

This brings us to the question: did Philip II., Pius V., or Gregory XIII. know beforehand of any plot to massacre the Huguenots? The answer is, in our opinion, unhesitatingly, No! We believe that the studies of Baumgarten and Philippson,[1] based on a careful examination of the despatches of the Spanish and Venetian Ambassadors and Papal Nuncios, are quite conclusive on this point. It is impossible to reproduce their arguments here. Suffice it to say that they show, with a wealth of detail, that Spain and the Papacy entertained the profoundest suspicion of Catherine's policy to the very last. They again and again appealed to her to keep the peace. This, of course, would have been absurd if they had known of any plan to get rid of the war-party. So fearful was Philip II. that France, impelled by the Admiral, would take the offensive, that as late as June, 1572, he countermanded his order for the fleet to sail against the Turk. In August, Gregory proposed a league with the Emperor and Venice to prevent a Franco-Spanish war. We do not suggest for a moment that Spain had not thought of the expediency of a massacre. On the contrary, on the 5th of August, the Papal Nuncio at Madrid reported that the King had remarked that

[1] *Vor der Bartholomäusnacht*, and *Die römische Curie und die Bartholomäusnacht.*

Charles IX. had his chance, now that the Admiral was in
Paris. Such, no doubt, would have been Philip's own policy;
but he did not suggest for a moment that it was Catherine's.
He certainly had no reason for thinking so, for when, in
February, 1570, his Ambassador had hinted that it would
be advisable to make away with Coligny and Montmorency,
she told him never to let her hear of such a proposal again.
And in July, 1572, she informed the Venetian Ambassador
that severe measures were impossible, adding that they had
been largely accountable for the unrest in the Low Countries.

Another problem which is intimately connected with the
massacre, is the question of its premeditation. It is generally
admitted that Catherine had several times—for instance, in
1563—considered the feasibility of Coligny's assassination.
But those most willing to grant this are the first to reject
the theory of the premeditation of the actual massacre of the
24th of August. Some writers, however, have affirmed that
the interview of Bayonne in 1565 and the massacre of St.
Bartholomew stood in the relation of cause and effect. " Hic
fructus est," wrote Sturm on the 10th of September, 1572,
" Baionensis conspirationis."[1] At the latter, so it was
maintained, Catherine agreed with Alva to exterminate the
Huguenot chiefs, and was only waiting for her opportunity
during the following seven years. But this theory has been
seriously undermined by the criticisms of de la Ferrière and
the later investigations of Erich Marcks.[2] They utterly deny,
and we believe with justice, that any such compact was ever
made. A more plausible theory was that the massacre of
St. Bartholomew was premeditated at least some time in
advance. This was the opinion of Lord Acton, whose article
was an able summing up of the materials actually at hand.
But he had no acquaintance with the bulk of the Spanish
papers, and only knew of the correspondence of the Nuncios
by a few stray despatches published by Mackintosh and
Theiner. It is just here that the work of Baumgarten and
Philippson is so useful. The latter insists that the plan to

---

[1] Ebeling, Arch. Beiträge, 216.

[2] L'Entrevue de Bayonne (*Revue des Q. Hist.*, vol. 34); *Die Zusammenkunft von Bayonne.*

assassinate the Admiral only took definite shape in the first ten days of August, while both agree that the massacre of St. Bartholomew was a sudden inspiration of the 22nd and 23rd, flowing naturally from the attempt on Coligny's life. A still later writer, Pio Rajna, in his comments on the letters of Corbinelli, is of the same opinion. Their arguments may be summarised as follows. Firstly, the peace of St. Germain in 1570 was sincere, and was concluded by the court without any *arrière pensée*. Secondly, Charles IX. induced Coligny to come to Blois in 1571, not with any desire to have him at his mercy, but rather to show his independence and escape from the maternal leading-strings. Thirdly, the court had agreed to hold the wedding of Henry of Navarre at Blois, and it was only in order to meet the wishes of Margaret of Valois that Paris was substituted,—a fact which disposes of the theory that the marriage in the capital was a carefully prepared trap. Fourthly, Cardinal Alessandrino's mission to France in 1572 was a total failure, and Lord Acton was wrong in supposing that Charles IX. on this occasion revealed a plot against Coligny and his followers. And lastly, the attempt to murder Coligny on the 22nd of August precludes the idea of a premeditated general massacre, for such a course would have been the best calculated to warn the rest of the intended victims.

These conclusions are, we believe, perfectly sound. The case for premeditation rests largely on the boastings of the Cardinal of Lorraine and the assertions of Cardinal Alessandrino, Petrucci, Sorbin, and others, who claimed that they knew of Catherine's plans years or months beforehand. But little credence can be attached to their statements; in every case they were made after the event. Philippson, indeed, is strongly of opinion that as late as the 21st of July, 1572, Catherine was still averse to violent measures. The first real hint of assassination is in a despatch of the 5th of August of Salviati, the only foreign representative, as the Queen Mother confessed later, to whom she revealed her plans. In it he remarked that Catherine would encourage trouble in the Netherlands; "at the same time she will keep her eyes on the hands of the Admiral . . . and will give him a rap over the knuckles, should anything else happen." And on the 11th he closed his despatch with the significant hope " that our Lord God may grant me the favour of one day being able to write you something which will bring joy and contentment to his Holiness."

This brings us to the exact share of the King in the events of the 22nd to 24th of August. The most reasonable theory is that Charles was ignorant of Catherine's attempt on the Admiral's life. All those in a position to know were of this opinion,—that is to say, the son of Marshal Tavannes, one of the conspirators; Anjou, and Margaret of Valois, brother and sister of the King; the Nuncio Salviati, and the Spanish Ambassador, who received his news from the conspirator and court favourite, Gondi. Margaret, indeed, stated in her Memoirs that her mother only revealed her plotting to the King on the evening of the 23rd of August. This testimony is supported from other quarters. It was only on the 23rd that Charles IX. agreed to a general massacre. Other evidence as to the King's attitude may be safely disregarded. It was not at first-hand. Therefore, though the opinions of de Thou, Hotman, Languet, Goulart, Barnaud, Sorbin, Capilupi, Michiel, Cavalli, Petrucci, Corbinelli, and the rest are interesting, and the most weighty, we believe, support the view we have taken, it would serve no useful purpose to quote them at length.

Another question which demands attention is the alleged Huguenot plot. It was one of the last facts marshalled by Catherine to convince her son. The great majority of modern historians were agreed that it had no foundation in fact, and was only put forward by Catherine to cover her own treachery. Kervyn de Lettenhove, however, in 1884, raised the whole question afresh and in the most uncompromising manner. " The Huguenot plot," he wrote, " is pointed out by Margaret of Valois and the Duke of Anjou. The Italian and Spanish despatches leave no doubt as to its existence, which has only been contested by the author of the Memoirs of Tavannes, writing long afterwards." [1] To this we would reply that the testimony of Margaret of Valois is quite worthless. The record of her own experiences and her views on the attitude

[1] *Les Huguenots et les Gueux*, ii. 554, note 1.

of her mother and brothers are interesting, but she was not in a position to judge of Huguenot intentions. The same may be said of the Duke of Anjou, even should we admit, as Philippson is inclined to do,[1] that the "Discours du Roy Henry troisième à un personnage d'honneur et de qualité sur les causes et motifs de la Saint Barthélemy"[2] is authentic. There are several other points in the views of Kervyn de Lettenhove equally open to question. It is difficult to believe, for instance, that his remark, that the Italian and Spanish despatches leave no doubt as to the existence of a Huguenot plot, was meant seriously. For, in the first place, they are by no means unanimous; and, in the second, it was to the interest of the Florentine and Spanish Ambassadors to throw odium on the common enemy. Then, again, to say that the existence of a plot is only contested by the author of the Memoirs of Tavannes, is far from the truth. It would be easy to name twenty writers of the time who ridiculed its existence. And finally, if the Memoirs of Tavannes are to be ruled out as having been written long afterwards, the Memoirs of Margaret of Valois and the "Discours" of Henry III. must share the same fate.

As is known, on the 24th of August, Charles IX. published to the world that the massacre was the work of the house of Guise. On the 25th the theory of a Huguenot plot was generally known. By the 26th the King had decided to acknowledge his own responsibility. Thenceforth the official rendering was that Charles IX. had merely anticipated an attack on himself. Curiously enough, the details of the alleged conspiracy were in a state of continual flux. They were given differently at different times,—in fact, were made to fit the occasion. Thus Catherine declared to Walsingham that the King only anticipated the rebels by a couple of hours; another version was that the plot was fixed for the 26th; Michiel gives the 6th of September. It was alleged that on the 22nd and 23rd of August, the Huguenots, after several meetings in the Rue de Béthisy, gave orders to Montgomery to collect 4000 men; then on the 26th the Huguenots were to enter the Louvre in small bodies so as to escape notice,

[1] *Westeuropa*, ii. 268.　　　　[2] Petitot Collection, xliv. 496.

and at midday, when the guard was careless, La Rochefoucauld was to present the King with an insulting memorial from Coligny, and when Charles had worked himself into a passion, he was to be slain, with his brothers, the Queen, the Queen Mother, and the rest of the court, every Catholic being apportioned to some Huguenot. Either to make the act appear more heinous, or to free Henry of Navarre from blame, it was even asserted that he was to be included among the victims. Other particulars and variations are also forthcoming. They are mostly of Spanish origin. One relates how Coligny, with fine dramatic sense, exclaimed to Henry of Navarre, that since he himself must die, he wished to leave him as heritage the kingdom of France. Another, and one of the most interesting, was confided to the unbelieving Elector Palatine by the future Henry III., then on his way to Poland. The Admiral, said he with rare aplomb, had conspired against the King, and had wished to be carried in a litter before the Louvre, where fifty armed Huguenots lay concealed ; when the deed had been done, he was to have retired, accompanied by five hundred horsemen who were near the city. The plan, he added, had been revealed, not by one only, but by thirty to forty Huguenots, many of whom were still living.[1]

Such was the case put forward by Catherine and her apologists. Fortunately for the memory of Coligny, it will not bear examination for a moment. In the first place, it is impossible to discover sufficient reason for a Huguenot conspiracy. Until the 22nd of August, the Admiral and his immediate followers undoubtedly trusted the King, and nothing which happened on that date shook their confidence. Charles showed himself thoroughly sympathetic. He was evidently sincerely desirous of discovering the criminals, and Montgomery expressed his faith in the royal intentions. The Huguenots believed that Guise was the guilty party. And, with a judicial commission sitting, they seemed in a fair way to humble the enemy. It is, therefore, to the last degree unlikely that they would have chosen that moment to attack a power which seemed to offer them the best means of slaking their vengeance. But even supposing that they had wished to

---

[1] *Monumenta pietatis et litteraria*, i. 311–318 (published 1701).

turn on the King, we may feel certain that they would never have chosen Paris as the scene of conspiracy. They may have been rash and hot-headed, but they were after all a part of soldiers. Three successive wars had made them alive to the fact that their strength lay in their cavalry. They were wholly unfit for street-fighting. An attack on the Louvre would have been the signal for 50,000 Parisians to spring to arms. To suppose that warriors like Pilles, Montgomery, Briquemault, and Coligny would have set such a trap for themselves, is inconceivable. Then, again, they were scattered. One large body was lodged to the south of the Seine, in the Faubourg St. Germain; the rest were on the north side. The one fact in favour of a conspiracy is that on the 23rd there was a large influx of Huguenots into the houses in the neighbourhood of the Rue de Béthisy. The reason for this was variously given. Petrucci, the Florentine, and the Huguenot Cornaton explain that it was done secretly. The Protestant author of the *Reveille - Matin* and the Florentine Cavriana, on the contrary, state expressly that it was the result of a royal command. It is somewhat difficult to decide between these two views, as all were in an excellent position to know the truth. But even admitting that it was done secretly, there is no reason to suppose that it was intended for any other purpose than to protect the Admiral's house. If, on the other hand, Charles IX. ordered it, the Huguenots are freed from all blame.

There is another point worth considering. The *Reveille-Matin* affirms that only a part of the Protestant gentlemen changed their lodgings. This precludes the idea of a plot; conspirators do not act in this haphazard manner. Then, again, the Huguenots asked for a guard for Coligny's lodging, surely the very last act of conspirators, for it was to put their leader into the hands of the enemy. Nor is it to be forgotten that at three o'clock of the morning of the 24th—that is to say, according to Catherine, within two hours of the time fixed for the conspiracy—Coligny was practically alone in his house. The Florentine Cavriana, in obvious forgetfulness of the official version, wrote that "every Huguenot tried to fly and save himself, for they were caught unprepared and without sufficient arms with which to make head." Catherine herself was even less happy. She explained to Walsingham that on the morning of the 24th Montgomery had appeared at the Pré-aux-Clercs, his intention being to help those who were to start the outbreak within the city. This was a serious *faux pas* on her part; nothing was so dangerous as to enter on details, for Walsingham was one of the few who knew the facts. He at once explained that he could correct her version from his own knowledge. He had sent to Montgomery that morning, and had found him and his followers practically unarmed. On receiving this unexpected reply, Catherine at once drew back, murmuring that Montgomery was less guilty than the rest. Another attempt of hers was equally a failure. She explained to Languet that compromising letters had fallen into the King's hands. Petrucci relates a somewhat similar fact. He asserts that a memoir of Coligny was found wherein the Huguenot murderers and their prospective victims were named, and that Catherine handed it over to Nevers. But this document never saw the light of day, for the simple reason, undoubtedly, that it had never existed. It is re-markable, too, that the alleged confessions of Bouchavannes, the supposed Huguenot traitor, were never published. The royal apologia was left to Charpentier, a nominal Protestant, whose testimony, one way or the other, is of little consequence.

It is hardly necessary to labour the question further. And the height of absurdity is reached when we remember that the alleged organiser of the plot was the Admiral, a man dangerously wounded and weak from loss of blood. Even had his friends succeeded, he could scarcely have hoped to escape with his life. Moreover, as the *De Furoribus Gallicis* relates, Paris was full of the wives and children of the Hugue-not lords and gentlemen. If, therefore, we accept the theory of a conspiracy, we have to suppose that the Protestant leaders were willing to risk the lives of those near and dear to them as well as their own!

In a word, no Huguenot plot ever existed. It was an in-vention of the busy brain of the Queen Mother, and was only accepted by the credulous or those who, like the Duke of Anjou, had interests at stake. Briquemault went to his death declaring it a fiction. Those best able to know rejected it with scorn. Among them were Walsingham, the son of Marshal Tavannes, and the Papal Nuncio, Salviati. And we may conclude in the words of the latter: " the official account of the trial says, in so many words, that the Admiral was of late conspiring against the persons of the King and his brothers, although this is most false, and it is a shame that it should be believed by men whose business it is to know something of the world." [1]

There are other problems connected with the massacre of St. Bartholomew which, though less important than those already treated of, are still more difficult to decide. Thus, we have given Maurevel as the man who attempted to assassinate Coligny on the 22nd, yet the evidence in favour of Bême, or even perhaps Tosinghi, is strong. Moreover, in describing the wound received by the Admiral, we have followed the author of the *Reveille-Matin*, who was personally present, Salviati, and the majority of the Spanish accounts. Yet Cornaton, who held up the wounded arm while Ambroise Paré was operating, says that it was shot through by two pellets. The same uncertainty exists everywhere. We feel confident that a Swiss gave Coligny the first blow on the 24th of August,[2] and not Bême, who is generally credited with the deed. Nevertheless, it is impossible to feel any certainty, for, as Salviati remarked satirically, the number of those who claimed the murder was so great, that if the room had been the Piazza Navona—one of the great squares in Rome—it would not have been half large enough to hold them all. The same doubt exists as to his last moments. The different accounts are almost bewildering: one was that he jumped out of the window and killed himself; another, that he feigned sleep; a third, that he fought most bravely with his sword and bedcover; a fourth, that when Bême asked him if he was the Admiral, he replied yes, and begged him to respect his age and grey hairs; and finally, that he said never a word—the rendering which we have accepted as being more in accordance with the probabilities of the case.

---

[1] Vatican, Nunz. di Francia, v. 146.
[2] We have here followed M. N. Weiss, *Bull. du prot. fr.*, 1896.

Moreover, the number of days that he lay dead in the neighbourhood of the Rue de Béthisy is given differently; we have followed the Journal of Jehan de la Fosse and the author of the *Reveille-Matin*. Even the position and ownership of the house where he was living has been debated, though everything points to it having belonged to the family of du Bourg and having been the second house (though the first door) on the left-hand side of the Rue de Béthisy, on entering it from the Rue de l'Arbre Sec.[1]

[1] Some idea of the enormous mass of material dealing directly or indirectly with the massacre of St. Bartholomew may be gauged from the notes in de la Ferrière's *La Saint Barthélemy*, Kervyn de Lettenhove's *Les Huguenots et les Gueux*, vol. ii., and Philippson's *Westeuropa*, ii. 255–272. Other despatches, works, articles, etc., which we would mention are : Guido Lolgi to Cardinal Farnese, Paris, 25th Aug. (Naples, Carte Farn., 186); Panicarola from Paris, 26th Aug. (Vatican, Armadio, 64, 31); advices from Paris, 24th, 27th, 28th Aug. (Vatican Library, Urbino, 1043, 129); summary of despatches of Ferraran representatives in Paris, 22nd, 24th, 28th Aug. (Modena Francia, 59); Mantuan Amb. from Paris (Mantua, Arch. Gonz., 656); notes of Walsingham of 7th Sept. (British Museum, Caligula C. iii. 404, 416); various accounts from Paris (Hansen's *Rheinische Akten zur Geschichte des jesuiten Ordens*); Languet's account published by Holländer (*Zeitschrift für die Geschichte des Oberrheins, neue Folge*, x.); Philippson's "Die römische Curie und die Bartholomäusnacht" (*Deutsche Zeitschrift für Geschichtswissenschaft*, 1892); Pio Rajna's publication of and comments on Corbinelli's account of St. Bartholomew (Archivio Storico Italiano, 1898); Weiss on the assassins of Coligny (*Bull. du prot. fr.*, 1896); Reade (*Hug. Soc. Publications*, vol. i.); Layard's *Massacre of St. Bartholomew*. Various articles and criticisms have also been written by B. Duhr, H. de L'Épinois, Tamizey de Larroque, and Léon Marlet (*Bull. du prot. fr.*, 1903, p. 345).

CHAPTER XVII

CAUSES OF THE RISE AND DECLINE OF THE HUGUENOT MOVEMENT

CAUSES OF RISE :—Corruption of Roman Church—Spirituality of Protestantism—Sternness and Ideas of Des Adrets—Attractive Forces of Protestantism—Number and Military Value of Huguenot Nobility—Importance of the Three Colignys—Huguenots and Princes of the Blood—The Constitutional and National Party—Support of the "Politiques"; its Value—Balancing Policy of the Crown—International Character of Protestantism—Huguenotism saved by England and Germany—Absence of large, highly-organised Royal Army—Strength of the Calvinistic System.

CAUSES OF DECLINE :—Desertions owing to Numerical Inferiority and Aristocratic Dependence on Royalty—Number of Protestants—Losses in War—Victims of St. Bartholomew ; Estimate of Number—Victory of Henry of Navarre, entails Defeat of Huguenotism—Reasons for Numerical Inferiority—Humanists, Royalty, People reject Huguenotism—Supposed anti-Monarchical and Disturbing Tendencies of Huguenotism—False Charges of anti-Royal Action—Huguenotism essentially a Disturbing Factor—Its Political Acts and Theories—The Catholic Reaction—Huguenot Excesses, Verbal and Military—Antagonism between Calvinism and Lutheranism—Hostility to Huguenotism of Peasantry and Legal Class—Huguenotism estimated.

THERE are few pages in history more melancholy than those of French Protestantism. It promised so much, and, in comparison with its indomitable efforts, effected so little. Beginning in persecution, it closed in persecution. Its dreams of victory, its heroic deeds, its laborious creation of a roll of martyrs, soldiers, and statesmen, seem almost so much effort wasted and in vain. At the end of the vista looms up the Revocation of the Edict of Nantes, and partial failure. And yet, one may ask, why had it declined so in spirit and numbers that Louis XIV., if not invited, was at least not deterred from giving it its seeming *coup de grâce*? What was its especial strength and weakness?

In France, as elsewhere, the reasons for the early growth of Protestantism are not far to seek. Firstly, it answered in a very real degree to a spiritual need. A series of half-pagan popes, a code of morals peculiarly of the Renaissance and Italian, a policy of nepotism and family aggrandisement, had made Rome a byword. " A good horse or a bad man," ran a sixteenth-century proverb, " were never the better for going to Rome." And unfortunately for Catholicism, spiritual paralysis was not confined to the Papal court. Each local church added to the sum-total faults peculiarly its own. As for France, she was in a state of religious anarchy. The Concordat between Francis I. and Leo X. had seemed to the King, by granting him the right to appoint to all ecclesiastical offices, a pleasant way out of his difficulties. It was none the less a disastrous experiment. There were one hundred and seventeen bishoprics, fifteen archbishoprics, and countless abbeys and priories, in the gift of the Crown, and one and all were looked upon as the legitimate spoil for favourites and ladies of the court. " All that is needed to have a benefice in France," remarked the Venetian Contarini, " is to be the first to ask." As a result, children like Odet of Châtillon were created arch-bishops; in 1556, the court were thinking of a cardinalate for the five-year-old Duke of Angoulême ; [1] among the high ecclesi-astics, preaching was an almost forgotten art ; [2] morality was lax ; the regular and mendicant orders were on the brink of internecine strife ; the parish priest, deserted and neglected by his superiors, imbibed little of the new learning, and remained stupid, ignorant, a mere mouther of ancient shibboleths : " they were the first," said the fanatical Catholic, Charles Hatton, of some of them, " to dance, play at skittles, and fence, indulging nightly in debauches in taverns and the streets like the wickedest of the countryside." In October, 1548, Charles, Cardinal of Guise, while conversing with the Papal Nuncio, drew a lamentable picture of the French Church. He declared that the bishops were ignorant and uncharitable, that a large number of the priests were worthless, that canons refused to obey their bishops and monks their abbots, and that benefices were held by absentees at the Papal court, who, out of the yearly income of thirty or forty crowns, took twenty-five and left the

---

[1] Paris, Bibl. Nat., filza i. B. 273.
[2] Les Prédicateurs de la Ligue, 33.

rest to some poor curé. The root of the evil, said he, lay in the dispensations granted by Rome.[1]

It was to a society thus divided and disillusioned that Protestantism made its appeal. Its success, if not immediate, was steady. It was in the end acclaimed by a section of the nobility. For a time it won the support of the scholars, who greeted it as one more blow for intellectual freedom. From the first it appealed to the craving for self-development of the bourgeois and artisan. To certain, at least, the greater familiarity of the new religion with the unseen, the more intimate ruling of daily life, the use of homely metaphor and the vulgar tongue, came as an inspiration after the dim mysticism of the Catholic faith. It is difficult to overestimate the power of the translation of the Psalms by the Catholic Marot which yet became the birthright as it were of French Protestantism, the appealing tenderness of the writings of Palissy, or the quiet strength of Beroald's Morning Prayer of the guard at the siege of Sancerre: " And seeing, O Heavenly Father, that those who dwell and sojourn in this town, after thee entrust themselves to the fidelity and watchfulness of us the guard, give us grace that we may so fulfil the demands of our charge, that through our cowardice or negligence no harm may befall. And that, finally, it may please thee, O great God of armies, so to change this miserable and unhappy hour into a time where all pity and justice reign, that we may no more need to stand in arms." It was with language such as this, if sometimes more uncouth, that the missionary band of Geneva awakened France. Their insistence too, on austerity of life, on sobriety in speech and dress, was not lost in a community suffering from a lax morality, and an Italian and Renaissance court. The courtiers stormed when, in March, 1563, the Sieur du Moulin was executed for adultery; and the young nobles, no doubt, did not appreciate the decision of the Huguenot National Assembly of the 25th of April, 1562, that "the churches shall warn the faithful, both men and women alike, to favour modesty, especially in that which concerns dress, so that all superfluities may be cut down and all excesses abolished."

But such discipline and such a moral code appealed to

[1] Letter of Nuncio, 23rd Oct.: Naples, Carte Farn., 690.

many. And what above all touched the public conscience
and made Huguenotism strong as death, was that their creed
was a living creed. Turn where one will, one is conscious of a high and serious tone. In the woods of Florida,
Le Challeux, the carpenter of Dieppe, comforted the fugitives
from Fort Caroline and Spanish vengeance with the question:
"Cannot He who has opened the sea to afford a path to His
people and swallow up His enemies lead us through the sylvan
places of this strange land?"[1] "Here are the enemy who
hasten to our deliverance," cried the minister Beaumont, as
the Catholic soldiery came running sword in hand to butcher
him and his little flock. "It is the will of God to receive us
by their arms. Let us hasten to present ourselves before His
face singing, 'Into Thy hands I commit my spirit, for Thou
hast redeemed me.'"[2] "Martini," cried a voice from the
crowd to one of the martyrs of Castres, "raise thine eyes
unto heaven and trust in the grace and mercy of God, who
will receive thee this day into His kingdom."[3] That stern
Calvinist, the Queen of Navarre, thus exclaimed against an
attempt to force a girl to attend Catholic services: "I believe
you know that I owe obedience to none; but if God had so
far afflicted me as to permit of them wishing to constrain me,
I would endure death first, obeying the Creator rather than
His creature."[4] The meditative Huguenot pasteur, Daniel
Toussaint, who had escaped the massacre of St. Bartholomew,
could still look calmly in the face of death, for in the grave
"nothing is lost but the infection and corruption, the which we
doe desire to loose. And our bodies shall rise againe glorious
bodies. For it is even as when a man melteth a great masse
or lumpe of copper to make a faire image of. Truelie then
is not the copper lost, but fined and set in honour."[5]

Even in many of its excesses there was a something
which marked off Huguenotism from the creed of the mere
spiller of blood. One of its most cruel leaders was the Baron

---

[1] Le Challeux, 29.   [2] D'Aubigné, iii. 88.   [3] Jacques Gaches, 2.

[4] Jeanne d'Albret à Madame de Langey, October, 1561: Rochambeau, *Lettres
d'Antoine de Bourbon*, etc., 243.

[5] *The Exercise of the faithfull soule*, Englished out of the French almost word
or word by Ferdenando Filding, and dedicated to the right worshipfull and his
especiall good master, Walter Raleigh, esquier, 1583.

des Adrets, whose methods Coligny viewed with disfavour. Throughout the first war of religion he upheld Protestantism in the stretch of country between Lyons and Avignon by ability and the terror of his name. Moving with incredible swiftness, wherever he appeared there was victory and a trail of blood. It is told how the rumour of his presence was sufficient to turn the scale in the battle of St. Gilles; and how, at Montbrison, in revenge for Catholic excesses at Orange, the garrison was precipitated from the rocks, one alone being spared, and that for a *bon mot*, " for, having stopped on the edge of the precipice, the Baron said to him, ' What! do you take twice to do it?' ' Sir,' said the soldier, ' you may take ten times.' " [1] Yet even the action of des Adrets does not lack a certain grandeur of its own. Fortunately, we have, from the pen of d'Aubigné, the scene where the Baron, no longer a Protestant, declared the motives which had guided him in his earlier career. Some of them, at least, are such as Cromwell, the stormer of Wexford and Drogheda, might have confessed to when in a worldly mood. " Being at Lyons on the return of the King from Poland,[2] I saw an usher, who gave me the *entrée*, refuse it to the old Count de Bennes and to the Baron des Adrets. When the latter retired to a seat in the hall, I got up and accosted him with great reverence. When he saw what I had done, he granted me the favour of asking him three things : why he had exhibited a cruelty which was unbecoming to his great valour; why he had left a party in which his influence had been so great; and lastly, why, since he had left that party and fought against it, nothing had succeeded with him. He replied to me on the first head, that to pay back cruelty in its own coin is no cruelty at all—it was justice. Then telling me the terrible tale of more than 4000 murders committed (by the enemy) in cold blood . . . he said that he had paid them back in kind, but less of it, with an eye on the past, and on the future : on the past, because he could not bear, unless he were a coward, the cutting up of his faithful companions; on the future, for two reasons, which no captain could disregard,

---

[1] D'Aubigné, ii. 56.

[2] Henry III., who had fled from Poland, was in Lyons, September, 1574.

one being that the only means to stop the barbarities of your enemies is to take your revenge. Whereupon he told me of the 300 horsemen sent back in waggons some time ago to the hostile army, each having a foot and a hand cut off, in order to change, as it did, a merciless into a courteous war. The other reason was that there was nothing so dangerous as to show himself to his followers a respecter of special rights and persons, for war made with deferences is made with bowed head and lack of courage, especially when the enemy boasts that he is acting in the King's name. In a word, the soldier cannot at the same time have his hand at his hat and on his sword. Moreover, as his heart was set on high and difficult enterprises, he had no wish to see his troops make for the rear when the occasion offered. When, however, all hope of pardon was gone, their only refuge was in the shadow of their flags, and their very life depended on victory.

"As to his reasons for leaving the party, they were that the Admiral wished to decide the war by maxims, and set the talkers as judges over the doers.

"When I pressed him hard with my third question, he answered briefly and with a sigh : ' Mon enfant,' said he, ' nothing is too warm for a captain whose interest in victory is shared by his soldiers. With the Huguenots I had soldiers fearful, yet undismayed, solaced with vengeance, passion, and honour ; now I have tradesmen who think only of money. As to the first, I needed only to give them their head ; with the last, I have to use my spurs.' " [1]

But apart from the spiritual appeal of Huguenotism, and the stern character it evoked, there were reasons more mundane which made it a power. To the bourgeois, especially as it developed after the massacre of St. Bartholomew, it offered a realisation of municipal ideals. It has even been alleged that it appeared to some of the lower strata of society as a possible escape from serfdom and feudal dues. To no insignificant number of the religious orders, even if it appealed spiritually, it none the less offered an escape from irksome vows. And it attracted some individuals, at least, with all the hazards and allurements of change. There were

[1] D'Aubigné, ii. 72–75.

cadets of families eager for a career; the nobles, Giovanni Michiel tells us, being more affected by the new doctrines than others, " especially those of forty and under." [1] Among them, too, were soldiers back from the wars; adventurers, such as at a later time were to be found equally in the camp of the King of Portugal and of the Moors; [2] captains, unemployed or unpaid, with real or imaginary grievances against the Guises; country gentlemen jealous of courtiers; perhaps, too, there may still have been some in the south who nursed a traditional aversion to Paris and that land of France beyond the Loire. [3] Then, too, there was a feeling of impatience amongst the nobility at the steady growth of the royal power. [4] In a word, those who had rancours, equally with those who had ambitions and ideals, hailed the new creed. To such, indeed, the real religious and political significance of Calvinism was often a closed book. They repeated its watchwords, but when awakened to its possible consequences, relapsed to the old faith. Still, for the time, it gained their allegiance. It is astonishing, remarks the Baron de Ruble, to watch the growth of the democratic ideals of Calvinism in Guienne, among a nobility far from the court, poor, ill-educated, and whose profession was that of arms. [5]

But, however won, the nobility was the backbone of the party. Condé gave its numbers as one-half of its class; Giovanni Corero in 1569 declared that perhaps he would not err should he say that it was a third; while another Venetian, Alvise Contarini, remarked in 1572 that it was a half. The estimate of Corero is probably correct. But of even more importance was the fact that the nobility was pre-eminently the warrior caste. It provided the cavalry in time of war, that peculiarly French arm of the sixteenth century. Huguenotism, therefore, largely recruited from its ranks, obtained a military importance altogether out of proportion to its mere numbers. Let one conceive the battle of St. Denis, and a hundred other

---

[1] Alberi, iii. 426.   [2] La Noue, 182.

[3] The native of Languedoc, Gascony, and Guienne still spoke of France as north of the Loire. See d'Aubigné, ii. 92 ; J. Gaches, 69; Bruslart, 165.

[4] A very interesting despatch was written from Paris by Luca Mannelli, 1st April, 1568, on the relations of the Crown and nobility : Naples, Carte Farn., 759.

[5] Jeanne d'Albret, 41.

fights, with its gentlemen become so many bourgeois footmen, or the host following Coligny so much infantry and so deprived of mobility, and one perceives the consequence of this aspect of the question.

Of almost equal importance with the predominance of the military element was the position of the Châtillons. Cardinal Odet, a member of the Council, was by character and training a courtier and diplomat: " I notice this fact and remind you of it," writes he, " that at court the most pressing are oftenest the most successful in their affairs."[1] Andelot was the warrior, the Colonel of French Infantry, and the Protestant *chevalier sans peur*. The two together brought to the party a combination of resource, intelligence, and high distinction which cannot be over-valued. But their claims to Huguenot gratitude were small in comparison with those of Coligny. A member of the aristocratic class, and trusted by that of the bourgeois and artisan, he was the one man who gave Huguenotism unity, the one man who gave it character; he did more, he saved it at a crisis. He alone could have brought it through the dark hours of 1569, when the court was singing Te Deums and hailing the end of opposition.

But in speaking of the Châtillons, we must not forget the attractive personalities of the Princes of the Blood. Many a young noble was swept along in the joyous train of the witty, brilliant, winning " Petit Homme," as they affectionately termed Louis of Bourbon, Prince of Condé;[2] while Henry of Navarre was universally accepted as the Admiral's successor,—of quite another character, it is true, but at least of equal abilities and with a more successful record in war. He was a prince " of the fine texture of which to make something great."[3] His energy, his lightness of soul, that vital force which lent his action so great a charm, marked him out as a leader of men. But quite apart from the question of mere talents, Navarre and the two Condés possessed what was of equal value:

[1] Odet to a representative at court, the 12th of March, 1551: Marlet's *Correspondance d'Odet de Coligny*.

[2] Bordier's *Le Chansonnier Huguenot*, 252.

[3] Discourse sent by Mornay to Walsingham, May, 1583: *Mémoires de Mornay*, ii. 239-241.

rights. They were able to throw over the doings of the party an air of legality. True, it was not until the death of Henry III. that this legality was in any sense real, but it none the less served. It gave the French rebel confidence, and Elizabeth and the German Princes an excuse.

In addition, however, to advancing the claims of the rights of Princes of the Blood, the Huguenots voiced public sentiment in other matters. They posed as the constitutional party. Their programme, which was an echo of traditions as read in the light of the new acquaintance with the histories of Greece and Rome, was ample enough. Its chief item was insistence on the importance in the constitution of the Estates General. Later, indeed, the League stole their cries, or rather the Jesuits developed a more radical theory,—that of the rights of the people,[1]—and the Huguenots in revenge fell back on hereditary and royal rights as exemplified in the person of Henry of Navarre. Still, in the early years, especially between 1559 and 1562, they were the first to set their sails to the breeze, and so gained the first impulse. And as they were the constitutional party, so were they, in some degree at least, the national party. This they showed in their undying hostility to Spain. Their attitude was equally national in opposition to Italianising influences. It was a protest in part against the system of politics as enunciated by Machiavelli in his works, "held dear and precious by the Italian and Italianised courtiers";[2] and in part against the Italian adventurers in France, and, after 1572, against Catherine herself. Here the Huguenots were on firm ground. In September, 1574, L'Estoile jotted down popular doggerel of a strongly anti-Italian character.[3] In 1575, Ogelin de Busbecq, the Imperial Ambassador, remarked, "The feeling against the Italians who are in the French service is very strong," for they "farm nearly all the taxes. There will be another St. Bartholomew if they do not take care, and they will be the victims."[4] The

---

[1] Otto Gierke, *Johannes Althusius und die Entwicklung der naturrechtlichen Staatstheorien.*

[2] Lord Acton in his Introduction to Burd's *Machiavelli.*

[3] L'Estoile's *Mémoires-Journaux*, i. 20.

[4] *Letters of Ogelin de Busbecq*, ii. 39–41.

expression of this hatred against an Italian and foreign element was congenial to Huguenot tastes, and they made it their own. In the negotiations of October, 1567,[1] in Hotman's *Franco-Gallia*, and a hundred other pamphlets, it is the subject of Huguenot complaint.

The strength, moral and material, thus gained was considerable. For their national and constitutional, together with their anti-Guise policy, won them the support of the "Politiques." This group was composed of two elements. There were firstly the political thinkers, such as the Chancellor L'Hôpital and the historian de Thou, whose support was as much moral as material, yet none the less valuable. They adopted very much the same attitude towards Huguenotism as did the Humanists before persecution and Calvin's preaching of a blind obedience to the Bible had dulled their sympathies.[2] They increased its intellectual and above all its polemical effectiveness in a polemical age. The eighteenth-century editor of the *Memoirs of Condé* remarked that " almost all the political writings of the sixteenth century which fell from Huguenot pens are better composed and better written than those published by the Catholics." We can readily believe it, since among Huguenot pamphleteers are to be found Hotman, Languet, Mornay. How much greater, then, does this superiority appear when we remember that for all practical purposes we can add the names of a Politique such as La Planche and of the authors of the *Satyre Ménippée*.

The second element among the Politiques was that of the men of action. The significance of their adhesion to the Protestant ranks did not, as is so often stated, largely or altogether lie in the fact that thereby there was a transference of so many influential personages from the royal camp to that of its opponents. The importance of the movement was due in great part to its introducing into politics a new geographical factor. A glance at the map will show that Languedoc in the hands of the Montmorencys, who were the real leaders of the " Politiques," served, when they were hostile, as a wedge

---

[1] Their attitude is interestingly given in an anti-Huguenot pamphlet, called *Discours sur les causes de l'execution faicte es personnes de ceux qui avoyent conjuré contre le Roy et son Estat*, 1572, p. 6.

[2] H. Hauser, " De l'Humanisme et de la Reforme en France," *Revue Hist.*, lxiv.

in the force of Protestantism, cutting off east from west, Dauphiné from Guienne, and so rendering concerted action impossible. But with that province friendly under Damville, a broad belt of Huguenot influence stretched from the Alps to the Atlantic, which Catholic effort, even in the campaign of 1586, could not materially pierce.

The position, too, of the Crown contributed not a little to Huguenot success. It could not afford to proceed to extremities. During the years of Charles IX.'s boyhood, at least, it was but one among contending factions, and was forced to temporise and balance. Complete success against the Protestant rebels would have meant a Guise dictatorship. In addition, Catherine de' Medici's own proclivities recommended this rôle. Her statecraft was the reflection of her character. Being a woman, she was " inclined to peace," and to " such measures as were farthest out of the power of fortune "; as a diplomatist " she knew how to accommodate herself to her circumstances."

But this was not the only strength which Huguenotism drew from an outside source. It was saved, time and again, by the general European situation. In the first place, the foreign wars of Francis I. and Henry II. gave it time to strike root; in the second, the Peace of Cateau Cambrésis opened the way for an invasion of Genevan missionaries; in the third, the Guises, when in power in 1559 and 1560, were so fully occupied elsewhere that they were unable to provide troops to repress the new movement in the provinces. And lastly, the exigencies of foreign politics were such, the need of the help of Protestant Germany so absolute, that the Crown was distracted in its crusade against heresy. And there is no persecution so futile as a persecution by fits and starts. Then, too, we must remember, French Protestantism had its allies. If this, its international character, religious as well as political, were ignored, we should fail to recognise one of the great secrets of its success.[1] At every crisis in its history Huguenotism had England or Germany to fall back on. In fact, its system of foreign alliances was a chief cause in saving it from exter-

---

[1] For international and religious character of civil wars, see interesting dictum quoted by Marcks in *Die Zusammenkunft von Bayonne*, 14.

mination. French historians,[1] indeed, are chiefly concerned in
dwelling on the pillage, the insubordination, and the not seldom
uselessness of the German mercenaries. Still, we have only to
name the campaign and battle of Dreux, Coligny's campaign in
Normandy, the march of the Protestants from Pont à Mousson
to Chartres, the battle of Moncontour, the Voyage of the
Princes, not to mention operations of later date, to find that
foreign succour was a prime military factor. Moreover, to the
Huguenots of France it meant something more than mere
subsidies received or soldiers added to the fighting force. In
many of their diplomatic ventures they had foreign support;
in their demands on the Valois kings they had in reserve
the possibility of foreign interference.

We have now passed under review some of the causes of
Huguenot influence; two remain: the absence of a large
regular royal army, and the peculiar characteristics of the
Calvinist system. If the Crown had had at its command a
national force such as was at the disposal of Louis XIV., and
if Huguenotism had been loosely organised, this latter, small
in numbers, could never have dictated terms. As a movement, indeed, it would probably have been suppressed at the
outset. As it was, the Crown had only a small army, and
Calvinism had its system. In France the religious movement
long deprecated the attribution to itself of any political
complexion. "Our confession," declared the Synod of La
Rochelle in 1571, "rejects the error of those who would
abolish the discipline of our Church by confounding it with
the civil and political government of the magistrates."[2] And
this was always true of Huguenotism in a sense. Thus the
political organisation which sprang into existence after the
massacre of St. Bartholomew, was founded, not on their church
polity, but on local and political divisions. Yet even here, as
at Montauban in 1581, the Synod constantly tended to
supersede the political assembly as the unit to be represented
in their Estates General. And it is equally certain that without Calvin's church system—even when it was not avowedly
political in tendency—Protestantism in France would never

---

[1] For instance, Anquez, *Henri IV. et l'Allemagne, passim.*
[2] Frossard, *Etude sur la discipline ecclé. des églises reformées,* 9.

have developed such extraordinary powers of resistance. " By means of their consistories," it was observed in 1568, "and by the forms of procedure of their religion, they raised funds, assembled men, arms, and munitions of war, and, in an hour, when they pleased, stirred up the provinces, and surprised the towns of your realm." [1]

Such, then, was Huguenotism. Its advantages, as we see, were many. And yet from the very outset it contained within itself seeds of decay. Brantôme tells us that when the Pope heard of the massacre of St. Bartholomew, he exclaimed, " So many souls lost who might have become Catholic ! " The remark itself is quite apocryphal, and we may pass it by. What is of interest is Brantôme's own reflection on the same : " He spoke the truth, for we have since seen many Huguenots converted and become good Catholics." We have here the secret of failure : Huguenotism was no longer a growing creed. It was wasting away by attrition, and at an accelerated speed. A new name was found for the process. Deserters were dubbed " Guillebedoins," a local term of Saintonge. In the early years of the religious wars, that is between 1562 and 1572, these backsliders swell to a formidable roll. There were several renegades at the fall of Lectoure in August, 1562, and still more at the fall of Bourges, such as Captain Laporte, St. Remy, Brion, and Saint Martin de Brichanteau, known as the Huguenot; then Genlis, with Joachim and Philippe de St. George, all of whom returned later; also Flogeac, Charles Chabot, Seigneur de Ste. Foy, Piennes, Belleville, Pierre du Bec-Crespin, Seigneur de Vardes, Louis de Bar, Jacques de Lorges, brother of Montgomery, Du Mortier, a member of the Council, the powerful de la Chesnaye, known as the King of Craon, the Sieur de Touchet, father of the mistress of Charles IX., Grammont, Bouchavannes, Jean de Beaumanoir, later created a marshal, and a host of others. In the last quarter of the century we have to number a son of Coligny and the grandson of Condé; while the seventeenth century was to witness the lapse of countless bearers of historic names, not the least being the great Turenne. Some of the reasons for this are not far to seek. Imaginary slights

[1] La Mothe-Fénelon, i. 28.

and private quarrels, the fascination of Catherine's "flying squadron" of maids of honour of easy morals, played their part. Again, Huguenot inferiority, once war had begun, was marked; and it is hard to be of the weaker side. But what weighed with the mass of individuals was that the King was hostile. La Noue summed up the question with his usual insight. "When in 1561," he remarked, "liberty of worship was granted at court, several, both great and small, took a taste for the religion. But it was like a fire of straw, all flame, and then collapse, for substance was wanting. When once the newness had worn off, their liking weakened, and they returned for the most part to the old cabal of the court. Even some of the Huguenots changed their coats to follow this track. Therefore, we must hold that in general the court is the true image of the Prince: as he is, so is his suite." The sixteenth century had opened with the partial transformation of mediæval chivalry, with its local associations, into an aristocracy dependent on royalty. In a word, the King had become the symbol of the race, his court the social centre. Even the comparative impotence of the last of the Valois could not materially weaken the tendency. It needed but a few years of Henry IV., the work of Richelieu, the pose of Louis XIV., to more than restore the old traditions. And the result? Huguenotism was struck to the heart. It was a party of aristocrats; in the development of French history it became one of courtiers; and with that inevitably, if gradually, ceased to be Protestant.

Even to a party numerically powerful, such desertions would have been serious; to Huguenotism they proved well-nigh fatal. Various estimates have been made of the Protestant strength. Monluc put its number at one in ten of the population in 1561, Prosper de Ste. Croix at one in eight or one in ten. About the same time Michele Soriano remarked that "not a tenth part of the kingdom is tainted," and in 1569 Giovanni Corero was of opinion that "of the lower classes not the thirtieth part is Huguenot," while Mézeray, with conscious exaggeration, stated later that "there were a hundred Catholics in France to every Huguenot." Thus, even at the highest estimate, which is probably the most accurate,—that is, one eighth or one tenth of the population,—

there was little margin for loss. Unhappily, quite apart from desertions, a process of wastage was going steadily on. About 1584, La Noue computed the slain in war alone as 200,000. Both sides suffered heavily, probably equally, say 100,000 each. But this was a loss which Protestantism, with its originally vast inferiority in numbers, could not face with eqanimity.

Of all their tragedies, perhaps the one which has affected the imagination most is the massacre of St. Bartholomew. Nothing is more difficult than to give the number of the victims. Crespin's *Histoire des Martyrs* reckoned the slain in Paris in thousands, though the number of names actually mentioned is small.[1] Giovanni Michiel, the Venetian Ambassador, gave the highest estimate as 4000, the lowest as 2000.[2] De Thou, who was also in Paris, stated that 2000 were killed on the first day alone.[3] Botzheim, writing shortly after the event, and drawing his information from other Germans actually present, put down the victims as 8000.[4] M. Weiss, one of the latest historians to deal with the subject, working on an interesting theory of the cost of burial, comes to the conclusion that 8000 is not too high a figure for the capital.[5] The same divergence of opinion was apparent in calculating the losses at Orleans, for d'Aubigné and three eye-witnesses of the massacre—the pasteur Toussaint, the student Botzheim, and the apothecary Claude Chrestien— gave them variously as 400, 700, 1500, and 2000.[6] When we come to estimate the total for the whole of France, the same uncertainty prevails. Hotman, writing in October, 1572, gave the round number of 50,000.[7] La Popelinière declared that more than 20,000 were slain,[8] while de Thou, on the other hand, was of opinion that 30,000 was an exaggeration.[9] Among modern writers who have dealt with the subject are Lord Acton [10] and the German Catholic, Duhr.[11]

---

[1] Edition of 1572, 712–717. [2] Layard, *The Massacre of St. Bartholomew*, 30.
[3] *Histoire Universelle*, iv. 595.
[4] Ebeling, *Archivalische Beiträge*, 120. [5] *Bulletin du prot. fr.*, 1897.
[6] *La Saint-Barthélemy à Orleans*, par B. de Puchesse, Mém. de la Soc. arch. de l'Orléanais, xii. 535.
[7] Ehinger's *Franz Hotmann*, 118. [8] *Histoire de France*, ii. 70.
[9] *Histoire Universelle*, iv. 607. [10] *North British Review*, 1869.
[11] *Stimmen aus Maria Laach*, xxix. 136.

The figure given by this latter—five thousand—is certainly too low. Ten to twenty thousand, we believe, would be more correct. But even at this very moderate estimate, it was a terrible catastrophe.

There is another point, too, in which St. Bartholomew was quite unique. The roll of the dead contained the names of their greatest and best: Coligny, Teligny, La Rochefoucauld, Pilles, Lavardin, Guerchy, François Nompar de Caumont, Pierre Ramus, La Place, the Marquis de Renel, and a few weeks later Cavagnes and Briquemault. Indeed, the history of Huguenotism is only too melancholy in its lavish sacrifice of human lives — holocaust on holocaust, bloody scene on scene. The author of the *Histoire Ecclésiastique*, in speaking of the Toulouse of May, 1562, related that "the common opinion is that in all this sedition the deaths on one side and the other amounted to three or four thousand." In dealing with Provence, the same work devoted some fifty pages to the executions of the Catholic leader, Sommerive. Nor was this all. From the very nature of the case, Huguenotism was at a disadvantage. In no province was it the dominant faction. In Poitou, Gascony, Guienne, Dauphiné, it was on an equality with Catholicism, but nothing more; in Brittany, Picardy, Champagne, even in Normandy, it was in a minority. The natural consequences followed. When war broke out, it disappeared, or became only a scattered remnant, north of the Loire. On the other hand, it was nowhere able, except in Navarre, to mete out to its enemies a like treatment.

It was an irony, too, of the situation that its very successes led to its undoing. No desire was dearer to the heart of every Huguenot than to see Henry of Navarre King. And yet the nearer they brought him to his goal, the more pressing the necessity for him, if he would reap the full fruits of victory, to say his "Mass." And there was another result equally unforeseen. Once Henry was on the throne, the *raison d'être* for the alliance between Huguenot and "Politique" was gone. They therefore fell apart. The latter was lost in the ranks of the Catholic party, while the former was left isolated.

So far we have dealt with some of the causes which led to a

constant thinning of the Huguenot ranks. We have now to
consider a more important, if more complex, question : why
did the Protestants in France never cease to be a minority?
We shall find an answer in the reason which was at the root
of the royal hostility, as well as of that of the Parlement and
of two-thirds of the nobility. It is true that Francis I. and
Henry II. were moved by more than one motive in clinging to
Rome. They were no doubt satisfied with the Concordat,
which, if it deprived them of ecclesiastical absolutism, left them
masters of the Church in France. They were equally alive to
the fact that a break with the Papacy would close for ever the
road to Italy.[1] They saw, too, that the people were sincerely
Catholic,[2] and that the Humanists refused to abandon
hedonism and free criticism to throw themselves into the
reform movement. But perhaps the most powerful motive in
deciding their attitude was their fear of the supposed anti-
monarchic and democratic tendencies of Calvinism. Brantôme
alleges that when Francis I. threatened to introduce Lutheranism, the Papal Nuncio retorted, " Sire, you will be the first to
regret it ; only harm would come of it, and you would lose
more than the Pope, for a new religion among the people soon
leads to a demand for a change of prince." This sentiment,
as we see, is the French variant of " no bishop, no king." It
was no mere empty platitude to Frenchmen or Catholics. It
was the expression of an instinct. This was the reason why
they would give no quarter to Protestantism.

The Huguenots, for their part, were well aware of these
fears. They were not slow to make an attempt to meet them.
" The most peaceable and loyal servants whom the King
hath," they pleaded with Catherine in 1560, " are those who
make a true profession of the Evangelical doctrine, seeing that
by it they are taught to render to him due subjection and
obedience, to live peaceably under his high power, to create
no disturbance, to pay all tailles and tributes to which they
are beholden, according to the ordinance of God." On the
24th of September, 1560, La Chasse, on behalf of the

[1] Decrue, *Anne de Montmorency*, i. 198.
[2] Some of the reasons for this are given by Polenz, *Geschichte des französischen
Calvinismus*, i. 183–185.

Protestants of Montpellier, protested obedience to the King and magistracy and horror of all Nicolaites, Libertines, and other seditious persons. Calvin in particular insisted on the duty of obedience to constituted authorities.[1] In July, 1561, Languet declared that princes were nowhere better obeyed than in Protestant Germany.

But protest as they might, the Huguenots could not disabuse Catholics of their suspicions. " It has always been the nature of such religion," remarked a writer, " to make war on superiors and overthrow the political order." [2] " Everywhere where they have begun their preaching," said Renon de France of Protestantism as it developed outside of Germany, " they have driven out their lords and magistrates, and have left no privilege to the nobles, nor authority to their prince." [3] Even the sympathetic L'Hôpital, in his address to the Parlement on the 18th of June, 1561, was forced to say that among the Reformers were some who threatened to refuse payment of tithes to the churches and dues to the King. Again, in giving details of the conspiracy of Amboise, the Florentine Alfonso Tornabuoni related that the rebels " came resolved to slay the King and his Council, and make a republic." [4] Michele Soriano, the Venetian, affirmed that " in some places they (the Huguenots) have been unwilling to permit the publication of the royal edicts; in others they have begun to spread among the populace the idea that the King has his authority from the people, and that the subject is not obliged to obey the Prince when he commands anything which is not to be found in the New Testament. And they are on the highroad to reduce that province to the condition of a democratic state like Switzerland, and to destroy the monarchy and the kingdom." In 1562, the Procureur General of the Parlement of Paris insisted that the Huguenot ideal was to turn the monarchy into an oligarchy, and then divide the kingdom into cantons. This belief, indeed, in the anarchic or at least anti-monarchic nature of Protestantism was widespread. It was

[1] Max Lossen, *Die Lehre vom Tyrannenmord in der christlichen Zeit*, 23.
[2] *Brieve remonstrance sur la morte de l'admiral*, Lyons, 1572.
[3] *Histoire des troubles des Pays Bas*, edited by Piot, 57.
[4] Desjardins, iii. 409.

expressed almost simultaneously by three statesmen in May and June of 1562 : by Girolamo della Rovere at Paris, by Duke Philibert of Savoy at Savigliano, and by Philip II. at Aranjuez.[1] In 1564, the rumour got abroad that the Huguenots were going to rise and cut the throats of the King and Queen, " in order to form a republic."[2]

It is worth noting that there was often a confusion in the minds of these critics between democratic and oligarchic tendencies. Moreover, the charges in great part had their basis in fears rather than facts. For instance, in 1567, "at the entry into St. Denis, when the keys of that place were borne to him (Condé), the cry went up, ' Long live the King, Louis of Bourbon,' that is to say, the Prince of Condé. But to-day one says that the cry was ' Long live the King and Louis of Bourbon.' "[3] It was also reported that Condé had had a medal struck with his own name engraved on it as King. M. Edmond Poullet is one of the latest scholars to reiterate this charge.[4] It has, however, no foundation in fact. The account of the Palatine Envoy, Zuleger, of his interview with Catherine shortly after the retreat of the Protestants from before Paris in the autumn of 1567, is conclusive on this point. " I again asked," he wrote, "if the Prince had had coins struck as King of France. The Queen replied, ' He has had coins struck in the former war, and perhaps in this one also, but with the name and inscription of the King, my son.' "[5] Then the heart of Francis II. and the busts of Louis XI. and Louis XII. at Orleans, the tombs of the ancestors of Francis I. at Angoulême and of the Bourbons at Vendôme, were either desecrated or destroyed. And the conclusion was drawn that a levelling spirit was at work. It may be so, for it is hard to dogmatise on questions of motive. But it might equally be held that we have here the mere lust for pillage or the blind rage of fanatics against everything of wood or

[1] Turin, Francia Lettere Ministri, i. ; Miscellanea di Storia Italiana, ix. 578 ; Naples, Carte Farn., 258.

[2] Monluc, v. 25.

[3] Petrucci, Paris, 8th Oct. 1567 : Desjardins, iii. 538.

[4] Editorial note, Corres. du Cardinal de Granvelle, iii. 85.

[5] König. bay. Akad. d. Wiss., hist. Klasse, Abhandlungen, 1870, ii. 197.

stone. Thus at Caen, in May, 1562, the tomb of William the Conqueror suffered equally with, but no more than, the statues of the Seven Liberal Arts.[1]

There is, in fact, no reason to believe that Calvinism, had it been accepted by the Crown and a majority of the nation, would have proved a disturbing factor. Such as we find it when first organised in France in 1559, and before it had been given a definite political complexion by outside forces, it was neither essentially anti-monarchical nor anti-national. It is quite possible to conceive of it as fitting into the framework of the then existing society, and aiding, not retarding, the centralising tendencies of the monarchy. Yet though much Catholic criticism was mere wild striking in the dark, their instincts did not wholly play them false. No religious ideal could be precipitated into the midst of the sixteenth-century state without its influence on politics. And when once Calvinism—democratic in its conceptions, oligarchic in its forms—had to force its way in opposition to, or at least unaided by, royalty, it was of the very breath of change. It was inevitably dragged into the political arena. It was forced to declare for or against Guise. It was equally forced to favour either the predominance of the Crown or the fast-disappearing privileges of noble, townsman, and province. Thus it came about that after 1572 Huguenotism gave expression to many of the forces telling in favour of localism and against centralisation. It represented municipal, feudal, and aristocratic reaction. And as a necessary corollary it often voiced anti-absolutist yearnings which were scarcely distinguishable from anti-monarchical tirades. The massacre of St. Bartholomew was the turning-point. Until that date, these tendencies, even when existent, were half-concealed. Calvin inculcated obedience to constituted authority; when there was rebellion, it was always claimed to be directed not against the King but against his advisers. Royal prerogatives were seldom discussed, save at odd moments, as when in 1562, in the consistory of Orleans, the question of the relative merits of elective and hereditary monarchy was raised. Huguenot aims were preponderatingly religious, their wars were religious

---

[1] Delarue, *Nouveaux essais sur Caen*, 575; Bourgueville de Bras, 253-258.

wars. All this was changed by the murder of Coligny and his fellow-victims. The nature of kingship was examined, its limitations set down ; popular rights were stated, even the power to depose was claimed ; ingenious theories of resistance —the germ is to be found in Calvin's *Institutio Christianæ Religionis*[1]—were elaborated, the right being variously said to reside in the Estates General or the magistrates. The most anarchic of these propositions are to be found in Mornay's *Vindiciæ contra Tyrannos* and the *Droit des magistrats sur les sujets*.[2] But there even lurked a danger for established forms in the seemingly innocent enthusiasm of Hotman for the true and ancient France, where " the government was the very same which the ancient philosophers, and among them Plato and Aristotle, judged to be best and most excellent in the world, as being made up and constituted of a mixture and just temperament of the three kinds of government—namely, the regal, noble, and popular."[3]

Nor was this mere theory. When Condé was chosen in the assembly of Milhau, 1574, " chief, governor-general, and protector, in the name and place and with the authority of the King of France, to rule with such lawful moderation as should befit a true judge of Israel chosen of God, and not a tyrant nor terrible and ungovernable prince,"[4] he was hedged about with so many restrictions that he had little power left. At a later date, Henry of Navarre was provided with a consultative council, while on the mere rumour of his possible apostasy the conference of St. Jean took into consideration the proposal to elect a new protector for their church.[5]

But it was not only against universal distrust that Huguenotism had to struggle. The Catholic reaction, as conducted by the Jesuits, had appeared. Its presence in Europe was soon evident in the changed attitude of the Emperor Maximilian, once the hope of Protestantism.[6] In

---

[1] Marcks' *Coligny*, 333.

[2] See Weill, *Les théories sur le pouvoir royal*, etc. ; and Armstrong, *English Hist. Review*, iv. 13.

[3] *Franco-Gallia*, 65 (English trans., 1711).

[4] Anquez, *Histoire des assem. pol.*, 13, 14.

[5] *Mémoires de Mornay*, iv. 426-430.

[6] Maurenbrecher, *Hist. Zeit.*, xxxii. 222

France it was already a force in 1562. It received a further
impetus during the course of the first civil war. " The latter,"
remarked the Venetian Corer, "brought out the innate
Catholicism of the people." From the very first Paris
became the centre of the movement. This was of immense
importance. Paris was France. La Rochelle, opulent as it
was, was a poor substitute. The population of the capital
was said to be 400,000, of which more than 20,000 were
scholars. And yet out of the whole city, says La Noue,
Condé in the spring of 1562 could not count on more
than 300 gentlemen, 300 soldiers, 400 scholars, and a few
bourgeois.

Another reason for Huguenot failure was the violence of its
partisans. In many instances violence was to be expected.
It was the retaliation for long years of persecution and wrong.
Still, there is no doubt that their character as combatants
steadily deteriorated. They fought the first war " in the guise
of angels," so ran the legend, " the second as men, and the
third as fiends incarnate." [1] Such deterioration was almost
inevitable ; it was equally apparent in the Catholic forces. It
nevertheless alienated many, and gave a certain point to the
diatribes of enemies. For instance, we have the Catholic poet
and soldier La Motte Messemé writing of the spirit of France
brooding with horror over the ways of the new sect.[2] " When
they passed from words to arms," declared a Venetian
Ambassador, "and with horrible cruelty began to rob, lay
waste, and slay, the poor people began to say, ' What religion
is this ? Are these not they who professed to understand the
gospel better than another ? But where find they that Christ
bids one steal his neighbour's goods and slay his fellow ? '
These and like considerations were the reason why one put
a curb on one's self and no longer threw one's self (into the
movement) as at first." [3]

Nor was their licence one of action only. Intemperance
of speech was a still older and more inherent vice. In dealing
with the Church of Rome, especially, they indulged in the
lowest forms of scurrility. The Pope was customarily branded

[1] D'Aubigné, iii. 390.   [2] *Les Honnestes Loisirs*, 62.
[3] Alberi, iv. 186.

as Antichrist. He was invoked in one Huguenot song with
the cry—

> " Dormoy tu?
> Dormoy tu, dy, grosse beste,
> Dormoy tu?"[1]

A treatise of the usually grave and self-contained Mornay
was given to the world under the title of *The Mystery of
Iniquity, that is to say, the History of the Papacy*. The
German scholar Botzheim, in relating the massacre of St.
Bartholomew at Orleans, mentioned incidentally a Madame
Coursière, "who was wont to detest, execrate, and curse the
Mass." The priest Mendoza averred that the Spanish in 1565
discovered in Fort Caroline packs of cards illustrated with rude
caricatures of the holiest objects of Catholic veneration. We
would not imply that the Huguenots were without excuse.
As they were the attacking force, self-repression was difficult,
and a certain fury of tone exhilarating. Moreover, they had
suffered much, and could not be expected to make too nice
a choice of words. And it is well to remember that their
enemies were at least equally guilty. Nevertheless, the fact
remains that these excesses kindled an undying hatred among
Catholics.

Unfortunately, too, this truculent tone accentuated the
differences between French and German Protestantism. These
differences were profound, and began early to be translated
into acts. Thus, when Anthony of Navarre proposed a
Protestant league, Johannes Brenz at once demanded his
opinion on the communion;[2] in the first war of religion part
of the royal mercenaries were raised in the Protestant
Ernestine Thuringia;[3] the Margrave Philip of Baden, the
Rhinegrave John Philip, and the Count of Westerburg
actually assisted Charles IX. against the Huguenots;[4] and
Alva, with pardonable exaggeration, declared that the hatred
of Protestant and Calvinist was greater than that of Protestant

---

[1] " Chanson contre le Pape," by Eustorg de Beaulieu, 1546, in Bordier's
Chansonnier Huguenot, 127.
[2] Kugler, *Christoph Herzog zu Wirtemberg*, ii. 293.
[3] Barthold, *Deutschland und die Huguenotten*, 375–398.
[4] Menzel, *Wolfgang von Zweibrücken*, 506.

and Catholic.[1] Yet the Calvinist and Lutheran divines,—
especially those of Wurtemberg and Saxony,—instead of
attempting to conciliate one another and bring about an
understanding, inflamed jealousies and created difficulties.
Calvin in this instance set a bad example. Vermilius wrote
to him in regard to the controversy with the Lutheran
Westphal: "Dolebunt hujus pugnæ tam cruentum fuisse
conflictum? Regeremus vicissim non potuisse aliâ ratione
Centauros et Cyclopes."[2] Calvin himself exclaimed in 1561:
"Interea Lutherani suis bacchanalibus indulgere non desi-
nunt."[3] The *odium theologicum* was a hard taskmaster.

So far we have mostly dealt with the general causes of
opposition to Huguenotism. There were others, however,
particular to special classes. The hostility of the mass of the
peasantry was exhibited in every quarter, in Perigord equally
with Normandy and Poitou. The reasons for this were
complex. To mention no others, they were the tillers of the
soil, and suffered heavily from marauding armies and bands
of Protestants; they were peasants, the Huguenots, in a
peculiar degree, the noblesse. Here is a sentence from La
Noue which throws a flood of light on the subject: "One will
find gentlemen who imagine, I believe, that the mark of
nobility is to intimidate, beat, and take what suits them from
their subjects, as though the latter were slaves."[4] And the
Papal Nuncio noted in 1570 that the nobility tyrannised over
the people.[5]

We need not dwell on the weakness to the Protestant
cause from this alienation of a whole section of the people.
Equally serious was the estrangement of the legal profession.
This latter was the champion of Gallican liberties, and looked
askance at the Reformers as interfering in a domain peculiarly
its own. They equally hated them as politicians, "persuaded
as they were that, if those of the religion came out on top,
they would have to run; otherwise, they would be made to
explain their judgments and mount the scaffold, in order to
correct the abuses of justice which are not less than those of

[1] Baumgarten, *Vor der Bart.*, 105.   [2] *Calvini Opera*, xvi. 35.
[3] *Calvini Opera*, xviii. 475.   [4] La Noue, 13.
[5] Paris, 22nd Aug.: Vatican, Nunz. di Francia, iv. 26.

the Roman Church. Moreover, if a true reformation came, they would have to face the loss of the big benefices which they and their children and other guardians were holding." [1] If we add to these words of La Planche the fact that the Parlements were rich with the spoils of Huguenot confiscations, that they were the champions of royalty against aristocratic privilege, that the Huguenots were soldiers with all the fine contempt for a class unused to arms, we can understand why there was war to the knife. When it was in their power, Condé, Coligny, and their followers heavily punished their enemies, as when in the first war of religion they executed Sapin, and in 1570 ravaged the homes of the Parlement of Toulouse. At other times they heaped ridicule on their pretensions and exposed their failings. Bernard Palissy, Huguenot, artist, craftsman, in one of his charming allegories of contemporary life thus satirically depicted the thoughts of one of the noblesse of the robe: " Then I told him quite simply that all who drink the milk and wear the fleece of the sheep and feed them not are accursed; and I quoted to him the passage written in Jeremiah the Prophet (chapter 34). At that, swelling with braggadocio and a mighty fury, he said, ' What? According to what you say there would be a great many damned and accursed of God, for I know that in our sovereign court and in all the courts of France there are very few councillors who do not possess a bit of a benefice which helps them supply their trappings, accoutrements, banquets, and petty cash of the home, and even acquire in time some noble place or office of greater honour and authority. Call you that folly? It is the highest wisdom,' said he. ' What is a great folly is to be hung and burnt for upholding the authority of the Bible.' " [2]

Hotman, again, in his *Franco-Gallia* described their history as one of craft and usurpation, and of a class living upon the spoils of the people, " promoting contributions and processes, just as of old a great number of Egyptians were employed by their tyrants in building pyramids and other such useless structures." [3]

[1] La Planche, 404. [2] Anatole France, *Les œuvres de Bernard Palissy*, 125.
[3] *Franco-Gallia*, 136.

Thus we see that Huguenotism, with certain advantages, was bound to fail. The France of the sixteenth century rejected it, as the Florence of the fifteenth century had rejected Savonarola. She rejected it with equal determination, and possibly with greater justification; for she seemed to have other means to work out her safety, while the passionate melancholy of the Italian was a more potent spell than the clear dogmatism of Geneva. The Calvinistic organisation, in truth, in which the religious stood apart from the political, or rather where the latter was directly or indirectly controlled by the former, prospered where, as in Scotland, it seemed the only way toward national unity. It failed in the England of the seventeenth century, where Parliament was an instrument ready forged.

So with France; a small Protestant bourgeoisie and a large section of the nobility did not offer a field for permanent success. Alter the circumstances which gave it a temporary impulse, and you have failure. Throw it into opposition to the King, as after Henry IV.'s abjuration, and it loses the strength which it derived from its position as advocate of patriotism and the national cause. What France craved was not so much moral and religious ideals, as national unity and, what for the time at least flowed from it, national strength. This the monarchy and Henry IV. could give.

Yet though one is inclined to believe that the course actually taken by France was the one marked out for her, that is not to say that it was the only one, or the one that offered most. When she turned her back on the Reform movement, she took a heavy responsibility. It has often been said that modern England is the outcome of her struggles for political and religious liberty. Modern France is equally the result of her rejection of Huguenotism and the Revocation of the Edict of Nantes. France, indeed, has responded times out of number to the generous appeals of humanity. She has shown less instinct to adopt a new ordering of daily life. And yet this latter is what the acceptance of Calvinism would have entailed. It would have meant much to her—above all, the bracing of the moral fibre. There can be no doubt that Protestantism was the moral force of the sixteenth century. In this respect, at least, the old faith had little to offer. The golden age of French Catholicism was yet to come, the age of St. François de Sales, Bossuet, Fénelon, Pascal. And more, Huguenotism contained within its ranks much that was best in France. This was inevitable. The very acceptance of a new faith was an intellectual effort ; it also told of the workings of conscience. The belief, too, in the direct responsibility of individual souls to God, and the facing through long years of infinite odds, created character. We can find no one among militant Catholics who can compare in those qualities which go to make up a rounded and impressive personality with Coligny, Beza, La Noue, Mornay. And the more closely Huguenots clung to their ideals, the more they deserve generous treatment. Henry IV.'s abjuration may have seemed sound policy; ethically, however, the censure of the act by d'Aubigné was of a higher order of ideas. " It was better," he exclaimed, " to be King of a corner of France, serving God, and assisted by those of tried fidelity and love, than reign precariously under the heel and domination and at the bidding of the Pope."

And lastly, French Protestantism in one aspect represented human progress. It was reason struggling to the light. Many of its political features, good and bad, find their parallel among the Catholic party. But it can claim two great advantages. It championed national opposition to Spain; and its history was a long struggle for toleration. That struggle may have been selfish in a sense. The true meaning of religious liberty may never have been fully grasped. Certainly Calvinism, when predominant elsewhere, was impatient of dissent. Nevertheless, the struggle initiated by Coligny and closed in victory almost forty years later was a milestone on the road to religious freedom. If that victory had been more frankly accepted, France would have suffered no such national catastrophe as the Revocation of the Edict of Nantes.

CHAPTER XVIII

COLIGNY AND THE NEW WORLD

Early French Exploration — Laudonnière's Exposition of Colonial Movement — Villegaignon's Expedition to Brazil — Ribaut's First Expedition to Florida — Expedition of Laudonnière—Ribaut's Second Expedition—Coming of Menéndez—Massacre of Huguenots—Coligny's Position—Expedition of de Gourgues—Massacre of Spaniards—Expedition of the Young Monluc—Expedition of La Mainguetière—Coligny's Colonial Policy Part of his General Policy—Reasons of Failure.

DURING the fifteenth century the Iberian peninsula was in the throes of a movement of expansion. Portugal was steadily creeping down the west coast of Africa. In 1492, Columbus discovered America for Spain. Within a few months the Holy See set itself to apportion the new heritage. Out of its pure liberality, and in the plenitude of its apostolic power, it conceded and consigned to the rulers of Castile and Leon "all islands and lands found and to be found, discovered and to be discovered, to the west and south, by making and drawing a line from the Arctic or North Pole to the Antarctic or South Pole, which line shall be distant an hundred leagues west and south of any of the islands which are commonly called the Azores or Cape de Verde."[1] Such was the decree. But it was not to be the last word on the New World. England and France, possessed of a new unity, and quickened by all that we sum up under the name of the Renaissance, had their ambitions. They had the need and energy to expand; the most fitting direction seemed over sea.

---

[1] Bull of Alexander VI. of the 4th of May, 1493 (Navarrete, ii. 32). It was withdrawn and superseded by a later one of the 25th of September of the same year. The two Iberian powers eventually agreed on a meridian 370 leagues west of the Cape de Verde, Spain taking all discoveries west, and Portugal all those east of the line.

France, at least, was already the heir of traditions.   Her
hardy mariners, so it is claimed, explored and traded as early
as the fourteenth century on the west coast of Africa.   Some
years before the voyage of Columbus, a French ship was said
to have been swept by the Gulf Stream to the shores of
Brazil.   Be that as it may, their pilots and captains—Gonne-
ville, Verrazano, and a host of others—by the middle of the
sixteenth century had built up a trade with Brazil, and
drawn upon the fisheries of Newfoundland.   Francis I. gave
them a benevolent if fitful protection.   With fine derision he
asked to be shown the article in the testament of Adam which
willed away the New World to the kings of Portugal and Spain,
and, in the spirit of his question, actively aided Verrazano in
his enterprises.   He was eager to partake of fabulous riches
and break down a monopoly ; he was doubtless not unwilling,
too, to injure his greatest adversary, Spain.   The death, however, of Verrazano, the great Italian captain in the French
service, " was the cause that this laudable enterprise was left
off untill the yeere 1534, at which time his Majestie (desiring
always to enlarge his kingdome, countreys and dominions, and
the advauncing the ease of his subjectes) sent thither a pilote
of S. Mallowes, a Breton named James Cartier, well seene in
the art and knowledge of navigation, and especially of the
North parts, commonly called the new lande, led by some
hope to finde passage that wayes to the South Seas." [1]

Jacques Cartier himself adds another end which he had in
view : " It seems to my feeble understanding," writes he to
the King, " though I cannot give the reason why, that it is the
will of God in His divine goodness, that even as all human
creatures dwelling upon the globe have seen and known this
sun, so shall they in time to come have knowledge of and
believe our holy faith."   His voyages to the " North Parts,"
or Canada, half religious, half secular, need not detain us here.
No permanent settlement resulted.   The supreme effort to
found a New France in America was yet to be made, and by
Coligny.   Let us then turn to the plain tale of his ventures
as expressed in the language and thoughts of the sixteenth
century.   There we shall find the reasons which impelled him

---

[1] Ribaut's *Terra Florida.*

to undertake the task, the ideas stirring in his breast and in the breasts of his contemporaries, his hopes, plans, and ultimate failure.

Laudonnière, Protestant, gentleman, the trusted friend of Coligny and captain of the second French expedition to Florida, thus gives us the philosophy and ethics of the colonial movement. " There are two things," writes he, " which according to mine opinion have bene the principall causes in consideration whereof aswell they of ancient times as those of our age have been induced to travell into farre and remote regions. The first hath beene the naturall desire which wee have to search out the commodities to live happily, plentifully, and at ease : be it whither one abandon his naturall Countrey altogether to dwell in a better, or bee it that men make voyage thither, there to search out and bring from thence such things as are there to be found, and are in greatest estimation and in most request in our Countreys. The second cause hath beene the multitude of people too fruitefull in generation, which being no longer able to dwell in their native soyles, have entred upon their neighbours limites, and oftentimes passing further have pearced even unto the uttermost regions. After this sort, the North climate, a fruitfull father of so many nations, hath oftentimes sent foorth this way and that way his valiant people and by this meane hath peopled infinite Countreys."[1] Then deprecating the lust of glory and dominion, and the Roman system of colonisation, which wore out the central power, he continues : " These are the effects and rewards of al such as being pricked forward with this Romane and tyrannical ambition will goe about thus to subdue strange people : effects, I say, contrary to the profit which those shall receive, which onely are affectioned to the common benefite, that is to say, to the generall policie of all men, and endeavour to unite them one to another, as well by trafficke and civill conversation, as also by military vertues, and force of armes, when as the Savages will not yeeld unto their endevours so much tending unto their profit.

" For this cause Princes have sent forth out of their Dominions certaine men of good activity to plant themselves in strange Countreys, there to make their profite to bring the

[1] Laudonnière, *Hakluyt*, iii. 367 (edit. of 1809-1812).

Countrey to civilitie, and if it might be, to reduce the inhabitants to the true knowledge of our God: an end so much more commendable, as it is farre from all tyrannical and cruel government: and so they have alwayes thrived in their enterprises, and by little and little gained the heartes of them which they have conquered or wonne unto them by any meanes."

The first expedition connected with the name of Coligny was that of Nicholas Durand, Seigneur of Villegaignon, a man of very eventful career. Born at Provans in Champagne, he was a contemporary of Calvin at the University of Paris. Entering the Order of St. John of Jerusalem, he was left for dead after the most heroic charge in the African campaign of Charles v. He fought the Turks in Hungary, and was present at the battle of Cerisole. By splendid daring, he brought Mary Queen of Scots safely to France; and in 1548 found himself Vice-Admiral of Brittany. In this position he was the energetic lieutenant of Coligny in the operations round Boulogne, and by his real abilities won the favour of the Admiral. Vain, restless, visionary, unstable, intelligent, brave, in sentiment a monk, by profession a soldier, he had just those qualities and those vices which might wreck a delicate undertaking. In the course of time, in Brittany, as elsewhere, he had his inevitable quarrel. " Finding himself at daggers drawn with the Captain of the château of Brest on a question of the fortifications, and in danger of losing his influence, he was seized with the idea of making a voyage to Brazil. He knew that Messire Gaspard de Coligny, who was Admiral of France, and favoured henceforth as far as he was able the Huguenot party, was in high favour with King Henry. Therefore to gain his ends, he told him that his sole object was to find and fortify some spot in America which would serve as a refuge for those of the religion who should wish to retire there. Little by little, declared he, they would people the country, and advance the church of God in bringing the inhabitants to a knowledge of the truth. It was a fine enterprise, and what was more, seemed feasible. The Admiral, therefore, explained to the King, not what concerned the kingdom of God, but the benefits which would accrue to him and his realm from those lands as it did to the Spaniards, and obtained two large vessels well freighted, and ten thousand livres to meet the first expenses." [1] The *personnel* of his company was not all that could be wished. He appealed for men fearing God. A few adventurers of the better sort and some Huguenots responded. For the rest he had to scour the gaols. On the 12th of July, 1555, his little fleet of three vessels set sail from Havre. He had with him six hundred souls—sailors, soldiers, gentlemen, and artisans. A combination of monkish prejudice and want of foresight had led him to exclude women. On the other hand, he carried with him a valuable library of theological works, which was later to prove a powerful engine against the heresiarchs from Geneva. Provisions were scanty, for he had lavishly squandered the sums entrusted to him. He was sailing, as he thought, to a country of golden promises, where there was abundance of everything. At length sighting land, they came on the 10th of November to where Rio Janeiro now stands, to their tired eyes surely a paradise. The air was soft, the quiet bay swept inward, the strange forests were shadows of a dream. Villegaignon's hopes were more than realised. Freighting his vessels, he sent them home to tell of the wonders of his land. He wrote to Coligny and Calvin in particular, imploring them to send him godly colonists and ministers to reclaim the heathen and build up a new and holy kingdom.

The spot finally selected for the settlement was an island, and so less open to attack. Here he set himself to build a fort to repel either natives or Portuguese. In honour of his protector, he called it Fort Coligny. Even the gentlemen, to whom manual labour was derogatory, were infected by his zeal, and fell to work. The ethics also were to be of Malta and of his Order. He had brought no women, yet an illicit connection with the natives was punishable with death. Though an excellent position for a fort, the island had no water; that had to be sought on the mainland. This was an oversight. It was also an oversight that no seed was sown. Still, for the moment provisions were plentiful; the

[1] *Histoire Ecclésiastique*, i. 184.

friendly Indians supplied them in return for trinkets. The fate of a colony worked on such a system can easily be imagined. All grew tired of work, not a few of so strict a morality. A formidable conspiracy of the less reputable element was detected only just in time. A greater danger threatened when Villegaignon instituted a *corvée* upon the aborigines to finish the fortifications. As a result, these latter silently disappeared; supplies ceased to flow. Things looked black indeed, when, on the 7th of March, 1557, sails appeared on the horizon. The fleet, so long waited for in vain, had come.

When Villegaignon's letters arrived in France, Coligny set about organising relief. Bois le Comte, nephew of Villegaignon, was given command of the expedition. He had few of the virtues of his uncle, all his failings, with some others peculiarly his own. Under him were 290 persons, Normans, men of Paris, and of Champagne. This time there were six girls, a too small quota if the new settlement was to be permanent. The pick of the company, however, were some French Huguenots, and especially fourteen Genevans, chosen by Calvin. Their leader was Dupont de Corguilleray, who had formerly been a neighbour of Coligny; the two ministers were Pierre Richer and Guillaume Chartier. Of the eleven others, the best known to fame is Jean de Léry, the inimitable historian of the voyage. Passing through Châtillon, they were gladly received by Coligny, who begged them to push on for Paris and the coast, and avoid delay. On the 19th of November, 1556, Bois le Comte put to sea. Every vessel met on the way was mercilessly pillaged. It was an evil beginning for an expedition which was to extend the bounds of the kingdom of God. On the 7th of March, 1557, as we have said, they were descried by the watchers of Fort Coligny in the offing.

Villegaignon, as may be supposed, received them with open arms. He promised the Huguenots the exercise of their religion. He wrote to Calvin to express his gratitude. He would not stray a hair's breadth, he declared, from the path marked out by the latter in his letters; these were to be his guide, and with this intent he had them registered in his "senate." Moreover, he had chosen a council of ten, to which he had delegated all his powers.[1]

Richer and Chartier were, on their side, no less enthusiastic over their reception in "Antarctic Gaul." "We have found," wrote they, "a father and brother in Nicholas Villegaignon— father, because he embraces, nourishes, and fosters us as sons; a brother, because with us he calls upon God the only Heavenly Father, and believes that Jesus Christ is the only mediator between God and man." And they go on to liken him to Solomon, and to tell how he partook of the Lord's Supper in the Genevan style, prayed, and made public confession of his faith.[2] This was an auspicious opening. A unity, however, so perfect could not last long. These letters were written in April. In May the rift had already appeared. The pretext of the quarrel were the rites of baptism. The real cause, no doubt, was that Villegaignon had never really accepted Calvinism, and was now at one and the same time alarmed at the effect which his coquetting with the new religion might have on his position in France, and jealous of the influence Richer and the Huguenot leaders were gaining in the little colony. Villegaignon did not at once proceed to extremities. He allowed Chartier to return to Europe on the 4th of June to refer the dispute to Calvin. When he was gone, however, a close study of the Fathers, the promptings of his jealous and autocratic nature, the not too wise influence of a priest, Jean Cointa, had their effect. He had forbidden Huguenot worship during Chartier's absence. He now indulged in a series of petty tyrannies. As a consequence, the Huguenots retired to the mainland. Finally, they obtained leave to start for Europe. This meant the ruin of the expedition, for all that was best was to be found in their ranks. On the 4th of January, 1558, they set sail in a Breton vessel. Five out of the twenty Genevans returned to Brazil when only a few days out; the ship was unseaworthy, and Villegaignon had taken care that it was badly provisioned. Of those who returned, he kept two in prison as heretics, the other three he hurled from the rocks. Huguenot writers

---

[1] A Latin letter of Villegaignon, *Calvini Opera*, xvi. 437.
[2] Latin Letters of Richer and Chartier, *Calvini Opera*, xvi. 433, 440-446.

ATTACK ON FORT COLIGNY (FORT DES FRANÇOYS) BY THE PORTUGUESE, 1560

(Thevet)

have designated his action as murder. It certainly was a harsh justice. Those who reached Europe fortunately escaped his ignoble vengeance. He had entrusted to them a sealed packet to be delivered to the first magistrates they should meet on landing. It was an order to imprison them as heretics. More humane than he, the magistrates refused to put his recommendation into execution. The rest is soon told. The colony was now ruined beyond redemption. Villegaignon sailed away to France at the end of 1558, and left it to its fate. It was not long in coming. In the early months of 1560, Fort Coligny was captured by the Portuguese governor of Bahia.

Yet though the history of New France in South America ends here, Coligny's career as a coloniser was only at its beginning. From being a secondary figure, a mere protector, he became the chief actor. For the moment he seems to have been tempted by other Portuguese possessions, by the rich and half-discovered lands beyond the Moluccas, and by the reputed gold mines on the upper waters of the Zambesi.[1] But eventually he turned to Florida,[2] a country discovered and claimed by Spain. His colonial policy was now a branch of his foreign policy—that is, a phase of his struggle with Philip II. " My Lord Admirall of Chastillon," so wrote Laudonnière, a member of the first expedition to Florida and the captain of the second, " a noble man more desirous of the publique then of his private benefite, understanding the pleasure of the King his prince, which was to discover new and strange Countreys, caused vessels fit for this purpose to be made ready with all diligence, and men to be levied meete for such an enterprise : among whom hee chose Captaine, John Ribault, a man in trueth expert in sea causes : which having received his charge, set himself to Sea the yeere 1562, the eighteenth of Februarie, accompanied onely with two of the Kings shippes, but so well furnished with Gentlemen (of whose number I myselfe was one) and with olde Souldiers, that he had meanes to atchieve some notable thing and

---

[1] Falgairolle : *Jean Nicot, Sa Correspondence*, 35, 71.

[2] The whole south-east coast of North America was known under the name of Florida.

worthy of eternall memorie." [1]   John Ribaut's own explanation
as to how he entered on the undertaking is more detailed,
states more clearly the religious aspect of early colonising,
and in its Elizabethan translation is still more delicate and
quaint.   "Where as in the yere of our Lorde God, 1562, it
pleased God to move your honour,[2] to choose and appoynt
us, to discover and vewe a certaine longe coast of the West
India, from the heade of the land called Laflorida, drawyng
toward the North part, unto the head of Brittons, distant from
the sayd head of Laflorida 900 leagues, or thereaboute : to the
end that we might certifie you and make true report of the
temperature, fertilitie, Ports, Havens, Ryvers, and generally of
all the commodities that be seen and found in that land, and
also to learne what people were there dwelling, which thing
you have long time ago desired, being stirred thereunto by this
zeale.   That France might one day through new discoveries
have knowledge of straunge countreys, and also thereof to
receyve (by means of continuall trafique) riche and inestimable
commodities as other nacions have done by taking in hand
such far navigations, bothe to the honour and prowesse of their
kinges and princes, and also to the encrease of great profit
and use to their common wealthes, countreys and dominions,
which is most of all without comparison to be considered and
esteemed.   It seemeth wel that we have been stirred hereunto
even of god above, and led to it by the hope and desiere you
have that a number of brutishe people and ignoraunt of Jesus
Christ, may by his grace come to some knowledge of his holy
lawes and ordinances.   So therefore it seemeth that it hath
pleased God by his godly providence to reserve the care which
he hath had of their salvation until this tyme, and wil bryng
them to our faith, at the time by himself alone foreseen and
ordeyned." [3]

With these thoughts in mind, Jean Ribaut set sail on the
12th of February, 1562.   With great daring he determined
on a new course, by steering straight for Florida and so
avoiding the Spanish Islands.   On " Thursday the laste of
Apryle at the breake of the daye, we discovered and clearly
perceyved a faire coast, stretchynge of a great length covered

[1] Laudonnière, *Hakluyt*, iii. 371.   [2] Coligny.   [3] Ribaut's *Terra Florida*.

with an infinite number of high and fayre trees.[2]   The next
day he resolved ...

LAUDONNIÈRE'S VISIT TO RIBAUT'S COLUMN OF OCCUPATION OF FLORIDA, THE ARMS OF FRANCE
BEING ENCIRCLED BY THE GRAND COLLAR OF THE ORDER OF ST. MICHAEL

(J. Le Moyne)

with an infinite number of high and fayre trees." [1]   The next
day he entered the river which he named the river May, and
which is now known as the St. John's.   Courteously received
by the natives, he took possession of the land in the name
of the King by raising a stone column, which Laudonnière,
two years later, found to be worshipped as an idol.[2]   Then
setting sail again, he coasted as far as Archer's Creek in South
Carolina.   Here he determined to found his colony.   Calling
the crews round him, he told them of his intention to navigate
farther north and then return to France for reinforcements.
Who, he asked, were willing to remain behind to form the
first settlement?   " I pray you therfore all to advise yourselves
thereof, and to declare your mindes freely unto mee, protesting that I will so well imprint your names in the kings eares
and the other princes, that your renowne shall hereafter shine
unquenchable through our Realme of France." [3]   After such
an appeal some twenty volunteered.   Thus was formed the
French colony of Charlesfort.   It was but another failure.
Ribaut started on his voyage for the north.   It was the last
they saw of him.   Arriving in France on the 20th of July,
he found his country plunged into civil war.   Another
expedition was impossible.   All he could do was to retire to
England and write his experiences.   For more than a year the
little camp on Archer's Creek waited for the ships that never
came.   At length, in 1563, disappointed and disillusioned,
they found their way back to Europe, landing in England.

It was at this very time that Coligny was at last free to
renew his efforts.   There was again peace in France, and in 1564
a royal proclamation had given him a respite of three years
from the charges of complicity in the murder of the Duke of
Guise.   Then " my lord Admiral de Chastillon shewed unto the
king, that he heard no newes at all of the men which Captaine
John Ribault had left in Florida, and that it were a pity to
suffer them to perish.   In which respect the king was content
he should cause 3 ships to be furnished, the one of six score

---

[1] Ribaut's *Terra Florida*.
[2] Narrative of Le Moyne, who accompanied the expedition under Laudonnière :
American edition, 1875.
[3] Laudonnière : *Hakluyt*, iii. 377.

tunnes, the other of 100, and the third of 60, to seeke them out, and to succour them."[1] "The Admiral the meanwhile, recommended to the king a nobleman of the name of Renaud de Laudonnière, a person well known at Court, and of varied abilities, though experienced not so much in military as in naval affairs. The king accordingly appointed him his own lieutenant, and appropriated for the expedition the sum of a hundred thousand francs. The admiral, who was a man endowed with all the virtues and eminent for Christian piety, was so zealous for the faithful doing of the king's business, as to give special instructions to Laudonnière, exhorting him in particular to use all manner of diligence in doing his duty, and first of all, since he professed to be a religious man, to select the right sort of men, and such as feared God, to be of his company. He would do well, in the next place, to engage as many skilled mechanics of all kinds as possible."[2] There was still the same fatal oversight as had ruined the expedition of Villegaignon: no agriculturists, no thought of sowing in the new land! In accordance, therefore, with instructions, Laudonnière embarked on the 22nd of April, 1564. On the 24th of June he cast anchor off the river May or St. John's, and after a cruise northward returned on the 29th. Here France made her second experiment in Floridan colonisation, and experienced her second failure. A fort which he named Fort Caroline was built on the south bank of the river, two leagues from its mouth. Two of the ships were sent back to France. Then the trouble began. There soon sprang up a party of dissatisfied adventurers who were to wreck the expedition. Laudonnière's seeming inability to ensure a constant flow of supplies, his readiness to listen to the mere talkers, his amiability—in fine, his lack of the highest qualities of leadership —was to give them their chance. At first some of the men proved unruly ; then followed active insubordination, a pardon, more trouble. Six or seven of the most factious were shipped off to Europe in a French vessel which had appeared. Thirteen sailors, left in their stead, became a nucleus of fresh discontent, and, joined by others, sailed off as pirates to the Antilles, where ultimately, forced by hunger, they entered the

---

[1] Laudonnière: *Hakluyt*, iii. 384. [2] Le Moyne, American edition, i.

harbour of Havana and disclosed all they knew of the French colony. In December the final conspiracy came. Laudonnière was deposed; two vessels which had been building were seized and manned. Then the conspirators disappeared, also bound for the Antilles. In course of time they were surprised by the Spaniards. The few who escaped returned to Fort Caroline, where four of the ringleaders were executed.

With the shedding of this looser element a period of prosperity might have been expected. But there were more difficulties ahead. Coligny had insisted on a humane treatment of the natives as essential for the success of New France. Laudonnière carried out his instructions to the letter. Unhappily, he allied himself with the less admirable, probably the weaker, of the two principal chiefs; then outraged all Indian sentiment by forcing his ally to restore his prisoners. As a result, there was coolness, followed by unconcealed hostility. As Laudonnière had not sown and did not fish, but dreamed of gold or new supplies from Europe, famine stared him in the face. To keep body and soul together, their former ally was seized and held to ransom in the form of provisions. As these were insufficient, raids were made on the Indian fields, and many French killed or wounded. A return to France now seemed the only alternative, and the carpenter was set to build a new vessel. But it was found that this would cause delay, and the men were impatient. Its construction, therefore, was abandoned, and a brigantine got ready, when the Englishman, Master John Hawkins, appeared with four sail on the 3rd of August, 1565. He was now near the conclusion of his second great voyage, having left Plymouth the year before. He at once offered to ship the French to Europe. Laudonnière, afraid that this was merely an English trick to dispossess them of the land, refused. But he gladly accepted Hawkins' handsome offer of provisions and the sale of a ship of fifty tons at a moderate price. In the relation of his voyage, Laudonnière bears eloquent testimony to the generosity of his benefactor. " I may say," writes he, " that we received as many courtesies of the Generall, as it was possible to receive of any man living. Wherein doubtlesse he hath wonne the

reputation of a good and charitable man, deserving to be
esteemed as much of us all as if he had saved our
lives." [1]   On the 7th of August, Hawkins left. On the
28th, Laudonnière was again ready to start, when a new
fleet appeared. It was that of Jean Ribaut.

Letters from Laudonnière had reached France, asking
for reinforcements, and at the same time had come the
malcontents and their charges against their late captain, of
tyranny, of writing and intriguing with other nobles, and,
what was especially offensive to the austere Admiral, of
living a dissolute life. Unfortunately, Coligny gave to the
latter too ready an ear. And while fitting out a new
expedition, he secretly determined on the recall of his
lieutenant at Fort Caroline. His appeal for men met with
a quick response. The failure of his colonising efforts
heretofore deterred but few. Volunteers came streaming in,
some led, remarks Le Challeux, a carpenter of the expedition,
by a devouring curiosity and thirst for knowledge, some by
hope of gain, and some by the restless spirit bred in the
civil wars. But what above all drew men was the alluring
picture given of this land as one of opulent promise, some
lost Atlantis of their dreams. " Florida promised full and
sufficient contentment of all earthly desires. It was a land
singularly favoured of heaven, where was neither frost nor
northern cold, nor any fierce, blistering, southern heat. The
fields, which needed neither to be worked nor in any way
prepared, produced a sufficient sustenance for such as should
dwell therein. It is enough, it seems, to have but diligent
and industrious men to make it the most rich and fertile
country in the whole circle of the world. There, too, the
grass sprouts and grows admirably tall ; everywhere are
animals, everywhere gold—a land, in fine, of spacious, well-
filled fields, of mountains of a just and moderate height, of
rivers marvellously pleasant, of divers trees exuding a sweet-
smelling gum. Considering all this, it would be strange
indeed if man did not draw therefrom great pleasure and
singular delectation." [2]   On the 22nd of May, 1565, the

---

[1] Laudonnière : *Hakluyt*, iii. 419.
[2] I have somewhat freely translated Le Challeux, 12 and 13.

expedition left Dieppe, a fleet of seven sail. It was the largest which had yet set out from France. It was under the command of the experienced sailor, Jean Ribaut, who had captained the first voyage to Florida in 1562, and who had now returned from England. Among his subordinates was to be found a relative of Coligny. On the 28th August, after having leisurely explored the coasts, they reached Fort Caroline. Laudonnière in his joy greeted them with a salvo of artillery. He did not take long to disabuse Ribaut of the false impressions he had received of his conduct. But when once he had read his recall, most considerately penned by the Admiral, he determined to return home. The generous offer of Ribaut to share the command did not shake his resolution. Events, however, were at hand which had not entered into their calculations. Ribaut had arrived on the 28th of August; on the 4th of September yet another fleet appeared. It was of five sail. But this time it was not Frenchmen nor the genial English slaver. It was the distinguished Spaniard, Menéndez de Avilés, a dark and fanatical spirit, come at the bidding of Philip II. to clear out this nest of heretics from New Spain. The port was sighted at two in the afternoon. Four of Ribaut's ships were riding lazily at anchor outside the bar. The Spaniards came on slowly. When still half a league away the wind died down, and they lay becalmed; then the rain fell in torrents, accompanied by thunder and lightning. By ten in the evening the storm passed, the stars came out, the wind freshened, and Pedro Menéndez was able to range alongside. His own ship cast anchor between the two largest of Ribaut's, hardly a pike-thrust away. It was now close on midnight. Suddenly a trumpet sounded. When the French replied, Menéndez, standing on the deck of the *San Pelayo*, called across to the enemy—

" Gentlemen, whence comes this fleet ? "

" From France," replied a voice.

" What are you doing here ? "

" We are bringing infantry, artillery, and supplies for a fort which the King of France possesses in this country and for others yet to build."

"Are you Catholics or Lutherans? Who is your general?"

"We are all Lutherans of the new religion, and our general is Jean Ribaut."

Then, in reply to their eager inquiries, he told them that he was Pedro Menéndez, come to burn and hang the Lutheran French. He would board them, said he, in the morning. Should any turn out to be Lutherans, he would execute justice on them as his King, Philip II. of Spain, had ordained. With one impulse the French hurled back insults and abuse. They jeered at him and his king. They challenged him to come on. If he were a brave man, cried they, he would not wait till the morning. This was mere bravado. They were not prepared for an attack. Ribaut and the majority of his followers were on shore. When Menéndez, roused by their insolence, got ready to close, they cut their cables, slipped out to sea, and easily evaded pursuit. In the morning the Spanish general returned. But he found it impossible to land: French soldiers were massed on the beach. It was equally impossible to force a passage, for inside the bar the smaller French vessels were drawn up across the river, and formed an effective barrier. He therefore turned south to San Agustin, now St. Augustine, where part of his force was already disembarking.

News of this was brought to Ribaut by three of the vessels which had fled from the Spaniards the night before. It at once suggested to him a bold move. He would attack them before they had time to entrench or receive reinforcements. His plan, however, met with unexpected opposition. Laudonnière warned him of the peril of the undertaking. He was able to attest from his own experience the danger arising from the sudden and violent storms of the coast. Other officers strongly advised setting up the cannon in Fort Caroline, strengthening the defences, and harassing the Spaniards should they march to the attack. It at least seemed expedient to await the return of the flagship, the *Trinity*, which had been blown out to sea. But all these objections were to no purpose. Ribaut insisted. He was fond, as Laudonnière says of him, of the devices of his own brain, " which sometimes he printed in his head so deeply that it was very hard to put them out." And now at this juncture he recalled the wording of the last written despatch of Coligny : " Captain Ribaut ! While in the act of closing this letter, I have received certain news that Don Pedro Menéndez is leaving Spain for the coast of New France. See that you do not suffer him to trouble us, any more than he would let us trouble them." This Ribaut read in the light of a command for instant action. And so on the 10th of September he sailed out with his larger vessels. He had with him the greater part of his own force, together with the pick of those of Laudonnière.

Though a hazardous undertaking, it promised well. And with ordinary good fortune Ribaut might have been credited with one of the most brilliant feats of French colonial enterprise. But wind and weather conspired against him. Two of the Spanish fleet were stealing off—one for Spain, the other for Havana—when the French closed in on San Agustin. Menéndez himself, with two boats and a sloop, lay becalmed some distance from land ; he seemed to offer an easy prey ; suddenly a light breeze sprang up, and he slipped in over the bar. The French, with their heavier vessels, could not follow. They therefore turned to the open sea—at least so reported Menéndez to Philip II.—and set out in pursuit of the Spanish galleon. But the prize escaped. One of the terrible hurricanes of those waters swept down and cast them up as hopeless wrecks on the coast far to the southward.

Menéndez watched them sail away, no doubt with grave misgivings. But the storm brought him his opportunity. He reasoned that the bulk of the Huguenot force must be on board. It would take them a long time to beat back. Meanwhile, Fort Caroline would be practically defenceless. He had only to march against it, and it was his. On the 16th according to the Chaplain Mendoza, or the 18th according to Menéndez' own letter, he set out. For two days he struggled on, like the great Conquistador he was, through rain and storm, across trackless wastes and swollen rivers, with a tired, grumbling, and half-mutinous soldiery. At dawn on the 20th he stood on the bluff fringing the river. The fort lay below him in the valley. His men rushed down the slope. There was no defence. The French were sleeping. It was little else than a massacre. A hundred and forty-two in all were slaughtered. Only the women and children and those under the age of fifteen were spared. Three light craft which were anchored close by were helpless, and had to witness the most revolting scenes of the tragedy. The Spanish soldiery, with appalling cruelty, came down to the water's edge, and, shouting their cries of victory, threw at them the eyes torn out of their victims. One of the vessels was sunk. The other two, the larger being under the command of the son of Jean Ribaut, escaped down the river and joined the rest of the fleet. Here, a remnant of fugitives, which had made its way painfully through the woods, was eventually picked up. They were twenty-six in number. Among them were Laudonnière, the geographer Le Moyne, who has left us a series of interesting illustrations of the expedition with explanatory text, and another historian of this French attempt at colonisation, Le Challeux, the carpenter of Dieppe. They had now to decide what was to be done. No news came of Ribaut, and yet it was impossible to remain on indefinitely. Two or three of the vessels, therefore, were scuttled, and on the 25th of September they left in the remaining two for Europe. Separated at sea, the one which carried Laudonnière arrived at Swansea in Wales, while the other, with the younger Ribaut, a selfish and cowardly sailor, who seems to have possessed none of the qualities of his father, reached La Rochelle. They had lost all their illusions. The grey-haired Le Challeux, who has written so eloquently of the marvellous wonders of La Florida, looked back on it all as an evil dream—

> " Qui veut aller à la Floride,
>   Qu'il y aille, j'y ay esté :
> Et revenu sec et aride,
>   Et abbatu de povreté." [1]

On the 24th of September, Menéndez had returned to San Agustin. On the 28th he heard for the first time that Jean

---

[1] *Relation de N. Le Challeux*, prefatory poem, " par ledit Autheur arrivé en sa maison en la ville de Dieppe, ayant faim."

Ribaut had been wrecked, and that the French were now a few leagues distant to the south. With his usual decision, he determined to strike at once. He arrived on the scene at night, having made the journey partly by boat and partly on foot. The French fires were seen burning brightly on the other side of an inlet of the sea. When dawn broke, Menéndez, accompanied only by one companion, sauntered down to the water's edge. He was disguised as a sailor, his men, to the number of fifty, lying in ambush. The French, half famished from want of food, were busy searching among the rocks for shellfish. One of them was induced to swim across. He told a sorrowful tale. They were part of the French force which had been shipwrecked far to the south. All they wished for now was a free passage to Fort Caroline. When he was told that it had fallen and its garrison had been executed as Lutherans, he begged for the lives of himself and companions. But Menéndez was adamant: he insisted on unconditional surrender. Then a lieutenant of Laudonnière and four others were sent, but with a like result. In the end the French consented to hand over their arms and trust to his mercy. The French accounts even assert—they are here, however, not too trustworthy—that their lives were promised them. Whether this be true or not, it is certain that they were hopeful. But Menéndez was a typical Spaniard, and his mercy was typically Spanish. No seaman ever sailed out of the port of Cadiz with a sincerer faith in the cold, inexorable teachings of the Inquisition. The French were brought over by boat in batches of eight to ten. Menéndez himself retired behind a sand-dune and out of sight of the landing. At his order, the leader and eight of his fellows were fed and their hands tied behind their backs; for, said he, his force was small and San Agustin was four leagues away. Each batch was treated in like manner, being in each instance hid from those coming over. Ten or twelve who professed themselves Christians, as the Chaplain Mendoza naïvely puts it, were spared. These were sent to San Agustin by boat. Then the rest started on foot on the return journey. The great Conquistador himself strode on in advance. But hardly had he gone a bowshot's distance when he made a mark in the sand. This was the signal for the tragedy. As each batch passed the fatal line they were knifed by their captors. When the butchery was ended, a hundred and eleven corpses lay on the sand. Then Menéndez resumed his march, and so ended the bloody 29th of September.

On the day after his return he received information of the existence of still another band of Frenchmen, and at the same spot as the first. He therefore again set out, and again the same tragedy was enacted to the minutest details. They were the crew of Ribaut's own ship. Seventy to eighty refused to yield, and fled southward; an equal number were butchered; five alone were spared. The gallant and unfortunate Ribaut met his fate chanting the psalm: "Domine Memento Mei." [1] "We are of earth," cried he, "and to earth we must return. Twenty years more or less can matter little."

Even with this Menéndez was not yet finished with his enemies. Twenty days later he set himself to fit out yet another expedition. Those of Ribaut's force who had fled southward had constructed a fort near Cape Canaveral and were putting together a vessel out of wreckage. The Spaniards came in the morning of All Saints' Day. But on this occasion the work of Menéndez was less thorough. He had neither the time to track them in the woods where they had fled, nor the wish to leave them behind. Their lives, therefore, were offered them. All, with the exception of four or five, surrendered, and finally found their way to the galleys.

The worst that can be justly charged against Ribaut is that he was unfortunate. The best that can be pleaded for Menéndez was said for him by himself, his brother-in-law Solis de Meras, and his chaplain Mendoza. Such as it is, it is a narrative of atrocious cruelty and wrong—a tale of the fountains of pity dried up, a revelation of the evil which religion can do when turned from its true functions. From highest to lowest the actors in the tragedy were tainted with moral blindness; it matters little whether it be Philip II. writing, "Tell him, as to those he has slain he has done well, as to those he has spared

---

[1] It has been remarked (*Hist. Gen. des Voyages*, xiv. 446) that the Spanish narrator meant to write: "Memento Domine David," and that Ribaut, no doubt, recited it in French.

let them be sent to the galleys," or Menéndez carrying out his plans by ruse and half-deceit, or the priest Mendoza exclaiming triumphantly, " The greatest profit of this victory is the triumph which our Lord has granted us whereby His holy gospel will be introduced into this country, a thing so needful for the saving of so many souls from perdition." The sixteenth century, elbow-deep in blood, was not squeamish on the question of atrocities. But there were some deeds which shocked even its dulled sensibilities; one was the massacre of St. Bartholomew, another was the slaughter of the French in Florida.

Europe, as may be supposed, was not at once in possession of these facts. But the French Ambassador at Madrid was full of forebodings. In December, 1565, he put the French claims before Alva, much as Catherine herself had done in a conversation with Francis d'Alava at Tours. They were: Florida was not Spanish, it had not been mentioned in the treaty of Cateau Cambrésis, and in ancient maps it had been marked down as the " coast of the Bretons." [1] But on the 17th of January, 1566, he warned his mistress that, should the Spaniards be victorious, she would receive piteous news. The following day Madrid was electrified by the rumour of the defeat of the French expedition. It was the first hint of the massacre of the defenders of Fort Caroline. Details were soon provided by a Biscayan who had landed at La Rochelle with the young Ribaut. Then Flores arrived with Menéndez' letter of the 15th of October,[2] and Europe for the first time was aware of the full extent of the calamity. Without wasting time in apologies, Philip II. boldly demanded the punishment of Coligny. For the moment Catherine seemed resolved to uphold the honour of France and insist in her turn on the punishment of Menéndez. She was beside herself with rage. But she restricted herself to diplomatic protest and appeals for the release of prisoners. Coligny, for his part, as he could do little else, was at least active in bringing to the royal notice the whereabouts and condition of these latter. And in a letter

[1] Douais, *Dépêches de Fourquevaulx*, 17; cf. *Lettres de Catherine de Médicis*, ii. 338.
[2] It is given in full in *Riudiaz y Caravia*, ii.

of the 18th of August, 1566, he implored the King to bestir himself over one of the better known of the captives.[1]

But what the Queen dared not and Coligny could not do was done by the Sieur de Gourgues, a Catholic gentleman of Gascony. In the course of a roving life he had been put to the galleys by the Spaniards. Henceforth he had been consumed by a steady hatred against his oppressors. In 1567 he determined to be his countrymen's avenger. Collecting a little fleet of three sail, manned by a hundred and eighty soldiers and sailors, he set out from Bordeaux on the 2nd of August. His presumed destination was the west coast of Africa. It was only when he arrived in the waters of Cuba that he divulged his plans. His companions to a man swore to follow him. Reaching the mainland, and sighting two forts which the Spaniards had built on each side of the mouth of the river May, he saluted and sailed out to sea. Then doubling back he entered a river farther to the north, known to the French as the river Seine. Here he found as allies an Indian tribe, who greeted him with snatches of Huguenot hymns. What was even better was the appearance of a young French boy who had escaped the massacre. From him and from the natives he obtained many details as to the strength of Fort Caroline, now christened San Mateo, and of the two forts at the mouth of the river May. De Gourgues then made his dispositions. Taking one hundred arquebusiers and sixty out of the eighty sailors in two boats, he left the three vessels under a lieutenant, to whom he also entrusted his keys. " This saddened greatly the heart of all, even of the mariners remaining to guard the ships, who could not check their tears. It was a parting to move one to compassion, to hear so many adieus from one to another, and so many charges and recommendations on the part of those who went, to their relatives, their friends, their wives, their allies, in case they should never return." [2]

The plan of de Gourgues was first to rush the two smaller forts, using the Indians as auxiliaries to prevent escape into the bush. After a toilsome march he found himself in the neighbourhood of the river May or St. John's. The surprise

[1] Paris, Bibl. Nat., 15882, cxlix.   [2] *La Reprise de la Floride.*

was complete.   The first fort was carried ; of the sixty
Spaniards a few were spared, " that there might be done unto
them according to that which they had done to the French."
Then, training the guns on the second fort, De Gourgues rowed
across the stream and cut off the Spanish retreat, while the
Indians attacked in force.   This onslaught was as successful
as the first.   Fifteen out of sixty of the enemy were spared.
The question of the next few days was how to reduce San
Mateo, which was held by at least three hundred.   It fell out
better than he could have hoped.   Advancing in loose order,
the Spaniards thought his troop was only the advance guard,
and determined to crush it.   Sixty of their picked men came
out against him.   He at once seized the opportunity.   Sending a small band between them and the fort, he attacked in
front.   Caught between two fires, they were killed to a man.
Their friends fled in wild panic to the woods.   But de
Gourgues, without wasting a moment, rushed through the fort
and issued out at the other side just as the Spaniards were
being driven back by the missiles of the Indians.   The rest
was a massacre.   Thirty alone of the two hundred and sixty
were spared.   Summoning them before him, he informed them
of their fate.   " Although," cried he, " you could not be
punished as you deserve, still there is need that you undergo
what the enemy can inflict on you honestly, so that by your
example others may learn to keep the peace and alliance
which you have so wickedly and unhappily violated."   With
this de Gourgues had them hung up to the trees, and had
engraved with a hot iron on a slab of fir the inscription : " This
I do not against Spaniards or Marannes,[1] but against traitors,
robbers, and murderers."   Then San Mateo or Fort Caroline
and the two smaller ones at the mouth of the river were
destroyed, and the thirty prisoners first captured hung.

When de Gourgues arrived in France, La Rochelle gave
him a popular ovation.   The country was seething with excitement.   In a voyage from Bordeaux to Paris, the Spaniard
Guerau de Spes was in imminent danger of his life, so intense

---

[1] *La Reprise de la Floride.*   The word " Maranne " was a term of opprobrium suggesting anyone who was supposed to have Jewish or Moorish blood, and so especially
insulting to a Spaniard.

was the hatred felt by Catholic and Protestant alike against Spain.[1] But these sentiments found little echo at court. Spain cried out for his punishment; the Cardinal of Lorraine was Philip's mouthpiece in the Council. It was only the determined championship of his cause by the Admiral that saved him from punishment.

Such was the expedition of this great captain of Gascony. But it was not the only one of these years. Twelve months earlier, from the same port of Bordeaux and in the same month of August, yet another Gascon had set sail. It was Pierre Bertrand de Monluc, son of the great Catholic leader, Blaise de Monluc. The Queen Mother, who got wind of the expedition, was full of fears. Monluc the father replied to her inquiries in a vein peculiarly Gascon and his own. " What will you ? " wrote he. " My children are not so cowardly of heart as to remain simple cadets of Gascony, content to eat the fat soup at their father's board. Their desire is rather to gain goods and honours, and in the winning of them to hazard freely their persons and lives, and even serve the Turk rather than remain idle. If they did otherwise, I should not look upon them as mine." [2] Unfortunately, brave words and brave intentions do not make an expedition. The destination of the young captain was Madagascar. Landing, however, at Madeira to get water, he fell in a fray with the Portuguese. When the survivors returned, Portugal demanded an exemplary punishment. But, as in the case of de Gourgues, Coligny intervened. " Monsieur l'Admiral," says Monluc, " loved and esteemed my son only too well. And testified to the King that there was not a prince or noble in France who could have fitted out in so short a time such an expedition, from his own means, and without any royal gift." [3] Therefore, now that he was dead, Coligny saw that his followers did not suffer, declaring in the Council that the treatment Portugal had meted out to the remnant left behind in Brazil by Villegaignon deprived her of all right of protest.

---

[1] Coleccion de doc. ined., xc. 127 (Guerau de Spes to Philip II., Paris, 19th July, 1568).

[2] De la Ferrière's *Deux Années de Mission à St. Petersbourg*, 231.

[3] Monluc, iii. 76.

Yet another expedition was to start from the shores of France. In the year 1571, the Admiral got ready several vessels "manned by good troops, and gave the command to La Mainguetière, an experienced seaman of great courage. His orders were to approach as near as he was able to the coast of America, and examine the ports and the lie of the land, so that while an attack was made on Flanders, a considerable diversion could be effected by ravaging the coasts of the Spanish possessions in the Western Isles, and so oblige the enemy to divide their forces. But avarice, that passion so natural to man, caused the enterprise to miscarry. Those who were sent to spy out the country, set themselves to pillage; the sweets of gain made them despise the peril, . . . so that they were surprised in Hispaniola and all butchered, not one escaping." [1]

This was the last attempt of the Admiral as a coloniser of the New World. In his series of efforts we remark two periods. The first was covered by the expedition of Villegaignon. Coligny was still in the background, a secondary figure; his ideas still indeterminate. He had certain instincts and tendencies, but little else. With the first voyage of Ribaut to Florida began a second period. He was now the great coloniser, because he had become the arch-antagonist of Spain. In a word, colonisation was a cardinal factor in his policy. And it is significant that it was no longer on the shores of New Portugal, but on those claimed by Spain, that he attempted a landing. Catherine de' Medici, equally an enemy of Spain, longed for colonies; yet, womanlike, hoped to avoid a conflict. Coligny had no such illusions. In fact, he anticipated a struggle, and no doubt wished for it. For a foreign war was the only antidote he knew for civil war. And even at its worst, a death-grip with Spain represented an economy in blood. "The tenth part of the men dead in the least of our civil wars," writes de Gourgues, "had been more than enough to have conquered there [2] a kingdom several times larger than our own." [3] Here de Gourgues but echoed the sentiments of Coligny.

---

[1] De Thou, iv. 492 ; cf. Barbot's *Histoire de la Rochelle, Arch. hist. de la Saintonge*, xviii. 374.

[2] In Florida.   [3] *La Reprise de la Floride*, 69.

Thus we see that two of the chief reasons in guiding the Admiral's colonial enterprises were hatred of Spain as the enemy of Protestantism and France, and a desire to substitute a foreign for a civil war. But there were others, which, taken together, were perhaps equally strong. There was, first of all, a keen sense of the value of a New France as a refuge for the persecuted followers of his faith. The *Histoire Ecclésiastique* declares that this influence was already a power and at work in suggesting the expedition of 1555, though Coligny was not yet a professed Huguenot. And it is significant that in the three voyages that follow the Huguenot element is everything, the rest nothing. Then there was the missionary character of these enterprises. "It was quite in keeping with the earnestness of English character," Professor Jebb has remarked, "that in our earliest colonising days such enterprise was regularly associated with the idea of enlarging the bounds of Christendom."[1] In reality, however, such earnestness was not peculiarly English. The Kings of France, of Portugal, of Spain, Jacques Cartier, Menéndez, de Gourgues, Coligny, Calvin, were all in their various degrees possessed of the same idea. Colonisation meant to each of them so many souls gained for Christ. Another motive which the Admiral shared with his contemporaries was the desire to tap for his country new sources of wealth. "I am looking about," writes he in 1564 on the eve of his second expedition to Florida, "to find new means whereby to traffic and make one's profit in foreign lands, and I hope so to manage that in a little while we may have the finest trade in Christendom."

But leaving aside this discussion of motive, the question at once arises: Why did Coligny so often and signally fail? Was it owing to ill fortune or lack of capacity? The answer seems to be, in some degree to both. There is no doubt that chance played a large part in these enterprises. The three expeditions to Florida certainly did not court failure at the outset. Jean Ribaut, in spite of his obstinacy, Laudonnière, in spite of a certain strain of weakness, were able captains. Their ships' company compared favourably in every way with those of other early navigators. In a word, their efforts, under

[1] Address at the Church Congress, 1898; see the *Guardian*, September.

ordinary circumstances, might have been crowned with a success at least equal to that of Portugal and Spain. Again, if Villegaignon's weakness had developed on slightly other lines, Brazil might not have been lost to France.

Yet Coligny as the organiser, and Ribaut and Laudonnière as his lieutenants, are not altogether free from blame. They one and all had set their heart on having a trading and military post, not, in the modern sense, a colony. It is true that such a mistake—if it can be called so in her case—was that of Spain. But it is more difficult to understand and condone when committed by a man who looked upon a colony as a permanent settlement for religious refugees. Even from his own standpoint Coligny is in some degree responsible for the repeated failures of all the expeditions to cultivate the land. Mechanics were plentiful, never tillers of the soil. Thus there was no guarantee of permanence. Their supplies had to come from the natives, and the least freak of the latter threatened them with starvation and extinction. This is not a criticism drawn from the experience of the nineteenth century; John Hawkins and his men, in their visit to Fort Caroline in 1565, saw the danger, and suggested the remedy. " Notwithstanding the great want that the Frenchmen had, the ground doth yeeld victuals sufficient, if they would have taken paines to get the same, but they being souldiers, desired to live by the sweat of other men's browes," whereas " to them that should inhabit the land it were requisite to have labourers to till and sowe the ground : for they having victuals of their owne, whereby they neither rob nor spoile the inhabitants, may live not onely quietly with them . . . but also shall have abundance of victuals profered them for nothing." [1]

Yet though from the very outset chance and a lack of foresight seemed fated to doom all the Admiral's enterprises, we cannot cease to regret his failure. If the colony of Fort Coligny or Fort Caroline had only lived out even a precarious existence, some of the faults we have noted would have worked themselves out. And the history of a South America dominated by a French and Protestant colony might surely have been happier, and at least very different to that of one

[1] The voyage made by John Hawkins : *Hakluyt*, iii. 614, 615.

22

moulded in the evil traditions of Spain, Portugal, and the Inquisition. Whether success would in the end have benefited France, is another matter. There is no doubt that the tendency of a Calvinistic, and in the issue almost of necessity republican settlement, would have been toward separation. Still, it would have been a powerful factor in the spread of French influence and of the French tongue. Coligny, for his part, if he did not see all, at least saw some of the possibilities of a colonial Empire. And his untiring and even passionate energy, his sentiment as Protestant and Frenchman, his clear perception of colonisation as part of a general scheme, his determination to strike at the overshadowing predominance of Spain in the New World, and so at the same time empty his own land of strife, all these mark him out as pre-eminently the first of the great colonial statesmen of France.[1]

[1] Most of the authorities for the colonisation of Brazil and Florida are indicated by Gaffarel in his *Histoire du Brésil français au seizième siècle* and his *Histoire de la Floride*, and by Parkman in his admirable *Pioneers of France in the New World*. We would add that the Spanish accounts of two eye-witnesses, Mendoza and Solis de Meras, the letters of Menéndez, with much other valuable material, are to be found in *Riudiaz y Caravia, La Florida, su conquista y colonización*, por Pedro Menéndez de Avilés, published in 1893.

CHAPTER XIX

COLIGNY'S LIFE AND CHARACTER

Hotman's Description of his Appearance and Daily Life—Other Details—His Culture—His Sternness and Solitary Nature—Reverence and Affection felt for him by his Followers—His Tact—His Power of Leadership and Dominating Personality—La Noue's Tribute—His European Standing—Coligny and Cromwell compared—Tendencies of French History—Warring Influences in Coligny's Life—His Policy and Ideals—Causes of his Failure.

IN the course of 1575, three short years after the death of Coligny, there appeared a slender little volume of a hundred and thirty odd pages, under the title of *Gasparis Colonii Castellonii, Magni Quondam Franciæ Admiralii, Vita.* Translated first into English and then into French, it did much to keep fresh the memory of the greatest of French Protestants. There can now be little doubt that the author was the distinguished legist, Francis Hotman. He knew the Admiral intimately; he had been with him at Orleans, and visited him at Châtillon. The sketch, therefore, of his friend's appearance and daily life, with which he concludes his work, is quite unique. It is drawn in part, as he tells us, from his own reminiscences.

"As soon as he had risen from bed, which was always at an early hour, he put on his gown, and, falling on his knees, made prayer and invocation to God on behalf of the whole company. And when the rest had kneeled down after his example, prayer was made in the manner usual in the churches in France. When it was ended, he employed the whole time before the sermon either in hearing the delegates of the churches which were sent to him, or in despatching other public business. The sermon was delivered on alternate days at a given sign, and was accompanied by the singing of a

psalm.   Business was then resumed until dinner-time.   When
it was ready, all the servants, except a few who were preparing
the food, assembled in the hall, where the table was laid.
And if there had been no sermon, a psalm was sung and the
accustomed blessing was said, the Admiral standing at the
board with his wife by his side.   This was his constant
practice, not only in his own house and when at ease, but in
the camp, as innumerable Frenchmen and many German
knights and captains who were often invited to dine with him
can testify.

"On the removal of the cloth, rising and standing with his
wife and the rest of the company, he either returned thanks,
or called on his minister to do so.   At supper-time the same
order of prayer and singing of psalms was followed.   And in
addition, since he perceived that it would be somewhat difficult
for all his servants to attend nightly prayers at bed-time, for
the hour was uncertain owing to their various duties, he gave
order that they should all be with him immediately after
supper, when, after singing a hymn, prayer was made.   It
cannot be told how many of the French nobility began to
establish this religious order in their families after his example,
the more so as he used often to admonish them that, for the
cultivation of true piety, it was not enough for the father of a
family to be present at services, and order his own private
ways as piety and religion demand, unless by his example he
brought his household and domestics to the same rule of life
as well.   And it is agreed that such was the admiration
entertained for his piety and holy life, even by those of the
Catholic party, that, but for the dread of tortures and
massacres which followed, a far greater number of the French
would have been converted to the same religion and discipline.

"When the time of the Lord's Supper was at hand, he
was wont to call his domestics and members of his household
about him, and make known unto them that he had to render
an account unto God, not only of his own mode of life but of
theirs.   If any discord had fallen among them, they were
reconciled.   If any man seemed insufficiently prepared for the
understanding and veneration of that great mystery, he caused
him to be more diligently instructed in religion.   If any seemed

more stubborn, he told them openly that he would rather be alone in his house than keep a following of the wicked.

" Moreover, he thought the institution of schools and discipline for youths a singular benefit from God, calling it the seminary of the church and training-ground of piety. And he held that the ignorance of letters had cast a mist, not only on the commonwealth but also on religion, and that in its shadow had been born and bred the tyranny of the Roman Pontiff, who had ruled by ignorance over the blind and lost, just as Father Dis—according to the poets—over darkness and night. This had led him to found and build at great cost a college in an agreeable and healthy site, hard by the castle of Châtillon. And there he maintained most learned expounders of the Hebrew, Greek, and Latin tongues, and many boys and youths as well.

" Furthermore, the strongest proof of his integrity was that, though he enjoyed the highest honours wherewith he might have furthered his own private interests and received great gain like other courtiers, he added not one acre or cottage to his hereditary domain. Though frugal in administering his household, he spent liberally in hospitality what he gained by saving, when leaders, nobles, and men of all kinds came to him on public business from all parts of France. As a consequence, as is well known, he left to his heirs and successors a burden of debt not less than 40,000 pounds, besides a yearly sum of 6000 pounds paid as interest to his creditors. Nor should we pass over in silence the incredible unity of mind, love, and good-will of the three Châtillon brothers. So great was it, that it seemed as though all three were kindled but by one soul.

" The Admiral lived three and fifty years, six months, and eight days. He was of middle stature, of a ruddy complexion, with regular and well-proportioned limbs. He had a calm and unclouded countenance, a soft and winning voice, though his utterance was somewhat hesitating and slow. His health was fairly good. He was graceful in gesture and bearing, especially when at home, dressed in his gown, and walking with his wife or friends. He was sparing of wine, ate and slept moderately, his rest covering at the most seven hours.

Since the time of the last pacification, he let no day slip by
without entering with his own hand in his diary, before going
to rest, such things as had happened and were worthy of
notice in the last civil wars. These memoranda, having been
found after his death, were taken to the King's Council, and
his calm and tranquil mind gained him the admiration even of
those who hated him most. Besides this, when the war was
over and he had betaken himself to La Rochelle, as has been
said before, he let no day pass without reading, morning and
evening, one of Calvin's sermons on the story of Job. And
oftentimes he would say that that story was the consolation of
his soul and sovereign remedy in distress."

Unfortunately, these daily notes of the Admiral were burned
by the Count de Retz. It was an irreparable loss. An introductory passage in Coligny's own description of his defence of
St. Quentin—remarkable for the splendid vigour of its style—
gives us an insight into the spirit in which he would have com-
mented on the civil wars. It runs—

"It seems to me that it is only reasonable that those who
are in positions of trust should themselves give a faithful
account of the same. This must be done, if for no other
reason than that it commonly happens that those who have
been on the spot speak without sufficient care: some to have
you think that nothing has been hidden from them, others
because they are so fond of talking that they are always ready
to give an account of things of which they know nothing.
Again, there are others who colour their accounts according
as they wish well or ill to those concerned. Further, there
are so many kinds of depreciators, especially foreigners, that
one must not be surprised if they are often ill-informed of
things which happen at a distance when even those at hand
differ for the reasons we have given. Wherefore, on due
consideration, it seems to me only reasonable that those who
know,[1] rather than others, should set down in writing the naked
truth without concealment or disguise."

Other particulars of Coligny's personal appearance and
habits have come down to us from other quarters. One of
them is the habitual toothpick. It was usually thrust into

[1] Coligny's phrase is " ceux qui tiennent la queue de la poële."

the beard, or carried on the ear or between the teeth. When in a brown-study he was accustomed to bite on it unconsciously. It was therefore seized on by the crowd as the symbol of his personality. " God save us," ran the popular legend, " from the toothpick of the Admiral." And when after his death the Paris rabble wished to express their derision of his effigy in straw, they stuck into its mouth a piece of lentisk-wood.[1] Hotman, too, has omitted several details which are of great interest. Beza, in his *Histoire Ecclésiastique*, describes how, on the 15th of April, 1563, shortly after the conclusion of the first civil war, the Admiral entered his court of justice, and, having prayed, ordained that thenceforth proceedings should begin with prayers according to a formulary which he shortly afterwards inscribed on a tablet and posted up. Then addressing those present, he declared that God had but lately delivered him from many dangers, and that to His glory he dedicated the rest of his life. And he exhorted his officers to act as honest men in the execution of their charges. He would pay them good wages, he said, so that they would have no need to administer justice for money ; but he would punish severely those who abused the forms of justice.

These were Coligny's more serious pursuits. But they by no means absorbed his energies. Other interests claimed him as well. He was an aristocrat of the highest culture. When Brantôme wished for an example of the typical educated man of action, his choice fell instinctively on Coligny. As nephew of the Constable, he had had exceptional opportunities. He had moved in the most refined and intelligent circles in Europe. He had the key to the literary and artistic wealth of the Renaissance. He had travelled in Italy. His brother the Cardinal was the patron of Rabelais and Ronsard. He himself had been taught by Bérauld, one of the most brilliant votaries

---

[1] The toothpick played a by no means unimportant part in the domestic economy of the sixteenth century. Thus the royal physician, Jacques de Lugerye, wrote from Paris to Mary Queen of Scots : " Monsieur de St. Cosme me promist en vostre faveur, dernierement qu'il partit de Rheims, se souvenir de diligement vous garder et vous presenter de ma part à son arrivée une fourchette d'or au manche de la quelle s'aproprie ung cure dent de mesme affin, madame, que la negligence de conserver voz dentz en leur perfection ne soyt excusée sur la rarité du lentisque de votre Royaulme."
—British Museum, 1940I, 86.

of the new learning. He wrote and understood Latin, and spoke it fluently. He was a lover of art and of all that gave life an ample and generous air. That form of Protestantism which affected gloom and developed so easily into an unreasoning hostility to humane culture, had not descended on Châtillon. Coligny and the typical Puritan were poles apart. Like all his contemporaries, from Catherine de' Medici to Anne of Montmorency, he was an enthusiastic art-collector and builder. In this connection we have a letter from his hand begging for a portrait of Edward VI. Besides surrounding his château with a bastioned wall, he built a wing in the style of the Renaissance with an elegant pavilion at either end. Its most striking feature was a vast gallery, where the great sculptor, Jean Goujon, was set to work, and where other artists decorated the walls with scenes from family history. When Hotman with two friends visited him in the spring of 1572, Coligny personally conducted them over the château and gardens. More than twenty years earlier, on the 14th of August, 1551, he had been able to announce to the Duke of Guise a present of melons and other fruits. Another reference to his country life belongs to the year 1567, when, on the court party sending to Châtillon, he was found peacefully tending his vines.

Perhaps his most personal trait — it struck friends and strangers alike—was what Beza in a letter to him described as his pensive and solitary nature. Translated into action, this self-contained and stoical attitude expressed itself by a sternness bordering on cruelty. In December, 1568, he put the Catholic garrison of the château of Mirebeau to the sword. Brantôme heard him confess that, if he could have laid his hands on the cowardly Huguenot captain of Lusignan in 1569, he would have cut off his head. We have already described his summary vengeance on the peasants of Perigord and on the property of the members of the Parlement of Toulouse. His was a character, in fine, not made after the humanitarian ideals of Rousseau and Bernardin de Saint Pierre, but which, none the less, did very well for its time. He had to deal with an unruly people. As he had no hold over his followers, and was considered a rebel by Catholics, and so not privileged to claim belligerent rights, he was often driven to impose his will

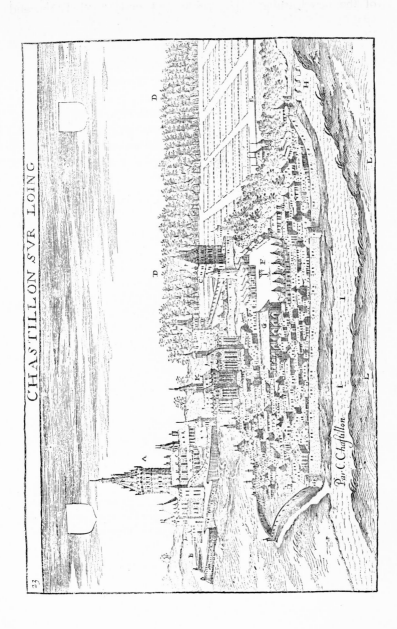

CHASTILLON SVR LOING

Par C. Chastillon

by intimidation.   Yet he was not naturally harsh.   He never acted from a vicious instinct.   He protested time and again, and with justice, that he loathed cruelty.   When he was pitiless, it was to gain some definite end, generally to wrest more humane methods from the enemy.   No one was more humane where mercy was possible.

As to his relations with his followers, these have been distorted out of all recognition.   It has been alleged that they chafed under his iron rule; that they were indignant at his melancholy ways and general air of dictation.   Yet all the evidence forthcoming is the flimsy judgment of Davila, who was only born in 1576, and the reports of a handful of Catholics whose policy and interest it was to discover friction where none existed.   As a matter of fact, it was a stormy age; conditions were shifting, times were dangerous, and leadership, to be effective, had to be arbitrary.   He had to impose his will.   But there is no reason to believe that his methods were resented.   On the contrary, the Protestant nobility were passionately attached to him.   Their insubordination during his illness in 1570 was only one of those momentary fits of impatience which obsess even the most loyal followers.   As a rule, they served him gladly.   No better instance can be imagined than the experience of two of their number, Puyviault and Genlis.   During the third civil war, on two of those rare occasions when he lost control of himself, he was with difficulty restrained from chastising them with his own hands.   Yet the one died with him in Paris, the other in forwarding his designs on the Netherlands.

This docility, no doubt, was in some degree owing to his manner.   He was quite unlike his uncle the Constable.   He rarely aroused personal antipathy.   We can instance no case of antagonism with any member of his party.   We seldom even hear of friction.   During his long career he had intimate and personal dealings with innumerable princes, captains, nobles, ambassadors, of almost every nationality: William of Orange, Louis of Nassau, Rollshausen, Mansfeld, Smith, Throckmorton, Walsingham, Anthony of Navarre, Joan of Navarre, Henry of Navarre, the two Condés, great Huguenot noblemen like La Rochefoucauld, Grammont, Portien, Rohan, and a host of others. He had, of course, many enemies, but they were political, not personal. The one possible exception was Francis Duke of Guise. Even the trouble with Catherine de' Medici was, in the first instance, a question of politics.

Then, too, he was a born leader. He had the instinct of command. He was endowed with character and a dominating personality. He had great natural powers, and had reaped all the advantages of a careful training, high position, and long experience. Even such an elementary gift as physical courage appealed with especial force to a party of soldiers. They were well able to appreciate an incident of the year 1566. There was talk of his assassination; when an Italian protested his innocence, Coligny replied ironically that he thought him the very last man to undertake the business. Add to this the fact that he was indomitable in face of disaster, that he identified himself with his followers' interests, that he was incorruptible,— court influence could not move him,—that he was free from the taint of personal ambition, that he was just, magnanimous, accessible to all, and we have the reason, not only for the love which the lower orders of Huguenotism bore him, but for the willing obedience of his equals. The prevailing sentiment among every class of Huguenot was one, not of discontent, but of affection and respect. It was expressed with simple pathos by one of their number. " If anyone," wrote La Noue, " in these lamentable wars has laboured greatly with both mind and body, it has been the Admiral. He has borne the greater part of the burden of affairs and military anxieties. He has treated the Princes his superiors with deference and his inferiors with modesty. He has always held piety in singular esteem. He has loved justice, and so been prized and honoured by those of the party he has embraced. Ambition has never moved him to seek honours and commands; he has fled them rather, but has been forced to take them because of his fitness and high qualities. He has shown himself in arms as skilful as any captain of his times. He has always exposed himself courageously to dangers. Great-hearted in adversity, and quick to find a way out, he has always been free from dissimulation and parade. In fine, he was a personage worthy to restore an unsound and enfeebled state."

This almost regal predominance in his party naturally re-acted on his place in Europe. His personality became a great international factor. His enemies recognised his importance by making him the centre of attack. They never committed the folly of under-rating his abilities. " He was held," wrote a hostile Italian, " to be a man of wisdom and sagacity, astute and dexterous in business. He had great experience of the world. He was patient, listened willingly, but expressed his ideas to few. In addition, he was sober, vigilant, strong, and of spotless integrity in public affairs." When, in the spring of 1566, Spain complained of the influence wielded by him, the French Ambassador Fourquevaulx retorted " that even were he a Jew or Turk, he would still deserve to be esteemed and had in favour." No one, not a ruler, ever occupied quite his unique position. The one career which may be compared with his is that of Oliver Cromwell. Coligny was the first, as the Lord Protector was the last, of the race of the great Protestant men of action. They were both leaders of a minority. They were able, in varying degrees, to win a victory for their opinions. If Coligny's success, both military and civil, was the more equivocal, it must be remembered that his resources were less, that the problems he had to face were more confusing, that he was entangled in a heritage of family feuds, that the necessity of calling in foreign aid prevented him from creating a common spirit in the army, and that in the nobility he had a more erratic force to depend on than Cromwell in the great English middle class. Nor was this resemblance between the two merely on the surface. It went deeper. It lay at the very base of their mental and moral being. The imperishable phrase in the testament of the greatest of Huguenots might equally well have come from the pen of the greatest of Puritans: " That which I desire the most is that God be served everywhere, and chiefly in this realm, in all purity and according to His ordinance, and, after, that this kingdom be preserved." They possessed in a marked degree that first essential of leadership: character. Their individuality had a certain massive quality. It impressed by its strength. Both, moreover, were instinctively conservative ; nor were they, in the modern sense, democratic. They had a keen sense of the value of monarchical institutions, which in the one case was reinforced by a peculiarly French reverence for the person of the King. But there was one fundamental difference produced by a difference in social status. Coligny, no doubt, owed not a little of his weakness to his high birth. It reared against him a barrier of rivalry and hate; it was in some degree responsible for the ignoble and personal aspect of the religious wars. None the less, he drew from it at the same time much of his strength. It gave him a wider outlook than Cromwell. In a word, he was more of a statesman. He was as little, perhaps less, of a theoriser. It is rare to find in his correspondence anything approaching to a philosophic view of government or action. His position and education made him satisfied with things as they were. He was practical, the man of action. When he saw an abuse, he struck at it, little influenced by the theoretical aspect of the question. When he attempted to found colonies, it was not to carry out any theory of politics or experiment in government, but to enlarge the bounds of France. Nevertheless, his attitude differed materially from that of Cromwell. Coligny started with a great advantage. He was reared in a court atmosphere. He was early introduced to the conduct of affairs. He had a wide knowledge of European politics. He was at home in dealing with complex problems; his views were clear and definite. Cromwell, on the other hand, was a country gentleman. He had little contact with the outer world until well on toward middle age. He stumbled on greatness. As a consequence, when compared with Coligny, his mind to some extent lacks grasp and clearness. Their foreign policy is a case in point. But nowhere is this more apparent than in their public utterances.

Why, then, it may be asked, with such advantages of character and training, was the Admiral's career a partial failure. To find an answer we must glance at the course of French history. The history of France was pre-eminently the history of the monarchy. For the instinct of the race tending finally to produce a symmetry in art, in manners, in literature, and state organisation, found in the King its representative and leader. From the battle of Bouvines to the time when the

Satyre Ménippée was to chant of Henry IV., the hero of the
people, and freedom from a foreign yoke, the King was the
centre of national sentiment.   Reaction was but the starting-
point of a fresh career.   Compared with the permanent effects
of a St. Louis or a Charles VII., an Etienne Marcel is a mere
political accident.   So inevitable was this centralising influence,
that Philip Augustus and Charles V., Louis XI. and Francis I.,
seem rather the instruments than the directors of a tendency.

Into such a France the young Coligny entered.   So far
the Crown had stood out the embodiment of a revived
nationality, the sole depository of power.   No force had as
yet appeared to set limits to its growth or shackle its freedom.
And, under favourable circumstances, the future Admiral
might have been known to posterity as the great nephew
of the Constable, the organiser of modern France, the
consolidator of kingly power.   But it was not to be.   The
Renaissance, followed by the Reformation, had breathed on
the dry-bones of mediævalism.   These, with the dependent
movements of the Counter-Reformation and militant Calvinism, were the chief forces of the sixteenth century.   Add to
them the rivalry between two great houses and aristocratic
reaction against monarchical centralisation, and we have the
essential factors of the situation in France.   Coligny was as
little able as others to stand aside.   He was caught into the
turbulent current of his age, sharing its emotion and seeming
confusion to the full.   Family traditions, patriotic instincts,
religious predilections, loyalty to the Crown, cross and recross
—a tangled skein.   Passionately national, he called to his
aid the hereditary foe.   Alive to the necessity of family
solidarity, he and the Constable were found in opposite camps.
Loyal by position and birth, his wars for the most part were
waged against the King.   No one was more conscious than he
of these seeming paradoxes.   They added one touch the more
to the melancholy of his character.   The English Ambassador
noted his fears at the thought of giving the stranger a foot-
hold in France.   One of his most stirring appeals was a letter
to Anne of Montmorency for family union.   The words of
Brantôme and La Noue, his life itself, were sufficient witness
of his horror of civil war.

But through all this seeming maze ran the great motive of his life: to harmonise patriotism and his Protestant ideals. On the one hand, he would see at home a France religiously renovated; on the other, he would himself lead her against the common enemy, Spain. The latter half of this programme— that is to say, a duel with Philip II.—had much to recommend it. It was patriotic; it meant working along traditional lines, for it was merely continuing, under new conditions, the old Hapsburg-Valois struggle. But its success became well-nigh impossible when coupled with his plan of seeing " that God be served everywhere, and chiefly in this realm, in all purity and according to His ordinance." Internal dissensions—family, personal, political, religious—became too keen. It may be doubted whether at any moment there were the elements in France for a moral or, shall we say, religious regeneration. Hostility to Rome, even in the Parlement, was platonic. In none of the three estates, clergy, nobility, and people, were interest and will so blended as to make a revolutionary class-policy possible. Again, the royal house and court, both by character and instinct, were hostile. In fine, France was not Huguenot, and for a good reason. In Geneva, Calvinism represented to some degree a revolt from the house of Savoy, and so the political movement supported the religious. Luther, again, was putting into action all the accumulated hate and desires of centuries. In England, too, the Reformation was partly political; it was the expression of her nationality. But in France there was no such craving. She had early taken up an independent position. She was now more Catholic, as in the early centuries she had been more Roman. And therefore Protestantism appealed neither to her political nor religious sense. It had no sufficient *raison d'être*.

And so Coligny's efforts, deeply influenced by the new religious movement, were foredoomed to failure. For success, it would have needed a France with another history and a king other than that prey to nervosity, Charles IX. The more popular manners of the Guises were well able to balance Coligny's more solid gifts. He impressed all, but appealed only to the few. France, or more truly Paris, rejected him and his policy. She slew him in her midst. His dead body was the object of her ignoble rage. The Parlement, representing the might of justice, proclaimed his children " base-born, vilein, peasants, unable to inherit," and ordered his coat of arms to be " broken and shattered by the executioner of high justice in sign of perpetual ignominy." Yet though debarred from becoming the popular hero, he has won the full appreciation of posterity. The jubilant and confident prophecy of Hotman has come true: " Justus sempiternâ memoriâ viget: neque unquam labefactabitur "—" the righteous is had in everlasting remembrance, nor shall he ever be moved."

FINIS

APPENDICES

APPENDIX I

THE HUGUENOTS AND THE TREATY OF HAMPTON COURT

NO action of the Admiral and Condé has been more severely criticised by modern writers than the treaty of Hampton Court. They have been held responsible for every one of its articles. The entry of the English soldiers into Havre has been described as a surrender of the town to the hereditary foe. Kervyn de Lettenhove compares the Prince's conduct to that of the Constable of Bourbon.[1] De Ruble takes the same view.[2] Froude, in telling how Condé offered to place Havre and Dieppe in Elizabeth's hands as security for Calais, adds that for a French prince to reintroduce the English into Normandy was a kind of treason.[3] The Duc d'Aumale[4] and the Comte de la Ferrière[5] agree in throwing doubt on the sincerity of the two leaders' protestations that it was without their knowledge and consent that an article was introduced into the treaty stipulating that Elizabeth was to hold Havre until she received the surrender of Calais. In this connection de la Ferrière remarks : "There is one point which is very strange. It relates to the contract made for the surrender of Havre to the English. The Admiral declares that he never saw it before his voyage into Normandy.[6] Yet he ratifies it without reading it, and makes all the lords of his suite do the same, to obtain the money destined for the reiters. And it is after this ratification that Throckmorton lets him see it." This is virtually a charge of sharp practice. In reading it over, one naturally draws the conclusion that Coligny was in a position to lay his hands on the treaty if he had so wished, but knowingly refrained. Nothing

---

[1] *Les Huguenots et les Gueux*, i. 100. [2] *Antoine de Bourbon*, iv. 328.
[3] Vol. vii. 421. [4] *Histoire des Princes de Condé*, i. 162, 163.
[5] *Le XVIᵉ siècle et les Valois*, 115. [6] In February, 1563.

23

is farther from the truth. According to Throckmorton, who was at Havre, and Middlemore, who was in the Huguenot camp, the Admiral's life was hanging by a thread; the reiters were in a mood to stop at nothing. At this juncture Throckmorton, as a preliminary to handing over their pay, sent to Coligny at Caen, between the 19th and 23rd of February, a document to sign. It was couched in general terms, and promised to observe the treaty of Hampton Court.[1] But the Admiral did not see a copy of the treaty itself, and had no means of seeing it. It remained in the hands of Throckmorton until the latter's arrival at Caen on the 27th of February. It was then for the first time that the Admiral had a chance of reading it as drawn up by Cecil and the Vidame de Chartres.

Unfortunately, this remark of de la Ferrière is only too characteristic of his treatment of the whole subject. When not incorrect, he is misleading. The editor of the *Calendar of State Papers*, Kervyn de Lettenhove, Ruble, and the Duc d'Aumale, are equally in error. Thus the latter (i. 379) prints what he calls "articles présentés à la reine d'Angleterre par le prince de Condé." This is a purely fancy title adumbrated by the Duc himself. The original in the Record Office is endorsed by Cecil as " Articles in French, etc., for Vidame," the name of the Vidame being represented by a cipher mark.[2]

If, therefore, we would gain a clear idea of the whole question, we must refer back to the originals in the British Museum and the Record Office. And the necessity for this is by no means lessened in reading an article written by M. N. Weiss in the January number of the *Bulletin de la société de l'histoire du protestantisme français* of 1900. It was the first serious attempt to combat the prevailing opinion of the guilt of the Admiral and Condé, and as such is interesting. But it is based solely on printed documents. And these are not only too few, but are not to be trusted. M. Weiss was thus not in a position to criticise actual statements of fact or the accuracy of the material he was using. Let us give a few instances of what we mean. In dealing with the negotiations before Paris in November and December of 1562, de la Ferrière asserts that Throckmorton had in his hands a copy of the treaty of Hampton Court.[3] If this were correct, Coligny's statement that he never knew of the article stipulating for the exchange of Havre for Calais until his arrival in Normandy would be a

---

[1] R.O. Chapter House, Diplomatic Documents, 1151. The catalogue wrongly dates it as of November 1562.

[2] R.O. xl. 293. (We have used the contraction R.O. for Record Office throughout this chapter.)

[3] *Lettres de Catherine de Médicis*, i. Intro. cxliii.

palpable falsehood; for he would certainly have been informed of it by Throckmorton in December. Again, in the *Calendar of State Papers* of 1563, No. 537 states that "although M. De Beauvois, by command of Admiral Coligny and Warwick, has commanded," etc. In face of this, the Huguenot leaders' case at once falls to the ground, for it rests on the assumption that Beauvoir-la-Nocle was not under the command of Warwick, but wholly independent. Fortunately for them, the document in the Record Office, of which No. 537 is supposed to be a correct abstract, runs as follows: "Whereas not onely Monsieur de Beauvois by the commandment of the Lord Admiral Chastillon but allso the right honorable Lord Erle of Warwycke . . . have gevinge in Charge and commandement," etc.—a very different thing![1] And finally, M. Weiss remarks that the articles published by the Duc d'Aumale on p. 379 of the first volume of his *Histoire des Princes de Condé* are the minutes of the instructions given by Condé, while No. 663 of the Calendar of 1562 contains the proposals of Elizabeth, the actual treaty of Hampton Court being a compromise between the two. We may reply to this, firstly, that the articles published by the Duc d'Aumale are certainly not the instructions given by Condé. A glance at a letter of de la Haye of the 29th of August will set this at rest.[2] From it we conclude that one of the demands in the instructions given by Condé was for a force of 10,000 men, and not 6000, as given in the document published by the Duc d'Aumale. And secondly, No. 663 of the *Calendar of State Papers* is not, as M. Weiss supposes, the demands of Elizabeth, but is an English translation of the actual treaty itself, and is endorsed by Cecil the 27th of September.[3]

In dealing, then, with the whole question, we propose in the first place to give a short sketch of the treaty of Hampton Court, and of the negotiations before and after. We shall then be better able to judge whether Coligny and Condé agreed to the inclusion of an article consenting to an English occupation of Havre until Calais was surrendered; whether at any time before the Admiral's arrival in Normandy in February, 1563, they were in a position to know of or suspect the inclusion of such an article; and lastly, whether even Throckmorton, the intermediary between Elizabeth and Condé, was cognisant of it before the battle of Dreux, when his connection with the Huguenots temporarily ceased.

---

[1] R.O. liii. 479. It is given correctly by Forbes (ii. 368), but of course, without reference to the R.O., it was impossible to tell which of the two—Forbes or the Calendar—was correct.

[2] Calendar, No. 545.   [3] R.O. xli. 486.

The first Huguenot agent to visit England was Séchelles, who arrived at the end of April.[1] About the same time Elizabeth and Catherine exchanged views through special ambassadors, Sir Henry Sidney and the Comte de Roussy. But all three embassies were more or less perfunctory. England as yet was not ready actively to interfere. But a new event suddenly changed the whole aspect of affairs. It was the occupation in the middle of May of Havre—or Newhaven, as the English called it—by Jean de Ferrières, Seigneur de Maligny, and Vidame de Chartres. The Huguenots, who had quietly taken possession of Dieppe soon after the massacre of Vassy, had now the two great harbours of Normandy in their hands. They were thus in an admirable position to receive loans and supplies from England. And to English statesmen they were now a party with which it was worth while to negotiate. By the treaty of Cateau Cambrésis of 1559, the French King was bound to deliver to England the town of Calais at the end of eight years, that is to say, in 1567, provided that the latter had not entered on hostilities against the former. If he should fail to deliver the city, he was to pay the sum of 500,000 écus or crowns; yet even after this payment England's rights on the town were still to hold good. Such was the treaty. But Englishmen generally were very doubtful of France's voluntary fulfilment of her pledges. Throckmorton, therefore, hailed the outbreak of the religious wars as an excellent opportunity of obtaining furthur guarantees for the immediate or ultimate surrender of Calais. And on the 19th of April he wrote to Cecil that they ought now to be able to obtain Calais, or Dieppe, or Havre, perhaps all three. The occupation of the latter by the Vidame brought the possibility, or rather the probability, of an Anglo-Huguenot alliance within the range of practical politics. But as yet the Admiral and Condé contented themselves with begging for a loan of 100,000 crowns. They were not ready to allow, much less to solicit, active interference. That was only to be done as a last resort, when the Triumvirate had set the example. They still clung to both the letter and spirit of Coligny's policy of not introducing foreign armed assistance. As late as the 21st of June, Armigil Waade reported a conversation between the Captain of Dieppe and Horsey, "whereby it semeth that they will admitt no straunge ayde ffor that the Prince of Condé hath so protestyd

---

[1] Two letters of Coligny and Condé of the 1st and 2nd of April, which speak of a mission of Briquemault to England, are to be found as Nos. 975 and 976 of the *Calendar of State Papers* of 1562. This is an error; they should have been placed among the despatches of the year 1563.

onless the adversary part begynne to call strangers to ayde."[1] England, therefore, had to be content with underhand intrigue in the Norman towns, engineered by Horsey, Waade, and others.

With the failure of the conference of Talcy, however, active negotiations were set on foot. Catherine at once saw the danger. She was especially alarmed by an intriguing mission entrusted to Sir Peter Mewtas, and a proposal to send two members of the English Privy Council, who would virtually play the rôle of arbitrators. She determined, therefore, to anticipate. Her choice of an ambassador fell on a moderate, Marshall Vieilleville, who arrived in London on the 5th of August. But he was too late. The Vidame de Chartres had crossed secretly three weeks earlier,[2] and had made and received various proposals. These can be gauged by memoranda drawn up by Cecil on the 17th of July,[3] and by a despatch of Horsey. The Vidame would seem to have demanded a loan and reinforcements to the number of 10,000, Elizabeth in return insisting on the occupation of Havre. Here was the difficulty. Without some such guarantee it was almost impossible for her to move, for, should she do so, she would lose her rights on Calais. On the other hand, the Huguenots were well aware that to admit her would be to lose popular support. The Vidame, therefore, on returning to France with the promise of the immediate appearance of ten English ships off the Norman coast, at once sent off post haste to Orleans. The upshot is clearly stated by Beza, who had lately left France for Germany, but again returned with Andelot in November. "It was finally concluded at Orleans by the Prince and his council, composed of the principal associates, that, if it were possible, one should get the Queen of England to be content with Fécamp or Dieppe. But in case she should persist in her demand for Havre, it should be handed over to her on well-defined conditions, namely, that those who should enter there or elsewhere should do nothing against the estate and crown of France, for whose preservation they had been called and for no other cause. On the other hand, the Prince and his associates promised, in return for having been succoured, that the said Queen should suffer no damage or prejudice to her rights on Calais. As to Havre, the inhabitants, natural subjects of the King, should remain in the hands and under the

---

[1] R.O. xxxviii. 159.

[2] Nos. 389, 455 of Calendar of 1562. Cf. letter of Alvarotto of 10th Sept. : Modena Francia, 37, and Lettenhove, *Relations politiques des P. B. & Angleterre*, iii. 87–89, 91.

[3] Calendar, Foreign, 1562, No. 331. This is now to be found in the R.O. among the Domestic Papers, xxiii. 55.

government of the Seigneur de Beauvoir, under the name and authority of the King, in the absence of the Admiral, Captain and Governor-in-Chief of the said town."[1] These, we believe, were the general lines of the instructions sent to the Vidame. And in so far as the treaty of Hampton Court differed from them, he alone was responsible. Robert de la Haye, a Master of Requests, was chosen to carry them—they were in writing[2] —to Normandy. He was also entrusted with a blank parchment which bore the signatures of the principal chiefs then in Orleans, and on which the treaty about to be negotiated was to be inscribed.[3] On the 15th of August, he, with the Vidame and other Huguenot emissaries, arrived in England.

The succeeding negotiations are manifestly difficult to follow, for the materials are scanty and often undated. But we believe they were somewhat as follows: The Vidame and de la Haye demanded firstly a succour of 10,000 men and a large loan as a return for the admission of English troops into Havre. To this, we believe, Cecil made reply in the terms of what he names a "first offer." It is to be found in a memorandum which the editor of the *State Papers* has placed among the documents of the month of July.[4] According to it, England, on the receipt of Havre,—which as a natural corollary would be garrisoned by English troops,—would provide a loan of 140,000 crowns, and would redeliver the town when the loan was repaid and Calais given back. The French negotiators, as was only natural, would not hear of this, as what they wanted above all were men.[5] Cecil then made his "second offer." 6000 men were to be sent, but only half of the former sum of money—that is to say, 70,000 crowns. But this was found little more acceptable than his "first offer." Unfortunately, the only thing which a somewhat confused[6] letter of the Vidame of the 25th of August leaves

---

[1] *Hist. Ecclés.*, ii. 863. Coligny, on the 4th of October, 1560, had succeeded La Mailleraie in the command of Havre: Bastard, *Vie de Jean de Ferrières*.

[2] See R.O. xl. 405 (Calendar of 1562, No. 545), where de la Haye writes: "Des dix pieces que le neveu (Condé) a cottés par *son memoyre*."

[3] 665 of Calendar of 1562.

[4] Calendar of 1562, No. 268 (R.O. Domestic, xxiv. 21).

[5] In his letter of the 17th of August, Cecil remarks: "I dowte muche of the q. ma^{ty}: yf succours of men cannot be gotten, I wish it might be in money."—R.O. xl. 364 (Calendar, No. 491).

[6] This confusion is increased by the faulty translation in the Calendar of 1562. Thus the phrase "puisque sa M. ne trouve par conseil prendre la protection elle ne vouldroit faire traité avec euls *qui* en lieu de les fortifier *fust* cause de la diminution des forces tant des étrangers que de ceuls de la nation," is rendered: "As the Queen is not advised to undertake their protection, she would not treat with *those who*, instead of strengthening, have been the cause of the diminution both of the foreign and native forces." This is obviously incorrect. "Qui" undoubtedly refers to "traité" and not to "euls."

beyond doubt is his discontent with the size of the loan. He
would seem also to have been troubled by the small number
of troops offered. Personally, also, we think a reference is
made to the English proposal to hold Havre until Calais was
surrendered in the phrase: " Monsieur pour plusieurs raisons . . .
je ne puis passer oultre à ce qui a esté devisé touts ces jours car
je voi . . . tant d'inconvenients pour ceuls que nous voudrions
ayder desquels nous rendrions la cause fort odieuse sans leur
donner secours et comfort notable."[1] Be that as it may, the
same day Cecil forwarded to Throckmorton for the Prince a
copy of a letter of de la Haye which had been written in cipher.
Its receipt was acknowledged by Throckmorton on the 9th of
September. As far as we can judge, it was repeated by Cecil
on the 29th, and is calendared as No. 545. In it de la Haye
informed Condé that the English would only consent to send
foot, and not more than 6000; moreover, they demanded Havre
(Le Coudre), and would only let him have a third of the
requested loan. From this we may gather that the money
which Condé asked for was either 420,000 or 210,000 crowns,
according to whether the third mentioned is the amount
contained in Cecil's "first" or "second offer." In addition to
this letter, de la Haye sent a messenger to Orleans who arrived
on the 9th of September. As the treaty of Hampton Court
is of the 20th of September, it is very improbable that the
Vidame heard from the Prince before signing—certainly not
before it had been drawn up.

But to return to England. In a letter of the 29th of August,
Cecil declared that an agreement had been arranged. The three
principal points mentioned formed, three weeks later, the basis
of the treaty of Hampton Court. They were: an aid of 6000
men, a loan of 140,000 crowns, and Havre to be restored "when
Calais shall." We feel inclined to place the document, incorrectly mentioned by M. Weiss as Condé's instructions, before
the writing of this letter of Cecil; but it might possibly have
followed it.

We have, in all, six forms or copies of the treaty of Hampton
Court. Two of them are in English. One is a rough résumé
of its articles drawn up by Smith before it was actually signed,[2]
the other being corrected and endorsed by Cecil on the 27th of
September.[3] The four remaining are in Latin. One of them[4]
is of little importance. Another is a finally corrected draft,

[1] R.O. xl. 394 (Calendar, No. 530).
[2] Cecil in endorsing it says it is by Smith: R.O. xli. 479 (No. 656 of Calendar).
Cf. R.O. xli. 475 (Calendar, No. 650), and British Museum, Lansdowne, 102, 17
(Cecil to Smith, 19th Sept.).
[3] R.O. xli. 486 (Calendar, No. 663).   [4] R.O. xli. 487 (Calendar, No. 664).

and is signed by the Vidame and de la Haye.[1] The other two are the actual treaty—namely, one signed by Elizabeth,[2] and the other written on the blank parchment which bore the signatures of Condé, Coligny signing as Chastillon, and the other chiefs.[3] All six forms contain the three principal points—namely, a loan of 140,000 crowns, a succour of 6000 men, and the English possession of Havre until the surrender of Calais.

We are now in a better position to judge as to whether the Prince and Admiral sanctioned or knew of the article dealing with the exchange of Havre for Calais. They both again and again insisted that the Vidame had gone beyond his instructions. Coligny is especially clear on this point in a conversation held with the English agent, Middlemore, on the 12th of May, 1563. "For any promesse," said he, "made by me or any letter wrytten by me to hir ma^te wherin she hathe to shew that she shulde kepe newhaven untill Cales were rendrid unto her, I doo not think I ever made any and wolde be gladde to see them yf her majestie have any such letters of myne to shew. As towching the contract you speak of, I protest I never knew nor understode what was in it nor never sawe it untill my comming into normandy. At what tyme monsr. de throkmorton shewyd it me, but I had first ratifyed it. And yf I did think before that there had bene any more conteynid in it then the assurance only unto the Q. ma^tie of such monny as she had and shulde lend unto us and that the ayd and succours which she had and shuld gyve unto us in this cause might not prove domeageable in no sorte to her right and interest to Calles God never doo me good. And to lett you understand more of that matter, and that you may thinke I had some reason to beleve so, monsr. de la haye wrot to me to Orleans soone after the contract was made in England that as towchinge the sayde contract yt was promysyd there unto him that it shuld be rendrid him when he wolde and so sayd he wolde send it over to me for that they had playnely answeryd him there that they coulde not serve themselves by it nor yt coulde stande them in no steade, which monsieur de la haye hathe here since confyrmid to be."[4]

This, we believe, was a true statement of the facts. In the first place, it agrees with Beza's relation in the *Histoire Ecclésiastique* of the instructions given to de la Haye. This is most important, for it was in no way incumbent on him to defend his two leaders, and in fact he frequently criticises them severely. But what is still more in favour of Coligny's version

[1] British Museum, Caligula, E. 5.   [2] Condé, iii. 689.
[3] R.O. Chapter House, Diplomatic Documents (Calendar, No. 665).
[4] R.O. lvii. 682 (Calendar of 1563, No. 753).

is the undoubted existence of written instructions. No one can doubt that the "memoir" mentioned by de la Haye on the 29th of August contained Condé's instructions to his delegates. And it is inconceivable that, if they had contradicted Condé's assertion of ignorance, the Vidame would not have produced them and shifted the responsibility. He did not do so because he could not. He was far too great a noble to have been restrained by fear. And the plea he addressed to Cecil on the 19th of November, 1564,[1] namely, that he dare not justify himself because of the strength of Condé's position as Prince of the Blood, is insincere. Moreover, in no document in the British Museum, Record Office, or at Hatfield, is there any statement of the Vidame that he had been actually authorised by the Prince.

Again, Smith had several long conversations with de la Haye in the spring of 1563, yet he never reports that the latter ever suggested or admitted that Condé's contentions were incorrect. Then, too, we find that Cecil, writing on the 17th of August, immediately after the arrival of the Vidame, mentions the main points of the latter's instructions, but never a word as to any power to negotiate for the holding of Havre until Calais was surrendered. That suggestion undoubtedly came from Elizabeth, and was never communicated, as far as we can judge, to Condé. It was certainly not mentioned in de la Haye's letter of the 29th of August, and we do not believe that it was imparted by the messenger who arrived in Orleans on the 9th of September. For in an interview between the two leaders and Throckmorton shortly after, the former complained in detail of the hard bargain which Elizabeth had driven, but never even hinted that a part of it was an engagement in regard to the surrender of Calais. And further, on the 14th of December, 1562, Cecil wrote to Throckmorton, "I have sent dyvers thyngs to Mr. Smyth to be sent yow, and amongst other II or III articles, wherunto I have the prynce of Condé seale, and the hands of the admyrall etc., and yet I did promiss la haye not to notify the same."[2] Now this unwillingness of de la Haye may have been dictated solely by a commendable caution. But it may equally have been owing to the knowledge that he and the Vidame had gone beyond their powers, and that this fact would at once be communicated to their leaders.

There are other facts, too, which all point in the same direction. Condé and Coligny never for a moment throughout the winter of 1562–63 hesitated to declare publicly that

[1] R.O. lxxv. 674 (Calendar of 1564, No. 803).
[2] R.O. xlvi. 975 (Calendar, No. 1250).

Elizabeth would retire from Havre, though they generally
added—in the sense of their instructions given to de la Haye,
and described in the *Histoire Ecclésiastique*—that she was
entitled to receive guarantees for the ultimate surrender of
Calais in accordance with the treaty of Cateau Cambrésis.
This was their attitude in the negotiations of November and
December before Paris, and is reflected in the despatches of
Throckmorton, and even in the subsequent correspondence of
Coligny with Elizabeth herself. On the 2nd of March, 1563,
too, Smith wrote that "the prince mainteineth still, and
hath from tyme to tyme allwais said that so sone as the
Queene doth accord to them for religion, your ma^{te} shall
delyver Newhaven and retire all your forces out of fraunce."[1]
And Condé was further strengthened in his opinion by a public
declaration issued by Elizabeth.[2]

In fact, the only two people who might have been supposed
to be in a position to enlighten Condé as to the exact details of
the treaty were the English Ambassadors Smith and Throckmorton. In dealing with this matter, Lettenhove remarks that
it is "un agent anglais nommé Thomas Smith qui est chargé
de remettre ce traité aux Huguenots."[3] And de la Ferrière, in
writing of the negotiations before Paris in the winter of 1562,
adds that "Condé désavouant les premiers engagements pris en
son nom avec Élisabeth prétendait n'avoir jamais donné l'ordre
de livrer le Havre, et pourtant Throckmorton avait en ses mains
la copie du traité ; Élisabeth la lui avait envoyée pour s'en servir
à l'occasion."[4] Both statements, it may be said at once, are
grossly inaccurate. They are the culmination of some very
loose historical writing. Kervyn de Lettenhove, for instance,
bases his remark on a letter of Smith of the 22nd of September,
1562. Yet on turning to this letter there is no mention whatever of the treaty. All that Smith took with him to France

---

[1] R.O. lii. 349 (Calendar, 385).

[2] It is No. 671 in the Calendar of 1562 (R.O. xli. 493) and in the *Harleian
Misc.*, iii. 185. The Latin form, published in 1562, is to be found in the British
Museum. The French translation, which was forwarded to Condé, is in the
Mémoires de Condé, iii. 700. In the English and Latin copies formal mention was
made of the English rights on Calais by the treaty of Cateau Cambrésis. Un-
fortunately, in the translation sent to Condé and printed at Orleans, all mention of
Calais was omitted. Yet it would be rash to suggest that this was owing to sharp
practice on the part of the Huguenots or even of the translator, for in a French
translation endorsed by Cecil (Calendar, No. 674) there is also no mention of Calais.
But however this difference between the various translations arose, it led to heated
arguments later between Smith and Coligny (R.O. liii. 489 and Calendar of 1563,
No. 548. Cf. Brit. Mus., Lansdowne, 102, 34). This declaration is not to be confused with the one issued by Elizabeth for her lieutenant on the 27th of Sept.
(Calendar of 1562, Nos. 707–709, and R.O. xli. 521–523).

[3] Vol. i. 100.　　　　　　[4] *Lettres de Catherine de Médicis*, i. Intro. cxliii.

was his cipher, his instructions, and a French translation of the declaration of Elizabeth.[1] And thus it was that on the 8th of November he wrote: "Ye se they (especially the Cardinal of Ferrara) canne tell me of articles betwixt the Queenes majestie and Condé, by occasion ye know somewhat I did se, but no more certain then my memorie could then beare awaie and yet then they were but in drawing so farre as I know and not concludid."[2] Writing four months later, on the 31st of March, 1563, he explained that he had told the Prince and Admiral that he was not privy to the treaty of Hampton Court, and tried, though vainly, to draw them out on the question of the exchange of Havre for Calais. He then went on to beg for a copy of the treaty,[3] a request with which Cecil finally complied.[4] These facts naturally dispose of Lettenhove's theory as to Smith. It is equally easy to point out the error of de la Ferrière. All that is necessary is to read Throckmorton's despatches of September to December. They never pretend to any acquaintance with the provisions of the treaty. And it was to give him a more exact idea that Cecil and Elizabeth, on the 14th of December, informed him that they were sending him a copy of two or three of its articles.[5] As is known, Throckmorton was taken prisoner on the 19th of December at the battle of Dreux, and consequently could not have received them while with Coligny.

The reasons which induced the Vidame to agree to the compromising article on Havre and Dieppe are easily explained. It is evident from the letters written by Killigrew from Normandy in August, 1562, that Jean de Ferrières was not far removed from nervous collapse—a state of mind very apparent in a letter of a later date from the Vidame himself. He felt himself irretrievably compromised; the only course which seemed left open to him was to go on. And in this connection it is worth while to point out that, when the rumour arrived of Condé's refusal to authorise the English occupation of Havre, things, as Cecil tells us, were soon set straight by assistance from another quarter.[6] Now this could only have been done by the Vidame on his own responsibility, and in deliberate defiance of the supposed wishes of the Prince.

We have, we believe, said enough to show that all the facts

---

[1] See Cecil to Smith, 19th Sept. : British Museum, Lansdowne, 102 ; Smith to Cecil, 21st Sept. : R.O. xli. 500 (Calendar, No. 679) ; Cecil to Smith, 22nd Sept. : R.O. xli. 501 (Calendar, No. 680) ; Smith to Cecil, 22nd Sept. : Forbes, ii. 51.
[2] R.O. xliv. 770 (Calendar, No. 1000).
[3] R.O. liii. 489 (Calendar, No. 548).
[4] British Museum, Lansdowne, 102, 33 (Cecil to Smith, 10th April, 1563).
[5] R.O. xlvi. 975 and 977 (Calendar, Nos. 1250 and 1252).
[6] Cecil, 11th Oct. : Wright, i. 99.

are overwhelmingly in favour of Condé's and Coligny's long and complete ignorance of the compromising nature of their treaty with England. If further proof is needed, it will be found in the position of Beauvoir-la-Nocle, the Admiral's representative as Governor of Havre. We may say at once that Condé undoubtedly did agree to the occupation of the town by England. There is, in fact, nothing to lead us to suppose that he denied his responsibility, though rumours were constantly set on foot to that effect; one of them arrived in England on the eve of the embarkation of the men for Havre.[1] But it must not be supposed for a moment that this occupation in any sense entailed a surrender of the town by the Huguenots. It was solely military. It was intended as a guarantee to Elizabeth that she would not suffer in her rights on Calais, and as a convenience to the Huguenots by allowing them to employ their troops elsewhere. The treaty itself—which on this point follows closely the instructions given by Condé—states this very clearly. It lays down that Elizabeth's lieutenant in Havre was to have no civil jurisdiction whatever over Charles IX.'s subjects. His power was solely military. The French inhabitants were answerable to Beauvoir alone, and the latter never for a moment allowed this point to remain in doubt. It was, in the words of an Englishman writing from Havre on the 17th of November, a "mixt governement."[2] It is only necessary to quote in this connection the explanation given by the Privy Council in a letter to Challoner of the 29th of May, 1563. It was in reference to the Spanish agent's complaint, "touching some shippes and marchandises of theirs taken upon the seas and brought into newhaven, by the Frenche and espetiallye a shippe with Alam, of which he earnestly desired restitucion : ffor answer and satisfaction of whom, yt was signified unto him at the begynneng, that the Quenes majestie had no jurisdiction or authoritye to mynister justice at newhaven for thinges concerning the frenche, according to her promesse, at the first delivery of that Towne into her majesties possession."[3]

Since this article was written, a document has been published by Abbé Métais in the *Bulletin historique et philologique*[4]

[1] Supposing this rumour to have been true, which we doubt, Condé's objection may only have been made on technical grounds—that is to say, that he was not in a position personally to authorise their entry.

[2] R.O. xlv. 823 (Calendar, No. 1060).

[3] British Museum, Galba, C. i. 91 ; cf. *Calendar of State Papers*, Simancas, 300 (Quadra to Philip II., 15th Feb. 1563). For the further elucidation of the position of Beauvoir, we would refer to R.O. xliv. 771 (Calendar of 1562, No. 1001); Forbes, ii. 181 ; R.O. xlv. 823 (Calendar of 1562, No. 1060); Forbes, ii. 205, 206, 368 ; de la Ferrière, *La Normandie à l'étranger*, 53.

[4] Nos. 3 and 4, year 1902, p. 440, etc.

of the *Comité des travaux historiques et scientifiques.* It claims attention. This is the text :—

Nous Loys de Bourbon, prince de Condé, duc d'Anguyen, pair de France, Gaspart conte de Colligny, admiral de France, François de Colligny, s^r d'Andelot, conte de Montfort, colonnel général de l'infanterie françoise, et François, conte de la Rochefoucault et de Roussy, prince de Marcillac:—Bien et deument advertiz des traictez et capitulations de nostre mandement faictes en l'année mil cinq cens soixante deux par nostre très cher et très amé cousin le vidame de Chartres, et maistre Robert de la Haye, m^e des requestes de l'hostel du Roy auec la Royne d'Angleterre, ayans esté commis et depputez par nous du conseil et consentement des s^{rs} estans lors prez de nous à Orléans pour aller traicter auec ladicte Royne sur le secours et assistance que nous demandions à ladicte dame pour la conseruation de l'estat et couronne de France, sur les moiens de seureté aussi requis par sa Maiesté pour faire descendre et accommoder son armée en France,— Aduouons et ratiffions lesdictz traictez et capitulations, faictes par nostred. cousin auec la Royne d'Angleterre, ensemble ce qui a esté faict par les sieurs de Beauuoir, gouuerneur du Havre de grace et de Faurs, gouuerneur de Dieppe soubz nostre authorité, recongnoissant le tout avoir esté faict par ledict vidame et ledict de la Haye de nostre mandement et du sceu des sieurs signez audict traicté et le tout aussi pour le seruice du roy monseigneur et pour le bien de ses affaires, et pour aprobation de tout ce que dessus nous auons signé la présente de nos mains. A *Vouzailles*, ce *vingtvniesme* jour de *Novembre*, l'an mil cinq cens soixante *huict*.[1]

LOYS DE BOURBON.

G. COLLIGNY.   F. DE COLLIGNY.   LAROCHEFF$_F$.

Par Monseigneur duc et pair de France.

ROBERT.

Abbé Métais would have us believe that this document points to a proposed mission of the Vidame de Chartres to arrange a replica of the treaty of Hampton Court, or in other words deliver up or favour the capture by England of Havre, Dieppe, and Rouen ; and that it is an irrefragable proof that Coligny and Condé in it approved of that treaty in all its terms, and among them the exchange of Havre for Calais. It

---

[1] The words in italics are in a different ink from the rest of the document, and therefore must have been added later ; see remark of Abbé Métais, p. 440.

is necessary, therefore, to deal with the questions raised by this document one by one.

Firstly, as to its date. It must have been drawn up some time in October–November, 1568, when the troops from north of the Loire under Andelot, Montgomery, and the Vidame de Chartres coalesced with the main army under Condé, Coligny, and La Rochefoucauld. It had certainly not been framed previously by the Vidame with the object of having it signed by his colleagues on a favourable opportunity as a vindication of his action in 1562. If it had, it would have contained the names of Montgomery, Grammont, and others, and not those of Andelot and La Rochefoucauld. The two latter had nothing whatever to do with the treaty of Hampton Court—a most important point wholly ignored by Abbé Métais and M. Baguenault de Puchesse.

We now come to the reason for the proposed mission of the Vidame to England in 1568. In this connection, Mr. E. G. Atkinson's study of *The Cardinal of Châtillon in England*, and various documents in the Record Office and the British Museum, contain certain facts of great interest. Cardinal Odet reached Dover on the 8th of September. On the 14th and 15th of the same month, Coligny and Condé wrote to Elizabeth, informing her that they were sending Cavaignes, though the latter was not expected in London before the 3rd of October. Two days earlier, two other French gentlemen had arrived from La Rochelle, but when they left France Odet's arrival in England was still unknown. On the 16th, Elizabeth issued a warrant for 20,000*l.*, but the payment was not actually made until the 6th of November. About the same time the Huguenots were also busy importuning the German Princes for troops. And on the 20th of October, Zweibrücken besought Elizabeth to provide funds for his proposed march on France.[1] These facts seem to supply the reason for the suggested mission of the Vidame. It was probably October before the Huguenot leaders knew of Odet's activity in England; it must have been another month at least before they heard of Elizabeth's willingness to aid with money; while the document of the 21st of November was probably signed before they received news that the 20,000*l.* had actually been paid over. Moreover, this sum was only a part of what they had asked for.[2] It was in the midst of this uncertainty, we believe, that they conceived the idea of despatching the Vidame. Cavaignes, though he had been empowered by them, was scarcely of sufficient

---

[1] British Museum, Galba, xi. 303.
[2] See the letter of Cecil, British Museum, Cal. E. vi. 56.

authority, and his success was in doubt. Odet naturally seemed the ideal negotiator; but he and they were hardly as yet in touch, and neither he nor Cavaignes was in a position to explain adequately Huguenot needs.

We submit, therefore, that it was intended to send Jean de Ferrières for money, and possibly munitions of war, and that only. For any mention or suggestion of negotiations for an English descent on Normandy and a repetition of the articles of the treaty of Hampton Court, we seek in vain. In the first place, all the probabilities seem to point to the intention of sending the Vidame to carry on negotiations already begun. And in these we can find no hint of an English descent on Normandy. On the 18th of October, Cecil, in writing to Leicester, discussed the question then at issue—but never a word of anything but of a grant of money.[1] This is curious, as in his letters of August–September, 1562, he invariably placed the subject of Havre and Calais in the forefront. Then again, if the proposed mission was to negotiate a new treaty of Hampton Court, how are we to explain the fact that when they were nearing the Loire, with the intention of joining hands, if possible, with William of Orange, they omitted in the end to send the Vidame, although that was the very moment to create a diversion? And, lastly, can we suppose that men of the acknowledged ability of Condé and Coligny could have thought of making such a proposal? The treaty of Hampton Court seemed, from the English and Huguenot standpoint, a not unstatesmanlike move in 1562; its replica in 1568 was little less than fantastic. It had brought England nothing but shame; Elizabeth would certainly be chary of repeating her disastrous experiment. It was self-evident that mere talk of intrigues in the Norman towns would not move her; nothing less than the full possession of Havre or Calais could conceivably satisfy her; and neither was Condé's to give. Indeed, the only facts that we can find which give any colour to Abbé Métais' contention—apart from his interpretation of the document signed at Vouzailles—are the assertion by Philip II.'s representative on the 9th of October, of the existence of a Huguenot plan to seize Havre,[2] a manifestly vague allusion by La Mothe-Fénelon to a deferred mission of the Vidame "pour venir renouveller et conclurre aulcunes leurs cappitulations par deça,"[3] and talk of intrigues in connection with Calais. They are a slender—too slender—basis on which to build a theory

---

[1] British Museum, Cal. E. vi. 56. [2] Navarrete, *Coleccion de doc. inea.*, xc. 137.
[3] 24th Jan. 1569 (*Correspondance*, i. 154).

that the Vidame was to arrange a treaty on the lines of that of Hampton Court.

Why, then, it may be asked, was the document of the 21st of November, 1568, ever drawn up? One answer at least is easy. The Huguenots were in urgent want of money, and the Vidame de Chartres seemed the most suitable person to obtain it. He was among the greatest of the Protestant nobles; he was intimately acquainted with England and English affairs; and he was, above all, a *persona grata* with Elizabeth.[1] No doubt, too, he had been able to convince his colleagues that he had done his best in very difficult circumstances in 1562, and had only given way on the question of the exchange of Havre for Calais under strong pressure. But there was one great objection. There had been a break between him and Condé, and, though a reconciliation had taken place, the Vidame himself, in a letter of the 19th of November, 1564, had let Cecil know that it was hollow and based on insincerity. If, therefore, he was to exert his full influence with Elizabeth as Condé's emissary, some striking expression of the latter's confidence was necessary. This could best be done by a general acknowledgment of the Vidame's services in the negotiations of 1562, as they had been the cause of estrangement between him and the Prince —hence the document signed at Vouzailles.

This brings us to the pith of the question: what relation does this document bear to the treaty of Hampton Court? It confirms that treaty—but in what sense and to what degree? The article of Abbé Métais suggests that it does so in all its terms. This, we believe, is contrary to the facts. We have pointed out that Condé and Coligny declared repeatedly, and with reason, that the article which stipulated that Havre was to be held by Elizabeth until Calais was surrendered had not been introduced into the treaty with their knowledge or consent, and *ipso facto* was void. But they never, as far as we are aware, rejected the treaty as a whole, and therefore Abbé Métais' statement that it existed no longer in 1568 has no force as regards them. On the contrary, they considered it still binding even after the capture of Havre in July, 1563; but it was the treaty such as they acknowledged it—that is to say, without the objectionable article of the exchange of Havre for Calais. This comes out very clearly in an interview which Coligny had with Smith, the English Ambassador, the 31st of December, 1563. As the latter knew that the Admiral rejected all responsibility for this article, he remarked that "as for things passed that

[1] Elizabeth to Palsgrave, etc., 23rd July, 1563: R.O. lxi. 963 (Cal. 1053).

cannot be amendid, thei must nedes be sufferid to passe." But
he begged him to exercise his influence in favour of the English
contention that the treaty of Cateau Cambrésis should form the
basis of the proposed peace with France, and demanded the
money which the Huguenots owed Elizabeth. To this Coligny
replied, that before his coming to Caen in 1563 he had not
known of any accord by which England had been promised
anything more than repayment of her loan. As to the treaty
of Cateau Cambrésis—the detaining of Havre by Elizabeth had
manifestly abolished it and entailed the forfeiture of Calais. As
to the loan, it would be repaid, even if he had to sell his shirt.[1]
It will thus be seen, that while Coligny stoutly reiterated his
absence of responsibility for the English retention of Havre,[2]
and his desire to reimburse Elizabeth, Smith recognised that
the question of Havre was over and done with, and turned all
his attention to the repayment of the loan. This became the
English official attitude, as is plain from the instructions to
Norris in November, 1566, where no mention is made of Havre,
but the repayment of the loan is again claimed. And we can
see no reason to believe that Coligny's and Condé's attitude of
1563–64 underwent a sudden change in 1568, or that they supposed that England would think it changed. The document of
November was a general ratification and acknowledgment of
the acts, treaties, and capitulations made during the first
religious war by the Vidame, de la Haye, Beauvoir-la-Nocle,
and de Faurs. It did not refer solely to the treaty of Hampton
Court, but to all treaties and capitulations; nor did it particularise as to the articles of that treaty. In a word, it was a mere
acknowledgment of the *bona fides* of the Vidame and his fellow-
negotiators. It cannot be taken as a ratification of the article
which stipulated for the exchange of Havre for Calais. That
question was over and done with. England knew that the
Huguenot chiefs rejected all responsibility on that head. If the
latter had wished to stultify themselves, they would undoubtedly
have referred to the article and appended their approval. Moreover, to suppose that they wished in this document to go back
on the attitude they had so long adopted is little less than
absurd. It would have been tantamount to saying to Elizabeth,
"We have lied to your agents and ambassadors time and again.
We have said that the article regarding the exchange of Havre
for Calais was introduced into the treaty of Hampton Court

---

[1] R.O. lvii. 6 (Cal. of 1564, No. 6).

[2] Condé adopted precisely the same attitude nearly a year later, for the Vidame
wrote of him on the 19th November, 1564: "Il estoit aussi difficile de tirer de luy une
confession contraire à celle qu'il avoit fait en mon absence comme de blanchir ung
More" (R.O. lxxv. 674).

24

without our consent; we have declared that to allow you to retain Havre was beyond our power, against our will, and treason to our King—all this we take back, and acknowledge to have been lies!" Such a step, of course, would have been the one best calculated to wreck the proposed embassy at the outset. If anything else were needed to prove that the Huguenot chiefs had no such intention, it is the presence in this document of the names of Andelot and La Rochefoucauld. Now, neither of them had anything whatever to do with the treaty of Hampton Court. Their names do not appear in it. When de la Haye carried away from Orleans the signed parchment on which the treaty was subsequently copied, Andelot was in Germany, La Rochefoucauld in the west. And in the spring of 1563, Andelot let Smith know what he thought of the article dealing with the exchange of Havre for Calais ; subjects, said he, cannot give away the towns of their prince.[1] It is impossible, therefore, to think that in 1568 he had either forgotten this or that conditions were such as to induce him to acknowledge an article for which he had had no responsibility and which had aroused his ire.

Thus this document of November, 1568, was primarily intended as a letter of credence. There is no reason to believe that it points to an intention to negotiate a replica of the treaty of Hampton Court. It would certainly have been more plausible to suggest that it was intended to serve as an acknowledgment of the Huguenot debt to Elizabeth of 100,000 crowns. For, in the first place, this loan does not appear to have been repaid ; and it is just possible that in the autumn of 1568, when English monetary aid seemed doubtful, Condé and his friends determined to despatch the Vidame to acknowledge the old debt as the only way to obtain a fresh loan. It is impossible, however, to build a theory on proofs or rather probabilities so slight, though future investigation may throw some light on the matter.

And now to recapitulate. The Vidame alone must be held responsible for the article in the treaty of Hampton Court by which Elizabeth was granted the privilege of holding Havre until such time as she could exchange it for Calais. Secondly, Condé and Coligny not only did not authorise the Vidame in this, but did not know, and were not in a position to know, of his action. Thirdly, Havre was never surrendered to the English, but was jointly occupied by them and the Huguenots, though for obvious reasons Elizabeth's lieutenant was given military command. Fourthly, in October–November, 1568, the monetary position of the Huguenots was such that the leaders determined to despatch the Vidame to England. His mission had for its

[1] Aumale, i. 481.

object the obtaining of financial supplies.   No sufficient evidence has been produced by Abbé Métais to lead us to suppose that the Huguenots wished to arrange a new descent on Normandy.   The document he has published, as far as we can see, does not suggest it, while the bulk of the evidence to be drawn from the general political situation is against it.   But even could it be shown that such was really their intention, it would not suggest, far less prove, that they were contemplating a fresh act of treason ; for, as we have shown, Condé and Coligny never proposed, nor ever knew of until too late, nor acknowledged, the objectionable article in the treaty of Hampton Court. And finally, since they had made it clear both to England and the Vidame himself that they could in no way be held responsible for this article, though they did not reject the treaty as a whole, and since England had ceased to insist on this article as no longer a living question, the document of the 21st of November, 1568, must be read in the light of these facts.[1]

[1] M. Weiss' criticism of the article of Abbé Métais (*Bull. de la Soc. de l'histoire du prot. fr.*, of this year), together with the reply of the latter and a further criticism by M. Weiss, reached us too late for treatment here.   The question of Coligny's signature, however, is referred to in note 3, page 11.

APPENDIX II

PAMPHLET PRESENTED BY COLIGNY TO CHARLES IX.
ON WAR WITH SPAIN, JULY, 1572

WE have used the MS. copy in the Bibliothèque Mazarine, No. 2079. M. Auguste Molinier is scarcely correct in stating in the catalogue that it is not the one sometimes attributed to Mornay and published in his Memoirs in 1624. The two are substantially the same.

The most serious omissions in the published form of 1624 is an examination of the probable attitude of the various states of Italy, and certain references to the finances and credit of Spain and the condition of her mines in the Indies. Moreover, it is without six and a half opening lines to be found in the MS. No. 2079, while it closes with a eulogium of how the King will be feared, instead of, as in MS. No. 2079, a warning on the necessity of anticipating a Spanish attack.

Though its authorship has been disputed, we believe that there can be little doubt that it is in the main, at least as regards its form, the work of Mornay. It is studded with the elaborate imagery of the professed litterateur. Moreover, it is not quite at one, in its references to the financial condition of Spain, with Coligny's own statement to Middlemore of the 10th of June. True, this might be explained by supposing that the Admiral changed his argument to suit his audience. But it is equally plausible to suppose that we have here the views of Mornay. Nor does Baumgarten's argument, that Coligny would scarcely have given so important a trust to one so young, carry weight. Mornay must have been known as a young man of extraordinary promise, and his late journey through the Low Countries marked him out as eminently fitted for the task.

On the other hand, there is every reason to believe that the pamphlet faithfully reflected the personal views of Coligny, and was only prepared, or at least finished, after conversations with him. In the first place, it shows an intimate knowledge with the military aspect of the question. Secondly, its references to

Genlis prove that it was drawn up in part after Mornay had come to Paris and was in touch with the Admiral. And thirdly, Corbinelli, to whom the MS. copy in the Bibliothèque Mazarine originally belonged, ascribed it to Coligny.[1] Now the former not only styled himself the great Huguenot's friend, but had an exact and accurate knowledge of affairs. It is therefore hardly credible that he would have attributed it to the Admiral if the latter had had no hand in drawing it up; nor would Coligny have put it before the King as his own.

[1] See also Archivio Stor. It., 1898, p. 83.

INDEX

Acier, Jacques de Crussol, Sr. d', 219.
Acton, Lord, 231 (note 2), 275, 276, 299.
Admiral of France, Gaspard, Count of Coligny, Seigneur of Châtillon, *passim*.
Admiralship of France, nature and limits of, 45 (and note 2), 46 (and note 1).
Adrets, François de Beaumont, Baron des, 256, 288–290.
Alava, Francès de, 211, 232 (note 3), 235, 331.
Albret, Joan of, Queen of Navarre. *See* Navarre.
Alençon, Francis, Duke of, 237, 244, 245, 257, 262.
Alessandrino, Cardinal, 241, 277.
Alva, Don Fernando Alvarez de Toledo, Duke of, 46, 126, 180, 182, 207–208, 246, 276, 331.
Alvarotto, importance of his correspondence, 5–6.
Ambassadors (Spanish), prejudiced observers, 7.
Amboise, conspiracy of, 78–84, 302.
Amboise, edict or peace of, 150–151, 169, 175, 178, 179, 186, 195.
Amiens, François d'Ailly, Vidame of, 48.
Angoulême, Duke of, (later Charles IX.), 286.
Angoulême, Henri d', Bastard, 266, 267.
Anjou, Henry, Duke of, (also Duke of Orleans and later Henry III.), 99, 182, 191, 194, 201, 203, 204, 206, 207, 215, 216, 217, 218, 220, 222, 223, 236, 237, 239, 241, 257, 258, 259, 262, 264, 265, 278, 279, 280, 282, 289.
Anthony of Navarre. *See* Bourbon.
Archives, 5–7.
Army, for military organisation and tactics. *See* Cornet, Ensign, Vanguard, "Battle," Ordinances, Regulations of Condé, Gendarmery, Reiters, battles of Dreux, St. Denis, Moncontour, Arnay-le-Duc, and pages 43 (note 7) and 193.
Arnay-le-Duc, battle of, 226–227.
Ascanio della Corgnia, 42.
Association, act or oath of, 11th April 1562, 111, 114.

Astarac, Bernard d', Baron of Montamat, 256.
Atkinson, E. G., 366.
Aubespine, Claude de l', Sec. of State, 86, 118, 121.
Aubespine, Sebastian de l', Bishop of Limoges, 215, 247, 248, 275.
Aubigné, Agrippa d', at Amboise, 82–83, 167; Coligny after Moncontour, 224; tribute to Joan of Navarre, 245; interview with des Adrets, 289–290; condemns Henry IV.'s abjuration, 311.
Aumale. *See* Lorraine.
Aumale, duc d' (1822–97), 201 (note 1), 208, 353, 354, 355.
Aussy, Denys d', 206 (note 3).
Austria, Don John of, 246.
Autricourt, Valeran d'Anglure, Sr. d', 222.
Avaray (or Avaret), de Besiade, Sr. d', 114, 142.
Avenelles, Pierre des, 82.
Avignon, Legation of, 14–15.

Babinet, Colonel, 216 (note 1), 219 (note 1), 221.
Baden, Philip, Margrave, 221, 223, 307.
Baguenault de Puchesse, 5, 366.
Bahia, Gov. of, 319.
Ban, arrière, 43 (and note 4).
Bar, Louis of, 128, 297.
Barnaud, Nicolas, (author of *Reveille-Matin*), 278, 281, 283.
Bassompierre, Christophe, Baron of, 220.
"Battle" (military term), 43 (note 7).
Baubigny, Sr. de, 138.
Baumgarten, H., 5, 275, 277, 372.
Bayonne, interview of, 180, 182, 276.
Beaudiné, Galiot de Crussol, Sr. of, 256.
Beaumont (minister), 288.
Beauville, Sr. de, 272.
Beauvoir-la-Nocle, Jean de la Fin, Sr. of, 256, 355, 364, 365, 369.
Bec-Crespin, Charles du, (Baron of Bourry), 256.
Bec-Crespin, Pierre du, (Sr. of Vardes), 297.

Printed by
MORRISON & GIBB LIMITED
Edinburgh

A CATALOGUE OF BOOKS
PUBLISHED BY METHUEN
AND COMPANY: LONDON
36 ESSEX STREET
W.C.

CONTENTS

MAY 1909

A CATALOGUE OF

MESSRS. METHUEN'S

PUBLICATIONS

In this Catalogue the order is according to authors. An asterisk denotes that the book is in the press.

Colonial Editions are published of all Messrs. METHUEN's Novels issued at a price above 2s. 6d., and similar editions are published of some works of General Literature. These are marked in the Catalogue. Colonial editions are only for circulation in the British Colonies and India.

All books marked net are not subject to discount, and cannot be bought at less than the published price. Books not marked net are subject to the discount which the bookseller allows.

Messrs. METHUEN's books are kept in stock by all good booksellers. If there is any difficulty in seeing copies, Messrs. Methuen will be very glad to have early information, and specimen copies of any books will be sent on receipt of the published price *plus* postage for net books, and of the published price for ordinary books.

I.P.L. represents Illustrated Pocket Library.

Part I.—General Literature

Abraham (George D.). THE COMPLETE MOUNTAINEER. With 75 Illustrations. *Second Edition. Demy 8vo. 15s. net.*
A Colonial Edition is also published.

Acatos (M. J.). See Junior School Books.

Adams (Frank). JACK SPRAT. With 24 Coloured Pictures. *Super Royal 16mo. 2s.*

Adeney (W. F.), M.A. See Bennett (W. H.)

Ady (Cecilia M.). A HISTORY OF MILAN UNDER THE SFORZA. With 20 Illustrations and a Map. *Demy 8vo. 10s. 6d. net.*

Æschylus. See Classical Translations.

Æsop. See I.P.L.

Ainsworth (W. Harrison). See I.P.L.

Aldis (Janet). THE QUEEN OF LETTER WRITERS, MARQUISE DE SÉVIGNÉ, DAME DE BOURBILLY, 1626-96. With 18 Illustrations. *Second Edition. Demy 8vo. 12s. 6d. net.*
A Colonial Edition is also published.

Alexander (William), D.D., Archbishop of Armagh. THOUGHTS AND COUNSELS OF MANY YEARS. *Demy 16mo. 2s. 6d.*

Alken (Henry). See I.P.L.

Allen (Charles C.). See Textbooks of Technology.

Allen (L. Jessie). See Little Books on Art.

Allen (J. Romilly), F.S.A. See Antiquary's Books.

Almack (E.), F.S.A. See Little Books on Art.

Amherst (Lady). A SKETCH OF EGYPTIAN HISTORY FROM THE EARLIEST TIMES TO THE PRESENT DAY. With many Illustrations and Maps. *A New and Cheaper Issue Demy 8vo. 7s. 6d. net.*

Anderson (F. M.). THE STORY OF THE BRITISH EMPIRE FOR CHILDREN. With 42 Illustrations. *Cr. 8vo. 2s.*

Anderson (J. G.), B.A., NOUVELLE GRAMMAIRE FRANÇAISE, A L'USAGE DES ÉCOLES ANGLAISES. *Crown 8vo. 2s.*
EXERCICES DE GRAMMAIRE FRANÇAISE. *Cr. 8vo. 1s. 6d.*

Andrewes (Bishop). PRECES PRIVATAE. Translated and edited, with Notes, by F. E. BRIGHTMAN. M.A., of Pusey House, Oxford. *Cr. 8vo. 6s.*
See also Library of Devotion.

'Anglo-Australian.' AFTER-GLOW MEMORIES. *Cr. 8vo. 6s.*

Anon. HEALTH, WEALTH, AND WISDOM. *Crown 8vo. 1s. net.*

Aristotle. THE ETHICS OF. Edited, with an Introduction and Notes by JOHN BURNET, M.A., *Cheaper issue. Demy 8vo. 10s. 6d. net.*

Asman (H. N.), M.A., B.D. See Junior School Books.

Atkins (H. G.). See Oxford Biographies.

Atkinson (C. M.). JEREMY BENTHAM. *Demy 8vo. 5s. net.*

*Atkinson (C. T.), M.A., Fellow of Exeter College, Oxford, sometime Demy of Magdalen College. A HISTORY OF GERMANY, from 1713 to 1815. With many Maps. *Demy 8vo. 15s. net.*

Atkinson (T. D.). ENGLISH ARCHITECTURE. With 196 Illustrations *Second Edition. Fcap. 8vo. 3s. 6d. net.*
A GLOSSARY OF TERMS USED IN ENGLISH ARCHITECTURE. With 265 Illustrations. *Second Edition. Fcap. 8vo. 3s. 6d. net.*

Auden (T.), M.A., F.S.A. See Ancient Cities.

Aurelius (Marcus). WORDS OF THE ANCIENT WISE. Thoughts from Epictetus and Marcus Aurelius. Edited by W. H. D. ROUSE, M.A., Litt. D. *Fcap. 8vo. 3s. 6d. net.*
See also Standard Library.

Austen (Jane). See Standard Library, Little Library and Mitton (G. E.).

Aves (Ernest). CO-OPERATIVE INDUSTRY. *Crown 8vo. 5s. net.*

Bacon (Francis). See Standard Library and Little Library.

Baden-Powell (R. S. S.) THE MATABELE CAMPAIGN, 1896. With nearly 100 Illustrations. *Fourth Edition. Large Cr. 8vo. 6s.*

Bagot (Richard). THE LAKES OF NORTHERN ITALY. With 37 Illustrations and a Map. *Fcap. 8vo. 5s. net.*

Bailey (J. C.), M.A. See Cowper (W.).

Baker (W. G.), M.A. See Junior Examination Series.

Baker (Julian L.), F.I.C., F.C.S. See Books on Business.

Balfour (Graham). THE LIFE OF ROBERT LOUIS STEVENSON. With a Portrait. *Fourth Edition in one Volume. Cr. 8vo. Buckram, 6s.*
A Colonial Edition is also published.

Ballard (A.), B.A., LL.D. See Antiquary's Books.

Bally (S. E.). See Commercial Series.

Banks (Elizabeth L.). THE AUTO-BIOGRAPHY OF A 'NEWSPAPER GIRL.' *Second Edition. Cr. 8vo. 6s.*

Barham (R. H.). See Little Library.

Baring (The Hon. Maurice). WITH THE RUSSIANS IN MANCHURIA. *Third Edition. Demy 8vo. 7s. 6d. net.*
A Colonial Edition is also published.

A YEAR IN RUSSIA. *Second Edition. Demy 8vo. 10s. 6d. net.*
A Colonial Edition is also published.

Baring-Gould (S.). THE LIFE OF NAPOLEON BONAPARTE. With nearly 200 Illustrations, including a Photogravure Frontispiece. *Second Edition. Wide Royal 8vo. 10s. 6d. net.*
A Colonial Edition is also published.

THE TRAGEDY OF THE CÆSARS: A STUDY OF THE CHARACTERS OF THE CÆSARS OF THE JULIAN AND CLAUDIAN HOUSES. With numerous Illustrations from Busts, Gems, Cameos, etc. *Sixth Edition. Royal 8vo. 10s. 6d. net.*

A BOOK OF FAIRY TALES. With numerous Illustrations by A. J. GASKIN. *Third Edition. Cr. 8vo. Buckram. 6s., also Demy 8vo. 6d.*

OLD ENGLISH FAIRY TALES. With numerous Illustrations by F. D. BEDFORD. *Third Edition. Cr. 8vo. Buckram. 6s.*

THE VICAR OF MORWENSTOW. Revised Edition. With a Portrait. *Third Edition. Cr. 8vo. 3s. 6d.*

OLD COUNTRY LIFE. With 69 Illustrations. *Fifth Edition. Large Crown 8vo. 6s.*

A GARLAND OF COUNTRY SONG: English Folk Songs with their Traditional Melodies. Collected and arranged by S. BARING-GOULD and H. F. SHEPPARD. *Demy 4to. 6s.*

SONGS OF THE WEST: Folk Songs of Devon and Cornwall. Collected from the Mouths of the People. By S. BARING-GOULD, M.A., and H. FLEETWOOD SHEPPARD, M.A. New and Revised Edition, under the musical editorship of CECIL J. SHARP. *Large Imperial 8vo. 5s. net.*

A BOOK OF NURSERY SONGS AND RHYMES. Edited by S. BARING-GOULD. Illustrated. *Second and Cheaper Edition. Large Cr. 8vo. 2s. 6d. net.*

STRANGE SURVIVALS: SOME CHAPTERS IN THE HISTORY OF MAN. Illustrated. *Third Edition. Cr. 8vo. 2s. 6d. net.*

YORKSHIRE ODDITIES: INCIDENTS AND STRANGE EVENTS. *Fifth Edition. Cr. 8vo. 2s. 6d. net.*

THE BARING-GOULD SELECTION READER. Arranged by G. H. ROSE. Illustrated. *Crown 8vo. 1s. 6d.*

THE BARING-GOULD CONTINUOUS READER. Arranged by G. H. ROSE. Illustrated. *Crown 8vo. 1s. 6d.*

A BOOK OF CORNWALL. With 33 Illustrations. *Second Edition. Cr. 8vo. 6s.*

A BOOK OF DARTMOOR. With 60 Illustrations. *Second Edition. Cr. 8vo. 6s.*

A BOOK OF DEVON. With 35 Illustrations. *Third Edition. Cr. 8vo. 6s.*

A BOOK OF NORTH WALES. With 49 Illustrations. *Cr. 8vo. 6s.*

A BOOK OF SOUTH WALES. With 57 Illustrations. *Cr. 8vo. 6s.*

A BOOK OF BRITTANY. With 69 Illustrations. *Cr. 8vo. 6s.*

A BOOK OF THE RHINE: From Cleve to Mainz. With 8 Illustrations in Colour by TREVOR HADDEN, and 48 other Illustrations. *Second Edition. Cr. 8vo. 6s.*
A Colonial Edition is also published.

A BOOK OF THE RIVIERA. With 40 Illustrations. *Cr. 8vo. 6s.*
A Colonial Edition is also published.

A BOOK OF THE PYRENEES. With 25 Illustrations. *Cr. 8vo. 6s.*
A Colonial Edition is also published.
See also Little Guides.

Barker (Aldred F.). See Textbooks of Technology.

Barker (E.), M.A. (Late) Fellow of Merton College, Oxford. THE POLITICAL THOUGHT OF PLATO AND ARISTOTLE. *Demy 8vo. 10s. 6d. net.*

Barnes (W. E.), D.D. See Churchman's Bible.

Barnett (Mrs. P. A.). See Little Library.

Baron (R. R. N.), M.A. FRENCH PROSE COMPOSITION. *Third Edition. Cr 8vo. 2s. 6d. Key, 3s. net.*
See also Junior School Books.

Barron (H. M.), M.A., Wadham College, Oxford. TEXTS FOR SERMONS. With a Preface by Canon SCOTT HOLLAND. *Cr. 8vo. 3s. 6d.*

Bartholomew (J. G.), F.R.S.E. See C. G. Robertson.

Bastable (C. F.), LL.D. THE COMMERCE OF NATIONS. *Fourth Ed. Cr. 8vo. 2s. 6d.*

Bastian (H. Charlton), M.A., M.D., F.R.S. THE EVOLUTION OF LIFE. With Diagrams and many Photomicrographs. *Demy 8vo. 7s. 6d. net.*

Batson (Mrs. Stephen). A CONCISE HANDBOOK OF GARDEN FLOWERS. *Fcap. 8vo. 3s. 6d.*

THE SUMMER GARDEN OF PLEASURE. With 36 Illustrations in Colour by OSMUND PITTMAN. *Wide Demy 8vo. 15s. net.*

Batten (Loring W.), Ph.D., S.T.D. THE HEBREW PROPHET. *Cr. 8vo. 3s. 6d. net.*

Bayley (R. Child). THE COMPLETE PHOTOGRAPHER. With over 100 Illustrations. *Third Edition. With Note on Direct Colour Process. Demy 8vo. 10s. 6d. net.*

A Colonial Edition is also published.

Beard (W. S.). EASY EXERCISES IN ALGEBRA FOR BEGINNERS. *Cr. 8vo. 1s. 6d.* With Answers. *1s. 9d.*

See also Junior Examination Series and Beginner's Books.

Beckford (Peter). THOUGHTS ON HUNTING. Edited by J. OTHO PAGET, and Illustrated by G. H. JALLAND. *Second Edition. Demy 8vo. 6s.*

Beckford (William). See Little Library.

Beeching (H. C.), M.A., Canon of Westminster. See Library of Devotion.

Beerbohm (Max). A BOOK OF CARICATURES. *Imperial 4to. 21s. net.*

Begbie (Harold). MASTER WORKERS. Illustrated. *Demy 8vo. 7s. 6d. net.*

Behmen (Jacob). DIALOGUES ON THE SUPERSENSUAL LIFE. Edited by BERNARD HOLLAND. *Fcap. 8vo. 3s. 6d.*

Bell (Mrs. Arthur G.). THE SKIRTS OF THE GREAT CITY. With 16 Illustrations in Colour by ARTHUR G. BELL, 17 other Illustrations, and a Map. *Second Edition. Cr. 8vo. 6s.*

Belloc (Hilaire), M.P. PARIS. With 7 Maps and a Frontispiece in Photogravure. *Second Edition, Revised. Cr. 8vo. 6s.*

HILLS AND THE SEA. *Second Edition. Crown 8vo. 6s.*

ON NOTHING AND KINDRED SUBJECTS. *Fcap. 8vo. 5s.*

A Colonial Edition is also published.

Bellot (H. H.L.), M.A. See Jones (L. A. A.).

Bennett (W. H.), M.A. A PRIMER OF THE BIBLE. With a concise Bibliography. *Fifth Edition. Cr. 8vo. 2s. 6d.*

Bennett (W. H.) and Adeney (W. F.). A BIBLICAL INTRODUCTION. *Fifth Edition. Cr. 8vo. 7s. 6d.*

Benson (Archbishop) GOD'S BOARD Communion Addresses. *Second Edition. Fcap. 8vo. 3s. 6d. net.*

Benson (A. C.), M.A. See Oxford Biographies.

Benson (R. M.). THE WAY OF HOLINESS: a Devotional Commentary on the 119th Psalm. *Cr. 8vo. 5s.*

Bernard (E. R.), M.A., Canon of Salisbury. THE ENGLISH SUNDAY: ITS ORIGINS AND ITS CLAIMS. *Fcap. 8vo. 1s. 6d.*

Bertouch (Baroness de). THE LIFE OF FATHER IGNATIUS. Illustrated. *Demy 8vo. 10s. 6d. net.*

Beruete (A. de). See Classics of Art.

Betham-Edwards (Miss). HOME LIFE IN FRANCE. With 20 Illustrations. *Fifth Edition. Crown 8vo. 6s.*

A Colonial Edition is also published.

Bethune-Baker (J. F.), M.A. See Handbooks of Theology.

Bidez (J.). See Byzantine Texts.

Biggs (C. R. D.), D.D. See Churchman's Bible.

Bindley (T. Herbert), B.D. THE OECUMENICAL DOCUMENTS OF THE FAITH. With Introductions and Notes. *Second Edition. Cr. 8vo. 6s. net.*

Binns (H. B.). THE LIFE OF WALT WHITMAN. Illustrated. *Demy 8vo. 10s. 6d. net.*

A Colonial Edition is also published.

Binyon (Mrs. Laurence). NINETEENTH CENTURY PROSE. Selected and arranged by. *Crown 8vo. 6s.*

Binyon (Laurence). THE DEATH OF ADAM AND OTHER POEMS. *Cr. 8vo. 3s. 6d. net.*

See also Blake (William).

Birch (Walter de Gray), LL.D., F.S.A. See Connoisseur's Library.

Birnstingl (Ethel). See Little Books on Art.

Blackmantle (Bernard). See I.P.L.

Blair (Robert). See I.P.L.

Blake (William). THE LETTERS OF WILLIAM BLAKE, TOGETHER WITH A LIFE BY FREDERICK TATHAM. Edited from the Original Manuscripts, with an Introduction and Notes, by ARCHIBALD G. B. RUSSELL. With 12 Illustrations. *Demy 8vo. 7s. 6d. net.*

ILLUSTRATIONS OF THE BOOK OF JOB. With General Introduction by LAURENCE BINYON. *Quarto. 21s. net.*

See also Blair (Robert), I.P.L., and Little Library.

Bloom (J. Harvey), M.A. SHAKESPEARE'S GARDEN. Illustrated. *Fcap. 8vo. 3s. 6d.; leather, 4s. 6d. net.*

See also Antiquary's Books.

Blouet (Henri). See Beginner's Books.

Boardman (T. H.), M.A. See French (W.)

Bodley (J. E. C.), Author of 'France.' THE CORONATION OF EDWARD VII. *Demy 8vo. 21s. net.* By Command of the King.

Body (George), D.D. THE SOUL'S PILGRIMAGE: Devotional Readings from the Published and Unpublished writings of George Body, D.D. Selected and arranged by J. H. BURN, B.D., F.R.S.E. *Demy 16mo. 2s. 6d.*

Bona (Cardinal). See Library of Devotion.

Boon (F. C.)., B.A. See Commercial Series.

Borrow (George). See Little Library.

Bos (J. Ritzema). AGRICULTURAL ZOOLOGY. Translated by J. R. AINSWORTH DAVIS, M.A. With 155 Illustrations. *Third Edition. Cr. 8vo. 3s. 6d.*

Botting (C. G.), B.A. EASY GREEK EXERCISES. *Cr. 8vo. 2s.*
See also Junior Examination Series.

Boulting (W.) TASSO AND HIS TIMES. With 24 Illustrations. *Demy 8vo. 10s. 6d. net.*

Boulton (E. S.), M.A. GEOMETRY ON MODERN LINES. *Cr. 8vo. 2s.*

Boulton (William B.). SIR JOSHUA REYNOLDS, P.R.A. With 49 Illustrations. *Demy 8vo. 7s. 6d. net.*

Bowden (E. M.). THE IMITATION OF BUDDHA : Being Quotations from Buddhist Literature for each Day in the Year. *Fifth Edition. Cr. 16mo. 2s. 6d.*

Boyle (W.). CHRISTMAS AT THE ZOO. With Verses by W. BOYLE and 24 Coloured Pictures by H. B. NEILSON. *Super Royal 16mo. 2s.*

Brabant (F. G.), M.A. See Little Guides.

Bradley (A. G.). ROUND ABOUT WILTSHIRE. With 14 Illustrations, in Colour by T. C. GOTCH, 16 other Illustrations, and a Map. *Second Edition. Cr. 8vo. 6s.*
A Colonial Edition is also published.

THE ROMANCE OF NORTHUMBERLAND. With 16 Illustrations in Colour by FRANK SOUTHGATE, R.B.A., and 12 from Photographs. *Second Edition. Demy 8vo 7s. 6d net.*
A Colonial Edition is also published.

Bradley (John W.). See Little Books on Art.

Braid (James), Open Champion, 1901, 1905 and 1906. ADVANCED GOLF. With 88 Photographs and Diagrams. *Fourth Edition. Demy 8vo. 10s. 6d. net.*
A Colonial Edition is also published.

Braid (James) and Others. GREAT GOLFERS IN THE MAKING. Edited by HENRY LEACH. With 24 Illustrations. *Second Edition. Demy 8vo. 7s. 6d. net.*
A Colonial Edition is also published.

Brailsford (H. N.). MACEDONIA : ITS RACES AND THEIR FUTURE. With Photographs and Maps. *Demy 8vo. 12s. 6d. net.*

Brodrick (Mary) and **Morton (A. Anderson).** A CONCISE DICTIONARY OF EGYPTIAN ARCHÆOLOGY. A Hand-Book for Students and Travellers. With 80 Illustrations and many Cartouches. *Cr. 8vo. 3s. 6d.*

Brooks (E. E.), B.Sc. (Lond), Leicester Municipal Technical School, and **James (W. H. N.),** A.R.C.S., A.M.I.E.E., Municipal School of Technology, Manchester. See Textbooks of Technology.

Brooks (E. W.). See Hamilton (F. J.)

Brown (P. H.), LL.D. SCOTLAND IN THE TIME OF QUEEN MARY. *Demy 8vo. 7s. 6d. net.*

Brown (S. E.), M.A., B.Sc., Senior Science Master at Uppingham. A PRACTICAL CHEMISTRY NOTE - BOOK FOR MATRICULATION AND ARMY CANDIDATES. Easy Experiments on the Commoner Substances. *Cr. 4to. 1s. 6d. net.*

Brown (J. Wood), M.A. THE BUILDERS OF FLORENCE. With 74 Illustrations by HERBERT RAILTON. *Demy 4to. 18s. net.*

Browne (Sir Thomas). See Standard Library.

Brownell (C. L.). THE HEART OF JAPAN. Illustrated. *Third Edition. Cr. 8vo. 6s. ; also Demy 8vo. 6d.*

Browning (Robert). See Little Library.

Bryant (Walter W.), B.A., F.R.A.S., F.R. Met. Soc., of the Royal Observatory, Greenwich. A HISTORY OF ASTRONOMY. With 35 Illustrations. *Demy 8vo. 7s. 6d. net.*

Buckland (Francis T.). CURIOSITIES OF NATURAL HISTORY. Illustrated by H. B. NEILSON. *Cr. 8vo. 3s. 6d.*

Buckton (A. M.) THE BURDEN OF ENGELA. *Second Edition. Cr. 8vo. 3s 6d. net.*

EAGER HEART : A Mystery Play. *Seventh Edition. Cr. 8vo. 1s. net.*

KINGS IN BABYLON : A Drama. *Cr. 8vo. 1s. net.*

SONGS OF JOY. *Cr. 8vo. 1s. net.*

Budge (E. A. Wallis). THE GODS OF THE EGYPTIANS. With over 100 Coloured Plates and many Illustrations. *Two Volumes. Royal 8vo. £3, 3s. net.*

Bull (Paul), Army Chaplain. GOD AND OUR SOLDIERS. *Second Edition. Cr. 8vo. 6s.*
A Colonial Edition is also published.

Bulley (Miss). See Dilke (Lady).

Bunyan (John). See Standard Library and Library of Devotion.

Burch (G. J.), M.A., F.R.S. A MANUAL OF ELECTRICAL SCIENCE. Illustrated. *Cr. 8vo. 3s.*

Burgess (Gelett). GOOPS AND HOW TO BE THEM. Illustrated. *Small 4to. 6s.*

Burke (Edmund). See Standard Library.

Burn (A. E.), D.D., Rector of Handsworth and Prebendary of Lichfield. See Handbooks of Theology.

Burn (J. H.), B.D., F.R.S.E. THE CHURCHMAN'S TREASURY OF SONG : Gathered from the Christian poetry of all ages. Edited by. *Fcap. 8vo. 3s. 6d. net.* See also Library of Devotion.

Burnand (Sir F. C.). RECORDS AND REMINISCENCES. With a Portrait by H. v. HERKOMER. *Cr. 8vo. Fourth and Cheaper Edition. 6s.*
A Colonial Edition is also published.

Burns (Robert), THE POEMS. Edited by ANDREW LANG and W. A. CRAIGIE. With Portrait. *Third Edition. Demy 8vo, gilt top. 6s.*
See also Standard Library.

Burnside (W. F.), M.A. OLD TESTA-
MENT HISTORY FOR USE IN
SCHOOLS. *Third Edition. Cr. 8vo. 3s. 6d.*
Burton (Alfred). See I.P.L.
Bussell (F. W.), D.D. CHRISTIAN
THEOLOGY AND SOCIAL PROGRESS
(The Bampton Lectures of 1905). *Demy
8vo. 10s. 6d. net.*
Butler (Joseph), D.D. See Standard
Library.
Caldecott (Alfred), D.D. See Handbooks
of Theology.
Calderwood (D. S.), Headmaster of the Nor-
mal School, Edinburgh. TEST CARDS
IN EUCLID AND ALGEBRA. In three
packets of 40, with Answers. *1s.* each. Or
in three Books, price *2d., 2d.,* and *3d.*
Canning (George). See Little Library.
Capey (E. F. H.). See Oxford Biographies.
Careless (John). See I.P.L.
Carlyle (Thomas). THE FRENCH
REVOLUTION. Edited by C. R. L.
FLETCHER, Fellow of Magdalen College,
Oxford. *Three Volumes. Cr. 8vo. 18s.*
THE LIFE AND LETTERS OF OLIVER
CROMWELL. With an Introduction
by C. H. FIRTH, M.A., and Notes and
Appendices by Mrs. S. C. LOMAS. *Three
Volumes. Demy 8vo. 18s. net.*
Carlyle (R. M. and A. J.), M.A. See
Leaders of Religion.
Carmichael (Philip). ALL ABOUT
PHILIPPINE. With 8 Illustrations.
Cr. 8vo. 2s. 6d.
Carpenter (Margaret Boyd). THE CHILD
IN ART. With 50 Illustrations. *Second
Edition. Large Cr. 8vo. 6s.*
Cavanagh (Francis), M.D. (Edin.). THE
CARE OF THE BODY. *Second Edition.
Demy 8vo. 7s. 6d. net.*
Celano (Thomas of). THE LIVES OF ST.
FRANCIS OF ASSISI. Translated into
English by A. G. FERRERS HOWELL. With
a Frontispiece. *Cr. 8vo. 5s. net.*
Channer (C. C.) and Roberts (M. E.).
LACEMAKING IN THE MIDLANDS,
PAST AND PRESENT. With 16 full-
page Illustrations. *Cr. 8vo. 2s. 6d.*
Chapman (S. J.). See Books on Business.
Chatterfield (Thomas). See Standard
Library.
Chesterfield (Lord), THE LETTERS OF,
TO HIS SON. Edited, with an Introduc-
tion by C. STRACHEY, with Notes by A.
CALTHROP. *Two Volumes. Cr. 8vo. 12s.*
Chesterton (G. K.). CHARLES DICKENS.
With two Portraits in Photogravure. *Fifth
Edition. Cr. 8vo. 6s.*
Childe (Charles P.), B.A., F.R.C.S. THE
CONTROL OF A SCOURGE : OR,
HOW CANCER IS CURABLE. *Demy 8vo.
7s. 6d. net.*
Christian (F. W.). THE CAROLINE
ISLANDS. With many Illustrations and
Maps. *Demy 8vo. 12s. 6d. net.*
Cicero. See Classical Translations.
Clapham (J. H.), Professor of Economics in
the University of Leeds. THE WOOL-

LEN AND WORSTED INDUSTRIES.
With 21 Illustrations and Diagrams. *Cr.
8vo. 6s.*
Clarke (F. A.), M.A. See Leaders of Religion.
Clausen (George), A.R.A., R.W.S. SIX
LECTURES ON PAINTING. With 19
Illustrations. *Third Edition. Large Post
8vo. 3s. 6d. net.*
AIMS AND IDEALS IN ART. Eight
Lectures delivered to the Students of the
Royal Academy of Arts. With 32 Illustra-
tions. *Second Edition. Large Post 8vo.
5s. net.*
Cleather (A. L.). See Wagner (R).
Clinch (G.), F.G.S. See Antiquary's Books
and Little Guides.
Clough (W. T.) and Dunstan (A. E.).
See Junior School Books and Textbooks of
Science.
Clouston (T. S.), M.D., C.C.D., F.R.S.E.
THE HYGIENE OF MIND. With 10
Illustrations. *Fifth Edition. Demy 8vo.
7s. 6d. net.*
Coast (W. G.), B.A. EXAMINATION
PAPERS IN VERGIL. *Cr. 8vo. 2s.*
Cobb (W. F.), M.A. THE BOOK OF
PSALMS : with a Commentary. *Demy 8vo.
10s. 6d. net.*
Coleridge (S. T.). POEMS. Selected and
Arranged by ARTHUR SYMONS. With a
Photogravure Frontispiece. *Fcap. 8vo.
2s. 6d. net.*
Collingwood (W. G.), M.A. THE LIFE
OF JOHN RUSKIN. With Portrait.
Sixth Edition. Cr. 8vo. 2s. 6d. net.
Collins (W. E.), M.A. See Churchman's
Library.
Combe (William). See I.P.L.
Conrad (Joseph). THE MIRROR OF
THE SEA : Memories and Impressions.
Third Edition. Cr. 8vo. 6s.
Cook (A. M.), M.A., and **Marchant (E. C.),**
M.A. PASSAGES FOR UNSEEN
TRANSLATION. Selected from Latin and
Greek Literature. *Fourth Ed. Cr. 8vo. 3s. 6d.*
LATIN PASSAGES FOR UNSEEN
TRANSLATION. *Third Ed. Cr. 8vo. 1s. 6d.*
Cooke-Taylor (R. W.). THE FACTORY
SYSTEM. *Cr. 8vo. 2s. 6d.*
Coolidge (W. A. B.), M.A. THE ALPS.
With many Illustrations. *Demy 8vo.
7s. 6d net.*
  A Colonial Edition is also published.
Corelli (Marie). THE PASSING OF THE
GREAT QUEEN. *Second Edition. Fcap.
4to. 1s.*
A CHRISTMAS GREETING. *Cr. 4to. 1s.*
Corkran (Alice). See Little Books on Art.
Cotes (Everard). SIGNS AND POR-
TENTS IN THE FAR EAST. With 35
Illustrations. *Second Edition. Demy 8vo.
7s. 6d. net.*
  A Colonial Edition is also published.
Cotes (Rosemary). DANTE'S GARDEN.
With a Frontispiece. *Second Edition.
Fcap. 8vo. 2s. 6d.; leather, 3s. 6d. net.*
BIBLE FLOWERS. With a Frontispiece
and Plan. *Fcap. 8vo. 2s. 6d. net.*

Cowley (Abraham). See Little Library.

Cowper (William). THE POEMS. Edited with an Introduction and Notes by J. C. BAILEY, M.A. Illustrated, including two unpublished designs by WILLIAM BLAKE. *Demy 8vo.* 10s. 6d. net.

Cox (J. Charles). See Ancient Cities, Antiquary's Books, and Little Guides.

Cox (Harold), B.A., M.P. LAND NATIONALIZATION AND LAND TAXATION. *Second Edition revised. Cr. 8vo.* 3s. 6d. net.

Crabbe (George). See Little Library.

Craik (Mrs.). See Little Library.

Crane (C. P.), D.S.O. See Little Guides.

Crane (Walter), R.W.S. AN ARTIST'S REMINISCENCES. With 123 Illustrations by the Author and others from Photographs. *Second Edition. Demy 8vo.* 18s. net.

A Colonial Edition is also published.

INDIA IMPRESSIONS. With 84 Illustrations from Sketches by the Author. *Second Edition. Demy 8vo.* 7s. 6d. net.

A Colonial Edition is also published.

Crashaw (Richard). See Little Library.

Crawford (F. G.). See Danson (Mary C.).

Crofts (T. R. N.), M.A., Modern Language Master at Merchant Taylors' School. See Simplified French Texts.

Cross (J. A.), M.A. THE FAITH OF THE BIBLE. *Fcap. 8vo.* 2s. 6d. net.

Cruikshank (G.). THE LOVING BALLAD OF LORD BATEMAN. With 11 Plates. *Cr. 16mo.* 1s. 6d. net.

Crump (B.). See Wagner (R.).

Cunliffe (Sir F. H. E.), Fellow of All Souls' College, Oxford. THE HISTORY OF THE BOER WAR. With many Illustrations, Plans, and Portraits. *In 2 vols. Quarto.* Vol. I. 15s.

Cunynghame (H. H.), C.B. See Connoisseur's Library.

Cutts (E. L.), D.D. See Leaders of Religion.

Daniell (G. W.), M.A. See Leaders of Religion.

Dante (Alighieri). LA COMMEDIA DI DANTE. The Italian Text edited by PAGET TOYNBEE, M.A., D.Litt. *Cr.8vo.* 6s.

THE DIVINE COMEDY. Translated by H. F. CARY. Edited with a Life of Dante and Introductory Notes by PAGET TOYNBEE, M.A., D.Litt. *Demy 8vo.* 6d.

THE PURGATORIO OF DANTE. Translated into Spenserian Prose by C. GORDON WRIGHT. With the Italian text. *Fcap. 8vo.* 2s. 6d. net.

See also Little Library, Toynbee (Paget), and Vernon (Hon. W. Warren).

Darley (George). See Little Library.

D'Arcy (R. F.), M.A. A NEW TRIGONOMETRY FOR BEGINNERS. With numerous diagrams. *Cr. 8vo.* 2s. 6d.

Davenport (Cyril). See Connoisseur's Library and Little Books on Art.

Davenport (James). THE WASHBOURNE FAMILY. With 15 Illustrations and a Map. *Royal 8vo.* 21s. net.

Davey (Richard). THE PAGEANT OF LONDON. With 40 Illustrations in Colour by JOHN FULLEYLOVE, R.I. *In Two Volumes. Demy 8vo.* 15s. net.

Davis (H. W. C.), M.A., Fellow and Tutor of Balliol College. ENGLAND UNDER THE NORMANS AND ANGEVINS: 1066-1272. With Maps and Illustrations. *Demy 8vo.* 10s. 6d. net.

Dawson (Nelson). See Connoisseur's Library.

Dawson (Mrs. Nelson). See Little Books on Art.

Deane (A. C.). See Little Library.

Deans (Storry R.). THE TRIALS OF FIVE QUEENS: KATHARINE OF ARAGON, ANNE BOLEYN, MARY QUEEN OF SCOTS, MARIE ANTOINETTE and CAROLINE OF BRUNSWICK. With 12 Illustrations. *Demy 8vo.* 10s. 6d. net.

A Colonial Edition is also published.

Dearmer (Mabel). A CHILD'S LIFE OF CHRIST. With 8 Illustrations in Colour by E. FORTESCUE-BRICKDALE. *Large Cr. 8vo.* 6s.

Delbos (Leon). THE METRIC SYSTEM. *Cr. 8vo.* 2s.

Demosthenes. AGAINST CONON AND CALLICLES. Edited by F. DARWIN SWIFT, M.A. *Second Edition. Fcap. 8vo.* 2s.

Dickens (Charles). See Little Library, I.P.L., and Chesterton (G. K.).

Dickinson (Emily). POEMS. *Cr. 8vo.* 4s. 6d. net.

Dickinson (G. L.), M.A., Fellow of King's College, Cambridge. THE GREEK VIEW OF LIFE. *Sixth Edition. Cr. 8vo.* 2s. 6d.

Dilke (Lady), Bulley (Miss), and **Whitley (Miss).** WOMEN'S WORK. *Cr. 8vo.* 2s. 6d.

Dillon (Edward), M.A. See Connoisseur's Library and Little Books on Art.

Ditchfield (P. H.), M.A., F.S.A. THE STORY OF OUR ENGLISH TOWNS. With an Introduction by AUGUSTUS JESSOPP, D.D. *Second Edition. Cr. 8vo.* 6s.

OLD ENGLISH CUSTOMS: Extant at the Present Time. *Cr. 8vo.* 6s.

ENGLISH VILLAGES. With 100 Illustrations. *Second Edition. Cr. 8vo.* 2s. 6d. net.

THE PARISH CLERK. With 31 Illustrations. *Third Edition. Demy 8vo.* 7s. 6d. net.

Dixon (W. M.), M.A. A PRIMER OF TENNYSON. *Second Edition. Cr. 8vo.* 2s. 6d.

ENGLISH POETRY FROM BLAKE TO BROWNING. *Second Edition. Cr. 8vo.* 2s. 6d.

Dobbs (W. J.), M.A. See Textbooks of Science.

Doney (May). SONGS OF THE REAL. *Cr. 8vo.* 3s. 6d. net.

Douglas (Hugh A.). VENICE ON FOOT. With the Itinerary of the Grand Canal. With 75 Illustrations and 11 Maps. *Fcap. 8vo.* 5s. net.

Douglas (James). THE MAN IN THE PULPIT. *Cr. 8vo.* 2s. 6d. net.

Dowden (J.), D.D., Lord Bishop of Edinburgh. FURTHER STUDIES IN THE PRAYER BOOK. *Cr. 8vo.* 6s.
See also Churchman's Library.

Drage (G.). See Books on Business.

Draper (F. W. M.). See Simplified French Texts.

Driver (S. R.), D.D., D.C.L., Regius Professor of Hebrew in the University of Oxford. SERMONS ON SUBJECTS CONNECTED WITH THE OLD TESTAMENT. *Cr. 8vo.* 6s.
See also Westminster Commentaries.

Dry (Wakeling). See Little Guides.

Dryhurst (A. R.). See Little Books on Art.

Du Buisson (J. C.), M.A. See Churchman's Bible.

Duguid (Charles). See Books on Business.

Dumas (Alexandre). THE CRIMES OF THE BORGIAS AND OTHERS. With an Introduction by R. S. GARNETT. With 9 Illustrations. *Cr. 8vo.* 6s.
THE CRIMES OF URBAIN GRANDIER AND OTHERS. With 8 Illustrations. *Cr. 8vo.* 6s.
THE CRIMES OF THE MARQUISE DE BRINVILLIERS AND OTHERS. With 8 Illustrations. *Cr. 8vo.* 6s.
THE CRIMES OF ALI PACHA AND OTHERS. With 8 Illustrations. *Cr. 8vo.* 6s.
Colonial Editions are also published.

MY MEMOIRS. Translated by E. M. WALLER. With an Introduction by ANDREW LANG. With Frontispieces in Photogravure. In six Volumes. *Cr. 8vo.* 6s. *each volume.*
A Colonial Edition is also published.
VOL. I. 1802-1821. VOL. III. 1826-1830.
VOL. II. 1822-1825. VOL. IV. 1830-1831.

Duncan (David), D.Sc., LL.D. THE LIFE AND LETTERS OF HERBERT SPENCER. With 15 Illustrations. *Demy 8vo.* 15s.

Dunn (J. T.), D.Sc., **and Mundella (V. A.).** GENERAL ELEMENTARY SCIENCE. With 114 Illustrations. *Second Edition.* *Cr. 8vo.* 3s. 6d.

Dunstan (A. E.), B.Sc. (Lond.), East Ham Technical College. See Textbooks of Science, and Junior School Books.

Durham (The Earl of). A REPORT ON CANADA. With an Introductory Note. *Demy 8vo.* 4s. 6d. net.

Dutt (W. A.). THE NORFOLK BROADS. With coloured Illustrations by FRANK SOUTHGATE, R.B.A. *Second Edition.* *Cr. 8vo.* 6s.
WILD LIFE IN EAST ANGLIA. With 16 Illustrations in colour by FRANK SOUTHGATE, R.B.A. *Second Edition.* *Demy 8vo.* 7s. 6d. net.
SOME LITERARY ASSOCIATIONS OF EAST ANGLIA. With 16 Illustrations in Colour by W. DEXTER, R.B.A., and 16 other Illustrations. *Demy 8vo.* 10s. 6d. net.
See also Little Guides.

Earle (John), Bishop of Salisbury. MICRO-COSMOGRAPHIE, OR A PIECE OF THE WORLD DISCOVERED. *Post 16mo.* 2s. net.

Edmonds (Major J. E.), R.E.; D.A.Q.-M.G. See Wood (W. Birkbeck).

Edwards (Clement), M.P. RAILWAY NATIONALIZATION. *Second Edition, Revised.* *Crown 8vo.* 2s. 6d. net.

Edwards (W. Douglas). See Commercial Series.

Edwardes (Tickner). THE LORE OF THE HONEY BEE. With many Illustrations. *Cr. 8vo.* 6s.

Egan (Pierce). See I.P.L.

Egerton (H. E.), M.A. A HISTORY OF BRITISH COLONIAL POLICY. A Cheaper Issue, with a supplementary chapter. *Second Ed., Revised.* *Demy 8vo.* 7s. 6d. net.
A Colonial Edition is also published.

Ellaby (C. G.). See Little Guides.

Ellerton (F. G.). See Stone (S. J.).

Epictetus. See Aurelius (Marcus).

Erasmus. A Book called in Latin EN-CHIRIDION MILITIS CHRISTIANI, and in English the Manual of the Christian Knight. *Fcap. 8vo.* 3s. 6d. net.

Ewald (Carl). TWO LEGS, AND OTHER STORIES. Translated from the Danish by ALEXANDER TEIXEIRA DE MATTOS. Illustrated by AUGUSTA GUEST. *Large Cr. 8vo.* 6s.

Fairbrother (W. H.), M.A. THE PHILO-SOPHY OF T. H. GREEN. *Second Edition.* *Cr. 8vo.* 3s. 6d.

Fea (Allan). SOME BEAUTIES OF THE SEVENTEENTH CENTURY. With 82 Illustrations. *Second Edition.* *Demy 8vo.* 12s. 6d. net.
THE FLIGHT OF THE KING. With over 70 Sketches and Photographs by the Author. *New and revised Edition.* *Demy 8vo.* 7s. 6d. net.
A Colonial Edition is also published.
SECRET CHAMBERS AND HIDING-PLACES. With 80 Illustrations. *New and revised Edition.* *Demy 8vo.* 7s. 6d. net.
A Colonial Edition is also published.

Ferrier (Susan). See Little Library.

Fidler (T. Claxton), M.Inst. C.E. See Books on Business.

Fielding (Henry). See Standard Library.

Finn (S. W.), M.A. See Junior Examination Series.

Firth (J. B.). See Little Guides.

Firth (C. H.), M.A., Regius Professor of Modern History at Oxford. CROMWELL'S ARMY: A History of the English Soldier during the Civil Wars, the Commonwealth, and the Protectorate. *Cr. 8vo.* 6s.

Firth (Edith E.). See Beginner's Books.

FitzGerald (Edward). THE RUBÁIYÁT OF OMAR KHAYYÁM. Printed from the Fifth and last Edition. With a Commentary by Mrs. STEPHEN BATSON, and a Biography of Omar by E. D. ROSS. *Cr. 8vo.* 6s. See also Miniature Library.

FitzGerald (H. P.). A CONCISE HAND-
BOOK OF CLIMBERS, TWINERS,
AND WALL SHRUBS. Illustrated.
Fcap. 8vo. 3s. 6d. net.
Fitzpatrick (S. A. O.). See Ancient Cities.
Flecker (W. H.), M.A., D.C.L., Headmaster
of the Dean Close School, Cheltenham.
THE STUDENT'S PRAYER BOOK.
THE TEXT OF MORNING AND EVENING
PRAYER AND LITANY. With an Introduc-
tion and Notes. *Cr. 8vo. 2s. 6d.*
Fletcher (J. S.). A BOOK OF YORK-
SHIRE. With 16 Illustrations in Colour
by WAL PAGET and FRANK SOUTHGATE,
R.B.A., and 12 from Photographs. *Demy
8vo. 7s. 6d. net.*
A Colonial Edition is also published.
Flux (A. W.), M.A., William Dow Professor
of Political Economy in M'Gill University,
Montreal. ECONOMIC PRINCIPLES.
Demy 8vo. 7s. 6d. net.
Foat (F. W. G.), D.Litt., M.A., Assistant
Master at the City of London School.
LONDON : A READER FOR YOUNG
CITIZENS. With Plans and Illustra-
tions. *Cr. 8vo. 1s. 6d.*
Ford (H. G.), M.A., Assistant Master at
Bristol Grammar School. See Junior School
Books.
Forel (A.). THE SENSES OF INSECTS.
Translated by MACLEOD YEARSLEY. With
2 Illustrations. *Demy 8vo. 10s. 6d. net.*
Fortescue (Mrs. G.). See Little Books on
Art.
Fraser (J. F.). ROUND THE WORLD
ON A WHEEL. With 100 Illustrations.
Fifth Edition Cr. 8vo. 6s.
A Colonial Edition is also published.
French (W.), M.A. See Textbooks of Science.
Freudenreich (Ed. von). DAIRY BAC-
TERIOLOGY. A Short Manual for
Students. Translated by J. R. AINSWORTH
DAVIS, M.A. *Second Edition. Revised.
Cr. 8vo. 2s. 6d.*
Fulford (H. W.), M.A. See Churchman's
Bible.
Fuller (W. P.), M.A. See Simplified French
Texts.
Fyvie (John). TRAGEDY QUEENS OF
THE GEORGIAN ERA. With 16 Illustra-
tions. *Second Ed. Demy 8vo. 12s. 6d. net.*
Gallaher (D.) and Stead (W. J.). THE
COMPLETE RUGBY FOOTBALLER,
ON THE NEW ZEALAND SYSTEM.
With 35 Illustrations. *Second Ed. Demy
8vo. 10s. 6d. net.*
A Colonial Edition is also published.
Gallichan (W. M.). See Little Guides.
Gambado (Geoffrey, Esq.). See I.P.L.
Gaskell (Mrs.). See Little Library, Stan-
dard Library and Sixpenny Novels.
Gasquet, the Right Rev. Abbot, O.S.B. See
Antiquary's Books.
George (H. B.), M.A., Fellow of New College,
Oxford. BATTLES OF ENGLISH HIS-
TORY. With numerous Plans. *Fourth
Edition. Cr. 8vo. 3s. 6d.*
A HISTORICAL GEOGRAPHY OF THE

BRITISH EMPIRE. *Third Edition.
Cr. 8vo. 3s. 6d.*
Gibbins (H. de B.), Litt.D., M.A. IN-
DUSTRY IN ENGLAND : HISTORI-
CAL OUTLINES. With 5 Maps. *Fifth
Edition. Demy 8vo. 10s. 6d.*
THE INDUSTRIAL HISTORY OF
ENGLAND. With Maps and Plans.
Fifteenth Edition, Revised. Cr. 8vo. 3s.
ENGLISH SOCIAL REFORMERS.
Second Edition. Cr. 8vo. 2s. 6d.
See also Hadfield (R. A.)., and Commer-
cial Series.
Gibbon (Edward). MEMOIRS OF MY
LIFE AND WRITINGS. Edited by
G. BIRKBECK HILL, LL.D *Cr. 8vo. 6s.*
THE DECLINE AND FALL OF THE
ROMAN EMPIRE. Edited, with Notes,
Appendices, and Maps, by J. B. BURY,
M.A., Litt.D., Regius Professor of Modern
History at Cambridge. *In Seven Volumes.
Demy 8vo. Gilt top. 8s. 6d. each. Also,
Crown 8vo. 6s. each.*
See also Standard Library.
Gibbs (Philip). THE ROMANCE OF
GEORGE VILLIERS : FIRST DUKE
OF BUCKINGHAM, AND SOME MEN
AND WOMEN OF THE STUART
COURT. With 20 Illustrations. *Second
Edition. Demy 8vo. 15s. net.*
A Colonial Edition is also published.
Gibson (E. C. S.), D.D., Lord Bishop of
Gloucester. See Westminster Commentaries,
Handbooks of Theology, and Oxford Bio-
graphies.
Gilbert (A. R.). See Little Books on Art.
Gloag (M. R.) and Wyatt (Kate M.). A
BOOK OF ENGLISH GARDENS.
With 24 Illustrations in Colour. *Demy
8vo. 10s. 6d. net.*
Godfrey (Elizabeth). A BOOK OF RE-
MEMBRANCE. Being Lyrical Selections
for every day in the Year. Arranged by.
Fcap. 8vo. 2s. 6d. net.
ENGLISH CHILDREN IN THE OLDEN
TIME. With 32 Illustrations. *Second
Edition. Demy 8vo. 7s. 6d. net.*
Godley (A. D.), M.A., Fellow of Magdalen
College, Oxford. LYRA FRIVOLA.
Fourth Edition. Fcap. 8vo. 2s. 6d.
VERSES TO ORDER. *Second Edition.
Fcap. 8vo. 2s. 6d.*
SECOND STRINGS. *Fcap. 8vo. 2s. 6d.*
Goldsmith (Oliver). THE VICAR OF
WAKEFIELD. With 10 Plates in
Photogravure by Tony Johannot. *Leather,
Fcap. 32mo. 2s. 6d. net.*
See also I.P.L. and Standard Library.
Gomme (G. L.). See Antiquary's Books.
Goodrich-Freer (A.). IN A SYRIAN
SADDLE. *Demy 8vo. 7s. 6d. net.*
A Colonial Edition is also published.
Gorst (Rt. Hon. Sir John). THE CHIL-
DREN OF THE NATION. *Second
Edition. Demy 8vo. 7s. 6d. net.*
Goudge (H. L.), M.A., Principal of Wells
Theological College. See Westminster Com-
mentaries.

A 2

Graham (P. Anderson). THE RURAL EXODUS. The Problem of the Village and the Town. *Cr. 8vo.* 2s. 6d.

Granger (F. S.), M.A., Litt.D. PSYCHOLOGY. *Third Edition. Cr. 8vo.* 2s. 6d.

THE SOUL OF A CHRISTIAN. *Cr. 8vo.* 6s.

Gray (E. M'Queen). GERMAN PASSAGES FOR UNSEEN TRANSLATION. *Cr. 8vo.* 2s. 6d.

Gray (P. L.), B.Sc. THE PRINCIPLES OF MAGNETISM AND ELECTRICITY. With 181 Diagrams. *Cr. 8vo.* 3s. 6d.

Green (G. Buckland), M.A., late Fellow of St. John's College, Oxon. NOTES ON GREEK AND LATIN SYNTAX. *Second Ed. revised. Crown 8vo.* 3s. 6d.

Greenidge (A.H. J.), M.A., D.Litt. A HISTORY OF ROME : From the Tribunate of Tiberius Gracchus to the end of the Jugurthine War, B.C. 133-104. *Demy 8vo.* 10s. 6d. net.

Greenwell (Dora). See Miniature Library.

Gregory (R. A.). THE VAULT OF HEAVEN. A Popular Introduction to Astronomy. Illustrated. *Cr. 8vo.* 2s. 6d.

Gregory (Miss E. C.). See Library of Devotion.

Grubb (H. C.). See Textbooks of Technology.

Hadfield (R. A.) and **Gibbins (H. de B).** A SHORTER WORKING DAY. *Cr. 8vo.* 2s. 6d.

Hall (Mary). A WOMAN'S TREK FROM THE CAPE TO CAIRO. With 64 Illustrations and 2 Maps. *Second Edition. Demy 8vo.* 16s. net.

Hall (R. N.) and Neal (W. G.). THE ANCIENT RUINS OF RHODESIA. Illustrated. *Second Edition, revised. Demy 8vo.* 10s. 6d. net.
A Colonial Edition is also published.

Hall (R. N.). GREAT ZIMBABWE. With numerous Plans and Illustrations. *Second Edition. Demy 8vo.* 10s. 6d. net.

Hamel (Frank). FAMOUS FRENCH SALONS. With 20 Illustrations. *Third Edition. Demy 8vo.* 12s. 6d. net.
A Colonial Edition is also published.

Hamilton (F. J.), D.D. See Byzantine Texts.

Hannay (D.). A SHORT HISTORY OF THE ROYAL NAVY, 1200-1688. Illustrated. *Demy 8vo.* 7s. 6d. net.

Hannay (James O.), M.A. THE SPIRIT AND ORIGIN OF CHRISTIAN MONASTICISM. *Cr. 8vo.* 6s.
THE WISDOM OF THE DESERT. *Fcap. 8vo.* 3s. 6d. net.

Hardie (Martin). See Connoisseur's Library.

Hare (A. T.), M.A. THE CONSTRUCTION OF LARGE INDUCTION COILS. With numerous Diagrams. *Demy 8vo.* 6s.

Harvey (Alfred), M.B. See Ancient Cities and Antiquary's Books.

Hawthorne (Nathaniel). See Little Library.

Heath (Frank R.). See Little Guides.

Heath (Dudley). See Connoisseur's Library.

Hello (Ernest). STUDIES IN SAINTSHIP. *Fcap 8vo.* 3s. 6d.

Henderson (B. W.), Fellow of Exeter College, Oxford. THE LIFE AND PRINCIPATE OF THE EMPEROR NERO. Illustrated. *New and cheaper issue. Demy 8vo.* 7s. 6d. net.
AT INTERVALS. *Fcap 8vo.* 2s. 6d. net.

Henderson (M. Sturge). GEORGE MEREDITH : NOVELIST, POET, REFORMER. With a Portrait in Photogravure. *Second Edition. Crown 8vo.* 6s.

Henderson (T. F.). See Little Library and Oxford Biographies.

Henderson (T. F.), and Watt (Francis). SCOTLAND OF TO-DAY. With 20 Illustrations in colour and 24 other Illustrations. *Second Edition. Cr. 8vo.* 6s.
A Colonial Edition is also published.

Henley (W. E.). ENGLISH LYRICS. CHAUCER TO POE, 1340-1849. *Second Edition. Cr. 8vo.* 2s. 6d. net.

Henley (W. E.) and **Whibley (C.)** A BOOK OF ENGLISH PROSE, CHARACTER, AND INCIDENT, 1387-1649. *Cr. 8vo.* 2s. 6d. net.

Henson (H. H.), B.D., Canon of Westminster. LIGHT AND LEAVEN : HISTORICAL AND SOCIAL SERMONS. *Cr. 8vo.* 6s.

Herbert (George). See Library of Devotion.

Herbert of Cherbury (Lord). See Miniature Library.

Hewins (W. A. S.), B.A. ENGLISH TRADE AND FINANCE IN THE SEVENTEENTH CENTURY. *Cr. 8vo.* 2s. 6d.

Hewitt (Ethel M.) A GOLDEN DIAL. A Day Book of Prose and Verse. *Fcap. 8vo.* 2s. 6d. net.

Hey (H.), Inspector, Surrey Education Committee, and **Rose (G. H.),** City and Guilds Woodwork Teacher. THE MANUAL TRAINING CLASSROOM : WOODWORK. Book I. *4to.* 1s.

Heywood (W.). See St. Francis of Assisi.

Hill (Clare). See Textbooks of Technology.

Hill (Henry), B.A., Headmaster of the Boy's High School, Worcester, Cape Colony. A SOUTH AFRICAN ARITHMETIC. *Cr. 8vo.* 3s. 6d.

Hind (C. Lewis). DAYS IN CORNWALL. With 16 Illustrations in Colour by WILLIAM PASCOE, and 20 other Illustrations and a Map. *Second Edition. Cr. 8vo.* 6s.

Hirst (F. W.) See Books on Business.

Hoare (J. Douglas). A HISTORY OF ARCTIC EXPLORATION. With 20 Illustrations & Maps. *Demy 8vo.* 7s. 6d. net.

Hobhouse (L. T.), late Fellow of C.C.C., Oxford. THE THEORY OF KNOWLEDGE. *Demy 8vo.* 10s. 6d. net.

Hobson (J. A.), M.A. INTERNATIONAL TRADE : A Study of Economic Principles. *Cr. 8vo.* 2s. 6d. net.
PROBLEMS OF POVERTY. An Inquiry into the Industrial Condition of the Poor. *Seventh Edition. Cr. 8vo.* 2s. 6d.

THE PROBLEM OF THE UNEMPLOYED. *Fourth Edition. Cr.8vo. 2s.6d.*

Hodgetts (E. A. Brayley). THE COURT OF RUSSIA IN THE NINETEENTH CENTURY. With 20 Illustrations. *Two Volumes. Demy 8vo. 24s. net.*
A Colonial Edition is also published.

Hodgkin (T.), D.C.L. See Leaders of Religion.

Hodgson (Mrs. W.) HOW TO IDENTIFY OLD CHINESE PORCELAIN. With 40 Illustrations. *Second Edition. Post 8vo. 6s.*

Holden-Stone (G. de). See Books on Business.

Holdich (Sir T. H.), K.C.I.E. THE INDIAN BORDERLAND: being a Personal Record of Twenty Years. Illustrated. *Demy 8vo. 10s. 6d. net.*
A Colonial Edition is also published.

Holdsworth (W. S.), M.A. A HISTORY OF ENGLISH LAW. *In Two Volumes. Vol. I. Demy 8vo. 10s. 6d. net.*

Holland (H. Scott), Canon of St. Paul's. See Newman (J. H.).

Hollway-Calthrop (H. C.), late of Balliol College, Oxford; Bursar of Eton College. PETRARCH: HIS LIFE, WORK, AND TIMES. With 24 Illustrations. *Demy 8vo. 12s. 6d. net.*
A Colonial Edition is also published.

Holt (Emily). THE SECRET OF POPULARITY: How to Achieve Social Success. *Cr. 8vo. 3s. 6d. net.*
A Colonial Edition is also published.

Holyoake (G. J.). THE CO-OPERATIVE MOVEMENT OF TO-DAY. *Fourth Ed. Cr. 8vo. 2s. 6d.*

Hone (Nathaniel J.). See Antiquary's Books.

Hook (A.) HUMANITY AND ITS PROBLEMS. *Cr. 8vo. 5s. net.*

Hoppner. See Little Galleries.

Horace. See Classical Translations.

Horsburgh (E. L. S.), M.A. WATERLOO: With Plans. *Second Edition. Cr. 8vo. 5s.*
See also Oxford Biographies.

Horth (A. C.). See Textbooks of Technology.

Horton (R. F.), D.D. See Leaders of Religion.

Hosie (Alexander). MANCHURIA. With Illustrations and a Map. *Second Edition. Demy 8vo. 7s. 6d. net.*
A Colonial Edition is also published.

How (F. D.). SIX GREAT SCHOOLMASTERS. With Portraits and Illustrations. *Second Edition. Demy 8vo. 7s. 6d.*

Howell (A. G. Ferrers). FRANCISCAN DAYS. Being Selections for every day in the year from ancient Franciscan writings. *Cr. 8vo. 3s. 6d. net.*

Howell (G.). TRADE UNIONISM—NEW AND OLD. *Fourth Edition. Cr. 8vo. 2s. 6d.*

Huggins (Sir William), K.C.B., O.M., D.C.L., F.R.S. THE ROYAL SOCIETY. With 25 Illustrations. *Wide Royal 8vo. 4s. 6d. net.*

Hughes (C. E.). THE PRAISE OF SHAKESPEARE. An English Anthology. With a Preface by SIDNEY LEE. *Demy 8vo. 3s. 6d. net.*

Hughes (Thomas). TOM BROWN'S SCHOOLDAYS. With an Introduction and Notes by VERNON RENDALL. *Leather. Royal 32mo. 2s. 6d. net.*

Hutchinson (Horace G.) THE NEW FOREST. Illustrated in colour with 50 Pictures by WALTER TYNDALE and 4 by LUCY KEMP-WELCH. *Third Edition. Cr. 8vo. 6s.*

Hutton (A. W.), M.A. See Leaders of Religion and Library of Devotion.

Hutton (Edward). THE CITIES OF UMBRIA. With 20 Illustrations in Colour by A. PISA, and 12 other Illustrations. *Third Edition. Cr. 8vo. 6s.*
A Colonial Edition is also published.

THE CITIES OF SPAIN. With 24 Illustrations in Colour, by A. W. RIMINGTON, 20 other Illustrations and a Map. *Third Edition. Cr. 8vo. 6s.*
A Colonial Edition is also published.

FLORENCE AND THE CITIES OF NORTHERN TUSCANY, WITH GENOA. With 16 Illustrations in Colour by WILLIAM PARKINSON, and 16 other Illustrations. *Second Edition. Cr. 8vo. 6s*
A Colonial Edition is also published.

ENGLISH LOVE POEMS. Edited with an Introduction. *Fcap. 8vo. 3s. 6d. net.*

Hutton (R. H.). See Leaders of Religion.

Hutton (W. H.), M.A. THE LIFE OF SIR THOMAS MORE. With Portraits after Drawings by HOLBEIN. *Second Ed. Cr. 8vo. 5s.*
See also Leaders of Religion.

Hyde (A. G.) GEORGE HERBERT AND HIS TIMES. With 32 Illustrations. *Demy 8vo. 10s. 6d. net.*

Hyett (F. A.). FLORENCE: HER HISTORY AND ART TO THE FALL OF THE REPUBLIC. *Demy 8vo. 7s. 6d. net.*

Ibsen (Henrik). BRAND. A Drama. Translated by WILLIAM WILSON. *Third Edition. Cr. 8vo. 3s. 6d.*

Inge (W. R.), M.A., Fellow and Tutor of Hertford College, Oxford. CHRISTIAN MYSTICISM. (The Bampton Lectures of 1899.) *Demy 8vo. 12s. 6d. net.*
See also Library of Devotion.

Ingham (B. P.). See Simplified French Texts.

Innes (A. D.), M.A. A HISTORY OF THE BRITISH IN INDIA. With Maps and Plans. *Cr. 8vo. 6s.*

ENGLAND UNDER THE TUDORS. With Maps. *Second Edition. Demy 8vo. 10s. 6d. net.*

Jackson (C. E.), B.A., Senior Physics Maste Bradford Grammar School. of Science.

Jackson (S.), M.A. See Commercial Series.

Jackson (F. Hamilton). See Little Guides.

Jacob (F.), M.A. See Junior Examination Series.

James (W. H. N.). See Brooks (E. E.).

Jeans (J. Stephen). TRUSTS, POOLS, AND CORNERS AS AFFECTING COMMERCE AND INDUSTRY. *Cr. 8vo. 2s. 6d.*
See also Books on Business.

Jebb (Camilla). A STAR OF THE SALONS: JULIE DE LESPINASSE. With 20 Illustrations. *Demy 8vo. 10s. 6d. net.*
A Colonial Edition is also published.

Jeffery (Reginald W.), M.A. THE THIRTEEN COLONIES OF NORTH AMERICA. With 8 Illustrations and a Map. *Demy 8vo. 7s. 6d. net.*
A Colonial Edition is also published.

Jeffreys (D. Gwyn). DOLLY'S THEATRICALS. *Super Royal 16mo. 2s. 6d.*

Jenks (E.), M.A., B.C.L. AN OUTLINE OF ENGLISH LOCAL GOVERNMENT. *Second Ed.* Revised by R. C. K. ENSOR, M.A. *Cr. 8vo. 2s. 6d.*

Jenner (Mrs. H.). See Little Books on Art.

Jennings (Oscar), M.D. EARLY WOODCUT INITIALS. *Demy 4to. 21s. net.*

Jessopp (Augustus), D.D. See Leaders of Religion.

Jevons (F. B.), M.A., Litt.D., Principal of Hatfield Hall, Durham. RELIGION IN EVOLUTION. *Cr. 8vo. 3s. 6d. net.*
See also Churchman's Library and Handbooks of Theology.

Johnson (Mrs. Barham). WILLIAM BODHAM DONNE AND HIS FRIENDS. Illustrated. *Demy 8vo. 10s. 6d. net.*

Johnston (Sir H. H.), K.C.B. BRITISH CENTRAL AFRICA. With nearly 200 Illustrations and Six Maps. *Third Edition. Cr. 4to. 18s. net.*
A Colonial Edition is also published.

Jones (H.). See Commercial Series.

Jones (H. F.). See Textbooks of Science.

Jones (L. A. Atherley), K.C., M.P., and **Bellot (Hugh H. L.), M.A., D.C.L.** THE MINER'S GUIDE TO THE COAL MINES REGULATION ACTS AND THE LAW OF EMPLOYERS AND WORKMEN. *Cr. 8vo. 2s. 6d. net.*
COMMERCE IN WAR. *Royal 8vo. 21s. net.*

Jones (R. Compton), M.A. POEMS OF THE INNER LIFE. Selected by. *Thirteenth Edition. Fcap. 8vo. 2s. 6d. net.*

Jonson (Ben). See Standard Library.

Juliana (Lady) of Norwich. REVELATIONS OF DIVINE LOVE. Ed. by GRACE WARRACK. *Third Ed. Cr. 8vo. 3s. 6d.*

Juvenal. See Classical Translations.

'Kappa.' LET YOUTH BUT KNOW: A Plea for Reason in Education. *Cr. 8vo. 3s. 6d. net.*

Kaufmann (M.), M.A. SOCIALISM AND MODERN THOUGHT. *Second Edition Revised and Enlarged. Cr. 8vo. 2s. 6d. net.*

Keats (John). THE POEMS. Edited with Introduction and Notes by E. de SELINCOURT, M.A. With a Frontispiece in Photogravure. *Second Edition Revised. Demy 8vo. 7s. 6d. net.*

REALMS OF GOLD. Selections from the Works of. *Fcap. 8vo. 3s. 6d. net.*
See also Little Library. and Standard Library.

Keble (John). THE CHRISTIAN YEAR. With an Introduction and Notes by W. LOCK, D.D., Warden of Keble College. Illustrated by R. ANNING BELL. *Third Edition. Fcap. 8vo. 3s. 6d.; padded morocco, 5s.*
See also Library of Devotion.

Kelynack (T. N.), M.D., M.R.C.P. THE DRINK PROBLEM IN ITS MEDICO-SOCIOLOGICAL ASPECT. By fourteen Medical Authorities. Edited by. With 2 Diagrams. *Demy 8vo. 7s. 6d. net.*

Kempis (Thomas à). THE IMITATION OF CHRIST. With an Introduction by DEAN FARRAR. Illustrated by C. M. GERE. *Third Edition. Fcap. 8vo. 3s. 6d.; padded morocco. 5s.*
Also Translated by C. BIGG, D.D. *Cr. 8vo. 3s. 6d.*
See also Montmorency (J. E. G. de)., Library of Devotion, and Standard Library.

Kennedy (Bart.). THE GREEN SPHINX. *Cr. 8vo. 3s. 6d. net.*

Kennedy (James Houghton), D.D., Assistant Lecturer in Divinity in the University of Dublin. ST. PAUL'S SECOND AND THIRD EPISTLES TO THE CORINTHIANS. With Introduction, Dissertations and Notes. *Cr. 8vo. 6s.*

Kimmins (C. W.), M.A. THE CHEMISTRY OF LIFE AND HEALTH. Illustrated. *Cr. 8vo. 2s. 6d.*

Kinglake (A. W.). See Little Library.

Kipling (Rudyard). BARRACK-ROOM BALLADS. *89th Thousand. Twenty-fifth Edition. Cr. 8vo. 6s. Also Leather. Fcap. 8vo. 5s.*
A Colonial Edition is also published.
THE SEVEN SEAS. *77th Thousand. Fourteenth Edition. Cr. 8vo. 6s. Also Leather. Fcap. 8vo. 5s.*
A Colonial Edition is also published.
THE FIVE NATIONS. *65th Thousand. Fourth Edition. Cr. 8vo. 6s. Also Leather. Fcap. 8vo. 5s.*
A Colonial Edition is also published.
DEPARTMENTAL DITTIES. *Seventeenth Edition. Cr. 8vo. 6s. Also Leather. Fcap. 8vo. 5s.*
A Colonial Edition is also published.

Knight (Albert E.). THE COMPLETE CRICKETER. With 50 Illustrations. *Demy 8vo. 7s. 6d. net.*
A Colonial Edition is also published.

Knight (H. J. C.), B.D. See Churchman's Bible.

Knowling (R. J.), M.A., Professor of New Testament Exegesis at King's College, London. See Westminster Commentaries.

Lamb (Charles and Mary), THE WORKS. Edited by E. V. LUCAS. Illustrated. *In Seven Volumes. Demy 8vo. 7s. 6d. each.*
See also Little Library and Lucas (E. V.)

Lambert (F. A. H.). See Little Guides.

Lambros (Professor S. P.). See Byzantine Texts.

Lane=Poole (Stanley). A HISTORY OF EGYPT IN THE MIDDLE AGES. Fully Illustrated. *Cr. 8vo. 6s.*

Langbridge (F.), M.A. BALLADS OF THE BRAVE : Poems of Chivalry, Enterprise, Courage, and Constancy. *Third Edition. Cr. 8vo. 2s. 6d.*

Law (William). See Library of Devotion and Standard Library.

Leach (Henry). THE DUKE OF DEVONSHIRE. A Biography. With 12 Illustrations. *Demy 8vo. 12s. 6d. net.*
THE SPIRIT OF THE LINKS. *Cr. 8vo. 6s.*
A Colonial Edition is also published.
See also Braid (James).

Le Braz (Anatole). THE LAND OF PARDONS. Translated by FRANCES M. GOSTLING. With 12 Illustrations in Colour by T. C. GOTCH, and 40 other Illustrations. *Third Edition. Crown 8vo. 6s.*

Lee (Captain L. Melville). A HISTORY OF POLICE IN ENGLAND. *Cr. 8vo. 3s. 6d. net.*

Lewes (V. B.), M.A. AIR AND WATER. Illustrated. *Cr. 8vo. 2s. 6d.*

Lewis (B. M. Gwyn). A CONCISE HANDBOOK OF GARDEN SHRUBS. With 20 Illustrations. *Fcap. 8vo. 3s. 6d. net.*

Lisle (Fortunéede). See Little Books on Art.

Littlehales (H.). See Antiquary's Books.

Llewellyn (Owen) and **Raven-Hill (L.).** THE SOUTH-BOUND CAR. With 85 Illustrations. *Crown 8vo. 6s.*

Lock (Walter), D.D., Warden of Keble College. ST. PAUL, THE MASTER-BUILDER. *Second Ed. Cr. 8vo. 3s. 6d.*
THE BIBLE AND CHRISTIAN LIFE. *Cr. 8vo. 6s.*
See also Keble (J.) and Leaders of Religion.

Locker (F.). See Little Library.

Lodge (Sir Oliver), F.R.S. THE SUBSTANCE OF FAITH ALLIED WITH SCIENCE : A Catechism for Parents and Teachers. *Ninth Ed. Cr. 8vo. 2s. net.*

Lofthouse (W. F.), M.A. ETHICS AND ATONEMENT. With a Frontispiece. *Demy 8vo. 5s. net.*

Longfellow (H. W.). See Little Library.

Lorimer (George Horace). LETTERS FROM A SELF-MADE MERCHANT TO HIS SON. *Seventeenth Edition. Cr. 8vo. 3s. 6d.*
A Colonial Edition is also published.
OLD GORGON GRAHAM. *Second Edition. Cr. 8vo. 6s.*
A Colonial Edition is also published.

Lover (Samuel). See I.P.L.

E. V. L. and **C. L. G.** ENGLAND DAY BY DAY : Or, The Englishman's Handbook to Efficiency. Illustrated by GEORGE MORROW. *Fourth Edition. Fcap. 4to. 1s. net.*

Lucas (E. V.). THE LIFE OF CHARLES LAMB. With 28 Illustrations. *Fourth and Revised Edition in One Volume. Demy 8vo. 7s. 6d. net.*
A Colonial Edition is also published.

A WANDERER IN HOLLAND. With 20 Illustrations in Colour by HERBERT MARSHALL, 34 Illustrations after old Dutch Masters, and a Map. *Ninth Edition. Cr. 8vo. 6s.*
A Colonial Edition is also published.

A WANDERER IN LONDON. With 16 Illustrations in Colour by NELSON DAWSON, 36 other Illustrations and a Map. *Sixth Edition. Cr. 8vo. 6s.*
A Colonial Edition is also published.

THE OPEN ROAD : a Little Book for Wayfarers. *Fourteenth Edition. Fcap. 8vo. 5s. ; India Paper, 7s. 6d.*

THE FRIENDLY TOWN : a Little Book for the Urbane. *Fourth Edition. Fcap. 8vo. 5s. ; India Paper, 7s. 6d.*

FIRESIDE AND SUNSHINE. *Fourth Edition. Fcap. 8vo. 5s.*

CHARACTER AND COMEDY. *Fourth Edition. Fcap. 8vo. 5s.*

THE GENTLEST ART. A Choice of Letters by Entertaining Hands. *Fifth Edition. Fcap. 8vo. 5s.*

A SWAN AND HER FRIENDS. With 24 Illustrations. *Demy 8vo. 12s. 6d. net.*
A Colonial Edition is also published.

Lucian. See Classical Translations.

Lyde (L. W.), M.A. See Commercial Series.

Lydon (Noel S.). See Junior School Books.

Lyttelton (Hon. Mrs. A.). WOMEN AND THEIR WORK. *Cr. 8vo. 2s. 6d.*

Macaulay (Lord). CRITICAL AND HISTORICAL ESSAYS. Edited by F. C. MONTAGUE, M.A. *Three Volumes. Cr. 8vo. 18s.*

M'Allen (J. E. B.), M.A. See Commercial Series.

MacCulloch (J. A.). See Churchman's Library.

MacCunn (Florence A.). MARY STUART. With 44 Illustrations, including a Frontispiece in Photogravure. *New and Cheaper Edition. Large Cr. 8vo. 6s.*
See also Leaders of Religion.

McDermott (E. R.). See Books on Business.

M'Dowall (A. S.). See Oxford Biographies.

Mackay (A. M.), B.A. See Churchman's Library.

Mackenzie (W. Leslie), M.A., M.D., D.P.H., etc. THE HEALTH OF THE SCHOOL CHILD. *Cr. 8vo. 2s. 6d.*

Macklin (Herbert W.), M.A. See Antiquary's Books.

M'Neile (A. H.), B.D. See Westminster Commentaries.

'Mdlle Mori' (Author of). ST. CATHERINE OF SIENA AND HER TIMES. With 28 Illustrations. *Second Edition. Demy 8vo. 7s. 6d. net.*

Magnus (Laurie), M.A. A PRIMER OF WORDSWORTH. *Cr. 8vo. 2s. 6d.*

Mahaffy (J. P.), Litt.D. A HISTORY OF THE EGYPT OF THE PTOLEMIES. Fully Illustrated. *Cr. 8vo. 6s.*

Maitland (F. W.), M.A., LL.D. ROMAN CANON LAW IN THE CHURCH OF ENGLAND. *Royal 8vo. 7s. 6d.*

Major (H.), B.A., B.Sc. A HEALTH AND TEMPERANCE READER. *Cr. 8vo.* 1s.

Malden (H. E.), M.A. ENGLISH RE-CORDS. A Companion to the History of England. *Cr. 8vo.* 3s. 6d.
THE RIGHTS AND DUTIES OF A CITIZEN. *Seventh Edition. Cr. 8vo.* 1s. 6d.
See also School Histories.

Marchant (E. C.), M.A., Fellow of Peter-house, Cambridge. A GREEK ANTHO-LOGY *Second Edition. Cr. 8vo.* 3s. 6d.
See also Cook (A. M.).

Marks (Jeannette), M.A. ENGLISH PASTORAL DRAMA from the Restora-tion to the date of the publication of the 'Lyrical Ballads' (1660-1798). *Cr. 8vo.* 5s. net.

Marr (J. E.), F.R.S., Fellow of St John's Col-lege, Cambridge. THE SCIENTIFIC STUDY OF SCENERY. *Third Edition.* Illustrated. *Cr. 8vo.* 6s.
AGRICULTURAL GEOLOGY. Illustrated. *Cr. 8vo.* 6s.

Marriott (J. A. R.), M.A. THE LIFE AND TIMES OF LORD FALKLAND. With 23 Illustrations. *Second Edition. Demy 8vo.* 7s. 6d. net.

Marvell (Andrew). See Little Library.

Masefield (John). SEA LIFE IN NEL-SON'S TIME. Illustrated. *Cr. 8vo.* 3s. 6d. net.
A Colonial Edition is also published.
ON THE SPANISH MAIN: or, SOME ENGLISH FORAYS IN THE ISTHMUS OF DARIEN. With 22 Illustrations and a Map. *Demy 8vo.* 10s. 6d. net.
A Colonial Edition is also published.
A SAILOR'S GARLAND. Selected and Edited by. *Second Ed. Cr. 8vo.* 3s. 6d. net.
AN ENGLISH PROSE MISCELLANY. Selected and Edited by. *Cr. 8vo.* 6s.

Maskell (A.). See Connoisseur's Library.

Mason (A. J.), D.D. See Leaders of Religion.

Masterman (C. F. G.), M.A., M.P. TENNYSON AS A RELIGIOUS TEACHER. *Cr. 8vo.* 6s.

Matheson (E. F.). COUNSELS OF LIFE. *Fcap. 8vo.* 2s. 6d. net.

May (Phil). THE PHIL MAY ALBUM. *Second Edition.* 4to. 1s. net.

Meakin (Annette M. B.), Fellow of the Anthropological Institute. WOMAN IN TRANSITION. *Cr. 8vo.* 6s.

Mellows (Emma S.). A SHORT STORY OF ENGLISH LITERATURE. *Cr. 8vo.* 3s. 6d.

Methuen (A. M. S.), M.A. THE TRAGEDY OF SOUTH AFRICA. *Cr. 8vo.* 2s. net. Also *Cr. 8vo.* 3d. net.
ENGLAND'S RUIN: DISCUSSED IN SIX-TEEN LETTERS TO A PROTECTIONIST. *Eighth Edition. Cr. 8vo.* 3d. net.

Miles (Eustace), M.A. LIFE AFTER LIFE: OR, THE THEORY OF REINCARNA-TION. *Cr. 8vo.* 2s. 6d. net.
THE POWER OF CONCENTRATION: HOW TO ACQUIRE IT. *Second Edition. Cr. 8vo.* 3s. 6d. net.

Millais (J. G.). THE LIFE AND LET-TERS OF SIR JOHN EVERETT MILLAIS, President of the Royal Academy. With many Illustrations, of which 2 are in Photogravure. *New Edition. Demy 8vo.* 7s. 6d. net.
See also Little Galleries.

Millin (G. F.). PICTORIAL GARDEN-ING. With 21 Illustrations. *Crown 8vo.* 3s. 6d. net.

Millis (C. T.), M.I.M.E. See Textbooks of Technology.

Milne (J. G.), M.A. A HISTORY OF EGYPT UNDER ROMAN RULE. Fully Illustrated. *Cr. 8vo.* 6s.

Milton (John). See Little Library and Standard Library.
A DAY BOOK OF MILTON. Edited by R. F. TOWNDROW. *Fcap. 8vo.* 2s. 6d. net.

Minchin (H. C.), M.A. See Peel (R.).

Mitchell (P. Chalmers), M.A. OUTLINES OF BIOLOGY. Illustrated. *Second Edi-tion. Cr. 8vo.* 6s.

Mitton (G. E.). JANE AUSTEN AND HER TIMES. With 21 Illustrations. *Second and Cheaper Edition Large Cr. 8vo.* 6s.
A Colonial Edition is also published.

Moffat (Mary M.). QUEEN LOUISA OF PRUSSIA. With 20 Illustrations. *Fourth Edition. Crown 8vo.* 6s.
A Colonial Edition is also published.

'Moil (A.).' See Books on Business.

Moir (D. M.). See Little Library.

Molinos (Dr. Michael de). See Library of Devotion.

Money (L. G. Chiozza), M.P. RICHES AND POVERTY. *Eighth Edition. Demy 8vo.* 5s. net. Also *Cr. 8vo.* 1s. net.
SOCIAL AND INDUSTRIAL PRO-BLEMS. *Demy 8vo.* 5s. net.

Montagu (Henry), Earl of Manchester. See Library of Devotion.

Montaigne. A DAY BOOK OF. Edited by C. F. POND. *Fcap. 8vo.* 2s. 6d. net.

Montgomery (H. B.) THE EMPIRE OF THE EAST. With a Frontispiece in Colour and 16 other Illustrations. *Second Edition. Demy 8vo.* 7s. 6d. net.
A Colonial Edition is also published.

Montmorency (J. E. G. de), B.A., LL.B. THOMAS À KEMPIS, HIS AGE AND BOOK. With 22 Illustrations. *Second Edition. Demy 8vo.* 7s. 6d. net.

Moore (H. E.). BACK TO THE LAND. *Cr. 8vo.* 2s. 6d.

Moorhouse (E. Hallam). NELSON'S LADY HAMILTON. With 51 Portraits. *Second Edition. Demy 8vo.* 7s. 6d. net.
A Colonial Edition is also published.

Moran (Clarence G.). See Books on Business.

More (Sir Thomas). See Standard Library.

Morfill (W. R.), Oriel College, Oxford. A HISTORY OF RUSSIA FROM PETER THE GREAT TO ALEXANDER II. With Maps and Plans. *Cr. 8vo.* 3s. 6d.

Morich (R. J.), late of Clifton College. See School Examination Series.

Morley (Margaret W.), Founded on. THE BEE PEOPLE. With 74 Illustrations. *Sq. Crown 8vo.* 2s. 6d.

LITTLE MITCHELL: THE STORY OF A MOUNTAIN SQUIRREL TOLD BY HIMSELF. With many Illustrations. *Sq. Cr. 8vo.* 2s.6d.

Morris (J.). THE MAKERS OF JAPAN. With 24 Illustrations. *Demy 8vo.* 12s. 6d. *net.*

Morris (Joseph E.). See Little Guides.

Morton (A. Anderson). See Brodrick (M.).

Moule (H. C. G.), D.D., Lord Bishop of Durham. See Leaders of Religion.

Muir (M. M. Pattison), M.A. THE CHEMISTRY OF FIRE. Illustrated. *Cr. 8vo.* 2s. 6d.

Mundella (V. A.), M.A. See Dunn (J. T.).

Munro (R.), M.A., LL.D. See Antiquary's Books.

Myers (A. Wallis), THE COMPLETE LAWN TENNIS PLAYER. With many Illustrations. *Second Edition. Demy 8vo.* 10s. 6d. *net.*

Naval Officer (A). See I. P. L.

Neal (W. G.). See Hall (R. N.).

Newman (Ernest). HUGO WOLF. With 13 Illustrations. *Demy 8vo.* 7s. 6d. *net.*

Newman (George), M.D.,D.P.H.,F.R.S.E., INFANT MORTALITY, A SOCIAL PROBLEM. With 16 Diagrams. *Demy 8vo.* 7s. 6d. *net.*

Newman (J. H.) and others. See Library of Devotion.

Newsholme (Arthur), M.D., F.R.C.P. THE PREVENTION OF TUBERCULOSIS. *Demy 8vo.* 10s. 6d. *net.*

Nichols (Bowyer). See Little Library.

Nicklin (T.), M.A. EXAMINATION PAPERS IN THUCYDIDES. *Cr. 8vo.* 2s.

Nimrod. See I. P. L.

Norgate (G. Le Grys). THE LIFE OF SIR WALTER SCOTT. With 53 Illustrations by JENNY WYLIE. *Demy 8vo.* 7s. 6d. *net.*

Norway (A. H.). NAPLES. PAST AND PRESENT. With 25 Coloured Illustrations by MAURICE GREIFFENHAGEN. *Third Edition. Cr. 8vo.* 6s.
A Colonial Edition is also published.

Novalis. THE DISCIPLES AT SAÏS AND OTHER FRAGMENTS. Edited by Miss UNA BIRCH. *Fcap. 8vo.* 3s. 6d. *net.*

Officer (An). See I. P. L.

Oldfield (W. J.), M.A., Prebendary of Lincoln. A PRIMER OF RELIGION. BASED ON THE CATECHISM OF THE CHURCH OF ENGLAND. *Crown 8vo.* 2s. 6d.

Oldham (F. M.), B.A. See Textbooks of Science.

Oliphant (Mrs.). See Leaders of Religion.

Oliver, Thomas, M.D. DISEASES OF OCCUPATION. With Illustrations. *Second Edition. Demy 8vo.* 10s. 6d. *net.*

Oman (C. W. C.), M.A., Fellow of All Souls', Oxford. A HISTORY OF THE ART OF WAR IN THE MIDDLE AGES. Illustrated. *Demy 8vo.* 10s. 6d. *net.*

Ottley (R. L.), D.D. See Handbooks of Theology and Leaders of Religion.

Overton (J. H.). See Leaders of Religion.

Owen (Douglas). See Books on Business.

Oxford (M. N.), of Guy's Hospital. A HANDBOOK OF NURSING. *Fourth Edition. Cr. 8vo.* 3s. 6d.

Pakes (W. C. C.). THE SCIENCE OF HYGIENE. Illustrated. *Demy 8vo.* 15s.

Parker (Gilbert), M.P. A LOVER'S DIARY. *Fcap. 8vo.* 5s.
A volume of poems.

Parkes (A. K.). SMALL LESSONS ON GREAT TRUTHS. *Fcap. 8vo.* 1s. 6d.

Parkinson (John). PARADISI IN SOLE PARADISUS TERRESTRIS, OR A GARDEN OF ALL SORTS OF PLEASANT FLOWERS. *Folio.* £3, 3s. *net.*

Parmenter (John). HELIO-TROPES, OR NEW POSIES FOR SUNDIALS. Edited by PERCIVAL LANDON. *Quarto.* 3s. 6d. *net.*

Parmentier (Prof. Leon). See Bidez (J.).

Parsons (Mrs. C.). GARRICK AND HIS CIRCLE. With 36 Illustrations. *Second Edition. Demy 8vo.* 12s. 6d. *net.*
A Colonial Edition is also published.

Pascal. See Library of Devotion.

Paston (George). SOCIAL CARICATURE IN THE EIGHTEENTH CENTURY. With over 200 Illustrations. *Imperial Quarto.* £2, 12s. 6d. *net.*

LADY MARY WORTLEY MONTAGU AND HER TIMES. With 24 Illustrations. *Second Edition. Demy 8vo.* 15s. *net.*
See also Little Books on Art and I.P.L.

Paterson (W. R.)(Benjamin Swift). LIFE'S QUESTIONINGS. *Cr. 8vo.* 3s. 6d. *net.*

Patterson (A. H.). NOTES OF AN EAST COAST NATURALIST. Illustrated in Colour by F. SOUTHGATE, R.B.A. *Second Edition. Cr. 8vo.* 6s.

NATURE IN EASTERN NORFOLK. With 12 Illustrations in Colour by FRANK SOUTHGATE, R.B.A. *Second Edition. Cr. 8vo.* 6s.

WILD LIFE ON A NORFOLK ESTUARY. With 40 Illustrations by the Author, and a Prefatory Note by Her Grace the DUCHESS OF BEDFORD. *Demy 8vo.* 10s. 6d. *net.*

Peacock (Netta). See Little Books on Art.

Patterson (J. B.). See Simplified French Texts.

Peake (C. M. A.), F.R.H.S. A CONCISE HANDBOOK OF GARDEN ANNUAL AND BIENNIAL PLANTS. With 24 Illustrations. *Fcap. 8vo.* 3s. 6d. *net.*

Peel (Robert), and **Minchin (H. C.)**, M.A. OXFORD. With 100 Illustrations in Colour. *Cr. 8vo.* 6s.
   A Colonial Edition is also published.
Peel (Sidney), late Fellow of Trinity College, Oxford, and Secretary to the Royal Commission on the Licensing Laws. PRACTICAL LICENSING REFORM. *Second Edition. Cr. 8vo.* 1s. 6d.
Petrie (W. M. Flinders), D.C.L., LL.D., Professor of Egyptology at University College. A HISTORY OF EGYPT. Fully Illustrated. *In six volumes. Cr. 8vo. 6s. each.*
VOL. I. FROM THE EARLIEST KINGS TO XVITH DYNASTY. *Sixth Edition.*
VOL. II. THE XVIITH AND XVIIITH DYNASTIES. *Fourth Edition.*
VOL. III. XIXTH TO XXXTH DYNASTIES.
VOL. IV. THE EGYPT OF THE PTOLEMIES. J. P. MAHAFFY, Litt.D.
VOL. V. ROMAN EGYPT. J. G. MILNE, M.A.
VOL. VI. EGYPT IN THE MIDDLE AGES. STANLEY LANE-POOLE, M.A.
RELIGION AND CONSCIENCE IN ANCIENT EGYPT. Lectures delivered at University College, London. Illustrated. *Cr. 8vo.* 2s. 6d.
SYRIA AND EGYPT, FROM THE TELL EL AMARNA TABLETS. *Cr. 8vo.* 2s. 6d.
EGYPTIAN TALES. Translated from the Papyri. First Series, IVth to XIIth Dynasty. Edited by W. M. FLINDERS PETRIE. Illustrated by TRISTRAM ELLIS. *Second Edition. Cr. 8vo.* 3s. 6d.
EGYPTIAN TALES. Translated from the Papyri. Second Series, XVIIIth to XIXth Dynasty. Illustrated by TRISTRAM ELLIS. *Crown 8vo.* 3s. 6d.
EGYPTIAN DECORATIVE ART. A Course of Lectures delivered at the Royal Institution. Illustrated. *Cr. 8vo.* 3s. 6d.
Phillips (W, A.). See Oxford Biographies.
Phillpotts (Eden). MY DEVON YEAR. With 38 Illustrations by J. LEY PETHYBRIDGE. *Second and Cheaper Edition. Large Cr. 8vo.* 6s.
UP ALONG AND DOWN ALONG. Illustrated by CLAUDE SHEPPERSON. *Cr. 4to.* 5s. net.
Phythian (J. Ernest). TREES IN NATURE, MYTH, AND ART. With 24 Illustrations. *Crown 8vo.* 6s.
Plarr (Victor G.). See School Histories.
Plato. See Standard Library.
Plautus. THE CAPTIVI. Edited, with an Introduction, Textual Notes, and a Commentary, by W. M. LINDSAY, Fell of Jesus College, Oxford. *Demy 8vo.* 10s. 6d. net.
Plowden-Wardlaw (J. T.), B.A., King's College, Cambridge. See School Examination Series.
Podmore (Frank). MODERN SPIRITUALISM. *Two Volumes. Demy 8vo.* 21s. net.
Pollard (Alice). See Little Books on Art.
Pollard (Eliza F.). See Little Books on Art.

Pollock (David), M.I.N.A. See Books on Business.
Potter (M. C.), M.A., F.L.S. AN ELEMENTARY TEXT-BOOK OF AGRICULTURAL BOTANY. Illustrated. *Third Edition. Cr. 8vo.* 4s. 6d.
Power (J. O'Connor). THE MAKING OF AN ORATOR. *Cr. 8vo.* 6s.
Prescott (O. L.). ABOUT MUSIC, AND WHAT IT IS MADE OF. *Cr. 8vo.* 3s. 6d. net.
Price (Eleanor C.). A PRINCESS OF THE OLD WORLD. With 21 Illustrations. *Demy 8vo.* 12s. 6d. net.
Price (L. L.), M.A., Fellow of Oriel College, Oxon. A HISTORY OF ENGLISH POLITICAL ECONOMY FROM ADAM SMITH TO ARNOLD TOYNBEE. *Fifth Edition. Cr. 8vo.* 2s. 6d.
Protheroe (Ernest). THE DOMINION OF MAN. GEOGRAPHY IN ITS HUMAN ASPECT. With 32 full-page Illustrations. *Second Edition. Cr. 8vo.* 2s.
Quevedo Villegas. See Miniature Library.
'Q' (A. T. Quiller Couch). THE GOLDEN POMP. A PROCESSION OF ENGLISH LYRICS FROM SURREY TO SHIRLEY. *Second and Cheaper Edition. Cr. 8vo.* 2s. 6d. net.
G. R. and E. S. MR. WOODHOUSE'S CORRESPONDENCE. *Cr. 8vo.* 6s.
   A Colonial Edition is also published.
Rackham (R. B.), M.A. See Westminster Commentaries.
Ragg (Laura M.). THE WOMEN ARTISTS OF BOLOGNA. With 20 Illustrations. *Demy 8vo.* 7s. 6d. net.
Ragg (Lonsdale). B.D., Oxon. DANTE AND HIS ITALY. With 32 Illustrations. *Demy 8vo.* 12s. 6d. net.
Rahtz (F. J.), M.A., B.Sc., Lecturer in English at Merchant Venturers' Technical College, Bristol. HIGHER ENGLISH. *Fourth Edition. Cr. 8vo.* 3s. 6d.
Randolph (B. W.), D.D. See Library of Devotion.
Rannie (D. W.), M.A. A STUDENT'S HISTORY OF SCOTLAND. *Cr. 8vo.* 3s. 6d.
WORDSWORTH AND HIS CIRCLE. With 20 Illustrations. *Demy 8vo.* 12s. 6d. net.
Rashdall (Hastings), M.A., Fellow and Tutor of New College, Oxford. DOCTRINE AND DEVELOPMENT. *Cr. 8vo.* 6s.
Raven (J. J.), D.D., F.S.A. See Antiquary's Books.
Raven-Hill (L.). See Llewellyn (Owen).
Rawstorne (Lawrence, Esq.). See I.P.L.
Raymond (Walter). See School Histories.
Rea (Lilian). MADAME DE LA FAYETTE. With many Illustrations. *Demy 8vo.* 10s. 6d. net.
Real Paddy (A). See I.P.L.
Reason (W.), M.A. UNIVERSITY AND SOCIAL SETTLEMENTS. Edited by. *Cr. 8vo.* 2s. 6d.

Redpath (H. A.), M.A., D.Litt. See West-minster Commentaries.

Rees (J. D.), C.I.E., M.P. THE REAL INDIA. *Second Edition. Demy 8vo. 10s. 6d. net.*
A Colonial Edition is also published.

*Reich (Emil), Doctor Juris. WOMAN THROUGH THE AGES. With 24 Illustrations. *Two Volumes. Demy 8vo. 21s. net.*
A Colonial Edition is also published.

Reynolds (Sir Joshua). See Little Galleries.

Rhoades (J. F.). See Simplified French Texts.

Rhodes (W. E.). See School Histories.

Rieu (H.), M.A. See Simplified French Texts.

Roberts (M. E.). See Channer (C. C.).

Robertson (A.), D.D., Lord Bishop of Exeter. REGNUM DEI. (The Bampton Lectures of 1901). *A New and Cheaper Edition. Demy 8vo. 7s. 6d. net.*

Robertson (C. Grant). M.A., Fellow of All Souls' College, Oxford. SELECT STATUTES, CASES, AND CONSTITUTIONAL DOCUMENTS, 1660-1832. *Demy 8vo. 10s. 6d. net.*

Robertson (C. Grant) and Bartholomew (J. G.), F.R.S.E., F.R.G.S. A HISTORICAL AND MODERN ATLAS OF THE BRITISH EMPIRE. *Demy Quarto. 4s. 6d. net.*

Robinson (A. W.), M.A. See Churchman's Bible.

Robinson (Cecilia). THE MINISTRY OF DEACONESSES. With an Introduction by the late Archbishop of Canterbury. *Cr. 8vo. 3s. 6d.*

Robinson (F. S.). See Connoisseur's Library.

Rochefoucauld (La). See Little Library.

Rodwell (G.), B.A. NEW TESTAMENT GREEK. A Course for Beginners. With a Preface by WALTER LOCK, D.D., Warden of Keble College. *Fcap. 8vo. 3s. 6d.*

Roe (Fred). OLD OAK FURNITURE. With many Illustrations by the Author, including a frontispiece in colour. *Second Edition. Demy 8vo. 10s. 6d. net.*

Rogers (A. G. L.), M.A. See Books on Business.

Romney (George). See Little Galleries.

Roscoe (E. S.). See Little Guides.

Rose (Edward). THE ROSE READER. Illustrated. *Cr. 8vo. 2s. 6d. Also in 4 Parts. Parts I. and II. 6d. each; Part III. 8d.; Part IV. 10d.*

Rose (G. H.). See Hey (H.)., and Baring-Gould (S.).

Rowntree (Joshua). THE IMPERIAL DRUG TRADE. A RE-STATEMENT OF THE OPIUM QUESTION. *Third Edition Revised. Cr. 8vo. 2s. net.*

Royde-Smith (N. G.). THE PILLOW BOOK: A GARNER OF MANY MOODS. Collected by. *Second Edition. Cr. 8vo. 4s. 6d. net.*
POETS OF OUR DAY. Selected, with an Introduction, by. *Fcap. 8vo. 5s.*

Rubie (A. E.), D.D. See Junior School Books.

Russell (Archibald G. B.). See Blake (William).

Russell (W. Clark). THE LIFE OF ADMIRAL LORD COLLINGWOOD. With Illustrations by F. BRANGWYN. *Fourth Edition. Cr. 8vo. 6s.*

Ryley (M. Beresford). QUEENS OF THE RENAISSANCE. With 24 Illustrations. *Demy 8vo. 10s. 6d. net.*

Sainsbury (Harrington), M.D., F.R.C.P. PRINCIPIA THERAPEUTICA. *Demy 8vo. 7s. 6d. net.*

St. Anselm. See Library of Devotion.

St. Augustine. See Library of Devotion.

St. Bernard. See Library of Devotion.

St. Cyres (Viscount). See Oxford Biographies.

St. Francis of Assisi. THE LITTLE FLOWERS OF THE GLORIOUS MESSER, AND OF HIS FRIARS. Done into English, with Notes by WILLIAM HEYWOOD. With 40 Illustrations from Italian Painters. *Demy 8vo. 5s. net.*
See also Wheldon (F. W.), Library of Devotion and Standard Library.

St. Francis de Sales. See Library of Devotion.

'Saki' (H. Munro). REGINALD. *Second Edition. Fcap. 8vo. 2s. 6d. net.*

Salmon (A. L.). See Little Guides.

Sathas (C.). See Byzantine Texts.

Schmitt (John). See Byzantine Texts.

Schofield (A. T.), M.D., Hon. Phys. Freidenham Hospital. FUNCTIONAL NERVE DISEASES. *Demy 8vo. 7s. 6d. net.*

Scudamore (Cyril). See Little Guides.

Sélincourt (E. de.) See Keats (John).

Sells (V. P.), M.A. THE MECHANICS OF DAILY LIFE. Illustrated. *Cr. 8vo. 2s. 6d.*

Selous (Edmund). TOMMY SMITH'S ANIMALS. Illustrated by G. W. ORD. *Tenth Edition. Fcap. 8vo. 2s. 6d. School Edition, 1s. 6d.*
TOMMY SMITH'S OTHER ANIMALS. Illustrated by AUGUSTA GUEST. *Fourth Edition. Fcap. 8vo. 2s 6d. School Edition, 1s. 6d.*

Senter (George), B.Sc. (Lond.), Ph.D. See Textbooks of Science.

Shakespeare (William).
THE FOUR FOLIOS, 1623; 1632; 1664; 1685. Each £4, 4s. *net*, or a complete set, £12, 12s. *net.*
Folios 3 and 4 are ready.
Folio 2 is nearly ready.
THE POEMS OF WILLIAM SHAKESPEARE. With an Introduction and Notes by GEORGE WYNDHAM. *Demy 8vo. Buckram, gilt top, 10s. 6d.*
See also Arden Shakespeare, Standard Library and Little Quarto Shakespeare.

Sharp (A.). VICTORIAN POETS. *Cr. 8vo.* 2s. 6d.

Sharp (Cecil). See Baring-Gould (S.).

Sharp (Elizabeth). See Little Books on Art.

Shedlock (J. S.) THE PIANOFORTE SONATA. *Cr. 8vo.* 5s.

Shelley (Percy B.). See Standard Library.

Sheppard (H. F.), M.A. See Baring-Gould (S.).

Sherwell (Arthur), M.A. LIFE IN WEST LONDON. *Third Edition. Cr. 8vo.* 2s. 6d.

Shipley (Mary E.). AN ENGLISH CHURCH HISTORY FOR CHILDREN. With a Preface by the Bishop of Gibraltar. With Maps and Illustrations. Part I. *Cr. 8vo.* 2s. 6d. net.

Sichel (Walter). See Oxford Biographies.

Sidgwick (Mrs. Alfred). HOME LIFE IN GERMANY. With 16 Illustrations. *Second Edition. Demy 8vo.* 10s. 6d. net.
A Colonial Edition is also published.

Sime (John). See Little Books on Art.

Simonson (G. A.). FRANCESCO GUARDI. With 41 Plates. *Imperial 4to.* £2, 2s. net.

Sketchley (R. E. D.). See Little Books on Art.

Skipton (H. P. K.). See Little Books on Art.

Sladen (Douglas). SICILY: The New Winter Resort. With over 200 Illustrations. *Second Edition. Cr. 8vo.* 5s. net.

Small (Evan), M.A. THE EARTH. An Introduction to Physiography. Illustrated. *Cr. 8vo.* 2s. 6d.

Smallwood (M. G.). See Little Books on Art.

Smedley (F. E.). See I.P.L.

Smith (Adam). THE WEALTH OF NATIONS. Edited with an Introduction and numerous Notes by EDWIN CANNAN, M.A. *Two volumes. Demy 8vo.* 21s. net.

Smith (H. Clifford). See Connoisseur's Library.

Smith (Horace and James). See Little Library.

Smith (H. Bompas), M.A. A NEW JUNIOR ARITHMETIC. *Crown 8vo.* Without Answers, 2s. With Answers, 2s. 6d.

Smith (R. Mudie). THOUGHTS FOR THE DAY. Edited by. *Fcap. 8vo.* 3s. 6d. net.

Smith (Nowell C.). See Wordsworth (W).

Smith (John Thomas). A BOOK FOR A RAINY DAY: Or, Recollections of the Events of the Years 1766-1833. Edited by WILFRED WHITTEN. Illustrated. *Wide Demy 8vo.* 12s. 6d. net.

Snell (F. J.). A BOOK OF EXMOOR. Illustrated. *Cr. 8vo.* 6s.

Snowden (C. E.). A HANDY DIGEST OF BRITISH HISTORY. *Demy 8vo.* 4s. 6d.

Sophocles. See Classical Translations.

Sornet (L. A.), and **Acatos (M. J.)** See Junior School Books.

South (E. Wilton), M.A. See Junior School Books

Southey (R.). ENGLISH SEAMEN Edited by DAVID HANNAY.
Vol. I. (Howard, Clifford, Hawkins, Drake, Cavendish). *Second Edition. Cr. 8vo.* 6s.
Vol. II. (Richard Hawkins, Grenville, Essex, and Raleigh). *Cr. 8vo.* 6s.
See also Standard Library.

Spence (C. H.), M.A. See School Examination Series.

Spicer (A. Dykes), M.A. THE PAPER TRADE. A Descriptive and Historical Survey. With Diagrams and Plans. *Demy 8vo.* 12s. 6d. net.

Spooner (W. A.), M.A. See Leaders of Religion.

Spragge (W. Horton), M.A. See Junior School Books.

Staley (Edgcumbe). THE GUILDS OF FLORENCE. Illustrated. *Second Edition. Royal 8vo.* 16s. net.

Stanbridge (J. W.), B.D. See Library of Devotion.

'Stancliffe.' GOLF DO'S AND DONT'S. *Second Edition. Fcap. 8vo.* 1s.

Stead (D. W.). See Gallaher (D.).

Stedman (A. M. M.), M.A.
INITIA LATINA: Easy Lessons on Elementary Accidence. *Eleventh Edition. Fcap. 8vo.* 1s.
FIRST LATIN LESSONS. *Eleventh Edition. Cr. 8vo.* 2s.
FIRST LATIN READER. With Notes adapted to the Shorter Latin Primer and Vocabulary. *Seventh Edition.* 18mo. 1s. 6d.
EASY SELECTIONS FROM CÆSAR. The Helvetian War. *Fourth Edition.* 18mo. 1s.
EASY SELECTIONS FROM LIVY. The Kings of Rome. *Second Edition.* 18mo. 1s. 6d.
EASY LATIN PASSAGES FOR UNSEEN TRANSLATION. *Twelfth Ed. Fcap. 8vo.* 1s. 6d.
EXEMPLA LATINA. First Exercises in Latin Accidence. With Vocabulary. *Fourth Edition. Cr. 8vo.* 1s.
EASY LATIN EXERCISES ON THE SYNTAX OF THE SHORTER AND REVISED LATIN PRIMER. With Vocabulary. *Twelfth and Cheaper Edition. Cr. 8vo.* 1s. 6d. KEY, 3s. net.
THE LATIN COMPOUND SENTENCE: Rules and Exercises. *Second Edition. Cr. 8vo.* 1s. 6d. With Vocabulary. 2s.
NOTANDA QUAEDAM: Miscellaneous Latin Exercises on Common Rules and Idioms. *Fifth Edition. Fcap. 8vo.* 1s. 6d. With Vocabulary. 2s. KEY, 2s. net.
LATIN VOCABULARIES FOR REPETITION: Arranged according to Subjects. *Sixteenth Edition. Fcap. 8vo.* 1s. 6d.
A VOCABULARY OF LATIN IDIOMS. 18mo. *Fourth Edition.* 1s.
STEPS TO GREEK. *Third Edition, revised.* 18mo. 1s.

A SHORTER GREEK PRIMER. *Third Edition. Cr. 8vo. 1s. 6d.*

EASY GREEK PASSAGES FOR UNSEEN TRANSLATION. *Fourth Edition, revised. Fcap. 8vo. 1s. 6d.*

GREEK VOCABULARIES FOR RE-PETITION. Arranged according to Subjects. *Fourth Edition. Fcap. 8vo. 1s. 6d.*

GREEK TESTAMENT SELECTIONS. For the use of Schools. With Introduction, Notes, and Vocabulary. *Fourth Edition. Fcap. 8vo. 2s. 6d.*

STEPS TO FRENCH. *Eighth Edition. 18mo. 8d.*

FIRST FRENCH LESSONS. *Ninth Edition. Cr. 8vo. 1s.*

EASY FRENCH PASSAGES FOR UN-SEEN TRANSLATION. *Sixth Edition. Fcap. 8vo. 1s. 6d.*

EASY FRENCH EXERCISES ON ELE-MENTARY SYNTAX. With Vocabulary. *Fourth Edition. Cr. 8vo. 2s. 6d.* KEY. *3s. net.*

FRENCH VOCABULARIES FOR RE-PETITION : Arranged according to Subjects. *Thirteenth Edition. Fcap. 8vo. 1s.* See also School Examination Series.

Steel (R. Elliott), M.A., F.C.S. THE WORLD OF SCIENCE. With 147 Illustrations. *Second Edition. Cr. 8vo. 2s. 6d.* See also School Examination Series.

Stephenson (C.), of the Technical College, Bradford, and **Suddards (F.)** of the Yorkshire College, Leeds. A TEXTBOOK DEALING WITH ORNAMENTAL DESIGN FOR WOVEN FABRICS. With 66 full-page Plates and numerous Diagrams in the Text. *Third Edition. Demy 8vo. 7s. 6d.*

Stephenson (J.), M.A. THE CHIEF TRUTHS OF THE CHRISTIAN FAITH. *Cr. 8vo. 3s. 6d.*

Sterne (Laurence). See Little Library.

Steuart (Katherine). BY ALLAN WATER. *Second Edition. Cr. 8vo. 6s.*

RICHARD KENNOWAY AND HIS FRIENDS. A Sequel to 'By Allan Water.' *Demy 8vo. 7s. 6d. net.*

Stevenson (R. L.) THE LETTERS OF ROBERT LOUIS STEVENSON TO HIS FAMILY AND FRIENDS. Selected and Edited by SIDNEY COLVIN. *Eighth Edition. 2 vols. Cr. 8vo. 12s.* LIBRARY EDITION. *2 vols. Demy 8vo. 25s. net.* A Colonial Edition is also published.

VAILIMA LETTERS. With an Etched Portrait by WILLIAM STRANG. *Seventh Edition. Cr. 8vo. Buckram. 6s.* A Colonial Edition is also published.

THE LIFE OF R. L. STEVENSON. See Balfour (G.).

Stevenson (M. I.). FROM SARANAC TO THE MARQUESAS. Being Letters written by Mrs. M. I. STEVENSON during 1887-8. *Cr. 8vo. 6s. net.* A Colonial Edition is also published.

LETTERS FROM SAMOA, 1891-95. Edited and arranged by M. C. BALFOUR. With

many Illustrations. *Second Edition Cr. 8vo. 6s. net.* A Colonial Edition is also published.

Stoddart (Anna M.). See Oxford Biographies.

Stokes (F. G.), B.A. HOURS WITH RABELAIS. From the translation of SIR T. URQUHART and P. A. MOTTEUX. With a Portrait in Photogravure. *Cr. 8vo. 3s. 6d. net.*

Stone (S. J.). POEMS AND HYMNS. With a Memoir by F. G. ELLERTON, M.A. With Portrait. *Cr. 8vo. 6s.*

Storr (Vernon F.), M.A., Canon of Winchester. DEVELOPMENT AND DIVINE PURPOSE. *Cr. 8vo. 5s. net.*

Story (Alfred T.). AMERICAN SHRINES IN ENGLAND. With many Illustrations, including two in Colour by A. R. QUINTON. *Crown 8vo. 6s.* See also Little Guides.

Straker (F.). See Books on Business.

Streane (A. W.), D.D. See Churchman's Bible.

Streatfeild (R. A.). MODERN MUSIC AND MUSICIANS. With 24 Illustrations. *Second Ed. Demy 8vo. 7s. 6d. net.*

Stroud (Henry), D.Sc., M.A. ELEMEN-TARY PRACTICAL PHYSICS. With 115 Diagrams. *Second Edit., revised. 4s. 6d.*

Sturch (F.), Staff Instructor to the Surrey County Council. MANUAL TRAINING DRAWING (WOODWORK). With Solutions to Examination Questions, Orthographic, Isometric and Oblique Projection. With 50 Plates and 140 Figures. *Foolscap. 5s. net.*

Suddards (F.). See Stephenson (C.).

Surtees (R. S.). See I.P.L.

Sutherland (William). OLD AGE PEN-SIONS IN THEORY AND PRACTICE, WITH SOME FOREIGN EXAMPLES. *Cr. 8vo. 3s. 6d. net.*

Symes (J. E.), M.A. THE FRENCH REVOLUTION. *Second Edition. Cr. 8vo. 2s. 6d.*

Sympson (E. Mansel), M.A., M.D. See Ancient Cities.

Tabor (Margaret E.). THE SAINTS IN ART. With 20 Illustrations. *Fcap. 8vo. 3s. 6d. net.*

Tacitus. AGRICOLA. Edited by R. F. DAVIS, M.A. *Fcap. 8vo. 2s.*

GERMANIA. By the same Editor. *Fcap. 8vo. 2s.* See also Classical Translations.

Tallack (W.). HOWARD LETTERS AND MEMORIES. *Demy 8vo. 10s. 6d. net.*

Tatham (Frederick). See Blake (William).

Tauler (J.). See Library of Devotion.

Taylor (A. E.). THE ELEMENTS OF METAPHYSICS. *Second Edition. Demy 8vo. 10s. 6d. net.*

Taylor (F. G.), M.A. See Commercial Series.

Taylor (I. A.). See Oxford Biographies.

Taylor (John W.). THE COMING OF THE SAINTS. With 26 Illustrations. *Demy 8vo. 7s. 6d. net.*

Taylor (T. M.), M.A., Fellow of Gonville and Caius College, Cambridge. A CONSTITUTIONAL AND POLITICAL HISTORY OF ROME. To the Reign of Domitian. *Cr. 8vo. 7s. 6d.*

Teasdale=Buckell (G. T.). THE COMPLETE SHOT. With 53 Illustrations. *Third Edition. Demy 8vo. 12s. 6d. net.*
A Colonial Edition is also published.

Tennyson (Alfred, Lord). EARLY POEMS. Edited, with Notes and an Introduction, by J. CHURTON COLLINS, M.A. *Cr. 8vo. 6s.*

IN MEMORIAM, MAUD, AND THE PRINCESS. Edited by J. CHURTON COLLINS, M.A. *Cr. 8vo. 6s.*
See also Little Library.

Terry (C. S.). See Oxford Biographies.

Thackeray (W. M.). See Little Library.

Theobald (F. V.), M.A. INSECT LIFE. Illustrated. *Second Edition Revised. Cr. 8vo. 2s. 6d.*

Thibaudeau (A. C.). BONAPARTE AND THE CONSULATE. Translated and Edited by G. K. FORTESQUE, LL.D. With 12 Illustrations. *Demy 8vo. 10s. 6d. net.*

Thompson (A. H.). See Little Guides.

Thompson (A. P.). See Textbooks of Technology.

Tileston (Mary W.). DAILY STRENGTH FOR DAILY NEEDS. *Fifteenth Edition. Medium 16mo. 2s. 6d. net.* Also an edition in superior binding, *6s.*

Tompkins (H. W.), F.R.H.S. See Little Books on Art and Little Guides.

Toynbee (Paget), M.A., D.Litt. IN THE FOOTPRINTS OF DANTE. A Treasury of Verse and Prose from the works of Dante. *Small Cr. 8vo. 4s. 6d. net.*
See also Oxford Biographies and Dante.

Trench (Herbert). DEIRDRE WEDDED AND OTHER POEMS. *Second and Revised Edition. Large Post 8vo. 6s.*

NEW POEMS. *Second Edition. Large Post 8vo. 6s.*

Trevelyan (G. M.), Fellow of Trinity College, Cambridge. ENGLAND UNDER THE STUARTS. With Maps and Plans. *Third Edition. Demy 8vo. 10s. 6d. net.*

Troutbeck (G. E.). See Little Guides.

Tyler (E. A.), B.A., F.C.S. See Junior School Books.

Tyrrell=Gill (Frances). See Little Books on Art.

Vardon (Harry). THE COMPLETE GOLFER. With 63 Illustrations. *Ninth Edition. Demy 8vo. 10s. 6d. net.*
A Colonial Edition is also published.

Vaughan (Henry). See Little Library.

Vaughan (Herbert M.), B.A. (Oxon.). THE LAST OF THE ROYAL STUARTS, HENRY STUART, CARDINAL, DUKE OF YORK. With 20 Illustrations. *Second Edition. Demy 8vo. 10s. 6d. net.*

THE NAPLES RIVIERA. With 25 Illustrations in Colour by MAURICE GREIFFENHAGEN. *Second Edition. Cr. 8vo. 6s.*

Vernon (Hon. W. Warren), M.A. READINGS ON THE INFERNO OF DANTE. With an Introduction by the Rev. Dr. MOORE. *In Two Volumes. Second Edition. Cr. 8vo. 15s. net.*

READINGS ON THE PURGATORIO OF DANTE. With an Introduction by the late DEAN CHURCH. *In Two Volumes. Third Edition. Cr. 8vo. 15s. net.*

Vincent (J. E.). THROUGH EAST ANGLIA IN A MOTOR CAR. With 16 Illustrations in Colour by FRANK SOUTHGATE, R.B.A., and a Map. *Cr. 8vo. 6s.*

Voegelin (A.), M.A. See Junior Examination Series.

Waddell (Col. L. A.), LL.D., C.B. LHASA AND ITS MYSTERIES. With a Record of the Expedition of 1903–1904. With 155 Illustrations and Maps. *Third and Cheaper Edition. Medium 8vo. 7s. 6d. net.*

Wade (G. W.), D.D. OLD TESTAMENT HISTORY. With Maps. *Fifth Edition. Cr. 8vo. 6s.*

Wade (G. W.), D.D., and **Wade (J. H.)**, M.A. See Little Guides.

Wagner (Richard). RICHARD WAGNER'S MUSIC DRAMAS : Interpretations, embodying Wagner's own explanations. By ALICE LEIGHTON CLEATHER and BASIL CRUMP. *In Three Volumes. Fcap 8vo. 2s. 6d. each.*
VOL. I.—THE RING OF THE NIBELUNG. *Third Edition.*
VOL. II.—PARSIFAL, LOHENGRIN, and THE HOLY GRAIL.
VOL. III.—TRISTAN AND ISOLDE.

Walkley (A. B.). DRAMA AND LIFE. *Cr. 8vo. 6s.*

Wall (J. C.). See Antiquary's Books.

Wallace-Hadrill (F.), Second Master at Herne Bay College. REVISION NOTES ON ENGLISH HISTORY. *Cr. 8vo. 1s.*

Walters (H. B.). See Little Books on Art and Classics of Art.

Walton (F. W.). See School Histories.

Walton (Izaak) and **Cotton (Charles).** See I.P.L.

Walton (Izaak). See Little Library.

Waterhouse (Elizabeth). WITH THE SIMPLE-HEARTED : Little Homilies to Women in Country Places. *Second Edition. Small Pott 8vo. 2s. net.*
See also Little Library.

Watt (Francis). See Henderson (T. F.).

Weatherhead (T. C.), M.A. EXAMINATION PAPERS IN HORACE. *Cr. 8vo. 2s.*
See also Junior Examination Series.

Webber (F. C.). See Textbooks of Technology.

Weir (Archibald), M.A. AN INTRODUCTION TO THE HISTORY OF MODERN EUROPE. *Cr. 8vo. 6s.*

Wells (Sidney H.) See Textbooks of Science.

Wells (J.), M.A., Fellow and Tutor of Wadham College. OXFORD AND OXFORD LIFE. *Third Edition. Cr. 8vo. 3s. 6d.*
A SHORT HISTORY OF ROME. *Ninth Edition.* With 3 Maps. *Cr. 8vo. 3s. 6d.*
See also Little Guides.

Wesley (John). See Library of Devotion.

Wheldon (F. W.). A LITTLE BROTHER TO THE BIRDS. The life-story of St. Francis retold for children. With 15 Illustrations, 7 of which are by A. H. BUCKLAND. *Large Cr. 8vo. 6s.*

Whibley (C.). See Henley (W. E.).

Whibley (L.), M.A., Fellow of Pembroke College, Cambridge. GREEK OLIGARCHIES : THEIR ORGANISATION AND CHARACTER. *Cr. 8vo. 6s.*

Whitaker (G. H.), M.A. See Churchman's Bible.

White (Gilbert). See Standard Library.

Whitfield (E. E.), M.A. See Commercial Series.

Whitehead (A. W.). GASPARD DE COLIGNY, ADMIRAL OF FRANCE. With Illustrations and Plans. *Demy 8vo. 12s. 6d. net.*

Whiteley (R. Lloyd), F.I.C., Principal of the Municipal Science School, West Bromwich. AN ELEMENTARY TEXT-BOOK OF INORGANIC CHEMISTRY. *Cr. 8vo. 2s. 6d.*

Whitley (Miss). See Dilke (Lady).

Whitling (Miss L.), late Staff Teacher of the National Training School of Cookery. THE COMPLETE COOK. With 42 Illustrations. *Demy 8vo. 7s. 6d. net.*
A Colonial edition is also published.

Whitten (W.). See Smith (John Thomas).

Whyte (A. G.), B.Sc. See Books on Business.

Wilberforce (Wilfrid). See Little Books on Art.

Wilde (Oscar). DE PROFUNDIS. *Twelfth Edition. Cr. 8vo. 5s. net.*
A Colonial Edition is also published.
THE WORKS.
A Uniform Edition. Demy 8vo. 12s. 6d. net each volume.
THE DUCHESS OF PADUA: A Play.
POEMS.
INTENTIONS and THE SOUL OF MAN.
SALOMÉ. A FLORENTINE TRAGEDY, and VERA; or, THE NIHILISTS.
LADY WINDERMERE'S FAN: A Play about a Good Woman.
A WOMAN OF NO IMPORTANCE: A Play.
AN IDEAL HUSBAND: A Play.
THE IMPORTANCE OF BEING EARNEST: A Trivial Comedy for Serious People.
A HOUSE OF POMEGRANATES, THE HAPPY PRINCE, and OTHER TALES.
LORD ARTHUR SAVILE'S CRIME and OTHER PROSE PIECES.
DE PROFUNDIS.

Wilkins (W. H.), B.A. THE ALIEN INVASION. *Cr. 8vo. 2s. 6d.*

Williams (A.). PETROL PETER: or Pretty Stories and Funny Pictures. Illustrated in Colour by A. W. MILLS. *Demy 4to. 3s. 6d. net.*

Williamson (M. G.), M.A. See Ancient Cities.

Williamson (W.), B.A. See Junior Examination Series, Junior School Books, and Beginner's Books.

Wilmot=Buxton (E. M.). MAKERS OF EUROPE. Outlines of European History for the Middle Forms of Schools. With 12 Maps. *Tenth Edition. Cr. 8vo. 3s. 6d.*
THE ANCIENT WORLD. With Maps and Illustrations. *Cr. 8vo. 3s. 6d.*
A BOOK OF NOBLE WOMEN. With 16 Illustrations. *Cr. 8vo. 3s. 6d.*
A HISTORY OF GREAT BRITAIN : FROM THE COMING OF THE ANGLES TO THE YEAR 1870. With 20 Maps. *Cr. 8vo. 3s. 6d.*
See also Beginner's Books.

Wilson (Bishop.). See Library of Devotion.

Wilson (A. J.). See Books on Business.

Wilson (H. A.). See Books on Business.

Wilson (J. A.). See Simplified French Texts.

Wilton (Richard), M.A. LYRA PASTORALIS : Songs of Nature, Church, and Home. *Pott 8vo. 2s. 6d.*

Winbolt (S. E.), M.A. EXERCISES IN LATIN ACCIDENCE. *Cr. 8vo. 1s. 6d.*
LATIN HEXAMETER VERSE: An Aid to Composition. *Cr. 8vo. 3s. 6d.* KEY, *5s. net.*

Windle (B. C. A.), D.Sc.,F.R.S.,F.S.A. See Antiquary's Books, Little Guides, Ancient Cities, and School Histories.

Wood (Sir Evelyn), F.-M., V.C., G.C.B., G.C.M.G. FROM MIDSHIPMAN TO FIELD-MARSHAL. With Illustrations, and 29 Maps. *Fifth and Cheaper Edition. Demy 8vo. 7s. 6d. net.*
A Colonial Edition is also published.

Wood (J. A. E.). See Textbooks of Technology.

Wood (J. Hickory). DAN LENO. Illustrated. *Third Edition. Cr. 8vo. 6s.*
A Colonial Edition is also published.

Wood (W. Birkbeck), M.A., late Scholar of Worcester College, Oxford, and **Edmonds (Major J. E.), R.E., D.A.Q.-M.G.** A HISTORY OF THE CIVIL WAR IN THE UNITED STATES. With an Introduction by H. SPENSER WILKINSON. With 24 Maps and Plans. *Second Edition. Demy 8vo. 12s. 6d. net.*

Wordsworth (Christopher), M.A. See Antiquary's Books.

Wordsworth (W.). THE POEMS OF. With an Introduction and Notes by NOWELL C. SMITH, late Fellow of New College, Oxford. *In Three Volumes. Demy 8vo. 15s. net.*
POEMS BY WILLIAM WORDSWORTH. Selected with an Introduction by STOPFORD

A. BROOKE. With 40 Illustrations by E.
H. NEW, including a Frontispiece in
Photogravure. *Cr. 8vo. 7s. 6d. net.*
See also Little Library.

Wordsworth (W.) and Coleridge (S. T.).
See Little Library.

Wright (Arthur), D.D., Fellow of Queen's
College, Cambridge. See Churchman's
Library.

Wright (C. Gordon). See Dante.

Wright (J. C.). TO-DAY. Thoughts on
Life for every day. *Demy 16mo. 1s. 6d. net.*

Wright (Sophie). GERMAN VOCABU-
LARIES FOR REPETITION. *Fcap. 8vo
1s. 6d.*

Wyatt (Kate M.). See Gloag (M. R.).

Wylde (A. B.). MODERN ABYSSINIA.
With a Map and a Portrait. *Demy 8vo.
15s. net.*

Wyllie (M. A.). NORWAY AND ITS
FJORDS. With 16 Illustrations, in Colour

by W. L. WYLLIE, R.A., and 17 other
Illustrations. *Crown 8vo. 6s.*
A Colonial Edition is also published.

Wyndham (George). See Shakespeare
(William).

Yeats (W. B.). A BOOK OF IRISH
VERSE. *Revised and Enlarged Edition.*
Cr. 8vo. 3s. 6d.

Young (Filson). THE COMPLETE
MOTORIST. With 138 Illustrations.
*New Edition (Seventh), with many addi-
tions. Demy. 8vo. 12s. 6d. net.*
A Colonial Edition is also published.
THE JOY OF THE ROAD : An Apprecia
tion of the Motor Car. With a Frontispiece in Photogravure. *Small Demy 8vo.
5s. net.*

Zimmern (Antonia). WHAT DO WE
KNOW CONCERNING ELECTRI-
CITY? *Fcap. 8vo. 1s. 6d. net.*

Ancient Cities

General Editor, B. C. A. WINDLE, D.Sc., F.R.S.

Cr. 8vo.   4s. 6d. net.

CHESTER. By B. C. A. Windle, D.Sc. F.R.S.
Illustrated by E. H. New.

SHREWSBURY. By T. Auden, M.A., F.S.A.
Illustrated by Katharine M. Roberts.

CANTERBURY. By J. C. Cox, LL.D., F.S.A.
Illustrated by B. C. Boulter.

EDINBURGH. By M. G. Williamson, M.A.
Illustrated by Herbert Railton.

LINCOLN. By E. Mansel Sympson, M.A.,
M.D. Illustrated by E. H. New.

BRISTOL. By Alfred Harvey, M.B. Illustrated by E. H. New.

DUBLIN. By S. A. O. Fitzpatrick. Illustrated
by W. C. Green.

The Antiquary's Books

General Editor, J. CHARLES COX, LL.D., F.S.A

Demy 8vo.   7s. 6d. net.

ENGLISH MONASTIC LIFE. By the Right
Rev. Abbot Gasquet, O.S.B. Illustrated.
Third Edition.

REMAINS OF THE PREHISTORIC AGE IN
ENGLAND. By B. C. A. Windle, D.Sc.,
F.R.S. With numerous Illustrations and
Plans.

OLD SERVICE BOOKS OF THE ENGLISH
CHURCH. By Christopher Wordsworth,
M.A., and Henry Littlehales. With
Coloured and other Illustrations.

CELTIC ART IN PAGAN AND CHRISTIAN
TIMES. By J. Romilly Allen, F.S.A.
With numerous Illustrations and Plans.

ARCHÆOLOGY AND FALSE ANTIQUITIES.
By R. Munro, LL.D. Illustrated.

SHRINES OF BRITISH SAINTS. By J. C. Wall.
With numerous Illustrations and Plans.

THE ROYAL FORESTS OF ENGLAND. By J.
C. Cox, LL.D., F.S.A. Illustrated.

THE MANOR AND MANORIAL RECORDS
By Nathaniel J. Hone. Illustrated.

ENGLISH SEALS. By J. Harvey Bloom.
Illustrated.

THE BELLS OF ENGLAND. By Canon J. J.
Raven, D.D., F.S.A. With Illustrations.
Second Edition.

PARISH LIFE IN MEDIÆVAL ENGLAND. By
the Right Rev. Abbott Gasquet, O.S.B.
With many Illustrations. *Second Edition.*

THE DOMESDAY INQUEST. By Adolphus
Ballard, B.A., LL.B. With 27 Illustrations.

THE BRASSES OF ENGLAND. By Herbert
W. Macklin, M.A. With many Illustrations.
Second Edition.

ENGLISH CHURCH FURNITURE. By J. C. Cox,
LL.D., F.S.A., and A. Harvey, M.B.
Second Edition.

FOLK-LORE AS AN HISTORICAL SCIENCE. By
G. L. Gomme. With many Illustrations.

*ENGLISH COSTUME. By George Clinch, F.G.S.
With many Illustrations

The Arden Shakespeare

Demy 8vo. 2s. 6d. net each volume.

An edition of Shakespeare in single Plays. Edited with a full Introduction, Textual Notes, and a Commentary at the foot of the page.

HAMLET. Edited by Edward Dowden. *Second Edition.*

ROMEO AND JULIET. Edited by Edward Dowden.

KING LEAR. Edited by W. J. Craig.

JULIUS CAESAR. Edited by M. Macmillan.

THE TEMPEST. Edited by Moreton Luce.

OTHELLO. Edited by H. C. Hart.

TITUS ANDRONICUS. Edited by H. B. Baildon.

CYMBELINE. Edited by Edward Dowden.

THE MERRY WIVES OF WINDSOR. Edited by H. C. Hart.

A MIDSUMMER NIGHT'S DREAM. Edited by H. Cuningham.

KING HENRY V. Edited by H. A. Evans.

ALL'S WELL THAT ENDS WELL. Edited by W.O. Brigstocke.

THE TAMING OF THE SHREW. Edited by R. Warwick Bond.

TIMON OF ATHENS. Edited by K. Deighton.

MEASURE FOR MEASURE. Edited by H. C. Hart.

TWELFTH NIGHT. Edited by Moreton Luce.

THE MERCHANT OF VENICE. Edited by C. Knox Pooler.

TROILUS AND CRESSIDA. Edited by K. Deighton.

THE TWO GENTLEMEN OF VERONA. Edited by R. Warwick Bond.

ANTONY AND CLEOPATRA. Edited by R. H. Case.

LOVE'S LABOUR'S LOST. Edited by H. C. Hart.

PERICLES. Edited by K. Deighton.

KING RICHARD III. Edited by A. H. Thompson.

THE LIFE AND DEATH OF KING JOHN. Edited by Ivor B. John.

THE COMEDY OF ERRORS. Edited by Henry Cuningham.

The Beginner's Books

Edited by W. WILLIAMSON, B.A.

EASY FRENCH RHYMES. By Henri Blouet. *Second Edition.* Illustrated. *Fcap. 8vo. 1s.*

EASY STORIES FROM ENGLISH HISTORY. By E. M. Wilmot-Buxton. *Fifth Edition. Cr. 8vo. 1s.*

STORIES FROM ROMAN HISTORY. By E. M. Wilmot-Buxton *Cr. 8vo. 1s. 6d.*

A FIRST HISTORY OF GREECE. By E. E. Firth. *Cr. 8vo. 1s. 6d.*

EASY EXERCISES IN ARITHMETIC. Arranged by W. S. Beard. *Third Edition. Fcap. 8vo.* Without Answers, 1s. With Answers. 1s. 3d.

EASY DICTATION AND SPELLING. By W. Williamson, B.A. *Seventh Ed. Fcap. 8vo. 1s.*

AN EASY POETRY BOOK. Selected and arranged by W. Williamson, B.A. *Second Edition. Cr. 8vo. 1s.*

Books on Business

Cr. 8vo. 2s. 6d. net.

PORTS AND DOCKS. By Douglas Owen.

RAILWAYS. By E. R. McDermott.

THE STOCK EXCHANGE. By Chas. Duguid. *Second Edition.*

THE BUSINESS OF INSURANCE. By A. J. Wilson.

THE ELECTRICAL INDUSTRY : LIGHTING, TRACTION, AND POWER. By A. G. Whyte, B.Sc.

THE SHIPBUILDING INDUSTRY : Its History, Practice, Science, and Finance. By David Pollock, M.I.N.A.

THE MONEY MARKET. By F. Straker.

THE BUSINESS SIDE OF AGRICULTURE. By A. G. L. Rogers, M.A.

LAW IN BUSINESS. By H. A. Wilson.

THE BREWING INDUSTRY. By Julian L. Baker, F.I.C., F.C.S. Illustrated.

THE AUTOMOBILE INDUSTRY. By G. de Holden-Stone.

MINING AND MINING INVESTMENTS. By 'A. Moil.'

THE BUSINESS OF ADVERTISING. By Clarence G. Moran, Barrister-at-Law. Illustrated.

TRADE UNIONS. By G. Drage.

CIVIL ENGINEERING. By T. Claxton Fidler, M.Inst. C.E. Illustrated.

THE IRON TRADE OF GREAT BRITAIN. By J. Stephen Jeans. Illustrated.

MONOPOLIES, TRUSTS, AND KARTELLS. By F. W. Hirst.

THE COTTON INDUSTRY AND TRADE. By Prof. S. J. Chapman, Dean of the Faculty of Commerce in the University of Manchester. Illustrated.

Byzantine Texts

Edited by J. B. BURY, M.A., Litt.D.

THE SYRIAC CHRONICLE KNOWN AS THAT OF ZACHARIAH OF MITYLENE. Translated by F. J. Hamilton, D.D., and E. W. Brooks. *Demy 8vo.* 12s. 6d. net.

EVAGRIUS. Edited by L. Bidez and Léon Parmentier. *Demy 8vo.* 10s. 6d. net.

THE HISTORY OF PSELLUS. Edited by C. Sathas. *Demy 8vo.* 15s. net.
ECTHESIS CHRONICA AND CHRONICON ATHENARUM. Edited by Professor S. P. Lambros. *Demy 8vo.* 7s. 6d. net.
THE CHRONICLE OF MOREA. Edited by John Schmitt. *Demy 8vo.* 15s. net.

The Churchman's Bible

General Editor, J. H. BURN, B.D., F.R.S.E.

Fcap. 8vo. 1s. 6d. net each.

THE EPISTLE OF ST. PAUL THE APOSTLE TO THE GALATIANS. Explained by A. W. Robinson, M.A. *Second Edition.*
ECCLESIASTES. Explained by A. W. Streane, D.D.
THE EPISTLE OF ST. PAUL THE APOSTLE TO THE PHILIPPIANS. Explained by C. R. D. Biggs, D.D. *Second Edition.*
THE EPISTLE OF ST. JAMES. Explained by H. W. Fulford M.A.

ISAIAH. Explained by W. E. Barnes, D.D. *Two Volumes.* With Map. 2s. net each.
THE EPISTLE OF ST. PAUL THE APOSTLE TO THE EPHESIANS. Explained by G. H. Whitaker, M.A.
THE GOSPEL ACCORDING TO ST. MARK. Explained by J. C. Du Buisson, M.A. 2s. 6d. net.
THE EPISTLE OF PAUL THE APOSTLE TO THE COLOSSIANS AND PHILEMON. Explained by H. J. C. Knight. 2s. net.

The Churchman's Library

General Editor, J. H. BURN, B.D., F.R.S.E.

Crown 8vo. 3s. 6d. each.

THE BEGINNINGS OF ENGLISH CHRISTIANITY. By W. E. Collins, M.A. With Map.
THE WORKMANSHIP OF THE PRAYER BOOK: Its Literary and Liturgical Aspects. By J. Dowden, D.D. *Second Edition, Revised and Enlarged.*
EVOLUTION. By F. B. Jevons, M.A., Litt.D.

SOME NEW TESTAMENT PROBLEMS. By Arthur Wright, D.D. 6s.
THE CHURCHMAN'S INTRODUCTION TO THE OLD TESTAMENT. By A. M. Mackay, B.A. *Second Edition.*
COMPARATIVE THEOLOGY. By J. A. MacCulloch. 6s.

Classical Translations

Crown 8vo.

ÆSCHYLUS—The Oresteian Trilogy (Agamemnon, Choëphoroe, Eumenides). Translated by Lewis Campbell, LL.D. 5s.
CICERO—De Oratore I. Translated by E. N. P. Moor, M.A. *Second Edition.* 3s. 6d.
CICERO—The Speeches against Cataline and Antony and for Murena and Milo. Translated by H. E. D. Blakiston, M.A. 5s.
CICERO—De Natura Deorum. Translated by F. Brooks, M.A. 3s. 6d.
CICERO—De Officiis. Translated by G. B. Gardiner, M.A. 2s. 6d.

HORACE—The Odes and Epodes. Translated by A. D. Godley, M.A. 2s.
LUCIAN—Six Dialogues Translated by S. T. Irwin, M.A. 3s. 6d.
SOPHOCLES—Ajax and Electra. Translated by E. D. Morshead, M.A. 2s. 6d.
TACITUS—Agricola and Germania. Translated by R. B. Townshend. 2s. 6d.
JUVENAL—Thirteen Satires. Translated by S. G. Owen, M.A. 2s. 6d.

Classics of Art

Edited by DR. J. H. W. LAING

THE ART OF THE GREEKS. By H. B. Walters. With 112 Plates and 18 Illustrations in the Text. *Wide Royal 8vo.* 12s. 6d. net.

VELAZQUEZ. By A. de Beruete. With 94 Plates. *Wide Royal 8vo.* 10s. 6d. net.

Commercial Series
Crown 8vo.

BRITISH COMMERCE AND COLONIES FROM ELIZABETH TO VICTORIA. By H. de B. Gibbins, Litt.D., M.A. *Fourth Edition.* 2s.

COMMERCIAL EXAMINATION PAPERS. By H. de B. Gibbins, Litt.D., M.A. 1s. 6d.

THE ECONOMICS OF COMMERCE, By H. de B. Gibbins, Litt.D., M.A. *Second Edition.* 1s. 6d.

A GERMAN COMMERCIAL READER. By S. E. Bally. With Vocabulary. 2s.

A COMMERCIAL GEOGRAPHY OF THE BRITISH EMPIRE. By L. W. Lyde, M.A. *Seventh Edition.* 2s.

A COMMERCIAL GEOGRAPHY OF FOREIGN NATIONS. By F. C. Boon, B.A. 2s.

A PRIMER OF BUSINESS. By S. Jackson, M.A. *Fourth Edition.* 1s. 6d.

A SHORT COMMERCIAL ARITHMETIC. By F. G. Taylor, M.A. *Fourth Edition.* 1s. 6d.

FRENCH COMMERCIAL CORRESPONDENCE. By S. E. Bally. With Vocabulary. *Fourth Edition.* 2s.

GERMAN COMMERCIAL CORRESPONDENCE. By S. E. Bally. With Vocabulary. *Second Edition.* 2s. 6d.

A FRENCH COMMERCIAL READER. By S. E. Bally. With Vocabulary. *Second Edition.* 2s.

PRECIS WRITING AND OFFICE CORRESPONDENCE. By E. E. Whitfield, M.A. *Second Edition.* 2s.

A ENTRANCE GUIDE TO PROFESSIONS AND BUSINESS. By H. Jones. 1s. 6d.

THE PRINCIPLES OF BOOK-KEEPING BY DOUBLE ENTRY. By J. E. B. M'Allen, M.A. 2s.

COMMERCIAL LAW. By W. Douglas Edwards. *Second Edition.* 2s.

The Connoisseur's Library
Wide Royal 8vo. 25s. *net.*

MEZZOTINTS. By Cyril Davenport. With 40 Plates in Photogravure.

PORCELAIN. By Edward Dillon. With 19 Plates in Colour, 20 in Collotype, and 5 in Photogravure.

MINIATURES. By Dudley Heath. With 9 Plates in Colour, 15 in Collotype, and 15 in Photogravure.

IVORIES. By A. Maskell. With 80 Plates in Collotype and Photogravure.

ENGLISH FURNITURE. By F. S. Robinson. With 160 Plates in Collotype and one in Photogravure. *Second Edition.*

ENGLISH COLOURED BOOKS. By Martin Hardie. With 28 Illustrations in Colour and Collotype.

EUROPEAN ENAMELS. By Henry H. Cunynghame, C.B. With 54 Plates in Collotype and Half-tone and 4 Plates in Colour.

GOLDSMITHS' AND SILVERSMITHS' WORK. By Nelson Dawson. With many Plates in Collotype and a Frontispiece in Photogravure. *Second Edition.*

GLASS. By Edward Dillon. With 37 Illustrations in Collotype and 12 in Colour.

SEALS. By Walter de Gray Birch. With 52 Illustrations in Collotype and a Frontispiece in Photogravure.

JEWELLERY. By H. Clifford Smith. With 50 Illustrations in Collotype, and 4 in Colour. *Second Edition.*

The Illustrated Pocket Library of Plain and Coloured Books
Fcap 8vo. 3s. 6d. *net each volume.*

COLOURED BOOKS

OLD COLOURED BOOKS. By George Paston. With 16 Coloured Plates. *Fcap. 8vo.* 2s. net.

THE LIFE AND DEATH OF JOHN MYTTON, ESQ. By Nimrod. With 18 Coloured Plates by Henry Alken and T. J. Rawlins. *Fourth Edition.*

THE LIFE OF A SPORTSMAN. By Nimrod. With 35 Coloured Plates by Henry Alken.

HANDLEY CROSS. By R. S. Surtees. With 17 Coloured Plates and 100 Woodcuts in the Text by John Leech. *Second Edition.*

MR. SPONGE'S SPORTING TOUR. By R. S. Surtees. With 13 Coloured Plates and 90 Woodcuts in the Text by John Leech.

JORROCKS' JAUNTS AND JOLLITIES. By R. S. Surtees. With 15 Coloured Plates by H. Alken. *Second Edition.*

ASK MAMMA. By R. S. Surtees. With 13 Coloured Plates and 70 Woodcuts in the Text by John Leech.

THE ANALYSIS OF THE HUNTING FIELD. By R. S. Surtees. With 7 Coloured Plates by Henry Alken, and 43 Illustrations on Wood.

THE TOUR OF DR. SYNTAX IN SEARCH OF THE PICTURESQUE. By William Combe. With 30 Coloured Plates by T. Rowlandson.

THE TOUR OF DOCTOR SYNTAX IN SEARCH OF CONSOLATION. By William Combe. With 24 Coloured Plates by T. Rowlandson.

THE THIRD TOUR OF DOCTOR SYNTAX IN SEARCH OF A WIFE. By William Combe. With 24 Coloured Plates by T. Rowlandson.

THE HISTORY OF JOHNNY QUAE GENUS: the Little Foundling of the late Dr. Syntax. By the Author of 'The Three Tours.' With 24 Coloured Plates by Rowlandson.

THE ENGLISH DANCE OF DEATH, from the Designs of T. Rowlandson, with Metrical Illustrations by the Author of 'Doctor Syntax.' *Two Volumes.*

This book contains 76 Coloured Plates.

[*Continued.*

ILLUSTRATED POCKET LIBRARY OF PLAIN AND COLOURED BOOKS—*continued.*

THE DANCE OF LIFE : A Poem. By the Author of 'Doctor Syntax.' Illustrated with 26 Coloured Engravings by T. Rowlandson.

LIFE IN LONDON : or, the Day and Night Scenes of Jerry Hawthorn, Esq., and his Elegant Friend, Corinthian Tom. By Pierce Egan. With 36 Coloured Plates by I. R. and G. Cruikshank. With numerous Designs on Wood.

REAL LIFE IN LONDON : or, the Rambles and Adventures of Bob Tallyho, Esq., and his Cousin, The Hon. Tom Dashall. By an Amateur (Pierce Egan). With 31 Coloured Plates by Alken and Rowlandson, etc. *Two Volumes.*

THE LIFE OF AN ACTOR. By Pierce Egan. With 27 Coloured Plates by Theodore Lane, and several Designs on Wood.

THE VICAR OF WAKEFIELD. By Oliver Goldsmith. With 24 Coloured Plates by T. Rowlandson.

THE MILITARY ADVENTURES OF JOHNNY NEWCOME. By an Officer. With 15 Coloured Plates by T. Rowlandson.

THE NATIONAL SPORTS OF GREAT BRITAIN. With Descriptions and 50 Coloured Plates by Henry Alken.

THE ADVENTURES OF A POST CAPTAIN. By A Naval Officer. With 24 Coloured Plates by Mr. Williams.

GAMONIA : or the Art of Preserving Game ; and an Improved Method of making Plantations and Covers, explained and illustrated by Lawrence Rawstorne, Esq. With 15 Coloured Plates by T. Rawlins.

AN ACADEMY FOR GROWN HORSEMEN : Containing the completest Instructions for Walking, Trotting, Cantering, Galloping, Stumbling, and Tumbling. Illustrated with 27 Coloured Plates, and adorned with a Portrait of the Author. By Geoffrey Gambado, Esq.

REAL LIFE IN IRELAND, or, the Day and Night Scenes of Brian Boru, Esq., and his Elegant Friend, Sir Shawn O'Dogherty. By a Real Paddy. With 19 Coloured Plates by Heath, Marks, etc.

THE ADVENTURES OF JOHNNY NEWCOME IN THE NAVY. By Alfred Burton. With 16 Coloured Plates by T. Rowlandson.

THE OLD ENGLISH SQUIRE : A Poem. By John Careless, Esq. With 20 Coloured Plates after the style of T. Rowlandson.

THE ENGLISH SPY. By Bernard Blackmantle. An original Work, Characteristic, Satirical, Humorous, comprising scenes and sketches in every Rank of Society, being Portraits of the Illustrious, Eminent, Eccentric, and Notorious. With 72 Coloured Plates by R. CRUIKSHANK, and many Illustrations on wood. *Two Volumes.* 7s. net.

PLAIN BOOKS

THE GRAVE : A Poem. By Robert Blair. Illustrated by 12 Etchings executed by Louis Schiavonetti from the original Inventions of William Blake. With an Engraved Title Page and a Portrait of Blake by T. Phillips, R.A. The illustrations are reproduced in photogravure.

ILLUSTRATIONS OF THE BOOK OF JOB. Invented and engraved by William Blake. These famous Illustrations—21 in number —are reproduced in photogravure.

WINDSOR CASTLE. By W. Harrison Ainsworth. With 22 Plates and 87 Woodcuts in the Text by George Cruikshank.

THE TOWER OF LONDON. By W. Harrison Ainsworth. With 40 Plates and 58 Woodcuts in the Text by George Cruikshank.

FRANK FAIRLEGH. By F. E. Smedley. With 30 Plates by George Cruikshank.

HANDY ANDY. By Samuel Lover. With 24 Illustrations by the Author.

THE COMPLEAT ANGLER. By Izaak Walton and Charles Cotton. With 14 Plates and 77 Woodcuts in the Text.

THE PICKWICK PAPERS. By Charles Dickens. With the 43 Illustrations by Seymour and Phiz, the two Buss Plates, and the 32 Contemporary Onwhyn Plates.

Junior Examination Series

Edited by A. M. M. STEDMAN, M.A. *Fcap. 8vo.* 1s.

JUNIOR FRENCH EXAMINATION PAPERS. By F. Jacob, M.A. *Second Edition.*

JUNIOR ENGLISH EXAMINATION PAPERS. By W. Williamson, B.A.

JUNIOR ARITHMETIC EXAMINATION PAPERS. By W. S. Beard. *Fifth Edition.*

JUNIOR ALGEBRA EXAMINATION PAPERS. By S. W Finn, M.A.

JUNIOR GREEK EXAMINATION PAPERS. By T. C. Weatherhead, M.A. KEY, 3s. 6d. net.

JUNIOR LATIN EXAMINATION PAPERS. By C. G. Botting, B.A. *Fifth Edition.* KEY, 3s. 6d. net.

JUNIOR GENERAL INFORMATION EXAMINATION PAPERS. By W. S. Beard. KEY, 3s. 6d. net.

JUNIOR GEOGRAPHY EXAMINATION PAPERS. By W. G. Baker, M.A.

JUNIOR GERMAN EXAMINATION PAPERS. By A. Voegelin, M.A.

Methuen's Junior School-Books

Edited by O. D. INSKIP, LL.D., and W. WILLIAMSON, B.A.

A CLASS-BOOK OF DICTATION PASSAGES. By W. Williamson, B.A. *Fourteenth Edition. Cr. 8vo. 1s. 6d.*

THE GOSPEL ACCORDING TO ST. MATTHEW. Edited by E. Wilton South, M.A. With Three Maps. *Cr. 8vo. 1s. 6d.*

THE GOSPEL ACCORDING TO ST. MARK. Edited by A. E. Rubie, D.D. With Three Maps. *Cr. 8vo. 1s. 6d.*

A JUNIOR ENGLISH GRAMMAR. By W. Williamson, B.A. With numerous passages for parsing and analysis, and a chapter on Essay Writing. *Fourth Edition. Cr. 8vo. 2s.*

A JUNIOR CHEMISTRY. By E. A. Tyler, B.A., F.C.S. With 78 Illustrations. *Fourth Edition. Cr. 8vo. 2s. 6d.*

THE ACTS OF THE APOSTLES. Edited by A. E. Rubie, D.D. *Cr. 8vo. 2s.*

A JUNIOR FRENCH GRAMMAR. By L. A. Sornet and M. J. Acatos. *Third Edition. Cr. 8vo. 2s.*

ELEMENTARY EXPERIMENTAL SCIENCE. PHYSICS by W. T. Clough, A.R.C.S. CHEMISTRY by A. E. Dunstan, B.Sc. With 2 Plates and 154 Diagrams. *Seventh Edition. Cr. 8vo. 2s. 6d.*

A JUNIOR GEOMETRY. By Noel S. Lydon. With 276 Diagrams. *Seventh Edition. Cr. 8vo. 2s.*

ELEMENTARY EXPERIMENTAL CHEMISTRY. By A. E. Dunstan, B.Sc. With 4 Plates and 109 Diagrams. *Third Edition. Cr. 8vo. 2s.*

A JUNIOR FRENCH PROSE. By R. R. N. Baron, M.A. *Third Edition. Cr. 8vo. 2s.*

THE GOSPEL ACCORDING TO ST. LUKE. With an Introduction and Notes by William Williamson, B.A. With Three Maps. *Cr. 8vo. 2s.*

THE FIRST BOOK OF KINGS. Edited by A. E. RUBIE, D.D. With Maps. *Cr. 8vo. 2s.*

A JUNIOR GREEK HISTORY. By W. H. Spragge, M.A. With 4 Illustrations and 5 Maps. *Cr. 8vo. 2s. 6d.*

A SCHOOL LATIN GRAMMAR. By H. G. Ford, M.A. *Cr. 8vo. 2s. 6d.*

A JUNIOR LATIN PROSE. By H. N. Asman, M.A., B.D. *Cr. 8vo. 2s. 6d.*

Leaders of Religion

Edited by H. C. BEECHING, M.A., Canon of Westminster. *With Portraits. Cr. 8vo. 2s. net.*

CARDINAL NEWMAN. By R. H. Hutton.

JOHN WESLEY. By J. H. Overton, M.A.

BISHOP WILBERFORCE. By G. W. Daniell, M.A.

CARDINAL MANNING. By A. W. Hutton, M.A.

CHARLES SIMEON. By H. C. G. Moule, D.D.

JOHN KNOX. By F. MacCunn. *Second Edition.*

JOHN HOWE. By R. F. Horton, D.D.

THOMAS KEN. By F. A. Clarke, M.A.

GEORGE FOX, THE QUAKER. By T. Hodgkin, D.C.L. *Third Edition.*

JOHN KEBLE. By Walter Lock, D.D.

THOMAS CHALMERS. By Mrs. Oliphant.

LANCELOT ANDREWES. By R. L. Ottley, D.D. *Second Edition.*

AUGUSTINE OF CANTERBURY. By E. L. Cutts, D.D.

WILLIAM LAUD. By W. H. Hutton, M.A. *Third Edition.*

JOHN DONNE. By Augustus Jessopp, D.D.

THOMAS CRANMER. By A. J. Mason, D.D.

BISHOP LATIMER. By R. M. Carlyle and A. J. Carlyle, M.A.

BISHOP BUTLER. By W. A. Spooner, M.A.

The Library of Devotion

With Introductions and (where necessary) Notes. *Small Pott 8vo, cloth, 2s. ; leather, 2s. 6d. net.*

THE CONFESSIONS OF ST. AUGUSTINE. Edited by C. Bigg, D.D. *Sixth Edition.*

THE IMITATION OF CHRIST : called also the Ecclesiastical Music. Edited by C. Bigg, D.D. *Fifth Edition.*

THE CHRISTIAN YEAR. Edited by Walter Lock, D.D. *Fourth Edition.*

LYRA INNOCENTIUM. Edited by Walter Lock, D.D. *Second Edition.*

THE TEMPLE. Edited by E. C. S. Gibson, D.D. *Second Edition.*

A BOOK OF DEVOTIONS. Edited by J. W. Stanbridge. B.D. *Second Edition.*

A SERIOUS CALL TO A DEVOUT AND HOLY LIFE. Edited by C. Bigg, D.D. *Fourth Ed.*

A GUIDE TO ETERNITY. Edited by J. W. Stanbridge, B.D.

THE INNER WAY. By J. Tauler. Edited by A. W. Hutton, M.A.

ON THE LOVE OF GOD. By St. Francis de Sales. Edited by W. J. Knox-Little, M.A.

THE PSALMS OF DAVID. Edited by B. W. Randolph, D.D.

LYRA APOSTOLICA. By Cardinal Newman and others. Edited by Canon Scott Holland, M.A., and Canon H. C. Beeching, M.A.

THE SONG OF SONGS. Edited by B. Blaxland, M.A.

THE THOUGHTS OF PASCAL. Edited by C. S. Jerram, M.A.

A MANUAL OF CONSOLATION FROM THE SAINTS AND FATHERS. Edited by J. H. Burn, B.D.

[Continued

THE LIBRARY OF DEVOTION—*continued.*

THE DEVOTIONS OF ST. ANSELM. Edited by C. C. J. Webb, M.A.

GRACE ABOUNDING TO THE CHIEF OF SINNERS. By John Bunyan. Edited by S. C. Freer, M.A.

BISHOP WILSON'S SACRA PRIVATA. Edited by A. E. Burn, B.D.

LYRA SACRA: A Book of Sacred Verse. Edited by Canon H. C. Beeching, M.A. *Second Edition, revised.*

A DAY BOOK FROM THE SAINTS AND FATHERS. Edited by J. H. Burn, B.D.

A LITTLE BOOK OF HEAVENLY WISDOM. A Selection from the English Mystics. Edited by E. C. Gregory.

LIGHT, LIFE, and LOVE. A Selection from the German Mystics. Edited by W. R. Inge, M.A.

AN INTRODUCTION TO THE DEVOUT LIFE. By St. Francis de Sales. Translated and Edited by T. Barns, M.A.

THE LITTLE FLOWERS OF THE GLORIOUS MESSER ST. FRANCIS AND OF HIS FRIARS. Done into English by W. Heywood. With an Introduction by A. G. Ferrers Howell.

MANCHESTER AL MONDO: a Contemplation of Death and Immortality. By Henry Montagu, Earl of Manchester. With an Introduction by Elizabeth Waterhouse, Editor of 'A Little Book of Life and Death.'

THE SPIRITUAL GUIDE, which Disentangles the Soul and brings it by the Inward Way to the Fruition of Perfect Contemplation, and the Rich Treasure of Internal Peace. Written by Dr. Michael de Molinos, Priest. Translated from the Italian copy, printed at Venice, 1685. Edited with an Introduction by Kathleen Lyttelton. And a Note by Canon Scott Holland.

DEVOTIONS FOR EVERY DAY OF THE WEEK AND THE GREAT FESTIVALS. By John Wesley. Edited, with an Introduction by Canon C. Bodington.

PRECES PRIVATÆ. By Lancelot Andrewes, Bishop of Winchester. Selections from the Translation by Canon F. E. Brightman. Edited, with an Introduction, by A. E. Burn, D.D.

Little Books on Art

With many Illustrations. Demy 16mo. 2s. 6d. net.

Each volume consists of about 200 pages, and contains from 30 to 40 Illustrations, including a Frontispiece in Photogravure.

GREEK ART. H. B. Walters. *Fourth Edition.*
BOOKPLATES. E. Almack.
REYNOLDS. J. Sime. *Second Edition.*
ROMNEY. George Paston.
WATTS. R. E. D. Sketchley.
LEIGHTON. Alice Corkran.
VELASQUEZ. Wilfrid Wilberforce and A. R. Gilbert.
GREUZE AND BOUCHER. Eliza F. Pollard.
VANDYCK. M. G. Smallwood.
TURNER. Frances Tyrrell-Gill.
DÜRER. Jessie Allen.
HOLBEIN. Mrs. G. Fortescue.
BURNE-JONES. Fortunée de Lisle. *Third Edition.*

HOPPNER. H. P. K. Skipton.
REMBRANDT. Mrs. E. A. Sharp.
COROT. Alice Pollard and Ethel Birnstingl.
RAPHAEL. A. R. Dryhurst.
MILLET. Netta Peacock.
ILLUMINATED MSS. J. W. Bradley.
CHRIST IN ART. Mrs. Henry Jenner.
JEWELLERY. Cyril Davenport.
CLAUDE. E. Dillon.
THE ARTS OF JAPAN. E. Dillon. *Second Ed.*
ENAMELS. Mrs. Nelson Dawson.
MINIATURES. C. Davenport.
CONSTABLE. H. W. Tompkins.
OUR LADY IN ART. Mrs. H. L. Jenner.

The Little Galleries

Demy 16mo. 2s. 6d. net.

Each volume contains 20 plates in Photogravure, together with a short outline of the life and work of the master to whom the book is devoted.

A LITTLE GALLERY OF REYNOLDS.
A LITTLE GALLERY OF ROMNEY.
A LITTLE GALLERY OF HOPPNER.

A LITTLE GALLERY OF MILLAIS.
A LITTLE GALLERY OF ENGLISH POETS.

The Little Guides

With many Illustrations by E. H. NEW and other artists, and from photographs.
Small Pott 8vo, cloth, 2s. 6d. net.; leather, 3s. 6d. net.

The main features of these Guides are (1) a handy and charming form; (2) illustrations from photographs and by well-known artists; (3) good plans and maps; (4) an adequate but compact presentation of everything that is interesting in the natural features, history, archæology, and architecture of the town or district treated.

CAMBRIDGE AND ITS COLLEGES. By A. Hamilton Thompson. *Second Edition.*
OXFORD AND ITS COLLEGES. By J. Wells, M.A. *Eighth Edition.*
ST. PAUL'S CATHEDRAL. By George Clinch.
WESTMINSTER ABBEY. By G. E. Troutbeck. *Second Edition.*

THE ENGLISH LAKES. By F. G. Brabant, M.A.
THE MALVERN COUNTRY. By B. C. A. Windle, D.Sc., F.R.S.
SHAKESPEARE'S COUNTRY. By B. C. A. Windle, D.Sc., F.R.S. *Third Edition.*

NORTH WALES. By A. T. Story.
BUCKINGHAMSHIRE. By E. S. Roscoe.
CHESHIRE. By W. M. Gallichan.
CORNWALL. By A. L. Salmon.
DERBYSHIRE. By J. Charles Cox, LL.D., F.S.A.
DEVON. By S. Baring-Gould.
DORSET. By Frank R. Heath. *Second Ed.*
HAMPSHIRE. By J. C. Cox, LL.D., F.S.A.

HERTFORDSHIRE. By H. W. Tompkins, F.R.H.S.
THE ISLE OF WIGHT. By G. Clinch.
KENT. By G. Clinch.
KERRY. By C. P. Crane.
MIDDLESEX. By John B. Firth.
NORFOLK. By W. A. Dutt.
NORTHAMPTONSHIRE. By Wakeling Dry.
OXFORDSHIRE. By F. G. Brabant, M.A.
SOMERSET. By G. W. and J. H. Wade.
SUFFOLK. By W. A. Dutt.
SURREY. By F. A. H. Lambert.
SUSSEX. By F. G. Brabant, M.A. *Second Edition.*
THE EAST RIDING OF YORKSHIRE. By J. E. Morris.
THE NORTH RIDING OF YORKSHIRE. By J. E. Morris.

BRITTANY. By S. Baring-Gould.
NORMANDY. By C. Scudamore.
ROME By C. G. Ellaby.
SICILY. By F. Hamilton Jackson.

The Little Library

With Introductions, Notes, and Photogravure Frontispieces.

Small Pott 8vo. Each Volume, cloth, 1s. 6d. net ; leather, 2s. 6d. net.

Anon. A LITTLE BOOK OF ENGLISH LYRICS.
Austen (Jane). PRIDE AND PREJUDICE. Edited by E. V. Lucas. *Two Vols.* NORTHANGER ABBEY. Edited by E. V. Lucas.
Bacon (Francis). THE ESSAYS OF LORD BACON. Edited by EDWARD WRIGHT.
Barham (R. H.). THE INGOLDSBY LEGENDS. Edited by J. B. ATLAY. *Two Volumes.*
Barnett (Mrs. P. A.). A LITTLE BOOK OF ENGLISH PROSE. *Second Edition.*
Beckford (William). THE HISTORY OF THE CALIPH VATHEK. Edited by E. DENISON ROSS.
Blake (William). SELECTIONS FROM WILLIAM BLAKE. Edited by M. PERUGINI.
Borrow (George). LAVENGRO. Edited by F. HINDES GROOME. *Two Volumes.* THE ROMANY RYE. Edited by JOHN SAMPSON.
Browning (Robert). SELECTIONS FROM THE EARLY POEMS OF ROBERT BROWNING. Edited by W. HALL GRIFFIN, M.A.
Canning (George). SELECTIONS FROM THE ANTI-JACOBIN : with GEORGE CANNING'S additional Poems. Edited by LLOYD SANDERS.
Cowley (Abraham). THE ESSAYS OF ABRAHAM COWLEY. Edited by H. C. MINCHIN.
Crabbe (George). SELECTIONS FROM GEORGE CRABBE. Edited by A. C. DEANE.

Craik (Mrs.). JOHN HALIFAX, GENTLEMAN. Edited by ANNIE MATHESON. *Two Volumes.*
Crashaw (Richard). THE ENGLISH POEMS OF RICHARD CRASHAW. Edited by EDWARD HUTTON.
Dante (Alighieri). THE INFERNO OF DANTE. Translated by H. F. CARY. Edited by PAGET TOYNBEE, M.A., D.Litt.
THE PURGATORIO OF DANTE. Translated by H. F. CARY. Edited by PAGET TOYNBEE, M.A., D.Litt.
THE PARADISO OF DANTE. Translated by H. F. CARY. Edited by PAGET TOYNBEE, M.A., D.Litt.
Darley (George). SELECTIONS FROM THE POEMS OF GEORGE DARLEY. Edited by R. A. STREATFEILD.
Deane (A. C.). A LITTLE BOOK OF LIGHT VERSE.
Dickens (Charles). CHRISTMAS BOOKS. *Two Volumes.*
Ferrier (Susan). MARRIAGE. Edited by A. GOODRICH - FREER and LORD IDDESLEIGH. *Two Volumes.* THE INHERITANCE. *Two Volumes.*
Gaskell (Mrs.). CRANFORD. Edited by E. V. LUCAS. *Second Edition.*
Hawthorne (Nathaniel). THE SCARLET LETTER. Edited by PERCY DEARMER.
Henderson (T. F.). A LITTLE BOOK OF SCOTTISH VERSE.
Keats (John). POEMS. With an Introduction by L. BINYON, and Notes by J. MASEFIELD.
Kinglake (A. W.). EOTHEN. With an Introduction and Notes. *Second Edition.*

[Continued.

THE LITTLE LIBRARY—*continued.*

Lamb (Charles). ELIA, AND THE LAST ESSAYS OF ELIA. Edited by E. V. LUCAS.

Locker (F.). LONDON LYRICS Edited by A. D. GODLEY, M.A. A reprint of the First Edition.

Longfellow (H. W.). SELECTIONS FROM LONGFELLOW. Edited by L. M. FAITHFULL.

Marvell (Andrew). THE POEMS OF ANDREW MARVELL. Edited by E. WRIGHT.

Milton (John). THE MINOR POEMS OF JOHN MILTON. Edited by H. C. BEECHING, M.A., Canon of Westminster.

Moir (D. M.). MANSIE WAUCH. Edited by T. F. HENDERSON.

Nichols (J. B. B.). A LITTLE BOOK OF ENGLISH SONNETS.

Rochefoucauld (La). THE MAXIMS OF LA ROCHEFOUCAULD. Translated by Dean STANHOPE. Edited by G. H. POWELL.

Smith (Horace and James). REJECTED ADDRESSES. Edited by A. D. GODLEY, M.A.

Sterne (Laurence). A SENTIMENTAL JOURNEY. Edited by H. W. PAUL.

Tennyson (Alfred, Lord). THE EARLY POEMS OF ALFRED, LORD TENNYSON. Edited by J. CHURTON COLLINS, M.A.
IN MEMORIAM. Edited by Canon H. C. BEECHING, M.A.
THE PRINCESS. Edited by ELIZABETH WORDSWORTH.
MAUD. Edited by ELIZABETH WORDSWORTH.

Thackeray (W. M.). VANITY FAIR. Edited by S. GWYNN. *Three Volumes.*
PENDENNIS. Edited by S. GWYNN. *Three Volumes.*
ESMOND. Edited by S. GWYNN.
CHRISTMAS BOOKS. Edited by S. GWYNN.

Vaughan (Henry). THE POEMS OF HENRY VAUGHAN. Edited by EDWARD HUTTON.

Walton (Izaak). THE COMPLEAT ANGLER. Edited by J. BUCHAN.

Waterhouse (Elizabeth). A LITTLE BOOK OF LIFE AND DEATH. Edited by. *Twelfth Edition.*

Wordsworth (W.). SELECTIONS FROM WORDSWORTH. Edited by NOWELL C. SMITH.

Wordsworth (W.) and Coleridge (S. T.). LYRICAL BALLADS. Edited by GEORGE SAMPSON.

The Little Quarto Shakespeare

Edited by W. J. CRAIG. With Introductions and Notes
Pott 16mo. *In* 40 *Volumes. Leather, price* 1s. *net each volume.*
Mahogany Revolving Book Case. 10s. *net.*

Miniature Library

Reprints in miniature of a few interesting books which have qualities of humanity, devotion, or literary genius.

EUPHRANOR: A Dialogue on Youth. By Edward FitzGerald. From the edition published by W. Pickering in 1851. *Demy* 32mo. *Leather,* 2s. *net.*

POLONIUS: or Wise Saws and Modern Instances. By Edward FitzGerald. From the edition published by W. Pickering in 1852. *Demy* 32mo. *Leather,* 2s. *net.*

THE RUBÁIYÁT OF OMAR KHAYYÁM. By Edward FitzGerald. From the 1st edition of 1859, *Fourth Edition. Leather,* 1s. *net.*

THE LIFE OF EDWARD, LORD HERBERT OF CHERBURY. Written by himself. From the edition printed at Strawberry Hill in the year 1764. *Demy* 32mo. *Leather,* 2s. *net.*

THE VISIONS OF DOM FRANCISCO QUEVEDO VILLEGAS, Knight of the Order of St. James. Made English by R. L. From the edition printed for H. Herringman, 1668. *Leather.* 2s. *net.*

POEMS. By Dora Greenwell. From the edition of 1848. *Leather,* 2s. *net*

Oxford Biographies

Fcap. 8vo. Each volume, cloth, 2s. 6d. *net ; leather,* 3s. 6d. *net.*

DANTE ALIGHIERI. By Paget Toynbee, M.A., D.Litt. With 12 Illustrations. *Third Edition.*

GIROLAMO SAVONAROLA. By E. L. S. Horsburgh, M.A. With 12 Illustrations. *Second Edition.*

JOHN HOWARD. By E. C. S. Gibson, D.D., Bishop of Gloucester. With 12 Illustrations.

ALFRED TENNYSON. By A. C. BENSON, M.A. With 9 Illustrations. *Second Edition.*

SIR WALTER RALEIGH. By I. A. Taylor. With 12 Illustrations.

ERASMUS. By E. F. H. Capey. With 12 Illustrations.

THE YOUNG PRETENDER. By C. S. Terry. With 12 Illustrations.

ROBERT BURNS. By T. F. Henderson. With 12 Illustrations.

CHATHAM. By A. S. M'Dowall. With 12 Illustrations.

FRANCIS OF ASSISI. By Anna M. Stoddart. With 16 Illustrations.

CANNING. By W. Alison Phillips. With 12 Illustrations.

BEACONSFIELD. By Walter Sichel. With 12 Illustrations.

JOHANN WOLFGANG GOETHE. By H. G. Atkins. With 16 Illustrations.

FRANÇOIS FENELON. By Viscount St Cyres. With 12 Illustrations.

School Examination Series

Edited by A. M. M. STEDMAN, M.A. *Cr. 8vo. 2s. 6d.*

FRENCH EXAMINATION PAPERS. By A. M. M. Stedman, M.A. *Fifteenth Edition.*
KEY. *Sixth Edition. 6s. net.*

LATIN EXAMINATION PAPERS. By A. M. M. Stedman, M.A. *Fourteenth Edition.*
KEY. *Sixth Edition. 6s. net.*

GREEK EXAMINATION PAPERS. By A. M. M. Stedman, M.A. *Ninth Edition.*
KEY. *Fourth Edition. 6s. net.*

GERMAN EXAMINATION PAPERS. By R. J. Morich. *Seventh Edition.*
KEY. *Third Edition. 6s. net.*

HISTORY AND GEOGRAPHY EXAMINATION PAPERS. By C. H. Spence, M.A. *Third Edition.*

PHYSICS EXAMINATION PAPERS. By R. E. Steel, M.A., F.C.S.

GENERAL KNOWLEDGE EXAMINATION PAPERS. By A. M. M. Stedman, M.A. *Sixth Edition.*
KEY. *Fourth Edition. 7s. net.*

EXAMINATION PAPERS IN ENGLISH HISTORY. By J. Tait Plowden-Wardlaw, B.A.

School Histories

Illustrated. Crown 8vo. 1s. 6d.

A SCHOOL HISTORY OF WARWICKSHIRE. By B. C. A. Windle, D.Sc., F.R.S.

A SCHOOL HISTORY OF SOMERSET. By Walter Raymond. *Second Edition.*

A SCHOOL HISTORY OF LANCASHIRE. By W. E. Rhodes.

A SCHOOL HISTORY OF SURREY. By H. E. Malden, M.A.

A SCHOOL HISTORY OF MIDDLESEX. By V. Plarr and F. W. Walton.

Methuen's Simplified French Texts

Edited by T. R. N. CROFTS, M.A.

One Shilling each.

L'HISTOIRE D'UNE TULIPE. Adapted by T. R. N. Crofts, M.A. *Second Edition.*

ABDALLAH. Adapted by J. A. Wilson.

LE DOCTEUR MATHÉUS. Adapted by W. P. Fuller.

LA BOUILLIE AU MIEL. Adapted by P. B. Ingham.

JEAN VALJEAN. Adapted by F. W. M. Draper.

LA CHANSON DE ROLAND. Adapted by H. Rieu, M.A. *Second Edition.*

MÉMOIRES DE CADICHON. Adapted by J. F. Rhoades.

L'EQUIPAGE DE LA BELLE-NIVERNAISE. Adapted by T. R. N. Crofts. *Second Ed.*

L'HISTOIRE DE PIERRE ET CAMILLE. Adapted by J. B. Patterson.

Methuen's Standard Library

Cloth, 1s. net; double volumes, 1s. 6d. net. Paper, 6d. net; double volume, 1s. net.

THE MEDITATIONS OF MARCUS AURELIUS. Translated by R. Graves.

SENSE AND SENSIBILITY. Jane Austen.

ESSAYS AND COUNSELS and THE NEW ATLANTIS. Francis Bacon, Lord Verulam.

RELIGIO MEDICI and URN BURIAL. Sir Thomas Browne. The text collated by A. R. Waller.

THE PILGRIM'S PROGRESS. John Bunyan.

REFLECTIONS ON THE FRENCH REVOLUTION. Edmund Burke.

THE POEMS AND SONGS OF ROBERT BURNS. Double Volume.

THE ANALOGY OF RELIGION, NATURAL AND REVEALED. Joseph Butler.

MISCELLANEOUS POEMS. T. CHATTERTON.

TOM JONES. Henry Fielding. Treble Vol.

CRANFORD. Mrs. Gaskell.

THE HISTORY OF THE DECLINE AND FALL OF THE ROMAN EMPIRE. E. Gibbon. Text and Notes revised by J. B. Bury. Seven double volumes.

THE CASE IS ALTERED. EVERY MAN IN HIS HUMOUR. EVERY MAN OUT OF HIS HUMOUR. Ben Jonson.

THE POEMS AND PLAYS OF OLIVER GOLDSMITH.

CYNTHIA'S REVELS. POETASTER. Ben Jonson.

THE POEMS OF JOHN KEATS. Double volume. The Text has been collated by E. de Sélincourt.

ON THE IMITATION OF CHRIST. By Thomas à Kempis. Translation by C. Bigg.

A SERIOUS CALL TO A DEVOUT AND HOLY LIFE. W. Law.

PARADISE LOST. John Milton.

EIKONOKLASTES AND THE TENURE OF KINGS AND MAGISTRATES. John Milton.

UTOPIA AND POEMS. Sir Thomas More.

THE REPUBLIC OF PLATO. Translated by Sydenham and Taylor. Double Volume. Translation revised by W. H. D. Rouse.

THE LITTLE FLOWERS OF ST. FRANCIS. Translated by W. Heywood.

THE WORKS OF WILLIAM SHAKESPEARE. In 10 volumes.

PRINCIPAL POEMS, 1815-1818. Percy Bysshe Shelley. With an Introduction by C. D. Locock.

THE LIFE OF NELSON. Robert Southey.

THE NATURAL HISTORY AND ANTIQUITIES OF SELBORNE. Gilbert White.

Textbooks of Science

Edited by G. F. GOODCHILD, M.A., B.Sc., and G. R. MILLS, M.A.

Fully Illustrated.

PRACTICAL MECHANICS. S. H. Wells. *Fourth Edition. Cr. 8vo. 3s. 6d.*

PRACTICAL CHEMISTRY. Part I. W. French, M.A. *Cr. 8vo. Fifth Edition. 1s. 6d.*

PRACTICAL CHEMISTRY. Part II. W. French and T. H. Boardman. *Cr. 8vo. 1s. 6d.*

EXAMPLES IN PHYSICS. By C. E. Jackson, B.A. *Cr. 8vo. 2s. 6d.*

TECHNICAL ARITHMETIC AND GEOMETRY. By C. T. Millis, M.I.M.E. *Cr. 8vo. 3s. 6d.*

PLANT LIFE, Studies in Garden and School. By Horace F. Jones, F.C.S. With 320 Diagrams. *Cr. 8vo. 3s. 6d.*

THE COMPLETE SCHOOL CHEMISTRY. By F. M. Oldham, B.A. With 126 Illustrations. *Second Edition. Cr. 8vo. 4s. 6d.*

ELEMENTARY SCIENCE FOR PUPIL TEACHERS. PHYSICS SECTION. By W. T. Clough,

A.R.C.S. (Lond.), F.C.S. CHEMISTRY SECTION. By A. E. Dunstan, B.Sc. (Lond.), F.C.S. With 2 Plates and 10 Diagrams. *Cr. 8vo. 2s.*

EXAMPLES IN ELEMENTARY MECHANICS, Practical, Graphical, and Theoretical. By W. J. Dobbs, M.A. With 51 Diagrams. *Cr. 8vo. 5s.*

OUTLINES OF PHYSICAL CHEMISTRY. By George Senter, B.Sc. (Lond.), Ph.D. With many Diagrams. *Cr. 8vo. 3s. 6d.*

AN ORGANIC CHEMISTRY FOR SCHOOLS AND TECHNICAL INSTITUTES. By A. E. Dunstan, B.Sc. (Lond.), F.C.S. With many Illustrations. *Cr. 8vo. 2s. 6d.*

FIRST YEAR PHYSICS. By C. E. Jackson, M.A. With 51 diagrams. *Cr. 8vo. 1s. 6d.*

Textbooks of Technology

Edited by G. F. GOODCHILD, M.A., B.Sc., and G. R. MILLS, M.A.

Fully Illustrated.

HOW TO MAKE A DRESS. By J. A. E. Wood. *Fourth Edition. Cr. 8vo. 1s. 6d.*

CARPENTRY AND JOINERY. By F. C. Webber. *Fifth Edition. Cr. 8vo. 3s. 6d.*

MILLINERY, THEORETICAL AND PRACTICAL. By Clare Hill. *Fourth Edition. Cr. 8vo. 2s.*

INSTRUCTION IN COOKERY. A. P. THOMSON. *2s. 6d.*

AN INTRODUCTION TO THE STUDY OF TEXTILE DESIGN. By Aldred F. Barker. *Demy 8vo. 7s. 6d.*

BUILDERS' QUANTITIES. By H. C. Grubb. *Cr. 8vo. 4s. 6d.*

RÉPOUSSÉ METAL WORK. By A. C. Horth. *Cr. 8vo. 2s. 6d.*

ELECTRIC LIGHT AND POWER: An Introduction to the Study of Electrical Engineering. By E. E. Brooks, B.Sc. (Lond.). and W. H. N. James, A.R.C.S., A.I.E.E. *Cr. 8vo. 4s. 6d.*

ENGINEERING WORKSHOP PRACTICE. By C. C. Allen. *Cr 8vo. 3s. 6d.*

Handbooks of Theology

THE XXXIX. ARTICLES OF THE CHURCH OF ENGLAND. Edited by E. C. S. Gibson, D.D. *Sixth Edition. Demy 8vo. 12s. 6d.*

AN INTRODUCTION TO THE HISTORY OF RELIGION. By F. B. Jevons. M.A., Litt.D. *Fourth Edition. Demy 8vo. 10s. 6d.*

THE DOCTRINE OF THE INCARNATION. By R. L. Ottley, D.D. *Fourth Edition revised. Demy 8vo. 12s. 6d.*

AN INTRODUCTION TO THE HISTORY OF THE CREEDS. By A. E. Burn, D.D. *Demy 8vo. 10s. 6d.*

THE PHILOSOPHY OF RELIGION IN ENGLAND AND AMERICA. By Alfred Caldecott, D.D. *Demy 8vo. 10s. 6d.*

A HISTORY OF EARLY CHRISTIAN DOCTRINE. By J. F. Bethune-Baker, M.A. *Demy 8vo. 10s. 6d.*

The Westminster Commentaries

General Editor, WALTER LOCK, D.D., Warden of Keble College, Dean Ireland's Professor of Exegesis in the University of Oxford.

THE BOOK OF GENESIS. Edited with Introduction and Notes by S. R. Driver, D.D. *Seventh Edition. Demy 8vo. 10s. 6d.*

THE BOOK OF JOB. Edited by E. C. S. Gibson, D.D. *Second Edition. Demy 8vo. 6s.*

THE ACTS OF THE APOSTLES. Edited by R. B. Rackham, M.A. *Demy 8vo. Fourth Edition. 10s. 6d.*

THE FIRST EPISTLE OF PAUL THE APOSTLE

TO THE CORINTHIANS. Edited by H. L. Goudge, M.A. *Second Ed. Demy 8vo. 6s.*

THE EPISTLE OF ST. JAMES. Edited with Introduction and Notes by R. J. Knowling, D.D. *Demy 8vo. 6s.*

THE BOOK OF EZEKIEL. Edited H. A. Redpath, M.A., D.Litt. *Demy 8vo. 10s. 6d.*

A COMMENTARY ON EXODUS. By A. H. M'Neile, B.D. With a Map and 3 Plans. *Demy 8vo. 10s. 6d.*

PART II.—FICTION

Albanesi (E. Maria). SUSANNAH AND ONE OTHER. *Fourth Edition.* Cr. 8vo. 6s.
THE BLUNDER OF AN INNOCENT. *Second Edition.* Cr. 8vo. 6s.
CAPRICIOUS CAROLINE. *Second Edition.* Cr. 8vo. 6s.
LOVE AND LOUISA. *Second Edition.* Cr. 8vo. 6s. Also *Medium* 8vo. 6d.
PETER, A PARASITE. Cr. 8vo. 6s.
THE BROWN EYES OF MARY. *Third Edition.* Cr. 8vo. 6s.
I KNOW A MAIDEN. *Third Edition.* Cr. 8vo. 6s. Also *Medium* 8vo. 6d.
Austen (Jane). PRIDE AND PREJUDICE. *Medium* 8vo. 6d.
Bagot (Richard). A ROMAN MYSTERY. *Third Edition.* Cr. 8vo. 6s. Also *Medium* 8vo. 6d.
THE PASSPORT. *Fourth Edition.* Cr. 8vo. 6s.
TEMPTATION. *Fifth Edition.* Cr. 8vo. 6s.
LOVE'S PROXY. *A New Edition.* Cr. 8vo. 6s.
DONNA DIANA. *Second Edition.* Cr. 8vo. 6s.
CASTING OF NETS. *Twelfth Edition.* Cr. 8vo. 6s. Also *Medium* 8vo. 6d.
Balfour (Andrew). BY STROKE OF SWORD. *Medium* 8vo. 6d.
Baring-Gould (S.). ARMINELL. *Fifth Edition.* Cr. 8vo. 6s.
URITH. *Fifth Edition.* Cr. 8vo. 6s. Also *Medium* 8vo. 6d.
IN THE ROAR OF THE SEA. *Seventh Edition.* Cr. 8vo. 6s. Also *Medium* 8vo. 6d.
MARGERY OF QUETHER. *Third Edition.* Cr. 8vo. 6s.
THE QUEEN OF LOVE. *Fifth Edition.* Cr. 8vo. 6s. Also *Medium* 8vo. 6d.
JACQUETTA. *Third Edition.* Cr. 8vo. 6s.
KITTY ALONE. *Fifth Edition.* Cr. 8vo. 6s. Also *Medium* 8vo. 6d.
NOÉMI. Illustrated. *Fourth Edition.* Cr. 8vo. 6s. Also *Medium* 8vo. 6d.
THE BROOM-SQUIRE. Illustrated. *Fifth Edition.* Cr. 8vo. 6s. Also *Medium* 8vo. 6d.
DARTMOOR IDYLLS. Cr. 8vo. 6s.
GUAVAS THE TINNER. Illustrated. *Second Edition.* Cr. 8vo. 6s.
BLADYS OF THE STEWPONEY. Illustrated. *Second Edition.* Cr. 8vo. 6s.
PABO THE PRIEST. Cr. 8vo. 6s.
WINEFRED. Illustrated. *Second Edition.* Cr. 8vo. 6s. Also *Medium* 8vo. 6d.
ROYAL GEORGIE. Illustrated. Cr. 8vo. 6s.
CHRIS OF ALL SORTS. Cr. 8vo. 6s.

IN DEWISLAND. *Second Ed.* Cr. 8vo. 6s.
THE FROBISHERS. *Crown* 8vo. 6s. Also *Medium* 8vo. 6d.
DOMITIA. Illus. *Second Ed.* Cr. 8vo. 6s.
MRS. CURGENVEN OF CURGENVEN. *Crown* 8vo. 6s.
LITTLE TU'PENNY. *A New Edition.* *Medium* 8vo. 6d.
FURZE BLOOM. *Medium* 8vo. 6d.
Barnett (Edith A.). A WILDERNESS WINNER. *Second Edition.* Cr. 8vo. 6s.
Barr (James). LAUGHING THROUGH A WILDERNESS. Cr. 8vo. 6s.
Barr (Robert). IN THE MIDST OF ALARMS. *Third Edition.* Cr. 8vo. 6s. Also *Medium* 8vo. 6d.
THE COUNTESS TEKLA. *Fourth Edition.* Cr. 8vo. 6s. Also *Medium* 8vo. 6d.
THE MUTABLE MANY. *Third Edition.* Cr. 8vo. 6s. Also *Medium* 8vo. 6d.
THE TEMPESTUOUS PETTICOAT. Illustrated. *Third Edition.* Cr. 8vo. 6s.
THE STRONG ARM. *Second Edition.* Cr. 8vo. 6s.
JENNIE BAXTER JOURNALIST. *Medium* 8vo. 6d.
Begbie (Harold). THE CURIOUS AND DIVERTING ADVENTURES OF SIR JOHN SPARROW; or, THE PROGRESS OF AN OPEN MIND. With a Frontispiece. *Second Edition.* Cr. 8vo. 6s.
Belloc(Hilaire), M.P. EMMANUEL BURDEN, MERCHANT. With 36 Illustrations by G. K. CHESTERTON. *Second Ed.* Cr. 8vo. 6s.
Benson(E. F.) DODO: A DETAIL OF THE DAY. *Fifteenth Edition.* Cr. 8vo. 6s. Also *Medium* 8vo. 6d.
THE VINTAGE. *Medium* 8vo. 6d.
Benson (Margaret). SUBJECT TO VANITY. Cr. 8vo. 3s. 6d.
Birmingham (George A.). THE BAD TIMES. *Second Edition.* Crown 8vo. 6s.
Bowles (G. Stewart). A GUN-ROOM DITTY BOX. *Second Ed.* Cr. 8vo. 1s. 6d.
Bretherton (Ralph Harold). THE MILL. Cr. 8vo. 6s.
Brontë (Charlotte). SHIRLEY. *Medium* 8vo. 6d.
Burke (Barbara). BARBARA GOES TO OXFORD. With 16 Illustrations. *Third Edition.* Cr. 8vo. 6s.
Burton (J. Bloundelle). ACROSS THE SALT SEAS. *Medium* 8vo. 6d.
Caffyn (Mrs.) ('Iota'). ANNE MAULEVERER. *Medium* 8vo. 6d.
Campbell (Mrs. Vere). FERRIBY. *Second Edition.* Cr. 8vo. 6s.

Capes (Bernard). THE EXTRAOR-
DINARY CONFESSIONS OF DIANA
PLEASE. *Third Edition. Cr. 8vo. 6s.*
A JAY OF ITALY. *Fourth Ed. Cr. 8vo. 6s.*
LOAVES AND FISHES. *Second Edition.
Cr. 8vo. 6s.*
A ROGUE'S TRAGEDY. *Second Edition.
Cr. 8vo. 6s.*
THE GREAT SKENE MYSTERY.
Second Edition. Cr. 8vo. 6s.
THE LAKE OF WINE. *Medium 8vo. 6d.*
Carey (Wymond). LOVE THE JUDGE.
Second Edition. Cr. 8vo. 6s.
Castle (Agnes and Egerton). FLOWER
O' THE ORANGE, and Other Tales.
With a Frontispiece in Colour by A. H.
Buckland. *Third Edition. Cr. 8vo. 6s.*
Charlton (Randal). M A V E. *Second
Edition. Cr. 8vo. 6s.*
THE VIRGIN WIDOW. *Cr. 8vo. 6s.*
Chesney (Weatherby). THE TRAGEDY
OF THE GREAT EMERALD *Cr.8vo. 6s.*
THE MYSTERY OF A BUNGALOW.
Second Edition. Cr. 8vo. 6s.
Clifford (Mrs. W. K.). THE GETTING
WELL OF DOROTHY. Illustrated by
GORDON BROWNE. *Second Edition. Cr. 8vo.
3s. 6d.*
A FLASH OF SUMMER. *Medium 8vo. 6d.*
MRS. KEITH'S CRIME. *Medium 8vo. 6d.*
Conrad (Joseph). THE SECRET AGENT:
A Simple Tale. *Fourth Ed. Cr. 8vo. 6s.*
Corbett (Julian). A BUSINESS IN
GREAT WATERS. *Medium 8vo. 6d.*
Corelli (Marie). A ROMANCE OF TWO
WORLDS. *Twenty-Ninth Ed. Cr.8vo. 6s.*
VENDETTA. *Twenty-Sixth Ed. Cr.8vo. 6s.*
THELMA. *Thirty-Ninth Ed. Cr. 8vo. 6s.*
ARDATH : THE STORY OF A DEAD
SELF. *Eighteenth Edition. Cr.8vo. 6s.*
THE SOUL OF LILITH. *Fifteenth Edi-
tion. Cr.8vo. 6s.*
WORMWOOD. *Sixteenth Ed. Cr.8vo. 6s.*
BARABBAS: A DREAM OF THE
WORLD'S TRAGEDY. *Forty-Third
Edition. Cr.8vo. 6s.*
THE SORROWS OF SATAN. *Fifty-Fourth
Edition. Cr.8vo. 6s.*
THE MASTER CHRISTIAN. *Twelfth
Edition. 177th Thousand. Cr.8vo. 6s.*
TEMPORAL POWER: A STUDY IN
SUPREMACY. *150th Thousand. Cr.8vo.6s*
GOD'S GOOD MAN: A SIMPLE LOVE
STORY. *Thirteenth Edition.* 150th Thou-
sand. *Cr.8vo. 6s.*
THE MIGHTY ATOM. *Twenty-seventh
Edition. Cr.8vo. 6s.*
BOY: a Sketch. *Tenth Edition. Cr.8vo. 6s.*
CAMEOS. *Thirteenth Edition. Cr. 8vo. 6s.*
Cotes (Mrs. Everard). See Sara Jeannette
Duncan.
Cotterell (Constance). THE VIRGIN
AND THE SCALES. Illustrated. *Second
Edition. Cr. 8vo. 6s.*
Crockett (S. R.), Author of 'The Raiders,'
etc. LOCHINVAR. Illustrated. *Third
Edition. Cr. 8vo. 6s.*
THE STANDARD BEARER. *Cr. 8vo. 6s.*

Croker (B. M.). THE OLD CANTON-
MENT. *Cr. 8vo. 6s.*
JOHANNA. *Second Edition. Cr. 8vo. 6s.*
Also *Medium 8vo. 6d.*
THE HAPPY VALLEY. *Fourth Edition.
Cr. 8vo. 6s.*
A NINE DAYS' WONDER. *Third
Edition. Cr. 8vo. 6s.*
PEGGY OF THE BARTONS. *Seventh
Ed. Cr. 8vo. 6s.* Also *Medium 8vo. 6d.*
ANGEL. *Fourth Edition. Cr. 8vo. 6s.*
Also *Medium 8vo. 6d.*
A STATE SECRET. *Third Edition. Cr.
8vo. 3s. 6d.* Also *Medium 8vo. 6d.*
Crosbie (Mary). DISCIPLES. *Second Ed.
Cr.8vo. 6s.*
Cuthell (Edith E.). ONLY A GUARD-
ROOM DOG. Illustrated by W. PARKIN-
SON. *Crown 8vo. 3s. 6d.*
Dawson (Warrington). THE SCAR.
Second Edition. Cr. 8vo. 6s.
THE SCOURGE *Cr. 8vo. 6s.*
Deakin (Dorothea). T H E YOUNG
COLUMBINE. With a Frontispiece by
LEWIS BAUMER. *Cr. 8vo. 6s.*
Deane (Mary). THE OTHER PAWN.
Cr. 8vo. 6s.
Doyle (A. Conan). ROUND THE RED
LAMP. *Eleventh Edition. Cr. 8vo. 6s.*
Also *Medium 8vo. 6d.*
Dumas (Alexandre). See page 39.
Duncan (Sara Jeannette) (Mrs. Everard
Cotes). T H O S E DELIGHTFUL
AMERICANS. *Medium 8vo. 6d.*
A VOYAGE OF CONSOLATION. Illus-
trated. *Third Edition. Cr. 8vo. 6s.*
Also *Medium 8vo. 6d.*
Eliot (George). THE MILL ON THE
FLOSS. *Medium 8vo. 6d.*
Erskine (Mrs. Steuart). THE MAGIC
PLUMES. *Cr. 8vo. 6s.*
Fenn (G. Manville). SYD BELTON ; or,
The Boy who would not go to Sea. Illus-
trated by GORDON BROWNE. *Second Ed.
Cr. 8vo. 3s. 6d.*
Findlater (J. H.). THE GREEN GRAVES
OF BALGOWRIE. *Fifth Edition.
Cr. 8vo. 6s.* Also *Medium 8vo. 6d.*
THE LADDER TO THE STARS. *Second
Edition. Cr. 8vo. 6s.*
Findlater (Mary). A NARROW WAY.
Third Edition. Cr. 8vo.. 6s.
OVER THE HILLS. *Cr. 8vo. 6s.*
THE ROSE OF JOY. *Third Edition.
Cr. 8vo. 6s.*
A BLIND BIRD'S NEST. With 8 Illus-
trations. *Second Edition. Cr. 8vo. 6s.*
Fitzpatrick (K.) THE WEANS AT
ROWALLAN. Illustrated. *Second Edi-
tion. Cr. 8vo. 6s.*
**Francis (M. E.). (Mrs. Francis Blun-
dell).** S T E P P I N G WESTWARD.
Second Edition. Cr. 8vo. 6s.
MARGERY O' THE MILL. *Third
Edition. Cr. 8vo. 6s.*
Fraser (Mrs. Hugh). THE SLAKING
OF THE SWORD. *Second Edition.
Cr. 8vo. 6s.*

IN THE SHADOW OF THE LORD. *Third Edition. Crown 8vo. 6s.*
Fry (B. and C.B.). A MOTHER'S SON. *Fifth Edition. Cr. 8vo. 6s.*
Fuller=Maitland (Ella). BLANCHE ESMEAD. *Second Edition. Cr. 8vo. 6s.*
Gallon (Tom). RICKERBY'S FOLLY. *Medium 8vo. 6d.*
Gaskell (Mrs.). CRANFORD. *Medium 8vo. 6d.*
MARY BARTON. *Medium 8vo. 6d.*
NORTH AND SOUTH. *Medium 8vo. 6d.*
Gates (Eleanor). THE PLOW-WOMAN. *Cr. 8vo. 6s.*
Gerard (Dorothea). HOLY MATRIMONY. *Medium 8vo 6d.*
MADE OF MONEY. *Cr. 8vo. 6s.*
Also *Medium 8vo. 6d.*
THE IMPROBABLE IDYL. *Third Edition. Cr. 8vo. 6s.*
THE BRIDGE OF LIFE. *Cr. 8vo. 6s.*
THE CONQUEST OF LONDON. *Medium 8vo. 6d.*
Gissing (George). THE TOWN TRAVELLER. *Second Edition. Cr. 8vo. 6s.*
Also *Medium 8vo. 6d.*
THE CROWN OF LIFE. *Cr. 8vo. 6s.*
Also *Medium 8vo. 6d.*
Glanville (Ernest). THE INCA'S TREASURE. Illustrated. *Cr. 8vo. 3s. 6d.*
Also *Medium 8vo. 6d.*
THE KLOOF BRIDE. Illustrated. *Cr. 8vo. 3s. 6d.* Also *Medium 8vo. 6d.*
Gleig (Charles). BUNTER'S CRUISE. Illustrated. *Cr. 8vo. 3s. 6d.*
Also *Medium 8vo. 6d.*
Grimm (The Brothers). GRIMM'S FAIRY TALES. Illustrated. *Medium 8vo. 6d.*
Hamliton (M.). THE FIRST CLAIM. *Second Edition. Cr. 8vo. 6s.*
Harraden (Beatrice). IN VARYING MOODS. *Fourteenth Edition. Cr. 8vo. 6s.*
THE SCHOLAR'S DAUGHTER. *Fourth Edition. Cr. 8vo. 6s.*
HILDA STRAFFORD and THE REMITTANCE MAN. *Twelfth Ed. Cr. 8vo. 6s.*
Harrod (F.) (Frances Forbes Robertson). THE TAMING OF THE BRUTE. *Cr. 8vo. 6s.*
Herbertson (Agnes G.). PATIENCE DEAN. *Cr. 8vo. 6s.*
Hichens (Robert). THE PROPHET OF BERKELEY SQUARE. *Second Edition. Cr. 8vo. 6s.*
TONGUES OF CONSCIENCE. *Third Edition. Cr. 8vo. 6s.*
FELIX. *Sixth Edition. Cr. 8vo. 6s.*
THE WOMAN WITH THE FAN. *Seventh Edition. Cr. 8vo. 6s.*
BYEWAYS. *Cr. 8vo. 6s.*
THE GARDEN OF ALLAH. *Seventeenth Edition. Cr. 8vo. 6s.*
THE BLACK SPANIEL. *Cr. 8vo. 6s.*
THE CALL OF THE BLOOD. *Seventh Edition. Cr. 8vo. 6s.*
Hope (Anthony). THE GOD IN THE CAR. *Eleventh Edition. Cr. 8vo. 6s.*

A CHANGE OF AIR. *Sixth Ed. Cr. 8vo. 6s.*
Also *Medium 8vo. 6d.*
A MAN OF MARK. *Fifth Ed. Cr. 8vo. 6s.*
Also *Medium 8vo. 6d.*
THE CHRONICLES OF COUNT ANTONIO. *Sixth Edition. Cr. 8vo. 6s.*
Also *Medium 8vo. 6d.*
PHROSO. Illustrated by H. R. MILLAR. *Seventh Edition. Cr. 8vo. 6s.*
Also *Medium 8vo. 6d.*
SIMON DALE. Illustrated. *Eighth Edition. Cr. 8vo. 6s.*
THE KING'S MIRROR. *Fourth Edition. Cr. 8vo. 6s.*
QUISANTE. *Fourth Edition. Cr. 8vo. 6s.*
THE DOLLY DIALOGUES. *Cr. 8vo. 6s.*
Also *Medium 8vo. 6d.*
A SERVANT OF THE PUBLIC. Illustrated. *Fourth Edition. Cr. 8vo. 6s.*
TALES OF TWO PEOPLE. With a Frontispiece by A. H. BUCKLAND. *Third Ed. Cr. 8vo. 6s.*
Hope (Graham). THE LADY OF LYTE. *Second Edition. Cr. 8vo. 6s.*
Hornung (E. W.). DEAD MEN TELL NO TALES. *Medium 8vo. 6d.*
Housman (Clemence). THE LIFE OF SIR AGLOVALE DE GALIS. *Cr. 8vo. 6s.*
Hueffer (Ford Madox). AN ENGLISH GIRL: A ROMANCE. *Second Edition. Cr. 8vo. 6s.*
Hutten (Baroness von). THE HALO. *Fifth Edition. Cr. 8vo. 6s.*
Hyne (C. J. Cutcliffe). MR. HORROCKS, PURSER. *Fourth Edition. Cr. 8vo. 6s.*
PRINCE RUPERT, THE BUCCANEER. Illustrated. *Third Edition. Cr. 8vo. 6s.*
Ingraham (J. H.). THE THRONE OF DAVID. *Medium 8vo. 6d.*
Jacobs (W. W.). MANY CARGOES. *Thirty-first Edition. Cr. 8vo. 3s. 6d.*
SEA URCHINS. *Fifteenth Edition.. Cr. 8vo. 3s. 6d.*
A MASTER OF CRAFT. Illustrated by WILL OWEN. *Eighth Edition. Cr. 8vo. 3s. 6d.*
LIGHT FREIGHTS. Illustrated by WILL OWEN and Others. *Seventh Edition. Cr. 8vo. 3s. 6d.*
THE SKIPPER'S WOOING. *Ninth Edition. Cr. 8vo. 3s. 6d.*
AT SUNWICH PORT. Illustrated by WILL OWEN. *Ninth Edition. Cr. 8vo. 3s. 6d.*
DIALSTONE LANE. Illustrated by WILL OWEN. *Seventh Edition. Cr. 8vo. 3s. 6d.*
ODD CRAFT. Illustrated by WILL OWEN. *Seventh Edition. Cr. 8vo. 3s. 6d.*
THE LADY OF THE BARGE. *Eighth Edition. Cr. 8vo. 3s. 6d.*
James (Henry). THE SOFT SIDE. *Second Edition. Cr. 8vo. 6s.*
THE AMBASSADORS. *Second Edition. Cr. 8vo. 6s.*
THE GOLDEN BOWL. *Third Edition. Cr. 8vo. 6s.*
Keays (H. A. Mitchell). HE THAT EATETH BREAD WITH ME. *Cr. 8vo. 6s.*

Kester (Vaughan). THE FORTUNES OF THE LANDRAYS. Illustrated. *Cr.8vo. 6s.*

Lawless (Hon. Emily). WITH ESSEX IN IRELAND. *Cr. 8vo. 6s.*

Le Queux (William). THE HUNCH-BACK OF WESTMINSTER. *Third Ed. Cr. 8vo. 6s.*
Also *Medium 8vo. 6d.*
THE CROOKED WAY. *Second Edition. Cr. 8vo. 6s.*
THE CLOSED BOOK. *Third Ed. Cr.8vo.6s.*
THE VALLEY OF THE SHADOW. Illustrated. *Third Edition. Cr. 8vo. 6s.*
BEHIND THE THRONE. *Third Edition. Cr. 8vo. 6s.*

Levett-Yeats (S. K.). ORRAIN. *Second Edition. Cr. 8vo. 6s.*
THE TRAITOR'S WAY. *Medium 8vo. 6d.*

Linton (E. Lynn). THE TRUE HISTORY OF JOSHUA DAVIDSON. *Medium 8vo. 6d.*

London (Jack). WHITE FANG. With a Frontispiece by CHARLES RIVINGSTON BULL. *Sixth Edition. Cr. 8vo. 6s.*

Lyall (Edna). DERRICK VAUGHAN, NOVELIST. *42nd Thousand. Cr. 8vo. 3s. 6d.* Also *Medium 8vo. 6d.*

Maartens (Maarten). THE NEW RELI-GION: A MODERN NOVEL. *Third Edition. Cr. 8vo. 6s.*

M'Carthy (Justin H.). THE LADY OF LOYALTY HOUSE. Illustrated. *Third Edition. Cr. 8vo. 6s.*
THE DRYAD. *Second Edition. Cr. 8vo. 6s.*
THE DUKE'S MOTTO. *Third Edition. Cr. 8vo. 6s.*

Macdonald (Ronald). A HUMAN TRINITY. *Second Edition. Cr. 8vo. 6s.*

Macnaughtan (S.). THE FORTUNE OF CHRISTINA M'NAB. *Fourth Edition. Cr. 8vo. 6s.*

Malet (Lucas). COLONEL ENDERBY'S WIFE. *Fourth Edition. Cr. 8vo. 6s.*
A COUNSEL OF PERFECTION. *New Edition. Cr. 8vo. 6s.*
Also *Medium 8vo. 6d.*
THE WAGES OF SIN. *Sixteenth Edition. Cr. 8vo. 6s.*
THE CARISSIMA. *Fifth Ed. Cr. 8vo. 6s.*
Also *Medium 8vo. 6d.*
THE GATELESS BARRIER. *Fifth Edition. Cr. 8vo. 6s.*
THE HISTORY OF SIR RICHARD CALMADY. *Seventh Edition. Cr.8vo. 6s.*

Mann (Mrs. M. E.). OLIVIA'S SUMMER. *Second Edition. Cr. 8vo. 6s.*
A LOST ESTATE. *A New Ed. Cr. 8vo. 6s.* Also *Medium 8vo. 6d.*
THE PARISH OF HILBY. *A New Edition. Cr. 8vo. 6s.*
THE PARISH NURSE. *Fourth Edition. Cr. 8vo. 6s.*
GRAN'MA'S JANE. *Cr. 8vo. 6s.*
MRS. PETER HOWARD. *Cr. 8vo. 6s.* Also *Medium 8vo. 6d.*
A WINTER'S TALE. *A New Edition. Cr. 8vo. 6s.*

ONE ANOTHER'S BURDENS. *A New Edition. Cr. 8vo. 6s.*
Also *Medium 8vo. 6d.*
ROSE AT HONEYPOT. *Third Ed. Cr. 8vo. 6s.*
THERE WAS ONCE A PRINCE. Illustrated by M. B. MANN. *Cr. 8vo. 3s. 6d.*
WHEN ARNOLD COMES HOME. Illustrated by M. B. MANN. *Cr. 8vo. 3s. 6d.*
THE EGLAMORE PORTRAITS. *Third Edition. Cr. 8vo. 6s.*
THE MEMORIES OF RONALD LOVE. *Cr. 8vo. 6s.*
THE SHEEP AND THE GOATS. *Third Edition. Cr. 8vo. 6s.*
A SHEAF OF CORN. *Second Edition. Cr. 8vo. 6s.*
THE CEDAR STAR. *Medium 8vo. 6d.*

Marchmont (A. W.). MISER HOAD-LEY'S SECRET. *Medium 8vo. 6d.*
A MOMENT'S ERROR. *Medium 8vo. 6d.*

Marriott (Charles). GENEVRA. *Second Edition. Cr. 8vo. 6s.*

Marryat (Captain). PETER SIMPLE *Medium 8vo. 6d.*
JACOB FAITHFUL. *Medium 8vo. 6d.*

Marsh (Richard). THE TWICKENHAM PEERAGE. *Second Edition. Cr. 8vo. 6s.*
Also *Medium 8vo. 6d.*
THE MARQUIS OF PUTNEY. *Second Edition. Cr. 8vo. 6s.*
IN THE SERVICE OF LOVE. *Third. Edition. Cr. 8vo. 6s.*
THE GIRL AND THE MIRACLE. *Third Edition. Cr. 8vo. 6s.*
THE COWARD BEHIND THE CUR-TAIN. *Cr. 8vo. 6s.*
A METAMORPHOSIS. *Medium 8vo. 6d.*
THE GODDESS. *Medium 8vo. 6d.*
THE JOSS. *Medium 8vo. 6d.*

Marshall (Archibald). MANY JUNES. *Second Edition. Cr. 8vo. 6s.*

Mason (A. E. W.). CLEMENTINA. Illustrated. *Second Edition. Cr. 8vo. 6s.*
Also *Medium 8vo. 6d.*

Mathers (Helen). HONEY. *Fourth Ed. Cr. 8vo. 6s.* Also *Medium 8vo. 6d.*
GRIFF OF GRIFFITHSCOURT. *Cr. 8vo. 6s.* Also *Medium 8vo. 6d.*
THE FERRYMAN *Second Edition. Cr. 8vo. 6s.*
TALLY-HO! *Fourth Edition. Cr. 8vo. 6s.*
SAM'S SWEETHEART. *Medium 8vo. 6d.*

Maxwell (W. B.). VIVIEN. *Ninth Edition. Cr. 8vo. 6s.*
THE RAGGED MESSENGER. *Third Edition. Cr. 8vo. 6s.*
FABULOUS FANCIES. *Cr. 8vo. 6s.*
THE GUARDED FLAME. *Seventh Edition. Cr. 8vo. 6s.*
ODD LENGTHS. *Second Ed. Cr. 8vo. 6s.*
THE COUNTESS OF MAYBURY: BE-TWEEN YOU AND I. Being the Intimate Conversations of the Right Hon. the Countess of Maybury. *Fourth Edition. Cr. 8vo. 6s.*